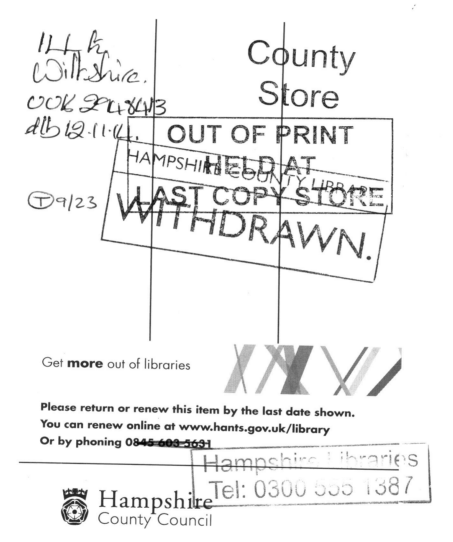

THE THIRD REICH
THEN AND NOW

These buildings of ours should not be conceived for the year 1940,
no, not for the year 2000, but like the cathedrals of our past
they shall stretch into the millennia of the future.

ADOLF HITLER, SEPTEMBER 7, 1937

GEBT MIR FUNF JAHRE
UND IHR WERDET
DEUTSCHLAND NICHT
WIEDER ERKENNEN
ADOLF HITLER

GIVE ME FIVE YEARS &
YOU WILL NOT
RECOGNIZE GERMANY
AGAIN

DELAWARE
SERVICE

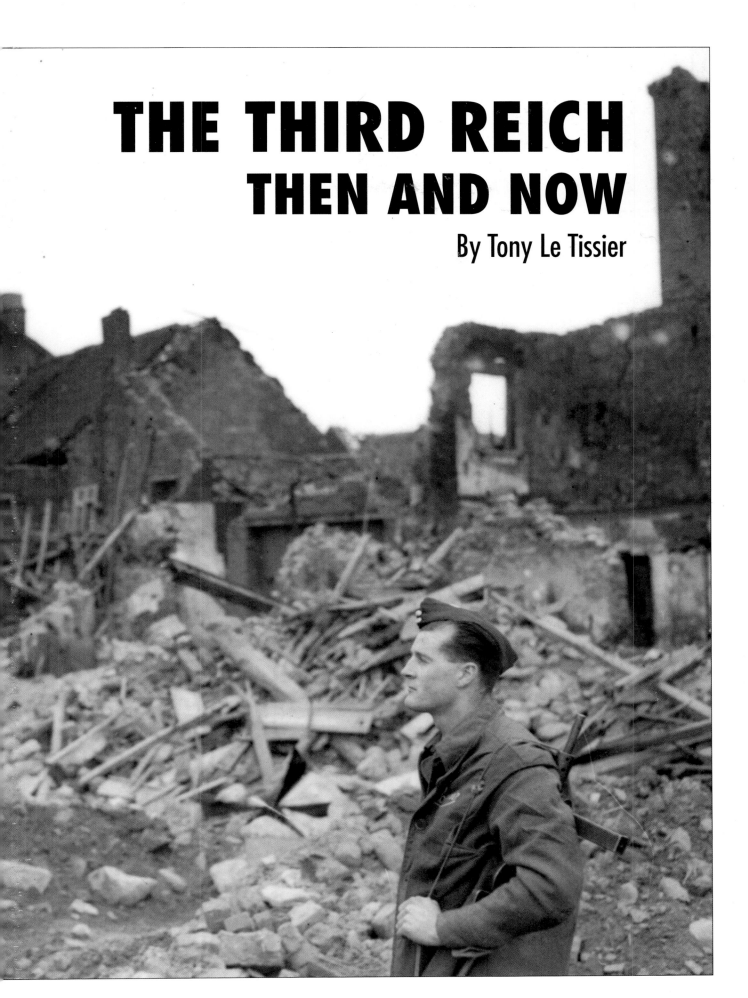

THE THIRD REICH
THEN AND NOW

By Tony Le Tissier

Credits

ISBN: 1 870067 56 8
© *After the Battle* 2005

PUBLISHERS
Battle of Britain International Ltd
Church House, Church Street,
London E15 3JA England

PRINTERS
Printed and bound in China
on behalf of Compass Press.

FRONT COVER: De-Nazification in Hamburg (see page 6). From a painting by George A. Campbell.

REAR COVER: Sergeant Bob Russell of the 2nd Devonshire Regiment takes the final salute from the balcony of the Reich Chancellery in Berlin.

FRONT AND REAR ENDPAPERS: Rewriting history in Berlin. These three plaques were erected at the Olympic Stadium to commemorate the Games in 1936 . . . but today the central one has been censored to remove any connection with the Third Reich.

PAGES 2-3: Hitler's pre-war prophecy comes true! Leading Aircraftman George Lockwood of Doncaster, a driver with an RAF photographic unit, studies a road sign erected by American forces between Aachen and Cologne.

PAGES 8-9: Hitler spricht! An extract from an address by Hitler given at a meeting of the NSDAP held in Weimar on November 6, 1938.

PAGES 58-59: Hitler with a mean bunch of Nazis at the parade held on November 9, 1938 in Munich to commemorate the deaths of the 16 Nazi martyrs in the putsch of 1923. Prominent in the front row are Wagner (Adolf), Amann, Streicher, Graf, von Brauchitsch, Raeder, Göring, Milch, Himmler and Frick.

PAGES 96-97: An SA unit in Munich on the Party Day in 1923.

PAGES 112-113: Dedication of the Horst Wessel Memorial at the graveside in Nikolai Cemetery in Berlin, January 1933.

PAGES 152-153: The Königsplatz in Munich — the symbolic heart of the Nazi Party, flanked by the twin Ehrentempel.

PAGES 166-167: Honouring the dead and dedication of the standards in the Luitpold Arena in Nuremberg on September 12, 1937.

PAGES 192-193: Torchlight processions were beloved to the Nazis. This is the Steinplatz in Bayreuth in March 1933.

PAGES 204-205: March 1933 — the SA parade through the Brandenburg Gate in Berlin.

PAGES 248-249: On Schlageter Memorial Day — May 26, 1938 — Hitler laid the foundation stone for the new factory to build his 'People's Car' — the Volkswagen.

PAGES 312-313: Such were the awful scenes at Belsen concentration camp when it was liberated by British troops in April 1945.

PAGES 354-355: Hitler the Warlord watches his troops go into battle.

PAGES 430-431
The peaceful setting of the present-day Luitpold Arena in Nuremberg, captured by American forces rather appropriately on April 20, 1945 — Hitler's birthday!

The seeds of unrest, which ultimately led to Adolf Hitler being installed as Chancellor of Germany and the birth of his Third Reich, were laid in 1919 with the signing of the Peace Treaty at Versailles. Here crowds in Berlin's Lustgaten protest at the action of the Weimar government on the 'Tag von Versailles': June 28.

Acknowledgements

The author is indebted to the following individuals and organisations for their assistance in the production of this volume.

Oberstleutnant Holger App, Sanitätsakademie der Bundeswehr, München; Professor Jay W. Baird, Columbia University, Ohio; Walter Bartl, Stadtarchiv Bayreuth; Florian Beierl, Zeitgeschichtliches Archiv Berchtesgaden; Roger Bell; Imme van den Berg; Robert Bierschneider, Staatsarchiv München; Margot Blank, Deutsch-Russisches Museum Karlshorst; Doris Bohm, Kreismuseum Wewelsburg; Herr Bömerl, Stadtmuseum München; Kapitänleutnant Dirk Brüne, Marineschule Mürwik, Flensburg; Fregattenkapitän Roland Bühner, Marineschule Mürwik, Flensburg; Hans-Peter Busch, Stadtarchiv Erwitte; Henk van Capelle; Dr Klaus Dettmer, Landesarchiv Berlin; Andreas Ehresmann, KZ-Gedenkstätte Neuengamme; Stefan Erichsen, Polizei Flensburg; Wilfried Engelbrecht, Historisches Museum Bayreuth; Helmuth Euler; Michael Foedrowitz; Willi Fischer; Frau Friedrich, Standesamt Halberstadt; Ulrich Fritz, KZ-Gedenkstätte Flossenbürg; Harko Gijsbers and René Kok of the Nederlands Instituut voor Oorlogsdocumentatie; Hauptmann Hartmut Happel, Generaloberst-Beck-Kaserne Sonthofen; Jan Heitmann; Ole Hertel, Olympiastadion, Berlin; Frau Hoffmann, KZ-Gedenkstätte Ravensbrück; Rob Hopmans; Monika Hövelmann, Stadtarchiv Wesel; Herr Huber, Friedhofverwaltung München; Herr Ingenpass, Stadtarchiv Essen; Klaus Janetzki, Landesarchiv Berlin; Frau Kahlefeld, Deutsches Historisches Museum, Berlin; Waltraud Käss, Bundesarchiv Berlin; Volker Knopf; E. Kremers, Stadtarchiv Krefeld; Dr Klaus Lankheit, Institut für Zeitgeschichte, München; Karl Heinz Leder; Saskia Lelieveld; Christoph Links, Ch. Links Verlag, Berlin; Oberstleutnant Uwe Löffler, Wehrbereichkommando IV (München); Andreas Matschenz, Landesarchiv Berlin; Bernd Mayer, Bayreuth; Frans Mekers; Heinrich Meyer, Stadtarchiv Kirchenlamitz; Andrew Mollo; Hauptbootsmann Ralph Neumann, Presse- unf Informationszentrum Marine, Glücksburg; Jean Paul Pallud; Peter Plenk; Sebastian Remus; Klaus Rheinfurth, Institut für Stadtgeschichte Frankfurt; Dr Martin Roelen, Stadtarchiv Kleve; Hans Jürgen Rolle; Rolf Sawinski; Herr Scheunemann, Olympiastadion Berlin; Christian Schmidt; Eberhard Schmidt, Wehrgeschichtliches Ausbildungszentrum, Marineschule Mürwik, Flensburg; 1ste Sergeant Chef Georg Schmitz, Kamp Vogelsang; Dr Dietmar Sedlaczek, KZ-Gedenkstätte Moringen; Frits Stol; Hans Swetlik, Fleinhausen; Bert Thisse, Stadtarchiv Kleve; Dr Bernhard Trefz, Stadtarchiv Backnang; Oberstleutnant Klaus Treude, Wehrbereichkommando IV (München); Andrea Trudewind, Stadtarchiv Düsseldorf; Bernd Wagner, Stadtarchiv Bielefeld, and not forgetting the late Bart Vanderveen.

5939

Contents

Introduction

Some sixty years have elapsed since the cataclysmic demise of Adolf Hitler and his Third Reich. In this book we trace the rise of Hitler, the Nazi Party and its ramifications, together with its deeds and accomplishments, during the twelve years that the Third Reich existed within today's boundaries of the Federal Republics of Germany and Austria.

The factors, circumstances, beliefs and feelings that engendered this extraordinary phase of European history have largely vanished in the course of time. Many of the Nazis' ideas sprang from the previous century, such as a consciousness of German unity, the development of a national pride, the belief in Teutonic racial supremacy, the need for the population explosion to be accommodated by expansion to the east, etc. The failure of the German High Command to publically acknowledge defeat in 1918 that gave rise to the 'stab in the back' theory, the collapse of the Hohenzollern and Habsburg dynasties, the rise of Communism, the punitive measures of the Versailles Treaty, and then the devastating effects of the Great Depression of the 1920s, all contributed to a great upheaval in the basic structure of German society that spawned the tenets of the Nazi Party. The losers of the First World War became the bully-boy beer hall warriors of the 1920s, and it was their families that came to pay the cost with the fear-

Left: **Hamburg, 1945. Paul Bebert, the Chairman of the Association of German Building Unions, symbolically removes the swastika and gear-wheel emblem on the former administrative building of the Deutsche Arbeitsfront.** *Right:* **Now the HQ of the Deutscher Gewerkschaftsbund (DGB — German Trade Unions Confederation).**

some losses on the battlefields of the Second World War, the bombing of the homeland and finally the enforced resettlement of millions.

In the immediate post-war period, the Allied Control Commissions failed to expunge Nazis entirely from the administration of these countries, because everyone had been involved and was tainted with the old system. Consequently those in authority were able to whitewash the immediate past with an

The building, located at Nos. 56-59 Besenbinderhof, close to the main railway station, was occupied by British troops on the first day of their arrival in Hamburg. On September 13, 1945, the British City Commandant Colonel Harry Armytage, handed Paul Bebert a hammer and chisel with the words: 'As an old trade unionist, strike the first blows against these symbols of National Socialism'.

educational tabu on the subject, but these people have now gone and the subsequent generations have had the opportunity to discover for themselves what their past entails.

Despite the continued existence of neo-Nazi groups in both countries, the majority of today's citizens of Germany and Austria hold little in common with the aspirations of their forebears, and find it hard to believe that they did what they did. Modern communications, freedom of the press and a democratic form of government answerable to the individual as much as to the mass have replaced the old ideas.

But if the emotional and political traces of the Third Reich have largely dissolved, many physical traces still survive, noticeably the autobahns and ubiquitous People's Car, the Volkswagen. Hitler's favourite hideaway, the Obersalzburg, has been largely stripped of anything that could promote a Nazi shrine and Martin Bormann's shelter tunnels have been converted into a Third Reich docmentation centre. The road up to the Kehlstein and the teahouse that he had built for Hitler now provide an opportunity for countless visitors from all over the world to view the magnificent scenery from what is now generally known as 'The Eagle's Nest'. But, as I experienced myself, a glimpse of two young men on the Kehlstein road, complete with Lederhosen, 1930's haircuts and calfskin-covered backpacks, can still jolt one back to a different era.

TONY LE TISSIER, 2005

Historical facts are suppressed in Germany, even when no swastika is involved. It seems that the name 'Adolf Hitler' itself is anathema as illustrated by the replacement of the panel commemorating the 1936 Olympic Games. Note how history has been rewritten: Hitler's name has gone as has that of the President of the German Olympic Committee, von Tschammer und Osten. On a second panel — see endpapers — Hitler's name has been replaced by the anonymous 'Reichsregierung' as the builder of the Reichssportfeld. Nazi minister Dr Frick and State Secretary Pfundtner as 'Gesamtleitung' (overall leadership) have become 'Reichsbauverwaltung' represented by Karl Reichle. Only March and Sponholz remain.

Expunging the swastika image was all part of the de-Nazification programme and today it is against the law to display the emblem in Germany. So one can imagine the reaction when, after reunification in 1990, this throwback to the 1930s was discovered in a forest at Zernikow in East Germany. The authorities lost no time in felling the offending trees.

ADOLF HITLER AND THE THIRD REICH

My faith in the German people has been wonderfully justified: I am so proud and happy that I can be your leader.

In these last weeks our German people has displayed just as splendid a picture of resolute determination as that which I came to know in the critical periods of the War: no nervousness, no haste, no uncertainty, no feeling of despair, but confidence, and loyal following of its leaders.

Every single man and every single woman knew that Fate might demand of us the supreme hazard. To this unity and to this calm we owe it that we were spared this supreme hazard.

Fate did not call us into the lists because it knew that we were strong. That knowledge we would take with us as our lesson for all time. Then nothing can harm our beloved Germany — not now, nor for all eternity. Germany, Sieg Heil!

ADOLF HITLER, WEIMAR, NOVEMBER 6, 1938

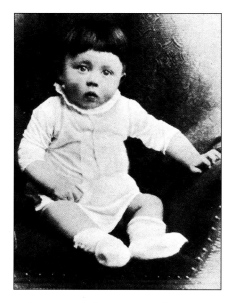

The Making of a Dictator

The Third Reich was the inspiration of one man, Adolf Hitler, who so came to dominate the German people that they 'worked toward the Führer' to make it possible. His dream was of a splendid and greater German empire, in which the German people would display their true heroic values as masters of their world and their fate. It would reverse all the ills and suffering of post Great War Germany and set them on a new course of glory. Unlike its predecessors, it would last a thousand years.

The First Reich, otherwise known as the Holy German Empire, had lasted from 962 to 1806. It had originated as a regal sub-division of Charlemagne's own vast empire of a hundred years earlier, achieving imperial status with the crowning as emperor of its elected King Otto I ('the Great') following the annexure of most of Italy with papal connivance. It ended with Napoleon's invasion of Prussia.

The Second Reich had been the achievement of Prussian Chancellor Otto von Bismarck, who managed to combine the various German states into waging a victorious war against the French that enabled him to have King Wilhelm I of Prussia proclaimed Emperor of Germany in the Hall of Mirrors at Versailles on January 18, 1871. It ended when Emperor Wilhelm II abdicated on November 9, 1918, following the defeat of the Germany Army in the field and widespread mutiny, revolt and revolution in the country.

Who then was this man that alone could inspire a dream that would turn the world upside down?

Adolf Hitler was born on April 20, 1889, in the Austrian village of Braunau, just across the river Inn from Germany. His father, born Alois Schicklgruber (1837-1903), had changed his name to Hitler in 1876, and his mother, Klara, née Pölzl (1860-1907), was Alois's third and much younger wife. Although of humble beginnings, Alois had made a successful career in the imperial Austrian customs service and was a typical civil servant of that time; an opinionated authoritarian and disciplinarian, pompous, humourless and, in his case, with little time for his family.

Klara, on the other hand, was a kindly, submissive woman, who had already lost three children of her marriage before Hitler was born. She subsequently bore two more children, Edmund, who also died in infancy, and Paula, who survived until 1960. Also in the household and well cared for and loved by Klara were Alois Jr. and Angela, children of Alois's previous marriage. Klara was supported in her duties by her unmarried sister, Johanna, and a living-in maidservant. The image of a comfortable middle-class existence, however, was marred by the intemperance of her brutal husband toward herself and particularly toward Adolf, who had inherited the same indomitable will and who was regularly beaten for his misdemeanours.

Top: **Birthplace of a dictator. On April 20, 1889, Klara Hitler gave birth to her son Adolf *(top left)* in this inn, the Gasthof des Josef Pommer, at No. 15 Salzburger Vorstadt in the Austrian border town of Braunau-am-Inn. At the time, Adolf's father Alois was a customs official at the border post with Germany, which lies just 500 metres away by the Inn river. The family rented a flat on the first floor. The household at this time consisted of six people: Alois and Klara; the two children from Alois' second marriage (Klara was his third wife), Adolf's half-brother Alois junior (born 1882) and half-sister Angela (born 1883); baby Adolf; and, living in with the family, Klara's unmarried sister Johanna Pölzl, known to all as 'Hannitante' (Auntie Hanna).**

Except for a few minor alterations, Hitler's birthplace stands unchanged. Salzburger Vorstadt is actually an extension beyond the old city gate of the town's central square.

Left: With the rise of the Nationalsozialistische Deutsche Arbeiterpartei (NSDAP, the German National Socialist Workers' Party), the house quickly became a Nazi shrine. In 1932, the German and Austrian Sturmabteilung (SA, Storm-troopers) organised a march past. The following year the Austrian NSDAP as a separate body was disbanded. *Above:* The building still remains standing on Salzberger Vorstadt.

Left: Having left Austria for Germany in 1913, Hitler (save for a few quick visits) did not return to his native country until after the Anschluss (union) of Austria with the German Reich which took place on March 12, 1938, by which time he had become Führer and Chancellor of Germany. First stop on his victorious journey to the capital Vienna, where he was to announce the 'return of his Heimat into the German Reich', was Braunau. That Saturday, following in the wake of the troops, he drove across the bridge over the Inn river that formed the border between the two countries and which leads directly on to the town's central Stadtplatz where he received a rapturous welcome from the ecstatic population. Hitler's motorcade slowly made its way past the house, although it did not stop. *Right:* The steel bridge, blown in 1945, has been replaced by a modern concrete span and the Inn river once again marks the border between Germany and Austria.

Ever since the war the municipality of Braunau has been uncomfortable over the dubious honour of hosting Hitler's birthplace and at a loss to know what to do about the building in which he was born. After 1945 it served in turn as a school, a bank and a library, and is currently a workshop for disabled people. In 1989, with fears of neo-Nazis planning to turn Hitler's upcoming 100th birthday into a demonstration, it was decided to erect a memorial in front of the house. The granite for the memorial came from the quarry at the former Mauthausen concentration camp, the inscription reading: 'For Peace, Freedom and Democracy. Never again Fascism. Millions of Dead serve as a Warning.' In 2000, still not happy with its legacy but wanting to show that Austria and Braunau are today prepared to confront their history head on, the town announced plans to turn the building into a Centre of International Understanding, where people can learn about the past and draw lessons from it.

In 1892, when Adolf was three, the family moved to Passau, on the German side of the border, where his father had been posted. After Alois' retirement from the Customs Service in 1895, the family moved back to Austria, settling in the hamlet of Hafeld (Fischlham community) near Lambach, where Alois had bought a farm and planned to increase his pension by starting up an inn and an apiary.

Alois's profession entailed frequent changes of residence, but by late 1898 the family had settled down in the small village of Leonding, just south-west of Linz, Alois (who by then had retired) having bought a small house at No. 16 Michaelsbergstrasse. These frequent moves had an effect on Adolf's attitude toward his schooling. He attended three

Decidedly unsuccessful at both, within two years he sold the farm *(above)* and moved to an intermediate house in Lambach.

Left: In late 1898, the family settled down in Leonding, a small village of 3,000 souls just south-west of Linz, where Alois had bought this small house at No. 16 Michaelsbergstrasse, with a nice garden where he could nurture his hives. By then the household counted seven persons. Klara had given birth to two more children, Edmund (born 1894 but died 1900) and Paula (born 1896), but 14-year-old Alois junior had fallen out with his tyrannical father and moved out. This meant Adolf now had to bear the brunt of his father's discipline and wrath. A scrubby,

thin-faced little rogue, he challenged his father to extremes of rudeness and consequently received a sound thrashing every day, while his protective mother (who sometimes got beaten up herself) tried to caress the boy and keep peace in the house. To offset the overheads, Alois let one room of the house to a woman named Elisabeth Plöckinger. *Right:* Standing directly across the street from the rear entrance of the village cemetery, the house on Michaelsbergstrasse has found a new use as the cemetery office.

different primary schools in turn, not making friends but tending to dominate and lead the other pupils. By the time he started his secondary education in 1900 at the Realschule in Linz he was becoming indifferent toward his teachers, one of whom later described him as 'a thin, pale youth, a boy not making full use of his talent, lacking in application, and unable to accommodate himself to school discipline.' In recollection of this time, Adolf was scathing of his teachers except for the history master, who had fired his imagination with tales of heroism from the German past, the German-nationalist feeling being particularly strong in Linz.

At the same time friction increased with his father, who wanted him to take up a career in the civil service, but to follow in his father's footsteps was anathema to Hitler, who announced that he wanted to be an artist, which only enraged his father further. Alois died suddenly in January 1903, the same year that Hitler was obliged to change schools because of his poor performance to one in Steyr, 18 miles away. There however, after only two years, Hitler left school at the age of sixteen without graduating.

Young Adolf, now nine, attended the local village school where this class photo was taken in 1899 (Hitler top row, centre). The following year, he went to the Realschule (secondary school) at nearby Linz.

Right: **Four decades later, on Sunday, March 13, 1938 (the day after he had passed through Braunau), Hitler made a stop at Leonding, not so much to see his childhood home but more to visit his parents' grave. Alois Hitler had died in 1903 and Klara Hitler in 1907 and both lay buried in the village churchyard. Together with his valet, Heinz Linge, Hitler walked to the grave with a wreath, then told Linge and the rest of his staff to retire telling them he wanted a few moments of his own. After placing the wreath against the gravestone, he stood in a contemplative stance, long enough for Heinrich Hoffmann, the Führer's personal photographer, to take several pictures.** *Below:* **Time has stood still in St Michael's Churchyard . . . at peace like any other cemetery. The Hitler family grave is still there, always well tended and adorned with flowers deposited by unknown hands.**

Left: **As Hitler drove away, Hoffmann pictured his Mercedes-Benz passing his old home.** *Right:* **How many people today would realise who once lived in this simple dwelling.**

13

Unlike primary school where he had done well right from the start, young Adolf performed poorly in secondary school, especially in mathematics, natural history and French. Consequently, early in 1904, due to continued bad marks, he was asked to leave. However, determined to give her boy a good education, his mother sent him to the next-nearest Realschule, which was at Steyr, 18 miles to the south. To pay for his boarding cost, she sold the house in Leonding and moved to Linz, to a two-room apartment on the third floor of No. 31 Humboldtstrasse (right). Nevertheless Hitler failed to make the grade at the new school and, when in addition he acquired a lung illness, his mother allowed him to quit school altogether and return home where for the next two years, coddled by her love, he indulged in idleness, doing little more than going out for walks, reading . . . drawing . . . enjoying the local theatre .

Hitler as a 16-year-old, sketched by his schoolmate F. Sturmberger.

The cost of living forced Klara to sell the Leonding house and in 1905 they moved to Linz, to a rented flat at No. 31 Humboldtstrasse, where Hitler then spent two years of indulged idleness, doing a little drawing, painting and reading, and attending the theatre or opera in the evenings, thereby developing a passion for Wagner. Typically, his reading was confined to works that confirmed his own preconceptions, and did nothing to improve or expand his knowledge. The indolence, fantasising and lack of discipline for systematic work that characterised this period in his life were all to be repeated in later years.

In September 1907 Hitler left home for Vienna with the intention of obtaining a place at the Academy of Visual Arts, despite the fact that his mother was dying from cancer. However, he twice failed the entrance examination and was advised that his future lay in architecture.

His mother died in 1907, leaving him enough money to support him for another year of indolence in Vienna, but for the following five years Hitler had to live off charity, odd jobs and the proceeds from peddling his drawings around the city's cafes. At first he took a room at No. 31 Stumpergasse, then in

November 1908 moved to No. 22 Felberstrasse near the Westbahnhof. He moved again to No. 58 Sechshäuser Strasse in August 1909 for a month before his money finally ran out. He disappeared in the underworld of poverty, wandering the streets of Vienna as a tramp and sleeping in parks, doorways and, when it got colder, in bars and dingy 'warming rooms'. By that Christmas he was in the new doss-house at No. 2 Asylallee in the Meidling district before eventually securing a place in the more congenial men's home at Nos. 25-27 Meldemannstrasse, where he was to remain for the rest of his time in Vienna.

In September 1907, at the age of 18, Hitler left the family home and moved to the capital Vienna with the ambition of enrolling in the Academy of Visual Arts and becoming an artist. He found a boarding room at No. 31 Stumpergasse in the Mariahilf shopping district. His landlady was Maria Zakreys, an unmarried Czech seamstress, whom he paid ten crowns a month for a ten-metre-square basement cubicle in the backyard, his room being Staircase No. 2, Basement Floor, Room No. 17. Rejected at the entrance examination to the Academy in early October, Hitler returned to Linz to nurse his mother, whose health had taken a

sudden turn for the worse. He remained there until she died on December 21, 1907. In February 1908, he returned to Vienna and Stumpergasse. Shortly after, at his insistent requests, his best friend from Linz, 18-year-old August Kubizek (right), arrived in Vienna to study music and moved in with Hitler, the two young men convincing Frau Zakreys to rent them a larger room. In his 1953 memoirs Adolf Hitler. Mein Jugendfreund, Kubizek mistakenly gave the house number as 29 instead of 31 and because of this many have photographed the wrong house. In our picture (left) No. 31 is on the right and No. 29 on the left.

In August 1908, Kubizek returned to Linz for the summer vacation, but with the understanding that they would keep the shared lodgings. The following month Hitler was again rejected by the Academy and on November 18, without notifying Kubizek, he moved to a new address, No. 22 Felberstrasse *(left)* in the 15th District, where he rented room No. 16 from Frau Helene Riedl. Here he would stay until August 20, 1909. Having already squandered the inheritance from his mother and loans from his 'Hannitante', by the late summer of 1909 Hitler's financial situation was getting desperate. On August 20, he moved to No. 58 Sechshäuser Strasse *(right)*, where he rented room No. 21 on the first floor from Frau Antonia Oberlechner. Four weeks later, unable to pay his rent, he fled from his lodgings. For the next five months he lived as a vagabond on the streets of Vienna, wearing tattered clothes and sleeping rough on park benches.

Above: **During the winter — mid-September 1909 to early February 1910 — he found a bed at the huge Asyl für Obdachlose (Asylum for the Homeless) at No. 2 Asylgasse in the Meidling district. Run by a philanthropic society whose principal supporter was the Jewish Epstein family, it was originally built in 1870 but had recently been extensively reconstructed and it had just re-opened the year before. Spotlessly clean and efficiently run, its facilities included spacious dormitories with numbered beds lined in military precision, numerous showers and toilets, and a large dining hall serving soup with bread. Each day applicants had to queue up at the entrance to gain a ticket, sometimes valid for just one night, sometimes for longer periods. It was during this period that Hitler began producing watercolours and picture postcards for a living. Striking a deal with another down and out, Reinhold Hanisch, he would paint while Hanisch would attempt to sell his works in cafes, the returns being shared fifty-fifty. Thus, slowly, Hitler began earning some money.**

Asylgasse is today named Kastanienallee. The former asylum is still in use as a hostel for homeless families.

Left: **By February 1910 the sales of his paintings had earned Hitler enough to enable him to rent a room in the huge Männerheim (Men's Home) at Nos. 25-27 Meldemannstrasse in the working-class district of Brigittenau in the north-western part of the city.**

Opened in 1905, the modern new facility could accommodate 544 single men. Here he stayed from February 9, 1910, to May 25, 1913. *Right:* **Now nearly a century old, the building on Melde-mannstrasse is today used as quarters for homeless men over 18.**

Above: **Unlike the other domiciles connected with his early life — in Braunau, Leonding, and later in Munich — none of Hitler's lodgings in Vienna were ever turned into shrines by Nazi propaganda during the Third Reich era. In fact, in what was clearly an attempt to cover up his time as a tramp in Vienna, right from the Anschluss Goebbels' propagandists began publicising a house where Hitler had never lived, No. 11 Simon-Denk-Gasse in the bourgeois 19th District, as the place where the Führer reputedly had had his lodgings as a young man. The house entrance was adorned with a wreath and a large portrait and Hitler Youth stood as guards of honour outside. This picture appeared on the front page of most illustrated newspapers. To erase traces of his true Viennese addresses, the NSDAP even confiscated all his original change-of-address notices from the city's registrar's office.**

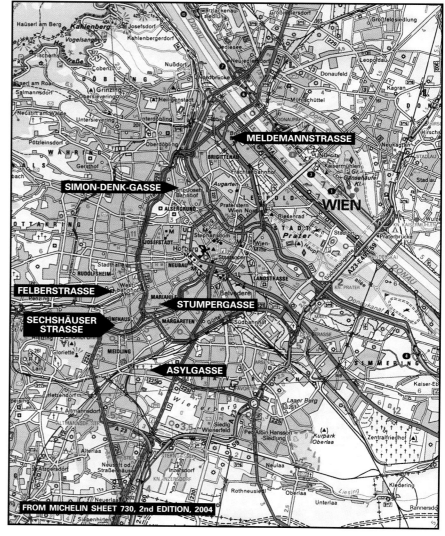

These are the locations associated with Hitler's five years' sojourn in Vienna.

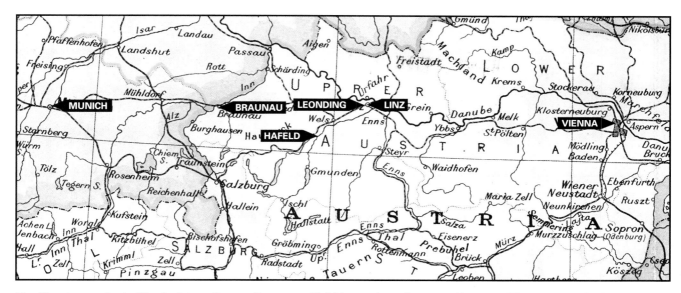

Significant stages in the life of a future dictator: Braunau to Hafeld . . . to Leonding . . . to Linz . . . to Vienna . . . and finally to Munich.

In May 1913 Hitler moved to Munich in order to avoid military service in the Austrian Army and continued his Bohemian existence there. He found accommodation at No. 34 Schleissheimer Strasse in a poor district in the northern part of the city, making a modest living out of the sales of his watercolours, and discussing politics with those he encountered in the cafes.

On January 18, 1914 he was shocked to receive a summons from Linz to answer charges for failing to register for military service. However, his apologetic attitude and desolate condition engaged some sympathy for his case and he was eventually released as unfit for duty.

Left: **Having decided to emigrate to Germany, Hitler quit Vienna and Austria for good on May 25, 1913. Together with a 20-year-old friend from the men's home, Rudolf Häusler, he travelled by train to Munich, where they rented a shared room on the third floor above Joseph Popp's tailor's shop situated at**

No. 34 Schleissheimer Strasse. Here the two men would live for the next nine months until Häusler was able to obtain a room of his own on February 15, 1914. *Right:* **The façade of No. 34 has been modernised, but the house on the right provides the link with the past.**

Above: One reason for Hitler's emigration from Austria was that he wanted to dodge military service in the Austrian Imperial Army. However, the Austrian authorities caught up with him and he was forced to report to Salzburg for a medical examination on February 15 (the same day that Häusler moved out), but he was rejected on grounds of poor health. Nevertheless, with the outbreak of the First World War on August 1, 1914, Hitler was one of a large enthusiastic crowd which assembled on Munich's Odeonsplatz to celebrate the declaration of war. Heinrich Hoffmann, then a local press photographer, recorded the event. Years later, when Hoffmann had become a close friend of Hitler, he told him that he had been there with his camera and, after a meticulous search, they picked him out. With an enlargement of Hitler inset in the corner, the picture was circulated widely in pre-war Germany. *Below:* Today Odeonsplatz remains completely unchanged.

Serving on the Western Front, in July 1916 Hitler was billeted at a butcher's shop at No.1345 Rue Faidherbe in the village of Fournes-en-Weppes.

On April 20, 1942, on the occasion of the Führer's 53rd birthday, a commemorative plaque was fixed to the front façade of the house. This was removed in 1944 and for years it stood stored and forgotten in the owner's garden shed but now it has been put on display in the war museum at nearby Fromelles which lies south-west of Lille in northern France.

Today the shop (at what is now No. 966) is closed with the windows bricked up but the four holes in the brickwork where the plaque was mounted can still be seen.

Seven months later, on August 2, 1914, he was one of the emotional crowd on the Odeonsplatz that greeted the declaration of war, going on to write a personal petition to King Ludwig III to serve as an Austrian in the Bavarian Army, which was approved. On August 16 he was called up and eventually assigned to Bavarian Reserve-Infanterie-Regiment 16, otherwise known as the Regiment List, which trained near Augsburg until sent to Flanders in late October, where it suffered 70 per cent casualties within the first week of active service.

In November 1914 Hitler was promoted corporal, his last promotion of the war, and assigned to the regimental staff as a runner, and one month later was awarded the Iron Cross Second Class. He was wounded in the left thigh by shell-fire in October 1916 and was away from his regiment for four months. Then on August 4, 1918, he was awarded the Iron Cross First Class for

delivering a message under exceptionally hazardous conditions. That October he became a victim to a mustard gas attack and was evacuated to Pasewalk

in Pomerania, where while recovering from temporary blindness he learned of Germany's defeat and the outbreak of revolution.

Hitler (seated on the right) pictured with some of his comrades in the garden of the local tax office which lay further down Rue Faidherbe and which was then in use as an infirmary.

Hitler revisited the house on June 26, 1940, during a sentimental tour of the World War I battlefields (see *After the Battle* No. 117). Heinrich Hoffmann pictured him posing in front of the same wall with two of his old comrades from Infanterie-Regiment 16, Ernst Schmied (left) and Max Amann (centre).

The exact spot where this well-known set of 'then and now' pictures had been taken proved elusive until Jean Paul Pallud found the site in 2002. Here, Françis Delattre and André Daumars of the Fromelles Museum, who helped him discover it, stand in for Schmied and Amann.

After he returned to Munich at the end of World War I, Hitler, still in the military, lived in the barracks of Infanterie-Regiment 2 at No. 29 Lothstrasse. Here he experienced the turmoil of the short-lived Communist revolution that was crushed by right-wing forces in May 1919. Arrested and questioned by the Communists, after his release, he became a spy and informer for the new military authority. It was at the Lothstrasse barracks that he first read a pamphlet of the fledgling Deutsche Arbeiterpartei (DAP) that later became the NSDAP, and he enrolled on September 12. Today, the barracks have been replaced by a modern office building, but the obelisk honouring the men of Infanterie-Regiment 2 still stands across the street.

He returned to a Munich seething with demobilising troops and in a state of political upheaval, the monarchy having been overthrown and a socialist interim government about to be replaced by a communist one only to be bloodily overthrown by the Reichswehr and Freikorps forces of the extreme right. He was first employed guarding a POW camp outside Munich until January 1919, before returning to become one of a group of 26 political instructors that the Army trained to indoctrinate returning prisoners of war and demobilising troops with anti-revolutionary, pro-national and anti-Semitic ideas. Hitler performed outstandingly well in this role, thus securing his position on the Army payroll until the end of March 1920. In August 1919 he was ordered to attend and report on a meeting of the Deutsche Arbeiterpartei (DAP — German Workers' Party) in the Sterneckerbräu inn, as a consequence of which he joined that party and soon became its leading speaker.

Hitler specialised as a propagandist, projecting what in effect were unoriginal ideas using simplicity of expression and repetition to ram his points home.

Left: **On April 1, 1920, Hitler — jobless but calling himself a writer — moved out of the barracks and into a sub-let room at No. 41 Thierschstrasse, where he would live for the next nine years — until then his longest stay in one place. His first room was a tiny unheated back cubicle on the first floor but later he moved to a somewhat larger room, though equally spartan, with just a bed, a makeshift bookshelf, a few drawings on the walls and worn linoleum on the floor. In 1933, a plaque was** affixed to the house which proclaimed that 'Adolf Hitler lived in this house from May 1 [sic],1920 to October 5, 1929'. (Ironically, the building at No. 41 was owned by a Jewish textile merchant, Hugo Erlanger. In 1935, the Nazis forced him to sell the property and during the 1938 Kristallnacht pogroms made him move out.) *Right:* **Although the plaque has gone, the house still stands practically unchanged. The former chemist shop on the ground floor is now a jeweller's.**

He wanted the Germans to expand their nationalistic consciousness to enable the reversal of the great 'betrayal' of November 1918 and the development of Germany into a world power. To achieve this, Germany's internal enemies had first to be destroyed, particularly the Jews, whom he never failed to attack in a most virulent manner.

As its most effective speaker, Hitler was soon able to impose his leadership and the leadership principle upon what became the Nationalsozialistische Deutsche Arbeiterpartei (NSDAP — National Socialist German Workers' Party), not hesitating to use histrionics to get his way. In July 1921 he even resigned his party membership as one of his ploys, only to rejoin two weeks later. He wanted the NSDAP, which was then only one of several minor Bavarian political parties, to be recognised and gladly accepted the notoriety associated with the beer hall violence that accompanied their meetings, and in August 1921 founded the strong-arm protection squad that was to evolve into the SA — the Sturm-Abteilung (Storm Detachment).

The expansion of the Party and the SA was greatly accelerated by the events of 1923. In January the French and Belgians occupied the Ruhr on the pretext of a default in reparation payments, a move that deeply offended nationalist sentiment. This was followed by the collapse of the currency, leading to the impoverishment and ruin of many; yet another intolerable experience for the German population. The anger and frustration this brought about led to considerable activity among the extreme right wing nationalist paramilitary groups, in which Hauptmann Ernst Röhm played a prominent role, eventually leading to the foundation of the Deutscher Kampfbund (German Combat League), which included the NSDAP and its SA, under the patronage of the Bavarian Reichswehr, which provided arms and military training. The League took centre stage at the Deutsche Tag (German Day) Rally of nationalist paramilitary organisations at Nuremberg in September 1923, when an estimated 100,000 attended and Hitler was one of the speakers. Significantly, Hitler was appointed the League's political leader, which brought him into top-level discussions at state and Reich level.

Despite there being a common nationalist cause that saw Bavaria saving Germany by removing the Berlin government by force, the key participants saw different ways of achieving this and even had different aims. It was this confused background, together with the lack of planning and preparation, that led to the collapse of Hitler's attempted 'putsch' of November 8/9, 1923 (see pages 98-111).

Hitler was arrested on the evening of November 11 and eventually taken to Landsberg Prison, where he was allotted Cell No. 7. The League's paramilitary organisations were disarmed and dissolved, but the triumvirate only lasted a few more months before a regular government took over in Munich.

'Speakers Corner' in Munich! This early picture of Hitler expounding his views was taken on the Marsfeld — the aptly-named Field of Mars — on January 28, 1923 during the first Party rally (see page 101). By now Hitler was the unchallenged leader of the NSDAP having ousted Anton Drexler as chairman two years before. Defying a ban on demonstrations by the Bavarian police president, he went ahead with the rally, the main theme being to protest against the French occupation of the Ruhr that had taken place two weeks before.

At his trial, Hitler was allowed to steal the limelight by a sympathetic court. On April 1, 1924, he was sentenced to five year's imprisonment for high treason, together with a fine of 200 Gold Marks.

His imprisonment involved no hardships, for Hitler was treated as an honoured guest by his jailors and was allowed considerable privileges, attended by his henchmen and entertaining numerable visitors. As before in his youth, he only read those books that confirmed his already existing convictions, and set to work on the first volume of his autobiographical political treatise *Mein Kampf.*

He was released at noon on December 20, 1924, and returned to his apartment at No. 41 Thierschstrasse in Munich. Hitler then remained politically inactive for a while as he waited for the ban on his speaking in public to be lifted, but he was now firmly resolved to pursue power legally through the otherwise detested democratic system, and this brought him into conflict with revolutionaries like Röhm of the SA, who felt obliged to leave.

This was a lean period for the Nazi Party as it struggled to expand. Although there were still some two million unemployed, American credits released by the Young Plan brought Germany relative prosperity for the first time since the Great War.

Looking from Marsfeld (now known as Marsplatz) into Marsstrasse today. The old Infantry School building visible in the background of the 1923 picture has been replaced by a new telecommunications building. The large building across the street is the Wittelsbacher Gymnasium.

In October 1929, by now having risen from a poor political agitator to a promising politician and enjoying the financial backing of rich industrialists, Hitler was able to move to one of the most fashionable parts of Munich, the Bogenhausen district on the east bank of the Isar river, where he rented a handsome flat at No. 16 Prinz-regentenplatz. His nine-room apartment covered the entire second floor of the building. To keep house for him, he brought along Frau Reichert, his landlady from the Thierschstrasse, and her mother, Frau Dachs. As cook he hired Frau Anni Winter.

It was here on September 18, 1931, that the body was found of 23-year-old Angelika ('Geli') Raubal, Hitler's niece (she was the daughter of his widowed half-sister Angela), who is generally assumed to have been the only woman with whom he ever really fell truly in love.

During the summer of 1926 Hitler moved to the Obersalzberg, a mountain summer retreat outside Berchtesgaden in the Bavarian Alps, to finish the second volume of his book, which was published in 1927. The book was later to become a record-breaking best-seller during the Third Reich, bringing him vast sums in royalties as it became a 'must' in every household. He first stayed at the Pension Moritz, then moved to the Marinehaus and finally to the Deutsches Haus hotel, where he was surrounded by his cronies, including Göring, who had returned from exile. Later on he was able to purchase Haus Wachenfeld, where he had previously stayed, and installed his half-sister Angela as housekeeper.

His ban on speaking in public was lifted in most German states during 1927 but persisted in Prussia, the largest, until the autumn of 1928. Attendance at his first public meetings was disappointing, for only the hard-core fanatics remained. A growing cult of idolatry brought about the adoption of the standard greeting of 'Heil Hitler!' at the first Party rally to be held in Nuremberg in August 1927. Then in the 1928 Reichstag elections, the first to be contested by the Nazis, they gained 12 seats. The following year 39 special trains brought in 25,000 SA and SS for the rally, as well as 1,500 Hitlerjugend. But it was the Wall Street crash of October 20, 1929, that brought about the crisis that Hitler needed in order to draw popular support.

The deepening chaos of the Depression saw a rapid expansion of Party and SA membership over the next two years, drawing support from a wide cross-section of the population, and in the September 1930 Reichstag elections the Party won a remarkable 107 seats.

But political success was temporarily marred by a personal crisis when on September 19, 1931, Geli Raubal was found dead in Hitler's apartment, shot by his own pistol. Hitler had moved into a spacious apartment at No. 16 Prinz-regentenplatz in Munich in 1929, taking his niece, Angela's daughter, with him as his housekeeper. From then on they were often seen in public together, and Hitler's possessiveness and domineer-

ing attitude toward her were noted. It was suspected that Geli was trying to break away from him and may in desperation have resorted to suicide, but the true facts of the case never emerged. Hitler was on his way to Nuremberg when he heard the news, and promptly raced back in great distress. His subsequent state of intense depression lasted several days before he returned to the political arena.

The apartment building on Prinzregentenplatz stands unaffected by time.

Born at Linz on June 4, 1908, Geli had come to Germany with her mother, whom Hitler had asked to become housekeeper of his newly rented villa at Berchtesgaden, in 1925. Four years later he took the pretty 21-year-old brunette into his home (just as 53 years earlier his father Alois had taken his 16-year-old niece and wife-to-be Klara into his house), giving her a room of her own in the Munich flat. Flattered and impressed by her now famous uncle, Geli enjoyed going out with him but suffered from his hypersensitive jealousy and domestic tyranny. Although the exact circumstances of her death were never satisfactorily explained, most likely she committed suicide after a

row with 'Uncle Alf', shooting herself with his pistol when he was away. Hitler was devastated by her death. For days he was inconsolable and his friends feared that he would take his own life. Geli's death was highly embarrassing and could easily have damaged his political career, but the Bavarian Minister of Justice Franz Gürtner, a covert sympathiser of the Nazi Party, helped smooth over the scandal. Geli was quickly and secretly buried in Munich's Ostfriedhof cemetery without any official coroner's inquest having been conducted, and Gürtner forbade all further inquiries into the case by the police or the public prosecutor's office.

Shortly afterwards, her remains were exhumed and transferred to Vienna to be buried in the Zentralfriedhof on Zimmeringer Hauptstrasse in Plot 23, Row II, Grave 73. The inscription on the headstone to her grave read: 'Here sleeps our beloved child Geli. She was our ray of sunshine. Born 4 June 1908 —

died 18 September 1931. The Raubal Family'. In 1966 the whole of this plot was cleared of all the gravestones and turned into a 'Park of Rest and Strength'. Thus, although the dead still lie beneath the well-tended turf, it is now very difficult to precisely identify individual graves.

Out on the city streets meanwhile, the battles between Nazis and Communists still went on as each pursued their vendettas of hate towards each other. *Left:* **On January 22, 1933 in Berlin — just a week before Hitler achieved his goal — the SA marched provocatively on the Communist headquarters located in the Karl Liebknecht House on the Bülowplatz (see also page 128).** *Right:* **The HQ is just hidden behind the Volksbühne Theatre on the left.**

Meanwhile Hitler remained master of the Nazi Party, riding the storms of internecine warfare that arose among the leadership. In 1930 he recalled Ernst Röhm to take over as Chief-of-Staff of the SA, then assumed overall command himself, demanding oaths of allegiance from the stormtroopers.

1932 brought a series of five massive election campaigns fought intensively by the Nazi Party. The first arose as Reich President Paul von Hindenburg's term of office came to an end. Hitler reluctantly decided to compete and came a close second to von Hindenburg in the two elections that were found necessary, gaining a massive 13 million votes. But in order to compete he had first to become a German citizen and that was achieved by appointing him a civil servant in the Braunschweig administration, for which he swore the oath on February 26, 1932.

A novel feature of these campaigns was that Hitler took to flying from city to city to deliver his speeches, attracting vast crowds that waited patiently in all weather conditions for his customary late arrival.

The Reichstag elections of July 31, 1932, brought the Nazi Party 230 seats, the largest party representation in the house, but in an interview on August 13, 1932, Reich President von Hindenburg refused point-blank to appoint the bitterly disappointed Hitler Reich Chancellor.

Another Reichstag election in the autumn of that year, with the Nazi Party's funds exhausted and a poor turn-out, saw the Nazis sustain a loss of 34 seats, but Hitler was not unduly dismayed and a major upheaval in the Party with the resignation of Gregor Strasser from all his offices only went to show the strength of Hitler's position.

Now in the fourth year of the Great Depression, Germany was in dire straits with over six million unemployed, and no firm government. Franz von Papen was replaced by General Kurt von Schleicher as Reich Chancellor on December 2, 1932, and immediately began intriguing for his successor's downfall, the final outcome being Hitler's appointment to that office on January 30, 1933. Hitler had achieved his aim by legal means after all and the drastic measures he promised were not long in coming.

The torchlight procession in Berlin on the night of Monday, January 30, 1933 — the crowning glory for the king of the Nazis.

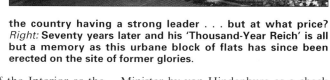

Left: **The evening of Monday, January 30, 1933 brought thousands of Berliners to the Wilhelmstrasse to applaud their new Chancellor, Adolf Hitler. After years of turmoil and political instability, at last there appeared to be the chance of** the country having a strong leader . . . but at what price? *Right:* **Seventy years later and his 'Thousand-Year Reich' is all but a memory as this urbane block of flats has since been erected on the site of former glories.**

His accession to power was celebrated by a massive torchlit parade of SA, SS and others through the streets of Berlin. His cabinet, with Hermann Göring as Minister without Portfolio and Wilhelm Frick as Minister of the Interior as the only other Nazi members, had von Papen as Vice Chancellor to add respectability. General Werner von Blomberg, who had been inserted in the role of Reichswehr Minister by von Hindenburg as a check on Hitler, proved to be a Nazi convert, and Hitler lost no time in gaining the army's support with the assurance that rearmament would be his first priority.

We are determined, as leaders of the nation, to fulfil as a national Government the task which has been allotted to us, swearing fidelity only to God, our conscience, and the nation.

The inheritance which has fallen to us is a terrible one. The task with which we are faced is the hardest which has fallen to German statesmen within the memory of man. But we are all filled with unbounded confidence, for we believe in our people and their imperishable virtues. Every class and every individual must help us to found the new Reich.

The National Government will regard it as their first and foremost duty to revive in the nation the spirit of unity and co-operation. They will preserve and defend those basic principles on which our nation has been built up. They regard Christianity as the foundation of our national morality, and the family as the basis of national life. They are determined, without regard for class and social status, to restore the nation to a consciousness of its political and national unity and of the duties consequent upon this realisation. They intend to make respect for our glorious past and pride in our ancient traditions the ground principles for the education of German youth. In this way they will wage *a pitiless warfare upon spiritual, political and cultural Nihilism. Germany must not, Germany shall not, go under in the chaos of Communism.*

Turbulent instincts must be replaced by a national discipline as the guiding principle of our national life. All those institutions which are the strongholds of the energy and vitality of our nation will be taken under the special care of the Government.

Fourteen years of Marxism have ruined Germany: one year of Bolshevism would destroy her. If, however, Germany is to experience this political and economic revival and conscientiously fulfil her duties towards the other nations, one decisive step is absolutely necessary first: the overcoming of the destroying menace of Communism in Germany.

May God Almighty give our work His blessing, strengthen our purpose and endow us with wisdom and the trust of our people, for we are fighting not for ourselves, but for Germany!

PROCLAMATION TO THE NATION, BERLIN, FEBRUARY 1, 1933

Having been appointed Reich Chancellor, Hitler poses with his 'cabinet of national concentration' which, although it included just three members of the NSDAP, was decidedly right-wing conservative. Standing L-R: Franz Seldte (Stahlhelm Party — the 'Steel Helmet' organisation of nationalistic war veterans) who was appointed Minister for Labour; Johann Ludwig Graf von Schwerin Krosigk (no party affiliation) became Finance Minister; Wilhelm Frick (NSDAP) was given the post of Minister for the Interior; Werner von Blomberg (unaffiliated) was the Defence Minister; and Alfred Hugenberg (Deutschnationale Volkspartei) took the office of Minister of Economics. Seated: Hermann Göring (NSDAP) as a Minister without Portfolio was commissioned the Interior Minister for Prussia and also Reich Commissioner for Aviation; Hitler (NSDAP), Chancellor; and Franz von Papen (currently unaffiliated, but before June 1932 belonged to Zentrumpartei). He became Vice-Chancellor and Reich Commissioner for Prussia.

Left: **Four weeks later, on February 27, Dutch anarchist Marinus van der Lubbe set fire to the Reichstag, the seat of the German parliament, this picture of the burning building being taken from beside the Brandenburg Gate. The Reichstag fire gave the Nazis** the excuse they needed to violently come down on Communists, Social Democrats and trade unions. *Right:* **Restored to its former glory and with Sir Norman Foster's spectacular glass dome completed in 1999, the building now houses the German Bundestag.**

However, his first task in office involved the dissolution of the Reichstag, the calling for new elections to confirm his position, and the passing of an Enabling Act that would allow him to govern without reference to either Parliament or President. The date of the new elections was fixed for March 5 and campaigning began immediately, but then on February 27, Marinus van der Lubbe set fire to the Reichstag, providing the opportunity for the Nazis to make a clean sweep of their political opponents.

Nazi thugs were already terrorising their opponents in those states already controlled by the Party, and particularly in Prussia, where Göring as Minister of the Interior was giving them every encouragement, but now the way was clear for the centralised persecution of their enemies. An emergency decree 'For the Protection of People and State' was promulgated the next morning, suspending indefinitely the rights of freedom of speech, of association, of the

press, and of the privacy of postal and telephone communications, and the Reich was given the authority to intervene in the autonomous Länder for the restoration of order. A massive round-up of Communists, Social Democrats, trade unionists and others began that was accompanied by savage beatings and even murder, but was accepted and even applauded by the majority of the population.

The election campaign was conducted under tremendous pressure, achieving a massive 88.8 per cent turnout of the electorate and giving the Nazis 43.9 per cent of the vote with 288 seats out of the total 647. By imprisoning the Communists (81 seats) and bullying the Social Democrats (120 seats), the Nazis hoped to get the necessary two-thirds majority for passing the Enabling Act.

The importance of propaganda as a tool of government was exemplified by the appointment of Joseph Goebbels as Minister of Popular Enlightenment and

Propaganda on March 13. Hitler himself was able to score a propaganda coup with Volkstrauertag (Remembrance Day) on Sunday, March 12, and what came to be known as 'The Day of Potsdam' on March 21, by demonstrating the union of the old Germany with the new, in having both Reichswehr and Party formations on parade with President von Hindenburg taking the salute in his uniform as a Generalfeldmarschall of the defunct Prussian Army, and using the old flags of the Second Reich instead of those of the Weimar Republic.

The very next day Himmler opened the first concentration camp at Dachau (see pages 314-321), a name that soon became dreaded throughout Germany, and on March 23 Hitler appeared in his Party uniform at the first session of the Reichstag in its new location at the Kroll Opera House to deliver a long speech in which he made electoral-type promises that were soon to be broken, but resulted in the passing of the vital Enabling Act with a majority of 441 votes to 91.

Left: **On March 21, the Nazis staged a 'Day of National Rising' at Potsdam, symbolic seat of the Prussian kings, to celebrate the birth of the Third Reich and the union of Reichswehr and Party. Here Hitler, together with von Papen and other cabinet** members, walks through the town to the main ceremony at the Garrison Church. *Right:* **One of the very few streets left untouched by the post-war changes in Potsdam, this is Schloss-Strasse with Am Neuen Markt in the right background.**

Left: **With the Reichstag a gutted shell, a new meeting place for Parliament was found at the New Opera House, better known as the Kroll Opera House, located at the other end of the large Königsplatz, directly opposite the Reichstag.** *Right:* **Heavily** **damaged in the war, the Krolloper was pulled down in March 1952 and for over four decades the site remained empty. Now, with Moltke-Strasse renamed Heinrich-von-Gagern-Strasse, the new Bundeskanzleramt (Chancellor's Office) dominates the view.**

The rapid pace of events continued as democracy as known under the Weimar Republic gave way to an authoritarian dictatorship. Meanwhile attacks on Jews, their property and institutions, had broken out all over the country, and a retaliatory threat of an international boycott of German goods by the American Jewish Congress led to a one-day German boycott of Jewish businesses on April 1. However, the German economy would not have been able to stand up to an international boycott, so the indefinite extension that had been threatened was called off. Nevertheless, the day was a portent of what the German Jews could expect from the new regime.

On April 7, 1933, the Law for the Restoration of the Professional Civil Service was promulgated, dismissing all Jews and political opponents from the civil service, although President von Hindenburg obtained an exemption for those Jews who had fought at the front. Other measures introduced that month discriminated against Jews being admitted to the legal profession, excluded them as doctors tending patients under the national insurance scheme, and limited the number of Jewish children in any school.

On May 2 all the trade unions were dissolved and replaced by the Deutsche Arbeitsfront (DAF — German Labour Front). This was followed by the banning of the Social Democratic Party and the other political parties dissolving themselves, leaving only the NSDAP, whose position was confirmed by the law of July 14, 1933, banning the formation of new political parties. During April Hitler appointed State Governors (Reichsstatthalter) to all the German Länder except Prussia, a role he later took on for himself, thus adding an undefined Party link to the existing structure that weakened the status of the Länder vis-a-vis the central government, in a process that was shortly to deprive them of their parliaments.

The process of Gleichschaltung (co-ordination) was well under way, bringing under the Party aegis every conceivable form of organised activity, most of it taking place voluntarily. There was a mad rush to join the NDSAP, especially by civil servants and teachers, and when the membership reached two and half million on May 1, 1933, a bar had to be placed taking on new members. It was in this feverish atmosphere that the burning of the books took place on May 10, when university faculties throughout the country attended the bonfires of books considered unacceptable to the new regime, by which time many distinguished academics had fled or been forced to retire, and the 'German Greeting' of 'Heil Hitler!' was in common use as the personality cult spread.

The first parliamentary session at the Kroll-Oper, suitably converted and adorned with a huge swastika backdrop, took place on March 21, the 'Tag von Potsdam', following the end of ceremonies there. Two days later, on March 23, Hitler addressed the new Parliament dressed in the brown shirt of the SA, calling for an 'Enabling Act' that would transfer the power to make laws from the Reichstag to himself as Chancellor. Parliament approved, thus legally putting an end to democracy.

The first year of a new government is a significant testing time for any administration, none the more so than for the National Socialists in 1933. Within ten years of failing miserably in his attempted coup d'etat in Munich, Hitler had achieved his goal in a bloodless legal revolution in Berlin. Dr Goebbels, the master of propaganda, hit on a new word from the Nazi dictionary to describe it: 'Machtergreifung' meaning 'Seizure of Power'. In Kiel on May 7, 1933 Hitler thanked the SA for their contribution in bringing him to power: 'You have been till now the Guard of the National Revolution; you have carried this Revolution to victory; with your name it will be associated for all time. You must be the guarantors of the victoriously completion of the Revolution, and it will be victoriously completed only if through your school a new German people is educated. If the army is the school of the German people in arms, you must form the political school so that one day from these two factors — the formation of the political will and the defence of the Fatherland — there will flow a great addition of strength. We have recognised that task and are resolved to fulfil it. You must fuse your will with mine.' It was back in May 1931 that Hitler explained what the initials 'SA' stood for — and he ought to know as it was his personal political army! 'In the beginning', said Hitler, 'the "SA" stood for "Saalschutzabteilung" — a corps for protecting the halls where National Socialist meetings were held — but later it stood for "Sport-Abteilung" before finally becoming, "Sturm-Abteilung" (Storm Detachment). However Hitler explained that 'these meanings of the letters SA were really irrelevant, for SA is a special conception and stands for itself: it has grown out of and beyond the original significations attached to the words'.

By the summer the whole outlook of the country had changed and there was a spirit of optimism about, partly engendered by an upswing in the economy that had nothing to do with the new government. A concordat had been signed with the Vatican by which the Roman Catholic clergy were to keep out of politics in exchange for tolerance from the government, stifling the basic resistance of the Catholics to the Nazi ethics and so enabling them to co-ordinate with the regime, although certain leading figures such as Bishop Clemens August von Galen of Münster continued to resist. An attempt to co-ordinate the various Protestant churches under a Reich Bishop proved an early failure and was not pursued.

A law enabling the sterilisation of persons liable to give birth to mentally retarded children or children with hereditary diseases that had been formulated the previous year was passed in July with the stipulation that the measure should be compulsory, resulting in some 400,000 persons being sterilised under this act during Hitler's reign.

Hitler took a summer break at Haus Wachenfeld on the Obersalzberg, where he was besieged by adoring tourists to the extent that Heinrich

Himmler, as police chief of Bavaria, had to introduce special traffic restrictions into the area.

By the autumn Hitler was able to turn his attention to international affairs with the removal of Germany from the League of Nations and the disarmament talks in Geneva. The failure of the western powers to react to this move led to Marshal Jozef Pilsudski of Poland suggesting an agreement with Germany, and on January 26, 1934, the two countries signed a ten-year non-aggression pact. This move, which was in effect an affront to France, went down particularly well in Germany, even with those still unfavourable to the Nazi Party, and when Hitler called for new elections for the Reichstag to be held on November 12, the NSDAP achieved a sweeping victory from a 95 per cent turn-out of the electorate. He further consolidated his position by having the Reichsrat, the Upper House, abolished on February 14, 1934.

Although still operating through a cabinet, Hitler had brought his Bavarian intimates to Berlin with him and it was noted that this sycophantic 'Chauffeureska' formed an almost impenetrable screen round him, only Goebbels, Göring and Himmler having direct access.

Hitler still had the big problem before him of settling the power controversy between the Reichswehr under its ageing and ailing commander-in-chief, President von Hindenburg, and the vast SA organisation under Ernst Röhm. The SA had been an essential instrument in the acquisition of power, but its continuing revolutionary aims were in direct conflict with the present need for the support of the Reichswehr in its traditional role as a prop for a stable government.

On a visit to the sick President on June 21, 1934, Hitler was advised to bring the revolutionary trouble-makers to reason, or the President would declare martial law and hand over control to the Reichswehr. He had no choice but to take action against Röhm. Eventually, with the connivance and persuasion of Göring and Himmler, Hitler led the raid on Röhm on June 30 that was to become known as 'The Night of the Long Knives'.

In the first half of 1934 matters came to a head between the Reichswehr and the SA. The professional 100,000-strong Reichswehr found its very existence under threat from the SA, whose numbers had been swollen to four and a half million with the recent absorption of the Stahlhelm. Organised on parallel

The SA bury one of their fallen comrades. This is the funeral in Berlin of Standarten-führer Peter Voss on April 6, 1934.

should hand over the responsibility for national defence and continue merely as a training organisation in support of the SA. The imposed threat was such that Blomberg, being anxious to secure Hitler's support for the Reichswehr, and acting on his own initiative, took counter-action by introducing the wearing of the Party's swastika emblem on armed service uniforms as a demonstration of the Reichswehr's loyalty to the new regime. He went further by having some 70 Jewish members of the officer corps discharged from the service. Only those 'non-Aryans' actively involved in the forthcoming 1936 Olympics were retained until after the event, when even those who had distinguished themselves were to be dismissed.

Then, in agreement with Hitler, the Reichswehr produced new guidelines for co-operation with the SA, which constricted the latter's activities to political, non-military matters, and which were announced in a speech made by Hitler on February 28, 1934, at a meeting of Reichswehr, SA and SS leaders. Until such time as the newly-proposed Wehrmacht should take form, the SA could temporarily be employed for

military lines under its notoriously homosexual Chief-of-Staff, Ernst Röhm, the SA now had political ramifactions that made it a considerable power in the land and the ambitious Röhm saw it as able of replacing the Reichswehr as a People's Militia.

At the Reich Party Rally in 1933, at which the SA had paraded en masse, Röhm had significantly stood alone beside Hitler, but his thinking was far from being in tune with the Party leader. In an article written in the June 1933 edition of the SA's monthly newspaper, in which Röhm's personality cult was being promoted to the exclusion of Hitler's, Röhm had written: 'The SA and the SS will not allow the German Revolution to fall asleep or be betrayed half-way there by the non-fighters. Whether they like it or not, we will carry on the struggle. If they finally grasp what it is about, with them! If they are not willing, without them! And if it has to be: against them!'

This revolutionary spirit was still very much alive among the junior ranks of the SA, many of whom were unemployed and struggling for an existence, in contrast to their seniors who had made the most of the opportunities opened to them with the acquisition of power. The continued unruly behaviour and hooliganism of its members had become an embarrassment to the government, but Hitler, who saw the revolution as complete, did nothing to either curtail them or rebuke Röhm. Instead, in December 1933, he appointed Röhm Minister without Portfolio in the government as a reward for his services. Röhm saw this merely as a step on the way toward acquiring an SA Ministry and then possibly the Ministry of Defence.

Then on February 1, 1934, Röhm had the effrontery to send Minister of Defence Blomberg a memorandum in which he suggested that the Reichswehr

> *My dear Chief-of-Staff,*
>
> *The fight of the National Socialist Movement and the National Socialist Revolution were rendered possible for me by the consistent suppression of the Red Terror by the SA. If the army has to guarantee the protection of the nation against the world beyond our frontiers, the task of the SA is to secure the victory of the National Socialist Revolution and the existence of the National Socialist State and the community of our people in the domestic sphere. When I summoned you to your present position, my dear Chief-of-Staff, the SA was passing through a serious crisis. It is primarily due to your services if after a few years this political instrument could develop that force which enabled me to face the final struggle for power and to succeed in laying low the Marxist opponent.*
>
> *At the close of the year of the National Socialist Revolution, therefore, I feel compelled to thank you, my dear Ernst Röhm, for the imperishable services which you have rendered to the National Socialist Movement and the German people, and to assure you how very grateful I am to Fate that I am able to call such men as you my friends and fellow-combatants.*
>
> *In true friendship and grateful regard,*
>
> *Your Adolf Hitler.*
>
> LETTER TO ERNST RÖHM, JANUARY 1, 1934

The cortège was photographed passing down Zietenstrasse as it neared the corner with Bülowstrasse in Schöneberg in the central part of the city.

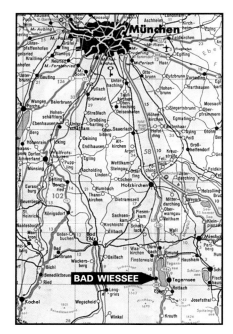

BAD WIESSEE

Within days of Hitler's glowing New Year tribute to the SA Chief-of-Staff, Röhm was manoeuvring to usurp the Reichswehr. Back in July 1933, Hitler had asserted that the SA could never take the place of, or enter into competition with, the army. And he is reported to have declared that he would act to supress any attempt to disturb the existing order as ruthlessly as he would deal with the so-called Second Revolution.

In June 1934 Hitler gave orders that the SA should go on leave for the month of July, the press release adding that Röhm was suffering from a painful nervous illness and was having time off for a cure. Meanwhile he agreed that there should be a conference of the SA leadership on June 30 to be held at a secluded hotel on the shore of the Wiessee, a lake some 50 kilometres south of Munich.

border security and pre-military training, but the Wehrmacht alone would be the nation's bearer of arms. At the conclusion of the meeting Blomberg and Röhm shook hands, but as soon as Hitler and the Reichswehr representatives had departed, Röhm was heard to say: 'What that ridiculous corporal said does not apply to us. Hitler is a traitor and should at very least be sent on leave. If we cannot get there with him, we will manage it without him!'

SA-Obergruppenführer Viktor Lutze reported this back to Hitler, who took note but was still not prepared to act, preferring to await developments. However, Göring and Rudolf Diels, the head of the Prussian Gestapo, were instructed to collect material on the SA's excesses, as did the Reichswehr on its own initiative. Then on April 20, 1934, Göring handed the Gestapo over to Himmler and the research intensified. The anti-SA conspiracy that then evolved was a co-operation between Göring, whose authority in Prussia was limited by the SA network, and Himmler, who wanted independent status for his SS from the SA. Their aim was Röhm's execution, and Reinhard Heydrich was tasked with providing the necessary evidence of high treason. At the same time the conspirators began drawing up death lists of those to be executed with Röhm.

The SA was not plotting high treason, it simply wanted to get Hitler to award it the recognition it felt it deserved as a military body in the service of the state, but Röhm's tactics of conducting a war of nerves against Hitler, touring his units with speeches about a second Nazi revolution, could not but alarm those hearing of it.

In May Hitler had cause to order the SA to stop their military exercises, which were posing an obstacle to his talks with the western powers on German rearmament, and then, after consultation with Röhm, sent the SA on leave from July 1 with orders to return to duty on August 1.

Then on June 17 Vice-Chancellor Franz von Papen made a speech at Marburg University in which he warned against a second revolution and attacked the selfishness, lack of character, insincerity, lack of chivalry and arrogance featured under the guise of the German revolution. His speech met with thunderous applause, but for Hitler this was an alarming signal that a conservative opposition still existed. Would such a candidate arise to oppose his taking over the presidential office when Hindenburg died?

Hindenburg had become seriously ill in May and retired to his estate at Neudeck in East Prussia, where Hitler went to see him on June 21. There Hitler was warned that urgent action was needed to restore peace in Germany and that if the government could not do it the President would declare martial law and call upon the Reichswehr to take over control.

Situated right on the lakeside, then it was called the Kurheim Hanselbauer but now it has been renamed the Kurhotel Lederer. The management shun anyone with interest in its former notorious history.

Röhm *(left)* **had an apartment in Munich at No. 10 Hohenzollern-strasse** *(centre). Right:* **Viktor Lutze was currently President of the Province of Hannover and also chief of police in the city.**

Hitler trusted Lutze who was privy to Röhm's aspirations and as a result he became the new leader-in-waiting of the SA. (He was killed in a road accident in May 1943.)

The situation indeed was serious. It was not just the lawlessness of the SA, but a genuine widespread distress over the continuing poor state of the economy, unemployment and the cost of food that propaganda alone could not solve. Hitler also felt himself threatened by the link between von Papen and Hindenburg. He had to act, and soon.

Next day he summoned Lutze from Hannover and told him in confidence that Röhm would have to be removed since he was holding SA leaders' conferences at which he was saying the SA would have to be armed to rescue him from the Reichswehr, whom Röhm had said were holding him prisoner.

SS and SD (Party Police) leaders were summoned to Berlin and briefed by Himmler and Heydrich on what to do should there be a revolt by the SA. Heydrich expected the danger areas to be

Bavaria, Berlin, Saxony and Silesia. The Reichswehr, now highly suspicious of the SA leadership, would provide backing for the SS with arms and transport.

Generalmajor Walter von Reichenau of the Reichswehr's Ministry Office worked out the details of the combined Reichswehr/SS plan to deal with the SA, or the 'Röhm putsch' as they now termed it. The Reichswehr was alerted and SS-Gruppenführer Josef 'Sepp' Dietrich commanding the Leibstandarte-SS 'Adolf Hitler' called to collect arms from the Ministry of Defence.

Heydrich proceeded to unleash a torrent of rumours and fabricated evidence directed at Hitler and the Reichswehr in support of the claim that Röhm was in fact planning a putsch. On June 26 the Abwehr (counter-intelligence) department of the Reichswehr received information that Röhm had issued orders to the SA for an attack on the Reichswehr.

Although the information was almost certainly false, it was passed on to Hitler with the rest.

It was while attending the wedding of Gauleiter Josef Terboven in Essen on June 28 with Göring and Lutze that Hitler received a message from Himmler that finally prompted him to take immediate action. It was to the effect that an audience had been arranged for von Papen with President von Hindeburg, and also added further anti-Röhm material to an alarmed Hitler. He returned to his room at the Hotel Kaiserhof in Essen and telephoned Röhm's adjutant summoning a meeting of the SA leaders at Bad Wiessee for 11 a.m. on the morning of June 30. At the same time the Reichswehr was placed on full alert and Göring sent back to Berlin by air to prepare for action against the SA and, if necessary, von Papen and his associates.

On June 21 Hitler had visited Göring's estate at Carinhall, north of Berlin, for the interment of the remains of Göring's first wife in a mausoleum which had been built in the grounds (see page 74). Then on the 28th he was in Essen with both Göring and

Lutze for the wedding of the local Gauleiter Josef Terboven *(left).* **Hitler and Co. were staying at the Kaiserhof Hotel which stood here at No. 6-8 Lindenallee. (Terboven blew himself up with explosives at the end of the war.)**

Next stop for Hitler was the Hotel Dreesen in Bad Godesberg on the Rhine. It would be here, three years later, that he would humiliate the British Prime Minister Neville Chamberlain during the Czechoslovakian crisis. But for the present it was one of Hitler's favourite watering holes although his stay was

rudely interrupted when news was given to him that the SA in Berlin were on the point of revolt and that demonstrations by them against his leadership were taking place — in Munich of all places. Out for revenge, Hitler immediately ordered that his aircraft be prepared for take-off.

Next morning Hitler inspected a Voluntary Labour Service Camp and sent a message to Berlin summoning 'Sepp' Dietrich to the Rheinhotel Dreesen at Bad Godesberg near Bonn, where Goebbels and Dietrich joined him that afternoon. Meanwhile rumours of unrest among the SA were being fed to Hitler by the SS, stoking the fire of his increasing anger.

Dietrich was ordered on to Munich and, when he reported his arrival there shortly after midnight, he was given further orders to take two companies of

the Leibstandarte that were due to arrive by rail at Landsberg-am-Lech, west of Munich, and be at Bad Wiessee by 11 a.m.

Meanwhile Hitler had been fed more false information regarding the SA, including a planned attack on government buildings in Berlin, when in fact most of the Berlin SA were already on leave, and their leader had gone on a cruise with his wife. He was also told that the SA had been demonstrating against the Führer and the Reichswehr on the streets of Munich. Some SA had

been out, apparently lured by some pamphlets of unknown origin, but were promptly ordered back home when their leaders heard of this.

Hitler flew to Munich in a towering rage at 2 a.m. and drove to the Bavarian Ministry of the Interior, where he sent for the local SA leaders Obergruppenführer August Schneidhuber and Gruppenführer Wilhelm Schmidt, and stripped them of their epaulettes, shouting: 'You are under arrest and will be shot!' before sending them off to Stadelheim Prison.

Arriving in Munich in the pre-dawn, he rushed straight to see Gauleiter Adolf Wagner (left), the Bavarian Minister of the Interior, at his office at No. 2 Salvatorplatz (right). By now

Hitler was in a towering rage, ordering the arrest of the first member of the SA that he set his eyes on: SA-Obergruppenführer Edmund Heines, the leader of the Upper Bavarian SA.

Without waiting for reinforcements to arrive, at 6 a.m. Sunday morning (July 1) Hitler, still seething, climbed in his Mercedes and ordered his driver Erich Kempka to head straight for Bad Wiessee. Secretary Christa Schröder and Goebbels sat in the back and two more cars brought up the rear. They covered the fifty kilometres to the Hanselbauer pension in less than an hour. *Right:* **Hitler led the way into the foyer which was deserted. When the landlady appeared she was amazed to come face to face with her Führer who immediately demanded that she lead the way up to Röhm's room.**

He then drove off in a convoy of three cars to Bad Wiessee, where Röhm and his companions were staying at the Pension Hanselbauer. Arriving at about 6.30 a.m., Hitler and his escort arrested the SA leaders, one of whom was found in bed with a young man, and confined them in the cellar until a bus could be found to take them to Stadelheim Prison. While they were waiting for the bus, Röhm's headquarters guard arrived on a truck, so Hitler stepped forward and ordered the men back to Munich. They set off but then stopped just outside the resort, presumably having second thoughts about their instructions, so Hitler took a long detour to the south to avoid them, reaching the Brown House in Munich at about 10 a.m.

There he instructed Goebbels to pass the code-word 'Kolibri' to Göring in Berlin, thus releasing the SS and the SD to the tasks of arrest and assassination contained in their sealed instructions.

At about 11 a.m. he appeared, still in a towering rage, before the SS leaders

that had not been arrested, and accused Röhm of having taken a 12-million Reichsmark bribe from the French Ambassador, saying that he would have Röhm and his six co-conspirators shot that evening.

Hitler then conferred with his close associates, including Lutze, now the new SA Chief-of-Staff, over the fate of the SA leaders. Hess wanted to shoot Röhm himself, but eventually at about 5 p.m. Hitler ordered Sepp Dietrich to form a firing squad of an officer and six men and supervise the executions at Stadelheim Prison. Bormann gave him a list of the SA prisoners, the six to be executed being marked with crosses. Röhm was not one of them.

However, when Hitler returned to Berlin at 10 p.m., Göring and Himmler were aghast at learning of Röhm's survival, which could easily have led to their own downfall, and put on the pressure for Röhm's execution and eventually prevailed on the afternoon of July 1. SS-Brigadeführer Theodor Eicke,

commandant of Dachau concentration camp, was tasked. Hitler still wanted to give his old friend a chance, so Röhm was left alone with a loaded pistol, but failed to take the 'honourable course', so Eicke stepped in and shot him dead.

The SS's country-wide rampage resulted in at least 83 known assassinations, some the result of mistaken identity, but many more casualties were suspected. Among the most prominent were Gustav von Kahr, who had blocked Hitler's putsch in 1923; two of von Papen's staff; Gregor Strasser; General Kurt von Schleicher, Hitler's predecessor as Reich Chancellor, together with his wife; and Generalmajor Ferdinand von Bredow, who was thought to have anonymously written a book that had upset the regime when it circulated in emigré circles in France. Von Papen had escaped with a scare, and the Reichswehr accepted its casualties without a murmur. Both Defence Minister General Blomberg and President von Hindenburg sent Hitler congratulatory messages.

Left: **His room No. 335 was on the landing of the second floor.** *Right:* **Pistol in hand, Hitler entered and accosted the bleary-eyed Röhm in bed: 'Ernst, you are under arrest!' Accusing him of being a traitor, Hitler brusquely ordered him to get dressed.**

Other rooms were searched and more SA men arrested as well as Röhm's cousin who was found sleeping with a young lady in another hotel down the road. When all were safely gathered in, the convoy set off for Munich.

The SA leaders who had been rounded up were taken to Munich's prison on Stadelheimer Strasse *(right)*. A list was drawn up and Hitler marked the six names of those who were to be executed first although initially he baulked at including Röhm who had been a colleague from the earliest days. The commander of Hitler's personal bodyguard, SS-Gruppenführer Josef 'Sepp' Dietrich *(above)* was charged with the executions which took place in the courtyard of the prison *(above right)*. Top of the list was SA-Obergruppenführer Edmund Heines and the Munich police president, SA-Obergruppenführer August Schneidhuber. Three SA-Gruppenführers were included: Hans Hayn, Hans Peter von Heydebreck and Wilhelm Schmidt. The last man whose name had been ticked by Hitler was Standartenführer Hans Joachim von Spreti-Weilbach although many more were to die over the next few days.

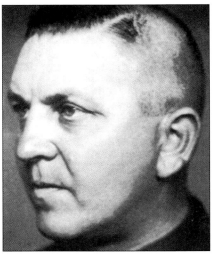

As far as Ernst Röhm was concerned, Hitler at first said he would pardon him because of his past services. However, when on the afternoon of July 1 he was finally persuaded by Göring and Himmler that Röhm must die, Hitler instructed SS-Brigadeführer Theodor Eicke *(right)*, the commander of Dachau concentration camp, to first give Röhm the chance of an honourable way out by committing suicide. A loaded pistol was given to Röhm in his cell (No. 474) *(left)* but when no shot was heard, 15 minutes later Eicke and two of his men opened the door and shot him dead.

On July 13, Hitler addressed the Reichstag and explained his actions. 'Chief-of-Staff Röhm, Gruppenführer Ernst, Obergruppenführer Heines, Hayn, and a number of others declared in the presence of witnesses that immediately there was to follow a conflict of the bloodiest kind, lasting several days, with their opponents. At the end of June I had made up my mind to put an end to this impossible development. At one o'clock in the night I received the last dispatches telling me of the alarm-summonses; at two o'clock in the morning I flew to Munich. Meanwhile Minister-President Göring had previously received from me the commission that if I proceeded to apply a purge he was to take similar measures at once in Berlin and in Prussia. With an iron fist he beat down the attack on the National Socialist State before it could develop. The necessity for acting with lightning speed meant that in this decisive hour I had very few men with me. In the presence of Minister Goebbels and of the new Chief-of-Staff [Lutze] the action was executed and brought to a close in Munich. Although only a few days before I had been prepared to exercise clemency, at this hour there was no place for any such consideration. Mutinies are suppressed in accordance with laws of iron which are eternally the same. If anyone approaches me and asks why I did not resort to the regular courts of justice for conviction of the offenders, then all that I can say to him is this: in this hour I was responsible for the fate of the German people, and thereby I became the supreme Justiciar of the German people! I did not wish to deliver up the young Reich to the fate of the old Reich. I gave the order to shoot those who were the ring-leaders in this treason, and I further gave the order to burn out down to the raw flesh the ulcers of this poisoning of the outside world. The penalty for these crimes was hard and severe. Nineteen higher SA leaders, thirty-one leaders and members of the SA were shot, and futher for complicity in the plot, three leaders of the SS, while thirteen SA leaders and civilians who attempted to resist arrest lost their lives. Three more committed suicide. Five who did not belong to the SA, but were members of the Party, were shot for taking part in the plot. Finally there were also shot three members of the SS who had been guilty of scandalous ill-treatment of those who had been taken into protective custody. In order to prevent political passion and exasperation venting itself in lynch justice on further offenders when the danger was removed and the revolt could be regarded as suppressed, as early as Sunday, July 1st strictest orders were given that all further retribution should cease.' Many more were eliminated than Hitler publicly admitted and the final death toll is believed to number well over a hundred. Röhm's grave (No. 1) lies in Row 3 of Plot 59 in Munich's Westfriedhof.

By the summer of 1934, 87-year-old Reich President Paul von Hindenburg, the man who had appointed Hitler Reich Chancellor *(left)*, was dying. Hitler visited the sick field-marshal at his Neudeck estate near Hohenstein in East Prussia several times.

Right: Here he is seen leaving the castle together with Oskar von Hindenburg, the president's son, on August 1 — one day before the field-marshal passed away. *Below:* Hindenburg lying in state flanked by two Reichswehr guards of honour.

Then on July 25, 1934, the Austrian NSDAP, which had been banned since the previous June, to Hitler's acute embarrassment murdered the Austrian Chancellor Engelbert Dollfuss in an attempted coup, but provided him with an outlet for von Papen, whom he sent to Vienna as ambassador.

Meanwhile von Hindenburg was near to death. Hitler flew out to Neudeck on August 1, but von Hindenburg failed to recognise him. That evening Hitler had his cabinet agree to a law combining the offices of Reich President with Reich Chancellor. Von Hindenburg died next day, August 2, 1934, and Hitler assumed the title of 'Führer and Reich Chancellor'.

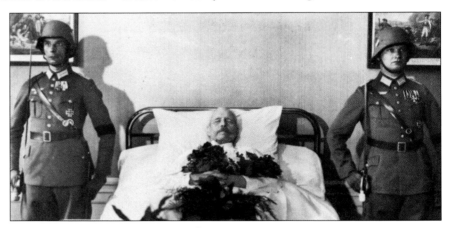

Although Hindenburg had expressed the wish to be buried at Neudeck, Hitler decided that the old warrior was to be laid to rest at the Tannenberg National Memorial, the huge monument in East Prussia commemorating Hindenburg's great victory over the Russian Second Army in August 1914. Built in the style of a Teutonic castle, it had been dedicated in September 1927.

On August 7, Hindenburg was buried at Tannenberg with full military honours in a dramatic ceremony masterminded by Albert Speer. Brought to Tannenberg the evening before, the coffin was placed on a bier in the centre of the Court of Honour which was filled with formations bearing the traditional flags of German regiments of WW I. Hitler (seen on the lectern behind the coffin) made a false start with his memorial address having been given the wrong text by his adjutant Julius Schaub.

General Blomberg arranged for every member of the armed forces throughout Germany to swear an oath of unconditional loyalty to the person of the Führer that same day. This move clearly involved prior preparation and presumably clearance with Hitler, but the initiative came from Blomberg in the hope of binding Hitler to the Reichswehr. It was to turn out the other way round.

Hitler then had von Hindenburg buried in a spectacular ceremony at the Tannenberg Memorial commemorating his great victory over the Russians of August 1914, despite the fact that von Hindenburg had expressed the wish to have a military funeral at the old Garrison Church in Potsdam, which held a particular place in his affections.

A subsequent plebiscite confirming Hitler's new powers produced a near 90 per cent approval from the German population. Hitler's position was now unchallengeable. He had secured total power and the 1934 Nuremberg Party Rally saw him in his element as Leni Riefenstahl filmed a propaganda masterpiece, *Triumph des Willens* (Triumph of the Will).

The next three and a half years saw the development of Hitler's chaotic form of government, 'working toward the will of the Führer', with overlapping organisations struggling for supremacy in their fields of competence, and the only arbiter an indifferent Führer as the basic structure of government crumbled away. Hitler lost all interest in domestic politics and reverted to the indolent lifestyle of his adolescence. All ministerial business was channelled to him through the Head of the Reich Chancellery, Hans-Heinrich Lammers, and Secretary of State Otto Meissner, but even they had the greatest difficulty attracting his attention. He rarely read the material they put before him before signing.

The Tannenberg memorial was blown up by German engineers on January 20, 1945, before the Red Army reached it, Hindenburg's sarcophagi having already been evacuated. After the war, the President and his wife were re-interred in the Chapel of St Elizabeth's in Marburg-an-der-Lahn. Today Tannenberg lies in Poland and has been renamed Olsztynek. All that remains of the memorial are small vestiges of its walls.

Left: The woman who would be Hitler's companion right up until the end was Eva Braun. One of three daughters of a Catholic schoolmaster, she was born on February 6, 1912 in a three-room apartment at No. 45 Isabellastrasse in Munich *(centre)*. In 1925 the Braun family moved to a much larger apartment on the second floor of No. 93 Hohenzollernstrasse *(right)*.

Eva met Hitler for the first time in October 1929 when she was 17. He paid a visit to Heinrich Hoffmann's photo shop at No. 50 Schellingstrasse in Munich where she worked as an office assistant, and this photo *(left)* is reputed to show their first meeting. The visitor was introduced to her as 'Herr Wolf' (she later claimed she had not realised he was the prominent politician Adolf Hitler). Hitler, who was then 40 years old, began courting her and she eventually fell madly in love with him and in early 1932, after the death of Geli Raubal, she became his mistress. Although many in Hitler's inner circle knew about their relationship, he kept her away from the public eye lest her presence lose him stature or support. An active young woman who followed fashion and loved sports, and with no interest in politics, Eva complained that Hitler did not spend enough time with her and she riled at his refusal to make her his official companion or to marry her. In despair, she twice tried to kill herself at her parents' home, once by a gunshot to her neck on November 1, 1932, and again three years later (May 29, 1935) when she took an overdose of sleeping pills.

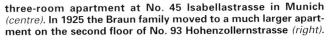

Left: After her second suicide attempt, judging that it would be better if Eva moved out from her parents who disapproved of the relationship, Hitler arranged for her to receive a place of her own at No. 12 Wasserburgstrasse, a quiet street in the fashionable Bogenhausen district of Munich, just north of his own apartment on Prinzregentenplatz, where she could live with her younger sister Gretl. Hitler did not buy the house personally but had Heinrich Hoffmann purchase it for 30,000 Reichsmarks. The two sisters moved in on March 30, 1936. Ownership of the property was formally transferred to Eva the following year. Eva enjoyed the house and the independence it gave her from her parents although Hitler rarely visited her there. *Right:* Wasserburgstrasse is today named Delpstrasse. The trees and bushes planted in the garden by Eva now almost hide No. 12 from view.

To introduce Hitler's next and probably best-known residence — his mountain retreat on the Obersalzberg mountain at Berchtesgaden in the Bavarian Alps — we have to take a step back in time to the early period when he had just emerged as leader of the new NSDAP. Hitler first came to the Obersalzberg in May 1923 when he visited his political and ideological mentor, the Nazi writer Dietrich Eckart. Financial sponsor and first editor of the NSDAP newspaper *Völkischer Beobachter*, Eckart was then being sought by the police for defamation of Weimar president Friedrich Ebert and was currently in hiding on the Obersalzberg in the Pension Moritz *(right)*. During the period that he spent on the mountain, Hitler stayed there as well.

By 1933, the Pension Moritz had been renamed the Platterhof and in March 1937, Martin Bormann was able to buy up the hotel for the Party for RM 260,000. The following summer, the old building was demolished and a completely new one erected in its place, also named the Platterhof Hotel. *Above left:* Opened in September 1941, every German who pilgrimaged to see the Führer could stay there one night for only RM 1. *Above right:* Untouched by the war, the Platterhof was exappropriated by the Americans in 1945 becoming the General Walker Hotel used as a recreation centre for US military personnel. *Right:* In 2000, the building was unceremoniously pulled down to become a car park for the new Obersalzberg Documentation Centre.

After his release from Landsberg prison in December 1924 (see page 111), and banned from delivering speeches in public, Hitler returned to the Obersalzberg, retreating to a small log cabin *(left)* belonging to the Pension Moritz. Apart from enjoying the simple life and wandering the hills wearing Lederhosen to take in the breathtaking scenic area, he was still politically active, and it was here that he dictated the second volume of *Mein Kampf* to Max Amann, his Army colleague from WW I and since 1922 director of the Party's publishing house Franz-Eher-Verlag GmbH. The book appeared in December 1926. He also spent his time writing long articles for the *Völkischer Beobachter* and discussing plans with his political cronies. They later called these years the 'Kampfzeit' (Battle Period) — hence the cabin was later referred to as the Kampfhäusl (Little Battle House). No trace of it is left today.

39

On October 15, 1928, Hitler rented a nearby country villa on the Obersalzberg, the Haus Wachenfeld. Owned by the widow of a Hamburg businessman, who was also a Party member, he occupied it for 100 Reichmarks per month.

It was even worse when he withdrew to the Obersalzberg, where he would rarely appear before a late lunch and then take an afternoon walk downhill to be picked up by car for the return journey, while all tourists were barred from the area, although some 2,000 were allowed to parade silently past his house each day. In the evenings he would watch a film. The company was almost invariably male, although sometimes Eva Braun brought female companions with her. Guests always took great pains against saying anything that would contradict or otherwise upset Hitler, or cause him to launch him into one of his lengthy monologues on subjects like the Great War.

Despite the frugality of his life-style, it was set in opulent surroundings. He was a millionaire from the sales of *Mein Kampf*, so could afford to live well, but his indifference to financial matters spurred corruption at all levels, and public money was poured freely into prestige enterprises. His Obersalzberg residence, Haus Wachenfeld, was expanded on a vast scale under Martin Bormann's direction as the Berghof to impress foreign dignitaries and the Kehlstein tea house constructed with no regard to cost. Also the Nazi elite could draw on copious salaries, all tax free, and amass gifts, donations and bribes to supplement their wealth, none better than Göring.

In June 1933 the income from the royalties from *Mein Kampf* enabled Hitler to purchase Haus Wachenfeld for RM 40,000. Two years later, judging that he needed a larger and more representative residence, he began an extensive rebuilding programme. Working from designs drawn up by Hitler personally, architect Roderich Fick incorporated the old house within the new building, adding another floor, a basement garage, and wide steps leading up to the front of the building. Renamed the Berghof (mountain homestead), the new house was finished in 1936.

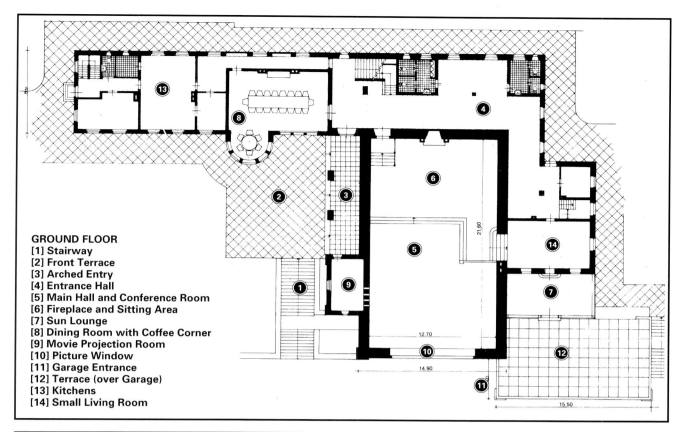

GROUND FLOOR
[1] Stairway
[2] Front Terrace
[3] Arched Entry
[4] Entrance Hall
[5] Main Hall and Conference Room
[6] Fireplace and Sitting Area
[7] Sun Lounge
[8] Dining Room with Coffee Corner
[9] Movie Projection Room
[10] Picture Window
[11] Garage Entrance
[12] Terrace (over Garage)
[13] Kitchens
[14] Small Living Room

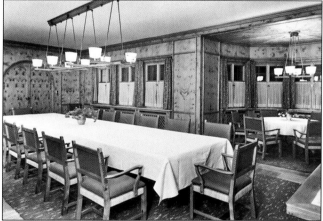

The dining room [8] in the eastern wing with its 24-seat table. The walls of the room were panelled with pine.

The spacious lounge [5-6] on the ground floor, furnished with Persian carpets and paintings, featured an open fireplace.

The large picture window [10], for which the Berghof is famous, could be lowered to permit an uninterrupted view of

the magnificent panorama of the mountains and valleys. It is seen here from the inside *(left)* and from the outside *(right)*.

Hitler's study [1] was on the first floor, its windows overlooking the Unterberg from where it was said the Emperor Charlemagne would one day arise to restore the past glories of the German Empire. Naturally Hitler latched onto the legend: 'It is no accident that I have my residence opposite it'. Meanwhile, on a practical level, Hitler was financially embarrassed as he had spent far too much on the extensions to his house: 'I've completely used up the income from my book, although Amann has given me a further advance of several hundred thousand marks. Even so there's not enough money, so

Bormann has told me today. The publishers are after me to release my second book, the 1928 one, for publication. [This book titled *Hitlers Zweite Buch. Ein Dokument aus dem Jahre 1928* was not published until 1961.] But I'm certainly glad this volume hasn't been published. What political complications it would make for me at the moment. On the other hand it would relieve me of all financial pressures at one stroke. Amann promised me a million just as an advance, and beyond that it would bring in millions. Perhaps later, when I'm further along. Now it's impossible.'

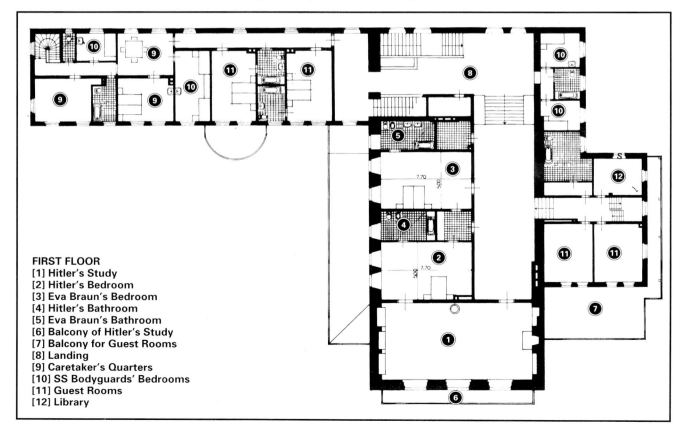

FIRST FLOOR
[1] Hitler's Study
[2] Hitler's Bedroom
[3] Eva Braun's Bedroom
[4] Hitler's Bathroom
[5] Eva Braun's Bathroom
[6] Balcony of Hitler's Study
[7] Balcony for Guest Rooms
[8] Landing
[9] Caretaker's Quarters
[10] SS Bodyguards' Bedrooms
[11] Guest Rooms
[12] Library

Above: **Every day hundreds of admirers would travel up the Obersalzberg and linger at the entrance to the Berghof hoping to get a glimpse of their beloved Führer. Their hopes were often fulfilled for it was not unusual for Hitler to come out to greet the crowds. Delegations of National Socialist organisations would parade past the house or be given the honour to march up the driveway to pay their respects, like this group of traditionally-dressed young farmers and their wives pictured in 1937.** *Right:* **Ruined by the Allied air raid on Berchtesgaden on April 25, 1945, the Berghof was later blown up on orders of the US occupation authorities on April 30, 1952 (see page 455). The garage, which remained largely intact, was razed by the Bavarian authorities in 1996.**

Innumerable pictures were taken on the stairway leading up to the front door of the Berghof. Heinrich Hoffmann took this shot during a visit of a delegation of the National-sozialistische Frauenschaft (NSF — National Socialist Women's Organisation) in 1938.

One side of the stairs and part of the Berghof's retaining wall is all that survives under the trees.

Left: **Across the valley from the Berghof but lower down on a rocky outcrop known as the Mooslahner Kopf, stood Hitler's Tea House. Designed by Professor Roderich Fick and completed in the autumn of 1937, its main room was a round pavilion of eight metres diameter. A half-hour's hike from the Berghof, the Mooslahner Teehaus was the traditional** destination of Hitler on his daily walk when residing on the Obersalzberg. (It is not to be confused with the much larger tea house on the Kehlstein mountain, the so-called Eagle's Nest.) *Right:* **The small Tea House was blown up by the Americans after the war, but its ruin remains until this day, tucked away and forgotten, far from the bustle of the tourist crowds.**

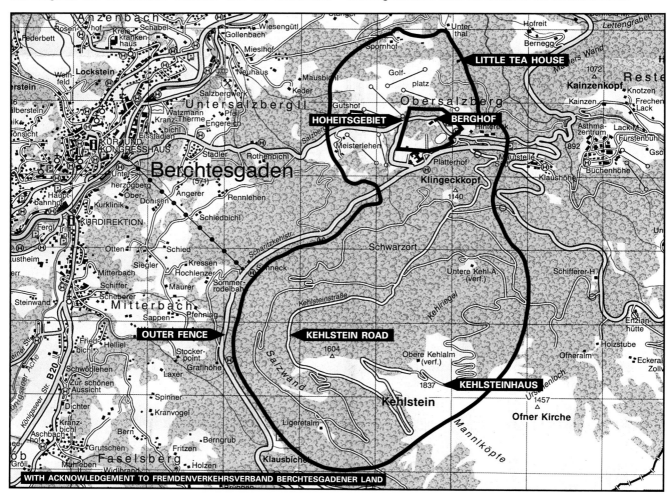

As war drew near, public access to the Obersalzberg was limited for security reasons. The whole area was declared 'Führersperrgebiet' (Führer Prohibited Area). Surrounded by a seven-foot fence, it was divided into two parts. The inner circle was the Hoheitsgebiet (Sovereign Area) which contained the Berghof and Martin Bormann's house. This area was guarded by SS sentries, the SS barracks being located inside the inner ring. The outer perimeter was guarded initially by civilian police, later replaced by the Reichssicherheitsdienst (RSD — State Security Service). Sentry boxes built of stone to blend in with their surroundings were erected at the entrances to the area, and passes had to be shown to obtain entry, one of Bormann's instructions being that 'a uniform is no authorisation to pass these gates'.

Left: In November 1936, Bormann (the man in charge of all building undertakings on the Obersalzberg) began a project to construct a scenic mountain road to the foot of the Kehlstein, a rocky mountain top (1,834 metres) towering high above the Berghof area. A major feat of engineering, the Kehlstein road was blasted out of virgin rock. With some 3,800 men working in shifts around the clock under the most dangerous and difficult conditions, the four-mile single-lane asphalt road, winding up very steeply through five tunnels and several spectacular hairpin bends, was ready in October 1938. This picture was taken by Heinrich Hoffmann shortly after its completion. *Right:* Our comparison was taken though the rear window of one of the shuttle buses that today take tourists up to the Kehlstein parking area and back down again.

Above: In April 1937, Bormann conceived the idea of constructing a tea house on top of the Kehlstein itself, to be presented to Hitler on his 50th birthday in April 1939. Perched on a rocky outcrop, the house was built in the record time of ten months, being completed in August 1938. The house had cost an estimated 6.3 million Reichsmarks, the total price tag of the whole project being a staggering 30 million. Ten labourers had died as a result of accidents during the construction. *Right:* Untouched by the Allied bombing, the Kehlstein house was confiscated by the Americans after the war and christened the Eagle's Nest. Turned over to the Bavarian government, and re-opened to the general public in April 1952, it has been a major tourist attraction ever since.

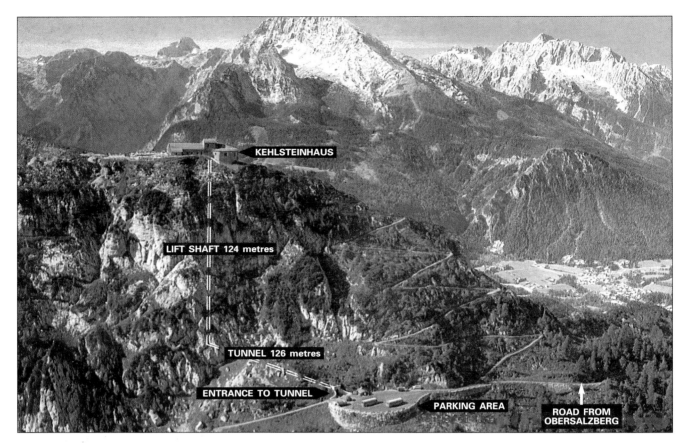

KEHLSTEINHAUS

LIFT SHAFT 124 metres

TUNNEL 126 metres

ENTRANCE TO TUNNEL

PARKING AREA

ROAD FROM OBERSALZBERG

To get from the Kehlstein parking area to the mountain peak above, a ten-foot-high marble-clad tunnel was driven 126 metres into the rock leading to a lobby from where a large gilded lift transported visitors 124 metres up to the interior of the Tea House.

The entrance to the tunnel — guarded by SS sentinels *(above)* — and *(below)* open to tourists today.

Hitler and Eva Braun with guests in the main sitting room of the Kehlsteinhaus.

Today the hall is in use as a restaurant, as are all the other large rooms.

Right: Hitler shows the newly completed tea house to Dr Robert Ley, chief of the Deutsche Arbeitsfront. L-R: Frau Ley and daughter, Ley, Hitler, Gauleiter Adolf Wagner of Munich–Upper Bavaria, Bormann (partly visible) and Hitler's personal adjutant, SS-Gruppenführer Julius Schaub. The footpath in the background leads up to the actual summit of the Kehlstein. Although he had visited the site of the Kehlstein tea house several times during the construction phase, Hitler rarely used the building after its completion, reputedly because of the thin air, but also because he had a fear of heights and he considered the lift a death trap. In all, Hitler made only 14 official visits to the house, nine of which occurred in September and October 1938, that is in the weeks immediately following its completion. His foreign guests included the Italian Foreign Minister Count Galeazzo Ciano and the French Ambassador François Poncet. During the war, he only visited the Kehlsteinhaus twice, the first time being October 17, 1940, when he showed it off to Italian crown princess Marie-José, the sister of King Leopold of Belgium. The number of Hitler's private visits to the Kehlsteinhaus is not recorded but Bormann used it regularly to receive and impress his own personal guests. Eva Braun was a great fan and went up there with friends as often as possible. The only real celebration that ever took place there was the wedding breakfast of Eva's sister Gretl when she married Himmler's liaison officer at Hitler's HQ, SS-Brigadeführer Hermann Fegelein, on June 3, 1944. This was also Hitler's last visit. *Centre right:* For once, one can be fairly certain that the tourists are aware that they are treading in the dictator's footsteps.

Hitler spends a moment in quiet contemplation on the sunny terrace which lies on the southern side of the building.

Today the large open windows have been fitted with glass panes. The door on the right leads to the restaurant's kitchen.

Meanwhile, Hitler moved forward apace with his political agenda. The return to the demilitarised Rhineland, where no German units had been permitted for 17 years, took place on March 7, 1936, when troops marched victoriously over the Hohenzollern Bridge spanning the Rhine in Cologne.

In January 1935 the Saarland, which had been put under the control of the League of Nations after the Great War under French stewardship, held a plebiscite over the possible return to Germany and voted over 90 per cent in favour after a propaganda campaign by Goebbels, the change of sovereignty to take place on March 1.

On February 3 a joint Anglo-French communiqué condemned unilateral rearmament and suggested having restrictions on arms levels and an international pact against aggression from the air. The German government responded with an invitation to the British for talks in Berlin on March 7, but the publication of a White Paper announcing an increase in British defence expenditure as a result of German rearmament created a furore in Germany and Hitler developed a diplomatic cold to postpone the meeting. Then on March 10 Göring revealed the existence of the Luftwaffe in flagrant breach of the Versailles Treaty, almost doubling the actual number of aircraft at its disposal to further impress diplomats.

The French had just renewed their military treaty with Belgium and now increased the duration of compulsory military service to two years. The Reichswehr leaders were also anxious for the promised increase in army strength based on the reintroduction of conscription, planning an immediate 24-division army expanding to a 36-division peacetime army, 550,000 strong, and capable of expansion to 63 divisions by 1939 should there be a war, but Hitler was awaiting the right moment to go ahead. On March 16, 1935, with the return of the Saarland having been greeted with a speech announcing no further claims on France behind him, he announced the introduction of conscription.

Destroyed in 1945 along with the two railway spans, the Hohenzollern's road span was never rebuilt.

The French and Italian governments were aghast at this development and protested forcibly, but the British only made a formal protest, asking whether the invitation for talks still stood. This showed Hitler that Germany's isolation was coming to an end, and on March 25 the British Foreign Secretary, Sir John Simon, and the Privy Seal, Anthony Eden, arrived in Berlin. They returned with the message that Hitler wanted parity in the air forces and a 35 per cent equivalent of British naval strength, i.e. naval parity with the French. Consequently the newly appointed Ambassador Extraordinary Joachim von Ribbentrop was sent to London in June to negotiate with the Admiralty. To his surprise, Sir John Simon opened the talks with the announcement that the British accepted Hitler's proposals. The Anglo-German Naval Agreement was signed on June 18 and von Ribbentrop returned in triumph with another breach in the Versailles Treaty.

Meanwhile Blomberg had been re-styled as Reich War Minister and appointed commander-in-chief of the Wehrmacht in the rank of Generalfeldmarschall.

On September 15 at the conclusion of the Nuremberg Party Rally, in which the Wehrmacht had participated for the first time, the Reichstag met in the city hall to pass a law making the Nazi swastika flag the official national one. At the very last minute Hitler introduced two hastily cobbled together bits of legislation that were to become notorious as 'The Nuremberg Laws'. The first was 'The Law of German Blood and German Honour', which forbade marriage and sexual intercourse between German citizens and Jews, and also forbade Jews from employing female German domestic servants under 45 years of age, or flying the new national flag. The second law, 'The Reich Citizenship Law', excluded all those not of 'German or kindred blood' from the right to German citizenship. However, these laws failed to define the term 'Jew', so after weeks of deliberation in the Party and State offices concerned, a Supplementary Decree was issued on November 14, laying down that no Jew could be a citizen of the Reich, and defined a Jew as being anyone descended of at least three grandparents of that race, and a 'Mischling', or part-Jew, being one descended from one or two Jewish grandparents.

Minister of the Interior Wilhelm Frick ordered the dismissal of all Jews from the civil service effective the end of the year. However, fears of a foreign boycott of the 1936 Winter Olympics to be held in Garmisch-Partenkirchen and the summer Olympic Games scheduled to be held in Berlin, and also concern to avoid disruption of the economy before rearmament was sufficiently advanced, now resulted in a relatively peaceful interlude for the Jewish population.

Meanwhile a severe domestic crisis and drop in Party and public morale had arisen through acute food shortages, rising prices and social tension. There were still some two and a half

At the Obersalzberg, Hitler began receiving an endless stream of distinguished visitors. His first official foreign guest after completion of the Berghof was David Lloyd George, leader of the British Liberal Party, who was received by Hitler on September 3, 1936.

Another noteworthy occasion was the visit of the Duke and Duchess of Windsor on October 22, 1937, seen here posing with Hitler and Dr Ley on the Berghof steps. The visit occurred one year after the Duke had abdicated to marry Mrs Wallis Simpson.

million out of work. Twice Hitler was obliged to divert large sums of foreign exchange from the purchase of raw materials for the armaments programme to the purchase of seed-oil to manufacture margarine for a population seriously lacking in fats.

Then, rightly sensing that neither France nor Britain would physically oppose his military reoccupation of the Rhineland, he sent his troops across the Hohenzollern Bridge before the assembled press on March 7, 1936, as he simultaneously addressed an ecstatic session of the Reichstag. His announcement was that Germany would be prepared to rejoin the League of Nations and enter into non-aggression pacts with France and Belgium, steps he had no intention of taking. At little risk Hitler had achieved a major triumph with this bold stroke. The Council of the League of Nations immediately condemned Germany as a treaty breaker, but Hitler simply dissolved the Reichstag and called for a plebiscite on his policies that brought a 98.8 per cent vote of approval from the electorate on March 29.

Then on July 2, while attending the Bayreuth Festival, a letter from Generalissimo Francisco Franco was delivered to him requesting assistance in flying North African troops across to Spain to fight the Communists. After consultation with Göring, he agreed to sending out part of the Luftwaffe's transport fleet, plus some experimental fighter and bomber units and a few anti-aircraft guns. This German contingent became known as the Condor Legion.

The opening of the Olympic Games in Berlin on August 1, 1936, was again a propaganda triumph for Hitler, duly filmed by Leni Riefenstahl. The anti-Jewish campaign was suspended and all anti-Jewish signs removed. Germany itself triumphed in the Games, winning the most gold, silver and bronze medals, and establishing a considerable lead in overall points over the USA in second place (see Berlin — The 1936 Olympic Games, see pages 218-226).

That summer Hitler produced a memorandum for Göring and Blomberg in which he contended that, as Germany was overpopulated and unable to feed

itself from its own resources, the only solution was expansion by force. Therefore the government would have to concentrate on resolving the problem of raw materials in order to make the country sufficiently self-reliant to enable the German economy and army to be ready to go to war in four years' time. This was followed up at the annual Party Rally in announcements of the launching of the Four Year Plan and an anti-Bolshevik campaign.

Meanwhile both Great Britain and Germany fostered good relations with a succession of distinguished visitors received by Hitler. The Great War Prime Minister, David Lloyd George, was one of them and was duly impressed by both Hitler and the Party Rally. The most prominent of these visitors were the Duke and Duchess of Windsor after the former's abdication as King Edward VIII. This had been a great disappointment for Hitler, for both Edward and his mistress Mrs Wallis Simpson were Nazi sympathisers, and they were given a big welcome on their visit to Germany in October 1937.

Dr Ley seeing the Duke and Duchess off at Berchtesgaden Station.

The bridge over the Ache river links past and present.

On September 25-29, 1937, the first official state visit of Italian dictator Benito Mussolini to Nazi Germany took place. Arriving by train at Munich's main station, the Duce, side by side with Hitler, inspected the Army and Party honour detachments drawn up on the station square, after which they rode in state to Hitler's apartment on Prinzregentenplatz for political talks. In the afternoon there was a ceremony and massive parade on the Königsplatz. The further programme included an inspection of army manoeuvres in Mecklenburg on the 26th, a visit to the Krupp munitions plant in Essen on the 27th and a triumphal drive through Berlin later that day. On the 28th Mussolini visited Potsdam, was received by Göring at his Carinhall estate and, after dark, spoke at a mass meeting at the Olympic Stadium. On the last day, he laid a wreath at the German War Memorial on Unter den Linden and watched another military parade before departing for Italy from Berlin's Lehrter Station in the afternoon.

Benito Mussolini, the Fascist dictator of Italy, was not at all happy with the Anglo-German relationship and in October 1936 the Duce sent his son-in-law, Count Galeazzo Ciano, who was also his Foreign Minister, to liaise what came to be known as the Axis Pact, formally allying Italy with Germany.

Hitler decided to back Generalissimo Franco more substantially and had a tactical ground support air unit operational in Spain by November, when he recognised Franco's regime as the legal government of Spain. However, Franco's war was not going that well and the new German liaison officer at his headquarters, General Wilhelm Faupel, returned to Berlin with an appeal for the commitment of three German infantry divisions. Hitler consulted with Faupel's predecessor, Oberstleutnant Walter Warlimont, who argued that this was a civil war that had to be won by Franco's troops alone and that the German assistance already given was sufficient to avoid defeat. Hitler agreed, saying that he would leave the honour of sending troops to Mussolini.

That same month, November 1936, he signed an Anti-Comintern Pact with Japan in mutual support against the Soviet Union. There was a lull on the international front until Mussolini paid a visit to Hitler in September 1937. Mussolini spoke German and they got on well together. No formal agreements were signed, but it was agreed that neither would draw close to Britain without the other party's approval and that Italy should have a free hand in the Mediterranean, and Hitler a free hand in Austria. The visit was a tremendous propaganda success for Hitler, also serving to show Mussolini the extent of his popularity in Germany and the strength of his position, for the first time appearing as the senior partner.

That autumn Hitler's sister Angela, with whom he was having problems over her disapproval of his mistress Eva Braun, gave up her post as housekeeper on the Obersalzberg and married a Professor Martin Hammitzsch in Leipzig. Hitler did not attend her wedding. Eva took over at the Berghof, where a suite was built for her next to Hitler's. With her came her two dogs, Stasi and Negus, who did not get on with Hitler's Alsation Blondi and had to be kept apart.

Hitler was having health problems with stomach cramps, wind, eczema and insomnia, and so at Eva's suggestion he engaged Dr Theo Morell as his personal physician. The treatment Morell gave him worked well and Morell was to be retained until the last, even though much of his later treatment can only be described as dubious.

Toward the end of 1937 von Blomberg married a woman of doubtful reputation, and Göring, who wanted his job, intrigued with Himmler to bring about his dismissal on January 27, 1938. For similar reasons Göring brought to Hitler's notice charges of homosexuality that had been raised against Generaloberst Werner von Fritsch, commander-in-chief of the army. During this crisis Hitler assumed personal command of the Wehrmacht, and forced von Fritsch to resign on February 2, replacing him with Generaloberst Walther von Brauchitsch, whom he bound to him with a gift of 80,000 Reichmarks to secure his divorce. Sixteen other generals were dismissed and Göring compensated by promotion to the rank of Generalfeldmarschall of the Luftwaffe. After investigation, the charges brought against von Fritsch were found to be false and, although he was reluctantly reinstated in the army by Hitler, his career was obviously at an end. As the honorary colonel of his old regiment, he chose to die honourably in battle leading it in the Polish campaign.

No crimson carpet to receive train arrivals outside Munich's Hauptbahnhof today. The view is south, the building in the background being the Le Meridien Hotel on Bayerstrasse.

March 1938 saw the Anschluss (unification) of Austria with Germany. Having announced a plebiscite for April 10, at which the Germans and Austrians could approve his actions, Hitler spent the first ten days of April electioneering in his homeland.

Wherever he went he was greeted as leader and saviour. On April 9, the day before the poll (at which 99 per cent would vote in favour of union), he visited Salzburg. Here his motorcade crosses the Staatsbrücke separating the Altstadt from the Neustadt.

Lord Halifax visited Hitler at the Berghof on November 19, 1937. He was there on behalf of the new cabinet headed by Neville Chamberlain to explain the British government's appeasement policy. In exchange for Germany's commitment to a permanent European peace settlement, the British were prepared to allow territorial concessions in Austria, Czechoslovakia and Danzig to be settled in accordance with German wishes. However, Hitler primarily wanted a free hand in the east and, although he would prefer to have an alliance with Britain, it was not essential to his plans.

Then on February 12, 1938, Hitler invited the Austrian Chancellor Kurt von Schuschnigg to the Berghof, where he bullied him into accepting an extremely one-sided agreement whereby the Austrian Nazis were to take part in the government with control of the Ministry of the Interior and therefore the police, and be free to conduct party activities. Schuschnigg thought he could counter this by announcing on March 9 a plebiscite three days later, but Hitler again bullied him into calling it off. Hitler then threatened to send in his troops if von Schuschnigg did not resign in favour of the Nazi leader Arthur Seyss-Inquart. Schuschnigg appealed to the western powers but got no response, and late on March 11 Hitler sent his troops in. They were met so enthusiastically that two days later he decided to absorb the whole of Austria into the Reich as the Ostmark. Britain condemned the manner in which the Anschluss had been achieved, but went on to recognise the new state of affairs.

The bridge across the Salzach has been widened but the façades of the buildings on the far bank remain unchanged.

After Austria came Czechoslovakia. In September 1938, the political crisis over German claims to the Sudeten region led to frantic diplomatic negotiations, culminating in the Munich Conference of September 29-30, at which the Western powers gave in to Hitler's demands. The conference took place at the newly completed Führerbau building (see page 158) on Munich's Arcisstrasse. Seated anti-clockwise around the fireplace are: British Prime Minister Neville Chamberlain, his advisor Sir Horace Wilson, Hitler, Mussolini, Italian Foreign Minister Galeazzo Ciano, French Premier Edouard Daladier, German Foreign Minister Joachim von Ribbentrop and his State Secretary Ernst von Weiszäcker.

Hitler decided to tackle the Czechoslovakian problem without delay. In February he instructed Goebbels to mount a propaganda campaign against the Czech government, accusing it of terrorising its German population, massing troops on the Sudetenland border and mistreating its Slav subjects. The latter reacted as expected by increasing their demands on the Czech government for independence. Then on March 28, 1938, Hitler instructed Konrad Henlein, the leader of the Sudeten German Party in that country, to increase his demands on the Czech government. By May 20 the situation had deteriorated to the extent that the Czechs mobilised in the belief that Germany was about to attack. Ten days later Hitler told the Wehrmacht that he was determined to crush the Czechs by military action and that the troops should be ready for action by October 1.

Everyone looked to Britain as the mediator, but Chamberlain's government were sticking to their policy of appeasement, believing that it was better to deal with Hitler direct than organising peripheral pacts against him, and on September 15, 1938, Chamberlain flew out to the Obersalzberg to discuss the matter of the Sudetenland. A week later at Bad Godesberg they met again with the British cabinet's approval of their agreement for the self-determination of the Sudeten Germans and the cession of that territory to Germany. However, Hitler now wanted to move in his troops prior to a plebiscite and to encourage Poland and Hungary to stake their own territorial claims on Czechoslovakia. Chamberlain left next day, unable to agree to these new demands, and asked Mussolini to use his good offices to avert war in Europe. Consequently a conference was scheduled for September 29 in Munich, where Mussolini put forward the proposal that the great powers would guarantee what remained of Czechoslovakia once the territorial concessions had been made. This was agreed next day, enabling Chamberlain to return to London waving the famous 'scrap of paper' proclaiming: 'Peace for our time!'

Hitler took over the Sudetenland on October 1, 1938, and promptly began planning the expansion of the German navy's surface fleet to a size capable of engaging the Royal Navy and for reoccupying former colonial territory as a challenge to the British Empire.

The historic conference room is now a simple classroom of Munich's State High School for Music.

52

On April 20, 1939, a massive parade was held in Berlin to mark Hitler's 50th birthday, some 50,000 troops of all arms marching or riding past the Führer for four hours. The parade was held on Berliner Strasse, which formed the western end of Berlin's new East-West Axis (see pages 230-233). The reviewing stand for Hitler and his guests was set up opposite the Technische Universität, from which this picture of motorised pontoon troops was taken.

Then on November 9, Goebbels's 'Kristallnacht' erupted, bringing world-wide condemnation. President Roosevelt recalled his ambassador. This pressure concentrated Hitler's attention on the Jewish question, and on January 29 in his sixth-anniversary speech to the Reichstag as Chancellor he went so far as to declare open war on 'World Jewry'. Only a few days before he had told the Czech Foreign Minister that no German guarantee would be given to a state that had not got rid of its Jews.

In January 1939 Hitler had a shock when Hjalmar Schacht as president of the Reichsbank handed him a memorandum countersigned by all the directors of that bank which read: 'The reckless expenditures of the Reich represent a most serious threat to the currency. The tremendous increase in such expenditures foils every attempt to draw up a regular budget; it is driving the finances of this country to the brink of ruin despite a great tightening of the tax screw, and by the same token it undermines the Reichsbank and the currency.' Despite this attack on his military and architectural spending, Hitler appears to have respected Schacht too much to do other than dismiss him from his post and even allowed him to go on extended holiday overseas.

A grand parade was held on April 20, 1939, in honour of Hitler's 50th birthday. Also present on the tribune opposite the Technical University was the elderly little Czech President, Dr Emil Hácha, who had apparently been invited just to be overawed by the display of military might. After the massed bands of the army, navy and air force came a formation of standard bearers carrying the flags and standards of every unit of the armed forces, followed by the goose-stepping Infanterie-Regiments 9 and 16, then the motorised infantry with the motorcycles and armoured cars of the reconnaissance

Most of the university building had to be pulled down after the war and rebuilt. We took our comparison from the fifth floor of the new edifice.

Hitler saluting the motorised infantry. Albert Speer, responsible for design of the East-West Axis, had widened Berliner Strasse as part of the road reconstruction. As a result, the two sections of the Charlottenburger Tor (visible in the background) had to be moved outwards.

units behind. Motorised signals and engineer troops came next before the mounted elements of the cavalry and artillery, led by their trumpeters. The horse-drawn batteries of light and heavy howitzers were followed by the motorised artillery and then the tanks. After the army came the navy with a marching element, then the Luftwaffe led by the Regiment 'General Göring' with a newly-raised parachute battalion, then signals and motorised anti-aircraft and searchlight units. A fly-past brought to a close the parade in which it was said some 50,000 troops had taken part.

Hitler was by no means finished with the question of Czechoslovakia, and on March 15, 1939, having approved the independence of Slovakia and bullied the aged Czech President into agreeing to his demands, he had his troops over-run the remainder of Czechoslovakia to establish the Reich Protectorate of Bohemia and Moravia.

However, this move showed Hitler in his true colours to the British and French public, whose governments responded by giving military guarantees to Poland, Romania, Greece and Turkey and entering into talks with the Soviets.

Meanwhile Hitler had taken over effective command of the Wehrmacht, establishing a new command organisation known as the Oberkommando der Wehrmacht (OKW) headed by General Wilhelm Keitel with Generalmajor Alfred Jodl as head of the planning department, a team that Hitler was to retain until the end. However, by subjecting the reorganised command to his own will, there remained a confusion of authority between the OKW and the army's Oberkommando des Heeres (OKH), the navy's Oberkommando der Kriegsmarine (OKM) and eventually the Waffen-SS, that was to have an adverse effect on the conduct of the war.

The Ost-West-Achse and Berliner Strasse were renamed Strasse des 17. Juni five days after the rising against the Communist regime in East Berlin in June 1953. Today the centre lane of the broad avenue is used as parking space for the university.

Bringing up the rear of the Army part of the birthday parade were the light tanks of the panzer units. Note the standard bearers lined up across the road.

The west wing of the Technical University (on the left) has survived in altered form while the building further down the street remains exactly as before.

From October 24, 1938, onwards, Germany had been trying hard to persuade Poland to join in an anti-Soviet alliance in return for the promise of territorial awards in the Ukraine, but on March 26, 1939, the day after the occupation of Czechoslovakia and three days after the occupation of Memel in Lithuania, Poland turned down Hitler's final offer. So, if Poland would not co-operate, then Poland would first have to be attacked to get to the Soviet Union.

Britain's guarantee of Polish independence on March 31 was intended as a warning to Hitler that he should enter into a general peace agreement. However, British hopes of an alliance with the Soviet Union foundered when Stalin, who himself was not ready for war, eventually opted for an alliance with Germany instead, and on August 23 von Ribbentrop and Soviet Foreign Minister Vasilii Molotov signed the German-Soviet Non-Aggression Pact in Moscow. The pact came as an incomprehensible shock to Nazis and Communists alike, but it brought Hitler vital oil, raw materials and grain to bolster his rearmament programme and gave Stalin the time he needed.

Meanwhile on April 28 Hitler made a speech before a vast audience that was also broadcast throughout Europe and even in the USA, in which he condemned the change in Great Britain's foreign policy, claiming that it negated the 1935 naval treaty between the two countries, and then attacked the Poles, declaring the non-aggression pact with Poland null and void as a result of Polish transgressions. Two international treaties were thus torn up in front of the world. The signal could not have been clearer.

On May 22 Italy and Germany signed the 'Pact of Steel' uniting their military efforts in case of war, and Hitler started working on Japan to join them. Next day he informed his Wehrmacht chiefs that he intended to invade and destroy Poland. The secret clauses of his non-aggression pact with the Soviet Union gave him a clear field of operations as far as the line of the Narva, Vistula and San rivers.

On April 28, 1939, Hitler delivered a landmark speech before the Reichstag at the Krolloper. No speech had ever had a larger audience for it was broadcast throughout Germany and most of Europe and carried by all the major networks in the United States. The address was Hitler's carefully staged response to an appeal made by US President Franklin Roosevelt to Hitler and Mussolini (who had just invaded Albania) on April 14 asking that they refrain from further aggression and assure the sovereignty of 30 named countries. The speech was a masterpiece of political propaganda, judged by many historians to be Hitler's most eloquent and brilliant ever. Starting out with his usual condemnation of the Versailles Treaty, he began by elaborately defending his foreign policy up to now, presenting himself as a servant to peace. Deploring Britain for its recent disrespect of German interests and Poland for its 'campaign of lies' against Germany, he surprised everyone by denouncing both the 1935 Naval Treaty with the former and the 1934 Non-Aggression Pact with the latter, slyly making a point of adding that the door to new negotiations was still open, provided it was on equal terms. Turning to the United States, he then, in a very effective display of irony and sarcasm, took up Roosevelt's message point by point, only to demolish each one in turn – which produced roars of laughter and applause from the house, the uproar being led by a delighted Hermann Göring who presided. Roosevelt — so ridiculed Hitler — believed that all problems could be solved around the conference table. However, the US had themselves been the first to refuse to join the League of Nations. Roosevelt was concerned about German intentions in Europe. But what would happen if Germany inquired about US intentions in Latin America? It would be referred to the Monroe Doctrine and told to mind its own business. And so Hitler went on, mocking each point in turn, all the while cleverly evading to answer Roosevelt's central question: would Germany invade yet another country?

The excuse for the attack on Poland was provided by Operation 'Himmler', a staged border incident in which a German radio station at Gleiwitz on the border was attacked and taken over by a German-speaking Pole who shouted anti-German slogans and called for conflict. Some dozen condemned convicts from a concentration camp were dressed up in Polish Army uniforms and then given lethal injections by an SS doctor before being given gunshot wounds and scattered around the area as if killed in the attack.

Left: On the evening of August 31, 1939, an SS team under SS-Sturmbannführer Alfred Naujocks staged a mock raid by 'Polish special forces' on the German radio transmitter station at Gleiwitz in Upper Silesia. This alleged Polish 'attack on the sovereign territory of the Reich' was used as a pretext for Germany's invasion of Poland at 4.45 a.m. the following morning. Right: Gleiwitz is today Gliwice in Poland, but the radio station and its wooden mast still stand.

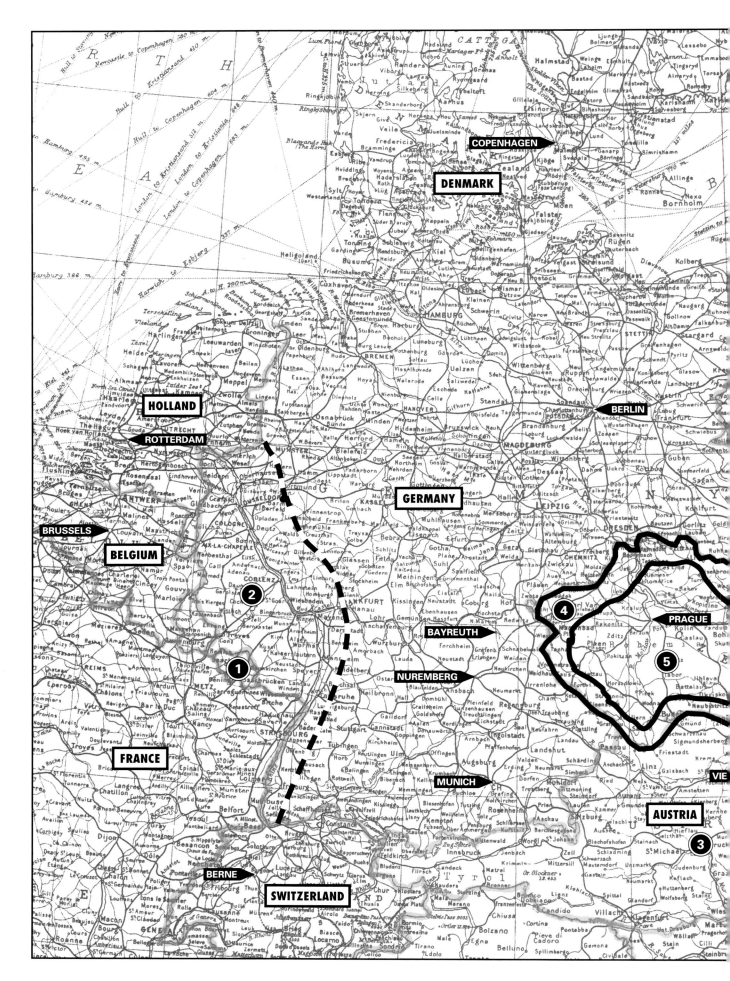

FREE PORT OF DANZIG

LITHUANIA

VILNIUS

EAST PRUSSIA

WARSAW

POLAND

CZECHOSLOVAKIA

BUDAPEST

HUNGARY

Hitler's empire in September 1939. These were his acquisitions during the previous five years:

The SAAR [1] returned to Germany from France after a plebiscite by Saarlanders on January 13, 1935. Hitler: 'We all wish to see in this act a first and decisive step on the way towards a gradual reconciliation between those who twenty years ago through unkind fates and human frailties stumbled into the most fearful and most fruitless struggle of all time. Your decision, German fellow-countrymen of the Saar, gives to me today the opportunity of stating that after the completion of your return the German Reich will make no further territorial claims on France.'

The RHINELAND [2] was established as a demilitarised buffer zone after the First World War to ensure that Germany could never again launch an attack on France. Allied troops were stationed in the zone but were withdrawn in stages: the US in March 1922; France in July 1925 with the last Allied forces leaving in June 1930. On March 7, 1936 Germany violated the Treaty of Versailles by occupying the Rhineland, Hitler repeating his statement: 'Germany has no further claims to make from France nor will she make any'.

AUSTRIA [3] was entered by German troops on March 11, 1938 and the country was formally annexed to Germany to form the Greater German Reich two days later. 'On Friday night', explained Hitler, 'I was asked to order German troops to march into Austria in order to prevent grave internal disorders in that country. Toward 10 p.m. troops were already crossing the frontier at numerous points. At 6 a.m. the next morning the main body began to march in. They were greeted with tremendous enthusiasm by the population, which was thus at last free. On Saturday, 13 March, at Linz, I decreed the incorporation of the Ostmark into the Reich and caused the members of the former Austrian Army to swear allegiance to me as the Commander-in-Chief of the German Forces.'

The SUDETENLAND [4] border region of Czech territory was added to Germany on March 29, 1938 with the agreement of the British, French and Italian governments. As far as Czechoslovakia was concerned, in Hitlers view 'the creation of this heterogeneous republic after the war was lunacy. It has none of the characteristics of a nation, whether from the standpoint of ethnology, strategy, economics, or language. To set an intellectually inferior handful of Czechs to rule over minorities belonging to races like the Germans, Poles, Hungarians, with a thousand years of culture behind them, was a work of folly and ignorance. The Sudeten Germans have no respect for the Czechs and will never accept their rule. After the war the Allied Powers declared that Germany was unworthy to govern blacks, yet at the same time they set second-rate people like the Czechs in authority over 3½ million Germans of the highest character and culture.'

BOHEMIA and MORAVIA [5] were occupied by Germany on March 15, 1939 and SLOVAKIA [6] was placed under German 'protection' the following day.

Finally MEMEL [7] was added to Hitler's portfolio when it was restored to Germany from Lithuania on March 21.

THE INNER CIRCLE

Direction must not be changed until the right men have been found for the change. More revolutions have been successful at the outset than have, when once successful, been arrested and brought to a standstill at the right moment.

ADOLF HITLER, JULY 6, 1933

Of all the top Nazis, Martin Bormann is probably the one whose traces in real estate have been erased most thoroughly, nearly all of the sites associated with his life having either gone or changed beyond recognition. *Above:* Bormann's birth house stood at No. 16 Sedanstrasse in Halberstadt. The house no longer exists, having been destroyed along with all the rest of the street in the final days of the war by the heavy US bomber raid on Halberstadt of April 8, 1945 which left most of the city in ruins. One of the first streets to be rebuilt, Sedanstrasse was renamed Thomas-Müntzer-Strasse, but the stretch between Nos. 6 and 24 was left open and made into a small park.

Martin Bormann

June 17, 1900 — May 2, 1945

Martin Bormann was born on June 17, 1900, in Halberstadt, where his father was serving as a musician with the cavalry. Bormann attended high school for only a year before leaving to take up agriculture on an estate in Mecklenburg until he was conscripted into Feld-Artillerie-Regiment 55 in 1918. After the war he went back to agriculture and also joined the Freikorps Rossbach. Along with Rudolf Höss, the future commandant of Auschwitz, he was involved in the murder of Walther Kadow, his former pri-

mary school teacher, for the alleged betrayal of Albert Schlageter (see page 114) to the French authorities, a crime for which Bormann served a year in Leipzig prison.

Bormann joined the Nazi Party and SA in 1927, rising rapidly in rank as a staff officer. Appointed regional press officer for Thuringia in 1927, he became the Gauleiter for that district the following year.

In 1929 he married Gerda Buch, an equally fanatical Nazi, and they produced ten children. Hitler was a witness at their wedding and godfather of their first child, who was named Adolf after him.

Bormann was appointed Hess's chief-of-staff in 1933 with the rank of Reichsleiter and a seat in the Reichstag. He then took over control of Hitler's personal finances, including the massive contributions from industrialists, and organised the purchase and development of property for Hitler and the Party on the Obersalzberg at Berchtesgaden, where he also established his own Landhaus Bormann. He also arranged the purchase of the house in which Hitler was born at Braunau-am-Inn (see pages 10-11) and the latter's parents' house at Leonding (see pages 12-13).

Left: In 1933, having risen to the position of chief-of-staff of Deputy Führer Rudolf Hess, Bormann was entrusted with the development of the Obersalzberg into a summer residence for Hitler's inner circle. Bormann went about his task with his usual cold efficiency, ruthlessly buying or driving out the farmers and townspeople who owned property on the mountain. As self-appointed 'Lord of the Obersalzberg', he mobilised huge funds, labour and raw materials to realise his plans, one of the most ambitious projects being the creation of the Kehlsteinhaus for Hitler. As the latter seldom used the tea house, Bormann used it for his own purposes. Here, he is seen on the Kehlsteinhaus terrace, the bulging right-hand pocket of his jacket betraying the revolver he always carried with him. Seated on the left is Propaganda Minister Joseph Goebbels (in light suit) in conversation with his private secretary, Dr Werner Naumann, and in the background, staring out across the mountains, is SS-Standartenführer Johann Rattenhuber, chief of the Reichssicherheitsdienst (RSD). This rare picture was taken by Wilhelm Schneider, a member of Hitler's servants' personnel staff. *Right:* Tourists relax with their drinks on the same terrace.

Above: In 1937, Bormann acquired his own residence on the mountain, when he took over an existing house, the villa of Dr Richard Seitz, located on a small hill overlooking Hitler's Berghof, commissioning architect Roderich Fick to expand it into a luxurious country home for his large and ever-growing family. *Below:* Like most buildings on the Obersalzberg, the Landhaus Bormann was destroyed by the Allied bomber raid on Berchtesgaden of April 25, 1945. Except for a few scattered bricks and stones, no trace of it remains today. Even the ground on which it stood was excavated to provide earth for a nearby car park. So far the site has been left undisturbed by the new development of the Obersalzberg.

BORMANN HOUSE

In 1936, one year before he got his hands on the Seitz villa, Bormann had already acquired a large family residence at Pullach, a southern suburb of Munich. Before the war, a housing estate consisting of 26 detached and semi-detached homes had been built in the north-east part of Pullach between Heilmannstrasse and the Munich—Wolfratshausen railway. Officially named Sonnenwald, but more commonly known as the 'Reich Settlement Rudolf Hess', it housed the families of Party functionaries working in the large Parteikanzlei (Party Staff) office block that stood in Margaretenstrasse at the southern end of the settlement. When the NSDAP staff vacated the premises to move to the new Führerbau and Verwaltungsbau headquarters in Munich's Arcisstrasse (see page 158), Bormann took over the building for his personal use as a family home. Hitler visited the Bormanns here in July 1939. During the war, Bormann

developed the 40-acre area into a stand-by Führerhauptquartier, ordering the construction of four large subterranean bunkers, fully equipped with all the necessary communications equipment. The FHQ site, code-named 'Hagen' (at times also 'Siegfried'), was never used as such. Captured intact by the Americans in April 1945, in 1947 it became the headquarters of the Organisation Gehlen, which later developed into the German Federal Republic's secret intelligence service, the Bundesnachrichtendienst. Right up to the present day, the BND site has been a top-secret facility, a blank spot on the map, closely guarded and completely sealed off by high walls from any public scrutiny. The BND has plans to move to Berlin, a transfer that is scheduled for 2008, but until then all photography around the complex is strictly forbidden. This is how it looked before the war.

Considering he also needed a family residence of stature in Munich itself, in 1939 Bormann bought a spacious villa at No. 26 Maria-Theresia-Strasse, in a very well-to-do part of the city. Again, although most other houses in the street survive, Bormann's former dwelling no longer exists, having been replaced with this modern block.

Two day's after Hess's flight to Scotland on May 10, 1941, Hitler abolished the post of Deputy Führer and gave Bormann charge of the newly-created Party Chancellery in the rank of Reich Minister, a position that in all but name made Bormann his private secretary. From now on Bormann became the power behind the throne, controlling access to the Führer and thereby wielding tremendous power, which he used to further his own interests to the detriment of other Nazi leaders such as Himmler and Göring. Through the Gauleiters and their subordinates, Bormann had full control over the Party apparatus and used it to strengthen the Party's influence vis-à-vis the Wehrmacht and SS.

This power came to its peak during the last days in the Führerbunker, when he even tried to manipulate Grossadmiral Karl Dönitz as Hitler's successor. Bormann took part in the break-out from the Reich Chancellery in his uniform of an SA-Obergruppenführer on May 2, 1945, but committed suicide in the vicinity of Lehrter Station, where his remains were discovered in 1972. Previously he was believed by many to have escaped, giving rise to all sorts of stories, and was even sentenced to death *in absentia* at the Nuremburg Trials.

Right: Even the spot where Bormann died on May 2, 1945, during the closing hours of the battle for Berlin, has been obliterated by the progress of time. Having got separated from the party with which they had escaped from the Führerbunker, and finding themselves trapped by Soviet forces on Invalidenstrasse, Bormann and SS-Standartenführer Dr Ludwig Stumpfegger, Hitler's physician, committed suicide by taking poison (see *Berlin Then and Now*, pages 266-267). After the war their bodies could not be found, giving rise to numerous rumours about Bormann's possible escape to South America or elsewhere. In 1965 an excavation was undertaken at a spot [1] along the S-Bahn just west of the Lehrter Bahnhof where it was suspected that the two bodies had been buried, but nothing was found. Seven years later workers digging a ditch for redevelopment work on the same piece of land accidentally discovered two skeletons at position [2].

Left: The 1965 excavation had been prompted by the testimony of retired post office official Albert Krumnow (with hat and walking stick) who had found and buried the two bodies on May 8, 1945. Considering that 20 years had elapsed, it was no wonder that he was off the mark by a few yards. *Right:* The remains found in December 1972 were examined by forensic specialists, and proven beyond doubt to be those of Bormann and Stumpfegger. In this shot, Bormann's skull is the one on the right and Stumpfegger's on the left. Thus, after 27 years, the myth that Bormann had escaped from Berlin was proved false. Another 27 years later, in August 1999, the German government announced that the ashes of Bormann's remains had been scattered over the Baltic Sea earlier that month — a deliberate move to avoid any grave becoming a shrine for neo-Nazis.

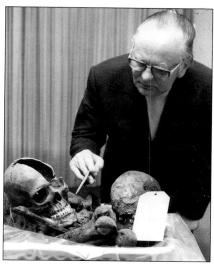

Left: The ditch where the skulls and bones of Bormann and Stumpfegger were found. *Right:* The site along Invalidenstrasse has long since been occupied by the Landesinstitut für Lebensmittel, but the massive re-development of Berlin has now also swept away the last link with the past. As part of the reinstatement of the Lehrter Bahnhof as the capital's central railway station, the former distinctive arches of the elevated S-Bahn have now been replaced with a modern-type overpass.

Joseph Goebbels was born in the Lower Rhineland textile city of Rheydt, at No. 186 Odenkirchener Strasse (today No. 202) *(centre)*. **In 1900, when Joseph was two, his father bought a house at No. 140 Dahlener Strasse (today No. 156),** *(right)*, **and this is where he grew up. Young Josef had his room in the loft.**

Joseph Goebbels

October 29, 1897 — May 1, 1945

Paul Joseph Goebbels was born on October 29, 1897, into a strict Roman Catholic working class family at Rheydt in the Ruhr. His intelligence was recognised at an early age, leading to his education at the local grammar and high schools and, while a deformed foot and permanent limp excluded him from military service in 1914, he obtained a grant that enabled him to study Germanics, history, literature and philosophy at various universities between 1917 and 1921, culminating with a doctorate in philosophy

Goebbels joined the Nazi Party in 1922 and two years later started a career in journalism as editor of the *Völkische*

Freiheit (Peoples' Freedom) in the Ruhr at Elberfeld. In 1925 he was made business manager of the Rhineland-North Gau and began working for Gregor Strasser as editor of *NS Briefe* (Nazi Party Letters), but then became embroiled in the critical Strasser-Hitler controversy over the degree of socialism in the movement, eventually switching to the complete support of Hitler. He was rewarded in 1926 with the appointment to Gauleiter of Berlin-Brandenburg, in which he made his mark as rabble-rouser and propagandist, encouraging beerhall brawls and the like in an area traditionally red in outlook. He founded and edited his own newspaper *Der Angriff* (The Attack) and scored a major political coup with the martyrdom of Horst Wessel in 1930.

He became a member of the Reichstag in 1928 as a Nazi representative for Berlin. One year later Hitler appointed

him head of the party's propaganda department, in which capacity Goebbels organised campaigns in support of Hitler's candidature as Reich President and election campaigns that doubled the Party's representation in the Reichstag, ultimately leading to Hitler's nomination as Chancellor.

On March 13, 1933, Goebbels was appointed Reich Minister for Propaganda and Popular Enlightenment with the major responsibility of co-ordinating all of the press, films, theatre, radio and sports into the Nazi fold, which he did with no respect for principles or morals. In 1931 he married the divorcee Magda Quandt, a devotee of Hitler by whom he had six children, but he was a notorious womaniser and his affairs with stage and film stars were widely publicised, one with the Czech actress Lida Baarova being so blatant that Hitler intervened to save the marriage.

In August 1924, aged 26, he left home and moved to Elberfeld (today a suburb of Wuppertal) in the nearby Ruhr, where in March 1925 he became the Geschäftsführer (manager) of the Nazi Party's newly activated Rhineland-North Gau. Its headquarters was in a five-room suite at No. 8 Auer Schulstrasse *(left)*.

Having reluctantly accepted the post of NSDAP-Gauleiter of the Berlin-Brandenburg district in November 1926, Goebbels' initial lodgings in the capital were at No. 5 Am Karlsbad. *Right:* **Today the new building which now stands on the site is occupied by an insurance company.**

In June 1927, Goebbels founded *Der Angriff* (The Attack), his own weekly newspaper for Berlin, the first edition of which appeared on July 4. From a poor start of selling only a few hundred copies in its first weeks of publication, it would grow to 31,000 copies in February 1928 and, after it became a daily in November 1930, to 68,000 copies in 1931, reaching a peak of 119,000 by February 1933. *Left:* The *Angriff* editorial offices were initially located at No. 10 Hedemannstrasse. *Right:* The corner building at No. 10 has gone but the identical premises next door survive.

It was in an attempt to regain favour with Hitler, that Goebbels launched the 'Reichskristallnacht' (Crystal Night) on November 9/10, 1938. Until then progress against the Jews had been suppressed on Hitler's instructions both for economic reasons and also because of international exposure with the 1936 Olympic Games in Berlin. But there was mounting pressure from the Party to take action, and the murder of a German diplomat in Paris by a Polish Jew two days earlier provided the excuse for action. That evening at a meeting of Party leaders commemorating the 1923 putsch, he announced that there had been anti-Jewish demonstrations in two towns in which shops had been demolished and synagogues burnt. The Führer had decided that such demonstrations were not to be prepared or organised by the Party, but neither were they to be discouraged if they originated spontaneously. The response was for the leaders to telephone their districts and initiate what came to be known as 'Kristallnacht' for the amount of glass that was spilled on to the streets.

Left: In October 1932 *Der Angriff* moved its offices to No. 106 Wilhelmstrasse, just round the corner from the old address, where it would stay until the spring of 1934. After that it moved to Zimmerstrasse. *Right:* The building on Wilhelmstrasse has gone but an historical sign board explains the relevance of the site to passers-by.

On December 19, 1931, Goebbels married Magda Quandt, the wedding taking place at Severin, the Quandt estate near Frauenmark in Mecklenburg.

The couple went to live at Magda's seven-room apartment at No. 2 Reichskanzlerplatz (now renamed Theodor-Heuss-Platz) in the Charlottenburg district of Berlin.

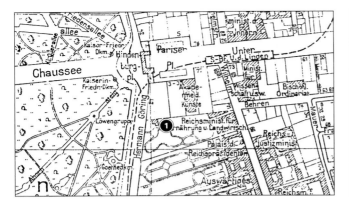

Left: In June 1933, by now Minister of Propaganda in the new Hitler government, Goebbels was assigned the villa at No. 20 Friedrich-Ebert-Strasse [1] (soon to be renamed Hermann-Göring-Strasse), as his official residence. Located in a secluded little park just south of the Brandenburg Gate and next to the US Embassy, it had formerly belonged to press tycoon and chairman of the Deutschnationale Volkspartei Alfred Hugenberg. In April 1938 Goebbels had the old palace pulled down and replaced by an entirely new dwelling, designed by Professor Paul Baumgarten, which was completed in August the following year. Costing 3.2 million Reichsmark, it had a marble-galleried banqueting hall on the ground floor and all the rooms, except the marbled bathrooms, were wood-panelled. *Right:* Today the site is occupied by the north-western corner of the new National Holocaust Memorial.

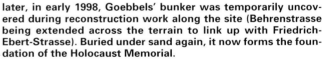

With the start of the Allied air attacks against Berlin in August 1940, Goebbels ordered the construction of an air raid shelter in the garden of his official residence. Designed by his private architect Hugo Bartels and completed in August 1941, it had a concrete roof and walls seven feet thick. Fifty-seven years later, in early 1998, Goebbels' bunker was temporarily uncovered during reconstruction work along the site (Behrenstrasse being extended across the terrain to link up with Friedrich-Ebert-Strasse). Buried under sand again, it now forms the foundation of the Holocaust Memorial.

In March 1936, by now with huge sums of money at his disposal, Goebbels was able to buy a luxurious red-brick villa at No. 8-10 Inselstrasse on Berlin-Schwanenwerder, a millionaire's paradise jutting into the Wannsee lake. Many houses in this exclusive suburb were Jewish-owned and in his *Angriff* days Goebbels had always inveighed against 'Schweinenwerder' (Isle of Pigs) as 'a Jew-boys' paradise'. The family moved into the lakeshore home just before Easter 1936. Today it is a station of the Berlin Water Police.

Nineteen months later, in October 1937, Goebbels also purchased the villa next door, No. 12-14 Inselstrasse. He acquired the property by having the mayor of Berlin, Dr Julius Lippert, put pressure on the Jewish owner, Samuel Goldschmidt, director of the Jewish Goldschmidt-Rothschild Bank, to sell the property to the city for only 117,000 marks. Once the deal was done, Goebbels surfaced as the real buyer. He used the house mainly to get some rest from his endless marital rows with Magda. Today, a forbidding gate prevents a close inspection of the villa.

Apart from the material damage inflicted, the action resulted in 91 Jewish deaths and the arrest of 20,000 for Himmler's concentration camps. Then, to add insult to injury, the Jews were ordered to effect immediate repairs to their property at their own expense, any claims against insurance to be confiscated for the Reich, and the Jewish community as a whole to pay a fine of one billion Reichsmarks!

The action caused considerable harm to Germany's reputation abroad, but in due course Goebbels became an intimate and close adviser of Hitler's, much to the annoyance of Göring and von Ribbentrop, both jealous of his influence.

Throughout the war Goebbels was responsible for the morale of the population with his highly effective propaganda organisation, in which control of the air waves with the death penalty for listening to foreign broadcasts played a significant role. It was mainly due to his efforts that the majority of the German people believed in Hitler's genius and in final victory right until the bitter end.

Shortly after the disaster of Stalingrad, he delivered a masterly speech in the Sportpalast in Berlin on February 18, 1943, calling for the waging of total war. However, it was not until after the July 1944 plot against Hitler, far too late, that he was appointed General Plenipotentiary for the Mobilisation of Total War, authorising him to mobilise all resources for the conduct of the final battle in defence of the Reich.

During the last days of the war Goebbels and his family moved from their home at No. 20 Hermann-Göring-Strasse (which had its own underground air raid shelter) into the Führerbunker at Hitler's invitation. After Hitler's suicide, Goebbels attempted — unsuccessfully over a 24-hour period — to obtain a cease-fire from the Russians to enable him to form the government dictated in Hitler's will. He then had his six children poisoned before committing suicide with his wife during the early hours of May 1, 1945.

In October 1936, on the occasion of his 39th birthday, the city of Berlin donated to Goebbels a large tract of land on the little and secluded Bogensee lake, located 20 miles north-east of the capital near the village of Lanke, for his personal use during his lifetime. Here, deep in the forest, he built a two-storey wood-framed house at the water's edge, which he would use as a love nest to entertain his various mistresses including Czech actress Lida Baarova. Today it is a forester's house.

In 1938 he acquired an 8,000-acre piece of woodland on the far side of the lake where in January 1939 he began construction of a much larger mansion to be used as a family country residence. Designed by Hugo Bartels, the imposing horseshoe-shaped Haus am Bogensee featured five bedrooms, a private cinema, a swimming pool, a guesthouse for two families, and such luxuries as large electrically-operated windows, a disappearing bar, an air-conditioned beer cellar and a refrigerated pastry-cooling table. It was ready for use in time for Goebbels' 42nd birthday in October 1939 although further work on it continued well into the war, the final cost running to three million Reichsmarks. Today it stands empty and unused.

Left: On May 1, 1945, after poisoning their six children, Goebbels and his wife committed suicide in the Führerbunker. Russian SMERSH (military counter-intelligence) troops found their horribly burned corpses the following day, and the dead children were found one day later. All corpses were taken to Plötzensee Prison for identification and then to the mortuary *(right)* at Buch Hospital in northern Berlin for forensic examination. (See pages 458-461 for what happened next.)

Hermann Göring was born in Germany but his parents did not live there. His father, Dr Heinrich Göring, was serving as German Consul-General and Minister-Resident at Port-au-Prince in Haiti when he was conceived, and his mother Franziska travelled back to Germany on her own to give birth. Hermann came into the world at the Marienbad-Sanatorium *(right)* at Rosenheim, 60 kilometres south-east of Munich, in southern Bavaria. No sooner was the baby weaned than Franziska returned to the Caribbean, leaving her newborn baby in the care of friends at Fürth. Not until 1896, when little Hermann was three, did his parents return to Germany. The former sanatorium at No. 52-54 Heilig-Geist-Strasse still exists, having since been converted to an apartment block.

Hermann Göring

January 12, 1893 – October 15, 1946

Hermann Wilhelm Göring was born at Rosenheim in Bavaria on January 12, 1893, the son of a senior German colonial official. His education terminated in December 1913 with his graduation as a second lieutenant from the prestigious Lichterfelde Academy in Berlin (later the home of the Leibstandarte-SS Adolf Hitler — see page 306).

He then joined Infanterie-Regiment 112 'Prinz Wilhelm', which fought in Alsace at the beginning of the First World War, and was awarded the Iron Cross Second Class within the first five weeks but then, after an illness, transferred to aviation, first as an observer and then as a fighter pilot, winning the Iron Cross First Class and then the coveted Pour le Mérite, otherwise known as 'the Blue Max'. He ended the war as commander of the famous Richthofen Squadron, but still only a substantive lieutenant. Later he persuaded his old regiment to discharge him in the rank of captain in exchange for renouncing his pension rights.

While earning his living flying in Scandinavia he met Carin Freiin von Kantzow, née Fock, the wife of a Swedish officer, with whom he fell madly in love. Their affair became so notorious that they were obliged to flee to Munich, where in 1922 he registered as a student of economics, but then heard Hitler speak and joined the Nazi Party. The acquisition of such a famous war hero was useful to Hitler, who gave him command of the SA.

Wounded in the groin during the Hitler putsch of November 8-9, 1923, he was smuggled into Austria, where morphine was used to combat the severe pain he was suffering, as a result of which he became an addict, a problem that was to haunt him for the rest of his life, twice being admitted to Swedish mental hospitals.

He returned to Germany in 1927 and was tasked by Hitler with gaining a foothold in Berlin society, for which his background was well suited. The following year he was given one of the Party's allocation of seats in the Reichstag, bringing him a regular income and

Below: **Young Hermann spent much of his youth at Burg Mauterndorf, a castle in Austria that was owned by a wealthy Jewish doctor and friend of the family, Dr Hermann von Epenstein. In later life, after Göring had risen to power, the castle became one of his favoured retreats. When Frau von Epenstein died in September 1939, she bequeathed the castle to Göring and this is where he would hide out in the final days of the Third Reich. After the war, Göring's widow Emmy claimed ownership of the property but this was contested by the Austrian republic and by relatives of Frau von Epenstein. In 1966 the castle was purchased by the Austrian government which has since restored and opened the building as a cultural centre.**

Above: **On February 3, 1922, Göring married Carin von Kantzow. After spending a few months living in a little hunting-box at Bayerischzell in the Bavarian Alps, the couple moved to a small house at No. 30 Döbereiner Strasse in the Munich suburb of Obermenzing. It was during this time that Göring met Adolf Hitler, joined the Nazi party and was appointed the first commander of the SA. The Görings lived at Obermenzing until the Hitler Putsch of November 1923 which resulted in Göring being severely wounded and forced to flee from Germany.**

In autumn 1927, amnesty was proclaimed for the 1923 putschists and Göring returned from Sweden, where he and Carin had lived since 1925, to make a fresh start in Germany. He settled down in Berlin, his first dwelling being an apartment at No. 16 Berchtesgadener Strasse *(left)*, on the corner with Apostel-Paulus-Strasse, in the respectable Wilmersdorf district. By spring 1928, his writing for newspapers and deals with aircraft firms was making him enough money to allow him to bring Carin over to join him. That May, Göring was elected a Reichstag member for the NSDAP, which brought more income and respectability. Within a year the couple moved a few blocks to a modern and more spacious flat at No. 7 Badensche Strasse *(right)* on the fourth storey. Here, they began a busy social life, forever entertaining guests and throwing receptions. The house also became a regular meeting place for leading Party members. Hitler, whenever he came to Berlin, always made sure he dropped in.

Carin died on October 17, 1931. Burying his grief in work, Göring moved into a stylish bachelor's apartment which once stood here at No. 34 Kaiserdamm in the fashionable Charlottenburg district.

Above: In January 1933 Göring became Interior Minister for Prussia in Hitler's first cabinet. The ceremonial raising of the swastika flag from the ministry building on Unter den Linden for the first time on March 13 (two weeks after the Reichstag fire) was good excuse for a march-past by SA troops, Göring viewing the parade from the balcony. *Below:* The post-war replacement at No. 70-72 today houses the Polish Embassy.

access to funding that enabled him and Carin to move from their first Berlin home at No. 16 Berchtesgadener Strasse to No. 7 Badensche Strasse, where they entertained on a grand scale. That autumn he was appointed Vice-President of the Reichstag.

Carin's death in October 1931 left Göring devastated. He gave up their flat and immersed himself in political work. In July 1932 he was elected President of the Reichstag, a catalytical role with direct access to President Hindenburg that eventually enabled him to announce to Hitler that he would be appointed Chancellor next day.

In Hitler's new government, Göring became Minister without Portfolio and Minister of the Interior of Prussia, thereby getting command of Germany's largest police force. Göring immediately began an energetic purge of all non-Nazi supporters in the police, replacing them with men from the SA and SS.

He also founded a 50,000-strong auxiliary police force of SA and SS, and established concentration camps at Oranienburg near Berlin and Papenburg (near the Dutch border) in which they could terrorise their political opponents.

Then on April 11 Hitler appointed him Prime Minister of Prussia, which gave Göring even greater powers that he wasted no time in exploiting. That same day, with Hitler's authority to control all wire-tapping throughout Germany, Göring founded the Forschungsamt (Research Office) with a core of code breakers. Housed in Schillerstrasse in the Charlottenburg district of Berlin, it expanded rapidly and proved of immense intelligence value to the Nazi leadership. Two weeks later Göring founded the Prussian Secret State Police, the dreaded Gestapo, as it was to become known and feared throughout Europe.

Meanwhile President Hindenburg had appointed him Reich Commissar for Aviation, so Göring began planning the establishment of the Luftwaffe, and in May his appointment was upgraded to Reich Minister for Aviation.

On August 31, 1933, President Hindenburg awarded Göring the rank of General der Infanterie, in exchange for which Göring gave him an estate in East Prussia before taking one for himself on the Schorfheide, the vast rolling forest region north-east of Berlin. There Göring had a Nordic hunting lodge built and named it Carinhall after his first wife, for whom a burial vault was pre-

In early 1933 Göring secured from the Prussian State Council a 100,000-acre plot of land in the vast Schorfheide Forest, some 50 kilometres north-east of Berlin. Here, on a ridge between the Grosser Döllnsee and the smaller Wuckersee lakes near Friedrichswalde, he planned to build a comfortable country house, to be named Carinhall in honour of his deceased first wife. Based on the hunting lodge of Carin's brother-in-law, Count Eric von Rosen, at Rockelstad Castle in Sweden, and finalised by architect Werner March, the T-shaped building was erected in ten months, being ceremoniously presented to Göring by the Prussian State Forestry in October 1933 and completed in May 1934. Of simple design, the ground floor consisted of a large rustic hall connected to a dining room plus kitchen and two closets, while on the first floor were Göring's study, two guest rooms and a bathroom.

pared in the grounds. A year later, on June 20, 1934, with Hitler as his guest of honour, Göring had Carin's coffin placed in the vault in an impressive ceremony attended by several hundred dignitaries.

With ever more heads of state and royal guests coming to the Schorfheide, Göring was no longer satisfied with his log cabin and in 1936-37 he rebuilt Carinhall on a grand scale, incorporating the old house. The new Carinhall, designed by architects Friedrich Hetzelt and Hermann Tuch, consisted of a main building with two wings arranged around an imposing courtyard. A gate connecting one of the wings with a perpendicular adjutant's wing formed a kind of forecourt. The Görings lived in the long central building, which had a 40-seat dining room (with the inevitable large window that could be lowered into the ground) on the ground floor; a cinema, bowling alley and old-style Bavarian beer hall in the basement, and Göring's large model railway in the attic. The new left wing contained a music room, library, gymnasium and indoor swimming pool, while the right wing housed guest rooms, a lounge, kitchen and the servants' quarters.

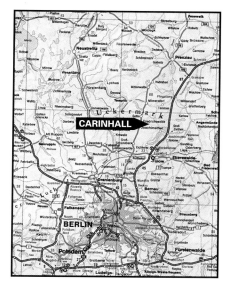

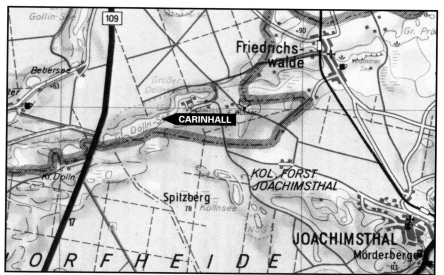

To get to Carinhall from Berlin, Göring would drive up the Reichsstrasse 109. Afraid of air attacks, he had shelters constructed at regular intervals along this road. In later years he would have used the new Berlin-Stettin autobahn.

Göring was a passionate huntsman, being a good shot and stalker and, now that he had the authority, he set out to reform the confusion of hunting laws that seemed to vary from estate to estate. As early as January 1934 he promulgated the Prussian Game Law, which was later adopted throughout Germany and still applies today.

On April 20, 1934, Göring handed over the Prussian police, including the Gestapo, to Himmler, as the price for obtaining the latter's co-operation in the elimination of the growing SA threat to the stability of the state. As Hitler acted on what was to become called 'The Night of the Long Knives', Göring and Himmler remained in Berlin, where they had spent the previous day and night listing persons to be dealt with throughout the country, and Göring himself led the raid on the Berlin SA headquarters.

Following Hindenburg's death in August 1934, Göring's prominent role in the consolidation of the Third Reich was formally acknowledged in December when Hitler signed two secret decrees, one naming Göring as his deputy in the now dual role of Reich President and Chancellor, and the second appointing him as his successor. Elated, Göring embarked on a vast expansion of Carinhall, which he would use to entertain and impress his guests, often appearing in the most fantastic of costumes, armed either with a spear or bejewelled daggers. Carinhall was eventually to cost the taxpayers 15 million Reichsmarks channelled equally between the Luftwaffe and Prussian State budgets.

The Reichsmarschall addressing a delegation of Japanese youth in the courtyard of Carinhall on July 7, 1938. The youngsters from Germany's Asiatic partner (the two countries were allies since the Anti-Comintern Pact of November 25, 1936) were on a tour of Germany.

Göring saying goodbye to the Yugoslav Minister President Milan Stojadinovic outside the new main entrance of Carinhall on January 15, 1938.

Left: Taking over the function of the rustic hall [1] of the old hunting lodge was this 'Great Hall' [2] built in 1936-37.

When Carinhall was extended again three years later, this hall became Göring's study. *Right:* The interior of the Great Hall.

Right: In 1939-40, Göring decided to extend Carinhall a second time, architects Hetzelt and Tuch adding yet another courtyard, another building, and another perpendicular wing [3]. The new building housed Göring's art gallery, while the new wing became the library, the old library being converted into guest rooms. The new extension doubled the size of the existing structure. Here the Reichsmarschall leads Japanese Foreign Minister Yosuke Matsuoka through the Galerie ([4] on the plan) during the latter's visit to Carinhall on March 29, 1941. Right from the start, Carinhall had been filled with tapestries, paintings and other treasures but, as the war progressed, Göring packed the house with ever more works of art that he had bought, confiscated or stolen from all over Nazi-occupied Europe.

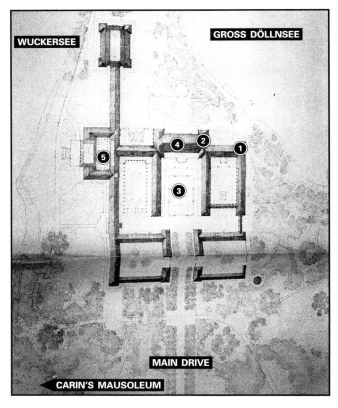

Above: Göring with Hitler on the terrace behind the original hunting lodge (now part of the larger house), which over-looked the Grosser Döllnsee. *Right:* On the occasion of his 52nd birthday, on January 12, 1945, Göring presented to his aston-ished guests his plans for a further extension [5] of Carinhall, which would once again double the size of the house. Sched-uled to be completed in 1953, in time for his 60th birthday, this would become the 'Hermann-Göring-Museum', housing North Germany's foremost art collection. In the event, his grandiose plans came to nought with the demise of the Third Reich.

WUCKERSEE

GROSS DÖLLNSEE

MAIN DRIVE

CARIN'S MAUSOLEUM

Above and right: **In late January 1945, special trains began to evacuate Carinhall's art treasures and valuable furniture to southern Germany. Göring himself left Carinhall for the last time on April 20, 1945, leaving personal orders for Luftwaffe engineers to blow up the house using aircraft bombs, which they did on the 28th when advance units of the Soviet Army had been spotted approaching. After the war, the site was cleared of the ruins, the stone being carted away to be utilised for other buildings in the area. Lying in East Germany and close to official guest houses of the DDR, the entire area was closed off by the East German Volksarmee in the early 1960s. Public access only became possible again after the demise of the Berlin Wall in 1989. (For the full story see** *After the Battle* **No. 71.)**

Today, the site of Göring's famous villa is just a large open clearing in the Schorfheide woods.

Right: From the beginning Göring had conceived Carinhall as a embodying the spirit of his dead wife Carin, who lay buried in the Fock family plot at Lovö Churchyard on Drottningholm Island, just west of Stockholm in Sweden. In 1933 Swedish anti-Nazis removed a swastika-shaped wreath that Göring had placed on her grave. Furious at the insult and desecration, the following year he had Carin's remains exhumed and transported to Carinhall to be placed in an underground crypt especially built for her in the grounds. Göring had personally planned every detail, including Carin's huge sarcophagus, which was designed to one day provide for his own body as well. A large group of mourners and dignitaries attended the ceremony in June 1934, Hitler and Göring leading the procession to the grave. The latter's enormous wreath of red roses bore a sash with the words: 'In constant love and loyalty and sincerest gratitude. Hermann'.

Göring and Hitler emerge from the underground tomb.

The interior of the vault.

Left behind unguarded at the end of the war, according to local rumours the sarcophagus was cut open in search for jewels and other valuables. In November 1950, a Swedish priest, Heribert Jansson, found Carin's bones strewn on the floor of the crypt so he repatriated them to her native Sweden to rest once more in the churchyard at Lovö.

Some time afterwards, the mausoleum was blown up by the East German army. This is what the site looks like today.

From the moment the Carinhall area became accessible again in 1990, rumours about Nazi treasures still hidden there attracted large numbers of gold-diggers. Several people claimed to have found silver bowls, rings, sculptures and other art treasures, and in July 1991 one group even claimed to have found Carin's body in a zinc coffin buried near the blown crypt! *Above left:* At the entrance to the estate, just outside Friedrichswalde, stand the two stone sentry boxes, the right-hand one bearing Göring's coat of arms. *Above right:* The two guardhouses on either side of the drive also survive. *Right:* To accommodate his important guests Göring had a special guest-house, known as the Schade-Haus, built on the west bank of the Grosser Döllnsee, across the lake from Carinhall. Undamaged by the war, it was used for the same purpose by the German Democratic Republic. Today the former guesthouse is the Spa-Hotel Döllnsee-Schorfheide.

One of the most interesting remains at Carinhall is the underground air raid shelter that Göring had constructed in 1940. Located to the west of the main house, it was accessible via a spiral staircase and a long corridor, with an escape tunnel leading to the bank of the Döllnsee lake. In 1993, German historian Volker Knopf thoroughly explored the accessible parts of the bunker, recovering numerous small fragments of marble, Greek vases, porcelain, etc. He initially secured permission to keep the bunker open and preserve it as a bat sanctuary, but in May 1998 the German forestry authorities decreed that the entrance should be sealed. Today all one can see are the three entry pipes for the bats.

Little known is that some of the bronze sculptures from Carinhall are preserved in public places. *Left:* The Riding Amazon by Franz von Stuck, cast in 1909, first stood in Carinhall's 'old' 1937 courtyard and later in the new 1939 courtyard. Today it stands in the Stadtpark at Eberswalde, 11 miles away. *Right:* The Red Deer by Johannes Darsow was commissioned by Göring for the 1937 International Hunting Exhibition in Berlin and later acquired by him for Carinhall. Representing a famous deer shot by Göring himself in East Prussia in 1936, it first stood in the park south of the guest wing and from 1939 at the western end of the Kastanienallee (chestnut avenue). From the mid-1950s to 1970 it stood in the palace park of Sansoucci at Potsdam, and since then in the Tierpark at Berlin-Friedrichsfelde.

On April 11, 1933, Göring had been appointed Prime Minister of Prussia. His official residence in Berlin was a luxurious palace at No. 11a Leipziger Platz.

The palace was pulled down after the war and today the site is an open plot behind the former Preussenhaus (now Bundesrat) and the Haus der Flieger (now House of Representatives).

In addition to Carinhall, Göring had a hunting villa at Rominten in East Prussia, a villa on the Obersalzberg built close to Hitler's, and a palace he had had constructed as President of Prussia at No. 11a Leipziger Strasse, Berlin, which he constantly kept altering. Like Carinhall, the palace displayed a vulgar opulence with fabulous tapestries, paintings and statuary, even special rooms to house gifts presented by or exacted from various individuals and institutions, and all carefully listed by the staff of their avaricious owner.

Barely nine months after Carin's death, Göring established relationships with Emmy Sonnemann, a blonde German actress who had separated from her husband, Karl Köstlin, but it was not until her divorce came through, and with some pressure from Hitler who attended as a witness, that they married in the Berlin Dom (cathedral) on April 10, 1935, in a ceremony that had regal overtones. Thirty thousand troops lined the streets for the occasion, which included a fly-past by 200 aircraft, and the oppulent wedding gifts filled two of Carinhall's spacious rooms. Although Göring was concerned that his groin injury would have rendered him impotent, their daughter Edda was born on June 2, 1938.

Göring's powers continued to expand as new appointments came his way. He was already involved in the problem of Germany's lack of oil, rubber and iron ore, and in 1935 Hitler made him responsible for petroleum and synthetic rubber production, followed by the task of arbitrating between the competing interests of agriculture and industry, eventually becoming Commissioner for Foreign Exchange and Raw Materials.

By April 1936 he had formed a team of experts culled from industry and the civil service to deal with these problems, their work eventually leading to Hitler's declaration of the Four Year Plan at Nuremberg that autumn, putting Göring firmly in charge of the German economy.

As the Four Year Plan progressed, Göring turned his attention to steel manufacture and had a vast plant built at Salzgitter in competition with the traditional industrialists of the Ruhr. The 'Hermann-Göring-Werke' under his direct control became one of the largest industrial concerns in Europe, constantly expanding and exerting tremendous commercial influence. Needless to say, this brought Göring even more personal wealth and funds with which to purchase the works of art and diamonds that he coveted.

Left: Despite his sorrow over Carin, within six months of her death Göring started an affair with the actress Emmy Sonnemann, a married woman. Under pressure from Hitler who, somewhat hypocritically, disapproved of such activities, Göring eventually married her. The wedding in Berlin on April 10, 1935, was a major social event with all the accoutrements of a royal wedding. The streets were decorated, all traffic in the inner city was suspended and 30,000 troops lined the streets and 200 military aircraft performed a fly-past while throngs cheered the couple as it drove down Unter den Linden to the Berlin Cathedral, emerging (left) as husband and wife. Right: The steps of the Berliner Dom as seen from the Lustgarten today.

Right: **Although Carinhall was clearly Göring's main estate, his status alone dictated that he also had to have a mansion on the Obersalzberg, in fact he was the first of the top Nazis to follow Hitler to the Bavarian mountain. In 1933 he bought the knoll known as the Eckerbichl just west and above Hitler's Berghof and the following year built a two-storied Landhaus in Bavarian style on top of it. It was a relatively small building but it had a heated 10 x 20 metre outdoor swimming pool in front, the first mansion in Berchtesgaden to possess such a luxury. The architect was Alois Degano who one year later would direct the conversion of Hitler's Haus Wachenfeld into the Berghof. Göring had his house enlarged several times, the last reconstruction taking place in 1941.**

However, energetic, ruthless and ambitious as he was, Göring could neither apply the necessary expertise nor the time to the individual elements of his vast empire, The initial dazzling success of 'Blitzkrieg' brought Göring promotion to Reichsmarschall but, as Hitler played out the role of 'The Greatest Field Commander of all Time', he relied heavily on the support of Göring's over-extended Luftwaffe and economic base, whose weaknesses became more and more apparent, especially as Göring and the General Staff had not planned on full-scale warfare beginning until the mid-1940s. Göring gradually lost influence and status as the deficiencies and failures came to light and were seized upon by his political enemies, Bormann in particular.

Eventually, believing that Hitler was about to be cut off in Berlin, on April 23, 1945, Göring sent a signal offering to take over, which Bormann presented to Hitler as evidence of betrayal. Göring was obliged to resign from all his offices and placed under house arrest. He later surrendered to the Americans and was put on trial at Nuremberg, where he committed suicide shortly before he was due to be executed.

Partly ruined by the Allied bombing raid of April 25, 1945, Göring's house was razed to the ground together with other Nazi buildings in 1952. For five decades 'Göring's Hill' remained a open plateau. Then in 2001 the Munich-based development company Gewerbegrund announced its intention to build a 140-bed, five-star spa hotel on the Obersalzberg for the London-based Brass Hotels and Resorts chain, the selected spot being Göring's knoll. The Intercontinental Resort Hotel was opened in 2005. In actual fact, the new building leaves the precise spot of Göring's house undisturbed, as shown by our picture which was taken from the site where the latter stood.

Having fled from Berchtesgaden to Mauterndorf Castle in Austria in late April 1945, Göring surrendered to the US 36th Infantry Division at Radstadt on May 8. Shortly afterwards, he was pictured at the 36th Division's headquarters at Kitzbühel, talking to Major General John E. Dahlquist, the division commander. On the right is Brigadier General Robert J. Stack, the division's assistant commander, who led the party sent to accept his surrender.

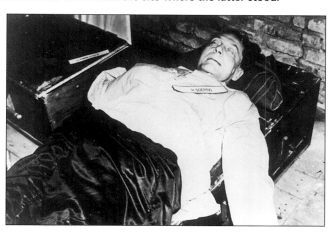

Brought to trial at the Nuremberg Tribunal, Göring cheated his executioners by swallowing cyanide in his cell in the evening of October 15, 1946, just a few hours before he was due to be hanged. The capsule containing the poison had been given to him by one of the American prison wardens, Lieutenant Jack G. Wheelis (see page 452), in exchange for the Reichsmarschall's wristwatch (see *After the Battle* No. 44).

Rudolf Hess was born in Alexandria, Egypt, where his father, Fritz Hess, was a prosperous merchant, but he received his secondary education in Germany. When Rudolf was 14, his father sent him to the Pädagogium *(above)* at Bad Godesberg, a Protestant boarding school for boys, which he attended from September 1908 to Easter 1911.

Rudolf Hess

April 26, 1894 – August 17, 1987

Rudolf Walther Richard Hess was born on April 26, 1894, in Alexandria's coastal suburb of Ibrahimieh in Egypt, and educated at German schools there and at Bad Godesberg near Bonn. As soon as war broke out in 1914 he enlisted in Bavarian Feld-Artillerie-Regiment 7, but a few weeks later was transferred to Bavarian Infanterie-Regiment 1 which was involved in the lengthy battles on the Somme and at Verdun. The following April he was awarded the Iron Cross Second Class. Later he fought with Bavarian Reserve-Infanterie-Regiment 18 in Rumania.

During convalescence after his second wound he was commissioned second lieutenant and decided to try his hand at flying, but qualified too late as a fighter pilot to take part in the final air battles.

When the war ended, Hess emerged an angry young man, brooding over the downfall of his country. He joined the Freikorps Epp, and then in 1920 enrolled at Munich University to study economics, and the same year joined the Nazi Party as Member No. 16.

In 1921 Hess became an active member of the SA and played an important part in Hitler's putsch of November 8-9, 1923, his role being to take several prominent members of the Bavarian Cabinet into the hills as hostages, for which he later received a light sentence that sent him to Landsberg Prison (see page 109), where he assisted Hitler with

the production of *Mein Kampf.* After their release, Hess wielded considerable influence in the early days of the party as Hitler's private secretary and adjutant, and also specialised in collecting funds for the party, being effective in obtaining considerable donations from leading industrialists. Based on the party headquarters in Munich, (from July 1930 established in the Brown House — see pages 154-155) his work took him all over Germany, so he incorporated his love of flying into the business and also encouraged Hitler to use this novel means of transport to get around the country on his vote-raising campaigns.

In December 1927 Hess married Ilse Pröhl. From 1930 to 1933 the couple occupied a third-floor apartment at No. 3 Löfftzstrasse in Munich but they soon acquired a substantial home at

Left: **Having married Ilse Pröhl in 1927, from 1930 to 1933 the couple lived at No. 3 Löfftzstrasse in northern Munich. This street was part of a newly built modern housing estate off Dachauer Strasse known as the Borstei, after its architect and owner Bernhard Borst. Built in 1924-1931 as Borst's private** development project, it comprised elegant 77 housing blocks with 773 rented houses in a secluded neighbourhood, which had its own shops, café, post office and kindergarten. *Right:* **The Hess's apartment on Löfftzstrasse was on the third floor, on the left-hand side of the central entrance.**

Its idyllic atmosphere was not enough to keep the Hess's in the Borstei and in 1933 — the year Hess was appointed Stellvertretender Parteiführer (Deputy Führer of the Nazi Party) — they moved to the other side of the city to a large villa at No. 48 Harthauser Strasse *(left)* in the well-to-do Harlaching district. Many prominent Nazis lived here. After Hess had flown to Britain in May 1941, his wife and son Wolf Rüdiger continued to live here until the house got bombed in 1944. *Above:* In 1945-46 Harlaching was taken over by the US Military Government, some 894 private houses being confiscated, their occupants told to move out, and the whole area being closed off with barbed-wire fence. In due course the Hess's villa was pulled down and plain Army utility buildings erected on the site. Today they are used for theatre rehearsals.

No. 48 Harthauser Strasse where in 1937 their son, Wolf Rüdiger Adolf Karl Hess, was born. Here also, on October 22 of that same year, they entertained the Duke and Duchess of Windsor on the latter's return from having tea with Hitler at Berchtesgaden. In addition, the family owned a holiday house at Reicholdsgrün in Upper Franconia.

With the Nazi seizure of power in 1933, Hess's career took a big leap forward. He became a member of the Reichstag and an honorary Obergruppenführer in the SS, whose black uniform he wore proudly on all public occasions, and that April Hitler appointed him Deputy Führer of the Nazi Party. This gave him a special staff of his own to help supervise all party offices, formations and affiliated organisations, with authority to reorganise them and issue rules and regulations. Gradually he brought all associations, clubs and professional organisations within the country under the Nazi Party's umbrella and control, banning all independent alternatives. Included in his achievements at this stage was the creation of the Deutsche Arbeitsfront (DAF — German Labour Front), an amalgamation and replacement of all the trade unions, under Robert Ley. Hess remained Hitler's intimate, but Martin Bormann as Hess's Chief-of-Staff, was gradually able to usurp Hess with his increasingly influential and powerful secretarial role.

On December 1, 1933, Hess was appointed Reich Minister without Portfolio, an appointment which was gradually developed to enable him to participate in the formation of legislation by all departments of the Reich and Länder Governments, as well as Hitler's own decrees. Thus Hess was directly involved in a series of laws aimed at opponents of the Nazi regime and the Jews. The same year his authority was extended down to local council level, and by 1937 no government official or Labour Service officer could be appointed without the consent of Hess or his authorised representative.

He took a prominent part in the 'Night of the Long Knives' in 1934, when he gave out a list of the names of 19 persons who were to be summarily executed, and then went on to make a public broadcast justifying the action taken against the leadership of the SA. Subsequently Hess went on to reorganise the SA with its new Chief-of-Staff Viktor Lutze.

He was also responsible for establishing the Euthanasia Committee under Philip Bouhler for the elimination of mentally and physically incapacitated persons that was empowered by a Hitler Decree in October 1939 and backdated to September 1 of that year. The committee's programme resulted in the deaths of some 100,000 to 275,000 persons (see pages 361-367) and was only curtailed in response to a strong protest by Protestant and Catholic church leaders when it became known that seriously wounded soldiers were also included.

After the conquest and division of Poland, Hess became involved in the administration of the occupied territories and the formulation of penal laws against their inhabitants. However, the focus was now on war and Hess's administrative apparatus was of no further interest to Hitler, with whom Hess was beginning to lose his influence, a catastrophe for one of such devotion.

The Hess family originally came from Wunsiedel in the Fichtel Mountains in northeast Bavaria, close to the border with Czechoslovakia. They also owned a holiday house *(above)* at Reicholdsgrün, a tiny farming village in the mountains 15 kilometres to the north of there. Built by Hess's father Fritz in 1907-08 at the southern entrance of the village, this is where Hess and his family spent most of their summer holidays. After the war, Hess's sister Margarete and her husband, retired Generalleutnant Erwin Rauch (who during the war had commanded the 123. Infanterie-Division on the Eastern and the 343. Infanterie-Division on the Western Front), lived in the house until the latter's death in 1969. For the subsequent fate of the house, see page 457.

On May 10, 1941, Hess made his momentous solo flight to Scotland as a self-appointed peace envoy, intending to arrange a peaceful settlement between Britain and Germany through the 14th Duke of Hamilton, whom he said he knew from the 1936 Olympic Games in Berlin. He took off from Augsburg airfield from where, despite Hitler's ban on his flying, he had been taking up aircraft of the Messerschmitt works to keep his eye in.

On July 19, 1940, Hitler had made a speech in the Reichstag offering peace to the British Empire, saying that only a small clique of British warmongers were keeping the war alive, while all the British people wanted was peace. Aware of Hitler's plan to invade the Soviet Union, Hess decided to secure the way for Germany's expansion to the east by neutralising the British opposition with a peace treaty. Such a coup would surely prove his worth to his Führer and recover his position at Hitler's side. He picked on the Duke of Hamilton, who had visited Berlin in 1936 for the Olympic Games, as a suitable contact, although they had never met.

Hess had continued to keep up his flying, and in 1934 he had even won the annual air race around the Zugspitze,

Germany's highest mountain. He had good contacts with the air industry and was thus able to have a twin-engined Messerschmitt 110 fitted out with special long-range tanks and placed at his disposal at Augsburg for training flights until circumstances were sufficiently favourable to attempt his mission to the

Duke's estate in Scotland, a flight that stretched both the aircraft and the pilot to the full extent of their capabilities.

He took off from Augsburg at 1725 hours, German Summer Time, on May 10, 1941, wearing the uniform of a Luftwaffe captain, and landed on Floors Farm, west of Eaglesham, Renfrewshire, at about 2310 hours local time, spraining his back and right ankle in the process. When he was helped to his feet by the head ploughman, he announced in English that he was Captain Alfred Horn of the Luftwaffe and had come with an important message for the Duke of Hamilton.

He was subsequently arrested and interrogated, but his message fell on deaf ears and Churchill ordered his detention until the termination of hostilities. So began a period of captivity that was to last until his death at the age of 93.

At 2000 hours on May 12, an announcement was read out on German radio, claiming that Hess had been mentally disturbed at the time of his flight. A BBC announcement acknowledging Hess's arrival followed the same evening.

After a 1,000-mile flight Hess took to his parachute over Floors Farm near Eaglesham, south of Glasgow, his Bf 110 aircraft crashing at nearby Bonnyton Farm. (For the full story see *After the Battle* Nos. 58 and 66.)

Detained by the British government, Hess spent the first year of his imprisonment at Mytchett Place, a country house near Aldershot. Known as 'Camp Z', it had been converted into a miniature fortress with trenches, machine gun posts and barbed wire especially to guard him.

With Hess showing increasing signs of mental instability, on May 25, 1942, he was transferred to Maidiff Court Hospital at Abergavenny in South Wales, where he remained under constant medical supervision. He was accommodated in two small adjoining rooms that led out to a walled exercise area.

Sentenced to life in September 1946, Hess spent the following 41 years in Spandau Allied Military Prison *(right)* at No. 23 Wilhelmstrasse in the borough of Spandau. After Hess's death in 1987, the prison was demolished to be replaced by the Britannia Centre, which until 1994 served the British garrison in Berlin. Today it is a shopping area for the local community, the former governors' and warders' quarters having been restored (see pages 450-451).

At the Nuremberg Trials, where Hess tried to simulate amnesia and mental illness, he was nevertheless found fit to plead and was sentenced to life imprisonment as one of the seven Nazi criminals awarded prison sentences and subsequently incarcerated at Spandau Allied Prison in Berlin.

From October 1, 1966, when the last two of the other six Nuremberg prisoners — Albert Speer and Baldur von Schirach — were released, he was the sole remaining inmate. In 1969 he was pictured during his daily walk in the prison garden.

On August 17, 1987, then aged 93, Hess committed suicide by hanging himself with a piece of electrical flex fastened to a window latch in the Portakabin that served as a summerhouse in the prison garden.

Following the release of Baldur von Schirach and Speer in 1966, Hess remained the sole prisoner there and all attempts to obtain a reprieve for him continued to be squashed by the Soviets, who had demanded the death penalty at his trial but been outvoted by the Western judges. Eventually, on August 17, 1987, after writing a farewell note to the family, he committed suicide in his garden pavilion, using an electric cable as a simple throttling loop around his neck. His body was then handed over to his family and he was finally buried in the family plot at Wunsiedel.

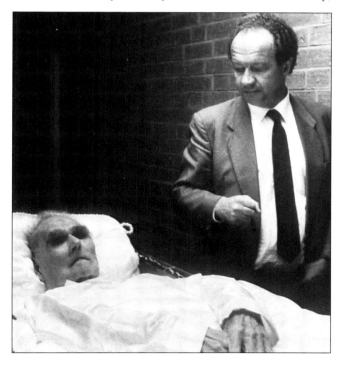

Left: After a post-mortem, Hess's body was released to the family who immediately had another autopsy carried out to get a second opinion on the cause of death. Here Wolf Rüdiger Hess poses beside his dead father. *Above:* Although it had been announced that Hess would be buried in the family grave at Wunsiedel, because of the huge media attention and fears of a neo-Nazi demonstrations on the day, he was initially buried at a secret location and only later re-interred at Wunsiedel. His wife Ilse, who died on September 7, 1995, now also rests there.

Heinrich Himmler came from a very respectable Munich bourgeois family. His father, Gebhard Himmler, was for many years tutor of a member of the Bavarian Royal Court, Crown Prince Heinrich of Wittelsbach. Named after the prince, Heinrich was born in a second-floor flat at No. 6 Hildegardstrasse, on the corner with Hochbrücken-strasse in the city centre. *Right:* The original house has disappeared, a modern office block now taking its place.

Heinrich Himmler

October 7, 1900 — May 23, 1945

Heinrich Himmler was born at No. 2 Hildegardstrasse, Munich, on October 7, 1900, in a highly respected, strongly Catholic family. He was a studious child, short-sighted and physically weak, but with a strong belief that adherence to order and discipline would bring him success. He joined the Bavarian Infanterie-Regiment 11 late in 1917 with ambitions of becoming a regular officer but was too late to do more than complete his basic training. After the war he served briefly in a small local Freikorps (Free Corps), but again saw no action. He then enrolled at Munich Technical University, obtaining his

diploma as an agricultural chemist in 1922. That same year he met Haupt-mann Ernst Röhm and enrolled in his Reichskriegsflagge paramilitary organisation. When Hitler staged his abortive putsch and marched on the Bavarian War Ministry on November 9, 1923, Himmler was the standard bearer with Röhm's organisation that had occupied that building on Hitler's instructions (see page 104), as a result of which he lost his job.

He then worked for Röhm as an unpaid secretary, after which he was taken on in a paid capacity at Landshut by Gregor Strasser, who recognised Himmler's organising ability. Himmler joined the Nazi Party and also the Schutzstaffel (SS), Hitler's personal bodyguard, with the SS number 186, in early 1925. When Strasser was sent off by Hitler to organise the Party in north-

ern Germany, Himmler remained behind as the District Organiser, touring around by motorcycle to deliver speeches.

In 1928 Himmler married Margarete Boden, the daughter of a West Prussian landowner, and set himself up as a poultry farmer on a property at No. 109 Wasserburger Landstrasse in Waltrude-ring, an eastern suburb of Munich, that she had purchased for that purpose with the proceeds of the sale of her clinic for homeopathic treatment in Berlin. From his wife he developed interests in home-opathy, mesmerism and herbalism, but neither the business nor the marriage proved a success, as his political activities increased. They had one daughter, Gudrun, and later adopted a boy, Ger-hard, but then separated. However, he continued to support them in their new home at Nos. 2-8 Kurstrasse in Gmund-

In 1922, Heinrich's father became director of the Wittelsbacher Gymnasium *(above)* at No. 8 Marsplatz (today No. 1). The family occupied an apartment on the second floor. Heinrich had just graduated at Munich Technical University and become a chemical fertiliser salesman for Stickstoff-Land GmbH.

In early July 1928, Heinrich married Margarete Boden, the daughter of a landowner from western Prussia, who was eight years his senior. Planning to begin a poultry farm, the couple bought a plot of land along Wasserburger Landstrasse at Waltrude-ring, on the eastern outskirts of Munich, where they built a small house. Himmler himself knocked together the chicken coop. The farm, with 50 hens, was a failure, due to persistent shortage of money to invest and Heinrich's increasing duties for the NSDAP. The farm at No. 109 Wasserburger Landstrasse no longer exists, the area between Nos. 51 and 133 now being open wasteland.

am-Tegernsee, even when he set up a separate establishment at Königsee for his secretary, Hedwig Potthast, by whom he had a son and a daughter.

On January 6, 1929, Hitler appointed Himmler as Reichsführer-SS. Starting with only 300 men under command, Himmler's ambitions soared, and he set out to expand his empire in total devotion to Hitler. Slight, sickly, squeamish and physically unimpressive, he wanted only pure, physical specimens of the Aryan race for the SS, which he saw as the elite order within the Nazi concept. One of his first steps was to take on Reinhard Heydrich, a dismissed naval officer cadet, to found the Sicherheitsdienst (SD) as an inner Party police and intelligence service.

When the Nazis came to power in 1933, Himmler became Acting Police President of Munich, which enabled him to establish the 'experimental' concentration camp for 5,000 prisoners on a disused factory site at Dachau. Then on April 1 of that year he became head of the Bavarian Political Police with Heydrich as his deputy.

Himmler's success in Bavaria led Minister of the Interior Willhelm Frick to give him command of the political police forces of all the other states except Prussia by January 1934, but three months later Göring also reluctantly handed over his Prussian police resources. This brought the implementation of terror and the remaining concentration camps of Oranienburg and Buchenwald under Himmler's central control, with new camps at Flossenburg, Mauthausen and Ravensbrück being opened before war broke out in 1939.

During 1933 the SS expanded dramatically to a strength of more than 50,000. Apart from the SS-Totenkopf-Verbände, or Death's Head units, guarding the concentration camps; Heydrich's expanding SD; the Allgemeine or General-SS; and Hitler's bodyguard now renamed the Leibstandarte-SS 'Adolf Hitler', there was also the Race and Resettlement Office under Richard Darré, Reich Minister for Food and Agriculture, who had produced the 'blood and soil' policy and had pronounced racial views, both of which strongly influenced Himmler. Darré was also helping to finance the SS with the high food prices he set.

The so-called 'Night of the Long Knives' of June 29/30, 1934, in which Himmler played a leading role, enabled the SS to gain independent status from the SA. Two years later Hitler appointed Himmler 'Reichsführer-SS and Chief of the German Police within the Ministry of the Interior', although Himmler and his SS continued to ignore Frick's superior status.

Himmler's dream continued to be the promotion of the SS as the elite order of the Nazi regime. His plans saw it as being comparable to the Jesuits within the Catholic Church, but Christianity was now abhorrent to him, and National Socialism had become the only ideology to be observed. The order was to be based on the Wewelsburg Castle (see pages 297-303), at Büren near Paderborn. He also founded a 'Friends of the

In 1933 Himmler bought a lakeside mansion at Gmund-am-Tegernsee, some 45 kilometres south of Munich, primarily to house his wife and their children Gudrun and Gerhard when his marriage broke down and he separated from Margarete. In 1936 he commissioned architect Alois Degano to reconstruct and enlarge the house, and in 1944 he had an air raid shelter added, using concentration camp inmates as the workforce. The property, at Nos. 2-8 Kurstrasse, survives unaltered, being used as offices by an organisation and communications consultants firm.

Reichsführer-SS' society for prominent citizens, who received honorary ranks in exchange for their generous donations, so that all manner of persons were to be seen wearing the black uniform, such as Hess, the Führer's Deputy.

In March 1935 Himmler obtained permission to form three regiments of SS reserve troops, the Verfügungstruppen, from his resources with funding from the Ministry of the Interior. Elements of these troops then led the reoccupation of the Rhineland on March 7, 1936, and took part in the annexation of Austria on March 12, 1938. Meanwhile Himmler insisted on political indoctrination to make his troops fanatical Nazis and also to make them abandon Christianity, which he regarded as effeminate and un-German.

The Jewish question remained foremost in Himmler's mind, and a special office was established under Heydrich and headed by Adolf Eichmann to consider the problems involved. On Hitler's instructions, progress against the Jews in Germany had stagnated because of the economic situation and also because of international exposure with the 1936 Olympic Games in Berlin. However, there was mounting pressure from Party activists, and Goebbels's instigated 'Reichskristallnacht' of November 9/10, 1938, resulted in 91 Jewish deaths and the arrest of 20,000 others for Himmler's concentration camps.

From 1941, Himmler's official residence as Reichsführer-SS in Munich was at No. 12a Möhlstrasse in the rich Bogenhausen district, one street away from Bormann's villa on Maria-Theresia-Strasse (see page 62) and close to Hitler's apartment on Prinzregentenplatz (page 22). Margarete and the children lived here until April 1945.

Himmler was then responsible for staging the incidents on the Polish border (see page 55) that provided the excuse for the invasion of Poland and the outbreak of the Second World War. His extermination squads (Einsatzgruppen) drawn from the SD, Gestapo and Ordnungspolizei then followed up the troops and cleared the rear areas of 'undesirables', while his Race and Resettlement Office plannned for the resettlement of millions of people in the areas affected by the secret protocol to the Soviet-German Non-Aggression Pact of August 23, 1939.

In October 1939 the title Waffen-SS was introduced and permission given for expansion into three motorised divisions in time for the invasion of the Netherlands, Belgium and France in May 1940.

With the invasion of the Soviet Union in June 1941, a frightful slaughter began behind the Eastern Front under Himmler's direction. The original Einsatzgruppen were later replaced by static Sicherheitsposten, which by the end of 1942 commanded some 15,000 German police and over 238,000 local auxiliaries, sometimes assisted by the Waffen-SS and even the Wehrmacht. The total death toll in the Soviet Union by these means is not known, but the elimination of 1,200,000 Jews was claimed.

But this was only part of the war being waged against the Jews, whose transportation from all over Europe to extermination camps in Poland had begun as early as October 1941, and on January 20, 1942, Heydrich convened a conference in a villa at Wannsee (see page 315) in Berlin to obtain full co-operation from various State organisations with Eichmann's diabolical plan for 'The Final Solution', the elimination of all the Jews in Europe.

In August 1943 Himmler replaced Frick as Minister of the Interior and also became head of the Reich Civil Service, further consolidating his personal powerbase.

Himmler's private residence in Berlin was at Nos. 8-10 Dohnenstieg in Dahlem.

The house no longer exists. The plot on which it stood is now bisected by Max-Eyth-Strasse, with No. 8-8a (above) **an apartment block on one corner and Nos. 10-10a comprising two modern villas on the other.**

The assassination attempt of July 20, 1944, which led Hitler to mistrust his generals even more, saw Himmler being appointed commander of the Replacement Army with total control over all of the Wehrmacht's remaining reserves and their supply facilities in Germany. Then in November, he was given command of the new Heeresgruppe Oberrhein (Upper Rhine) in Alsace, a role in which Himmler delighted, playing a mainly paper war from his remote headquarters in the Black Forest.

Left: **When Hitler in late January 1945 appointed Himmler to the command of Heeresgruppe Weichsel, tasked with defending the northern sector of the Eastern Front (a function for which the Reichsführer-SS was totally unsuited), Himmler established his command post in the woods outside Prenzlau, some 90 kilometres north of Berlin, in a mansion at No. 5 Birkenhain. Many accounts describe the house as if it was Himmler's own private property but it had in fact been requisitioned from the Ohnesorge family, who rented out just two rooms to Himmler. The actual command post was probably in Himmler's special train, which stood parked in the woods on a single-track railway branching off the Berlin-Prenzlau main line a short distance south of the Ohnesorge house. The HQ area further comprised a wooden conference hut and a stone building that served as barracks for the SS. Both these structures still stand. The mansion is today once again owned by the Ohnesorge family, Frau Sielmann (a daughter of the wartime owner) having bought back the house in 1994.**

Right: **In these last months of the war, shirking from his duties, engaged in fantasies of negotiations for a separate peace with the western Allies, and suffering from a vague 'illness' (some said he had angina, others spoke of tonsillitis, still others said he just had the flu), Himmler withdrew more and more to the private sanatorium of his boyhood friend (and chief SS doctor) SS-Obergruppenführer Professor Dr Karl Gebhardt at Hohenlychen, near the town of Lychen, 35 kilometres south-west of Prenzlau. The retreat became his unofficial headquarters. Overworked and listless, he spent much of his time in bed. On February 12, and again on April 2 and 21, he received Count Folke Bernadotte of the Swedish Red Cross for talks about the possible release of Scandinavian concentration camp inmates to Sweden, a move that Himmler hoped would create him goodwill with the western Allies. On March 20, army chief-of-staff Generaloberst Heinz Guderian persuaded him that with all his other burdens as head of the SS, chief of all police forces, Minister of the Interior and commander of the Home Army, he would do better to give up the army group post. Himmler, glad to be rid of the responsibility, agreed and next day Hitler appointed Generaloberst Gotthard Heinrici in his place. Today the Hohenlychen sanatorium stands empty and boarded up.**

Following the collapse of the German front facing the Vistula bridgeheads in January 1945, Himmler was then given command of Heeresgruppe Weichsel (Vistula) in Pomerania and set off to take command in his private train without even a map and only one member of his SS staff with any military experience. However this proved too much for him, he retired to bed with a common cold at Hohenlychen Sanatorium, 75 kilometres north of Berlin, where he was found by Generaloberst Heinz Guderian, who persuaded him to apply to be relieved.

On April 28, 1945, the unbelievable happened. 'Faithful Heinie' was reported by Reuters to be have offered the Western Allies the capitulation of Germany. Hitler was beside himself with rage at this totally unexpected treachery and ordered his execution. Himmler headed for Grossadmiral Karl Dönitz's headquarters, but the latter, having succeeded Hitler as Head of State, dismissed Himmler from all his posts.

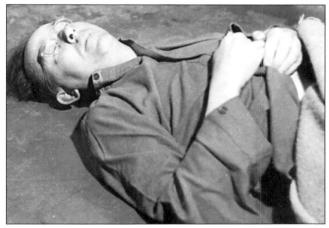

Left: **No. 31a Uelzener Strasse where Himmler, having been captured by the British, committed suicide on May 23, 1945** *(right).*

Three days after his death, on May 26, a four-men party led by Major Norman Whittaker and Sergeant-Major Edwin Austin of Second Army Defence Company buried Himmler in a secret grave on Lüneburg Heath. Thirty-two years later, in May 1977, *After the Battle*'s Editor-in-Chief Winston Ramsey took the two surviving grave-diggers, former Sergeants Bill Ottery (left) and Ray Weston (right), back to Germany and they pointed out the burial place, an unobtrusive spot at the foot of a tree in a forest. Although we published pictures in *After the Battle* No. 17 *(right)*, we did not disclose the grave location for precisely the same reason why the British Army buried Himmler in secret in 1945: to avoid the site becoming a shrine or rallying point for Nazi sympathisers. Now all four men present at the burial have passed away, leaving us the guardians of the secret. (For the full story of Himmler's capture, death and burial see *After the Battle* Nos. 14 and 17.)

Himmler then left Flensburg and drove south with several others, all in uniforms stripped of insignia and bearing documents showing them to be discharged members of the Secret Field Police, not realising that their forged documents placed them in an automatic arrest category.

With his moustache shaved off and wearing a black patch over one eye, Himmler was arrested as 'Sergeant Hitzinger' along with two escorts at Bremervörde on May 22, but was not recognised until he revealed his identity the next morning. He subsequently underwent two detailed body searches before the poison capsule hidden in his teeth was spotted by a doctor in a third search at No. 31a Uelzener Strasse in Lüneburg. Himmler noticed the doctor's reaction and promptly bit through the capsule, dying immediately.

His body was then buried secretly in an unmarked grave in a wood outside the town limits.

Albert Speer came from Mannheim, the small industrial town on the right bank of the Rhine, where his father, Albert Friedrich Speer, was a prosperous architect. The family — father, mother Luise and sons Hermann, Albert and Ernst — lived at No. 19 Prinz-Wilhelm-Strasse *(right)*, a grand house in a respectable street just off the town's central Friedrichsplatz, one of several houses owned by his father. The family occupied 14 rooms on three floors with seven servants living in the basement. Built in 1900, the house survived the Allied bombing that laid much of the historic city in ruins (most of the damage was done in the two RAF night raids of April 16/17 and September 5/6, 1943). Today, Prinz-Wilhelm-Strasse has been renamed Gustav-Stresemann-Strasse. The property at No. 19 is now an apartment building but surprisingly it still has ties with the Speer family, two of the present-day tenants being of that name.

Albert Speer

March 19, 1905 – September 1, 1981

Albert Speer was born in Mannheim, at No. 19 Prinz-Wilhelm-Strasse on March 19, 1905, the son of an architect. He himself studied architecture and was employed as an assistant architect in Berlin from 1928 to 1932. He married Margarete Weber, known as Gretel, in Berlin on August 28, 1928, and between 1934 and 1943 they produced four boys and two girls.

He joined the SA in 1931, going on to join the Nazi Party and the SS the following year. Then, as an independent architect, he obtained several minor contracts from Goebbels's office as Gauleiter of Berlin, eventually being commissioned to provide the technical effects for a mass parade on the Tempelhof Field on May 1, 1933. His use of flags and special lighting effects was so successful that they became standard features of Nazi mass functions.

His work attracted Hitler's attention as a frustrated architect himself, and in 1934 Speer was made head of the department responsible for town planning in Rudolf Hess's office as Deputy Führer. In 1935 he was responsible for adding Hitler's saluting balcony to the old Reich Chancellery in Wilhelmstrasse. Then in 1937 Speer was appointed Inspector General of Works with the special task of planning the reconstruction of Berlin as a capital city suited to the new Third Reich, a project that fascinated Hitler, who spent many hours studying Speer's plans and models, and earned Speer the coveted Party Badge in Gold (see pages 228-237).

Another similar project that brought them together many times over the years was Hitler's idea of making his home town Linz into the artistic capital of Europe as a competitor to Vienna, which he detested. Hitler produced numerous drawings from which Professor Hermann Giesler made the plans, but Speer was a close consultant, and a model was made that was kept in the

From 1934, Speer (second from left) was Hitler's favourite architect.

cellars of the Reich Chancellery for Hitler to study from time to time. Similar plans also existed for the cities of Cologne, Hamburg and Munich.

As a result of their growing association over architectural plans, Speer rented a small hunting lodge in a village near Berchtesgaden, close enough to be on call, but far enough away to retain some independence. Then in mid-1935 Hitler put the large Bechstein Villa, on the Obersalzberg itself a few hundred yards below the Berghof, at Speer's disposal, the house being shared with Hitler's personal physician, Dr Karl Brandt and his wife. In 1937 Speer rented a large villa further down the Obersalzberg from the actor Gustav Fröhlich for his family (No. 2 Antenbergweg) and built a separate architect's studio for himself 100 metres lower down (No. 1 Antenbergweg).

By 1935, with more and more assignments from Hitler and other prominent Nazis coming his way, Speer needed a dwelling in Berlin, so in that year he built himself a house at No. 21 Kronprinzessinnenweg, on the east bank of the Grosser Wannsee lake in south-west Berlin. Compared to the lavish residences of the others in Hitler's inner circle, the mansion was distinctly modest. It survives intact to this day.

Inevitably, Speer had to have a residence on or near Hitler's mountain retreat on the Obersalzberg. In 1934 the Speers rented a small hunting lodge in a village in the Oster valley near Berchtesgaden, big enough to set up drawing boards and with just enough room to accommodate his family and a few associates. However, Hitler wanted his favourite architect closer to hand and in mid-1935 he put a large house — the Bechstein Villa (above) — at Speer's disposal which was only minutes away from the Berghof. Two other families, including that of Hitler's personal physician, Dr Karl Brandt, were already billeted there. The house was destroyed by the Allied bombing raid of April 29, 1945 and no trace of it remains today.

Two years later, in May 1937, the Speers moved to large comfortable old house of their own on the other side of the Obersalzberg, the Waltenberger Heim, which Speer always said they had rented from the actor Gustav Fröhlich (in actual fact the Nazi Party had purchased the house for them). This was a short 15-minute walk away from the Berghof but being situated outside the Obersalzberg security perimeter (see page 44), it was just distant enough to give the Speers some privacy and independence. Five of the six Speer children were born here and the family lived there for most of the war until April 1945. The house at what is now No. 2 Antenbergweg is today privately owned.

Above: Just downhill from the villa, Speer built himself a studio where he and his associates could work on his many architectural projects and where he could present his designs to Hitler. Taken over by the Americans after the war as part of their Armed Forces Recreation Center, it was used as a guesthouse for high-ranking officers until 1995. Of all the buildings erected on the Obersalzberg during the Nazi period, Speer's studio is now one of only two originals to survive (the other one is the Luftwaffe-Adjudantur building below 'Göring's Hill'). All other structures were either destroyed by the RAF raid of April 1945, razed to the ground in the 1952 clearance, or demolished by the Bavarian authorities in its more recent programme to expunge all original traces of the Third Reich from the mountain. Speer's atelier escaped this fate, probably because it lies lower down on the mountain, and off the tourist track.

Ironically, when we pictured the Speer studio in the summer of 2003, it was being used by Kochta Architekten and the Projektbüro Resorthotel, the very architect's firm and development agency responsible for building the new five-star hotel on the Obersalzberg (see page 77).

On January 11, 1938 Hitler entrusted Speer with the construction of the new Reich Chancellery for completion by January 10, 1939, a seemingly impossible task, but nevertheless completed on time (see pages 238-245). In fact the plans for it had already been drawn and only required a few minor amendments during construction.

In 1941 Speer became the Member of the Reichstag for West Berlin. Then, following the death of Dr Fritz Todt in an aircraft accident on February 8, 1942, Hitler appointed Speer his successor as Minister for Arms and Ammunition and Head of the Organisation Todt, the Reich's principal construction agency. On September 2, 1943 Speer became Minister for Armament and War Production, by which time he was also in charge of the Nationalsozialistische Kraftfahrer-Korps (NSKK, Nazi Transport Corps), and a member of the Central Planning Office.

Speer proved a brilliant technical organiser and, despite interference from competing Nazi war-lords and the Allied bombing campaign, raised war production levels to unprecedented heights with the extensive use of slave labour. Nevertheless, by 1944 he began to realise that there was no chance of Germany winning the war, and he began taking active steps to prevent the implementation of Hitler's scorched earth orders which were to leave chaos and destruction in its wake. During his trial at Nuremberg he actually claimed a thwarted attempt to assassinate Hitler and his entourage by introducing poison gas into the Führerbunker's ventilation system.

Speer's unusual relationship with Hitler, the nearest possible to friendship in Hitler's case, was demonstrated by having himself flown back into the besieged city on April 23, 1945, to apologise to Hitler for not having carried out the orders for demolition. Although Hitler was accusing everyone around him of betrayal at this time, he excused Speer while depriving him of his now meaningless appointments. Speer flew out again and reported to Grossadmiral Dönitz at Flensburg, who

Right: **For his years as Minister for Armament and War production — here he is seen at the inauguration of the rebuilt Möhne dam (breached in the attack by No. 617 Squadron on May 16/17, 1943) on October 3, 1943 — Speer was sentenced to 20 years' imprisonment. After his release from Spandau in 1966, he went to live with his wife Margarete at No. 50 Schlosswolfsbrunnenweg *(right)*, the large family villa on the steep slope behind Heidelberg Castle. Owned by the family since 1905, until 1914 the property had been the family's holiday house, but with life at Mannheim during World War I becoming more dangerous, it had been vastly enlarged to become the family home in 1918. Speer had spent his teenage years there and his parents had lived there until their death (his father died in 1947, his mother in 1952). After the Americans, who had requisitioned the house, released it, his wife and five children moved into it, letting the top floor and a cottage in the garden to students to provide extra income. By the time Speer joined his wife there, all the children had moved out.**

appointed him Minister for Economics and Production in his new administration (see page 416). Speer was subsequently arrested with the other members of Dönitz's government.

The Allied Military Tribunal at Nuremberg, acknowledging Speer's admittance of guilt for the war crimes and crimes against humanity with which he was charged — the only plea of guilty from any of the accused — sentenced him to 20 years' imprisonment, which he served at Spandau Allied Prison until his release on October 1, 1966.

Settling in Heidelberg where the Speer family had their home at No. 50 Schlosswolfsbrunnenweg he then published his book *Inside the Third Reich*, revealing some of the complexities of Hitler's system of government that no way resembled the outward appearance of a monolithic totalitarian state.

Speer died of a heart attack during a visit to London on September 1, 1981, where he was staying as a guest of the BBC prior to taking part in a television programme, and was buried in the Bergfriedhof cemetery at Heidelberg.

Speer's grave at the Bergfriedhof in Heidelberg. The grave is located on the right-hand side of the main path leading into the cemetery from the Steigerweg gate.

Joachim von Ribbentrop was born at No. 453 Hohe Strasse in the Rhineland town of Wesel. The original house *(centre)* was destroyed during the war. Street numbers have since been changed and its replacement, a health shop *(right)*, is now at No. 4.

Joachim von Ribbentrop

April 30, 1893 – October 16, 1946

Joachim Ribbentrop was born in Wesel on April 30, 1893, the son of a Prussian officer. After leaving school, he emigrated to Canada, where he trained in banking before opening his own trading company. He returned to Germany as a volunteer during the First World War and attained the rank of lieutenant of the reserve. He at first served on the Eastern Front, then in 1915 was attached to the German military mission in Turkey. It is said that his award of the Iron Cross First Class was awarded retrospectively as a result of his own petition.

After the war he joined the demimonde of Berlin café society, but then found his feet with marriage to Anneliese Henkell, the heiress of Germany's richest sekt wine producer Otto Henkell, for whom he became the firm's representative in Berlin. In 1925 a change in the law enabled him to obtain adoption by a distant cousin and so add the honorific 'von' to his name.

He joined the Nazi Party late — on May 1, 1932 — and became an honorary member of the SS as a Standartenführer being promoted Obergruppenführer in 1940. He was regarded by other leading Nazis as an ambitious upstart, and thoroughly disliked for his vanity and arrogance. Goebbels said of him: 'Von Ribbentrop bought his name, married his money.'

However, he made a good impression on Hitler, to whom he was utterly subservient, and Hitler used Ribbentrop's palatial villa at No. 7-9 Lentzeallee in Berlin-Dahlem as a rendezvous during the negotiations leading to the formation of his first cabinet. He became Hitler's adviser on foreign affairs, setting up the Ribbentrop Bureau, as part of Rudolf Hess's organisation, that acted as a rival to the Foreign Office, which was far too conservative for Hitler's taste. In this capacity he took great pains to ensure that his expressed views were entirely in keeping with those of Hitler.

In 1933 he was made a member of the Reichstag for Potsdam. A year later Hitler appointed him Special Commissioner for Disarmament and sent him on a tour of foreign capitals to prepare the way for German rearmament, that culminated in him joining the German delegation to the Geneva Peace Conference in 1934. Then, as Ambassador-at-Large, von Ribbentrop went on to negotiate the Anglo-German Naval Agreement of June 18, 1935, which opened the way for the construction of a German battle fleet. The following

Left: **His marriage to Anneliese Henkell, heiress of the immensely rich Henkell family, in July 1920 enabled him to buy a grand villa at No. 7-9 Lenzteallee in the plush Dahlem suburb of Berlin. The house witnessed a key moment in the birth of the Third Reich for it was here that Hitler had his secret talks with Franz von Papen on January 18, 1933, and again with von Papen and Reich President von Hindenburg's son Oskar on January 22, that led to him becoming Chancellor on the 30th.** *Above:* **The Ribbentrop villa no longer exists, the triangular site on the corner of Lenzteallee and Schweinfurthstrasse now being wholly occupied by modern new dwellings.**

Hitler honours the Ribbentrops with a visit at their Dahlem residence on the occasion of his Foreign Minister's 48th birthday, April 30, 1941. The children (the Ribbentrops had five) are Ursula, eight years old, and Adolf, five. On the left are Ribbentrop's father Richard and stepmother Olga-Margarethe von Prittwitz und Gaffron (Ribbentrop's mother, Sophie, had died in 1902 when he was eight).

year von Ribbentrop was appointed Ambassador to Great Britain, with whom Hitler was hoping to establish an understanding that would enable him to pursue his ambitions on the Continent without interference. His mission failed partly because of his own outrageous and tactless behaviour, such as greeting the King with a Nazi salute. Rejected by British society, he became a pronounced anglophobe and next turned his attention to the formation of the Berlin-Rome-Tokyo Axis Pact.

During a cabinet reshuffle on February 4, 1938, von Ribbentrop was at last appointed Foreign Minister in succession to Konstantin von Neurath, a role that enabled him to give misleading advice about British reaction to Hitler's aggressive plans, and had the former Reich President's Palace in Berlin (see page 209) converted to his own use.

In addition to his villa in Berlin-

Dahlem, Ribbentrop maintained residences at Fuschl Castle on Fuschl Lake, east of Salzburg, and at Sonnenburg manor, north-east of Berlin. To satisfy

his hobbies, he also kept a horse-breeding farm near Düren in the Rhineland, a lodge for chamois hunting near Kitzbühel in Austria, and a hunting estate in Slovakia.

His part in the Munich conference of September 1939 was minor, Hitler being predominant, but he continued to bring diplomatic pressure with the object of occupying the rest of Czechoslovakia.

In early August 1939, von Ribbentrop wrote offering the Soviets a settlement treaty over areas of influence from the Baltic to the Black Sea, returning areas previously ruled by the Tsar and lost during the Revolution. This appealed to Stalin and eventually von Ribbentrop flew to Moscow to negotiate a non-aggression treaty with a secret protocol on the spheres of influence. The invasion of Poland took place on September 1, 1939 and on the 28th von Ribbentrop flew to Moscow once more to negotiate the future boundaries between the German and Soviet forces.

Above: Ribbentrop exploited his position as Foreign Minister to satisfy his greed for real estate. In 1936 he appropriated Sonnenburg manor, a 19th-Century country estate on the small Schiebelsee lake just south of Bad Freienwalde in eastern Brandenburg, some 60 kilometres north-east of Berlin. *Below:* The Puppenhaus (puppet house) he built as a plaything for his children still survives in the estate garden.

An overgrown air raid bunker in front of the house, connected to it by an underground passage, blocks the view today. After the war, the tunnel was blown up and the estate expropriated and divided up between small farmers and refugees from the East. In DDR times, it became a state agricultural farm.

In 1938, shortly after the Anschluss with Austria, Ribbentrop took possession of Schloss Fuschl, a beautiful little castle overlooking Lake Fuschl, 15 kilometres east of Salzburg. The owner of the castle, which dated back to the 15th Century, was expropriated, the castle confiscated, with Ribbentrop paying 300,000 Reichsmarks into a foundation as compensation for the take-over.

After this brief moment of triumph, he gradually lost influence, the role of the Foreign Office diminishing with the progress of the war, but he had it give full support to the 'Final Solution to the Jewish Question'.

Von Ribbentrop was tried, condemned and executed at Nuremberg for war crimes.

Left: Schloss Fuschl was Ribbentrop's favourite venue for receiving his official foreign guests. Here, he sees off Dr Ante Pavelic, leader of the Croatian Ustacha fascists and since April 1941 head of the 'independent state' of Croatia. *Right:* From 1945 to 1950, the US Military Government used the castle as a recreation centre for US personnel. Thereafter, it became a hotel, seeing a short return to the limelight in 1957-58 when the castle and its grounds became the film set for the romantic *Sissi* movies starring Romy Schneider and Karl-Heinz Böhm. Today Schloss Fuschl is a five-star hotel run by the Arabella-Sheraton chain. The head waiter kindly allowed us to take this comparison at the front door.

Left: At war's end, Ribbentrop realised that he would be a wanted man so found himself a hiding place in Hamburg, renting a humble room on the fifth floor of a big housing block, and endeavoured to disappear into anonymity. Found asleep in bed and arrested by British military police on June 14, 1945, he was sent to Nuremberg for trial. Pictured in his cell, he retained none of his former haughtiness. *Right:* Sentenced to death, he was hanged on October 16, 1946 (see page 446).

Julius Streicher

February 12, 1885 – October 16, 1946

Julius Streicher was born on February 12, 1885 in the village of Fleinhausen near Augsburg in Upper Bavaria. After serving in the First World War, being awarded with the Iron Cross First and Second Class and attaining the rank of lieutenant, he resumed his work as a primary school teacher, but was later suspended for alleged immorality. Having moved to Nuremberg, he was a founding member of the Deutsch-Sozialistische Partei (DSP — German Socialist Party), which he transferred across en masse to the Nazi Party in 1921 to form the Nuremberg group.

As a result of his participation in Hitler's abortive putsch, he lost his job as a schoolteacher in 1923 and began producing *Der Stürmer*, a violently anti-Semitic newspaper. Headquarters of the paper was at No. 19 Pfannschmiedegasse. Originally published with the sub-title of the *Nürnberger Wochenblatt* (Nuremberg Weekly), this often porno-

Julius Streicher came from Fleinhausen, a small village 20 kilometres south-west of Augsburg in Upper Bavaria, where his father was a schoolteacher. The Streicher family lived in a house *(right)* that was attached to the school building. *Below:* The house and school on St Nikolaus-Gasse were pulled down in 1998, its place taken by a new building housing the municipal fire brigade and community hall.

graphic, crude and scurrilous newspaper became the *Deutsche Wochenblatt* (German Weekly) in 1933, expanding its circulation from about 28,000 to 500,000 copies nation-wide. It invari-

ably contained cartoons depicting Jewish depravity, tales of sexual scandals, and exaggerated praise for Hitler and Nazism. Streicher bought the newspaper after the death of the publisher in

Left: **Appointed Gauleiter of Central Franconia in 1930, with headquarters in Nuremberg, Streicher achieved a position of absolute dictatorship in his province after the Nazis attained power in 1933. From 1937 his Gau headquarters was in a new building at No. 5 Marienplatz. The plot of land on which it was erected was a gift by the city of Nuremberg to the Nazi Party on the occasion of Streicher's 50th birthday in 1935. The villa that originally stood on the site occupied by a Jewish hops merchant, was pulled**

down. **A true example of Nazi architecture and designed by Franz Ruff (also responsible, among other things, for the Grosse Kongresshalle of the Nuremberg Party Rally Grounds — see pages 186-187), the new building came to be known as the 'Frankenhaus'.** *Right:* **Marienplatz is today named Willy-Brandt-Platz but the former 'Gau-Haus', as it was also known, stands unchanged at what is now Nos. 11-13. Today it accommodates the editorial offices of the *Nürnberger Nachrichten* newspaper.**

Removed from office in February 1940, Streicher withdrew to his farm estate, the Pleikershof, outside the village of Steinbach near Cadolzburg, 12 kilometres west of Nuremberg. Begun in 1933, the farm was intended to become a model agricultural establishment. Architect Julius Schulte-Frohlinde designed a horseshoe-shaped facility circling around a square courtyard. However, when Streicher was ousted, the farmhouse was not yet ready, so he moved into quarters improvised above one of the stables. From 1945 to 1948, the US Military Government used the Pleikershof to house Jewish survivors from the Nazi death camps awaiting emigration to Palestine. With supreme irony, the new tenants made the farm into 'Kibbutz Nilli' providing agricultural training for future emigrants. Today, the property is in private hands, the estate having been divided into two farms.

1935 and thereafter named Hitler as the publisher, although this was without the latter's permission and it was never officially accepted as a Nazi Party organ. However, Streicher often claimed that his was the only newspaper that Hitler read from cover to cover. The newspaper was frequently confiscated and prosecuted under the Weimar Republic, and was banned for two months in 1931. Even the Nazis had problems with it, for Goebbels banned it on one occasion in 1938 and it was attacked by the Gestapo in 1934 after the infamous 'ritual murder' issue.

Streicher was a Member of the Bavarian Parliament from 1924-1932 and then became a Member of the Reichstag for Thuringia on January 12, 1933. In 1925 Hitler charged him with rebuilding the NSDAP in Franconia, which led to Streicher calling himself the 'Frankenführer.' In 1930 he was appointed Gauleiter of Central Franconia and in 1936 of all Franconia, based on Nuremberg (with headquarters at No. 5 Marienplatz), and later he was given the rank of Obergruppenführer in the SA.

In 1933 he became leader of the 'Cen-

tral Committee for Countering Jewish Atrocity Tales and Boycotts', formed in response to a boycott of German goods in other countries after learning of the atrocities being committed against Jews in Germany. Then in the summer of 1935 he started a virulent campaign for a pogrom against the Jews, which led to the hasty drafting of the so-called 'Nuremberg Laws' passed unanimously by the Reichstag in session at Nuremberg on the occasion of the Reich Party Day on September 15, 1935.

These laws, with the titles of 'The Reich Citizenship Law' and 'The Law for the Protection of German Blood and German Honour', complied with the Nazi Party programme of 1920, and defined the words 'Jew', 'Half-Jew' and 'Part-Jew'. German citizenship was withdrawn from persons of non-German blood, automatically depriving all Jewish civil servants of their posts, although those that had served in the First World War were allowed to stay on until the end of the year.

Streicher was a sadistic bully, brutal and violent, with a sexual appetite bordering on the psychopathic. He ruled his province in savage style, carrying a

riding whip wherever he went and not hesitating to beat up people in the presence of witnesses. At the same time he acquired a fortune by appropriating Jewish properties at a fraction of their value.

A master rabble-rouser, he urged his audiences and readers in endless speeches and articles to fight the Jews, and in 1938 went on to publish a book demanding their total elimination.

However, once Hitler had consolidated his power, Streicher's behaviour became an embarrassment and Party officials began to complain. Hitler banned him from speaking in public, but then in 1939 Göring appointed a commission to examine Streicher's life and business transactions with the result that Streicher was dismissed from all his posts in February 1940. Streicher withdrew from public life to his Pleikershof farm estate, west of Nuremberg, however retaining his title of Gauleiter. He continued to behave as before and was completely unrepentant.

He was tried for crimes against humanity by the Allied Military Tribunal at Nuremberg in 1946, condemned and executed.

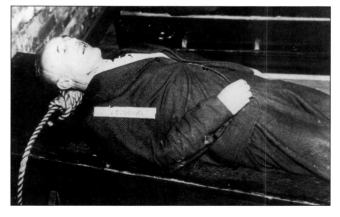

Left: At the war's end Streicher tried to escape captivity. He let his short haircut grow out, grew a beard and moved to a farmhouse near Waidring in the Bavarian Alps, where he disguised himself as a painter. On May 23, 1945, after an anonymous phone call, the S-2 (intelligence) team of the 502nd Parachute Infantry, US 101st Airborne Division — Major Henry Plitt, Captain Hugh Roberts, Corporal Victor Nelson and Pfc Howard Hardley — went to investigate. Although at first claiming to be

an innocent artist by the name of Sailer, when confronted, Streicher admitted his real identity. Here he is seen listening to Lieutenant Colonel Paul Danahy, G-2 of the 101st, after being brought in. On the right is German-speaking Lieutenant Peter Frank of the 502nd Parachute Infantry's POW Interrogation Team. *Right:* Sent to Nuremberg — the city where he had ruled for seven years — to be tried, Streicher ended up one of the ten Nazis who were hanged in October 1946 (see page 448).

HANS BAUR
Personal Pilot 1897-1993

ORT NICOLAUS VON BELOW
Luftwaffe Adjutant 1907-1983

ALBERT BORMANN
Adjutant 1902-1945

Hitler's Courtiers

Beyond Hitler's inner circle lay the members of his staff, a mixed bag comprising some old comrades — the Alte Kämpfer as they were called — like Julius Schaub who was an early member of the NSDAP succeeding Wilhelm Brückner as the Führer's personal adjutant when the latter was peremptorily sacked in 1940.

Julius Schreck was another early Party member serving as Hitler's chauffeur until he died from meningitis in 1936. Erich Kempka took over his driving duties, serving his master until the final act of setting fire to the corpse of his employer. We have also featured four of Hitler's secretaries: Gerda Christian, Gertrude 'Traudl' Junge, Christa Schröder and Johanna Wolf, all of whom stuck loyally with him to the bitter end in the Berlin bunker.

His two doctors, Karl Brandt and Theodor Morell, are included although the ministrations of the latter are said to have done Hitler more harm than good.

Heinz Linge was a constant in Hitler's life as his valet from 1939 to 1945 when he carried out his last duty to burn and bury the bodies in the Chancellery garden.

Karl Krause was Hitler's personal orderly and bodyguard during the prewar years but was dismissed in 1939.

Later he returned as an aide in the Reich Chancellery.

Otto Günsche was another personal adjutant and was injured in the July 1944 bomb explosion at Hitler's HQ on the Eastern Front. He, too, was present in the bunker at the end.

Rudolf Schmundt, his chief adjutant from the armed services, was also a casualty in the assassination attempt and he died from his wounds in October 1944.

Both Schulze brothers served, Richard first as an SS adjutant and later as commander of the SS-Junkerschule at Bad Tölz (see pages 310-311), and his younger brother Hansgeorg who was SS liaison officer to the Führer until he was killed in Russia in 1941.

DR KARL BRANDT
Physician 1904-1948

WILHELM BRÜCKNER
Chief Personal Adjutant 1884-1954

GERDA CHRISTIAN
Secretary 1913-1997

GERHARD ENGEL
Army Adjutant 1906-1976

OTTO GÜNSCHE
Personal Adjutant 1917-2003

HEINRICH HOFFMANN
Photographer 1885-1957

GERTRUDE 'TRAUDL' JUNGE
Secretary 1920-2002

ERICH KEMPKA
Chauffeur 1910-1975

KARL-WILHELM KRAUSE
Personal Orderly and Bodyguard 1911-

HEINZ LINGE
Valet 1913-1981

DR THEODOR MORELL
Physician 1886-1948

KARL-JESKO VON PUTTKAMER
Naval Adjutant 1900-1981

JULIUS SCHAUB
Chief Personal Adjutant 1898-1967

RUDOLF SCHMUNDT
Chief Military Adjutant 1896-1944

JULIUS SCHRECK
Chauffeur 1898-1936

CHRISTA SCHRÖDER
Personal Secretary 1908-1984

HANSGEORG SCHULZE
SS-Ordnance Liaison Officer 1917-1941

JOHANNA WOLF
Chief Private Secretary 1900-1985

THE EARLY BEGINNINGS

One thing indeed I know: all decisions have been for me easier than the one which I made on the 8th of November 1923. For the first time one had the conviction that it was not one's personal fate which was at stake, but the fate of the whole German people.

ADOLF HITLER, NOVEMBER 8, 1935

The Munich Putsch

After its brief but bloody experience with the post-war revolution, Bavaria had settled back into being a right-wing authoritarian regime. However, Minister President Gustav Ritter von Kahr despised Germany's weak central government and was keen to have the Weimar democracy replaced by one representing true national values. As early as May 14, 1921, he invited Hitler to meet with him to discuss the political

The birthplace of the Nazi Party. The Sterneckerbräu pub at No. 54 Tal in the centre of Munich was the watering hole of the Deutsche Arbeiterpartei, one of the many right-wing anti-Semitic splinter groups that were formed in Germany in the turmoil years after the First World War. On September 12, 1919, Hitler, who was then still in the army and acting as political spy for the military, was ordered to attend one of their meetings. After listening to a speech by one of the party's foremen, Gottfried Feder, Hitler drew attention on himself by speaking out at the subsequent discussion. Impressed by one of their pamphlets he decided to go to the group's next meeting. Although he wanted to form his own party, his Army superiors, interested in fostering the DAP, ordered him to join, which he did, and he soon rose to become their leading speaker.

situation. Next day Rudolf Hess, who had also been present at the meeting, wrote von Kahr a letter in which he described Hitler in terms that gave the very image Hitler was trying to project of 'an unusually decent, sincere character, full of kind-heartedness, religious, a good Catholic.'

Left: **He immediately set up a party office in the cafe's former tap room, a small vaulted room that could be entered by a side alley, the Sternecker Gasse. This would be the DAP headquarters for the next three months. The Sterneckerbräu closed in 1921, its premises taken over by a social-democrat co-operative association, but the café reopened in 1930. By then the Nazis were well on their way to power and the movement's birth cradle became a place of pilgrimage. Visitors had to pay 20 Pfennig to see the 'Gründungszimmer' (Foundation Room)**

which was adorned with swastikas and portraits of the founding members. On November 8, 1933, Hitler himself opened what was known as the Partei-Museum at the café. Also from that year onwards, on every anniversary of the 1923 Putsch, the Party's 'Alte Kämpfer' (Old Fighters) would meet at the café for a beer-swilling reunion. *Right:* **The Sterneckerbräu stood close to the Isartor gate in Munich's inner city. The building survives basically intact, but is now a furniture shop and the street numbers have been altered, No. 54 today being No. 38.**

On October 16, 1919, the DAP held its first mass meeting at the Hofbräukeller beer hall *(left)* at No. 19 Innere Wiener Strasse, across the Isar river from the Sterneckerbräu. It was here that Hitler for the first time in his life held a political speech before a larger audience, some 70 having turned up for the event.

Right: As he remembered it in *Mein Kampf*: 'I spoke for 30 minutes and what before I had simply felt within me, without in any way knowing it, was now proved by reality: I could speak! The people in the small room were electrified and their enthusiasm was expressed by donations of 300 marks.'

However, von Kahr resigned in September 1921 as a result of a row with the Reich Government, which was demanding that the Bavarians give up their arms, and he was replaced as Minister President by Hugo Graf Lerchenfeld-Koefering, an arch-conservative, who then became a target for Nazi abuse.

On August 16, 1922, Hitler spoke alongside the leaders of other nationalist associations on the Königsplatz in Munich. This was the first occasion that the SA paraded in public under its own banners, but they were heavily outnumbered by the other private armies fielded that day, including Hauptmann Ernst Röhm's 'Reichskriegsflagge'. There was talk of a 'putsch' (revolt) against Minister President Lerchenfeld at a rally to be held on August 25, but the police got to know of it and the rally was banned. Nevertheless, the Nazi element assembled on Karolinenplatz before 5,000 of their number moved on to the Kindlkeller beer hall at No. 18-22 Rosenheimer Strasse where they were besieged by Communists until the latter were dispersed by the police, who simply appealed to Hitler to calm things down, which he did. The political situation was now such that the Württemberg ambassador reported to Stuttgart: 'The National Socialists especially were gaining enormous support and were capable of anything. The leader Hitler must be quite a fascinating personality. So it is not impossible that they will try a putsch here before long, using the mounting inflation as an excuse.'

Mussolini's 'March on Rome' of October 28, 1922, was seized upon by the Nazis as an example to be emulated. Hitler would be their Mussolini, as Hermann Esser, the Party's first chief of propaganda, proclaimed at a meeting in the Hofbräuhaus beer hall at No. 9 Platzl on November 3. The idea of a march on Berlin, with Hitler acquiring power much as Mussolini had done, appealed to the Party membership, among whom a cult of heroic leadership was beginning to emerge.

With Hitler's demagogic talents bringing in an influx of new members, the DAP soon found need for a larger office and in January 1920 it moved house to another café a few streets away, the Gasthaus Cornelius at No. 12 Corneliusstrasse, where they had rented four side rooms, one of which had an office-window. This would remain the party's headquarters until November 1923 when, renamed the NSDAP, it was banned because of Hitler's failed coup.

The building has seen considerable change since the early 1920s and the former café is now a coin and stamp dealer.

On February 24, 1920, the DAP held another mass meeting in yet another beer hall, the Hofbräuhaus at No. 9 Platzl, in the centre of the inner city. It was here that Hitler first outlined the 25-point programme of his party, which included such points as the creation of a Greater Germany, abolition of the Versailles Treaty, removal of all Jews from office and the removal of their German citizenship, abolition of democracy, introduction of press censorship, etc. After speaking over hoots and catcalls, his speech was ultimately cheered thunderously by about 2,000 in attendance. That same day, the DAP changed its name to Nationalsozialistische Deutsche Arbeiter-Partei (NSDAP). After this first success with the crowds, the Hofbräuhaus became the venue for almost weekly NSDAP mass meetings, invariably with Hitler (party leader since July 1921) as the main speaker. From 1934 onwards,

every year the founding of the NSDAP at the Hofbräuhaus was commemorated at a festive meeting on February 24, attended by Party bigwigs and Alte Kämpfer and with Hitler delivering the main speech. This picture was taken at the 20th anniversary in 1940. By then a large plaque commemorating the historic first meeting had been mounted behind the speaker's rostrum: 'From this spot Adolf Hitler announced the programme of the National Socialist German Workers' Party on February 24, 1920'. What the plaque did not record was that the Hofbräuhaus was also generally hailed as the birthplace of the SA, the massive brawl between storm-troopers and party opponents that occurred in the hall on November 4, 1921, this being seen both as the hour of its birth and baptism of fire. The present whereabouts of the plaque, or even whether it still survives, is unknown.

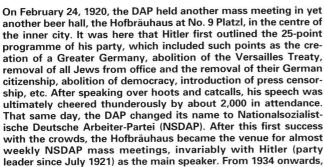

The crowds salute the Führer during the Party's 21st anniversary in 1941. The yearly commemorations continued right up to the end of the war. However, by February 1945 the Hofbräuhaus's main hall had been ruined by the Allied bombing raids on Munich, so the 25th — and last — celebration was instead held at the Hofbräukeller on Innere Wiener Strasse.

Restored to its former glory, the Hofbräuhaus continues to serve as the most famous beer hall in the world. A commercial enterprise sponsored by the State of Bavaria, it has absolutely no wish to be remembered because of its links with Nazi history and we were refused permission to take comparisons inside. This is how the main hall looks today.

On January 27-29, 1923, the NSDAP organised its first national Party Rally to be held in Munich. The undertaking narrowly escaped failure as a police ban was only avoided at the last minute after Hitler promised General Otto von Lossow, the military commander of Bavaria, that he would not stage a revolt. The main event was a massed parade on the Marsfeld on January 28 at which the standards of SA units were dedicated. It was a cold winter's day with snow on the ground; nevertheless over 6,000 of the Party's 15,000 members turned out. Hitler spoke (see page 21) and then reviewed a march-past of SA troops. Thus the rally was turned into a major success for the Party.

The occupation of the Ruhr by French and Belgian troops on January 11, 1923, when Germany failed to meet the full extent of the impossible reparations demands made on it at the Treaty of Versailles, brought an immediate political outcry throughout Germany. The situation was further exacerbated by the collapse of the currency, which brought distress, ruin and starvation to many, and by late September saw 142 million Reichsmarks equal to one American dollar.

The first Nazi 'Reich Party Rally' was scheduled to take place in Munich on January 27-29, 1923, but the Bavarian Government took fright at the possibility of a putsch and declared a state of emergency in Munich. Hitler was beside himself with rage at the news, for a ban would be a severe blow to his prestige. Röhm came to the rescue and a meeting was arranged between Hitler and General Otto von Lossow, the local Army commander, at which Hitler guaranteed that his rally would be conducted peacefully. Von Lossow, himself a Bavarian, regarded his 7. Division more as an independent Bavarian Army as of old than as an integral part of the greatly reduced, 100,000-strong Reichswehr, and therefore had considerable local influence. Hitler then went to see von Kahr, who was currently Minister President of Upper Bavaria, and Police President Eduard Nortz with the same assurances, as a result of which the Bavarian Government backed down. Hitler received permission to go ahead with a dozen mass meetings, all planned for the same evening, and for a parade on Munich's Marsfeld at which the SA standards were dedicated in a theatrical ceremony before 6,000 uniformed stormtroopers, thus according Hitler a major political triumph. The theme at the mass

meetings was to introduce him in a heroic mode as the country's forthcoming saviour.

Nevertheless, Hitler suffered a serious set-back over May Day 1923. It was the anniversary of the overturning of the revolution in Munich in 1919, and Hitler planned to stage a demonstration in commemoration. However, the Socialists had already booked a trade union march through the city streets for that day and obtained police permission. Hitler wanted conflict, so requested the arming of the nationalist paramilitary organisations by the Reichswehr for self-defence purposes, but General von Lossow refused to comply. The police then defused the situation by cancelling the march and

offering the use of the large Theresienwiese park near the city centre for a Socialist demonstration and the smaller Oberwiesenfeld park for the Nazis. Hitler was furious but, apart from a few minor clashes in the city later, both events passed off peacefully under strong police supervision.

That evening Hitler addressed a packed Circus Krone and announced the formation of the Arbeitsgemeinschaft der Vaterländischen Kampfverbände (Working Community of Patriotic Fighting Associations). This had been formed by Röhm, bringing the SA into league with other nationalistic paramilitary organisations, including his own 'Reichsflagge', under the overall leadership of Oberstleutnant Hermann Kriebel for the purpose of obtaining military training from the 7. Division, ostensibly in preparation for driving the French and Belgians out of the Ruhr, but in fact in anticipation of a possible conflict with the central government.

A first step was seen as an attack on the Communists in Thuringia before marching on to Berlin, to where the 'Weimar Republic' had moved in 1920. The SA was by no means the predominant partner in this organisation, which did not please Hitler, as he no longer had full control over it, but Röhm persuaded him to participate in the political leadership and to define its political aims. In this role Hitler even met the commander of the Reichswehr, General Hans von Seeckt, although the latter failed to be impressed by him.

Hitler managed to recover his political losses from the May Day fiasco at the rally held at Nuremberg on September 1 commemorating Deutscher Tag (German Day), the anniversary of the defeat of the French at Sedan in 1870. An estimated 100,000 nationalist paramilitary organisations attended, including the SA. Hitler was by far the most effective of the two speakers and stood on the podium alongside General Ludendorff, Prince Ludwig Ferdinand of Bavaria, and Oberstleutnant Kriebel during the two-hour march past.

Today, the Marsfeld (now Marsplatz) is hardly recognisable as the parade ground it once was, having been turned into an ordinary thoroughfare with most of the old expanse fenced off as a car park. The tall building in the centre background is the Wittelsbacher Gymnasium (where Heinrich Himmler's father was headmaster at the time of the 1923 rally) while just visible on the left is the famous indoor Circus Krone.

By November 1923, with both the Bavarian State leadership (a triumvirate under minister president Gustav von Kahr, General Otto von Lossow, the military commander, and Hans von Seisser, the police chief) and the Nazis under Hitler planning a coup d'etât against the government, Hitler was first to act. What became known as the 'Beer Hall Putsch' started at the Bürgerbräukeller at No. 29 Rosenheimer Strasse. Here on the evening of November 8, a pistol-brandishing Hitler interrupted a speech by von Kahr before a mass audience and had his SA men under Göring seal off the building, declaring that he was taking over power in Bavaria, and demanded that von Kahr and his triumvirate join his action.

With the change of Reich Chancellor to Gustav Stresemann on August 13, 1923, as head of a new coalition government, steps were taken to put down the Communist insurrections in Saxony and Thuringia by sending in the troops, thus forestalling a coup directed from Moscow. Then on September 26, Stresemann announced the end of passive resistance to the occupation of the Ruhr and the resumption of reparations payments. This was to lead to international acceptance of the German state, but was internal dynamite, and

Reich President Friedrich Ebert declared a state of emergency throughout Germany. That same day the Bavarian Cabinet proclaimed its own state of emergency and appointed the former Minister President von Kahr General-

staatskommissar (State Commissioner-General). The result was that Bavaria was now run by the triumvirate of von Kahr, head of the Bavarian State Police Oberst Hans von Seisser, and General von Lossow of the 7. Division.

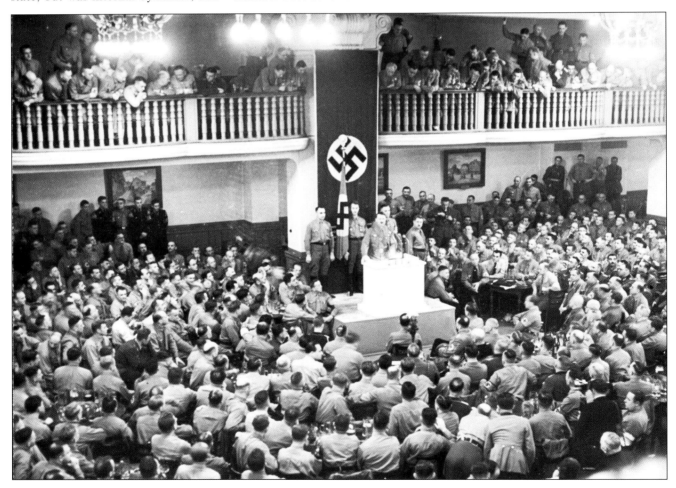

As far as is known, no photographs were taken at the Bürgerbräukeller on the night of the putsch. However, anniversary celebrations to commemorate the failed coup of 1923 were held there every year after 1933, with Hitler always present to address his old comrades, this picture being taken at the anniversary in November 1938. (After the bomb attempt on Hitler's life by Georg Elser on the 15th anniversary in 1939, which ruined the main hall, the celebrations had to be transferred to the Löwenbräukeller on the other side of town — see pages 368-371 and 391).

The situation then arose that the triumvirate wanted to install a nationalist dictatorship in Berlin based on a directorate, with or without von Kahr as a member, but certainly not including either Ludendorff or Hitler, and resting on the support of the Reichswehr. The Kampfbund leadership on the other hand wanted a directorate in Munich centring on Ludendorff and Hitler, but definitely without von Kahr, which would take Berlin by force with its own forces backed by the Reichswehr.

Von Seisser went to Berlin at the beginning of November to discuss the issue with leading figures and was told quite firmly by General von Seeckt that the Reichswehr would not move against the government. The triumvirate were prepared to wait and see how things developed, but Hitler and his supporters were impatient for action.

When it was discovered that the triumvirate would be present at a meeting to be held at the Bürgerbräukeller beer hall at No. 29 Rosenheimer Strasse on the evening of November 8, Hitler decided to attend and force a decision from them either to join in a coup d'état or be arrested. As a distraction from his true intentions, Hitler arranged for a Nazi Party meeting to be held at the Löwenbräukeller beer hall at No. 4 Nymphenburger Strasse that same evening, where his main force could congregate.

When Hitler and his close entourage accompanied by armed storm-troopers arrived at the Bürgerbräukeller, which was packed with about 3,000 people, von Kahr had already been talking for half an hour. He broke off his speech when he saw the steel-helmeted SA troopers enter, pushing a heavy machine gun into the hall. Hitler advanced escorted by two bodyguards with their pistols pointing at the ceiling and people stood on their chairs to try and see what was happening. Hitler stood on a chair and fired a shot into the ceiling to attract attention in the uproar. He announced that the national revolution had broken out and that 600 armed men were surrounding the hall. If there was trouble, they would bring a machine gun into the gallery. The Bavarian Government was deposed and a provisional Reich Government was to be formed. He then asked von Kahr, von Seisser and von Lossow to accompany him into the adjoining room, guaranteeing their safety.

Göring managed to calm down some of the bedlam in the hall by asking the crowd to sit down and enjoy their beer. Meanwhile Hitler was addressing the triumvirate, excitedly waving his pistol around, saying that no one would leave without his permission. He declared the formation of a new Reich Government with himself as the head. Ludendorff would be in charge of the Army with von Lossow as Reichswehr Minister, Seisser Police Minister, and von Kahr head of Bavaria with Ernst Pöhner, a prominent Nazi and former chief of police in Munich, as Minister President with dictatorial powers. He apologised for having to force the pace, but action was needed. If things should go wrong, he had four rounds in his pistol, one each for them and one for himself.

Provisionally repaired, the Bürgerbräukeller was used during the war as a depot for dairy products. Munich was entered by the Americans on April 30, 1945, the building soon being looted by the hungry population. From 1945 to 1957 it was a service club for US military personnel before reverting to a public beer hall. This is how it looked when we pictured it in 1974.

In September 1979 the historic beer hall was pulled down to make way for the new Munich City Hilton Hotel and the adjoining GEMA (municipal electricity company) building.

The Munich City Hilton at No. 29 Rosenheimer Strasse as it looks today.

Prime among the buildings captured by the putschists was the Bavarian Kriegsministerium (War Ministry) at No. 14 Ludwigstrasse. At the time it housed the headquarters of Wehrkreis (Military District) VII of the Reichswehr and also that of the 7. Division (which until three weeks before the putsch had been commanded by General Otto von Lossow, a Hitler sympathiser, and now a member of von Kahr's triumvirate). At about 11 p.m. on November 8, a force of 186 armed men from the Reichskriegsflagge (Reich War Flag) paramilitary group under Hauptmann Ernst Röhm — who had been on Lossow's staff and knew the ministry well — occupied the building, only to be surrounded by army and police forces loyal to the government. They had been sent in by von Lossow, who had put his allegiance to the triumvirate above his sympathy for Hitler. Two of Röhm's men, Theodor Casella and Martin Faust, were killed in the skirmishes. Among those defending the besieged building was 23-year-old Heinrich Himmler, here seen holding the Kaiser's War Flag behind the barricade outside the ministry. This is an oft-published picture but almost invariably Himmler is the only person identified. Few people realise that Röhm himself is also in it — he is the one dressed in the fur-collared coat (and smoking a cigar) on the right. The men on the left (with the shouldered carbines) are Privates Weikert and Kitzinger and, standing between Himmler and Röhm, is Hauptmann Joseph Seydel.

Hitler returned to the main hall after about ten minutes and addressed the crowd, saying that the action was not against the police and the Reichswehr, but 'solely at the Berlin Jew government and the November criminals of 1918'. He told them of his proposals for the new governments in Berlin and Munich, now mentioning Ludendorff, who had meanwhile appeared in full uniform, as nominated head of the German national army. He said that things were taking longer than expected, as von Kahr, von Lossow and Seisser were still 'struggling to reach a decision' and asked if the crowd would support them, for which he got a roar of approval. He went on dramatically: 'I can say this to you: either the German revolution begins tonight, or we will all be dead by dawn!'

The triumvirate then returned to the podium with Hitler and Ludendorff. Von Kahr spoke first, saying that he agreed to serve Bavaria as regent for the monarchy, for which he received tumultuous applause. Hitler shook his hand, saying that he would direct the policy of the new Reich Government. Ludendorff spoke next, expressing his surprise at the whole business. Lossow and Seisser were urged by Hitler to speak, then Pöhner promised full co-operation with von Kahr, and Hitler

shook hands with them all. He was in his element. Hess then read out a list of names given to him by Hitler of those to be arrested, and those members of the Bavarian Government present tamely

stepped forward and were taken off by Hess as hostages.

News of the successful coup was passed to the Kampfbund at the Löwenbräukeller, and Röhm set off to take over the Reichswehr headquarters (Bavarian Kriegsministerium) at No. 14 Ludwigstrasse, but then omitted to seize the military telephone exchange. Frick and Pöhner took over the Police Headquarters at No. 5 Ettstrasse. From this point on things began to go badly wrong. Hitler's precipitate decision to take action that evening had not allowed sufficient time for proper planning, and the putschists failed to take all their objectives.

Hearing of difficulties they were encountering at the Engineers' Barracks, Hitler left the Bürgerbräukeller to assist, leaving Ludendorff in charge, who then let the triumvirate depart, having taken them at their word as officers. They promptly reneged on their promises, feeling free to do so as they had been obtained from them at pistol point, and took counter-action.

By late evening the triumvirate were able to assure the state authorities that they had repudiated the putsch. Von Lossow was able to summon troops to Munich from the outlying garrisons, and the police were put on full alert.

Back at the Bürgerbräukeller nobody seemed to know what was happening as the leaders discussed the situation endlessly among themselves, and the mood became more and more dispirited. For hours no orders were given to the Kampfbund troops, and some of them began to drift away. At about 8 a.m. (November 9) Hitler sent some SA men to seize bundles of 50 billion Reichsmark notes from the printing press in order to pay his men. Later on he and Ludendorff decided upon a demonstration march through the city to the relief of Röhm, whom they had learnt was besieged in the Reichswehr headquarters and, as Hitler later said: 'We went to the city to win the people to our

The corner of Ludwigstrasse and Schönfeldstrasse today. The former Kriegsministerium building (today numbered 12-14 and housing the Bavarian Main State Archive) is actually outside the picture, just off on the left, the building on the right being Ludwigstrasse Nos. 8-10.

At noon on November 9, after a confusing night, the putchists prepared to march from the Bürgerbräukeller to the centre of Munich to rescue Röhm and his men under siege at the Bavarian war ministry. Among those taking position with Hitler in the front row were (L-R) General Erich von Ludendorff, hero of the First World War and proposed as Supreme Army Commander in Hitler's new government; Dr Friedrich Weber (with glasses), veterinary and leader of the Bund Oberland; and Hermann Göring, then chief of the SA.

Forming up behind the leading figures were some 2,000 supporters — Hitler's 100-man SA bodyguard, the Munich SA regiment, members of the Bund Oberland and elements of other nationalistic paramilitary organisations active in Bavaria. A large contingent was provided by cadets from the Munich Infantry School who had been persuaded to join the uprising by Oberleutnant Gerhard Rossbach (right), former leader of the Freikorps Rossbach, here pictured with Rudolf Hess (centre) at the entrance to the Bürgerbräukeller.

side, to see how public opinion would react, and to see how Kahr, Lossow and Seisser would react to public opinion. After all, those gentlemen would hardly be foolish enough to use machine guns against a general uprising of the people. That is how the march into the city was decided upon.'

At about 11.30 that morning, dull and overcast with flurries of snow, the Kampfbund storm-troopers began forming up outside the Bürgerbräukeller on the Rosenheimer Strasse. There were about 2,000 of them when they set off at about noon led by eight standard bearers, with the leaders immediately behind, then the troops 12 abreast in three parallel columns with Hitler's own 100-man Stosstrupp bodyguard on the left, the Munich SA in the centre and the Bund Oberland on the right. There was no band, for it had deserted earlier that morning. The group of leaders consisted of Hitler with Ludendorff on his left and Max Erwin von Scheubner-Richter on his right. Also present were Oberstleutnant Hermann Kriebel, the parade commander; Ulrich Graf, Hitler's personal bodyguard; Göring, as commander of the SA; Dr Friedrich Weber; Alfred Rosenberg; Wilhelm Brückner and other Nazi officials.

Marching up Rosenheimer Strasse, they came to the Ludwigsbrücke over the Isar river where a small police cordon had been set up. The police commander called upon them to halt or be fired on, but Göring bluffed that if they were fired on, hostages held at the rear of the column would be shot, so they were let through to the cheers of a gathering crowd. Swastika flags appeared and the support given by the crowd encouraged the marchers to break into song, their breath forming a mist in the cold air as they marched up Zweibrückenstrasse and through the Isartor gate into the old city.

A perfect match, looking back from Ludwigsbrücke to the beginning of Rosenheimer Strasse (see map page 106).

No pictures of the actual march that Friday appear to exist, but the Nazis made up for that after they came to power in 1933 by staging a symbolic re-enactment of the march every November 9, with all the surviving main protagonists taking part. We will see more of those anniversary processions later on, but this photo taken during the 1934 march serves to illustrate the original one of 1923. It was here on Ludwigsbrücke, the bridge across the Isar, that the marchers overran a small police detachment that attempted to halt the rebels at gunpoint.

Marching across the Isar and down Tal, the ever-growing procession arrived at Marienplatz, Munich's central square, where Julius Streicher, standing on top of his newspaper lorry, was trying to drum up further support from the crowds that had congregated there. On the right is the Neues Rathaus (New Town Hall) where earlier that morning the rebels had arrested members of the city council after which Rudolf Hess raised the swastika flag on the roof.

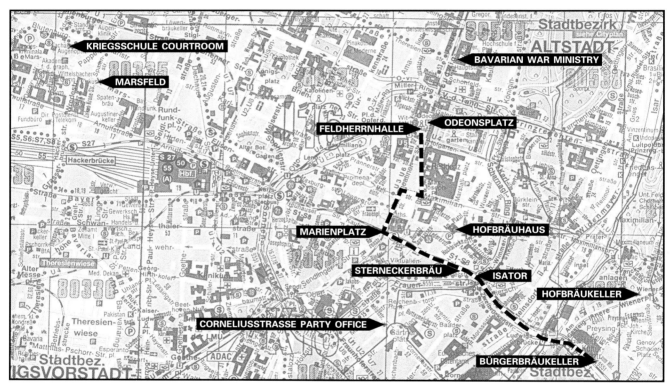

The route of the November 9 march and the various sites associated with the early history of the Nazi party.

Lorry-borne storm-troopers enter Marienplatz. They belong to SA units arriving from outside the city to reinforce the revolt.

Marienplatz was and still is the throbbing heart of Munich. Where rebels once marched, shoppers and tourists now reign.

Turning north from Marienplatz, the marchers found themselves funnelled into Residenzstrasse, which leads to the Odeonsplatz and on to Ludwigstrasse. As they reached the Feldherrnhalle, the arcaded war memorial that dominates the Odeonsplatz, they were confronted by a force of Bavarian State Police and soldiers armed with machine guns and an armoured car.

Continuing along Tal they reached Marienplatz, where Julius Streicher was addressing a large crowd. This market square was still decorated with Nazi bunting from recent rallies.

Streicher fell into line behind Hitler as they wheeled right into Weinstrasse, heading for the War Ministry where Röhm was under siege. A road-block further down the street forced them to wheel right again into Perusastrasse and then left into the converging Residenz-strasse, only to be confronted by another police cordon blocking access to the Odeonsplatz, the tall buildings on either side of the street boxing them in like a canyon, with only enough room for eight men abreast. As they came up to the police cordon, Graf stepped forward and shouted to a police leutnant, Michael Freiherr von Godin: 'Don't shoot! His Excellency Ludendorff is coming!'

Godin used his rifle to parry bayonets directed at him, whereupon a shot was fired, killing a sergeant behind him. There was a split second of silence before the police opened fire. The first volley brought down von Scheubner-Richter, who grabbed Hitler so violently as he fell that he dislocated Hitler's arm. Graf leapt in front of Hitler to protect him, only to fall gravely wounded. Göring also fell wounded with a bullet in his thigh, but Ludendorff and his adjutant, Major Strech, marched on calmly to the police line, which let them through unharmed.

Fourteen of the marchers were killed in this incident, and two in the defence of the War Ministry, bringing the Nazi death toll to 16. The police had lost four dead.

Right: **Despite its doubtful artistic value and historical reliability, the painting still makes for a good comparison.**

A short fire-fight broke out in which four policemen and 14 of the rebels were killed. Göring fell seriously wounded; Hitler was floored by his bodyguard, Ulrich Graf, and then bundled away with a dislocated arm to a car and taken to a safe address; and only Ludendorff walked on, reporting to the commanding police officer and allowing himself to be arrested. (However Robert Murphy, a US diplomat who witnessed the confrontation, categoricaly stated in his autobiography *Diplomat among Warriors* that both Hitler and Ludendorff, like any battle-hardened soldiers, fell flat to escape the hail of bullets.) Thus the putsch collapsed in blood and chaos. This contemporary painting by Schmitt portrays the legend created by Nazi propaganda of Hitler courageously giving the Nazi salute in the face of bullets.

Mounted police clearing the Odeonsplatz after the shoot-out. The building in the background is the Leuchtenberg Palace.

Looking from Odeonsplatz towards Wittelbacherplatz. The Leuchtenberg Palace today houses the Bavarian Finance Ministry.

The subsequent trial of Hitler, Ludendorff and eight other putschists ran from February 26 to March 27, 1924. Because none of the courtrooms in Munich was large enough to cater for the great public and Press interest, it was held in a lecture hall of the Kriegsschule (War School) at No. 3 Blutenburgstrasse. Hitler shrewdly assumed all responsibility for the putsch, knowing that such a stance would gain him sympathy and national recognition. The judge, Georg Neithardt, gave him every opportunity to state his political views, and passed out mild sentences. Hitler and three others were sentenced to five years, but eligible for parole after six months; five others got 18 months suspended and Ludendorff was acquitted.

Although many of the leaders were immediately arrested, Hitler got away, assisted by Dr Walter Schultze, chief of the Munich SA medical corps, who pushed him into his car that was parked nearby and drove off at speed. He was eventually taken to Ernst 'Putzi' Hanf-staengl's house in Uffing, south of Munich, where he was found and arrested by the police on the evening of November 11. He was then taken, dressed in a white nightshirt and with his arm in a sling, to the prison in the fortress of Landsberg-am-Lech.

The main defendants pose on the steps of the Infantry School after the trial (front row, L-R): Leutnant Heinz Pernet, Ludendorff's stepson; Friedrich Weber, leader of the Bund Oberland; Wilhelm Frick, chief of the Political Section of the Munich Police who had sided with Hitler during the Putsch (in 1933 he would become Interior Minister in Hitler's first cabinet and in 1943 Reich Protector of Bohemia and Moravia); Oberstleutnant Hermann Kriebel, a professional soldier who had been on Ludendorff's staff during World War I and had formed up the march formation at the Bürgerbräukeller; General Ludendorff; Hitler; Leutnant Wilhelm Brückner, who had led the Munich SA regiment during the march (in 1930 he would become one of Hitler's adjutants); Hauptmann Röhm; and Leutnant Robert Wagner, who had commanded the Infantry School cadets that joined the rebellion (in 1925 Hitler would appoint him Gauleiter of Baden).

Left: The courtroom building no longer exists, the only original part of the Kriegsschule still standing being its south wing at

No. 14 Pappenheimstrasse, now a kindergarten. Right: The site at No. 3 Blutenburgstrasse is now occupied by a primary school.

HITLER'S CELL

MAIN GATE

The fortress prison at Landsberg-am-Lech, 65 kilometres west of Munich. We have arrowed Hitler's cell.

The main gate of the Landesstrafvollzugsanstalt (state penitentiary) — then . . . and now.

Left: Hitler's sentence at Landsberg prison was comfortable and gave him ample time to begin the writing and dictation of his book *Mein Kampf.* Here he sits in the prisoners' common room with (L-R): Emil Maurice, his friend and chauffeur (who wrote down the preliminary notes for the book); Hermann Kriebel; Rudolf Hess (to whom he dictated the book's main text); and Friedrich Weber. Hess had escaped the November arrests and arrived at Landsberg later. Ilse Pröhl, Hess's fiancée, smuggled in the camera that took this and other prison pictures like the one *(right)* of Hitler wearing traditional Bavarian attire.

In 1934, on the tenth anniversary of his release, having by then achieved the leadership of Germany, Hitler returned to Landsberg prison for a nostalgic visit. His personal photographer Heinrich Hoffmann went along with him and pictured him talking to the prison priest *(left)*, entering his cell block *(centre)* and inspecting his old cell No. 7 *(right)*.

Left: The return visit gave Hoffmann the opportunity for a good 'then and now' comparison photograph. This picture of Hitler in his cell had been taken in 1923 by an obliging prison warden using Hoffmann's own camera which the latter had illegally brought in during one of his visits. *Right:* Hoffmann's comparison photo taken ten years later. *Below left:* In due course, Hitler's cell was turned into a shrine, with a portrait of him on the wall, a copy of *Mein Kampf* on the table, and flowers everywhere. A bronze plaque over the door *(below right)* recorded the cell's role in history, although the claim that 'Germany's greatest son' was imprisoned here from November 11, 1923 to December 24, 1924, was not quite accurate as, for the duration of the trial, Hitler had been detained in a cell at No. 18 Blutenburgstrasse in Munich. Removed by Colonel Donovan P. Yeuell of the 411th Infantry Regiment in April 1945, the historic plaque is now on display in the Kentucky Military History Museum.

Left: On the outside wall, cell No. 7 was marked with a wreath and swastika flag. *Above:* Although one is not really supposed to take photographs from this spot, we matched the picture overlooking the fence of the prison's sports field. From 1945 to 1955, Landsberg prison was in use by the US Military Government as the Allied Military Prison in their zone of occupation (the other prisons being at Wittlich in the French zone, Werl in the British zone — see *After the Battle* No. 118 — and Spandau in Berlin). Today Landsberg is once again a Bavarian state prison.

Left: Hitler actually spent only little over a year in prison, being released on December 20, 1924. He was met by Adolf Müller, the proprietor of the Munich Publishing House (printer of the *Völkischer Beobachter*), in his Daimler-Benz. Hoffmann had come along but was forbidden to take pictures of Hitler coming out of the prison. Instead he took this shot at what would still convey something of a prison atmosphere. *Right:* The old city gate, the Bayertor, on Münchener Strasse today.

Very soon the big Daimler-Benz drew up outside Landsberg Fortress. I got out and prepared my camera. .Then I heard a grinding noise — the gates were being opened. The historic moment, apparently, was upon us! But in reality, it was not! It was only the uniformed gate-keeper, who drew my attention to the fact that all photography was forbidden. I retorted that he was exceeding his authority, which did not stretch beyond the confines of the fortress itself; to which he replied quite calmly that if I ignored his warning, he would confiscate my camera. This was more than I was prepared to stand, and I demanded to see the Director. The Director was friendly, but quite firm, 'Instructions from the Government', he said. 'Hitler is not to be photographed as he leaves the fortress.' And that was that.

Angrily I returned to the car. 'I have no luck with Hitler', I yelled in Muller's ear. 'First of all he himself wouldn't let me photograph him, and now other people forbid it.' And I told him of my interview with the Director. At that moment Hitler came out through the gateway. With a terse greeting, he stepped swiftly into the car, and we drove off.

'I'm glad that you have come along', he said, turning to me; 'now you can photograph me without let or hindrance.'

I haven't noticed it', I retorted and I told him of my passage of arms with the fortress authorities. It seemed to me essential that a photograph to mark the occasion should be taken in Landsberg itself; and if that were not possible in front of the fortress, then I must take one elsewhere. I suggested that we stop by the old city gates, where we would still retain something of the fortress atmosphere. To this Hitler agreed, and I took several pictures.

HEINRICH HOFFMANN, 1955

Another 'then and now' for the Führer's personal photo album, taken during his return visit to Landsberg in 1934.

THE MARTYRS

In the ranks of those whose lives were thus sacrificed there stood also Horst Wessel, the singer who gave to the Movement its song, never dreaming that he would join those spirits who march and have marched with us.

ADOLF HITLER, FEBRUARY 12, 1936

Throughout history, martyrdom for a cause has always been a fine ideal and the Nazi Party capitalised on those who had lost their lives in the furtherance of its aims. The 'Ehrenliste der Blut-Opfer der Bewegung' — the Roll of Honour for those who sacrificed their blood for the Movement — listed 441 names, the majority (130) dying in 1934. The list begins with the names of the 16 men shot during the abortive putsch on November 9, 1923 although there are three earlier casualties: Karl Winter killed in Steinen on February 26 that year; Daniel Sauer on May 1 in Sickershausen and Albert Schlageter. He was executed by a French firing squad on May 26 and was subsequently accorded to the highest honour by the NSDAP as was Horst Wessel, who penned the Party anthem, and Herbert Norkus, a 15-year-old member of the Hitler Youth who became a symbol of dedicated sacrifice when he was brutally murdered. Symbolism and sacrifice were key elements in the doctrine of the Nazi Party and their dead were elevated to the level of sainthood. Here, overlooking the village where he was born, stands the monument to Albert Leo Schlageter, photographed *(above)* in 1933. *Below:* Today, 70 years later, only the base remains.

Albert Schlageter

August 12, 1894 – May 26, 1923

Albert Leo Schlageter was born in Schönau/Baden in the Black Forest on August 12, 1894, one of six children of a Catholic farming family. An intelligent boy, blond-haired and blue-eyed, he attended the village school in Schönau and went on to the Berthold Gymnasium in Freiburg-im-Breisgau, where he matriculated after gaining persistently high marks throughout his time there.

In 1914 he volunteered for military service with Feld-Artillerie-Regiment 76. After basic training he served on the Western Front, where he showed considerable aptitude as a gunner and rapidly gained promotion through the ranks. He saw service in several sectors from Flanders to the Vosges and was wounded fighting at Verdun in 1916. He was then awarded the Iron Cross Second Class and commissioned as a 2nd lieutenant of the reserve. In February 1918 he was awarded the Iron Cross First Class after his battery destroyed six British tanks in the fighting near Arras. Although dissolution and revolutionary unrest began to spread throughout the army, Schlageter's battery survived intact during the retreat through Belgium to reach their disbandment point at Freiburg.

Schlageter then enrolled as a student at Freiburg University but rapidly became disillusioned with his professors and fellow students in the contrast between their attitudes and those that had front-line experience. He also resented the bourgeois attitudes he encountered outside in the country in general. Having completed his studies

It was the occupation of the Ruhr in 1923 by France following default by Germany on the reparations imposed at the Treaty of Versailles which directly led to the arrest of Albert Schlageter for subversive activities. French troops were sent in on January 11 and this detachment is pictured entering Essen, the home of the mighty Krupp works. And it was also the Essen Detachment of the Freikorps to which Schlageter belonged during its campaign to disrupt rail traffic of supplies — primarily coal — to France.

> At that moment the French moved into the city. I heard their trumpets blowing, and hurried down to the street and watched. I saw the arrogance of the victors, the elegance and the smiles of contempt which bespoke punishment and revenge. The city was delivered to the will of the enemy, its honour sullied, and it was unbearable for those of us who had to suffer through it. Elemental proletarian rage rushed through me. To think that they could march in their military splendour while we stood there humiliated, that set my heart on fire with rage. The whole morning I walked through the city, totally beside myself.
>
> ERNST VON SALOMON, *DIE GEÄCHTETEN*, 1930

The French horse are passing the Essen Hauptbahnhof, continuing on into Hettwiger Strasse. The old railway station was destroyed in the Allied bombing raid of March 11, 1945. Its replacement was completed in November 1959.

in economics and unable to find civil employment, he joined the Freikorps von Medem as a way of both earning a livelihood and combating the threat of Communism.

In the spring of 1919 he took part in a campaign against the Bolsheviks in the Baltic region, where, under the overall command of General Rüdiger Graf von der Goltz, the Freikorps von Medem took part in the successful counter-offensive that liberated Riga on May 22, 1919. Schlageter received a special mention in the regimental history for having led a lightning thrust into the city.

Schlageter then transferred to the Freikorps von Petersdorf and in August 1919 took part in the Freikorps mutiny that resulted in the formation of the German Legion under the Russian Prince Pavel Avaloff-Bermondt as part of the White Russian Army in the west. However, this then became engaged in a series of disastrous defensive actions resulting in the total collapse of the Baltic Front in July of the same year. Schlageter managed to get away to East Prussia, hoping for further military employment.

By this time the newly-formed German Socialist government felt sufficiently confident to withdraw its clandestine support of the various Freikorps movement, and to begin maligning their efforts to secure the state from complete collapse in the immediate postwar period. Nevertheless, the Freikorps continued their existence and in the spring of 1920 Schlageter's unit was attached to Marine-Brigade 3 Löwenfeld in the neutralisation of Communist insurgents in the Ruhr. However, once that task was completed later in the year, the brigade was disbanded by the government.

Schlageter then went back to Lithuania to assist in the fighting against the Poles and was one of those that escaped when the Entente powers brought pressure against the Lithuanians to intern the so-called Baltic Germans. The following year Schlageter joined the Sturmbataillon Heinz as part of the Spezialpolizei (Special Police) in Upper Silesia, where trouble had broken out with the Poles in an area mandated to the French by the League of Nations. The Sturmbataillon Heinz, commanded by Heinz Oskar Hauenstein, was in fact a secret counter-sabotage unit operating in a situation in which terror and counter-terror were commonplace. In one notable operation in which Schlageter took part, 21 Germans were released from a prison in Kosel.

A plebiscite in this area in March 1921 gave the Germans a convincing victory but also brought about a third Polish insurrection and an invasion of Upper Silesia by the Poles. This was repulsed by Freikorps units, including Sturmbataillon Heinz, and Schlageter took part in the victory over the Poles at Annaberg on May 3, 1921, which the Nazis were to celebrate as an heroic event.

Sturmbataillon Heinz, although now officially banned by the German government, continued to operate as Organisation Heinz. Schlageter was tasked by Hauenstein to penetrate the Polish underground in Danzig. Acting

Lieutenant Albert Schlageter distinguished himself fighting on the Western Front and, like so many servicemen returning after suffering the privations of trench warfare, he was appalled at the attitude he found on enrolling at Freiburg University. He became a rebel student and early in 1919 joined the Freikorps — the semi-autonomous volunteer units, usually comprising the remnants of famous regiments led by officers dedicated to defending Germany from communists and insurgents. Although unofficially supported by the socialist administration, by 1920 one government minister described them as 'Praetorian hordes who have become a plague upon the land'.

as a disaffected agent prepared to sell German War Ministry secrets to the Poles, Schlageter became over-confident and his cover was blown. As a consequence, he was lucky to get away from the city without being arrested.

Schlageter then went to work for Hauenstein in Berlin, where the latter set up an import/export business, which was in fact a convenient cover for the illicit storing of, and trading in, illegal arms and ammunition for use in the Freikorps. During his stay in Berlin Schlageter is alleged to have joined the Nazi Party in 1922, but there is no evidence that he took an active part in their activities.

Then in January 1923 one Belgian and five French divisions invaded the Ruhr in retaliation for the failure of the Germans to meet war reparation pay-ments. This was met by widespread passive resistance that soon escalated into bloody conflict. In one incident at the Krupp plant in Essen, 13 unarmed workers were gunned down by French troops and another 30 wounded. Hatred against the French increased when they tried to establish a separate state in the Rhineland. Matters were not improved by rapid inflation of the currency.

Organisation Heinz was reactivated and Schlageter was assigned command of the Essen Detachment, where for over two months he directed sabotage and intelligence-gathering operations against the French in the Ruhr. The main activity was the dynamiting of railway lines to prevent the removal of coal to France, culminating in the blowing of a railway bridge on the main line between Düsseldorf and Duisburg.

Left: **Three weeks after this railway bridge was blown at Calcum (sometimes also spelt as Kalcum) between Duisburg and Düsseldorf, the French authorities, undoubtedly acting on information received, issued this statement via the local police: 'On the evening of March 15, 1923, at 8 p.m., the railway bridge over the Haarbach river near Calcum was blown up. This was probably perpetrated by two young men with the following descriptions. Family name probably Fr. v. Krampe or von Krause and Albert Leo Schlagstein or Schlageter, who is 20-25 years old, 1,60 tall, lanky, dark blond, without a beard, good looking with a confident** upright bearing. **Speaks with a foreign accent (not a Rhinelander), wearing black boots, brown sport stockings, grey trench coat and light sports cap. As a result of the deed, several respected citizens have been arrested as hostages by the occupation forces, who will not be set free until the perpetrators are put behind bars. Information is urgently requested which will lead swiftly to the arrest of the guilty parties.'** *Right:* **Two days later on April 7, Schlageter was traced to the Union Hotel at No. 2 Theaterplatz in Essen where he had somewhat unwisely registered in his own name. A new building now occupies the site.**

On April 5, 1923, the Prussian authorities in Kaiserswerth, Düsseldorf, at the behest of the French issued a warrant for Schlageter's arrest. A few days later he was picked up by the French at the Union Hotel in Essen and explosives found in his room. Several others of Organisation Heinz were also rounded up at this time. (Later on May 12 the German authorities were to arrest Heinz Hauenstein together with most of the remainder of his organisation.) During the three weeks leading up to his trial, Schlageter was subjected to a series of interrogations without success. An attempt to spring him failed when he was suddenly moved from Werden Prison to a new one at Düsseldorf-Derendorf, where he was kept in solitary confinement and denied exercise.

Schlageter and his fellow prisoners were brought before a French military court on May 10, 1923. Due to the fear of public disorder, the proceedings were conducted in some haste. They were accused of four crimes: the bombing of railway lines, abetting crimes against the French occupation forces, acts of sabotage, and plotting against German agents. The accused had little to say. At the conclusion of his examination in court, Schlageter stated: 'I take full responsibility for everything that I have done.' The prosecution called for the severest punishment possible. Schlageter was sentenced to death and his companions to prison sentences varying from five years to hard labour for life.

The news caused considerable controversy in Germany. Schlageter was a hero to the nationalists, but a right-wing bandit to the left. Many Germans living in French-occupied areas felt that the judgements of the court were invalid because the French occupation of the Ruhr was contrary to international law. As time passed an increasing number of prominent persons called for clemency, including the Pope, the Archbishop of Cologne, the Red Cross and the Queen of Sweden. The German Government also tried to bring pressure upon the French, but all in vain. Shortly before midnight on May 26, 1923, the French military authorities in Düsseldorf received instructions to carry out the death sentence.

Incriminating explosives were found in his hotel room and he was arrested. His trial before a French military court took place in Düsseldorf in the courthouse on Mühlenstrasse *(above).* **On May 10 Schlageter admitted that 'I take full responsibility for everything I have done'. The death penalty sparked off a heated public debate for while he was a hero to the nationalists, in the eyes of the socialists Schlageter was a terrorist. 'From the German standpoint', wrote the Editor of the *Kölnische Zeitung*, 'the judgements in Düsseldorf simply cannot be recognised, because the French military court was the result of an illegal entry upon German territory and therefore is devoid of any legal justification. We do not approve of the bombing of railways and if those responsible are indeed guilty, nevertheless their acts are understandable in human terms. The French have shown at many points a ruthlessness, an open hatred, as if they were not facing an equal cultured nation, but instead barbaric tribes of some dark continent. If this brutal treatment causes Germans to well up with a wild hatred against the invaders and forces them to answer illegal violence with illegal violence, then the French have only themselves to thank.'**

'I am about to go to my death', wrote Schlageter to his family from his cell in Derendorf prison. 'I will be able to take confession and communion. Farewell until our happy reunion in heaven. Greetings to you all again, Father, Mother and all those in the homeland.' The order to carry out the sentence had been confirmed by the French Prime Minister Raymond Poincaré and was received by the military in Düsseldorf just after midnight on Saturday May 26. An execution site had already been prepared less than two kilometres away, conveniently located near the Nordfriedhof (North Cemetery) at Golzheim. The site was later marked with this simple memorial and was also included on the 1930 street plan of Düsseldorf.

Schlageter made his confession to a priest and received communion before being driven out to the place of execution near the Nordfriedhof on the outskirts of Düsseldorf. An infantry company and a squadron of cavalry guarded the site as he was executed at dawn by a 12-man French firing squad in a stone quarry on the Golzheim Heath. Unusu-

ally, after being blindfolded and tied to a stake, he was forced into a kneeling position. The squad fired a salvo into his body, after which an NCO came forward and fired a coup de grâce into his head. For some reason this last gesture was taken by some of the German population as evidence that Schlageter had been murdered.

Schlageter was hastily buried in an unmarked grave in the nearby cemetery but this was considered adding insult to injury. Within days, the body had been exhumed and borne with full honours to his home in the Black Forest (below left). **Travelling via Freiburg where Schlageter had attended the university, he was buried in the churchyard at Schönau** (below).

The grave was a focal point of clashes between neo-Nazis and left-wing groups on the May anniversary of Schlageter's death, particularly during the 1970s when the gravestone was damaged. Now only the bottom section remains. In the background is the hill where the memorial on page 114 stood.

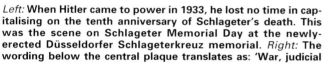

Left: When Hitler came to power in 1933, he lost no time in capitalising on the tenth anniversary of Schlageter's death. This was the scene on Schlageter Memorial Day at the newly-erected Düsseldorfer Schlageterkreuz memorial. *Right:* The wording below the central plaque translates as: 'War, judicial arbitrariness, expulsions, transgressions by foreign soldiers, greediness for economic power brought the most serious disaster to a country of peaceful labour. In spite of the hardest economic and social distress all levels of the population stood in an heroic struggle solidly behind the Reich.'

Schlageter's body was then handed over to the German authorities, who had him buried in the Nordfriedhof in a pauper's grave. This further incensed the nationalists, who felt that he should have been buried in a place of honour. A delegation of his old comrades arranged for the body to be removed, placed in a German coffin and transported to the village cemetery at his home in Schönau, a process that took some seven days to carry out.

Although there is no positive evidence that Schlageter belonged to the embryo Nazi party, nevertheless they claimed him as one of their own, listing him as number three on their Roll of Honour behind Karl Winter and Daniel Sauer. However, because of this link with the National Socialism of the Hitler era, the memorial at the execution site has since been swept away in the ongoing programme to eliminate that part of Germany's history. The large circular space that formed part of the memorial is still recognisable today, the sculpture that stands in its centre being Düsseldorf's monument to the victims of two world wars. Yet something quite extraordinary does still survive; we will see it in our final chapter.

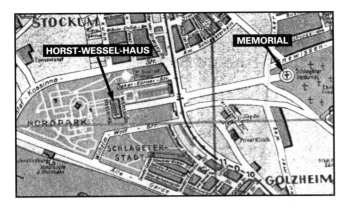

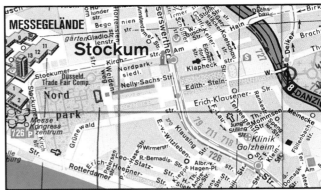

Left: **The Nazis constructed a processional avenue one kilometre long leading from the memorial to the local NSDAP Kreis (district) and Gau (provincial) headquarters: the Horst-Wessel-Haus**

(below) **named after our next martyr. The local area was even renamed Schlageter-Stadt.** *Right:* **An attempt has been made to eliminate the avenue which has been renamed Edith-Stein-Weg.**

The body in its new coffin was first moved to the Stadthalle in Elberfelde in what became a triumphal progress to Schönau. Crowds flocked to see the flag-draped coffin. A special train, laden with wreaths, made its slow way from town to town, being greeted by hundreds to thousands of mourners at each stop. Organisations and military units paraded and gun salutes were fired in scenes dominated by the Reichskriegsflagge — the German War Flag which was forbidden to be flown in the Weimar Republic. At Freiburg University some 30,000 people gathered to greet the coffin, including members of his old Artillerie-Regiment 76. He was eventually buried in the presence of his parents at Schönau on June 10, 1923.

A memorial was erected on Golzheim Heath with the inscription: 'Here fell, shot on the orders of the French on May 26, 1923, Albert Leo Schlageter for Liberty and Peace.'

In the Third Reich, Schlageter was remembered as a hero who had made the ultimate blood sacrifice for the rebirth of Germany. May 26 was declared 'Schlageter Memorial Day' as an annual event in the Nazi calendar, when ceremonies were held in his honour at Schönau, Düsseldorf and Munich.

The man alleged to have betrayed Schlageter to the French, Walther Kadow, was later murdered by a hit squad alleged to have included Martin Bormann and Rudolf Franz Höss, the future commandant of Auschwitz concentration camp.

The Horst-Wessel-Haus no longer survives having been replaced in 1987 by a modern building housing the town's

Aqua 200 and Nature Museum, but the horse statues still guard the original processional avenue.

120

Horst Wessel

October 9, 1907 – February 23, 1930

Horst Wessel, son of a prominent Lutheran preacher who had been a chaplain at Generalfeldmarschall von Hindenburg's headquarters during the Great War, was born in Bielefeld on October 9, 1907. After the war the family moved to Berlin, where the father's last appointment was at the St Nikolai Church on Poststrasse. The family home was nearby, at No. 51-52 Jüdenstrasse.

Wessel matriculated as a law student at the University of Berlin, but soon found that he much preferred politics to studying. He had already been active in the Bismarckbund, the paramilitary youth section of the Deutschnationale Volkspartei (DNVP, German National Peoples' Party) as well as the Viking-jugend, the youth section of the Frei-korps Ehrhardt, and soon after his father died in 1926, Wessel abandoned his studies and gave up his bourgeois background to live among the workers in the strongly Communist district of Friedrichshain, where he worked variously as both a taxi driver and a builder's labourer, and became an active member of the Nazi Party and the SA. In 1929 he reached the rank of SA-Sturmführer.

Many of the SA members were former Communists, for both parties had similar aims and methods, with the ends justifying the means, and a marked disdain for parliamentary procedures. On May Day 1929 the two parties had actually marched side by side through the streets in a joint protest against the police ban on marching demonstrations. Wessel displayed considerable skill in winning over Red Front sympathisers and even Red Front fighters to the Nazi cause. His enthusiasm, organisational

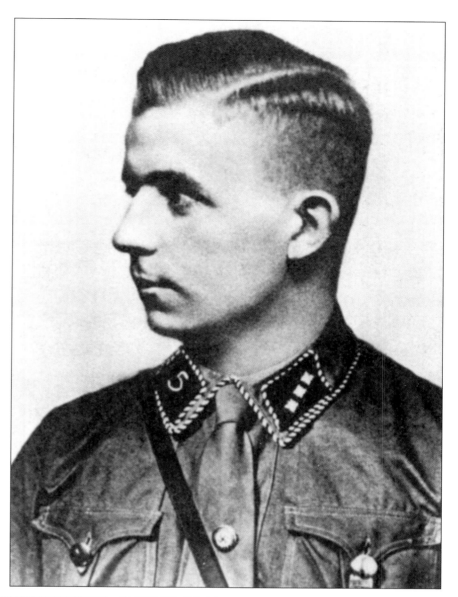

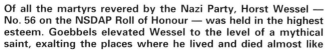

Of all the martyrs revered by the Nazi Party, Horst Wessel — No. 56 on the NSDAP Roll of Honour — was held in the highest esteem. Goebbels elevated Wessel to the level of a mythical saint, exalting the places where he lived and died almost like

'Stations of the Cross'. *Left:* This is the house where he was born in Bielefeld — No. 37 Kaiserstrasse — now renamed August-Bebel-Strasse. The Germans frequently name streets after people which means that names change when regimes change.

The SA (the abbreviation is pronounced 'Ess-R' in German), was the uniformed political army of the National Socialist Party, as Hitler explains on page 28. This picture features Wessel leading his SA-Sturm 5 during a parade for the Reichsparteitag held in Nuremberg in August 1929. The statue is the Prinzregentendenkmal — Prince Luitpold, the third son of Ludwig I of Bavaria.

ability, personal courage and flair as an orator enabled his political career to flourish, and he was rapidly promoted through the ranks to Sturmführer of SA-Sturm 5, which he soon increased in strength to 250 men, and became the Party's leading orator in Berlin after Goebbels.

From their Sturmlokale, the SA bar meeting points known as the 'Kegelerheim' on Peterburger Strasse and the 'Möwe' on Grosse Frankfurter Strasse, Wessel's SA-Sturm 5 took on the massive Communist presence in Friedrichshain, spreading out in all directions, agitating for the Nazi cause. Terror and counter-terror became a way of life for SA-Sturm 5.

Wessel organised a wind instrument band similar to those used by the Communists that proved very useful in attracting public attention. He wrote a poem *Die Fahnen hoch!*, which was published in Goebbels's newspaper *Der Angriff* and subsequently set to music.

Then one night in 1929 on his way back to his lodgings after the usual evening's clashes at the head of his storm-troopers, Wessel was passing the Café Mexico off Alexanderplatz, when he saw a young girl being molested, and went to the rescue. She was Erna Jaenicke, an 18-year-old prostitute, who was having problems with a potential client that had turned violent on her. Wessel immediately fell madly in love

with her and she gave up her role and pimp to live with him in his lodgings with the 29-year-old widow Elisabeth Salm in a garret at No. 62 Grosse Frankfurter Allee, where love took charge and his political activities went into a marked decline.

However, problems arose over the non-payment of rent, the holding of political meetings in their apartment, and the sharing of the kitchen, as a result of which on January 14, 1930, Frau Salm consulted her dead husband's old comrades of the 2. Bereit-

Seventy years have passed by and the Bahnhofplatz outside the main railway station (the Hauptbahnhof) has moved into another century while the horseman has ridden off into the sunset.

schaft (Squad) of the Rotfront-kämpferbund (Red Front Fighters' League). By this time, Horst Wessel was a marked man for the Communists, who had even issued leaflets warning their comrades to take note of his face, so they listened to her with interest. They called for reinforcements from the neighbouring 3. Bereitschaft and a group of 12 of them set off to confront him, their leader, 33-year-old Max Jambrowski assuring Frau Salm that they would give him a 'proletarian drubbing'.

Three of them climbed the four flights of stairs to the garret, 26-year-old Erwin Rückert, leader of the 2. Bereitschaft, and his deputy, 31-year-old Albrecht 'Ali' Höhler, both of whom were armed, and 27-year-old Josef Kandulski. When Wessel opened the door in answer to the bell and saw these unknown visitors, he reached into his pocket, but Höhler, who already had 16

It was about the time of the Nuremberg rally that Wessel met and fell madly in love with a Berlin prostitute, Erna Jaenicke. His recently widowed mother disapproved of the relationship so Horst moved out of the family apartment at No. 51-52 Jüdenstrasse (left). *Right:* **Formerly part of East Berlin, the street was totally expunged from the map by the Communist regime.**

criminal convictions, including some for serious assault, drew a pistol from his raincoat pocket and fired several times shouting: 'You know what this is for!' Hit in the mouth, Wessel collapsed, the bullet having removed his upper front teeth, ripped his tongue and shattered his palate. The Communists fled.

Wessel's SA comrades were called to help but he lay there untended on the floor for over an hour until the SA-Oberarzt Dr Leonardo Conti arrived, as they refused to call in a nearby doctor because he was Jewish. Meanwhile they had been searching the apartment for compromising documents before the police arrived.

Wessel was eventually taken to the nearby Friedrichshain Hospital, where he clung on to life for another 41 days before succumbing to blood poisoning, dying on the night of February 23, 1930.

Attempts were made by the Communists to cover up the shooting, claiming that it had been nothing but a squabble between two pimps. Höhler was smuggled out of Germany to Prague, where he was ordered to claim that Erna Jaenicke had been his lover and that when she left him for Horst Wessel he had shot the latter out of jealousy. They also pressurised Frau Salm to maintain this cover story.

Wessel's new lodgings were close to his SA headquarters in Friedrichshain — a predominantly communist district. In September he rented a room at No. 62 Grosse Frankfurter Allee and moved in with his girl friend but within a couple of months he had fallen out with the landlady. Her political persuasions were directly opposed to those of her lodger and in January 1930 she contacted friends of her late husband and asked them to sort Wessel out. On the 14th, a Tuesday, a Communist hit-squad

climbed the stairs to his room and gunned him down in front of Erna. *Left:* **No. 62 became a Nazi shrine but it, too, was swept away during a programme by the German Democratic Republic to transform the road into a wide parade avenue. The saluting base lay on the left within a stone's throw of where Wessel was shot.** *Right:* **Our comparison was taken during Communist days complete with the ubiquitous Trabants! This was then Karl-Marx-Allee but it has now reverted to Frankfurter Allee.**

After Wessel died from his wounds on February 23, Goebbels stage-managed his funeral for maximum propaganda effect.

However, this was the kind of propaganda opportunity that Goebbels had been waiting for. His newspaper gave daily accounts of the victim, whom he up-graded to status of a saviour: 'Leaving his mother and home, he took to living among those who scorned and spat at him. Out there in a proletarian neighbourhood he made his young, modest existence — a socialist Christ, one who appealed to others through his deeds.'

This campaign was greatly aided by Wessel's own poem, now set to music, that Goebbels had had sung at the conclusion of a meeting at the Sportpalast, thereby formally introducing it into the Party ritual. When Wessel eventually died, Goebbels wrote: 'His spirit has risen in order to live on in all of us. He is marching in our ranks.''

Goebbels planned an extravagant funeral at which Hitler would deliver the main speech, but Hitler declined, judging the situation in Berlin to be too explosive to take part. The Nazi Party was still too weak, with only 12 representatives in the Reichstag, to risk stirring up a major riot in Berlin with himself as the centre-piece.

The body was first taken from the hospital to the family home in Jüdenstrasse, where it was guarded overnight by an honour guard of SA storm-troopers and other uniformed representatives.

Next day, the SA-escorted cortège, their numbers severely limited by the police, had to pass through an enormous crowd of about 30,000 excited people gathered along the route to watch the funeral procession. The Communists in the crowd tried to disrupt the proceedings with singing and hurling insults, and at one point surged forward in an unsuccessful attempt to overturn the funeral carriage and snatch the swastika flag from the coffin. Shots were fired and a measure of order was only established with the arrival of riot police armoured cars. The procession continued with great difficulty along Prenzlauer Strasse to the gates of the St Marien und Nikolai Cemetery, where 'A final Heil Hitler to the pimp Horst Wessel!' was found to have been daubed on the walls.

The Wessel family grave was located in the Nikolaifriedhof where Horst's father had been buried only the previous May.

The pall bearers were six of the eldest SA-Sturmführers in Berlin — here they unload the coffin on reaching the cemetery.

Horst Wessel-Lied

Die Fahne hoch, die Reihen dicht geschlossen,
S.A. marschiert mit mutig festem Schritt,
|: Kam'raden, die Rot Front u. Reaktion erschossen,
Marschieren im Geist in unsern Reihen mit. :|

Die Straße frei den braunen Bataillonen!
Die Straße frei dem Sturmabteilungsmann!
|: Es schaun aufs Hakenkreuz voll Hoffnung schon Mil-
Der Tag für Freiheit und für Brot bricht an. :| lionen,

Zum letzten Mal wird zum Appell geblasen,
Zum Kampfe stehn wir alle schon bereit.
|: Bald flattern Hitlerfahnen über alle Straßen
Die Knechtschaft dauert nur noch kurze Zeit. :|

Die Fahne hoch, die Reihen dicht geschlossen,
S.A. marschiert mit mutig festem Schritt,
|: Kam'raden, die Rot Front u. Reaktion erschossen,
Marschieen im Geist in unsern Reihen mit. :|

Die Fah-ne hoch/die Reihen dicht geschlossen/ S.A. mar-schiert mit mutig festem Schritt/ |: Kam-ra-Den Die Rot Front u. Re-ak-tion er-schos-sen/ mar-schieru im Geist in un-sern Rei-hen m

Detachments of the SA, the Hitler-jugend and the Stahlhelm were drawn up inside the grounds. The SA Chief-of-Staff, Hauptsturmführer Salomon von Pfeffer, laid a wreath on behalf of the Führer, and Hermann Göring laid Horst Wessel's SA kepi on the coffin. When the pastor began conducting the burial service, he was violently interrupted by the mob outside, and mourners were scattered by a shower of rocks and stones coming over the wall, although the SA honour guard stood firm.

Then, under a leadened sky Goebbels began to speak: 'When in the future, in a German Germany, workers and students march along together, then they will sing his song, and he will march with them . . . The brown-shirt soldiers are already singing it in every corner of the country. In ten years, children in the schools, workers in their factories, and soldiers along the roads will sing it. His song has made him immortal! . . . Soldier of the German revolution! Just as always, hand on his belt, proud and upright, with his youthful smile, striking out ahead, leading his comrades, always ready to sacrifice his life, he will remain with us in this way.

'I can see columns marching, endless, endless. A humiliated people rise up and begin to stir . . . It joins in step behind the standards . . . The flags wave, drums resound, the pipes are jubilant; and a million flutes join in the song of the German revolution: *Die Fahnen hoch!*'

No sooner had he uttered these words then, as if an omen, the dark clouds parted, the sun shone on the mourners and a light breeze ruffled the swastika flags. From this point on the myth of Horst Wessel passed into the repertoire of Nazi propaganda. But Goebbels's imagination did not stop there. In his report in *Der Angriff*, he wrote: 'As the coffin came to rest in the cool ground, a depraved cry arose from the sub-humans outside the gates. The departed, still with us, raised his weary hand and beckoned into the shimmering distance: "Forward over the graves! At the end of the road lies Germany!"'

The theatrical martyrdom masterminded by Goebbels acted as a perfect recruiting campaign for the Party, and the adoption of Wessel's song *Raise High the Flag* was a perfect counter to the Communist's *The Red Flag*. Renamed the *Horst Wessel Lied*, it became the Nazi Party anthem, so furthering the canonisation of Wessel in the eyes of the converted.

Fearing his presence would do more harm than good, Hitler stayed away from the funeral but three years later it was a different story. In January 1933, the Nazis were poised to take office so, instead of waiting until the anniversary of Wessel's

death in February, he advanced the inauguration of Horst Wessel Memorial day to Sunday, January 22 as a deliberate political statement. According to reports, Mrs Wessel deliberately arrived late in protest at his failure to attend her son's funeral.

Veterans of SA-Sturm 5 continued to honour Horst Wessel Memorial Day with a graveside parade on the actual day of his death. This is the 20th anniversary on February 23, 1943.

On September 23, 1930, Albrecht Höhler and his companions were brought to trial at the Assize Court in Moabit. Höhler and his accomplice, Erwin Rückert, each received sentences of six years and one month imprisonment. Josef Kandulski was awarded five years and one month imprisonment, and Frau Salm 18 months. Of course,

Right: **The tell-tale cornerstone indicates the position of the grave.**

Left: **The ornate grave marker with its fallen flag symbolism which was installed by the Nazis was no doubt destroyed by the Soviets. What marks the position of the grave today** *(right)* is most probably the original headstone placed after Horst's father's death on May 9, 1923 because the inscription which remains reads: 'PFARRER [Pastor] LUDWIG WE----- 5.7.1879—9.'

Once in power, the Nazis memorialised every building assoc-iated with Wessel, in fact there was such a proliferation of monuments and memorial ceremonies that Goebbels had to issue instructions in October 1939 specifically banning all such ceremonies save those held on the anniversary of his death. *Above:* The parade held for the unveiling of a painted inscrip-tion on the facade of No. 51-52 Jüdenstrasse. It read: 'In this house Horst and Werner Wessel [his brother, also a member in the Berlin SA, who was killed in a skiing accident in December 1929] became fighters for Germany's honour and freedom'.

The building where Horst lived for a while in Vienna back in 1928 — No. 36 Humboldtgasse — then and now.

this was not good enough for the Nazis and they swore their revenge. In September 1933, the year the Nazis came to power, Höhler's body was discovered by a forester in some woods near Berlin; he had been removed from his cell and assassinated.

Then in June 1934, three Communists that had accompanied Höhler on that fateful occasion to Frau Salm's, although they had not opened fire nor even entered Horst Wessel's room, were belatedly brought to trial. Two of them, Sally Epstein, aged 28, and Hans Ziegler, aged 31, were nevertheless sentenced to death and executed by decapitation on April 10, 1935. The third went to a concentration camp.

During the years of Nazi rule, Horst Wessel was developed into a folk hero. Some 250 biographies, novels and plays were written about him, numerous statues were erected in his honour, and streets and squares named after him. Even the district of Friedrichshain was re-named after him. So too was the Communist headquarters building, known as the Karl-Liebknecht-Haus on Weydinger Strasse.

However, undoubtedly the most significant tribute was the playing of his song as the second national anthem.

From 1926 to 1933 the Karl-Liebknecht-Haus — named after a Communist martyr killed in 1918 — was the Communist Party HQ in Germany. Consequently it was the focal point of clashes with the Nazis. *Left:* This demonstration was held on the Bülowplatz in front of the building as events escalated to boiling point in January 1933. *Right:* On assuming power, the NSDAP quickly took the building over to claim it as its own. The square was renamed Horst-Wessel-Platz, the road name changed from Weydinger Strasse to Horst-Wessel-Strasse while a memorial park was laid out opposite.

A few of the Horst Wessel trees still survive in what has now been renamed Rosa-Luxemburg-Platz after another Communist who was murdered at the same time as Karl Liebknecht and who became one of their martyrs.

Left: In 1933 the building had been taken over from the Communists by SA Troop 6/6 to become the HQ for the Berlin-Brandenburg district. This picture shows the standard of the Berlin SA being paraded to the Sportpalast in March 1938 to celebrate the incorporation of Austria into what was then called the Greater German Reich. Note how a second entrance has been cut in the building which became a shrine for Wessel, buried just 200-odd metres down the road. By now Wessel had become an inspiration which far ascended his actual achievements. Goebbels even went as far as openly declaring: 'I feel it

in my bones — I'm absolutely sure of it — his soul was resurrected, to live among us all, and he is marching with our columns'. *Right:* When the Communist Party was resurrected after the war in the guise of the Sozialistische Einheitspartei Deutschlands (SED) they took back the building, returning it to its pre-Nazi appearance by blocking up the second doorway and changing the name back to the Karl-Liebknecht-Haus. Since the re-unification of Germany, the building has been taken over by the direct successor of the disbanded SED, the Partei des Demokratischen Sozialismus (PDS).

In AD9, an alliance of Germanic tribes led by Arminius (known in Germany as Hermann) ambushed and wiped out a Roman army in the Battle of the Teutoburg Forest. The Roman force was led by Publius Quinctilius Varus — hence the battle is known to Germans as the Varusschlacht — and the victory established the Rhine as the boundary between the Romans and Germans, hence the present-day division of the Romance language in France and the Germanic language. The battle was always believed to have been fought in the forest south of Osnabrück so when the battle was resurrected in the 19th century as a symbol of German nationalism and pride, a memorial — the Hermannsdenkmal — was erected in Detmold in 1875. (In fact recent archaeological research indicates that the battlefield was 50 kilometres *north* of Osnabrück at Kalkriese.) Seeking to elevate Horst Wessel on a par with Gemany's past heroes, the National Socialists had this monument erected in the narrow strip of Teutoburger Forest that runs through the southern part of Bielefeld, the town where Wessel was born.

The Horst-Wessel-Stein was dedicated on October 8, 1933. It stood on the Kammweg (Crest Route), today named Hermannsweg, in the forest west of Buschkampstrasse on a height between Togdrang and Ebberg hill. The stone was blown up by the Allies in 1945 and absolutely no trace of it remains today.

in addition to its political aspects, and young Herbert became a devoted member. He also joined the naval section, which offered the opportunity of working in boats off Teltow Park.

As a known Hitler Youth he was in frequent clashes with Communist youngsters of the Rote Jungfront. On one occasion he was caught by them and threatened with death if he did not join them within a week. However, his death came about in more complicated circumstances.

In early 1932 Walter Stennes, the leader of the SA in eastern regions of Germany, was in dispute with Hitler over the means of assuming power for the Nazi Party. He was prepared to risk doing so by force, whereas Hitler insisted on following legal means. There was an atmosphere of revolt within the SA in Berlin, and the Stennes faction was prepared to collaborate with the Communist Rotkämpferbund to achieve its aims. Stennes's section chief in Berlin, Bernhard Lichtenberg, had an SA man working as an apprentice in the same bakery as Gerhard Mondt, leader of the Moabit Hitlerjugend, who was keeping Lichtenberg informed of Mondt's and SA-Sturm 32's activities, as a result of which he learned of the intention to conduct a propaganda blitz at dawn the next Sunday, January 24, 1932. Acting without his chief's knowledge, Lichtenberg called for an assault on the Moabit Hitlerjugend on the morning. The informant was told to pass this information to Georg Stolt, head of the Moabit Rotkämpferbund, with the promise of ten mugs of beer each for Stolt's men if they killed Mondt.

Herbert Norkus

July 26, 1916 – January 24, 1932

Herbert Norkus was born in Berlin on July 26, 1916, the eldest son of Grenadier Ludwig Norkus, who became a member of SA-Sturm 6 in 1929. His mother died in a mental hospital in 1931 as the result of repeated Communist attacks on the dairy shop that she had run in order to keep the family going in the unstable post-war years. He lived with his father and younger brother in modest quarters in the factory grounds where his father worked off the Spandau Canal in the tough Westhafen area of Moabit known as Beusselkietz. Later on he attended the Luisen-Gymnasium on Zwinglistrasse in the centre of Moabit.

While the great majority of the Moabit youth supported the Communists, Herbert Norkus followed his father's example and joined the Hitlerjugend in 1931 at the age of 14. The Hitlerjugend offered attractions like sports, hiking, singing and playing in the great outdoors

Herbert's father Ludwig was a disillusioned war veteran who had joined the Berlin SA in 1929, his wife dying two years later. Without a mother Herbert loved the comradeship of the Hitlerjugend centred on the local combined headquarters for the HJ (pronounced in German 'Ha-Yot') and SA at No. 23 Hüttenstrasse *(above)*. Their leader was Scharführer Gerhard Mondt.

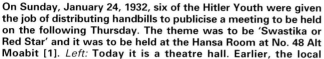

On Sunday, January 24, 1932, six of the Hitler Youth were given the job of distributing handbills to publicise a meeting to be held on the following Thursday. The theme was to be 'Swastika or Red Star' and it was to be held at the Hansa Room at No. 48 Alt Moabit [1]. *Left:* Today it is a theatre hall. Earlier, the local

Communist chief was tipped-off that Mondt's HJ were planning to leaflet in his territory — something he could not countenance — so retribution was planned. On Saturday night, some 50 members of the banned Red Front Fighters League assembled in the pub at No. 10 Oldenburgstrasse [2] *(right)* to plan the attack.

On the night of Saturday, January 23, Stolt put three of his teams on the alert. Fifty young men and youths spent the night in Otto Marx's pub on Oldenburgstrasse being instructed in how to run the ambush. They had no guns but were armed with knives and the usual weapons used in street-fighting. Then, under cover of darkness,

they deployed throughout the Beusselkietz area to await the arrival of their victims.

At dawn on the 24th, six Hitler Youths under the command of Scharführer Mondt started moving rapidly through the area distributing leaflets advertising a Nazi Party meeting. Within minutes they had been spotted

and the Communists gave chase. Mondt fired several blanks from his pistol, which gave some of the boys a chance to escape. Herbert Norkus's companion, Johannes Kirsch, managed to hide behind a large dustbin in an apartment building, but Herbert ran down Gotzkowskystrasse and turned into Zwinglistrasse.

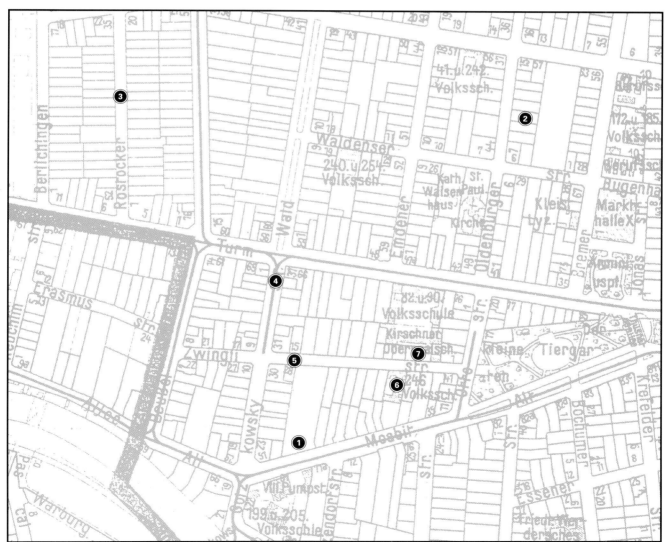

Escorted by their leader, Scharführer Mondt, the boys set out before dawn. They were going to start leafleting the tenement buildings in the strong Communist street of Rostocker Strasse [3] but when a motorcyclist who they recognised as a communist spotted them, Mondt decided to give that particular street a miss.

But it was too late . . . the Red Fighter boys were ready and waiting. The HJs split up as Mondt threatened their attackers with a blank-firing pistol. Herbert Norkus made his escape south down Gotzkowskystrasse [4], turning left into Zwinglistrasse [5] *(above)*.

But the gang were closing on him and he desperately looked for a way to escape even trying the door of his old school but it was locked. *Left:* The Luisen-Gymnasium building [6] still stands on the right-hand side of the road at No. 37 although it is now called the Wartburg-Schule. *Right:* Parking bays have now narrowed the street from how it looked 70 years ago.

He first tried to hide in a wholesale milk establishment, but the night watchman would not let him in. Ten of his pursuers then pounced on him, knocking him to the ground. He managed to get away and started running for his life, looking for shelter in several buildings along the street but without success. Once more he was surrounded and knocked down, stabbed and kicked. Again he struggled to his feet and ran off, leaving a trail of blood. He eventually collapsed in the entrance to No. 4 Zwinglistrasse, a small cleaning establishment, whose inhabitants came to his rescue. He was rushed to the Moabit Municipal Hospital by taxi, but died shortly afterwards.

Left: Running across the road, he was caught and surrounded. Norkus was repeatedly stabbed and beaten to the ground but managed to get to his feet and stagger a few yards before he collapsed in the doorway of this cleaners' shop [7]. *Right:* No. 4 has changed its face over the intervening years.

The police immediately set up a large-scale inquiry and within a few days were able to piece together an accurate description of the circumstances surrounding the murder. They put up wanted notices offering a reward of 500 Reichsmarks for information leading to the arrest of the alleged perpetrators: Willi Simon, Bernhard Klingbeil and Harry Tack, all Communist Party supporters, who had been spirited away by their organisation. Several months later at a sensational trial of some of the individuals involved in the crime, three of the accused were sentenced to three years imprisonment each, one was sentenced to one year, and three others released. Years later it was discovered that the three main suspects had been smuggled safely out of Germany to the Soviet Union.

Goebbels was addressing a rally in the Sportpalast when news of the murder was passed to him. He immediately used it to his advantage and followed up with an article in *Der Angriff*.

An elaborately staged funeral offered Goebbels an opportunity to focus on the heroic death theme so beloved of the Nazi movement. The body in an open casket was attended for 24 hours by a guard of honour of Hitler Youths at the Dorotheenstädtische Gemeinde on Hannoversche Strasse. On the afternoon of January 29, 1932, the coffin, draped with the flags of the Hitlerjugend and Marine-Jungschar, was escorted to the Neue-Johannes-Friedhof at Plötzensee, where Goebbels delivered the funeral oration to the Party elite and units of the Hitler Youth, SA and SS.

The cleaner Marie Jobs was awoken by the commotion and went to her door only to find the dying Norkus lying outside. He was rushed to Moabit Hospital *(above)* by taxi but he very soon succumbed from his injuries.

The political turmoil in Berlin continued and only ten days after the murder of Herbert Norkus another Hitler Youth, 18-year-old Georg Preiser, was killed in the city, bringing tension to a new high.

A few days later Hitler addressed the Berlin Hitlerjugend in the Tennishalle am Westen, personally greeting Norkus's comrades from Moabit. Reichsjugendführer Baldur von Schirach placed Herbert Norkus's name at the top of the list of the youthful Immortals, declaring January 24 as a national day of remembrance for all fallen Hitler Youths, and this became another important anniversary on the Nazi Party calendar. Norkus's unit flag became the Blood Flag of the Hitlerjugend, plaques were erected in his honour and pilgrimages made to his grave. Every New Year's Day von Schirach would address the youth of the nation in a broadcast from Norkus's grave.

Left: He was buried in the Neue-Johannes-Friedhof at Plötzensee and his grave No. 32 in Plot LII, Row 20 became another shrine in the annals of the Nazi Party. Here Baldur von Schirach, the leader of the Hitlerjugend, gives his New Year's Day speech in 1934 to the nation from the graveside. *Above:* After the war, the graves from this part of the cemetery were levelled and turned into a park.

FELIX ALLFARTH
Kaufmann
*5. Juli 1901

ANDREAS BAURIEDL
Hutmacher
*4. Mai 1879

THEODOR CASELLA
Bankbeamter
*8. August 1900

WILHELM EHRLICH
Bankbeamter
*19. August 1894

The Feldherrnhalle 16 — 'Die Neunte Elfte'

When Hitler came to power in 1933, it was in the fulfilment of his aims of November 1923, this time achieved by legal means. However, the commemoration of his abortive putsch was to become the high point in the Nazi liturgical calendar, with the original participants retracing their steps in solemn tribute to the 16 that had fallen that day. Fourteen of the victims had been participants in the march to the Feldherrnhalle: Felix Allfarth, a businessman; Andreas Bauriedl (standard bearer), a hatmaker; Wilhelm Ehrlich, a bank clerk; Anton Hechenberger (standard bearer), a locksmith; Oskar Körner, a merchant; Karl Kuhn, a head waiter (later said to have been an innocent bystander); Karl Laforce, an engineering student; Kurt Neubauer (Ludendorff's orderly); Klaus von Pape, a businessman; Theodor von der Pfordten, a councillor in the Superior Provincial Court; Johann Rickmers, a retired cavalry captain; Max Erwin von Scheubner-Richter, an engineer; Lorenz Ritter von Stransky, an engineer; and Wilhelm Wolf, a businessman. Two of the 16 had been killed at the War Ministry on Ludwigstrasse: Leutnant Theodor Casella and Schütze Martin Faust, both bank clerks and members of the Reichskriegflagge.

Since the Revolution of November 1918 had broken the laws which were formerly in force, it could not be expected of us that we should regard the Revolution as a legal constitution. So in November 1923 we marched, filled with the faith that we should succeed in overthrowing those who were responsible for November 1918, in annihilating the men who were responsible for the untold misfortune of our people.

But then Fate decided otherwise; today, after ten years, we can consider that time dispassionately. We know that we all stood under this command of Fate, that we were assuredly but the instruments of a Higher Power. It was not right that it should succeed: the time was not yet ripe. That which then pained us most was the division which arose between those forces in whose ranks we, too, once had stood and the forces which the nation needed for its liberation.

Ten years have passed, and for me today my greatest happiness lies in the fact that the hope of those days is fulfilled and that we now stand side by side — the representatives of our army and the representatives of our people, that we have become one and that this unity in Germany will never break in pieces.

Could our dead of the 9th of November rise again they would weep for joy that now the German army and the awakened German people have found their way to unity. Because today we are binding into one the whole strength of the nation we can now give to the dead their eternal rest.

ADOLF HITLER, NOVEMBER 9, 1933

MARTIN FAUST
Bankbeamter
*27. Januar 1901

ANTON HECHENBERGER
Schlosser
*28. September 1902

OSKAR KÖRNER
Kaufmann
*4. Januar 1875

KARL KUHN
Oberkellner
*26. Juli 1897

KARL LAFORCE
stud. ing.
*28. Oktober 1904

KURT NEUBAUER
Diener
*27. März 1899

KLAUS VON PAPE
Kaufmann
*16. August 1904

THEODOR VON DER PFORDTEN
Rat am obersten Landesgericht
*14. Mai 1873

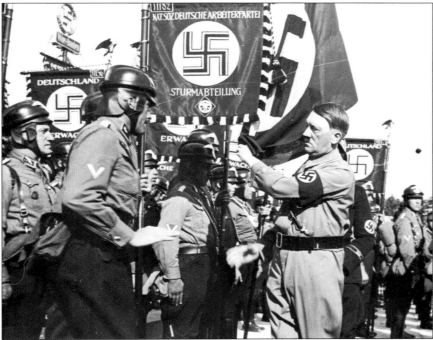

In later years, there was much argument in the Nazi Party as to who had carried the flag at the head of the column, the banner which became the symbolic *Blutfahne* — the Blood Flag. Exhaustive investigations established that it had been carried by Heinrich Trambauer. This was his testimony: 'Despite my many years at the front it was a tremendous feeling of joy and pride to carry the first flag of our Führer Adolf Hitler to victory. After making the bend through the Theatinerstrasse, we came into the Residenzstrasse, heading for the Feldherrnhalle. A state policeman surged from the Residence Guard, ready to do battle. At that point, we struck up the *Deutschlandlied* but the shooting which claimed our first heroes was the response to our song.

Von Stransky, Bauriedl, and Hechenberger were killed in my group. Taking cover, I immediately fell to the ground, the flag under me. Catching my breath, I lay there momentarily, waiting for the right time to escape, because saving the flag meant more to me than my life.' Trambauer kept it safe and the SA gave it to Hitler on his release from prison. He handed it over to Reichsführer-SS Josef Berchtold at the rally in Weimar in July 1926. Later it was installed at the NSDAP headquarters in Munich. As a revered symbol of 'Die Neunte Elfte' — as Friday November 9 became known — it was later ceremoniously carried on parades by SS-Standartenführer Jakob Grimminger *(right)* who had taken part in the putsch. (He died on January 28, 1969.)

JOHANN RICKMERS
Rittmeister a. D.
*7. Mai 1881

Dr. M. E. V. SCHEUBNER-RICHTER
Ingenieur
*9. Januar 1884

LORENZ RITTER VON STRANSKY
Ingenieur
*14. März 1899

WILHELM WOLF
Kaufmann
*19. Oktober 1898

The Nazis had wanted the 16 to be buried in a mass grave, but the city authorities would not allow it, insisting upon individual burial in their respective parishes in accordance with German law. Felix Allfarth, Theodor Casella, Martin Faust, Karl Laforce, Klaus von Pape, Dr Max Erwin von Scheubner-Richter and Lorenz Ritter von Stransky were buried in the Waldfriedhof; Andreas Bauriedl, Oskar Körner and Theodor von der Pfordten in the Nordfriedhof, and Anton Hechenberger, Karl Kuhn and Wilhelm Wolf in the Ostfriedhof. Wilhelm Ehrlich, Kurt Neubauer and Johann Rickmers were buried in their home towns.

The city authorities also later banned a commemorative ceremony that the Nazis planned for Sunday, November 8, 1925, on the grounds that past experience showed it would be used to glorify the putsch and would lead to marching and demonstrations in the streets.

Further controversy surrounded the order of precedence in the front row of the column in the annual re-enactment. Obviously most of those who had marched alongside Hitler were dead but a row broke out when Hermann Kriebel wrote to Rudolf Hess, the Deputy Führer, complaining that he should have the right to march beside Hitler. 'In 1933 I marched in the place where I did in 1923 — next to the Führer. In 1935 Graf demanded that he march next to the Führer, where he marched in 1923. Since the parade was already formed and the Führer had taken his position, I did not want to make a scene and I quietly relented. Then in 1937 Graf demanded that he march in the place to which he had no right, and I gave in again out of deference to Graf's deed at the Feldherrnhalle.' To try to settle the argument, Ulrich Graf was asked to

comment: 'In 1937, as I arrived with the Führer and also greeted Leutnant Kriebel, he said to me smirking, "Herr Graf, we should form up like we did in 1923" whereupon I laughed and said "Yes, Herr Oberstleutnant, but then the head of the parade will have to be changed." Then Kriebel said to me, "But I belong to the left of the Führer." Then I said, "No, in 1923 I was next to the Führer." And he said, "Göring doesn't belong over there either." I remained next to the Führer. We started to march and during the whole parade, Kriebel just pouted. I suggest that to clear up the matter, the Führer should be asked where I should march in future.' *Above:* This is the 1934 march — easily recognisable because Göring is wearing a greatcoat (the same one he wore in 1923). Kriebel is on Hitler's left with Graf beside him. (See also page 105.)

Heinrich Wilhelm Trambauer, who had rescued his Nazi banner from the front rank of the parade, hid it for several months before handing it over to his SA sergeant major, who then handed it personally to Hitler when he was released from prison. Hitler then gave it for safekeeping to Reichsführer-SS Josef Berchtold at the Party rally in July 1926, and later it was displayed in the Hall of Honour in the Brown House in Munich when it became Party Headquarters.

In this shot from the 1935 march we can see that Graf is now standing alongside Hitler which must have been his position in 1923 as he dislocated Hitler's left arm as he pulled him to the ground, taking the bullets meant for Hitler in the process.

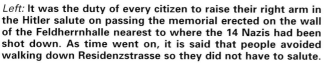

Left: **It was the duty of every citizen to raise their right arm in the Hitler salute on passing the memorial erected on the wall of the Feldherrnhalle nearest to where the 14 Nazis had been shot down. As time went on, it is said that people avoided walking down Residenzstrasse so they did not have to salute.**

Right: **In 1946, the Allied Control Council issued a directive that every monument in Germany was to be de-Nazified by January 1947. Consequently the Bavarian Minister of Culture, Franz Fendt, issued instructions for the memorial to be dismantled. Its fate is uncertain.**

Early in 1933 Hitler tasked his favourite architect, Professor Paul Ludwig Troost, with drawing plans for a suitable memorial to the 16 martyrs. The design was then entrusted to a young SA man, Kurt Schmid-Ehmen, for execution. It was mounted on the four-metre-high east-facing curtain wall of the Feldherrnhalle memorial and consisted of a bronze plaque bearing the names of the 16 martyrs under the inscription: 'On November 9, 1923, at the Feldherrnhalle and in the yard at the War Ministry the following men died believing firmly in the resurrection of their people.' Above this was a block with the letters N.S.D.A.P. surmounted by an eagle perched on a wreath containing a bold swastika. There was also another smaller bronze plaque beneath it on the wall itself flanked by hooks for hanging pine wreaths that Hitler ordered to to be maintained fresh.

General Walther von Reichenau, the Commander-in-Chief of Wehrkreis VII, at the oath-giving ceremony on November 7, 1935.

Hitler then had the Blutorden (Blood Medal) struck for all those that had participated in the march. It was of silver, oxidised so as to give it a dull finish, and suspended on a broad blood-red ribbon edged in thin black and white stripes and was worn on the right breast. The obverse had an eagle in flight carrying a wreathed '9. Nov.' with the inscription 'München 1923-1933' and the reverse an engraving of the Feldherrnhalle crowned by a radiating swastika. Around and just inside the upper rim of the reverse were the words 'Und ihr habt doch gesiegt' (And yet you won). At the base of the design was impressed the number of the medal issued to the recipient, who was given a small red-linen certificate with his name, photograph and the number of the medal, which he carried at all times. Although the original medal was restricted to those who had taken part in the 1923 putsch, its use was later extended for outstanding service to the Party, and even retrospective awards were made. A total of 436 posthumous awards of the medal were made, the last being to Reinhard Heydrich on June 4, 1942.

The Blutorden medal was instituted by Hitler in March 1933 to honour those who had participated in the putsch. Qualifying for it were members of the SA, Reichskriegsflagge or Bund Oberland who had 'participated in a battle' on November 9, 1923, but also those who had been refrained from doing so by the police or Reichswehr. NSDAP members could apply for the medal themselves or be put forward by Party officials, but the final decision for the award rested with Hitler alone. Each medal had the wearer's Party number engraved on the rear. (It is interesting to note that in 1924 the Nazi's themselves only commemorated 14 'putsch martyrs', Allfarth and Ehrlich being omitted from the official listing.)

ready to gate-crash. Professor Bruno Goldschmitt was entrusted with the visual effects of this vast propaganda exercise, and allocated the decoration of the streets from the Bürgerbräukeller to Odeonsplatz, and also all the beer halls to be used for the Old Fighters' celebrations. Accommodation had to be organised for the various categories of participants from first-class hotels for the families of the martyrs to straw-filled barns for the lesser brethren, and a whole round of festivities were planned. Special performances were arranged at the Nationaltheater of *Lohengrin*, at the Prinzregententheater of *Alle gegen Einer, Einer für Alle*, and at the Residenztheater of *Magdelena*.

Below: **Although the picture was taken outside the Bürgerbräukeller, we are looking at the building opposite. This was the site of the Kindlkeller beer hall at Nos. 18-22 Rosenheimer Strasse.**

Above: **The faithful assemble on the morning of November 9 — in this case it is the parade of 1938. Hitler wears the Blutorden on his right breast pocket. Behind him stands Ulrich Graf, his bodyguard in 1923 who took the bullets meant for Hitler. (He died in 1950.) He is talking to Adolf Wagner, the Gauleiter of Munich and Upper Bavaria. (Wagner suffered a stroke in 1942 and died two years later.) In the left background is Christian Weber who had the responsibility for Hitler's security at the annual parade. (He was killed in April 1945.)**

Hitler took a personal interest in the preparations for the tenth anniversary and set up a special office under SS-Brigadeführer Christian Weber to supervise them. Great pains were taken to ensure that only those that had genuinely been on the 1923 march would participate in the re-enactment, for there were many opportunists

The flags of the Freikorps are ceremoniously handed over to the SA-Stabschef Ernst Röhm.

Police measures included the the closure of all shops and businesses in the vicinity between 8 a.m. and 2 p.m., the banning of deliveries and the use of automobiles in the city centre. Additional police resources were brought in to cope with the heavy security and control commitments involved.

On the evening of the first day, November 8, Ernst Röhm, SA Chief-of-Staff, conducted a ceremony on Königsplatz denoting the demise of the old Freikorps and Kampfbund organisations now having been amalgamated into the Nazi system. Their banners were handed over to the SA to be marched solemnly across to the Brown House for installation in the Hall of Honour. The participants then dispersed to the various beer halls arranged for their reunions.

At 6 p.m. Hitler appeared at a reunion of 1920 founding members of the Party being held at the Sterneckerbräu inn at No. 54 Tal, leaving two hours later to attend the reunion of the 1923 participants at the Bürgerbräukeller.

Meanwhile Goebbels was addressing a packed Circus Krone on Marsstrasse. Then thousands of students carrying blazing torches marched along the deliberately darkened streets from the university buildings on Ludwigstrasse to Königsplatz via Odeonsplatz to meet up with the SA and SS formations awaiting them for a Grosser Zapfenstreich

(a Beating of Retreat-type ceremony) conducted by the Reichswehr. This was attended by Reichsstatthalter Ritter von Epp, Interior Minister Adolf Wagner, Ernst Röhm and his SA staff, Polizeigeneral Heinrich Doehla and other senior army and police officers, and included a speech by Göring, who had come across from the Bürgerbräukeller party.

Hitler at the 'old boys' reunion in the Bürgerbräukeller.

Promptly at noon the Old Fighters — the Alte Kämpfer — set off on the two-kilometre march in silence as there was no band in 1923.

Elaborate arrangements had been made for the radio broadcast of the occasion throughout Germany to ensure the maximum emotional propaganda value from dawn on the 9th to beyond midnight, the progress of the commemorative march being presented in the style of 'Stations of the Cross' as it passed pillars topped by blazing urns and bearing the names of individual martyrs in gold spaced out along the route. As in 1923, no band accompanied the march, and the participants wore brown shirts with no coats or hats.

Left: Julius Streicher, who had joined Hitler at the Marienplatz in 1923 (see page 106), was given pride of place at the head of the column. Here he leads down Rosenheimer Strasse towards the Ludwigsbrücke (right). These two comparisons (below) were deliberately taken at exactly the correct time on November 9, in this case on the 64th anniversary.

While Hitler appears to be deep in thought, his mind no doubt having drifted back through the years, can we sense the animosity between Graf, the stocky ex-wrestler, and the aloof Kriebel? As we have seen he was aggrieved that he was not next to Hitler because, as military commander of the Deutscher Kampfbund in 1923, he considered himself of greater importance as Hitler's immediate subordinate and also as a fellow prisoner in Landsberg (see page 109). Between them in the row behind is Alfred Rosenberg the so-called 'chief ideologist of the NSDAP'. The column has had to squeeze through the Isar Gate which forms the entrance to the inner city. Then, trams ran through and along the street called Tal; now, the road circles around the tower. All along the route, memorial pillars topped with flaming urns recorded the name of a Nazi martyr who had lost his life for the party.

The oily smoke added to the Wagnerian atmosphere, the silence broken only by the tramp of the jackboots.

Hitler: 'I had meant the Munich Putsch to be the beginning of a "March on Berlin" which should carry us straight to power. From its failure I learnt the lesson that each country must evolve its own type and methods of national regeneration.' He explained in 1933 that 'this evening and this day [November 9, 1923] made it possible for us afterwards to fight a battle for ten years by legal means: for make no mistake, if we had not acted then I should never have been able to found a revolutionary Movement, to form

Marienplatz then . . . and Marienplatz now. In the background the Altes Rathaus (old Town Hall).

it and keep it in being and yet all the time maintain legality. One could have said to me with justice: "You talk like the others and you will act just as little as the others." But this day, this decision later made it possible for me, in spite of all opposition, to perse-vere for nine years. I could say: "We are a revolutionary move-ment, and shall win power, we shall break this state in pieces and subdue it to our will, and yet we refuse to desert the path of legal-ity. Apparently a contradiction, but the sequel has justified us".'

This is also where Julius Streicher, the publisher of the *Der Stürmer* newspaper, joined the group.

The three horizontal runes on the flags which lined the route were called the 'Opfergedanke' — the symbols of sacrifice. Here in this picture of the 1938 ceremony, the Alte Kämpfer have retraced their route down Residenzstrasse and the parade is about to halt in front of the memorial on the Feld-hernhalle. Note the press photographers on the left and the soldiers holding the wreaths about to be laid at the memorial. (It was only in 2001 that it was revealed that the red dye for the Nazi flag — known as 'polar red' — was made for the Germans by the Swiss firm Geigy!)

Back to the first march in November 1933. This tenth anniversary parade must have been an emotional experience for the participants as they halted at the exact spot where blood had been spilled. Hitler explains here how he came to adopt the straight arm salute. (The army were allowed to give their normal salute until July 24, 1944 when, in response to the attempt to kill Hitler four days earlier, Göring issued instructions that henceforth the army must adopt the German — or Nazi — salute.)

They marched in silence between rows of saluting spectators. When they reached Marienplatz the Glockenspiel on the Town Hall played the tune of the Horst Wessel Song, and when they reached the point on Residenzstrasse where the confrontation with the police had taken place, a cannon in the Hofgarten fired once to be answered by other artillery pieces deployed throughout the city. There then followed a minute's silence, during which all movement was stilled.

The military salute is not a fortunate gesture. I imposed the German salute for the following reason. I'd given orders, at the beginning, that in the Army I should not be greeted with the German salute. But many people forgot. Fritsch drew his conclusions, and punished all who forgot to give me the military salute, with 14 days' confinement to barracks. I, in turn, drew my conclusions and introduced the German salute likewise into the Army.

On parades, when mounted officers give the military salute, what a wretched figure they cut! The raised arm of the German salute, that has quite a different style! I made it the salute of the Party long after the Duce had adopted it. I'd read the description of the sitting of the Diet of Worms, in the course of which Luther was greeted with the German salute. It was to show him that he was not being confronted with arms, but with peaceful intentions.

In the days of Frederick the Great, people still saluted with their hats, with pompous gestures. In the Middle Ages the serfs humbly doffed their bonnets, whilst the noblemen gave the German salute. It was in the Ratskeller at Bremen, about the year 1921, that I first saw this style of salute. It must be regarded as a survival of an ancient custom, which originally signified: 'See, I have no weapon in my hand!'

I introduced the salute into the Party at our first meeting in Weimar. The SS at once gave it a soldierly style. It's from that moment that our opponents honoured us with the epithet 'dogs of Fascists'.

ADOLF HITLER, JANUARY 3/4, 1942

For several decades, Residenzstrasse looked much like it did in 1923, only the white line and vehicles betraying this shot as having been taken in the 1970s.

Now the powers that be have closed off the street to all but pedestrians and cyclists . . . but did they realise that the bollards stand as silent sentinels to the memory of the Alte Kämpfer!

The Feldherrnhalle, or Field-Marshals' Hall, facing the Odeons-platz dated from 1844 and was erected to commemorate the deeds of the Bavarian Army and two of its illustrious generals. Perhaps it is fitting therefore to include these shots from the 1938 parade as the front rank is now joined by representatives of the armed forces: Grossadmiral Erich Raeder (C-in-C Kriegsmarine);

Generalfeldmarschall Walther von Brauchitsch (just appointed C-in-C Heer); Generalfeldmarschall Wilhelm Keitel (Chief of OKW — the German High Command); and Generalfeldmarschall Erhard Milch, the Luftwaffe chief. Note the temporary pillars topped with flaming oil at the rear of the monument bearing the names of the fallen 16 plus the legend: 'Zum Appell' (On parade).

Above: **The SA parade on the Odeons-platz November 9, 1934. Nymphenburger Strasse leading to the Königsplatz can be seen on the left — a view virtually unchanged in 70 years** *(right).*

A column of SA standard bearers, 195 strong, had formed up at the Feld-herrnhalle an hour previously and been joined by 20,000 SA marching through the Siegestor (Triumphal Arch) and up Ludwigstrasse six abreast in two columns, and then by columns from other organisations of the Kampfzeit, all converging on Odeonsplatz.

Meanwhile the deaths of Leutnant Theodor Casella and Schütze Martin Faust had been commemorated at the Bavarian War Ministry in a ceremony involving Röhm, Himmler, and the Minister of Defence, General Werner von Blomberg.

The 1938 parade has just crossed Karolinenplatz with its obelisk erected in 1833 in remembrance of the 300,000 Bavarians who participated and were killed in Napoleon's campaign

in Russia in 1812. The marchers are now level with the Brown House — the NSDAP headquarters just out of the photo on the left. Within a few yards they will enter the Königsplatz.

In the 18th century, under the enlightened rule of the Kings of Bavaria, Munich was enriched with monuments and buildings in the Classical style. As soon as he came to power, Hitler immediately embarked on his own impressive plans for the embellishment of the Königsplatz to make it the symbolic heart of the movement. The Party had alreay acquired the Barlow-Palast [1], between the square and the Karolinenplatz [2], in 1928 for a national headquarters for the NSDAP and it was renamed 'Das Braune Haus' in 1931. Hitler's chosen architect, Professor Paul Troost, remodelled the Brown House as befitted the new regime, and then immediately set about erecting two

open-topped temples alongside to hold the exhumed remains of the 16 martyrs. These two temples — the Ehrentempel or Ehrenmal [3 and 4] — each containing eight bronze sarcophagi, were later flanked by two new Nazi administrative buildings. The Führerbau [5], where the Munich agreement was signed, lay on the north-east corner of the Königsplatz with a matching building, the Verwaltungsbau [6], to the south-east. Having transformed the eastern side into a mecca of Nazism, the whole square was then paved to become a massive parade ground, offset by the Glyptothek museum [7] Propyläen arch [8] and Kunstausstellungsgebäude museum [9] of the Ludwig I era.

The pattern had been set for future anniversaries of the 1923 putsch, but no commemorative parade took place in 1934, being too close on the heels of the purge of Röhm and the SA leadership. Nevertheless, Hitler made his usual appearance and speech at the Bürgerbräukeller.

The three days of events planned for 1935 were even grander than those of two years earlier, for Hitler had commissioned Professor Troost to build the twin Ehrentempel (Temples of Honour) on Königsplatz for the 16 martyrs. Troost died while they were still under construction, but his young widow Gerdy completed the task. Of neoclassical design, they were built in marble, surrounded by pillars and open to the sky. Studio Troost also supplied the bronze sarcophagi to hold the martyrs' remains.

By November 7, 1935, the bodies had been disinterred from the various Munich cemeteries and placed under SA watch. An SA guard of honour met the coffins of Wilhelm Ehrlich, Kurt Neubauer and Johann Rickmers when they arrived by train at the main station and escorted them to the King's room in the Wittelsbach Residenz.

Then on the night of November 8/9, horse-drawn caissons of the Wehrmacht brought them to the Siegestor on Leopoldstrasse to the accompaniment of muffled drums along darkened streets lined by the SA carrying flaming torches. Waiting for them were a host of SA, SS and senior Party members, backed by a sea of flags.

In his Bürgerbräukeller speech in 1934, Hitler said of the Party's martyrs: 'They, too, in the spirit are in our ranks: in the other world they will know that their fight was not in vain. The blood which they shed has become for the Reich the water of baptism.' Although no formal parade was held that year in case there was a backlash from the recent elimination of SA leader Ernst Röhm, greater things were in the pipeline for 1935. Hitler's plans for transforming the Königsplatz into a shrine for the martyrs culminated with the ceremonial re-interrment of the 16 men in twin temples.

Soon after 11 p.m. the Old Guard arrived, having marched there from their Bürgerbräukeller reunion. The procession then set off for the Feldherrnhalle, where the Old Guard carried the sarcophagi up the steps one at a time to lay them before a large smoking urn on a column backed by a huge blood-red flag. The first verse of the Horst Wessel Song was then sung as a funereal dirge, and 10,000 SA men marched on to Odeonsplatz. Hitler then went up alone into the Feldherrnhalle to commune with the dead, being followed after a while by some of his closest colleagues. That night 16 Hitler Youths kept vigil in the Feldherrnhalle, a gesture that was repeated throughout Germany at the graves of all the over 400 Nazis that had been killed in the cause.

Draped with what was by now the Geman National Flag (which had been officially brought into being at the Nuremberg Party Rally just two months earlier), on the night of Friday, November 8, the 16 coffins were brought to lie in state in the Feldherrnhalle before the serried ranks of the SA drawn up on the Odeonsplatz.

From the gun carriages . . . to the draped catafalques . . . to the bronze sarcophagus within the Ehrentempel — the Temples of Honour. In his inaugural speech Hitler declared that for many years he had vowed that if ever he came to power he would take these comrades from the cemeteries where they were buried, would do them honour and show them to the nation. 'That determination I have now fulfilled', said Hitler. 'They now pass into the German immortality. In their own time they could not yet see the Reich of today: they could only dimly envisage it. Fate has forbidden them to experience this Reich. But though they might neither see nor experience this Reich we will take care that this Reich shall see them. And therefore we have laid them in no crypt and beneath no dome. No, just as once they marched, their breast open to the air, so now shall they lie in wind and weather, in storm and snow, under God's free heaven, a perpetual reminder for the German nation. For us they are not dead: these temples are no crypts: they are an eternal guard-post. Here they stand for Germany and keep guard over our people. Here they lie as true witnesses to our movement.'

where the caskets were unloaded on to a platform in front of the Temples of Honour, where the relatives of the dead were waiting. The elaborate ceremony continued with a 'Final Roll Call' conducted by Gauleiter Adolf Wagner.

Once the caskets had been placed in the temples, Hitler went in to lay wreaths on each one and then the SS-Standarte 'Grossdeutschland' marched on to take on the honour guard duty that it was to maintain until the end of the Third Reich. Finally Baldur von Schirach conducted a swearing-in ceremony for 1,200 boys and 600 girls entering the Hitlerjugend, symbolising the handing over of the torch to the new generation.

Left: **The Führerbau building still survives in the guise of the State High School for Music** *(below)* **— minus of course the eagles over the porticos — but the Ehrentempel have gone — we shall see their demise later on.**

At noon next day (November 9) the marchers assembled once more outside the Bürgerbräukeller, this time the Blood Flag being escorted by members of the SA, as was to be the case in future years. Large blood-red flags were suspended over the route and spaced out at regular intervals were columns topped with smoking urns, each named after one of the dead and guarded by representatives of his home region. As Hitler went past, the name of the martyr was read out on loudspeakers and repeated on the broadcasting system.

Upon arrival at the Feldherrnhalle a 16-gun salute was fired, and one by one the caskets were loaded on to their caissons. The procession then moved along Brienner Strasse toward Königsplatz,

These picture show the ceremonial in 1938 — the salute to the fallen. Adolf Wagner, the Gauleiter of Munich, was given the role of calling out the 16 names, his amplified voice echoing around the square as he summoned the dead 'Zum letzten Appel'. As each name was read out, the massed contingents would answer each call with a shouted: 'Hier!'

However, as the years went by the ceremonies lost some of their impact, and the rise of the SS and decline of the SA became more marked. By 1938 the SS outnumbered the SA by four to one on Königsplatz, parading immediately behind the Blood Flag, while the SA were banished to the flanks of the massed Party organisations. That year Himmler invited thousands of guests that he particularly wished to impress to the swearing-in ceremony for the SS-Verfügungstruppe and SS-TotenkopfVerbände recruits on Odeonsplatz, where Hitler arrived to receive their oaths at midnight on the 9th.

Left: **The wives and mothers are warmly greeted by Hitler and Wagner.** *Below:* **The following day the general public were permitted to pay their respects.**

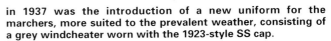

In 1936 a highly effective film called *Für Uns* (For Us) was produced on the November ceremonies that was widely used in the education of the young in Nazi ideology. An innovation in 1937 was the introduction of a new uniform for the marchers, more suited to the prevalent weather, consisting of a grey windcheater worn with the 1923-style SS cap.

Left: **After the war, to disguise the sunken tombs, each was filled with earth — this picture shows the bed newly planted with** shrubs in 1975. *Right:* **Another thirty years later, both the Ehrentempel have disappeared beneath a veritable forest!**

MUNICH

Today we stand in the midst of our spring battle against the night of winter, and the mission of this the oldest city of our Movement, which was the starting point of the new German redemption, is this: it must be the central point from which shall be waged the battle for Germany's great future. Munich has a greater task than that of any other city. This city as the central point of the Party must ever again and again let new life foam up. Munich is not merely in theory the capital of the National Socialist Party, it is so in fact and spiritually in the best sense of the word.

ADOLF HITLER, MARCH 19, 1934

'Hauptstadt der Bewegung' — The Capital of the Movement

Munich was known throughout the time of Third Reich as the 'Hauptstadt der Bewegung', the 'capital of the movement', for it was not only the birthplace of the NSDAP but remained the Party's administrative centre. The Nazi era was to leave some indelible scars behind it.

Architecture was Hitler's private passion, his hobby as a relief from matters of state, and his first opportunity to engage himself in this field arose with the adaptation of the former Barlow Palace on Munich's elegant Brienner Strasse for use as the NSDAP Party Headquarters, known thereafter as the Braune Haus (Brown House). Set slightly back from the road, with extensive gardens to the rear and tall gates in front, the new office building faced the official residence of Monsignor Pacelli, the Vatican's representative to Catholic Bavaria.

Nearly three quarters of a million marks had been raised by special levy on Party members to cover the cost of remodelling the palace ballrooms and reception area into efficient offices for propaganda, membership and culture. Hitler directed the renovation personally. By wedding classicism to modernism he hoped to create an example for future Party buildings to follow. The result was tasteful, even luxurious but hardly revolutionary: cream-coloured walls, brass fixtures, imitation teak panelling. The ubiquitous swastika was repeated everywhere, on widow panes,

The National Socialist Party was given birth in Bavaria so it was only natural for its capital to be located in Munich. Here the embryo movement had tried to seize power and here the Party gave honour to its revered dead. Central to that aim was the King's parade ground — the Königsplatz — burial place of the Party's putsch martyrs just a few yards from its headquarters: the Brown House at No. 45 Brienner Strasse. The building, originally known as the Barlow Palace, was erected in 1828 and the Nazi Party purchased it on July 5, 1930. This picture was one of a series taken in November 1938 during the annual 'Neunte Elfte' commemorations (see also pages 58-59). The entrance to the northernmost Ehrenmal can be seen on the left.

draperies, even on the faces of clocks. Hitler's architectural advisor had decorated a fleet of North German Lloyd liners, and wags called the result on Brienner Strasse a cross between a steamship stateroom and a Pullman sleeper.

The building was easily recognisable from the street by the tremendous red banner billowing from its roof top and the heavy bronze doors beneath a lintel with the battle cry 'Deutschland Erwache!'('Germany Awake!') Two young sentries in black breeches and brown shirts scrutinised each visitor, be he peasant lad, dusty despatch rider or elegant former officer. Inside, a third sentry gave the Hitler salute and requested the visitor's identification papers. A reception bureau recorded this information and checked the newcomer through to his destination by telephone. Security was tight, as befitted a political citadel.

From the lobby a magnificent staircase rose to the second floor and the structure's showpiece, the Party Senate Chamber. The Chamber, measuring 60 by 150 feet, enclosed a double row of 42 red-leather chairs set in a gigantic semicircle facing the Leader's throne. Twice daily, tours filed up the staircase and past Hitler's corner suite to the Chamber's entrance, flanked on either side by commemorative tablets listing the names of the Party's first martyrs, the dead of the Beer Hall Putsch. Their memory was kept alive daily by the addition of fresh garlands of cut evergreens.

Flags and standards and a bust of Dietrich Eckart, Hitler's mentor and spiritual 'North Star', greeted visitors to the Brown House. It was Eckart who coined the phrase 'Deutschland Erwache!' (Germany Awake!) in one of his poems.

Eventually, offices for Agriculture and Economic Planning took over a neighbouring building, while in the garden at the rear a rambling wooden structure was erected to house the legion of typists and stenographers. There were departments for bookkeeping and dues collection and a statistical department that could compute in an instant the party strength anywhere in Germany by means of a Hollerith machine. Steel filing cabinets as heavy as bank safes and proof against shellfire and Bolshevik invasion held the photographs and case histories of every one of the movement's 600,000 registered voters. In the basement a cosy *völkisch* canteen dispensed *Weißwurst*, *Leberknödel* and vegetarian dishes to the 140 employees of the Braunes Haus from Herr Hitler down to the lowliest office boy.

So just where was the Braune Haus? For more than 40 years places like Munich and Nuremberg wanted to sweep the Nazi years under the carpet but now a more enlightened age has dawned. History is history, however unpalatable, and one does a disservice to the generations which follow to try to expunge the years between 1933 and 1945. In recent years, informative signs have sprung up in many German cities, some even including 'then' photographs to compare with the view today. This notice stands within yards of the Brown House front door. (We will see the end of the building in our final chapter.)

But before we move on we should illustrate two earlier NSDAP head offices. We saw the first meeting place in the Sterneckerbräu on page 98 and the second on page 99. An unnofficial party HQ was then set up in the office of the *Völkischer Beobachter* newspaper at No. 15 Thierschstrasse (today No. 11) which was used from 1923 to 1925. The parent company was Franz-Eher-Verlag and it was the publisher, Max Amann, Hitler's sergeant-major during the war, who brought out his book in two volumes in 1925 and 1926. Originally titled *A Four and a Half Year Struggle against Lies, Stupidity and Cowardice*, Amann persuaded Hitler to adopt the more marketable title: *Mein Kampf* (My Struggle). Eher-Verlag had world rights and by the time of Hitler's death, eight million copies had been sold. The English rights were purchased by Hurst and Blackett for £350 and an abridged version was brought out in 1933. (The book is still banned in Germany.)

Then, with the release of Hitler from prison in December 1924, new premises had to be found and Heinrich Hoffmann suggested they use the building behind his photographic shop at No. 50 Schellingstrasse. This remained the Party headquarters from April 1925 to September 1931 when it moved to the converted Barlow Palace. *Above:* At the top table in August 1928 (L-R): Alfred Rosenberg, editor of the *Völkischer Beobachter* who became head of the Party's Foreign Affairs Office; Walter Buch who headed the odd-sounding Committee for Investigation and Settlement — a body created to hush up crimes by Party members; Franz Xaver Schwarz, an accountant at Munich's City Hall who became the Party's Treasurer; Gregor Strasser, the Reich Organisation Leader who lost his life in the Röhm purge; and Himmler who was to take over the leadership of the SS in 1929.

Hoffmann's shop now sells interior decorations but note the headless eagle still perched over the garage on the right.

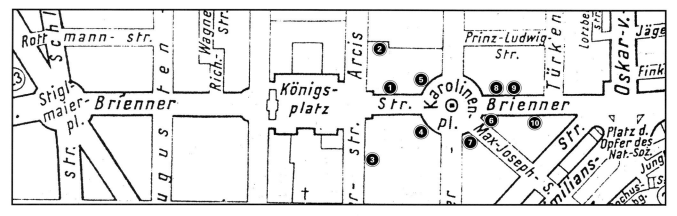

Brienner Strasse became the heart of Nazi administration. [1] The Brown House. [2] Führerbau [3] Verwaltungsbau.

With the acquisition of power, funds became readily available for reinforcing the Party's position within the city. Properties were acquired, sometimes whole sections of streets for Party use. For instance, on Karolinenplatz, No. 1 was taken over by Hans Frank's Reichsrechtsamt (State Law Office); No. 2 by the NS-Frauenschaft (the Party's women's organisation) under Gertrud Scholtz-Klink; No. 3 by the Party's main treasury offices under Franz Xaver Schwarz; No. 4 by the Party's high court under SS-Obergruppenführer Walter Buch, Martin Bormann's father-in-law; No. 6 by Dr Robert Ley's Deutsche

[4] The site of the NSDAP Treasury.

Arbeitsfront (DAF, German Labour Front), whose offices also extended to No. 28 Brienner Strasse. Again next door at No. 26 Brienner Strasse, the Kraft durch Freude (Strength through Joy) offices of the DAF were located, while No. 23 became the Haus der deutschen Ärzte (German Doctors' House) and No. 20 Gestapo Headquarters. Similarly in Arcisstrasse (today Meiserstrasse), Nos. 6-12 on one side of the street and Nos. 5-11 on the other were taken over by various Party offices. Barer Strasse was completely taken over, SA headquarters occupying Nos. 7-11, as was Karlstrasse, where the SS were located at No. 10.

[5] The NSDAP High Court building.

[6] The Reichsrechtsamt building. [7] Nationalsozialistische Frauenschaft office (right).

[8] HQ of the Deutsche Arbeitsfront.

[9] The Kraft durch Freude HQ.

[10] Haus der Deutschen Ärzte.

Left: **The Führerbau or Führerhaus (Leader's Building) was the National Socialist headquarters in Munich. Designed by Paul Ludwig Troost and built facing the Königsplatz by his company Atelier Troost, its formal address was No. 12 Arcisstrasse (but** since renamed No. 10 Meiserstrasse). *Right:* **Shorn of its Nazi impedimenta, the building survives intact as the High School for Music. The patched up holes for the supports for the eagle still show in the stonework over the doorway.**

It was completed together with its twin, the Verwaltungsbau, (then housing Nazi administration but now the Bavarian State **Graphics Archive) and the two Ehrentempel within two years and was dedicated on November 3, 1935 (see also page 147).**

The Königsplatz was paved with granite slabs, one metre square, to create the Nazi Party's most revered parade ground.

The building beyond is the Kunstausstellungsgebäude — a long word simply meaning art gallery — dating from 1848.

No. 12a Möhlstrasse was acquired for Heinrich Himmler and the plot of No. 12 Arcisstrasse for Hitler, where the 'Führerbau', an office for his use when visiting Munich, was constructed. It was here that the 1938 Munich agreement was signed (see *After the Battle* No. 62) and where Hitler met Mussolini again shortly after the defeat of France. This building and an identical one opposite, No. 10 Meiserstrasse, which was a Party administration building, were both designed by Professor Paul Ludwig Troost, who was then tasked with Hitler with designing twin 'Ehrentempel' (Temples of Honour) to be built between these two buildings for the 16 Nazis killed in the 1923 abortive putsch. The area around the twin buildings was cleared of trees so as to give an open aspect on to the Königsplatz, which Hitler had paved in granite to serve as a parade ground.

The paving remained right up to 1987 when it was torn up to reinstate the square to its original design of 1806.

The Haus der Deutschen Kunst was another design by Troost *(left)* and very dear to Hitler's heart. At the ceremony to lay the foundation stone on October 15, 1933, he said: 'We cannot conceive of any restoration of the German people unless the culture of Germany — above all the art of Germany — rises afresh. Young Germany builds for its art its own house. And in giving this building for German art to the city of Munich it professes its allegiance to the spirit of him [Ludwig II] who as King of Bavaria made of this city a home of German art.' *Right:* Hitler inspects the construction with Professor Leonard Gall and Albert Speer. Professor Troost died suddenly on January 21, 1934 when his wife Gerdy, also an accomplished architect, took over.

On October 15, 1933, Hitler laid the cornerstone of the Haus der Deutschen Kunst at No. 1 Prinzregentenstrasse. The hammer broke during the ceremony, which was taken as an ill omen, and within a month the architect, Professor Troost, was dead. Hitler returned on July 18, 1937, to open the building in grand style with the architect's young widow, Gerdy Troost. The exhibition of German art on view contained many modern paintings that Hitler found degenerate and disapproved of. Gerdy had been one of the judges making the selection and had a violent argument with Hitler about it prior to the opening that concluded with her resignation from the committee. Despite this, Hitler continued to visit the Troost studios, whose work he greatly admired. The evening of the opening there was a grand procession celebrating 2,000 years of German culture.

Left: The museum was completed by 1937 and opened on July 18. Annual exhibitions of German art were held each July, this being the parade for the second one in 1938. In his speech Hitler declared: 'The German people of this 20th century are the people of a newly awakened affirmation of life, seized with admiration for strength and beauty and therefore for that which is healthy and vigorous. Strength and beauty — these are the fanfares sounded by this new age, clarity and logic dominate its effort. He who would be an artist in this century must dedicate himself to this century. For the Neanderthal men of art there is no place in the twentieth century — at least not in National Socialist Gemany.' *Right:* Our 21st century comparison.

Above: **July 18, 1939 — the Third Exhibition of German Art — at which Hitler explained that 'it was only in January 1933 that it could be determined whether the Movement would do justice to its mission or whether it would fail in perpetuating its work in the field of culture.' He expressed the hope that 'in the future individual outstanding artists might turn their thought to the experiences, the events and the fundamental ideas of the present. For however numerous in their thousand-fold variety may be the historical visions or the other impressions which life may make upon the artist and which enrich him for his creative work, which rise before his mind and awake his enthusiasm, yet over and above them all stands the present-day splendour of his own time which need not fear comparison with the grandest epochs in our German history.'** *Above right:* **The terrace on the front of the building has now been cut back to the line of the pillars. Hitler would surely not approve of the desecration of his pride and joy** *(right).*

On the Tag der Deutschen Kunst, Hitler made a pilgrimage to the grave of the man whose architecture he admired the most: Paul Ludwig Troost in Munich's Nordfriedhof. Although Gerdy

Troost had taken up her husband's mantle, in due course Hitler fell out with her, giving Albert Speer a free hand to satisfy the Führer's grand designs for Germany.

Right: **Many existing buildings were given 'make-overs' to convert them for use by the Nazi Party. The Prinz-Karl-Palais on Königstrasse, directly across the street from the Haus der Deutschen Kunst, is a good example. Previously an art gallery, it was reconstructed in 1936-39 by architect Fritz Gablonsky to serve as a guesthouse for important Party members and visiting statesmen. This is where Mussolini stayed during his five-day state visit to Germany in September 1937** *(below)* **— the first time that the two fascist leaders had conferred on German soil. (They had first met each other when the Führer flew to Venice on June 14, 1934.) Mussolini arrived in Munich on September 25 where he was treated to a whistle-stop tour of the Nazi tourist spots — the Feldherrnhalle, Ehrentempel, Königsplatz and the Haus der Deutschen Kunst, etc, guided by Hitler personally. He then lunched with the Alte Kämpfer at the Führerbau and that evening departed by train for Mecklenburg.**

Today the Prinz-Karl-Palais is the personal fiefdom of the Minister-President of Bavaria.

New barracks for the SS-Standarte 'Grossdeutschland' were specially built for the regiment on Ingolstädter Strasse.

Left: Anton Mussert, the leader of the Dutch Nazi Party — the Nationaal-Socialistische Beweging — is given a conducted tour by SS chief Heinrich Himmler. Mussert was arrested on May 7, 1945, found guilty of treason, and shot exactly one year later.

Taken over by US forces in 1945, today the Ernst-von-Begemann Kaserne is the home of the Bundeswehr Medical Academy.

Above: **This building, seen during the flag ceremony on December 5, 1937, was specially constructed for the Luftgaukommando VII headquarters (the district command of the air force). It still stands at Nos. 24-28 Prinzregentenstrasse** (right).

The SS-Standarte 'Grossdeutschland' had a completely new barracks complex constructed for them in 1935-38 at No. 193 Ingolstädter Strasse in the Freimann district, including officers' married quarters. The barracks also contained a small satellite of Dachau concentration camp to provide labour for the administrative authorities.

A new headquarters building for Luftgaukommando VII was constructed at No. 24-28 Prinzregentenstrasse with a 225-metre-long facade to a design by architect German Bestelmeyer and opened in 1938. A feature of this facade were the steel-helmet crowned windows of the upper storey and Luftwaffe eagles flanking the portico of the main entrance.

Left: **The Reichszeugmeisterei (Reich Quartermaster) complex was opened at Nos. 202-204 Tegernseer Landstrasse to control** the design of uniforms, insignia and standards for the myriad Party organisations. Right: **It, too, still stands.**

Munich's memorial to those killed in the war of 1914-1918 lies in the Hofgarten. Its foundation stone was laid on November 4, 1923, the ceremony attended by Hitler just five days before the putsch. *Above:* It was unveiled on December 14 the following year, the building in the background being the Bavarian Parliament building — the Neue Staatskanzlei. *Below:* One has to descend to the crypt to lay a wreath on the prostrate form of a dead soldier — the Töter Krieger. This picture is dated August 8, 1936 so Lloyd George, Britain's Prime Minister during the latter part of the war, would have then seen the red marmor figure by Bernhard Bleeker but this was replaced in 1972 by a bronze replica by Hans Wimmer. (The original is now in the Bavarian Army Museum in Ingolstadt.)

NUREMBERG

In no other city could even future generations establish that magical association of the heritage of a past of unexampled richness with the clear evidences of a glorious present and of a future which were no less unique.

In a single section — in the coming into being of the new Nuremberg — one may recognize the growth of our Movement, the development of Germany. A gigantic forum is being constructed: the spaces for our parades are the greatest in the world. Tomorrow there is to be laid the foundation stone of a stadium such as the world has never seen. In two years at least the structure of the colossus of our Congress Hall will stand completed and as our first granite monument will bear witness to the greatness of the idea which inspired it and bear witness also to the greatness of the whole layout of the new city.

ADOLF HITLER, SEPTEMBER 7, 1937

All political parties hold annual rallies to publicise their policies, encourage their delegates, and fire up their supporters, but none have surpassed the huge National Socialist gathering in Nuremberg in the 1930s. The first Nazi Party rally was held in Munich in 1923 (January 27-29) but not repeated until Weimar in 1926 (July 3-4), and from 1927 onwards they were always staged in Nuremberg. According to one report, it was Julius Streicher with his Nuremberg background (see pages 92-93) who was instrumental in promoting *his* city as a venue for the annual Party congress. The old medieval city with its beautiful walled old town — the Altstadt — and castle were steeped in Teutonic legend, something which always appealed to the Nazi ideologists, and so Nuremberg became the Hauptstadt der Partei — the NSDAP capital — with the first Reichsparteitag being held from August 19-21, 1927.

The saluting base for the street parade was Hitler's car parked in the market place — the Marktplatz, naturally renamed the Adolf-Hitler-Platz in 1933. In this shot from the 1927 event, Pfeffer von Salomon (the SA commander since November 1926) takes the salute with Hitler. The bald-headed Streicher, then Gauleiter of Nuremberg-Fürth, stands beside the Mercedes. In August 1930 Hitler himself assumed command of the SA after repeated conflicts with von Salomon. When Ernst Röhm was appointed in his place, instead of being given the title of Oberster Führer der SA, he (and Lutze after him) was only given the lesser title of Stabschef (Chief-of-Staff) which no doubt reflected a change in attitude on Hitler's part after the rebellion of the SA in Berlin in September 1930. (Von Salomon fell out of favour, and was later sent to a concentration camp. He survived the war and died in April 1968.)

'Hauptstadt der Partei' – The Capital of the Party

Top: The SA parade route is marked on this contemporary plan. [1] Kaiserburg. [2] Burgfreiung. [3] Reichsjugendherberge 'Luginsland' (Kaiserstallung). [4] Albrecht-Dürer-Haus. [5] Fembo-Haus. [6] Topler-Haus. [7] Groland-Haus. [8] Peller-Haus. [9] Egidienkirche. [10] Laufer Schlagturm. [11] Rathaus. [12] St Sebalduskirche. [13] Bratwurstglöcklein. [14] Schöner Brunnen. [15] Bratwurst Herzlein. [16] Henkersteg. [17] Heilig-Geist-Spital. [18] Schuldturm. [19] Meistersinger-Kirche. [20] St Lorenz-Kirche. [21] Nassauer-Haus. [22] Polizeipräsidium. [23] Weisser Turm. [24] Jakobskirche. [25] Mauthalle. [26] Germanisches Museum. [27] Opernhaus. [28] Deutscher Hof Hotel. [29] Das Braune Haus in Franken. [30] Gauhaus. *Above left:* Looking in the opposite direction towards the Fleischbrücke compared to later rallies, the one in 1927 was a very simple occasion with delegates meeting on Friday afternoon (August 19) followed by the formal opening of the congress on Saturday with brass band concerts and parades. The main event was on Sunday when the ceremonial consecration of the flags took place in the Luitpoldhain arena. *Above right:* The old town was badly knocked about before and during the battle for the city and all the buildings visible are new post-war constructions.

Although one further Party rally was held from August 1-4 in 1929, not until Hitler became Chancellor was he able to issue instructions for the extensive building works which were to transform the Nuremberg skyline. The Luitpoldhain — literally the 'Holy Forest of Luitpold' in German — was a grassy park where the First World War memorial designed by Fritz Mayer had been dedicated in 1930.

landed in his third airship in 1909 and which were now used as a picnic area.

The Luidpoldhain had been used by the Nazis for their rallies since the early 1920s. It now contained a war memorial, the Ehrenmal, which had been designed by Fritz Mayer and built between 1928 and 1930. For their 1933 rally the triumphant Nazis erected a huge wooden grandstand surrounded by three wooden towers, each 96 feet high, on top of which were mounted large flags, 78 by 18 feet in size. Other flagpoles erected around the arena were 105 feet high. The speaker's platform was 18 feet high and able to accommodate 1,000 honoured guests, while the grandstands could seat 50,000 spectators. To one side was a stand for the press capable of taking 1,500. The amplification system comprised 82 loudspeakers. These preparations were completed by a workforce of 1,500 in very short time, during which Hitler made an inspection of the site on August 19.

With the appointment of Hitler as Chancellor in 1933, the Nazi Party rallies grew into national events of great significance, for which he decided to build a gigantic stage on the outskirts of Nuremberg.

The site selected was the Luitpoldhain, named after a Bavarian king, that had been laid out as exhibition grounds in 1906. Nearby was the sports stadium built by the city between 1923 and 1928, and also the Zeppelinwiese, the meadows upon which Graf Zeppelin had

Right: **The only permanent alteration that could be carried out in time for the 1933 rally scheduled to run from August 31 to September 3 was to add seven stone pillars on either side on which pans of oil could be placed to create the 'flaming urn' effect beloved of the Nazis.**

Within a year the arena had been transformed with the addition of a paved pathway — Die Strasse des Führers — nearly 60 feet wide and 240 yards in length linking the war memorial with a speaker's tribune on the opposite side of the park.

Grandstands had been added on three sides seating 50,000. Now the stage was set for one of the most dramatic spectacles of all — the Day of the SA and SS on Sunday, September 9, 1934. (The rally ran from September 5-10.)

What was most significant in the 1934 parade was the public demonstration of the acendancy of the SS. *Above:* In 1933, Ernst Röhm had marched beside Hitler, across what was then still turf, to give the tribute to the fallen. *Below left:* Now Heinrich Himmler representing the SS had achieved a place on Hitler's right alongside the new SA Chief-of-Staff Viktor Lutze. Henceforth the SA was to become a very minor player and would soon be completely overshadowed by the SS. In a complete role reversal, what had once been a small unit within the SA was now to become its master.

From 1933 . . . to 2003 . . . a timeless comparison.

Adolf Hitler: 'Nuremberg has become the expression in stone of German strength and German greatness in a new German Reich'. Professor Kurt Schmid-Ehmen (1901-1968) was the Third Reich's 'eagle man' producing many versions of the Hoheitszeichen, the national emblem. *Right:* **The bronze eagles in situ for the 1935 rally held from September 10-16.**

Work on a more permanent basis was carried out for the following year's rally. A workforce of 620 was employed to erect two gigantic reviewing stands 500 feet long, together with a speaker's stand, again 18 feet high, backed by four metal flagpoles 130 feet high, and flanked by stands for the press between two enormous stone towers topped by the Party eagles. These eagles, 19 feet high and with a wingspan of 23 feet, were designed and manufactured in a film studio by Kurt Schmid-Ehmen, who had them transported to the site on five trucks for assembly on the site. Earth was spread all over the six square miles of parade grounds at Nuremberg so as to be able to seed them with grass.

The eagles were replaced in 1935 with similar ones cast in bronze, and by 1937 the grass parade ground before the stands had been laid with paving in the first step to covering the whole area, so turning the Luitpoldhain into a vast stone edifice. The granite path connecting the tribune with the war memorial opposite was 54 feet wide and 720 long. Eventually the whole area extended over five square miles and could accommodate 150,000 participants and 50,000 spectators.

When Nuremberg fell to American forces in April 1945, the Luitpold Arena was initially used as a parking area. Later it was a venue for forces concerts but in 1959-60, the Third Reich constructions were all demolished . . . save for the 14 pillars in front of the war memorial. Now, once again, it is a peaceful expanse of parkland.

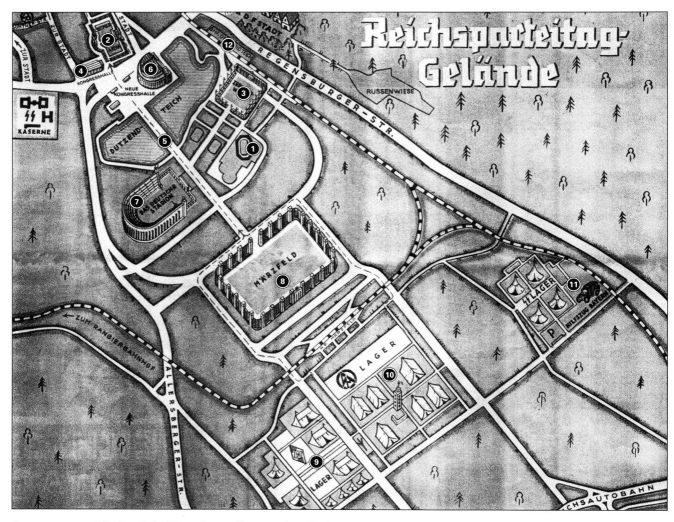

A contemporary SA plan of the Nuremberg rally grounds — both in existence and projected. (The reference numbers are our additions.) [1] Existing Municipal Stadium used by Hitler Youth. [2] Luitpoldhain. [3] Zeppelinwiese. [4] Luitpoldhalle. [5] Processional avenue. [6] New Congress Hall (never completed). [7] New German Stadium (never completed). [8] Märzfeld (never completed). [9] HJ and RAD camping ground. [10] SA camping ground. [11] SS camping ground. [12] Dutzendteich railway station.

As early as 1929 the Luitpoldhain had proved too small to accommodate the constantly increasing number of participants, so it was decided to use one or more of the adjacent fields for larger demonstrations. A number of stands capable of seating 350,000 spectators were set up on the Zeppelinwiese (Zeppelin Meadow) for the 1933 congress, and the following year a special railway station was built nearby to facilitate the movement of spectators and participants to and from the area. Then an underground tramway was built in 1938 partly in concrete tunnels and partly between cuttings between the Oskar-von-Müller-Strasse, Tristanstrasse and Tiroler Strasse to avoid traffic jams during the parades.

The Zeppelinwiese arena in 1933. The temporary tribune was backed by the framework eagle. The Hitler Youth Stadium can be seen in the background. The 1933 event was the first to be held under a title 'Reichsparteitag des Sieges' (Reich Party Rally of Victory), and although Hitler had decreed that the city would host all future rallies, Nuremberg was not officially given the title 'Stadt der Reichsparteitage' until July 1936.

As we have seen, Professor Troost was the chief architect of the Third Reich but when he died in 1934 a replacement had to be found. *Left:* Hitler chose a young 28-year-old architect, Albert Speer, right, who had already been applauded for the special effects he had employed at a parade in Berlin the previous year. *Right:* His first major commission was to design a permanent grandstand for the Zeppelinwiese and he openly admitted in later years that he based his design on the ancient Doric architecture of the Pergamum Altar in Turkey. It was more or less finished for the 1936 rally held from September 8-14 although the huge swastika over the central tribune had yet to be installed as well as the large flaming urns at each end. Speer cleverly disguised the absence of marble cladding on the brickwork by using decorative swastika banners.

Early in 1934 Hitler summoned Albert Speer, an architect whose work he increasingly admired, and asked him to submit a design for permanent stone structures for the Zeppelinwiese. Speer hit on the idea of a mighty flight of stairs topped and enclosed by a long colonnade, flanked on both sides by stone abutments. A model was made and then shown with some trepidation to Hitler. Speer, fully aware of Hitler's over-riding passion for architecture and building, watched anxiously as Hitler impassively studied the model and drawings from every angle. Finally, with a single word he approved the design and departed abruptly.

This was the turning point in Speer's architectural career that was to lead to the design of Germania, the revamp of Berlin as capital of the Third Reich. With other architects Hitler would call for revisions several times, but from then on Hitler respected Speer's plans and let him proceed without interference.

The work began immediately in order to have at least the platform ready for the September rally. The Nuremberg tram depot had to be demolished, as were a neighbouring sportsfield and some tennis courts in order to incorporate their space in the Zeppelinwiese, thereby enlarging it by a third and increasing its capacity to 400,000 people. (The population of Nuremberg at this time was 420,000.) However, the task was not completed until the 1936 rally, by which time the field had been expanded to allow sufficient space for manoeuvres by the armed forces and for political meetings, with an avenue 72 feet wide connecting it to the main concourse.

The new grandstand on the north-eastern side of the field was 80 feet high and 1,300 feet long. At first, until the brickwork faced by stone cladding could be completed, the back of the tribune and the steps leading to the VIP stands were temporarily made out of

Hitler's triumphal entry into the arena would be greeted with a tumultuous roar, drowning out the Wagnerian music — like the Rienze Overture — which would help build up the tension in the crowd before his gladiatorial entrance. Here we see Speer's transformation from the flag-bedecked backdrop (left) of 1935 to the stone pillars of 1936 (right).

wood. At the rear, iron scaffolding 120 feet high was topped by a huge eagle and several large flags. For the 1935 rally another large eagle was mounted on eight poles, but this was replaced the following year with a vast gold swastika.

By July 1936 the rear of the grandstand facing the street had been covered with marble tiles and 170 stone pillars formed background screens to the spectator stands flanking the tribune. The actual parade ground now measured 960 by 870 feet and was paved with stone. Stone grandstands 20 feet high, incorporating 34 towers, each carrying six flagpoles, enclosed the field on three sides, all ready for the rally in September.

Years later Hitler confided to his close retinue that 'the most difficult effort comes at the march-past when one has to remain motionless for hours. On several occasions it has happened to me to be seized by dizziness. Can anyone imagine what a torture it is to remain so long standing up, motionless, with the knees pressed together? And on top of that, to salute with outstretched arm? Last time, I was compelled to cheat a little. I also have to make the effort of looking each man in the eyes, for the men marching past are all trying to catch my glance.' Left: Here he salutes the men of the German Labour Corps — the Reichsarbeitsdienst — at the 1935 rally. Right: The RAD leader was Konstantin Hierl on the right. The other RAD officer is unidentified but in front are Wilhelm Frick and Rudolf Hess. (Hierl died in 1955 after having served a five-year term in prison.)

Albert Speer was also made responsible for the decor of the buildings in which Hitler would appear during the course of these rallies and for special effects. He would have the thousands of flags of the various organisations parading for an evening event to be kept out of sight until they could be marched on into the spotlights that would bring out the colours of the flags and the gold of the eagles to maximum effect. The colours of the national flag, sometimes enhanced with gold, lent themselves to the purpose. He also devised the spectacular 'cathedral of light' by requisitioning 130 searchlights from the Luftwaffe, which were then positioned around the stadium area to shine vertically to a height of over 20,000 feet. The reflection could be seen at Frankfurt over 100 miles away. At first Göring had objected to the number required, protesting that they were revealing almost their entire strategic reserve, but Hitler won him over by saying: 'If we use them in such large numbers for a thing like this, people will think that we are swimming in searchlights!' Speer himself described the effect: 'The feeling was of a vast room, with the beams, the mighty pillars of infinitely high outer walls.'

Perhaps one of the most striking effects at an arena event — the 'Cathedral of Light' introduced by Speer at the 1936 rally.

In addition, 1,200 spotlights were used to illuminate the pillars at the back of the stand, and 50 powerful kleig lights were used for the tribune, the flagpoles and the field itself, consuming 40,000 kilowatts in an evening. A special stone building housed the transformers producing the electricity for this purpose.

An American reporter for *The New York Times* was mesmerised by the spectacle. 'At 8.30 a trumpet fanfare following a roar of cheers outside the arena constantly coming nearer announced Hitler's arrival. Then he appeared, a lone figure atop the wide steps at the far side of the arena, where the wide lane ended. Awaiting him on the steps was a great gathering of high Nazi officials, all, like himself, in brown uniform. As he appeared there shone upward from a hidden circle of 150 (*sic*) army searchlights behind the grandstands as many spears of light to the central point above. It was the same device employed at the closing ceremony of the Olympic Games, but it was greatly improved and infinitely larger. In this bright light Hitler walked down the steps through the group awaiting him and slowly a procession with him at the head marched across the field to the tribune.

The thunderous cheers quite drowned the music of the massed bands playing him in. He ascended the tribune and stood there waiting until there was complete silence. Then suddenly there appeared far in the distance a mass of advancing red color. It was the 25,000 banners of Nazi organizations in all parts of Germany. The color bearers marched with them across the rear of the brown columns on the field. Then they came forward, six abreast in the narrower lanes and 20 abreast in the wide center aisle, so there was presented the spectacle of a great tide of crimson seeping through the lanes between the solid blocs of brown. Simultaneously the minor searchlights along the pillared rim above the grandstands were turned down on the field, lighting up the gilded eagles on the standards, so the flood of red was flecked with gold. The effect was indescribably beautiful.'

The final touches were added in 1937. The spectators' wooden seats were replaced with stone ones and pedestals were placed on the walls flanking the grandstand, on which large metal bowls were placed containing open fires that burned for the duration of the rally. The floor in front of the grandstand was decorated with tile mosaic and a granite terrace built at the rear with steps leading down to street level. Nearly 40,000 oak trees, the ancient Germanic symbol of strength, were planted around the Zeppelinwiese to add some greenery to the stone surroundings. Accommodation for the German Post Office and Red Cross was also provided.

However, the blinding effect of the natural Jurrasic limestone used for the construction gave rise to the nickname 'Weisse Würstchen Wiese' (White Sausage Meadow), probably inspired by the rows of white pillars behind the tribune.

Above: **The Zeppelinwiese grandstand with the final touches added, the gas-fired bronze urns and the golden swastika wreath . . . ready for the 1937 rally** *(below)* **held from September 6-13.**

Move our time machine on through half a century . . . and this is the sorry sight today with Speer's masterpiece vandalised and used as a race track. We will see what happened to it in the intervening period in our last chapter.

The third arena taken over for the Party rallies was the existing municipal stadium which was used for the ceremony for swearing in the Hitler Youth. The 'Tag der Hitlerjugend' (Day of the Hitler Youth) was a fixed and important part of the rallies programme.

The sports stadium that was the venue for all the Hitlerjugend events during the party rallies already existed when the Nazis came to power. Planned since 1921 and designed by architect Otto Ernst Schweizer and landscape gardener Alfred Hensel, it had been built between 1926 and 1928 and — with its swimming pool and tennis courts, cafés, gardens and greens — was regarded as one of the most modern sports facilities of the Weimar period.

Below: **One essential alteration was the addition of a rostrum for the Führer.**

The Nazis needed few alterations to make the stadium fit their purposes, the only constructional work being the addition of two wooden towers opposite the main grandstand. Known as the Altes Stadion (old stadium) to distinguish it from Speer's planned but never completed Deutsches Stadion (German Stadium), the facility was also referred to as the 'Stadion der Hitlerjugend.'

The same players entrance on the left still exists from the days of the Hitler Youth although now the ground has been renamed the Franken-Stadion. It was used by the US Army after the war and the Glenn Miller orchestra gave a concert here on July 1, 1945. Reconstructed in 1953 and 1964 and completely modernised in 1988-89, the stadium now has a capacity of 60,000 and is the home of the FC Nürnberg football club.

179

Speer loved flags and he draped the front of the Luitpold Hall with rows of hanging banners. The Luitpoldhain arena can be seen over on the right.

In 1906 the Nuremberg city authorities had erected a large pavilion as an exhibition hall near the Zeppelinwiese on the occasion of the 100th anniversary of the state of Bavaria and named it the Luitpoldhalle. It was of steel construction with large windows and skylights. The main hall was 540 feet long, 150 feet wide and 50 feet high. During the First World War it had been used as a warehouse, but the Nazis later took it over and called it the Kongresshalle (Congress Hall).

The Luitpoldhalle was destroyed by Allied bombing and the ruins cleared away in 1950 although the steps in front of the entrance have been left in situ.

'When we all meet once a year at the Party Rally at Nuremberg', recounted Hitler in one of his regular lengthy after-dinner discourses, 'it always gives me the impression of being just one huge family gathering. The Party Rally has, however, been not only a quite unique occasion in the life of the NSDAP but also in many respects a valuable preparation for war. Each rally requires the organisation of no fewer than 4,000 special trains. As these trains stretched from Munich to Halle, the railway authorities were given first-class practice in the military problem of handling mass troop transportation. Nor will the Rally lose its significance in the future. Indeed, I have given orders that the venue of the rally is to be enlarged to acccommodate a minimum of two million for the future — as compared to the million to a million and a half today. The German Stadium alone will accommodate 400,000 people and is on a scale which has no comparison on earth.'

Above: The interior of the hall seen here being used as a grain store in 1915 and *(right)* after having been given the Speer make-over. The Luitpold Hall was the venue for all the main speeches during the rallies.

In 1933 the Party had its art nouveau facades replaced by more-sober rectangular walls, decorated with huge swastika flags. The interior posts and walls were covered with fabric and the posts decorated with flowers. The hall had a seating capacity of 20,000 and room on the stage for 130 musicians as well as 750 Party functionaries. Seventy-six loudspeakers were deployed around the hall and two flanking stands reserved for the press. Forty-two spotlights aimed at the ceiling provided illumination, later to be replaced by neon tubes in 1935 when they were first introduced. An air-cooling system was installed along the ceiling the same year. One of the largest electric organs ever built, with 4,000 pipes ranging from 2 to 48 feet in height, was installed behind the speaker's stand.

However, the chairs in the hall were hard, making sitting through the invariably long speeches extremely uncomfortable, and smoking was prohibited.

It is well known that Hitler was a dedicated film buff and no doubt he greatly admired the German actress Leni Riefenstahl. She was also an accomplished film director and she claimed that Hitler first invited her to meet him in 1932 after the release of her film *Das Blaue Licht* (The Blue Light). 'Very soon now I am going to be the leader of Germany', Hitler told her. 'And when I am, I want you to make pictures just for me, just about me and the Movement.' Although it was an anathema to Nazi officials to have a woman in charge, all the more so because she was not a member of the Party, nevertheless, no doubt at Hitler's insistance, Goebbels commissioned her in June 1933 to make a documentary of the forthcoming rally in Nuremberg. *Sieg des Glaubens* (Victory of Faith) received its premiere in Berlin on December 1 but it would appear that because Röhm appears prominently in the film, all copies were subsequently destroyed as only one exists today. Its success however, led to greater things in 1934. *Triumph des Willens* (Triumph of the Will) became a priceless tool in the propaganda armoury of the Nazi Party when it was premiered on March 29, 1935.

In 1934 Hitler invited Leni Reifenstahl, a talented ballet dancer, film actress, director and producer, who had just won a golden medal at the Venice film Festival for her film *Das Blaue Licht* (The Blue Light), to film that year's Party Rally. Armed with this cachet, she was able to site her cameras to the best advantage during the meticulous planning for the event. The resultant film *Triumph des Willens* (Triumph of the Will) was a masterpiece of propaganda for the Nazi cause and won her another gold medal at Venice and a Grand Prix in Paris, apart from a national state prize in Berlin. The film was a remarkable, awe-inspiring tribute to Hitler. An extract from a condensed outline of the script reads:

''The Führer approaches through the clouds, his plane weaving through the white masses. The music is soft and romantic, the effect godlike. Nuremberg appears below. The Horst Wessel anthem starts. The shadow of Hitler's plane passes up a long line of marching men in the street below. Shot by shot, we descend nearer to the streets and the city full of marching columns.

'The airport. The plane taxis in. The welcoming crowds crane forward, their arms a sea of Nazi salutes. The Führer emerges. The crowd surges with enthusiasm. Goebbels in a raincoat follows the Führer grinning with pleasure.

'The drive into Nuremberg. The camera is behind Hitler in the car, angled up, concentrating on his arm extended in salute. Montage of Hitler's arm and the crowd as the car drives along the endless streets thronged with people. The music builds, reflecting the emotion of welcome. Hitler's car stops for a mother and her little girl to present flowers to the Führer. During the journey there are frequent shots of people in the crowds, people at the windows above, even a cat on a beflagged balcony.

Hitler simply dominated the screen. He occupied about a third of the film footage, and extracts from his speeches a fifth of the soundtrack with over two-thirds of the entire verbal content.

After *Triumph des Willens*, no further films were made featuring him. This was indeed Hitler at his zenith.

Julius Streicher, the local gauleiter, put a large house in the city at Riefenstahl's disposal for use as a production office. She assembled a crew of 120, many of whom she had worked with before including the outstanding cameramen Sepp Allgeier, Franz Weihmayr and Walter Frentz (who later achieved fame for filming Hitler's jig at the Wolfsschlucht Führerhauptquartier when the news arrived of the fall of France in June 1940). In all, 16 cameramen and three assistants were employed on the film and 30 cameras were used, some mounted on the extended ladders of fire engines for high-angle shots or on wheeled trolleys. Camera platforms were constructed both along the city march route and on the rally fields to give uninterrupted views, one of the most remarkable being a camera pod which could be raised up one of the tall flagpoles at the rear of the Luitpoldhain. There were four complete sound-recording trucks and a large number of spot and arc lights. To create the wide variety of camera angles seen in the film, both wide-angle and telephoto lenses were used to juxtapose the scenes of the huge parades with close-ups of the reactions on people's faces. The highlight of Frentz's work was to be given permission to film from the Führer's car as it drove through the crowds to the Deutscher Hof Hotel.

The sequence showing the massed review of the SA and SS in the Luitpold arena on Sunday, September 9 are probably the most impressive in the film. Reifenstahl's cameramen *(above and below)* were dressed in SA uniforms to blend with the parade.

Right: Close-up of the ceremony of blessing the standards from the touch of the Blood Flag, being held here by Grimminger in the steel helmet. The elevating camera pod on the flagpole can be seen in the background.

Albert Speer: 'In the autumn of 1934 I was ordered to accompany Hitler to Nuremberg. More major constructions for the Party rallies was wanted: a field for military exercises, a large stadium, a hall for Hitler's cultural addresses and for concerts as well. I thought, why not concentrate all that together with what already existed into a great centre? Until then I had not ventured to take the initiative on such questions, for Hitler kept this sort of decision for himself. I therefore went about drafting this plan with some hesitation.' This is Speer's model which was exhibited at the World Fair in Paris in 1937. The existing facilities are [1] the Luitpoldhain; [2] Zeppelinwiese; [3] Hitler Youth Stadium and [4] Luitpold Hall. Speer's new proposals were the Märzfeld [5], the Kongresshalle [6], the German Stadium [7] and the processional avenue [8].

In 1935 Hitler asked Professor Paul Schulze-Naumberg to submit plans for a giant complex of stadiums, halls and rally grounds at Nuremberg, but his plans were rejected and Albert Speer called in to fill the breach. Speer's plans were approved during a drive to Nuremberg, where Hitler was to consider plans submitted by the municipal authorities. Speer's plan involved the expenditure of the equivalent of £300 million, and a governing body called the Association for the Nuremberg Rally Site was established to administer the project.

A model of the completed area was exhibited at the 1937 World Fair in Paris and won the Grand Prize.

Four major constructions were involved, the Märzfeld, the new Kongresshalle already designed by Ludwig Ruff in 1933, the giant German Stadium, which was to be the largest stadium in the world and holding 400,000 persons, and a processional avenue a mile and a quarter long to link all the facilities.

The towers of the Märzfeld under construction.

The overall cost was estimated at three billion Reichsmarks — a massive sum which probably equates to around £6.75 billion in today's money. Speer's schedule gave a completion date of 1945 but the war curbed work on all the new additions. This is how the uncompleted Field of Mars looked at the end of the war, only 11 of the projected 24 towers having been completed.

The Märzfeld, named after Mars the god of War, was sited nearest to the railway station and was an enormous army parade ground 3,400 by 2,300 feet in size and large enough for the staging of manoeuvres. Stands surrounding the area were to accommodate 160,000 spectators, behind which would rise 24 towers, each 130 feet high, and among the stands would be a platform of honour crowned by the sculpture of a woman nearly 200 feet high.

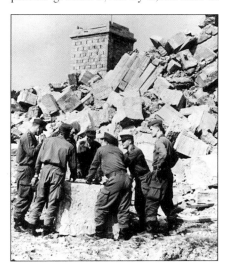

Falling within the US Zone of Occupation, the Nuremberg facilites were taken over by American forces and the Märzfeld was used for training and storage. *Left:* Then in April 1966, engineers of the post-war German army — the Bundeswehr — began blowing up the first five towers, completing the job the following year when the area was cleared . . . or was it? *Right:* In the summer of 2002, labourers doing ground work discovered that part of the base of one of the towers (the one circled on the model opposite) still survives alongside Hermann-Thiele-Weg in the Langwasser-Nord district.

This new Kongresshalle was to be 670 feet wide, 870 feet long and 150 feet high, 1.3 times the length and 1.7 times the width of the Roman Colosseum. The cost of construction was estimated at approximately £25 million. The hall was to provide seats for 40,000 people and standing room for a further 8,000. The walls were to be decorated with 1,000 flags, while the roof was to be supported by 83 columns, each of them 51 feet high. The whole project would cover 160,000 square feet.

An extensive network of railway tracks was laid around the whole site to facilitate the transportation of building materials, an estimated 150 freight trains being used daily for shipments. In 1935-36 the sides of the Dutzendteich, a large lake adjoining the site, were dammed in order to keep the grounds dry.

The Kongresshalle was one of Hitler's favourite projects and work continued on it until the winter of 1942-43, when other priorities took over. The building was about half-completed when the work stopped, the roof, second storey, interior construction and stage remaining unfinished.

The Congress Hall *(left)* **was the only building not designed by Speer as the commission had been awarded to Ludwig and Franz Ruff.** *Right:* **At the cornerstone-laying ceremony for the Kongresshalle in 1935, Hitler saw Speer standing in the second row of saluting dignitaries. He was so overcome when Hitler stepped forward to shake his hand that he let his hand fall with a smack on the top of the bald head of Julius Streicher in the front row!**

Apart from the model *(top left)*, a same-size section was erected on site. It can be seen on the left in this picture taken looking across the Grosse Dutzendteich lake.

The Congress Hall project was dear to Hitler's heart and construction work continued on it long after other cultural projects had to be abandoned. This is how the unfinished building looked in 1945.

The incomplete new Kongresshalle presented a problem to the civic authorities, as the cost of its removal would have been prohibitive. The discussion as to what possible employment could be found for the massive building continued for many years. An early idea to use it for trade and industries fairs was soon shelved. Another plan, launched in 1955, to complete it as a football stadium never materialised. In 1963, the Nuremberg Symphony Orchestra began using the building's southern wing for rehearsals. Other parts of the building and the inner courtyard were taken into use as storage facilities by the municipality and commercial firms. A fitting use of at least part of the building was finally found in November 2001 when a permanent museum exhibition on the Nazi Party Rallies and its legacy in stone — the Dokumentationszentrum Reichsparteigelände — opened in the northern wing on Bayernstrasse.

Left: **The Kongresshalle claimed to be the largest structure of all the Third Reich buildings which remain standing in Germany today (but see pages 252-253). While the cost of demolishing it would be prohibitive, the idea of completing it according to Ruff's original concept was also a political non-starter.** *Right:* **Instead, Günter Domenigs was brought in to design and convert the northern wing of the building into what the German's like to call, 'a documentation centre'. The brochure to the exhibition explains that 'a glass and steel gangway penetrates the Congress Hall like a shaft [and] makes, a clear contemporary architectural statement'. That it certainly does although the 'statement' it makes is anyone's guess!**

Completely dwarfing the Great Pyramids of Egypt, Hitler intended to outdo even the Circus Maximus in Rome with his German Stadium built to hold 400,000. Speer adopted an Athenian horseshoe shape facing east with the new processional avenue (seen in the foreground of the photo of the model), running north-south linking the various venues.

The German Stadium was intended to be the largest stadium ever built. At that time the largest had a maximum capacity of 100,000, while the Circus Maximus of Roman times had held nearly 200,000, but Hitler's was to accommodate twice this number and its volume would have absorbed three times that of the Cheops pyramid in Egypt in its horseshoe shape.

The cornerstone was laid during the 1937 rally on September 9, and the construction was to be completed by 1945. Ground was broken in 1938 and in 1939 a gigantic pit was dug for the foundations and railway tracks laid for the transporting of building materials. A temporary tower was then constructed in the centre of the site to accommodate the supervising engineers, who could then direct the work over loudspeakers.

When the Americans captured the city in 1945, they disconnected a large diesel pump that had been keeping the German Stadium site dry with the result that the area flooded and is now known as the Silbersee (Silver Lake). The stockpiled building materials were later used to form rockeries in the surrounding Dutzendteich Park.

Above left: **The processional avenue — Die Grosse Strasse. This ran for over a mile, crossing the Dutzendteich lake to link the Luitpoldhain at its northern end with the Märzfeld.** *Above right:* **The concrete surface shows where the wartime granite slabs finished.**

A processional avenue a mile and a quarter long was to link the Märzfeld with the other arenas. It was to be 264 feet wide and paved with heavy granite slabs, both to bear the weight of tanks and to echo the stamp of marching boots. The avenue was to be lined with stone steps for spectators and a saluting base was to be erected half way along in front of the projected German Stadium. A tunnel was constructed to take the Zeppelinstrasse where it crossed the avenue.

No rallies were held in Nuremberg after 1938. The one planned for September 2, 1939, was cancelled on August 26 on the eve of the invasion of Poland. However, construction work continued and in September 1941 orders went out for millions of cubic yards of cut and uncut granite to be provided by the stone industries of the occupied countries, while Sweden had a ten-year contract in this respect. It was only in 1943 that Hitler reluctantly brought the work to a halt.

Below left: **Up until 1968 it provided a useful landing strip for liaison aircraft of the US Army.** *Below right:* **The overgrown steps which would have seated thousands of spectators watching at parades remain, overgrown with weeds.**

The rally building site under the microscope of the RAF in 1941. [1] Luitpoldhain. [2] Zeppelinwiese. [3] Grosse Kongresshalle. [4] Deutsches Stadion. [5] Grosse Strasse.

Hitler always stayed in the Hotel Deutscher Hof in rooms 104 and 105, one of which was furnished as a bedroom and the other as a sitting room. Before his ascent to power, the Grand

Hotel opposite the station would not take him as a guest, so after 1933 he continued to patronise the Deutscher Hof and would take the salute from the hotel balcony.

Like a Roman emperor Hitler rode into this mediaeval town at sundown today past solid phalanxes of wildly cheering Nazis who packed the narrow streets. Tens of thousands of swastika flags blot out the Gothic beauties of the place, the façades of the old houses, the gabled roofs. The streets, hardly wider than alleys, are a sea of brown and black uniforms. I got my first glimpse of Hitler as he drove by our hotel, the Württemberger Hof, to his headquarters down the street at the Deutscher Hof, a favourite old hotel of his, which has been remodelled for him. He fumbled his cap with his left hand as he stood in his car acknowledging the delirious welcome with somewhat feeble Nazi salutes from his right arm. He was clad in a rather worn gaberdine trench-coat, his face had no particular expression at all — I expected it to be stronger — and for the life of me I could not quite comprehend what hidden springs he undoubtedly unloosed in the hysterical mob which was greeting him so wildly.

About ten o'clock tonight I got caught in a mob of ten thousand hysterics who jammed the moat in front of Hitler's hotel shouting: 'We want our Führer.' I was a little shocked at the faces, especially those of the women, when Hitler finally appeared on the balcony for a moment. They reminded me of the crazed expressions I saw once in the back country of Louisiana on the faces of some Holy Rollers who were about to hit the trail. They looked up at him as if he were a Messiah, their faces transformed into something positively inhuman. If he had remained in sight for more then a few moments, I think many of the women would have swooned from excitement.

Later I pushed my way into the lobby of the Deutscher Hof. I recognised Julius Streicher, whom they call here the Uncrowned Czar of Franconia. In Berlin he is known more as the number-one Jew-baiter and editor of the vulgar and pornographic anti-Semitic sheet the Stürmer. His head was shaved, and this seemed to augment the sadism of his face. As he walked about, he brandished a short whip.

WILLIAM SHIRER, *BERLIN DIARY*,
SEPTEMBER 4, 1934

The hotel on Frauentorgraben still stands. Then it posessed 300 beds and was exclusively for members of the NSDAP. Hitler's balcony *(left)* lay at the Essenweinstrasse end which was bombed during the war. It was rebuilt as an office block without the balcony *(right)* leaving the hotel occupying the original remaining section on the corner of Weidenkellerstrasse.

Left: **Lesser mortals had to be content to be put up in the NSDAP guest house at No. 3 Bahnhofplatz.** *Right:* **Today it is the Bavarian American Hotel.**

Left: **From 1938 the SS had their own accommodation in purpose-built barracks lying between Frankenstrasse and Ingolstädter Strasse, designed by Franz Ruff.** *Right:* **Occupied by the Americans** **in 1945, today the barracks are in the hands of the state office responsible for refugees and asylum seekers. The eagle has flown from its perch!**

The SA camping ground was completed with wooden huts and asphalt roads in 1935-36, making a convenient camp for displaced persons during the period 1949-60, but the whole area has now been built over as part of the suburb of Langwasser. The SS barracks built in 1938 between the Frankenstrasse and Ingolstädter Strasse to a design by Franz Ruff were described by Hitler as 'the gateway to the Party Rally Grounds'. They were damaged by bombing, but were later occupied by American troops. Today they are known as the Süd-Kaserne (Southern Barracks).

And so to the anticipation of Reichsparteitage. *Left:* **Enthusiastic crowds arrive at Bahnhof Dutzenteich — the special station built to service the rally grounds. This was conveniently situated just north of the Zeppelin arena (see page 174).** *Right:* **Still a station but devoid of the feverish excitement of** **yesteryear. Even Hitler said that 'on the day following the end of the Bayreuth Festival (next chapter) and on the Tuesday that marks the end of the Nuremberg Congress, 'I'm gripped by a great sadness — as when one strips the Christmas tree of its ornaments.'**

BAYREUTH

Songs go with us from our childhood to old age. They live in us and with us and it matters not where we be. Songs bring back to our eyes the homeland from which we came — Germany and the German Reich.

ADOLF HITLER, AUGUST 1, 1937

'Hauptstadt der Kultur' – The Cultural Capital

Hitler's fascination with Richard Wagner's music had begun with his misspent youth in Linz, when he had been so stirred by a performance of Wagner's early work *Rienzi* that he had taken his friend August Kubizek on a long nocturnal ramble up the Freinberg mountain and lectured him on the signifi-

cance of what they had seen in a state of near-ecstasy. The plot concerned a Roman tribune who restored the empire, a theme that ran close to his own expectations.

Once he could afford to attend the annual Bayreuth Wagner Festival, he seldom missed it. The Bechsteins,

whom he had met at Berchtesgaden, introduced him to the bizarre and complicated Wagner family in October 1923, shortly before his abortive putsch. Richard Wagner, who had founded the festival and built the Festspielhaus in which his operas were performed, had died in 1883, but his wife Cosima

Left: **Richard Wagner, German composer, born May 22, 1813, died February 13, 1883. 'For me', said Hitler, 'Wagner is someone godly and his music is my religion. I go to concerts as others go to church'.** *Top:* **Wagner settled in Bayreuth in April 1872 since when his works have been inexorably linked with the city. Here 'guests of the Führer' march past the timbered Golden Swan guesthouse and over the Ludwigsbrücke returning from the Bayreuth Festival.** *Above:* **The whole block, destroyed during the war, has been rebuilt; this is the junction of the Bahnhofstrasse and Hohenzollernring.**

Born in Leipzig, into a theatrical family, Richard was given a classical education and began composing at 17. His first opera, composed in 1833, was *Die Feen* (The Fairies) in the true German romantic style which was followed by *Das Liebesverbot* (The Ban on Love) and *Rienzi* which was performed in Dresden in 1842. It was so successful that the following year he was made musical director of the Dresden Theatre. *Tannhäuser* and *Lohengrin* followed — based like all his future works on German legends — but he became preoccupied with politics and wrote a number of articles advocating social revolution. In 1849 he took part in the Dresden uprising and when it failed was forced to flee Germany to avoid arrest. He missed the first performance of *Lohengrin* in August 1850 which was given instead by his friend Franz Liszt. In Switzerland he began work

on producing an opera based on the legend of Siegfried titled *Ring der Nibelungen* (The Ring of Nibelung), a major three-part composition which would take over 20 years to bring to fruition. The first two parts, *Das Rheingold* (The Rhinegold) and *Die Walküre* (The Valkerie) were completed between 1853 and 1856 but *Siegfrieds Tod* (Siegfried's Death) — later renamed *Götterdämmerung* (The Twilight of the Gods) — was not finished until 1874. It was given its premiere in Bayreuth in a brand new purpose-built Festival Theatre which had been built specifically for performing Wagner's works. *Left:* The Festspielhaus opened in August 1876 for the Bayreuth Festival — the first of what was to become and annual event. *Right:* Largely built of wood, the building claims to be one of the largest free-standing timber structures in the world.

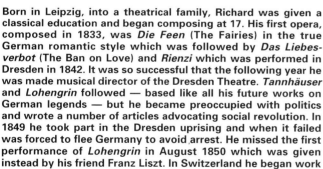

Although Richard Wagner had died six years before Hitler was born, his compositions had a profound effect on the young Adolf who found in the composer similar ideals to his own: both were nationalists with a dream of a greater Germany; both believed in the superiority of the Aryan, while both had an abiding hatred of the Jewish race. Wagner's operas represented the fullest expression of German romanticism;

he called them music-dramas and although in his lifetime he faced much opposition, he achieved lasting fame in the 20th century, not least through Hitler's devoted admiration. Wagner's works were seen as attachments to the Nazi creed and Bayreuth was elevated to the status of the cultural capital of the Third Reich. This is the Siegfried-Wagner-Allee leading up to the Festspielhaus — then and now.

'generally unscrupulous behaviour largely due to his blind artistic self-centredness'. Wagner's tempestuous private life was even reflected in his music, *Tristan und Isolde*, performed in 1865, being based on his hopeless love affair 13 years earlier with Mathilde Wesendonk which led to the break-up of his marriage to actress Minna Planer. He then stole Cosima, the wife of Hans von Bülow, the first great Wagner conductor. She was the illegitimate daughter of his friend Franz Liszt and she bore Richard Wagner three children: Isolde born in 1865; Eva in 1867 and Siegfried in 1869, all before her divorce in 1870 and marriage to Wagner the same year. (Minna died in 1866.) *Right:* In 1872 Wagner moved with Cosima to the villa in Bayreuth that he called Wahnfried (Peace from Illusion). on what is now Richard-Wagner-Strasse.

In 1925, the Bechsteins [the famous piano manu-facturers] *had invited me to stay with them in Bayreuth. They lived in a villa in the Lisztstrasse (I think this was the name of the street), within a few yards of Wahnfried. I had hesitated to go there, for I was afraid of thus increasing the difficulties of Siegfried Wagner, who was somewhat in the hands of the Jews.*

I arrived in Bayreuth towards eleven o'clock in the evening. Lotte Bechstein was still up, but her relatives were in bed. Next morning, Cosima Wagner came and brought me some flowers. What a bustle there was in Bayreuth for the Festival! There exist a few photographs of that period, in which I figure, taken by Lotte Bechstein.

I used to spend the day in leather shorts. In the evening, I would put on a dinner jacket or tails to go to the opera. We made excursions by car into the Fichtelgebirge and into Franconian mountains. From all points of view, those were marvellous days. When I went to the cabaret of the Chouette, *I found myself immediately in sympathy with the artistes.*

Dietrich Eckart, who had been a critic in Bayreuth, had always told me of the extraordinary atmosphere prevailing there. He told me that one morning they had broken into the Chouette, *and had gone, in company with the artistes, into the meadow behind the theatre, to play the* Miracle of Good Friday *there.*

At the first performance of Parsifal
Bayreuth, Cleving was still singing. What a stature, and what a magnificent voice! I'd already been present at performances of Parsifal *in Munich. That same year, I was also present at the* Ring *and the* Meistersinger
the Jew Schorr was allowed to sing the rôle of Wotan had the effect of a profanation on me. Why couldn't they have got Rode from Munich? But there was Braun, an artiste of exceptional quality.

For years I was unable to attend the Festival, and I'd been very distressed about it. Cosima Wagner also lamented my absence. She often urged me to come, by letter or by telephone. But I never passed through Bayreuth without paying her a visit.

It's Cosima Wagner's merit to have created the link between Bayreuth and National Socialism. Siegfried was a personal friend of mine, but he was a political neutral. He couldn't have been anything else, or the Jews would have ruined him. Now the spell is broken. Siegfried has regained his independence, and one again hears works by him. Those dirty Yids had succeeded in demolishing him! I heard, in my youth, his Bärenhäuter
Schmied von Marienburg is his best work. I still have a lot of things to see and hear!

ADOLF HITLER, MARCH 1, 1942.

When Richard Wagner died in 1883, Cosima continued to promote his works in the annual Bayreuth Festivals, and their son Siegfried became a talented composer and conductor in his own right. *Left:* Hitler was a frequent visitor. *Right:* The bust is that of King Ludwig II, one of Wagner's most fanatical admirers.

In 1864, aged 18, Ludwig had just ascended to the throne of Bavaria and he rescued Wagner who was currently living in abject poverty in Switzerland having run out on his creditors. The King invited Wagner to Munich with a pension and patronage which finally set him on the road to lasting fame.

When Cosima died in 1930 she was buried beside Richard in the garden of Wahnfried. Siegfried died the same year leaving the torch of the Bayreuth Festival in the hands of his widow, Winifred, seen *(above)* greeting Hitler in one of his many visits. The bouquet belies the Führer's ulterior motive — he was madly in love with her and had come a-courtin'.

continued to manage the festival until 1906, when their son Siegfried took over. The latter's English-born but German-raised wife, Winifred, was immediately captivated by Hitler, whom she saw as the future saviour of Germany. She promptly invited him to visit them next day at their home, the Haus Wahnfried, where she showed him the tombs of his hero Richard Wagner and his wife Cosima in the garden before introducing her own children, Wieland, Friedelind, Wolfgang and Verena, for whom she and her recluse husband in fact had little time.

Winifred was the daughter of a Welsh journalist and theatre critic John Williams and his German-born wife Emily Karop. Her parents died when she was two so she was brought up in an orphanage in Hastings, Sussex, before being adopted by relatives of her mother living in Berlin. They were musicians and friends of Cosima. Winifred had met Siegfried, 28 years her senior, when she was 17. The following year — 1915 — they married, but when Siegfried died Hitler stepped into his shoes.

It was a love affair born of their mutual admiration of Wagner's operas. She was captivated by Hitler, writing in one letter: 'You provide happiness which is beyond words'. *Left:* Here Winifred walks with Hitler towards the house he used when in Bayreuth which adjoined the front garden of Wahnfried.

In the end Wini turned the Führer down . . . but he still had more fish to fry! It was in 1933, while an art student in Munich, that the 19-year-old Lady Unity Mitford met and fell in love with Hitler. One of six daughters of Lord and Lady Redesdale, she was a lively girl, full of life and vitality and Hitler obviously delighted to be in her company. Her parents disapproved of the friendship and cut off her allowance but she eaked out an existance in Munich just to remain near Hitler. In December 1935 she confided to her sister, Lady Jessica, that 'I love him more and more each time though it doesn't seem possible to love him any more than I always did'. The Bayreuth Festival was one of their meeting places although they both look rather glum in this picture taken in the garden of Wahnfried. It was at the festival in August 1939 that Unity told her sister Diana, the wife of the British Fascist leader Sir Oswald Mosley: 'If it comes to war, I shall kill myself'. Following in the path of Hitler's former loves — Geli (page 23) and Eva (page 38), when war was declared on September 3, Unity tried to shoot herself in the head with a small-calibre pistol. The bullet lodged in her temple but it was decided that it was too dangerous to remove it. Hitler sent Unity home via Switzerland to Britain where she died from the wound in 1948.

Hitler missed the 1924 festival by being locked up in Landsberg prison, but Winifred, now a fanatical supporter, maintained contact and he was back in 1925. Encouraged by her, he often spent the night at Haus Wahnfried when travelling between Munich and Berlin, and established a warm contact with the children, who were allowed to call him 'Wolf', while he called Winifred 'Wini', in a sort of surrogate relationship with a family and wife he clearly missed not having.

Siegfried died during the 1930 festival, and Winifred took over at the age of 33, with the result that when Hitler became Chancellor the 1933 festival became more of a tribute to Hitler than Wagner. Visitors to the festival found the town decked with Nazi flags, the road leading to the Festspielhaus renamed Adolf-Hitler-Strasse and the

streets lined with SS and SA storm-troopers hailing the arrival of the Nazi leaders, for whom attendance was now 'de rigeur'. In the Festspielhaus, upon Hitler's instructions, spectators were issued with a pamphlet requesting them not to sing the national anthem or the *Horst Wessel Song* at the end of the opera, but the intervals were used for his public acclaim, and afterwards he would attend the receptions at the Haus Wahnfried that would often go on into the small hours.

The Nazi Party exploited the festival to the full, arousing the romantic and mythological feelings of the Germans with their intrinsic paranoia and sense of inferiority to replace them through Wagner's music with an exalted conviction of uniqueness and superiority. Winifred received generous financial support as well as the resources of the

Prussian State Theatre, so that productions were often planned and rehearsed in Berlin before moving to Bayreuth, and achieved particularly high standards in their music and scenery. The 1936 performance of *Lohengrin* was outstanding in the history of the festival for its excellence, and Hitler even suggested to King Edward VIII that he send the whole production, cast and musicians, to London's Covent Garden as a gift for the coronation, an impracticable gesture that was saved by Edward's abdication.

During the 1937 festival, Winifred suggested she invite Unity Mitford and her sister Diana (married to Oswald Mosley, leader of the British Union of Fascists) to join them for luncheon, which pleased Hitler immensely, for he admired Unity. Then in 1939 he invited his old school friend August Kubizek to

'Tea or coffee ladies?' Snapshot, probably taken by Hoffmann personally, on the terrace of Haus Wahnfried. L-R: Albert Speer,

Frau Hoffmann (Heinrich's second wife), Magda Goebbels, and Mary, a friend of Unity.

There was always excitement in the air when Hitler arrived in Bayreuth. This mixed party, including an older boy from the Hitlerjugend and girls from the Bund Deutscher Mädel, wait outside the entrance to Hitler's house in Wahnfriedstrasse to present him with their gifts.

attend every performance, but did not see him until after the final performance of *Götterdämmerung* on August 3, when he sent an SS officer to bring him back to the Haus Wahnfried. Kubizek produced a large pack of picture postcards of the Führer, which he persuaded Hitler to sign for friends back in Austria. Afterwards Hitler took him into the garden to show him Wagner's tomb, saying: 'I am happy that we have both met once more on this spot which always was the most venerable place for us both.'

Siegfried had married Winifred, so we are told, for the express purpose of producing heirs to continue the Wagner dynasty. She had four children: two boys, Wieland born in 1917 and Wolfgang in 1919, and two girls, Friedelind in 1918 and Verena in 1920. Thereafter her husband reverted to his preferred homosexual lifestyle — much to her anguish and no doubt a catylist for her close association with Hitler.

Left: During his earlier visits in 1933 and 1934, Hitler had the use of this house in Parkstrasse. It was owned by Fritz Böhner who rented it to the Führer for 36 Reichsmarks per day. Note the state policemen on duty beside the gate. It was in 1936

that he moved into the grander — and far more convenient — premises situated right next to the Wagner home on Richard-Wagner-Strasse. *Right:* Now No. 4 Parkstrasse is the home of Dr Hamm and the Reihl family.

The Bayreuth Festival continued after the outbreak of war. This is the tumultuous welcome given to the Führer at the 1940 Festspiel. The balcony of the Festival Hall can be seen on the left in the pictures below.

Winifred expected the festival to be suspended for the duration of the war, but Hitler insisted it continue and even asked for the lists of singers, musicians and stage-hands so that they could be exempted from military service. He also had Wieland Wagner, 22 in 1939, excused from military service and free to choose his own career, eventually being appointed chief operatic producer at Altenburg by Goebbels. Hitler then used the opportunity to open the festival to all classes of persons, replacing the wealthy cosmopolitan clientele that had attended hitherto with 'Guests of the Führer', organised by the Arbeitfront's 'Kraft durch Freude'. This department had servicemen and war industry workers brought in by rail, fed and accommodated overnight in barracks, given pamphlets on Wagner and a briefing in the morning on the opera they were about to see and then shipped out again that night to make way for the next batch. Although unable to attend, Hitler remained in close touch with events at Bayreuth and continued to be consulted on the content of programmes by Winifred.

Apart from the Festspielhaus [1], concerts were also held in the Opera House *(above)* on Opernstrasse [2]. Hitler's Parkstrasse house is [3] and Haus Wahnfried [4].

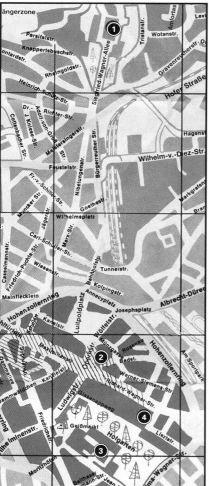

Bayreuth was bombed four times in April 1945, sustaining considerable damage. Haus Wahnfried was one of the casualties but the Festspielhaus escaped unharmed. Post-war Winifred had a hard time with the de-Nazification process which eventually obliged her to hand over control of the business to her sons Wolfgang and Wieland in 1951, when the festival was resumed. She continued to display her Nazi sympathies to the embarassment of her sons, and had Edda Göring, Göring's daughter, Ilse Hess and relatives of other high Nazi officials sit with her in the family box at the Festspielhaus. Wieland died in 1966 and Winifred in 1980. A successor to Wolfgang has been bitterly contested, his preferred choice being his second wife Gudrun.

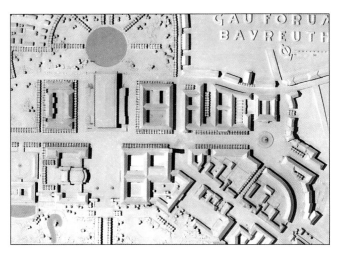

Before we leave Bayreuth, we should mention Hitler's plans for enlarging and reconstructing the Festspielhaus which only had accommodation for an audience of 2,000. (Even today the waiting list for tickets for the festival can be measured in years!) *Left:* It was in 1939 that Hitler came up with some grandiose ideas. The town was to have a great new civic forum, enormous meeting halls, and a stadium, the whole effect domi-

nated by a vastly enlarged Festspielhaus on its hill. Hitler had Rudolf Emil Mewes produce a design for the latter, which would incorporate the core of the existing wood-lined building because of its excellent acoustic values, but construction was eventually deferred by the outbreak of war. *Right:* L-R: Architect Hans Reissinger, Hitler, Wieland Wagner, and Bayreuth gauleiter Fritz Wächtler.

One building that was completed — although not directly relevant to the Festival — was the office block for the National Socialist Teacher's League (Nationalsozialistische Lehrerbund). The foundation stone was laid *(centre)* on September 24, 1933. Its mentor was Hans Schemm *(above)*, the Bavarian Minister of Culture, who had been the Gauleiter of Upper Franconia since 1928. Born in Bayreuth in October 1891, he trained in the teaching profession before being called up during the war. He served as a medical orderly but contracted tuberculosis and was invalided out shortly before the armistice. He returned to teaching, becoming a lecturer in National Sciences at the Adult Learning Institute in the city. He became an ardent member of the NSDAP and founded the Teacher's League in 1929. Later he was appointed Bavarian Cultural Minister. *Right:* The building had been designed in true Third Reich style by Hans Reissinger, its formal description being the Haus der Deutschen Erziehung.

Hans Schemm was killed in a plane crash on March 5, 1935 and Hitler (marked on this contemporary photo with a little white 'x') travelled to Bayreuth for his funeral service on the 9th. Coming just five years after the death of Cosima, it must have brought back sad memories which he shared with close colleagues: 'Nobody like Wagner has had the luck to be entirely understood by a woman. Those are things that life does not owe a man, but it's magnificent when it happens. In addition to all Wagner's gifts, Cosima was femininity personified, and her charm had its effect on all who visited Wahnfried. After Wagner's death, the atmosphere at Wahnfried remained what it had been during his lifetime. Cosima was inconsolable, and never ceased to wear mourning. She had wanted her own ashes to be scattered over her husband's tomb, but she was refused this satisfaction. Nevertheless, her ashes were collected in an urn, and this urn was placed in the tomb. Thus death has not separated these two beings, whom destiny had wished to live side by side!'

The square was renamed the Hans-Schemm-Platz in his memory but today it has reverted back to its original name of Luitpoldplatz.

BERLIN

It is therefore my unalterable will and determination to provide Berlin with those streets, buildings, and public spaces which will make it appear for all time fit and worthy to be the capital of the German Reich. The magnitude of these constructions and these works is not to be measured by the needs of the years 1937, 1938, 1939 or 1940. It is to be determined by recognising that our task is to give to a people, which has existed for a thousand years, with its millennial past of history and civilization for the limitless future which lies before it a city worthy of that future — a millennial city. Therefore of set purpose we withhold from the criticism of our own day the work which must be achieved in Berlin during the next twenty years: we submit it only to the judgement of those generations who one day shall come after us. Whatever that judgement may prove to be, one claim the future will allow for our justification: in this work we have thought not of ourselves, but of posterity.

ADOLF HITLER, SEPTEMBER 6, 1938

'Reichshauptstadt' — The Capital of the Reich

Wilhelmstrasse — the 'Whitehall' of Berlin. Here were gathered all the offices of the German State. *Top:* A New Year Honour Guard in January 1935 formed up outside the old Reich Chancellery at No. 77 (on the left). On the opposite side of the road is the Propaganda Ministry, the preserve of Joseph Goebbels. *Above:* Much of the street was redeveloped with nondescript buildings by the German Democratic Republic which held sway in the Soviet Sector of Berlin until 1990. The Communists renamed the street Otto-Grotewohl-Strasse in tribute to the former GDR Premier who died in September 1984, but it has since reverted to Wilhelmstrasse, originally named in honour of the Kaiser.

January 30, 1933. Having been appointed Reich Chancellor, Hitler leaves No. 77 Wilhelmstrasse.

Berlin remained the administrative capital of the Third Reich, where the normal instruments of government, the Reich ministries, were all to be found grouped tightly together in what was known as the Regierungsviertel (Government Quarter) based on Wilhelmstrasse around the Reich President's Palace and the Reich Chancellery.

On Wilhelmstrasse itself were to be found the Ministries of Finance at No. 60-61, Justice at No. 65, Food and Agriculture at No. 72, Foreign Affairs at Nos. 74-76, and Traffic at Nos. 79-80.

The old Reichskanzler-Palais lay here but now a new street called An den Kolonnade has been cut through at this point to service the flats. The signboard on the corner explains the former use of the site.

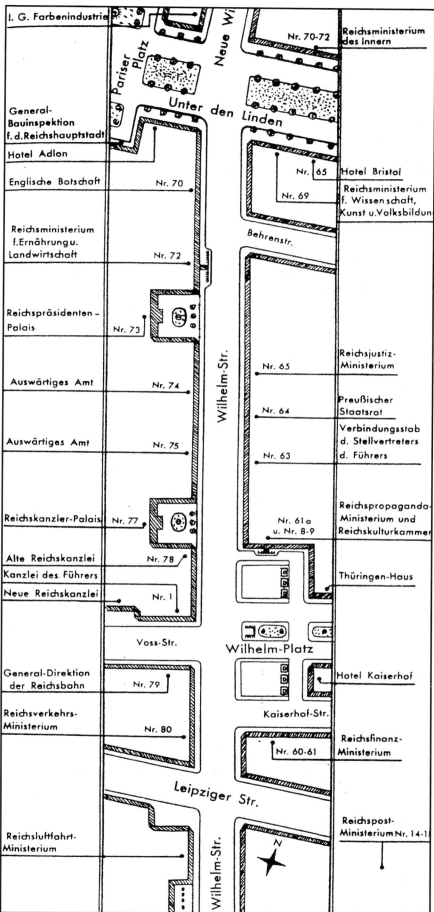

This plan illustrates the use of each building as at 1939.

Moving southwards down Wilhelmstrasse from Unter den Linden (which translates as Beneath the Lime Trees), on the northwestern corner at No. 70 lay the magnificent British Embassy *(above)*, an imposing classical building dating from 1884. *Below:* Can one honestly say that the hodge-podge replacement is remotely in the same class?

Left: At No. 72 lay the Ministry for Food and Agriculture, formerly the Palais Görne of the Princess Alexander and George. *Right:* Now the plot has been taken over by faceless blocks of flats built during the days of the German Democratic Republic. In the background, an extension of Behrenstrasse has been cut through to link up with Ebertstrasse.

Left: More New Year greetings to Hitler this time outside the Reich President's Palace next door at No. 73. Beside him on the balcony is Konstantin Freiherr von Neurath, until 1938 the German Foreign Minister. *Above:* This building has also gone the way of the others yet the balcony has been preserved on the façade of No. 4 Bahnhofstrasse in the eastern suburb of Köpenick — just a plain housing block without any special distinction.

Left: The German Foreign Ministry (No. 75-76), scene of so much activity in the run up to war. *Above:* Very unusual for Berlin streets, the plots have been renumbered, No. 75-76 now being the flats at Nos. 87-89.

The Wilhelmplatz looking south-west. Running from right to left one can see the Borsig Palace on the corner of Voss-strasse with the Ministry of Traffic (Reichsverkehrsministerium) on the opposite corner with blocks of the modern Air Ministry (Reichsluftfahrtministerium) beyond. The building on the left of the picture is the Treasury (Reichsfinanzministerium) at Nos. 60-61. The photograph was taken on February 20, 1938 — a very significant day in the history of the Third Reich for several reasons. This was the day that Hitler gave a long speech — a milestone-speech — to the Reichstag. It had been postponed from January 30 because of the fall-out following the marriage on January 12 of the Minister of War, Generalfeldmarschall Werner von Blomberg. Hitler and Göring had been invited to act as witnesses but it was later revealed that the bride was a lady of dubious reputation. Hitler was incensed that he had been inveigled into giving his support to one of his ministers marrying a prostitute and demanded an annulment. When Blomberg refused, Hitler sacked him on the spot. The logical successor to the post, General Werner Freiherr von Fritsch, was also fired when Hitler received fabricated evidence of his involvement with two young boys. All this led to his decision to personally take over the supreme command of the armed forces with Generalfeldmarschall Wilhelm Keitel as his chief-of-staff. The change-over was implemented on February 4. The Reichstag speech on February 20 also came right in the middle of Hitler's machinations towards both Austria and Czechoslovakia.

> *There is in Germany no problem of the relation between the National Socialist State and the National Socialist Party, or any problem of the relation between the National Socialist Party and the National Socialist army. In this Reich everyone who holds a responsible position is a National Socialist.*
>
> ADOLF HITLER, FEBRUARY 20, 1938

The decree of February 4, 1938 created the Oberkommando der Wehrmacht (OKW), with Keitel being given the grandiose title of Chief of the High Command of the Armed Forces although he was still subservient to Hitler. We shall see its headquarters building a few pages on (page 215) but here in the distance is the largest major Third Reich building remaining intact in Berlin today — Herman Göring's Air Ministry.

Göring had hoped to succeed Generalfeldmarschall von Blomberg as Minister of War but Hitler is reported to have rejected his candidacy on the grounds that 'Göring doesn't even know how to hold an inspection. I know more about it than he does!' The Reichsluftfahrtministerium designed by Ernst Sagebiel was built in 1935-36. It actually has entrances on both Wilhelmstrasse (on the left at No. 83) and Leipziger Strasse, (the turning on the right), where it is Nos. 5-9.

The building survived both the bombing and the 1945 battle so it provided very useful accommodation for the incoming Soviet administration of East Berlin. It was occupied by several ministries of the puppet German Democratic Republic and was taken over by the Bonn government in 1991. Today it houses the Bundesfinanzministerium — Germany's Treasury.

But surely Hitler was somewhat adrift over Göring's inspection capabilities . . . this looks like a pretty snappy parade in 1937. The occasion was the second anniversary of Wehrfreiheit Day — March 16, 1935 when Hitler repudiated the Treaty of Versailles and introduced military conscription under the proclamation of the 'Law for the Reconstruction of the National Defence Forces'. The old German army (the Reichswehr) permitted under the treaty to a maximum strength of ten divisions — 100,000 men — was to be expanded to 36 divisions and the name for the armed forces in general changed to Wehrmacht which more accurately translates as 'Defence Force'. (The army itself is called the 'Heer'.)

All photography in the courtyard of the Finance Ministry is now strictly verboten!

When Göring was appointed Air Minister in 1933, expansion of the air force — under the day-to-day control of his deputy Erhard Milch (currently the head of the German civilian airline Lufthansa) — had to be carried out behind the scenes. However all that changed in March 1935 when Hitler came out into the open and announced the establishment of the Luftwaffe. The new German air force needed a headquarters which is how the new building came into being.

Here, with our backs to the Air Ministry, we are looking across the junction of Wilhelmstrasse (straight on) to Leipziger Strasse.

Other significant buildings on the eastern side of the street were the Propaganda Ministry. This is the rear on Mauerstrasse.

The office of the Prussian Secretary of State (No. 63 Wilhelm-strasse) became the State Chancellery of the NSDAP in 1944. After the war the East Germans used it for a main office for their state publishing offices but now it has been taken over by the Consumer Protection Agency for Food and Agriculture (Verbraucherschutz Ernährung und Landwirtschaft).

And virtually unchanged the Ministry of Science and Education at No. 68 — then in 1943 *(left)* and now in 2003 *(right)*.

A few hundred metres west of Wilhelmstrasse lay the War Ministry overlooking the Landwehr canal. Parts of the building survived the war virtually intact and it appears much the same today *(right)* as it did during the Third Reich period *(left)*. From 1919 to 1935 it was the Reichswehrministerium at which point the Oberkommando der Wehrmacht took the building over. Its address then was Nos. 72-76 Tirpitzufer with its vehicle entrance on Bendlerstrasse — hence its nick-name 'Bendlerblock'.

On the Unter den Linden at Nos. 74-76 was the Ministry of the Interior, at No. 63 the Ministry for the Occupied Territories, and at No. 69 the Ministry for Science, Education and National Training, while the Ministry for War Production was located at No. 3 Pariser Platz from the time Speer took over in 1942.

The Ministry for Economic Affairs was nearby at Nos. 43-45 Behrenstrasse, the Ministry for Forests at No. 1 Leipziger Platz and the Ministry for Post at Nos. 12-18 Leipziger Strasse. The Ministry for Labour was furthest away at Nos. 90-102 Saarlandstrasse.

Of these only the buildings of the former Ministries of Justice and Air Transport remain on Wilhelmstrasse, with the rear part of the Ministry of Propaganda on Mauerstrasse. The Ministry for Post building on Leipziger Strasse has been restored as a postal museum. However, the sites of the important buildings along Wilhelmstrasse have now been signed with a brief description of their function and history.

The normal peacetime location of the OKW, OKH and OKM headquarters were in the Bendlerblock at Nos. 72-76 Tirpitzufer (now Reichpietschufer), but both the OKW and OKH moved to Wünsdorf, south of Berlin, during the war. The headquarters of the Reserve Army remained in the Bendlerblock and became the centre of the conspiracy for the July 20, 1944, plot against Hitler. It now houses the Gedenkstätte Deutscher Widerstand (German Resistance Memorial and Museum) as well as offices of the Federal Ministry of Defence.

Also at some stage during the war, U-Boat headquarters were set up in the Hotel am Steinplatz at No. 179 Uhlandstrasse, just off the Steinplatz in Charlottenburg. Today the hotel is a retirement home.

Once again the street name along the canal has changed — it is now Reichpietschufer and the building today houses the German Defence Ministry. The former Bendlerstrasse part of the building has been turned into a shrine for those officers who set out to assassinate Hitler on July 20, 1944, several of whom were shot by firing squad in the courtyard. (See page 399.)

The Sportpalast on Potsdamer Strasse was the main venue for Hitler's public speeches in Berlin. Its place in history was assured in 1938 as it was here that he spoke on March 28 about Austria ('The small country has more murdered National Socialists than the whole of Germany') and where later that year he delivered his famous speech on the Czechoslovakian crisis. It was on September 12 that he first called for justice for the Sudeten Germans which became the catalyst for open demonstrations in the Sudetenland against the Czech President Eduard Beneš for self-determination. On the 15th the British Prime Minister met Hitler at the Berghof to try to find a solution, Chamberlain privately declaring that it would be wrong to let the decision between war and peace be decided by the ruler of another country and a lunatic at that! More behind-the-scenes diplomacy followed over the next week before Chamberlain returned to Germany on the 21st. But now Hitler had made up his mind, telling the Prime Minister that 'I can no longer discuss these matters'.

William Shirer was present in the Sportpalast on September 26 to report for CBS. Heinrich Hoffmann took the photos.

The question which in these last months and weeks has moved us so profoundly has long been familiar to us: it is not so much Czechoslovakia: it is rather Mr Beneš. In this name is concentrated all that which today moves millions, which causes them to despair or fills them with a fanatical resolution.

I have demanded that now now after twenty years Mr Beneš should at last be compelled to come to terms with the truth. On October 1 he will have to hand over to us this area.

And then I can say only one thing: now two men stand arrayed one against the other: there is Mr Beneš and here stand I. We are two men of a different make-up. In the great struggle of the peoples, while Mr. Beneš was sneaking about through the world, I as a decent German soldier did my duty.

I have only a few statements still to make: I am grateful to Mr Chamberlain for all his efforts. I have assured him that the German people desires nothing else than peace but I have also told him that I cannot go back behind the limits set to our patience. I have assured him, that when this problem is solved there is no further territorial problem in Europe.

But in the same way I desire to state before the German people that with regard to the problem of the Sudeten Germans my patience is now at an end! I have made Mr Beneš an offer which is nothing but the carrying into effect of what he himself has promised. The decision now lies in his hands: Peace or War! He will either accept this offer and now at last give to the Germans their freedom or we will go and fetch this freedom for ourselves.

In this hour the whole German people will unite with me! It will feel my will to be its will. Just as in my eyes it is its future and its fate which give me the commission for my action.

Then there gathered close about me a band of brave men and brave women, and they went with me. And so I ask you my German people to take your stand behind me, man by man, and woman by woman. We are determined!

Now let Mr Beneš make his choice!

ADOLF HITLER, SPORTPALAST,
SEPTEMBER 26, 1938.

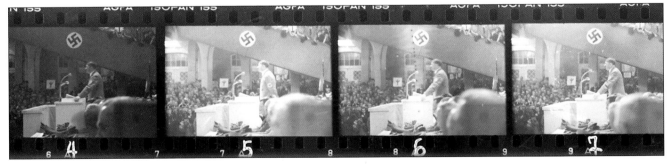

Today the historic Sportpalast — the Palace of Sport — is no more. It was demolished in 1974 and was replaced by these faceless blocks of flats. Hitler's speech there in September 1938 was one of the important milestones along the road to another world war. Britain's immediate response was that 'if France, in fulfilment of her treaty obligations, should become actively involved in hostilities against Germany, the United Kingdom would deem itself obliged to support France'. In the event it didn't come to that . . . yet. Three days later, the leaders of Britain, France and Germany, with Italy as peace-broker, met in the Führerbau in Munich (see page 158) to thrash out a deal — over the heads of the Czechs who were sold down the river. Peace had been bought but at a price. Each of the statesmen received a heroes welcome on return home and on October 9 Hitler publicly thanked the three men who 'with us have concluded that agreement which for many millions of Germans has secured their rights and, for the world has safeguarded peace'.

Hitler has finally burned his last bridges. Shouting and shrieking in the worst state of excitement I've ever seen him in, he stated in the Sportpalast tonight that he would have his Sudetenland by October 1 — next Saturday, today being Monday. If Beneš doesn't hand it over to him he will go to war, this Saturday. Curious audience, the fifteen thousand party Bonzen packed into the hall. They applauded his words with the usual enthusiasm. Yet there was no war fever. The crowd was good-natured, as if it didn't realise what his words meant. The old man full of more venom than even he has ever shown, hurling personal insults at Beneš. Twice Hitler screamed that this is absolutely his last territorial demand in Europe. Speaking of his assurances to Chamberlain, he said: 'I further assured him that when the Czechs have reconciled themselves with their other minorities, the Czech state no longer interests me and that, if you please, I would give him another guarantee: We do not want any Czechs.' At the end Hitler had the impudence to place responsibility for peace or war exclusively on Beneš!

I broadcast the scene from a seat in the balcony just above Hitler. He's still got that nervous tic. All during his speech he kept cocking his shoulder, and the opposite leg from the knee down would bounce up. Audience couldn't see it, but I could. As a matter of fact, for the first time in all the years I've observed him he seemed tonight to have completely lost control of himself. When he sat down after his talk, Goebbels sprang up and shouted: 'One thing is sure: 1918 will never be repeated!' Hitler looked up to him, a wild eager expression in his eyes, as if those were the words which he had been searching for all evening and hadn't quite found. He leaped to his feet and with a fanatical fire in his eyes that I shall never forget, brought his right hand, after a grand sweep, pounding down on the table and yelled with all the power in his mighty lungs: 'Ja!' Then he slumped into his chair exhausted.

WILLIAM SHIRER, *BERLIN DIARY*,
SEPTEMBER 26, 1938.

The 1936 Olympics had been allocated to Berlin by the International Olympic Committee in 1931, and by the time Hitler came to power the plans for the provision of facilities were so far advanced that they could not be changed to any great extent. The main location selected was on a small plateau and had originally been a racecourse well-served by public transport with its

It was Frenchman Baron Pierre de Coubertin who conceived the revival of the ancient Greek tradition of competitive championships with the founding of the International Olympic Committee (IOC) in 1894. His vision was of 'a four-yearly festival of the springtime of mankind' and the first games took place in Athens in 1896. Following Paris in 1900, St Louis in 1904, London in 1908 and Stockholm in 1912, Berlin missed out on the VIth Games scheduled for 1916 for obvious reasons. In May 1930, the German Olympic Committee presented their case to the IOC with forceful arguments as to why the XIth Olympic Games should be held in Berlin in 1936, having missed out 20 years earlier, but it was not until April 1931 that the IOC met in Barcelona (the other city shortlisted) to give its decision. When the votes were counted there were 43 for Berlin, 16 for Barcelona but 80 abstentions — a disturbing aspect which indicated that opinions were still divided against the former agressor. In the end, after a straw poll, Berlin was confirmed. And as the country hosting the summer games had the right to choose whether or not to stage the Winter Sports, Germany elected to hold the IVth Winter Olympic Games at Garmisch-Partenkirchen (above).

Twenty-eight nations took part from February 6-16: here the Canadian participants crowd Hitler and Goebbels (left) for their autographs.

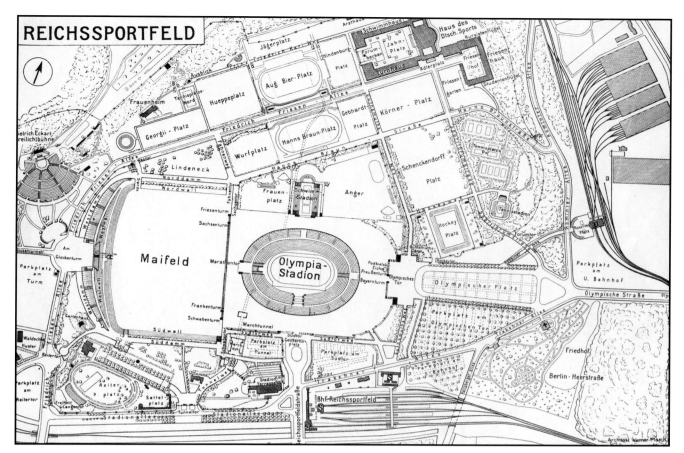

REICHSSPORTFELD

Hitler must have been overjoyed to be able to host such a prestigious event in Germany, giving him a perfect opportunity to show off his new regime to a world audience. Coming just a few months after he had taken back the Rhineland (see page 48), Hitler was concerned that there should be a maximum effort to portray Germany as a peace-loving nation to the foreign visitors. Construction work on the venue for the Berlin Olympics — centred on the old German Stadium built by Otto March in 1912-13 west of the city at Grunewald — was already well underway when Hitler became Chancellor but he took an immediate dislike to the plans drawn up by Otto's son Werner. Hitler thought it was still not large enough but there was worse as Albert Speer explains: 'March had designed a concrete structure with glass partition walls, similar to the Vienna Stadium. Hitler went to inspect the site and came back in a state of anger and agitation. Having been summoned to discuss some plans with him, I was present when he curtly informed State Secretary Hans Pfundtner of the Ministry of the Interior to cancel the Olympic Games. They could not take place without his presence, he said, since the Chief of State must open them, but he would never set foot inside a modern glass box like that. Overnight I made a sketch showing how the steel skeleton already built could be clad in natural stone and have more massive cornices added. The glass partitions were eliminated, and Hitler was content. He saw to the financing of the increased costs; Professor March agreed to the changes, and the Olympic Games were held in Berlin after all.'

Hitler inspected the Olympic Stadium while it was still under construction but did not like Werner March's idea of using glass screens, so seized on Albert Speer's suggestion to clad the steel framework with natural stone, thus providing it with a durability that was to prove valuable toward the end of the Second World War, when it housed both a field hospital and a factory manufacturing aircraft parts for Blaupunkt.

The complex included the numerous sports facilities and gymnasia of the National College of Physical Education, which under the Nazis became the Haus des Deutschen Sports directed by the Reichssportführer Hans von Tschammer und Osten. The adjacent swimming pool had permanent seating for 7,600 spectators and was temporarily expanded to take 16,000 for the Games.

Above: **The Haus des Deutschen Sports — another March design. The corner-stone was laid by President Hindenburg in 1925 for what was then to be called the College of Physical Exercise. It included indoor and outdoor swimming pools, gymnasiums and tennis courts, as well as serving as the central administration for all Germany's sport clubs.** *Right:* **From 1936 . . . to 2003**

own S- and U-Bahn stations. It even had a stadium, the Deutsche Stadion, which had been built by architect Otto March for the 1916 Olympics, prevented from taking place by the First World War, but this no longer met the 1936 standards. His son, Werner, designed a new stadium, oval in shape, with a sunken central arena, providing seating for 65,000 spectators and standing room for a further 35,000.

At the end of the war, the whole of the Olympic complex fell within the British Sector, and from 1945-1990 the House of German Sport served as the headquarters of the British Military Government in Berlin. Thereafter it was the HQ of the British Garrison until the Allies quit the German capital in 1994. The Olympic Bell, engraved with the slogan: 'I call the youth of the world', was shot out of the Glockenturm (Bell Tower) by an over-eager German anti-aircraft gunner during an air raid. It was then buried by British troops but later exhumed and set up beside the southern gate to the stadium. It has since been moved again and can be seen on the left. (For the full 'bell' story, see *Berlin Then and Now*.)

Left: **High diving champions (L-R): Kate Köhler (Germany), Bronze; Velma Dunn (USA), Silver; Dorothy Poynton-Hill (USA), Gold.**

Above: **The magnificent Olympic pool was split into two: a 20 × 20-metre diving and a 50-metre swimming pool beyond.**

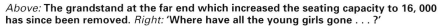

Above: **The grandstand at the far end which increased the seating capacity to 16, 000 has since been removed.** *Right:* **'Where have all the young girls gone . . . ?'**

Left: **Beauty and the beast! Jeannette Campbell (Argentina), silver medalist in the 100-metre freestyle.** *Above:* **The 'beast' aged 68, courtesy of sculptor Georg Kolbe.**

Other facilities included tennis [1], hockey [2] and riding [3] stadiums, with capacities for 3,000, 20,000 and 10,000 spectators respectively, and an open-air amphitheatre, then known as the Dietrich-Eckart-Freilichtbühne [4] and later as the Waldbühne, with seating for 20,000 spectators.

The largest spectator area, with room for 250,000 people, was provided by the Maifeld [5], which was actually constructed as a polo ground, and was dominated by the Glockenturm [6] (bell tower), which also contained the Langemarckhalle [7] memorial to the student battalions that had taken part in that battle in the First World War on November 10, 1914.

Access to the Olympic Stadium was served by road and rail. The S-Bahn Station Reichssportfeld [8] had 14 platforms and, together with the adjacent Pichelsberg Station could cope with up to 84,000 persons per hour, the U-Bahn Station Olympia-Stadion [9] 25,000 per hour with trains arriving at two-minute intervals, the latter having a tunnel link under the road to enable pedestrians to reach the stadium without impeding vehicular traffic. From central Berlin road access over Adolf-Hitler-Platz either continued with bus and tram services to stops on the Heerstrasse, or forked off down the Reichsstrasse to Steubenplatz, from where the statue of a naked boy on horseback pointed the

way down Olympiastrasse to Olympia-platz and the stadium. Public car parks were provided south of the stadium, but VIPs could use a broad tunnel leading under the stadium to the Haus des Deutschen Sports. This tunnel could provide parking for 100 cars and gave easy access to the VIP boxes. It was also used for marshalling sporting and military participants before they marched into the stadium.

Ticket sales arrangements could cope with 80,000 tickets per hour, and the exit arrangements were planned to be able to disgorge 100,000 people in 15 minutes. In all some four million tickets were sold, yielding ten million marks.

Left: **The amphitheatre named after Dietrich Eckart (see pages 39 and 155) hosted gymnastics . . but now it's pop concerts** *(right).*

The Langemarck-Ehrenhalle — the Hall of Honour for the fallen at Langemarck — lies beneath the Glockenturm.

In October 1914, untried and untested young students belonging to the Reserve-Korps of the German army were thrown into battle at Langemarck in Belgium and cut down in their thousands by the more experienced British and French troops. This sacrifice of the youth of Germany was exalted in post-war literature and commemorated by November 11 being declared Langemarck Day. Dedicated students from the University of Berlin set about creating a fitting monument which was unveiled in 1932. The sacrifice of 'the Heroes of Langemarck' passed into Third Reich folklore and the Hall of Honour became a shrine of remembrance. *Above:* This picture was taken on May 2, 1943 when the ashes of Reichssportführer Hans von Tschammer und Osten, who had died on March 25, were transferred to the Langemarck-halle. It was the tenth anniversary of Tschammer's appointment, and May 2 would from now on be Tschammer Memorial Day on the Nazi calendar.

The Olympic Village was built by the army on the Döberitz Training Area immediately west of the city with direct road and S-Bahn access to the stadium. It could house 4,500 athletes in 161 separate buildings, providing a post office, banks, shopping centre and customs post, and was staffed by 300 stewards provided by the Lloyds Shipping Company from Bremen. Each national contingent was allocated a young army officer for liaison purposes. There was also a swimming pool, a Finnish sauna and a gymnasium. The accommodation blocks were all named after German cities and contained a welcoming notice in every room that read:

'Welcome to the Olympic Village! This is your home for the moment. Here are your friends and competitors, a community of comrades serving the common ideal, and delighted to see you, to live with you and to enjoy a happy time together. Everything provided here is for your comfort and well-being, and

Hitler had been very pleased with Leni Riefenstahl's work on *Triumph of the Will* (pages 182-183) so he asked her to produce a film of the Games. This was released in 1938 as a two-part documentary titled *Olympia* which received world-wide acclaim.

even the rules are designed to ensure your undisturbed enjoyment of this facility. The Olympic Flag and the flags of your countries fly over this village, and every morning you will hear the bells ring out the Olympic Hymn. May the Olympic Spirit and Olympic Peace be with you from the first day to the last. Help us to honour and keep this peace. The German Army has built this village for our Olympic guests. It has done this gladly for sport, for it is itself sporting and true to the Olympic Ideal. Both the German people and the German Army extend to you a warm welcome!'

The officer supervising the organisation of the village and its final arrangements was Hauptmann Wolfgang Fürster but he was relieved immediately before the arrival of the first contestants as he was a Jew. He shot himself after attending the welcoming dinner for his successor, Oberstleutnant Werner von und zu Gilza.

Left: As Hitler drives to the stadium, Leni's camera on its prepared tracking is ready to film him crossing the Maifield *(right).* The athletes from the 49 countries competing were kept waiting while he first paid homage to the Heroes of Langemarck in the memorial where flags and standards were displayed in their shrine below the bell tower.

Hitler: 'Ich erkläre die Spiele in Berlin zur Feier der XI. Olympiade neuer Zeitrechnung als eröffnet.'

The Games were opened by Hitler as the head of the International Olympic Committee on the steps of the Pergamon Museum. Hitler then drove to the Glockenturm, where he symbolically first visited the Langemarckhalle memorial before proceeding on foot to the stadium with the International Olympic Committee between the formed up teams of the various countries participating. Following behind him were the King of Bulgaria, the Crown Princes of Greece, Italy and Sweden, and Mussolini's sons.

Upon entering the stadium through the tunnel they were greeted by a fanfare from 30 trumpets followed by the playing and singing of *Deutschland über Alles*, the *Horst Wessel Song* and the *Olympic Hymn*, which Straus had composed especially for the occasion.

The opening ceremonies ended that evening under a 'temple of light', an effect produced by massed searchlights under Albert Speer's direction, by which the spectators were treated to a ballet performance in Spartan costume led by Harald Kreutzberg and Mary

Wigman entitled 'The country's greatest gift — to die willingly for it when necessary'. The performance won such acclaim from the audience that they had to give three encores. This theme was the idea of Carl Diem, the organiser of the Games and secretary of the German Olympic Committee, who in March 1945 was to exhort members of the Hitlerjugend and Volkssturm assembled in the Kuppelsaal of the Haus des Deutschen Sports to sacrifice themselves for their country in the image of Sparta.

The large American team during the opening ceremony. The French athletes rather blotted their copybook by giving the Nazi salute as they marched past Hitler although it sent the Germans in the stadium into wild jubilation.

Although Germany won the most medals it peeved Hitler that Jesse Owens of America won four Golds, winning the 100 metres (10.3 seconds) *(left)*; the 200 metres (20.7 seconds); the 4×100-metre relay (39.8 seconds); and the long jump at 8.06 metres *(right)*. According to Baldur von Schirach, when Hitler explained why he refused to meet Owens, he said: 'Do you really think I would allow myself to be photographed shaking hands with a negro?'

Hitler followed the games with great interest. However, as a result of missing the end of a late event, for which he should have presented the medals as he had done until then, the Olympic Committee warned him that he should present all the awards or none at all. Hitler elected for the latter, consequently failing to shake hands with the fabulous coloured American athlete Jesse Owens, who won four gold medals. This gave birth to the rumour that he had refused to do so, but Jesse claimed that Hitler waved to him when he was collecting a medal from the committee.

Although the successes of some of the non-Aryan competitors caused a certain amount of heartache among the Nazi leadership, the overall results were a major triumph for the German national team, which included the Jews Helene Mayer, a fencer, and Rudi Ball, a hockey star, and won the most of all categories of medals, including 33 gold, coming well ahead of the Americans in second place. The Wehrmacht had taken a strong personal interest in the games, contributing strongly to the national team and winning 12 of the gold, six of the silver and 30 of the bronze medals in all. Two of the military medallists were rewarded with

Had Jesse Owens still been alive (he died in 1980), he would certainly have had the last laugh as his name remains for all time carved in stone . . .

instant commissions. However, the strong favourite for the discus, who had been given the national flag to carry on the opening parade, was put so out of condition by this experience that he only came eighth.

. . . and is memorialised on maps in the renaming of Stadion-allee as Jesse-Owens-Allee whereas Hitler's name has been expunged completely (see page 7).

After the Games finished on August 16, the Olympic Stadium was another perfect setting for Nazi gatherings. Speer records a rather humorous comment by Hitler some time later when talking about the new German Stadium in Nuremberg (see page 188). 'We talked about the Olympic Games', wrote Speer, 'and I pointed out, as I had done several times before, that my athletic field did not have the prescribed Olympic proportions. Without any change of tone, as if it were a matter settled beyond the possibility of discussion, Hitler observed: "No matter. In 1940 the Olympic Games will take place in Tokyo. But thereafter they will take place in Germany for all time to come, in this stadium and then we will determine the measurements of the athletic field!"'

But it was not to be! Now the Berlin stadium has been extensively altered during a four-year restoration which included adding a roof. It reopened to public inspection in August 2004 . . . but with Hitler's podium reduced in size!

The end of a Berlin dream. Pariser Platz pictured in a sorry state in July 1945. The Hotel Adlon is on the far left and next to the building used by Speer when working on his designs for the new Berlin as General-Bau-Inspektor für die Reichshaupt- stadt, where he was frequently visited by Hitler. In the centre is Speer's offices in his later capacity as Minister for Armaments and Munitions, and on the right, with the entrance in line with the telegraph pole, the remains of the American Embassy.

Hitler had not been greatly impressed with the efforts of the Berlin authorities in improving the appearance of the city. He had his own grand concepts for converting it into a capital city befitting his Thousand Year Reich. Everything would eventually be bigger and better, wider or taller than its equivalent in any other capital city. So in 1937 a law was passed on the 'restructuring' of Berlin, Hamburg, Munich and the Gau capitals, maximum priority being given to Berlin.

Albert Speer was appointed Inspector General of Building in Berlin, with a status equivalent to State Secretary, his office in the Academy of Arts building on Pariser Platz coming directly under Hitler, and totally eclipsing the municipal planning authorities.

Right: Speer addresses the staff of the Armaments Ministry assembled on the forecourt in a snowstorm on February 9, 1942 having just been appointed as the replacement for Fritz Todt who had been killed in a plane crash the previous day.

Left: For over 40 years, the site of Speer's office remained empty following the creation of a 'forbidden zone' next to the Berlin

Wall at the Brandenburg Gate. *Right:* Now the new Adlon Hotel stands on its original site next to a new office construction.

In 1938 a competition was held for the design of the University City to be constructed astride the Heerstrasse and to incorporate the Reichssportfeld for the university's sporting facilities, the competition acting as a trawl for recruiting suitable architects for the overall concept. As it was, the ideological-political situation in the Third Reich was already promoting the construction of commercial and public buildings uninhibited by the normal cost constraints, enabling many architects to make their names at this time. For example, Goebbels had promoted the construction of the Exhibition Halls around the Funkturm, which were designed by Richard Ermisch and built during 1934-36, and the nearby Deutschlandhalle, designed by Fritz Wiemer and Paul Tewes, had been erected in 1935 on so vast a scale that Hanna Reitsch was able to fly an autogyro indoors there in February 1938.

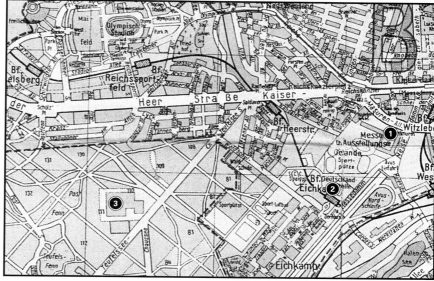

One of the first areas to be targeted in Hitler's concept for a new Berlin was 'University City'. Apart from the Reichssportfeld which we have seen, the Funkturm (Radio Tower) [1] *(left)* **is the only construction which survives from that time** *(above right)*. **The Deutschlandhalle [2]** *(below left)*, **completed in 1935, was gutted during an RAF raid in January 1943 although the building today** *(below right)* **bears the same characteristics.**

Hitler did lay the foundation stone in November 1937 for a huge technical academy for the armed forces [3] but having been destroyed by the Red Army in 1945, the remains were cleared in 1960 to form the basis of the huge mound of blitz rubble known as the Teufelsberg. Because of its height, this later became an ideal location for the establishment of a combined British-American listening post during the Cold War.

The only part of the University City actually to be built was the Wehrtechnische Fakultät (War College), designed by Hans Malwitz, whose groundstone was laid by Hitler in the Grunewald on February 27, 1937, but this was still not complete in 1945 and is now well and truly buried under the Teufelsberg, the 120-metre-high mountain of rubble removed from the ruins of the city after the war. It was intended that the University City would be made imposing as Berlin's western entrance with the style and size of its buildings, the largest of which would be the Langemarckhalle commemorating the sacrifice of the volunteer student regiments of the First World War. A site was also sought here for the University Clinic (hospital), which was to be moved from the city centre.

Also in the vicinity was planned the construction of a Reichsforstamt (State Forestry Office) and Jagdmuseum (Hunting Museum), and the relocation of the Zoological Gardens from their present site.

The western part of the East-West-Axis took priority in preparation for the big parade to be held on April 20, 1939 for Hitler's 50th birthday. As a memorial to the Second Reich, the Siegessäule (Victory Column), commemorating Prussian victories over the Austrians, Danes and French, was removed from in front of the Reichstag and re-sited on the Grosser Stern roundabout in the Tiergarten. On Hitler's direction, an 11-metre-high section was inserted into the column to make it more imposing. The statues of Bismarck, Moltke and Roon were brought along to enhance the site, as were all the white marble statues of the Siegesallee, which had previously run south into the Tiergarten from the column's Königsplatz site, and were replaced in the Neue Siegesallee running south-east through the Tiergarten from the new one.

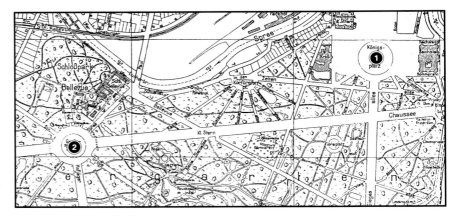

Speer started his main work in changing the face of Berlin outside the Reichstag. *Below left:* The Victory Column had stood on the Königsplatz [1] since 1873 but it was moved to the centre of the Grosser Stern [2] *(right)*, a roundabout mid-way along the Charlottenburger Chaussee, which was itself renamed the Ost-West (East-West) Axis.

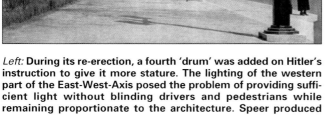

Left: During its re-erection, a fourth 'drum' was added on Hitler's instruction to give it more stature. The lighting of the western part of the East-West-Axis posed the problem of providing sufficient light without blinding drivers and pedestrians while remaining proportionate to the architecture. Speer produced a design, which he tested to Hitler's satisfaction in the Reich Chancellery garden, and then put into practise. *Right:* Some of the lamp standards still remain but they had to be removed east of the Victory Column for the improvisation of an emergency landing strip in April 1945.

Reconstructing the Charlottenburger Chausee without the aid of modern plant in little over eight months was a considerable **accomplishment as it had to be ready for Hitler's 50th birthday parade to be held on April 20, 1939.**

Further along the S-Bahn bridge had to be widened, and the 1906 Charlottenburg Gate's sections moved further apart. All the buildings on the north side of the street from the Technical University were demolished to make room for Hitler's tribune and the main spectator stands (see page 54).

From here the widened street climbed up to the Adolf-Hitler-Platz traffic roundabout before dipping down westwards to the Havel river as the Heerstrasse up which the troops would have to march from the Döberitz Training Area beyond Spandau. The plans for this 1929 roundabout, with the problem

of modern commercial office blocks on the south side and turn-of-the-century apartment blocks on the north, was to erect a memorial flanked by two semi-circular ten-metre-high colonnades. It was planned to rename the square Mussoliniplatz and also name the Heerstrasse S-Bahn station after him.

The five-mile section from the Brandenburg Gate to the Adolf-Hitler-Platz was completed and opened the previous evening.

Left: **The Brandenburg Gate is the symbol by which Berlin is known throughout the world. It has stood at the top of Unter den Linden since the 1790s with the Quadriga being mounted two years later. (Napoleon removed it as spoils of war in 1806 but it** was returned in triumph in 1814.) *Right:* **The archways, although wide enough to take a vehicle, have always caused a bottleneck so Speer's plan was to dismantle the twin guardhouses and move them sideways so traffic could circumvent the gate.**

Speer's basic concept for Berlin envisaged an autobahn ring, the outermost of four ring roads, enclosing the extended limits of the city with an East-West-Axis and a North-South-Axis crossing near the Brandenburg Gate, whose arms would extend beyond the autobahn ring to external airports, while other main roads and green belts of fields, parks and forests radiated outwards from this backbone. Also tied in with this was the railway system, which would have two mainline stations in Wedding and Tempelhof at either end of the seven-kilometre-long Prachtstrasse (Prestige Street), the central section of the North-South-Axis. Within this concept, Speer was also concerned with the lakes, rivers and canals that formed such a large part of the Berlin landscape.

East of the Brandenburg Gate, where the prestigious Unter den Linden had already been widened and its trees replanted for the 1936 Olympics, it was proposed to replant the trees yet again to balance the effect with that west of the Gate.

In order to facilitate the flow of traffic here, it was appreciated that the proportions of the arches through the Gate could not be altered without spoiling this historic structure, so it was decided to demolish the buildings on either side and re-site the Gate's guardrooms on the far side of the new traffic lanes thus made possible.

A new building designed by Paul Mebes was started in 1938 on the corner of Pariser Platz and Wilhelmstrasse opposite the Hotel Adlon to accommodate the administrative headquarters of IG Farben as an extension of the Deutsche Landesbank, but was still incomplete when it was destroyed during the war.

Further east, where Kaiser-Wilhelm-Strasse (now Karl-Liebknecht-Strasse) began east of the Spree, plans were made for constructing massive buildings either side of the street, leaving only the Marienkirche intact. On the north side next to the river would be the new Chamber of Commerce designed by Schwebes and Ullrich. Next to it would come a building housing the Post Office

Telephone Accounts Department, then the Städtische Kunsthalle (City Arts Hall), designed by Richard Ermisch and Gotthold Nestler, opposite the Marienkirche, from where on commercial office blocks would fill both sides of the street. Opposite the Chamber of Commerce would be a building of similar appearance but designed by Wilhelm Weygandt and Kurt Reichle for the State Labour Exchange offices.

There were already municipal plans in existence for the improvement and extension of the Museum Island complex, but these were all taken over by Speer's office with his team's far more radical ideas for giving Berlin's historical centre a more prestigious impact based on the lines of the Spree with streets and promenades following the river banks.

The whole residential area of Friedrich-, Johannis- and Oranienburger Strasse, as well as the University Clinic, was now to go. The Montbijou

Palace was originally to be transplanted to Pfaueninsel (Peacock Island) on the Havel, but in 1941 Hitler accepted Speer's suggestion that it should instead be moved to the grounds of the Charlottenburg Palace. As it happened, the war saw that it was destroyed in situ.

On these sites on the north bank of the Spree were to be constructed a 19th Century Museum, a new Museum for Egyptian and Near East Collections, and a German Museum, all three designed by Wilhelm Kreis. Opposite on the south bank would be a new Volkerkundemuseum with the purpose of explaining the Nazi racial theories to the public, for which Hanns Dustmann, Reichsarchitekt der Hitlerjugend, in consultation with the Party's expert on this subject, Alfred Rosenberg, was entrusted with the design. Next to it, the Zeughaus (Arsenal) would be extended in accordance with plans also drawn up by Wilhelm Kreis.

Faced with the same problem 60 years later following the removal of the wall dividing East and West Berlin, it was a pity that this same solution was not implemented in the post-reunification reconstruction of Pariser Platz. At least Speer could have claimed to have kicked the ball into touch!

None of the Hitler-Speer planning east of the Brandenburg Gate was completed and very little started other than the widening of Unter den Linden *(above)* for a parade route. *Right:* Now dual carriageways on either side have left the central strip a pedestrian area. The statue in the background is Frederick II on horseback. It was removed by the Communists in 1950 but 30 years later it was re-erected in its rightful place outside the Krönprinzen-Palais. *Below left:* Further down the road lay the Lustgarten facing the Schloss — the old King's Palace. It was badly damaged during the battle for Berlin and although it could have been restored, the Schloss was torn down in 1950 by the newly-created German Democratic Republic as a political statement. *Below right:* In its place they built their own Palace of the Republic. With the fall of the GDR in 1990, the West Germans wanted *it* demolished although 14 years on it is still standing. Now there is a groundswell of nostalgia for the way things were and a campaign is underway to retain the GDR building although bankrupt Berlin still have a desire to reconstruct the Kaiser's castle.

However, the largest concentration of planning was on the seven-kilometre-long central core of the North-South-Axis, for which the final plans were not approved by Hitler until 1942, although certain aspects had received prior approval and work on them was in progress. The entire project was to be completed by 1950.

From the north, the northern mainline railway station [1] was to be constructed above Perleberger Strasse in Moabit, the intervening area down to the existing Lehrter Station to be converted into a vast rectangular lake [2] 1,200 metres long and 400 metres wide, which would be lined on the long western side by a new town hall [3] designed by Richard Ermisch, flanked by a new Oberkommando der Kriegsmarine building designed by Paul Donatz and Kurt Dübbers, and a new Police Presidium [4].

Some parkland across the southern end of the lake would then allow the necessary lineal adjustment for the Great Hall [5] facing away due south down the main axis. Speer's plans for this gigantic structure encompassed a building 315 metres square and 290 metres high that would be capable of accommodating 150,000 to 180,000 people. The circular interior would be 250 metres in diameter and 220 metres high, far exceeding the dimensions of the Capitol in Washington or St Peter's in Rome. The building's dome would be capped by a glazed lantern in light metal, over which an eagle would be perched on top of a swastika, but in the spring of 1939 Hitler altered this to an eagle on a globe.

The siting of the Great Hall entailed firstly the demolition of the Diplomatic Quarter on the north side of Königsplatz (today Platz der Republik), the embassies being offered alternative sites on the southern edge of the Tiergarten, and secondly the diversion of the course of the Spree at this point by cutting twin tunnels under the square. A new U-Bahn line would also be cut across under the square to service a station to be built on the west side of the Great Hall.

Hitler decided to retain the Reichstag [6], presumably as an historical object, for he had previously spoken disparagingly of it. The Kroll Opera on the west side of the square would be removed to make way for the 'Führerpalais' [7] or 'Adolf-Hitler-Palais', for which Speer allocated two million square metres ground space. Next to it on the south side of the square would be the building for the Oberkommando der Wehrmacht [8].

The area of Königsplatz was intended as a pedestrian zone, so the junction of the East-West-Axis with the North-South-Axis [9] immediately to the south would be in the form of a 'T' and not a crossroads. Tunnels were therefore dug to enable traffic to enter and leave the East-West-Axis at this point, and these still exist near the Soviet War Memorial.

Kemperplatz [10] was to be enlarged and renamed Skagerrakplatz after the First World War naval battle, which the British call Jutland and which both sides claimed as victories. Flanking either side of the North-South Axis immed-

The real architectural megalomania of 'Germania' centred on the new North-South Axis which was planned to cross the East-West Axis with its repositioned Victory Column [16] just east of the Brandenburg Gate [17].

iately south of Skagerrakplatz east and west repectively were to be the massive structures of the Reichsmarschallamt [11] designed by Albert Speer and the Soldatenhalle [12] designed by Wilhelm Kreis.

Then would come the Runderplatz [13], a circular square immediately north of the Landwehr Canal. The site was cleared and the Haus des Fremdenverkehrs (Travel Bureau) constructed with its facade forming a concave quarter circle on the south-west side, but it was seriously damaged during the war and later demolished.

The continuation southwards of the North-South-Axis from Königsplatz would contain ministerial buildings, the head offices of Party organisations and major firms, and recreational facilities such as theatres, an opera house, a new

Philharmonic concert hall, a vast cinema for launching new films, hotels and restaurants, and the Thermenanlage (Thermal Baths) by Cäsar Pinnau.

Then came the Triumphal Arch [14], which Speer designed from original drawings produced by Hitler in the 1920s. The arch was to be 170 metres wide by 119 metres deep, and 117 metres high with an opening 80 metres high. Speer considered this construction disproportionate in scale to the other buildings in its vicinity but was unable to persuade Hitler otherwise.

Finally came the southern mainline railway station [15] to be built on the site of Schöneberg S-Bahn station to Speer's design. Further in towards the city centre, the Anhalter railway station would remain, but the Potsdamer station would go.

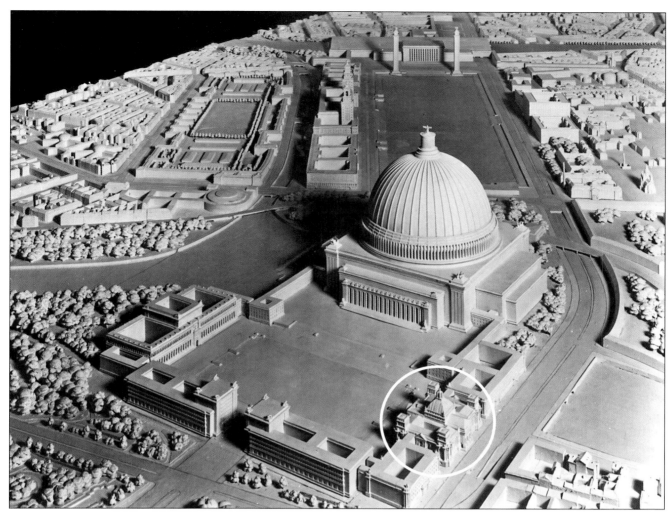

The Volkshalle, or People's Hall, was to be the centrepiece of the new Berlin which Speer advised could be finished by 1950. Completely dwarfing the Reichstag (circled), it was to be larger than St Peter's in Rome and as tall as the Eiffel Tower, and was designed to provide standing room for 150,000 people. Speer: 'Our model city was set up in the former exhibition rooms of the Berlin Academy of Arts. These rooms were kept under careful guard and no one was allowed to inspect the grand plan for the rebuilding of Berlin without Hitler's express permission. There was keen excitement when a new model was set up and illumiated by brilliant spots from the direction in which the sun would fall on the actual buildings. Hitler was particularly excited over the large model of the grand boulevard on a scale of 1:1000 which extended for a length of about a hundred feet. He loved to "enter his avenue" at various points and take measure of the future effect. For example, he assumed the point of view of a traveller emerging from the south station or admired the great hall *(above)* as it looked from the heart of the avenue. To do so, he bent down almost kneeling, his eye an inch or so above the level of the model, in order to have the right perspective.'

Despite unemployment there was a dearth of skilled labour in the building industry, and workers had to be brought in from the Protectorate of Bohemia and Moravia, part of the former Czechoslovakia, to fill the gap. The labour requirement was forecast as rising from 39,000 to 182,500 after the war, including 43,800 masons, 14,600 plasterers, 27,375 carpenters and 70,000 labourers. As late as December 1941 Speer wrote to the new Deputy Reich Protector in Prague, Reinhard Heydrich, asking for the dispatch of the promised 15,000 Czech workers and for an annual consignment of 50,000 young Czechs with extended labour service commitments after the war.

For transportation of building materials, Speer's organisation had a fleet of hundreds of trucks run by the NSKK (Nazi Transport Corps) 'Transportstandarte Speer' and 1,000 canal barges. Europe was scoured for building materials, contracts for stone being placed

A special work camp, the 'Arbeitslager Grosse Halle', was constructed on Schönwalderallee in the north-west outskirts of Spandau to the design of Carl Christoph Lörcher to accommodate 8,000 workers committed to the Great Hall project. Today the village is shared by two hospital complexes.

Hitler was very dissatisfied with Berlin's War Memorial established by the Weimar Republic on Unter den Linden. While Britain and France had been the first to establish national memorials after the war by interring an unknown warrior to symbolise all those who had died, it was not until 1931 that Germany set up the Reichsehrenmal war memorial in its capital.

with French, Italian, Swedish and Norwegian firms, while 16,000 tons of granite was ordered from Finland. Also the SS undertook to supply stone from the quarries worked by the slave labour of their concentration camps, and the notorious Klinkerwerk (brick works) was opened at Sachsenhausen for this purpose. In April 1941 Speer informed Göring that he would be requiring 70,000 tons of steel per month from the Second Four Year Plan's production.

How these grand schemes were to financed was left in the hands of Providence. The 1937 Restructuring Law provided a budget of 60,000 million Reichsmarks that barely covered planning costs. Speer's own monthly architectural fees alone amounted to 30,000 Reichsmarks in respect of the Great Hall, 15,000 for the Triumphal Arch, 10,000 for Hitler's palace, and 5,000 for the OKW building — some 60,000 Reichsmarks in all!

It utilised the Royal Guard House in which a black stone cube topped by a wreath placed in a central position with the simple inscription '1914-1918'.

Hitler described the existing Reichsehrenmal as paltry and undignified for a great nation. He was obviously greatly impressed by France's Arc de Triomphe, beneath which its unknown soldier rests with its eternal flame, and he prepared his own design when he was in prison in 1925. Hitler's arch was to be twice as high as the Paris monument and it would be engraved with the names of Germany's 1,800,000 dead. When he handed over his sketches for his Triumphal Arch and Great

Hall to Speer, Hitler told him that 'I saved them because I never doubted that some day I would build them. At least that will be a worthy monument to our dead of the world war.' *Right:* However this is all that was built: a ten-metre-diameter, load-bearing core which would have served as a foundation for the eastern side of the arch. It can still be seen next to the Kolonnen Bridge on Dudenstrasse in Berlin-Schöneberg. This alone cost 400,000 Reichsmarks!

So back to reality. The East Germans replaced the Weimar stone with a contemporary glass structure and re-opened it with a new title: 'The Memorial for the Victims of Fascism and Militarism'.

A very smart permanent guard of honour from the Nationale Volksarmee was established but when the NVA was disbanded in October 1990, the guard was withdrawn.

The interior to the Neue Wache was changed again by the West Germans. Now the central memorial for the Bundesrepublik

Deutschland, the sculpture is a 'Mother and her dead son' by Käthe Kollwitz.

While 'Germania' remained largely a pipe-dream, Albert Speer's greatest challenge was yet to come — the construction of a brand new Reich Chancellery. We saw on page 207 the old Chancellor's Palace which existed in 1933 at No. 77 Wilhelmstrasse. On the evening of January 30, the only way Hitler could acknowledge the cheers of the huge crowd was to look out of a first-floor window in the modern office extension (see page 25) which had been built in 1929-30. This was obviously far from satisfactory. 'I could not be seen from all sides', Hitler told Speer. 'After all, I could not very well lean out.'

Toward the end of January 1938 Speer was summoned by Hitler and abruptly given the task of producing a new Reich Chancellery by January 10, 1939, the day when Hitler would give his next New Year reception for the Diplomatic Corps. Given the immense scale of the proposed building — some 1,400 feet long — and the almost impossible timetable, this was to prove Speer's greatest achievement.

The Chancellery that Hitler had inherited on becoming Reich Chancellor was relatively new, having been erected as late as 1928-30, but Hitler described it as only being 'fit for a soap company', and Speer had already had to add a balcony to the structure.

So the first alteration externally was to add a balcony overlooking the Wilhelmplatz. In 1934, with the merging of the office of Chancellor and President, extensive alterations were carried out to the rooms to try to make them more suitable for Hitler's enlarged retinue and staff but it could still only be a temporary solution.

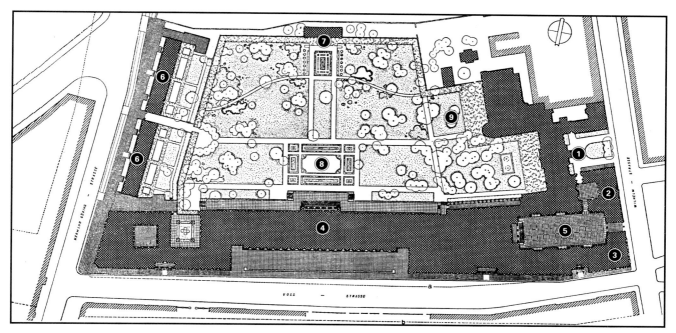

These alterations sufficed as a stop-gap for the next four years until January 1938. Hitler explains the two events which led to his instruction to build a new enlarged Chancellery: 'To ease the traffic flow through Berlin from east to west, it had been intended to extend the Jägerstrasse and to project it through the Ministerial garden and the Tiergarten and thus create a further link with the Tiergartenstrasse. I considered that these plans worked out by the existing Berlin Urban Building Directorate were faulty, and commissioned Professor Speer to ensure that the necessary relief for the traffic on the Leipziger Strasse and Unter den Linden would be better solved in a straight line west from the Wilhelmplatz. However this meant that the Voss-strasse would have to cease to be a bottleneck and become a main thoroughfare. Since for obvious reasons this widening could not be achieved at the expense of losing the Wertheim department store [on the south side], this was better achieved on the other side of the street where the Reichs Chancellery park was located. The need to demolish the whole of this side, and rebuild thus followed as a matter of course. Then, during December and January 1937-38, I had decided to solve the Austrian question, and thereby set up a Greater German State. Both for its official duties and for its representative functions necessarily linked to these, the old Reichs Chancellery would now no longer be adequate under any circumstances. On the 11th January 1938 I therfore entrusted the General-Bau-Inspektor, Professor Speer, with the task of rebuilding the Reichs Chancellery in the Voss-strasse and fixed the completion date for this as the 10th January 1939.' [1] Old Reichskanzlei. [2] Extension built 1929-30. [3] Borsig Palace. [4] New Reich Chancellery. [5] Ehrenhof. [6] Living quarters for SS-'Leibstandarte' guards. [7] Greenhouse. [8] Ornamental pond. The location where the Führerbunker was later built is [9].

The building stood on the Wilhelmstrasse, sandwiched between the Presidential Palace and the Borsig Palace, which formed the corner with Vossstrasse, and which had previously been used by Vice-Chancellor von Papen and was now occupied by Hitler's Deputy, Rudolf Hess. Speer decided to incorporate the old Chancellery building and Borsig Palace into the new structure.

By the evening of the first day Speer produced a list of deadlines for Hitler's approval. Work began immediately on clearing the site. The complexity of the task can be imagined, for not only had the structural and interior aspects of the design to be worked out in detail to Hitler's satisfaction, but the materials, fittings and furnishings had to be ordered so that the delivery dates fitted precisely into the completion programme.

Speer said that: 'Even at a later stage of the work I had to order many components before the architectural data had been definitely settled. For example, the longest delivery times were required for the enormous hand-knotted rugs which were to be used in several large salons. I decided their sizes and colours before I knew what the rooms they were meant for would look like. In fact the rooms were more or less designed around these rugs.'

The first part of the new buildings to be completed were the air raid shelters beneath. Whether this was the full complement that existed at the end of the war — less of course the Führerbunker, which was not built until 1944 — is not clear, but even at this stage the requirement was foreseen.

The aim was to impress and awe distinguished visitors with the power and might of the Third Reich. Speer's plan was therefore to use this elongated site to produce a series of imposing halls and galleries through which the visitor would have to pass before being admitted to the Führer — a walk of nearly 250 yards.

At first sight the task Hitler had given to Speer was impossible, his agreement being, he wrote later, 'the most thoughtless promise of my life. I decided to forgo any complicated organisational plan and schedule, since these would only have revealed that the project could not possibly be carried out within the time limit.'

The magnificence of the building can barely be appreciated through photographs but, more to the point, it is the unbelievable time scale in which it was constructed using the finest of materials which is difficult to comprehend. Not only was the building work finished 48 hours ahead of its hand-over date but it was complete with specially-made fabrics, furnishings and furniture — an incredible achievement in less than a year. *Above:* The length of the frontage on Voss-strasse was almost 1,400 feet. The terrace overlooking the garden *(below)* was over 600 feet long.

Speer started by creating the Ehrenhof (Courtyard of Honour). An entry passage was knocked through the left-hand end of the old Chancellery building next to the Borsig Palace and masked with two tall portals, through which the visitors would be driven. An outdoor staircase then led into a medium-sized lobby, from which 17-feet-high double doors led into the Mosaiksaal, a large hall lined in red marble inlaid with double-eagle motive mosaics and illuminated from above by a large skylight. At the far end another massive door led into the circular Runder Saal, similarly decorated to the Mosaiksaal, but a necessary device to connect it with the different alignment of the rest of the building. Next came the Marmorgalerie (Marble Gallery), nearly 500 feet long and twice as long as the Hall of Mirrors at Versailles. This was illuminated by tall, deeply inset windows overlooking the Voss-strasse on the left. A door at the far end led to the Grosser Emp-fangssaal (Great Reception Hall) and five doors were set at regular intervals in the right-hand wall, the third leading directly into Hitler's office. This was about 90 feet long by 50 feet wide and was illuminated by five French windows leading on to a long terrace overlooking the garden. Hitler's desk and a large map table were designed by Speer himself.

A visitor to the Chancellery would enter the Ehrenhof *(above)* via the heavy bronze doors which opened onto Wilhelmstrasse. *Below:* This Court of Honour was open to the sky. From here a flight of nine steps led to the west door which was flanked by two statues by Arno Breker representing the Party, left, and the Armed Forces, right.

The Ehrenhof measured 68 metres by 26 metres (220 feet by 85 feet) and was built of Jura dolomite.

1. Ehrenhof (Courtyard of Honour)
2. Vorhalle (Ante-room)
3. Mosaiksaal (Hall of Mosaics)
4. Runder Saal (Round Salon)
5. Marmorgalerie (Marble Hall)
6. Arbeitszimmer des Führers (Hitler's Office)
7. Reichskabinettssaal (State Cabinet Office)
8. Grosser Empfangssaal (Reception Hall)
9. Speisesaal (Dining Room)

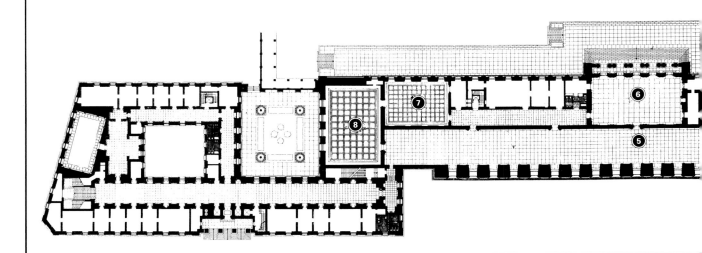

Arguably the two most spectacular halls — one can hardly call them rooms because of their size — were the beautiful Mosaiksaal *(below)* and the magnificent Marmorgalerie *(opposite)*. The Hall of Mosaics covered an area 46.2 metres × 19.2 metres — nearly 10,000 square feet — and was faced with dark red Austrian marble inlaid with ten large mosaics by Professor Hermann Kaspar. Because Speer was anxious to maintain even lighting, the natural light from the skylight was supplemented by artificial lighting both from above and in the grooves of the ceiling.

Kurt Schmid-Ehmen provided the bronze eagles above the doorways at either end. The eagle has been the national emblem of Germany ever since Charlemagne, King of the Franks, was crowned in Rome in AD 800. He adopted the Roman eagle for his coat-of-arms and in various forms and attitudes it was borne by successive German emperors. The Second Reich of 1871-1918 and the Weimar Republic after 1919 both used the single-headed spread-eagle and Hitler continued the tradition with the addition of the swastika wreath held in its talons.

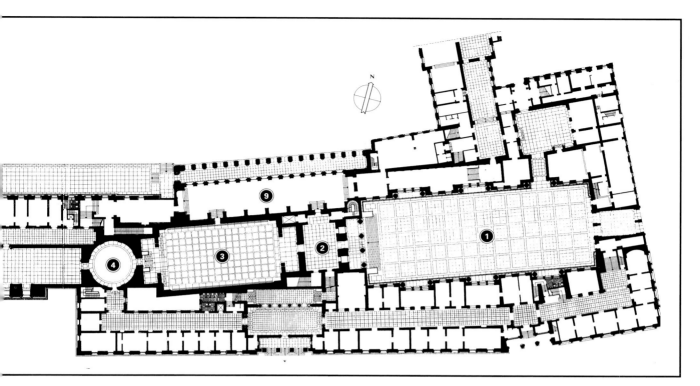

Hitler wanted to outdo Versailles so his Marble Gallery at 146 metres — nearly 500 feet — was nearly double the length of the Hall of Mirrors. The windows on the left looked out onto Voss-strasse (also with supplemental artificial light built in), while the rooms on the right were dominated by Hitler's office, the doorway crowned by a monogrammed shield. The only carpets were for the waiting areas outside each door as Hitler liked the idea of the mirror-bright floor which, he said, would enable his diplomatic visitors to practise walking on slippery surfaces!

To reach this point a visitor would have had to walk very nearly 250 yards to reach the holy of holies. A contemporary description of this gallery was of 'a picture of lively and beautiful colours as a result of the groups of furniture that are arranged on carpets between the doors in the long wall. Tapestries hang between the doors. The furniture designed by Albert Speer, comprises brilliant examples of German furniture-manufacture with beautiful marquetry and costly coverings. The room's splendid colour effects are further intensified by the choice of flowers and plants.'

The same commentator, Wilhelm Lotz, contributing to Speer's illustrated book *Die Neue Reichskanzlei* wrote this account describing the interior of Hitler's office: 'The Führer's office looks out to the garden terrace through five French windows six metres high and two metres wide. Five similar bays to those formed by the French windows are repeated on the opposite wall, constructed with fine, inlaid panels. In the middle bay on this side is the entrance door leading in from the Marmorgalerie. (There are two more doors on each of the narrow sides leading to the State Cabinet Room and to the areas where the adjutants' rooms are located.) The office, which is 27 metres long and 14.5 metres wide, has walls consisting of a dark red marble from Austria known as Limbacher. With a height of 9.75 metres, the room has a panelled ceiling with beams of darker wood that is a splendid feat of joinery. On the floor made of Ruhpolding marbles lies a single large carpet. The furnishings and layout are designed to be completely subordinate to the main spacial effects. On the narrow eastern side a marble fireplace measuring 2.7 metres high and 3.25 metres wide has been built of the same marble as the walls, for which Richard Klein has devised fine panels made of cast iron with figurative reliefs. The shields above the side doors are also the work of Richard Klein, while the national emblem above the entrance door, which is made of carved and gilded wood, was devised by Kurt Schmid-Ehmen. Albert Speer has designed the new furniture for this room: the Führer's big writing desk, the credenza unit on the west wall, and the large map table in front of the centre window, which consists of an especially fine piece of marble from Austria quarried and dressed from a single slab measuring 5 by 1.6 metres. The pattern for the inlay work was designed by Hermann Kaspar. Over the fireplace hangs Lenbach's famous portrait of Bismarck. The basic colours of this room come from a combination of the beautiful brown shades of wood and the red-brown of the marble, the fine materials used creating a colour synthesis that is severe but filled with restrained strength.'

Only by having work going on around the clock, with 4,500 workers operating in two shifts, was it possible to meet the deadline, and on August 1, 1938, the topping-out ceremony was held as planned, after only four months of construction work. Next day Hitler addressed the assembled staff and workforce in the Deutschlandhalle, praising their efforts and those of Albert Speer in particular.

The task was actually completed 48 hours ahead of schedule. The whole workforce, including all those that had contributed their efforts from all over the country, were invited to inspect the finished result. Afterwards Hitler addressed them in the Sportpalast:

'I stand here as a representative of the German people. And whenever I receive anyone in the Chancellery, it is not the private individual Adolf Hitler who receives him, but the Leader of the German Nation — and therefore it is not I who receive him, but Germany through me. For that reason I want these rooms to be in keeping with their high mission. Every individual has contributed to a structure that will outlast the centuries and will speak to posterity of our times. This is the first architectural creation of the new, great German Reich!'

True to his promise, the New Reich Chancellery was ready for the reception held in the Grosser Empfangssaal on January 11, 1939.

Hitler was delighted with the building and rewarded Speer with the Golden Party Badge for his achievement.

Whether it was Hitler returning from his triumph in Munich in 1938 *(left)* or victory over France in 1940 *(right)*, the scenes outside the New Reich Chancellery echoed the supreme adulation with which the Führer was held at this time.

The Reichskanzlei stood in all its magnificence for a brief five or so years . . . and by 1950 it was gone. We shall see its end in our final chapter. Meanwhile this is the same view today.

(For those waiting to read a more detailed account about the Chancellery, see *After the Battle* No. 61, or more of Berlin's history, see Tony Le Tissier's *Berlin Then and Now*.)

The military expansion, the development of the Luftwaffe, preparation for war and the consequences of waging war, brought about a considerable amount of military construction in the Berlin area.

Outside Speer's direct control were two important structures built to the designs of Ernst Sagebiel, Göring's Luftfahrtministerium (Air Traffic Ministry) on Wilhelmstrasse built in 1935-36 with its 2,000 offices, conference rooms, etc. which were to later serve the East German government for a consortium of ministries and now houses the Federal Ministry of Finance (see pages 210-211). Sagebiel then went on to design the new Tempelhof Airport complex in the shape of a spread eagle with its vast concave frontage nearly a kilometre long and an overhanging roof enabling aircraft to park under cover for the disembarkation and embarkation of passengers. Built in 1936-39 the airport, then the most advanced in the world, finally closed in the summer of 2004.

With the creation of the Luftwaffe, Göring's Air Traffic Ministry building on Wilhemstrasse came out into the open as the Air Ministry and headquarters of the Luftwaffe. Meanwhile a barracks complex with underground command facilities for the Luftwaffe Headquarters was established south of Potsdam in the Wildpark-West area. These barracks are now known as the Henning-von-Tresckow-Kaserne and accommodate the headquarters of IV. Armeekorps of the Bundeswehr.

The Berlin Luftgaukommando III headquarters were built in 1937 on Kronprinzenallee (today Clayallee) in Dahlem, and were taken over after the war as the headquarters of the American Sector.

As early as 1934-35 a Luftwaffentechnische Akademie was constructed in Gatow on the Havel side of the Kladower Damm. Today this accommodates the Havelhöhe TB Hospital. A year later work was begun across the road on the

In the 1930s, analysts abroad tried to work out how the Nazi regime managed financially and *The Banker* — the organ of British banking — published a survey covering four years of National Socialism in their edition of February 1937. Initially the German government ignored the findings but the repercussions in the British and foreign press soon made it change its mind. On February 10 the Institute for Business Research, a German government office, published an attack on the article. A fortnight later *The Banker* was banned in Germany, and in the middle of March the *Völkischer Beobachter* published an extremely irritated and violent attack although it carefully refrained from entering into a discussion regarding the validity of its statements and deductions. *The Banker* article had explained that 'when Herr Hitler became Chancellor the German [financial] crisis had been overcome six months previously. Production touched its nadir in August 1932, and by December of that year it had risen by approximately 10 per cent (during the same period in 1931 it had fallen by about 20 per cent). The index of share prices, at the same time, rose by over 20 per cent. But while business during those months was undoubtedly on the upgrade, the condition of the population was not improving. Indeed, hourly wages according to the official index declined from June to December, 1932 by 1 per cent, while unemployment, under seasonal pressure, increased from 5.5 to 5.8 millions. The first task of the Hitler Government, therefore, was to reduce unemployment. Work had to be "created"; the problem was what kind? It was no use producing goods which depended for their sale upon an increasing purchasing power of the population. The ideal kind of work was the production of goods which would not apppear on the market. Roads, land amelioration schemes, military goods, such as barracks, guns, aeroplanes, etc., can be produced without any danger of flooding a market dependent upon the purchasing power of the masses.' A good example of creating work was the construction of the new terminal building at Tempelhof airfield, Berlin's main airport. *Above:* The current terminal had been designed by Paul and Klaus Engler and built in 1929. It was already very modern by the standards of the day but nevertheless Ernst Sagebiel was commissioned to produce a vast new concourse *(below)*.

The Banker: 'But the employment problem had another angle, dictated by finance. It was necessary to find work which would employ the maximum of labour at the minimum of cost. Herr Hitler's complete task, therefore, was to "create" work which, on the one hand, would not disturb the equilibrium of the market and which, on the other hand, would employ nearly everybody; whether skilled or not. These considerations determined the projects which were undertaken first — the construction of roads, barracks, fortifications, etc. The amount of money involved for purposes other than wages in this type of work, even if it is carried out on a gigantic scale, is not unduly large. It is doubtful, for instance, whether during the first year of the Hitler regime much work was "created" which involved direct labour costs of less than 50 per cent of the total. At the same time most of the workers engaged in public works earned less than 800 marks per annum. If we assume that direct labour costs were, on the average slightly less than 50 per cent, we arrive at the total expenditure of about 2,000 million marks per annum in order to employ one million workers. The number of employed during the first year of the Hitler regime increased by about 2.2 millions.' *Above:* This is another Sagebiel creation — the Luftkriegsschule at Gatow. The occasion: the swearing in of new recruits on the 18th anniversary of the death of Manfred von Richthofen — the Red Baron.

Luftkriegsschule (Air War Academy) and Fliegerhorst (Air Base) Gatow. This was taken over by the Royal Air Force in 1945 and played a prominent role in the Berlin Airlift of 1947-48. Today as the General-Steinhoff-Kaserne it accommodates headquarters of the 4. Luftdivision, the band of the 3. Luftdivision and the Luftwaffenmuseum with a wide-ranging collection of NATO and Warsaw Pact aircraft on display, but the airfield itself has been decommissioned.

New Luftwaffe barracks were also built during the period 1936-37 for Flak-Bataillon 32 on the Ruppiner Chaussee in the Heiligensee suburb of Berlin, and are now used by the Berlin Police, and another for the I. Bataillon, Luftgau-Nachrichten-Regiment 3 on the Hottengrund in Kladow, which later accommodated a British infantry battalion under the title of Montgomery Barracks until the reunification, since when they have housed Jägerbataillon 1 'Berlin'.

The most attractive of the barrack complexes in Berlin was the General-Göring-Kaserne, built for the Regiment 'General Göring' in Reinickendorf on the site of a former airship unit at a cost of 86 million Reichsmarks. Work began in 1936 and the barracks were occupied the following year, although work was not completed until 1939 on the other 120 buildings, including the officers' mess, indoor and outdoor swimming pools, gymnasia and a sports stadium.

Gatow was used by the RAF from 1945 to 1994, the Aviation War School of the Third Reich now the location of the Luftwaffe Museum.

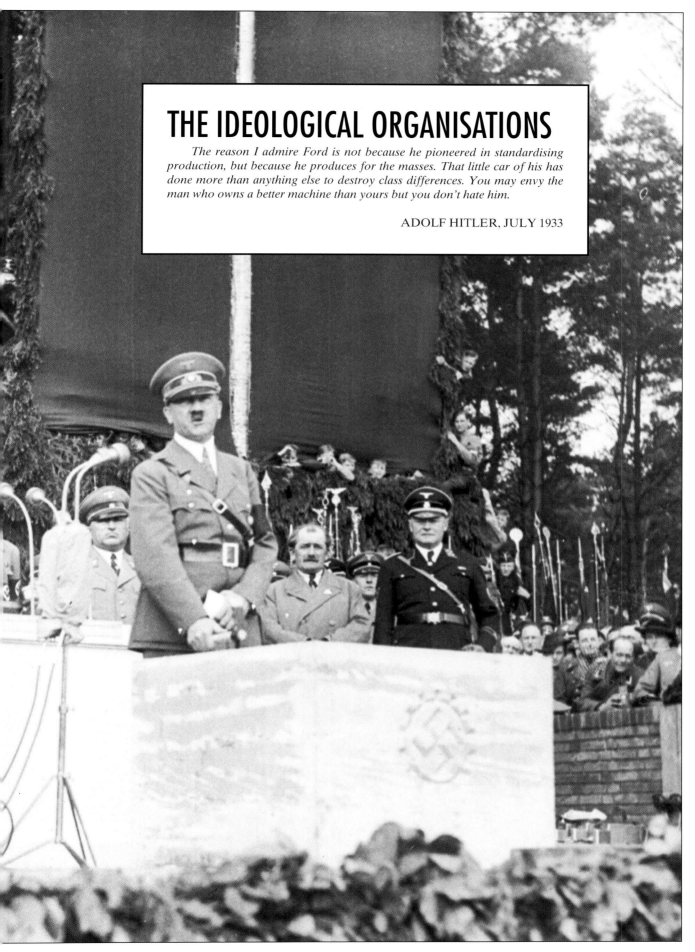

THE IDEOLOGICAL ORGANISATIONS

The reason I admire Ford is not because he pioneered in standardising production, but because he produces for the masses. That little car of his has done more than anything else to destroy class differences. You may envy the man who owns a better machine than yours but you don't hate him.

ADOLF HITLER, JULY 1933

Labour and Welfare

The traditional Socialist festival on May Day was taken over by the Nazis as a public holiday in 1933, when Hitler addressed the workers of the nation. Next day all trade union offices were closed down, their funds seized and their leaders detained, to be succeeded by the establishment of the Deutsche Arbeitsfront (DAF — German Labour Front) under Dr Robert Ley on May 10, covering all production and white-collar workers, as well as management staff, and offering voluntary membership.

Then on May 19 the Law on Trustees of Labour was passed, appointing 12 Reich Trustees of Labour for the regulation of wages and labour contracts within the various regions that had previously been negotiated between unions and employers. This was followed by the Law on the Organisation of National Labour of June 16, 1934, which fixed wages at the lowest rates reached during the depression, and continued to control wages as part of the regime's labour policy.

However, living standards slowly revived as more workers were taken on and businesses that had been close to

Left: **Dr Robert Ley had served in the German air arm during the war and had been captured by the French. He joined the NSDAP in 1925 when he became Gauleiter for Rhineland South. In 1933 he founded the Deutsche Arbeitsfront — basically a national trade union to which all workers had to belong.** *Above:* **Fehrbelliner Platz in Berlin could almost be called DAF-Platz due to the concentration of Labour Front buildings there. Building [1] was the Reichsleitung der DAF (managerial HQ); [2] housed the Verwaltungsbüro (administrative staff); [3] the Reichsgetreidestelle (Reich Corn Office) and [4] more of the DAF-Verwaltung. We have already seen how *The Banker* explained that Hitler had to create work and how incensed the Nazis were to its report. In February 1938 Hitler answered back in a long speech detailing the economic achievements of his regime: 'The total membership of the German Labour Front for 1937 is 17,973,000. After five years of National Socialist constructive work: 7,000 wage schedules, clearly defined legal relations, no hard-and-fast agreements, but minimum basic rates, wage scales according to performance, no class war with strikes and lock-outs, no wages under log standard, effective protection of all social interests, social settlement through the German Labour Front, social peace all round.'**

bankruptcy began to benefit from the revival of the economy and extended hours of work. Compulsory membership of the Reich Economic Chamber ensured that each branch of trade and industry was organised into groups centred on Industrial, Trade, Banking, Insurance, Energy, Artisan Trades or Transport Economic Groups. The state supervised and regulated overseas trade, capital investment and the supply of raw materials, as well as prices and wages.

Radios and loudspeakers were installed in all places of work so that Hitler's speeches could be broadcast

live and reach all the workers. Whenever he spoke the factory sirens would sound 'Cease Work' and the workers be obliged to listen dutifully under the eyes of Gestapo informers.

By the end of the 1930s, pressure from employers and the authorities made membership of the DAF virtually obligatory for all workers, and the DAF was enjoying an income over three times that of the Nazi Party. It also acquired a large business empire of its own with banks, insurance companies, housing associations and even a car plant, the Volkswagen-Werk at Wolfsburg.

One block away, at Nos. 174-177 Hohenzollerndamm, was the building occupied by the German Labour Front's life insurance department — the Versicherungsgebäude.

Now, with the swastika and gear wheel insignia of the DAF removed from above the entrance, the same building is used by the Berlin Senate.

Hitler went on to describe the improved working conditions in Germany: 'Holidays before the National Socialist regime were mostly at the worker's own expense, no legal claim, long period of waiting before the first holiday granted, insufficient holiday period, at the most five days. After five years of National Socialist constructive work, each working individual has a claim to holiday with pay, minimum, and not maximum holiday fixed, grading of holidays according to length of service in firm, age, number of years employed and difficulty of work; a short period of waiting, as a rule only six months, before the first holiday is granted, increased holiday period up to 18 days for young persons, holidays also for seasonal workers, healthy recreation by means of cheap Kraft durch Freude tours.' Hitler was referring here to the 'Strength through Joy' branch of the DAF which encouraged and promoted positive leisure activities. The department had its own cruise liners to take KdF members on holiday breaks and this picture shows the *Robert Ley*, left, and *Wilhelm Gustloff*, right.

In November 1933 Ley established two new departments within the DAF. The first was 'Schönheit der Arbeit' (Beauty of Labour), which was designed to persuade employers to improve the working conditions within their factories, while the second, 'Kraft durch Freude' (Strength through Joy), usually abbreviated to 'KdF', was intended to organise the free time of the labour force with sport and leisure activities. Physical exercise in the workplace was encouraged and youngsters expected to spend two hours a week doing it. These measures were also intended to encourage a spirit of community and egalitarianism with organised holidays within Germany as well as affordable sea cruises and the chance to own a motor car that had previously been only available to the rich. The ultimate aim was to engage all the worker's free time when he was not sleeping. Regular subscriptions toward the purchase of a KdF-Wagen, later known as the Volkswagen, also mopped up money available to the German consumer, which he would otherwise have sought to spend on goods the government could not supply in its drive for rearmament. By 1940 some 130,000 members of the Labour Front had registered their names for the car.

For the year 1937 Dr Ley could boast that the KdF had laid on over 7,000 theatrical performances, engaged seven million participants in organised sport, nine million in travel and rambling, 24 million in cultural and other activities, and had sent 180,000 on sea cruises. For the latter, the KdF purchased the liners *Der Deutsche*, *Sierra Cordóba* and *Stuttgart* from Norddeutsche Lloyd and chartered others, while having the *Wilhelm Gustloff* and *Robert Ley* especially built, although these last two were not ready until 1939 and soon afterwards were converted into hospital ships. By the time war broke out some 690,000 people had gone on KdF cruises, much to the envy of workers of other nations, visiting places as far afield as the Canary Islands. The cruises were used to educate the passengers in the Nazi concept, while Gestapo agents looked out for dissidents.

The KdF having signed an agreement with the Wehrmacht in 1935 to cater for the servicemen's free time, during the war the KdF provided entertainment behind the lines for the troops, including a theatre group travelling around in its own special train.

The ships, of course, would have an important role during war as troop transports, hospital ships and Kriegsmarine billet ships, and on January 30, 1945 the *Wilhelm Gustloff* was sunk in the Baltic by a Soviet submarine while evacuating people fleeing from the Red Army. Over 9,000 souls lost their lives in the attack.

Travel, hiking, and the organisation of holidays have developed considerably', explained Hitler. 'Cruises have been made to Norway, Madeira, the Azores and Italy. Since 1934 altogether 384 cruises with 490,000 participants, over 60,000 land trips with over 19 million participants, and 113,000 walking tours with some three million participants have been carried out. The German Labour Front has nine large ocean steamers at its disposal, four of which it owns. Expenditure up to date for the KdF fleet alone amounts to over 21 million Reichsmark. The total expenditure since 1934 for KdF, without investments and shipbuilding, amounts to approximately RM 77 million. Since the founding of KdF in 1934 a total of 155 million participants in the programmes has been counted. At the seaside resorts about 350,000 people were afforded an opportunity for sport. Over 4,500 sports instructors are in charge of sports activities. When has more ever been done for the worker?'

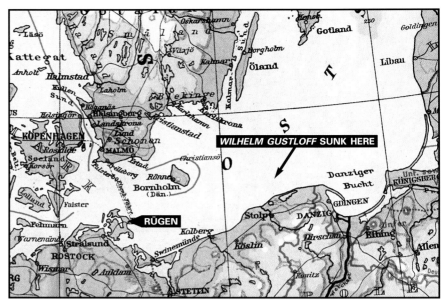

However the KdF's greatest material project was the construction of the KdF-Seebad Rügen on an eight-kilometre stretch of the Schmale Heide overlooking the Baltic at Prora. This massive sea bathing resort was intended to accommodate 20,000 holiday makers and 2,000 staff. The announced aim was to provide the German worker here with food, accommodation, bathing costume, towel and beach chair, for just two marks per day. 'The furnishing of the rooms would be simple, but modern. All bedrooms and living rooms would face the sea, be 2.2 x 4.75 metres in size, and equipped with two beds, a wash basin with running water, wardrobe and a sitting area with a table, chairs and an upholstered settee. All rooms would have central heating. Cafés and terraces, writing, reading and games rooms, bowling alleys, billiard rooms and covered relaxation areas would ensure that this was a first-class bathing resort and one that can be described as the most modern ever built.' The design eventually accepted by Ley was that of Clemens August Klotz, who had previously designed the Krössinsee and Vogelsang Ordensburgen (see pages 284-293).

In the centre a 600-metre-wide square, from which the complex would be administered, was flanked by two accommodation wings, each two kilometres long, giving an overall frontage of over 4½ kilometres. These accommodation wings were four storeys high, each wing being divided into four sections by cross-projecting buildings, ten in all, accommodating the staircases and lifts, as well as bathing and showering facilities, staff rooms, and shafts for the disposing of dirty linen and rubbish. Restaurants and other recreational facilities were located in the 100-metre-long seaward end of these projections. The ground floor of the accommodation blocks was used for children's rooms,

The holiday development designed by Clemens Klotz for the KdF at Prora on the island of Rügen in the Baltic was massive by any standards. The architect's model (above left) **and artist's impression** (above) **hardly convey the enormity of the main hotel block which ran for 4½ kilometres (over 2½ miles) . . . so no need for towels on deckchairs at KdF-Seebad Rügen!**

Surely the largest holiday hotel in the world. Rügen under construction in 1939. All rooms would have a sea view and cost two Reichsmarks per day per person.

After the war the Soviet Army occupied part of the northern wing and used the area and adjacent ruins for training purposes, including demolition exercises, but the basic structure proved surprisingly resistant. In the 1950s construction work was resumed on three parts of the southern and two parts of the northern wings with a view to providing holiday accommodation for the workforce of the German Democratic Republic. When the Nationale Volksarmee was founded in 1956, part of the northern wing was taken over to accommodate the 8. Motorschützendivision (8th Motor Rifle Division) of three motor rifle regiments, an armoured regiment and an artillery regiment, plus supporting chemical, transport, supply and rocket battalions, involving about 15,000 men. These were later joined by the DDR's only parachute battalion. Various training establishments were also set up here, including a secret one for training foreign guerillas, as well as a military hospital and holiday facilities.

offices and staff accommodation, and also provided wide throughways from the beach to the rear. The complex had its own railway station, while garages for 3,000 cars, and a quay with two piers, 300 and 800 metres long respectively, were proposed to enable ships to dock opposite the central square.

The foundation stone was laid on May 2, 1936, and 48 construction firms were involved, employing some 5,000 workers accommodated in hutted camps, but work came to an abrupt halt with the outbreak of war on September 1, 1939. By this time the foundations had been completed and the basic structure of most buildings up to roof level, but there were no staircases or windows. During the course of the war Russian slave labour was used to provisionally complete some of the southern wing's dormitory accommodation in order to house bombed-out families from Hamburg. These refugees, and others later from the east, were also accommodated in the staff quarters and workers' camps.

Rügen island lay within the Soviet zone of Germany and became a restricted military area but, with the demise of the German Democratic Republic, the military have withdrawn from the site. Today, small parts of the massive complex are in use, but most of it stands empty and derelict. With tourism to the Baltic shores on the increase, there have been several ambitious plans for a new development of the property allthough none of these have led to anything substantial. In September 2004, part of the complex was sold at an auction for 625,000 euros.

STADT DES KdF-WAGENS

Together with Dr Ferdinand Porsche, the designer of his 'People's Car', Hitler examines the model of the Volkswagen factory to be built at a new town just west of Fallersleben which was to be known as Stadt des KdF-Wagens. (The name was changed to Wolfsburg after a local geographical feature on July 26, 1945.)

In 1933 the German production of motor cars was ludicrously small in comparison not only with the United States, but also with other European countries — a paltry 46,000 per annum. The first step towards making Germany motor-minded was to free people from the earlier conception that the motor vehicle was an article of luxury. That is natural enough, if in a country there are only two, three, or four hundred thousand motor vehicles on the roads. But in the case of the German people there is a demand for six or seven million motor cars! Here the only decisive factor is that the cost of the production and maintenance of this most modern means of transport shall be brought into conformity with the people's income. 'That is impossible!' was the objection raised in 1933. To this I could give only one answer: 'What is possible in other countries shall be possible in Germany as well!'.

The motor car, then, must become the people's means of transport! Since this goal could not be reached with car prices as they were then, I had already determined before I came into power, that immediately the government fell into our hands I would begin the preliminary work for the production of a car whose price would enable it to become a real means of transport for the great mass of the people. By this means the motor car would at least cease to be an instrument of class division.

The significance of this factory in its wider effects is still today recognised by very few. The People's Car will not be a rival to other automobile manufacturers. For he who purchases this car and not a Mercedes does not do so because he is an enemy of the Daimler factory but merely because he cannot buy a Mercedes. It is very simple, sober considerations which compel folk to turn to the cheaper makes. He who can afford to buy the dearer car will do so in any event, but the great mass of people cannot do so. It is for the great mass of people that this car has been designed. Its purpose is to answer their needs in transport and it is intended to give them joy.

It shall therefore be named after the National Socialist organisation Kraft durch Freude the 'KdF-Car'. And together with the building of the factory there will be constructed a model German workingmen's town which shall be a school for the art of town planning and of social settlement. We want through the construction of this town to show how National Socialism views these problems, how it attacks them and how it solves them. This factory shall be a symbol of the National Socialist German Community of the People.

ADOLF HITLER, MAY 26, 1938

The acquisition by the DAF of the Volkswagen factory at Wolfsburg came about as a result of Hitler's desire for a 'People's Car' that would be accessible to the masses. On May 11, 1933, he met Dr Ferdinand Porsche at the Kaiserhof Hotel in Berlin and was delighted to learn that Porsche had already done some work for the NSU company on the design of a cheap car. Porsche's design met Hitler's specifications for a four-seater able to travel at up to 100 kilometres per hour on the autobahns (construction of which Hitler had announced only at the beginning of the month) and be air-cooled because of the severe winter conditions and shortage of garages. The only discrepancies were in the fuel consumption of seven litres of petrol per 100 kilometres (roughly 40 mpg), when Porche's model required eight, and the sales price, which Hitler set at no more than 1,000 RM (then the equivalent of £50).

'In a few years, however, the vast additional results of the Four Years Plan will supplement these successes', claimed Hitler, and in a direct jibe at *The Banker* article: 'What, in view of a world achievement of this scope, is the purpose of the absurd comments of critics at home and abroad, of the scribbling of half-witted or ill-intentioned journalists or parliamentary incapables? Is it not finally a joke of history when in those very countries which are themselves suffering from depressions, people consider it necessary to criticise us and to give us good advice. Without advice and above all without help from others, we have attempted to over- come a state of distress in the face of which many another country is still helpless. I should now like to present to the German people the results in some other fields of our work. In 1932 there were 56,400 motorcycles, 41,000 passenger vehicles and 7,000 commercial vehicles. Now in 1937 there are [respectively] 234,000, 216,000 and 59,600. Altogether 5½ years ago Germany had 1½ million motor vehicles, as compared with three million to-day. The Volkswagen [People's Car] will, however, supply very different figures in a few years time.' *Above:* Porsche shows Hitler a model of the VW (pronounced in German 'Fow-Vay').

At the Berlin Motor Show in 1934, Hitler announced that 'due to the superb designer Porsche and his staff, we have succeeded in completing preliminary design for the German People's Car.' The first three hand-made models, then known as the Volksauto, began their road trials on October 12, 1936, and by that Christmas had completed 30,000 miles. The main fault discovered was the weakness of the cast crankshaft, which was replaced by a forged one.

While this was going on, Dr Porsche was touring the plants of the major car manufacturers in the United States, as he realised that the only way to lower the price to Hitler's specification was through the use of mass production methods. In America he even managed to recruit 20 experienced workers of German descent to return to Germany with him to help set up his factory.

By January 1938 a 10,000-acre site had been acquired near Schloss Wolfsburg, about 50 miles east of Hannover. This lay astride the main railway line to Berlin and alongside the Mittelland Canal, important for the carriage of heavy goods. The mile-long factory along the north side of the canal was designed by four of Germany's leading industrial architects: Emil Mewes, Fritz Schlupp, Martin Kremmer and Karl Kohlbecker.

The KdF Saver Card. Hitler admitted that it was necessary to guide the purchasing power of the German people because if they spent all their money on foodstuffs, etc, — which could not be produced in sufficient quantity to go round — it would lead to a catastrophe. Instead the People's Car would serve as an object which they could spend their money on which would at the same time bring in hundreds of millions of marks each year in investment in German industry.

Left: **The foundation stone to the KdF factory was laid on May 26, 1938 (see also pages 248-249).** *Right:* **When we first visited the factory in 1976 while researching the feature in** *After the*

Battle **No. 12 we were told that the foundation stone had been broken up. But lo and behold it was unearthed in 1998 and is now displayed in the factory museum.**

In the middle of the Czechoslovakian crisis, Hitler took time off to lay the foundation stone before a 70,000-strong crowd on May 26, 1938. The stone had to be sealed without the intended capsule containing copies of the plans of the factory, as the latter were not yet ready, but three prototypes were on display for the ceremony out of the 60 that had been hand-built at the Daimler-Benz plant in Stuttgart. In his speech Hitler used the term KdF-Wagen, much to Dr Porche's surprise, for the car was already commonly known as the Volkswagen and one of the engine designers, Francis Reimspiess, on his own initiative had even designed the now famous VW badge for it. On leaving, Hitler had Porsche's son, Ferry, drive him in one of the prototypes to the station.

A town for the proposed 90,000 factory workforce was to be constructed on the south side of the canal, but there was a shortage of local labour, which Hitler eventually resolved by asking Mussolini to send him some unemployed Italians, who were then housed in hutted camps. The first thousand workers soon arrived, but by the outbreak of war the factory had yet to produce a single car. The 210 KdF-Wagens that had been produced elsewhere were either written off during testing or given to Nazi Party officials.

However, Hitler's intention was that within ten years every German worker would be able to own a KdF-Wagen, and he had the whole scheme assigned to the KdF organisation, which became resposible for overseeing the construc-

tion and running of the factory. Then on August 1, 1938, an ingenious stamp saving scheme was introduced, whereby workers could order and subscribe to a KdF-Wagen at an easily affordable price of 5RM per week. Altogether 336,686 people applied and eventually the sum of 280 million marks was raised, although no cars were ever delivered.

When building operations ceased at the end of 1940, only 2,690,000 square feet of the planned 6 million square feet of the factory had been completed. The town, known as KdF-Stadt but unmarked on the maps, had flats for 2,358 families. The Italian workers gradually dispersed and were replaced by Belgian, French, Danish, Dutch and Russian forced labourers, eventually totalling 17,365 in 1944. The factory produced

Hitler enjoying the prototype of the cabriolet version of the Volkswagen (seen in the top picture), with Dr Porsche holding **the wheel. The latter's son Ferry would take over and drive the Führer to the station.**

In the event, the war intervened and no cars were ever delivered to KdF savers. The factory was turned over to war production and was badly damaged during several bombing raids. Wolfsburg fell within the British zone and Major Ivan

Hurst *(left)* was given the job of seeing if the plant could be switched to production of the Volkswagen — initially to provide vehicles for the British occupation forces. Major Hurst and his staff worked a miracle and the rest, as they say, is history.

two military versions of the car during the war: the cross-country four-seater Kübelwagen, which was light enought to be manhandled if it became stuck for lack of four-wheel drive, and the Schwimmwagen amphibious version with a retractable propeller. Output amounted to 55,000 Kübelwagens and 15,000 Schwimmwagens, but this involved only a small part of the factory space, which also produced Ju 88 aircraft, mines, heating stoves and handgrenades, as well as providing facilities for airframe repairs and even assembling V1 flying bombs later on in the war.

The factory was bombed four times in 1944, sustaining over 2,000 hits with 55

killed and 160 wounded in all. By May 1945, 58 per cent of the factory was in ruins and 200 machines had been removed at the last minute to mine shafts at Longwy to save them from the advancing Russians, but it was American troops that discovered the factory after the forced labourers began looting the town when their SS guards fled. A Wehrmacht padre and an English-speaking French priest drove to the nearest American-occupied location at Fallersleben to appeal to the American troops to restore order, which they did when they learned that 30 American children of the German-American workers recruited before the war were in danger.

When the British Army took over the area as part of the British Zone of Occupation, the factory was placed under guard and then taken over as a vehicle repair workshop. In August 1945 the town's name was changed to Wolfsburg and the British Military Government assigned Major Ivan Hirst, REME, to the factory with a view to resuming car production. By the end of the month Kübelwagens were being assembled once more from remaining parts. A month later credit was made available for the production of the Volkswagen car, of which 58 had been produced by the end of the year, and 9,871 by the end of 1946. Eventually the factory was handed over to the German authorities on October 8, 1949.

In October 1949 the factory was handed over to the trusteeship of the new West German government and ten years later it became a public company. Some 280 million Reichsmarks had been paid in by the KdF savers during the Nazi era but it was not until October 1961 that a settlement was agreed in that savers could exchange their card — if fully paid up — for a credit of 600 Deutschmarks towards a new VW which were being retailed at DM 5,450. From then on sales of Hitler's People's Car went from strength to strength. The 100,000 mark had been passed in March 1950 and the 500,000 in July 1953.

By 1955 a million 'Beetles' had been produced *(left)* and with the completion of the 15,007,034th car on February 17, 1972, the production record held by the Model T Ford was overtaken. Manufacturing of the car ceased at Wolfsburg two years later but continued at a subsidiary factory at Emden until January 1978 whereupon production of thousands of more cars continued in Belgium and Mexico. *Right:* The very last KdF-Wagen came off the assembly line in Puebla, Mexico, on July 30, 2003. By then 21,529,464 People's Cars had been produced — surely the most enduring legacy from the Third Reich.

257

Robert Ley, left, worked closely with Baldur von Schirach, the young people's leader, as boys were drafted into the RAD at age 18.

Upon leaving school boys in Germany were directed to employment regardless of individual choice, often away from home and under communal apprenticeship arrangements with strictly disciplined conditions, and upon attaining the age of 18 both sexes became eligible for compulsory labour service in the Reichsarbeitsdienst (RAD). For males this entailed six months of endless drilling and route marches with highly polished shovels, apart from being employed on any work task in hand. The RAD leadership corps consisted predominently of men who had failed in life and been rejected by the Wehrmacht even in its reconstruction phase, a despicable and corrupt group that took spiteful delight in terrorising their young charges. Later on during the war the youngsters were also subjected to considerable pressure to volunteer for the Waffen-SS, which was not provided for under the National Conscription Law and consequently had to rely on volunteers to fill its ranks. Military conscription took place at 19 years of age until 1940, then dropped to 18 for 1941-42, and then to 17½. In the autumn of 1944 a major campaign was launched encouraging 16-year-olds to volunteer, and allegedly claimed 70 per cent success. The remainder were conscripted in February 1945, and those born in 1929 on March 5.

RAD service for females was voluntary until 1939, when a compulsory term of six months was introduced, the emphasis being on training them as future mothers and homemakers, and also as farmers' wives in keeping with the Nazi ideals of a vast agricultural community spreading out to the East, for which their primary task was to keep fit.

Over nine million RAD girls were mobilised for agricultural work in 1939, and others employed in armament factories. From 1940 onwards teams were also sent East to assist the SS-Rasse-

Books and magazines extolled the virtues of the labour corps: 'The closed marching ranks give a picture of sturdy strength. A new nation has arisen. On the effort of the individual will depend the success of the whole. The nation has realised that distress and adversity can only be overcome if each one ceases to do as he pleases and instead is prepared and willing to do his utmost when called upon. The spade of the Labour Service symbolises reconstruction of the Reich.'

und Siedlungshauptamt (Race and Resettlement Head Office) resettlement programme by preparing requisitioned properties for occupation by German settlers and establishing schools for their children.

Then in August 1941 a further six months' War Service was added to their RAD time for work with the Wehrmacht, government offices, hospitals and medical or social institutions. Although the Nazis were opposed to the militarisation of women, in practice the lives of the Wehrmacht auxiliaries became increasingly regimented, since they lived in hostels under the supervision of Nationalsozialistische Frauenschaft (NSF — National Socialist Women's Organisation) personnel. From mid-1943 onwards women were employed in servicing, but not firing, anti-aircraft batteries, taking over the manning of searchlights the following year. Eventually some 50,000 women were employed in the anti-aircraft defence operations and a further 30,000 on searchlights. In addition there were about 470,000 female auxiliaries with the Wehrmacht, mainly with the Replacement Army, 20,000 as signallers and staff personnel with the field armies, 130,000 with the Luftwaffe and 20,000 with the Kriegsmarine.

Throughout the war foreign workers were employed on a large scale to make up for the numbers of Germans that had been drafted into the Wehrmacht or employed in the armament industry. The economy needed an additional 500,000 agricultural workers, 300,000 metal workers, 140,000 construction workers and 50,000 miners. By the autumn of 1944 there were almost eight million foreign workers in Germany, of whom a quarter were prisoners of war. Some 2.8 million came from the Soviet

Union, 1.7 million from Poland, 1.3 million from France and 600,000 from Italy. About half the Soviet and Polish workers were women with an average age of 20. In addition there were some 650,000 concentration camp inmates, mainly Jews, employed in the armament industry.

In 1942 Fritz Sauckel was charged by Hitler to mobilise labour from the occupied territories. More than five million foreign workers were press-ganged into his labour camps and he has been described as the most notorious slave-driver in history. Thousands of workers died under his harsh jurisdiction and Sauckel was tried and found guilty of war crimes at Nuremberg. He was executed on October 10, 1946.

Prisoners of war were primarily employed in agriculture, where there had been a tremendous shortfall of labour even before the war. Then they were employed improving the transport network in the East and building air raid shelters in the cities, where the organisation of prisoner of war glazier and roofing battalions proved a great success in restoring bomb-damaged buildings. Gradually more and more were utilised in the manufacture of war material.

On March 21, 1942 Fritz Sauckel, Gauleiter of Thuringia, was appointed General Plenipotentiary for Labour Assignment. He began by having factories inspected to ensure that they had no excess of skilled labour and that a sufficient number of women were being employed in suitable jobs. He then extended the working week to a minimum 54 hours, and ordered that working conditions and wages for volunteer workers from occupied territories should be the same as for Germans. The latter did not apply to either Soviets or Poles, and was not out of any sense of humanity, but simply a realistic appraisal of the situation ensuring maximum productivity. Hitherto employers had preferred employing foreign labour as the same regulatory conditions of pay and working conditions did not apply to them as they did to Germans.

Attempts to attract volunteer workers from the occupied territories eventually produced only 200,000 of the five million that were employed, and conditions for the enforced slave labour were appallingly primitive and pay abysmal, with typhus and other illnesses wreaking havoc among the undernourished workers. Conditions in the Ruhr coal mines and the Krupp armament work camps were particularly bad.

Hitler's first great pronouncement to German workers took place on National Labour Day — May 1, 1933. A reputed two million were gathered at the Tempelhof Field in Berlin to listen to his major speech in which he announced the introduction of compulsory labour service. He said it was 'to teach the German nation once more that manual labour does not degrade or dishonour but rather does honour to everyone who performs it faithfully and conscientiously. The motto for the day must be "Honour work and respect the worker". Further it is our intention to start in a large way the public provision of work this year [the job creation discussed earlier in *The Banker* article]. We have made a programme of road building, a gigantic task which will demand millions.' Thus the network of Reichsautobahns was born.

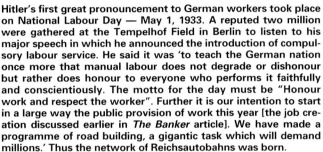

The construction plan for the Reich's new dedicated network of motor roads — the autobahns — was first announced by Hitler at a rally held on the Tempelhofer Feld in Berlin on May 1, 1933. He had already given encouragement to the German motor car industry on February 11 at the opening of the Automobile Exhibition in Berlin, which he had substantiated by abolishing the motor tax on new vehicles on April 10. Then on April 6 he had discussed the subject with Willy Hof, the racing car enthusiast and chief proponent of the autobahn plan. Hof was managing director of the Hafraba Company, which had been established in 1926 to investigate the possibility of establishing a motor road that would link Lübeck, Hamburg, Hannover, Kassel, Frankfurt-am-Main, Karlsruhe and Basel, with possible further extensions to Zürich, Airolo, Lugano, Milan and Genoa, thus connecting with the new Italian autostrada system. In August 1932 the company had applied for the construction of the first stretch of 99.8 kilometres, 'Main-Neckar', from Wiesbaden and Frankfurt/Main via Darmstadt to Mannheim and Heidelberg. Construction cost was estimated at 30.5 million marks, but the question of whether this should be privately funded against road tolls or be a public way had yet to be resolved by the Reich Traffic Ministry.

Dr Fritz Todt, who had joined the Party in 1922, was appointed to oversee the huge project to construct the German autobahn network, holding the official title of Generalinspektor für das deutsche Strassenwesen.

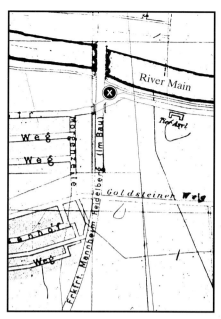

Four months later Hitler turned the first sod. In his speech on September 23 inaugurating work on the Frankfurt to Heidelberg section, he said that 'the significance of the vast work on which they were entering would be fully appreciated only in later decades. They were creating new arteries for traffic. Six thousand four hundred kilometres of new motor roads were planned as a first step in the fight against unemployment. The fight must be waged to remove its present distress. The best possible way to bring the German people back into work is, as I see it, to set German economic life once more in motion through great monumental works.' The position of the sod-bustin' operation just short of the River Main is marked [X].

Centre: The spot where the first spadeful of earth was turned was later memorialised in true Nazi fashion . . . but what happened to the ceremonial spade? *Left:* After research with the historical archives in Frankfurt, we found the spot — or what was left of it — as there is nothing now to mark its significance, save for a fragment of stone. The road is the entry/exit on the eastern side of the Frankfurt to Darmstadt autobahn.

A fast highway had already been constructed between Bonn and Cologne in 1929 under the patronage of Konrad Adenauer, then Lord Mayor of Cologne (and later to become the first Chancellor of the German Federal Republic), but it lacked a central dividing strip. There was also the AVUS, the dual-purpose automobile road and racetrack that had been built in Berlin between 1909 and 1921, although it had not been foreseen as part of the national road network, and was not incorporated as an autobahn until 1940.

Hitler regarded it as imperative to go in for the construction of the whole network, which he saw as opening up a new era in replacing the outmoded system of long-distance roads in existence. He also saw it providing jobs for 300,000 of the unemployed. The Reichswehr expressed fears that such prominent landmarks would serve to guide enemy aircraft and wanted none constructed near the country's boundaries in case they should serve as easy invasion routes, and the Reichsbahn (State Railways) objected for fear of competition with the conveyance of goods traffic. These objections found no sympathetic hearing.

The 1933 plan put before Hitler envisaged a seven-year construction programme once the specifics of the autobahns had been determined, the latter involving such matters as lane widths, connections to the normal road system, parking areas, petrol stations, restaurants, maintenance depots, etc, for which existing examples in Italy could be studied. The country's existing roads amounted to 300,000 kilometres, of which 25,000 kilometres involved long-distance traffic. The autobahn network was planned to add a further 6,400 kilometres to the system while blending with the landscape as far as possible.

On June 23, 1933, the establishment of the Reichsautobahnen Project was announced under the chairmanship of Generaldirektor Julius Dorpmüller of the Reich Traffic Ministry, who was to become Reich Traffic Minister in 1937, and with Willy Hof as the Managing Director. At the same time Dr Fritz Todt was appointed Inspector General of German Road Traffic, the project overseer directly responsible to the Cabinet. The State Railways provided the 50 million marks founding capital.

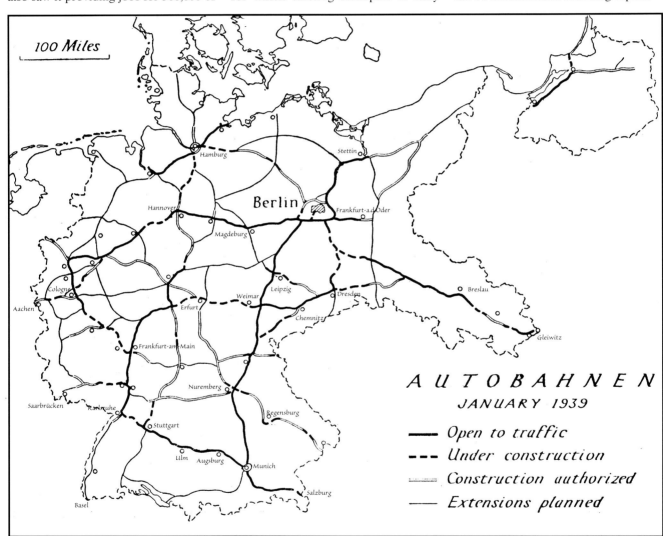

The project originally provided for 4,500 miles of road but this was later extended by another 2,000 miles. Construction rate was to be 650 miles per year with a labour force of 150-200,000. The initial plan was for six principal autobahns. These comprised two running across the country from north to south, three from west to east, and one from north-west to south-east. The first north-south route runs from Hamburg to Hannover, Frankfurt and Basel, and the second route runs from Stettin to Berlin, Leipzig, Nuremberg, Munich and so to the Austrian frontier near Salzburg. This route indirectly serves the Brenner Pass. The west-east roads run from Aachen on the Dutch and Belgian frontiers to Cologne, Hannover, Magdeburg, Berlin, Frankfurt-an-der-Oder and then to the Polish frontier west of Posen; **from Saarbrücken to Frankfurt-am-Main, Erfurt, Weimar, Chemnitz, Dresden, Breslau and to Gleiwitz and Beuthen on the Polish frontier; and from Karlsruhe to Stuttgart, Ulm, Augsburg and Munich. The diagonal road from north-west to south-east follows the line of the lower Elbe and upper Oder valleys from Hamburg to Berlin and Breslau. The new highways began and ended at strategic points on the frontiers of the country and served all the important industrial areas and regional administrative centres. All cities and other built-up areas were avoided, the autobahns usually passing at a distance of from two to eight miles from their outskirts, so that high-speed long-distance traffic might avoid the congested streets of all the great cities. The map shows the state of play in 1939.**

Dr Todt based the selection and survey of routes on considerations of traffic flow, both actual and potential, economic requirements and topographical details. He also decided the basic standards of design, but modifications were made to meet local conditions, and these were controlled from 15 provincial offices. It is significant that the scheme was operated by railway engineers rather than by civil engineers, and the autobahnen incorporated several characteristic features of railway lay-out, such as separated tracks and long uninterrupted stretches for high speed. The new roads were designed for 100 mph requiring a minimum sight distance of about 1,000 ft in flat country, depending on the gradient. Curves were similarly governed by gradient and speed. The completed road consisted of two carriageways each with a nominal width of 24 ft 9 in, separated by a central grass strip 16-20 ft. wide. This strip was sometimes planted with trees or shrubs which helped to prevent dazzle from headlights, or in some cases in forested areas to mask the road from oblique angles in the air. In the mountainous areas the lanes were either at different levels or completely separated, which served a similar purpose in eliminating headlamp glare. In addition, the centre of each carriageway was provided with a strip of luminous paint to guide drivers during mist and fog. *Right:* Special machinery was used at all stages of construction including an electrically-operated concrete construction train, stretching the whole width of the road moving on rails. The mixers were replenished by means of narrow-gauge railway. About 240 yards of concrete could be laid in this way per day in a single shift, though higher figures were recorded.

The surface of the concrete was finished with great precision to obtain a fine grain, first by machines and then by hand. The limit of error allowed was four millimetres in four metres. In order to prevent the concrete from drying too quickly in wind or sun and to prevent damage by rain, portable tents mounted on the rails were used to cover the surface, followed by a layer of wet sand, moist straw or woven straw mats. It was usually four weeks or more before the road was opened to traffic.

The first surfacing work began in July 1934 between Frankfurt and Darmstadt and this became the first autobahn opened by Hitler on May 19, 1935.

Hitler turned the first symbolic sod near Frankfurt-Goldstein on September 3, 1933, but little practical progress was made until the following year, when work began on March 21, 1934, near Unterhaching on the Munich-Salzburg stretch that would link Hitler's favourite locations. On the same day Göring initiated work on the Berlin-Stettin autobahn at Finowfurt, while Hess did the same on the unique canal barge lift at Niederfinow nearby. Already 15,000 workers were engaged on 22 locations throughout the Reich. In fact no more than 124,483 workers came to be engaged at any one time, although about the same number were employed in the administrative side of the project.

On May 19, 1935, Hitler was able to open the first completed stretch of autobahn between Frankfurt-am-Main and Darmstadt. A snag soon arose when cars using the new autobahns found that they were overheating, not having been designed to sustain high speeds for long periods, which provided a new problem for the motor industry.

We apologise for no comparison but this stretch is probably the busiest in Germany. Not only has it now been widened to eight lanes but the bridges seen in the photos with 'Frankfurt' and 'Darmstadt' painted on them have gone. And it is really dangerous to stop and take photographs . . . apart from being an offence. One cannot help hearing the echo of Hitler's words as one drives along: 'A mammoth work must give witness to our will, our dilligence, our talent and our strength of purpose.' So the German autobahn network is another direct legacy from the Third Reich. In Hitler's long statement to the Reichstag on February 20, 1938 concerning the economic progress made by the National Socialist state at the end of the first Four Year Plan, he announced that 1,500 miles were under construction. 'The system of autobahns is the largest building undertaking in the world', he said, 'and already, with a displacement of 240 million cubic metres of earth, by far exceeds the building achievement of the Panama Canal. Also approximately 3,400 bridges have been built in connexion with the new motor roads.'

So before we close this section on the Reichsarbeitsdienst, it is important to realise that Dr Todt's work did not just concern the autobahns. There were basically three different classes of roads: the Reichsstrassen (25,675 miles): Landstrassen 1. Ordnung (First Class roads — 52,354 miles) and Landstrassen 2. Ordnung (Second Class roads — 54,155 miles). Finally there were 61,000 miles of Gemeindestrassen or country lanes linking rural communities. On November 16, 1935, Dr Todt announced that in order to bring about a standardisation in the Reich's roads, a model section was being prepared to the new standard of eight to ten metres. Reichstrasse 86 is akin to Route 66 in the

USA: a great trunk route from Pomerania in the north via Berlin and Munich to Garmisch-Partenkirchen on the Austrian border. 'Section No. 2/86 will always be illustrious in the annals of road-making in Germany', said Dr Todt. 'It is the first time that a 60-mile-long road has been simultaneously and throughout its length regulated and reconstructed. The Munich-Garmisch road will be a model section and an examplar for other roads.' *Above:* Reichsstrasse 8 crossing the Mangfall river valley on a prototype bridge designed by German Bestelmeyer which was used in many other locations. This particular bridge was blown up in 1945 and has since been rebuilt in a different style *(below).*

As it was essential that Nazi Party functionaries were instilled with the National Socialist doctrine and creed, training establishments were set up all over the Reich. The central college for the Deutsche Arbeitsfront was located in the grounds of an old castle at Erwitte, just east of the Ruhr. Under the direction of Dr Ley, the property was requisitioned to become Reichsschulungsburg Erwitte.

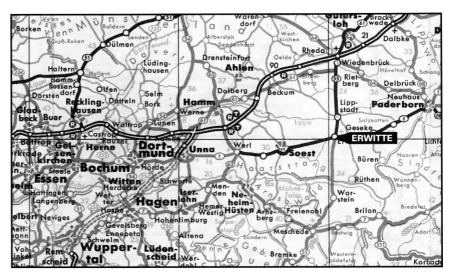

By 1934 a proliferation of Nazi Party training schools had been established at area (Gau) and district (Kreis) level throughout the Third Reich. As Reich Organisations Leader, Dr Robert Ley was anxious to ensure a degree of conformity within the system and therefore decided to establish a central training establishment for higher Party officials. The site chosen was that of the old moated castle at Erwitte, near Lippstadt

in Westphalia. Erwitte was then only a village of about 2,000 inhabitants, but was about to receive urban status with its 1,100th anniversary in March 1936, when Hitler accepted the offer of honorary citizenship.

The walls and moat of the ancient castle had all but disappeared, leaving only a stately mansion built in 1700 that was in dire need of renovation, and a large adjacent outbuilding for the administration of the estate. These two buildings and seven acres of accompanying land were purchased by the Gau of Westphalia South in January 1934 with the intention of setting up a local training establishment for regional party officials. However, the following July the project was taken over by the Deutsche Arbeitsfront, which lifted the school to a national level, and by November of that year it had acquired the title of Reichsschulungsburg Erwitte under Ley's auspices. A further ten and then seven acres were later added to the site.

Above: **This is the old mansion as it was when taken over by the DAF and converted into their training school.**

The main building at Erwitte is now a hotel.

Many of the buildings erected for the school remain virtually unchanged — like the guardhouse at the main gate.

A team of 50 members of the Voluntary Labour Service had established a camp in the grounds in 1933, these numbers being increased to 216 with the introduction of the compulsory Labour Service later that year, and work on the renovation of the mansion began under the direction of Julius Schulte-Frohlinde, including the construction of a new bridge connecting it with the town. The entrance hall was converted into a 'Hall of Honour' with a large eagle and a memorial plaque to the Feldherrnhalle 16. The building's four floors provided class and conference rooms, a library, reading and writing rooms, with bedrooms and dormitories above and a canteen and ablutions in the cellars. Dr Ley also had a room permantly reserved for his use within the building, as he frequently visited the establishment.

The estate administrative building (Renteigebäude) was converted into the main dining hall and kitchen with sleeping accommodation above. A new L-shaped administrative building was built nearby to contain the guardroom, administrative offices, the warden's appartment and more sleeping and ablutions facilities. A flag staff and parade ground were set in the angle formed by this building. Parallel to the foot of the L another new building accommodated the commandant and four other apartments were provided for married staff.

Four open-air classroom areas were set out and the last acquisition of land was used to accommodate an open-air swimming pool, whose facilities were shared with the local community. Later additions to the establishment included the Horst Wessel Memorial Hall, which was opened in August 1938, a ten-metre-high memorial, three semi-detached, half-timbered housing blocks for the staff, and a garage and workshop complex. A mock tower was constructed at the south-east corner of the estate to house a transformer. Finally, the old avenue leading from the west gate to the mansion was replanted with chestnuts.

On November 24, 1935, Ley officially opened the new Reichsschulungsburg Erwitte in a festive inauguration ceremony.

The retention of National Socialist insignia on buildings or memorials was forbidden by the Allies after the war (we will discuss this in detail in our final chapter) so it is very rare to find a Nazi-era eagle (by Willy Meller) still in place even if it has been de-Nazified by the removal of the swastika. *Below:* **This is the former Horst Wessel Hall today . . .**

. . . **although this bird has flown from his perch! Naturally it was another of Kurt Schmid-Ehmen's eagles.**

Above: **Another adler greeted visitors as they arrived in the main entrance hall to 'Schloss Erwitte'.** *Right:* **It, too, has now disappeared.**

Originally, Erwitte was just one of several training establishments run by the Deutsche Arbeitsfront and intended primarily as a training school for DAF officials, but this was soon widened to encompass leading functionaries from all branches of the Party. This higher status was officially recognised in 1941 when the school's name was changed from 'Reichsschulungsburg der DAF' to 'Reichsschulungsburg der NSDAP'.

The school's first commandant was Gottfried Joest, formerly the deputy head of education for the Gau of Westphalia South. Training courses began in 1935 and continued right up until 1945. During these ten years a total of at least 8,000 trainees passed through the school. In this respect, Erwitte was an

incomparably more important training establishment than the much-publicised Ordensburgen at Krössinsee, Vogelsang and Sonthofen, which in name were the Party's chief ideological schools but in practice handled far less students and had their courses virtually stopped short by the outbreak of war.

The courses at Erwitte were usually of two to three weeks duration with 200-300 participants. For the students the day began at 6.45 a.m. with a bout of physical training, followed by showers and breakfast. They then paraded for the flag-raising ceremony at 7.55 a.m. before beginning a morning of 'preaching the national socialist word'. After lunch came more sport and lectures using film and slides, a route march or practice on the miniature shooting range. One hour per day was given over

Above: **A ceremony just below the eagle pillar to remember the dead. Note from the comparison opposite that the three stone memorial tablets no longer remain beneath the oak tree.** Below: **Parade of the political leaders of the SA and SS.**

to singing patriotic songs. The evenings were free for private study and reading newspapers and books from the extensive library. 'Lights out' was at 10 p.m.. There were excursions three times a week, either for walking out in Erwitte or for visiting such local attractions such as the Hermann Memorial. The establishment brochure read: 'Hearty comradeship binds the participants. Each leaves the castle rich with inner experience, doubly prepared to serve his people as a soldier of the Führer.'

Upon leaving the establishment the students were assessed on their behaviour and discipline, physical ability, comradeliness, characteristics, spiritual ability, general and special knowledge, strength of ideology, speaking ability, overall quality, and special remarks.

With the outbreak of war the mansion and new administrative building were used as a field hospital, but this was cleared for Party use in October 1940, only to be reinstated as a field hospital in March 1941, soon being overfilled with wounded soldiers. Nevertheless, the basic function as a

Party training establishment continued on a reduced basis throughout the war, particular emphasis beging given to the education of the Volksdeutsche, German emigrants from the conquered territories.

Left: **Dr Ley on an inspection tour. Erwitte was captured by the Americans at the beginning of April 1945, the school being handed over to British jurisdiction in 1946. Belgian troops were quartered there until 1948 when it became a rehabilitation unit**

for war wounded. The Bundeswehr occupied Erwitte from 1959 until 1993 when it was handed over to the town council. Today, apart from the Schloss Hotel, the complex is used as a hospital and physiotherapy clinic.

The Hitler Youth officially came into being at the Weimar rally in July 1926 when Kurt Gruber was appointed Reichsführer der Hitlerjugend, although embryo sections for those aged 14-18 had been formed in the Party as far back as 1921. The age limit was reduced to ten in 1928 and a girls' section added the following year, named the Bund Deutscher Mädel (BDM), the League of German Maidens, in 1930. Although at first sight the organisation might give the impression they were akin to scouting, in fact it went far deeper. As Hitler stated some years later: 'The youth of today is ever the people of tomorrow. For this reason we have set before ourselves the task of inoculating our youth with the spirit of this community of the people at a very early age; at an age when human beings are still unperverted and therefore unspoiled.'

Schools and Colleges

Left: **Baldur von Schirach was appointed the Party's Reichsjugendführer in October 1930 with Dr Adrian von Renteln** *(right)* **under him as Reichsführer der Hitlerjugend from November 1931.**

The Nazis seized on the youth of their country as a prime motivation of their cause. Education, sport and culture were all used for political purposes, for propaganda and for the physical and mental development of an Aryan race that would provide warriors and colonial settlers for the expansion to the East. Great emphasis was placed on healthy physical development, and all children and adults were encouraged to compete for the Reich Sport Badge, especially in connection with the 1936 Olympics.

Children were taught to idolise Hitler as in this song performed at the beginning of each day at a school in Cologne:

Führer, my Führer, bequeathed to me by the Lord,
Protect and preserve me as long as I live!
Thou hast rescued Germany from deepest distress,
I thank thee today for my daily bread.
Abide then long with me, forsake me not.
Führer, my Führer, my faith and my light!
Heil, my Führer!

Teachers flocked to join the Nationalsozialistische Lehrerbund (NSLB — National Socialist Teachers' League), as membership became a virtual criterium for the job. Lessons on race and German history reflected the ideological imperatives of the regime. The Party's open hostility toward intellectuals led to a marked drop in the numbers going on to

university, where the further education of women was discouraged.

Outside school all activities were organised by the Hitlerjugend (HJ — The Hitler Youth), membership of which was compulsory from December 1936. Boys and girls aged 10 to 14 were organised into units of the Deutsches Jungvolk (DJ — the young boys' sec-

tion of the Hitler Youth) and Jungmädelbund (JM — Young Maiden's League) respectively, going on to the Hitlerjugend proper and Bund Deutscher Mädel (BDM — League of German Maidens, the girls' organisation in the Hitler Youth) from 14 to 18, all units forming part of a framework within the Party Gau system.

In June 1932 von Schirach took over direct control. At that time numbers were around 35,000 but this had increased to six million by 1936 when membership became compulsory. Outdoor sports catered for the physical side of the National Socialist youth programme while new Adolf Hitler Schools would indoctrinate the mind.

On June 11, 1933 a large parade was held in Berlin's Grunewaldstadion; six days later von Schirach, seen *(left)* taking the salute, was appointed Jugendführer des Deutschen Reiches. Then on July 1 the Hitlerjugend and Bund Deutscher Mädel *(right)* were reorganised to compulsorily encompass all youth from six years upwards.

Some limited political education was combined with sports activities, camping and cross-country hikes that removed the children from the often strict disciplinary background at home to a more independent existence in which the development of leadership qualities was encouraged and discipline enforced by themselves. The Hitler Youth also included motorised, mounted, naval, air and signals branches. Participation in mass parades and rallies provided a means of excitement and involvement with the community as a whole. Boys received a certain amount of paramilitary training, including map reading and small-bore rifle shooting, and both sexes were given the exciting experience of gliding when possible. Attendance was compulsory and absence was checked on by the police.

Left: In this overhead view, von Schirach can be seen standing in the motor car on the left. Note how the Olympic Stadium, seen in our comparison *(right)*, has not yet been built (refer back to page 219). In September that year Hitler addressed more than 80,000 members of the Hitler Youth at Nuremberg: 'On the youth of Germany are set all our hopes, our people's confidence, and our faith. You are the living Germany of the future not an empty idea, no mere formula: you are blood of our blood, flesh of our flesh, spirit of our spirit, you are our people's future. Youth must take a "holy vow" that "never again for all time shall the German people tear itself asunder; never again shall its unity be broken up: it shall be in truth a people of brothers which no distress and no danger shall henceforth divide".'

With the publication of the law in December 1936 making membership of the Hitler Youth compulsory, the following month the Führer announced 'the establishment of the Adolf Hitler Schools as an organisation forming part of the Hitler-jugend.' These boys were pictured outside Witzleben station in Berlin, obviously about to entrain for camp.

Suitable children were selected to attend the Party's elite schools, where they were given special physical and political training for their future roles. These were the Adolf Hitler Schools set up in 1937 as a joint venture by Reichs-jugendführer (Reich Youth Leader) Baldur von Schirach and Reichsleiter Dr Robert Ley, who was also responsible for the Ordensburgen. The schools were rated as HJ units and came under von Schirach's administration and not under the normal state educational system, the teachers and staff being all members of the HJ and the pupils wearing DJ uniforms. In order to ensure the required standard of teaching, selected HJ and DJ leaders that had passed their Abitur (school-leaving exam) were sent to the HJ's own Erzieher-Akademie (teacher academy) for four half-year terms before going on to a further four to six half-year terms at university.

The future of the German people depends on its youth. The entire German youth must therefore be prepared for its future duties. The Government of the Reich has accordingly approved the following Law, which is hereby published:

1. *The entire German youth within the territory of the Reich is united in the Hitler Youth.*

2. *The entire German youth — apart from the education within the home and in school — is to be educated physically, mentally, and morally in the spirit of National Socialism for the service of the people and for the community of the people.*

3. *The task of educating the entire German youth in the Hitler Youth is entrusted to the Reich Youth Leader of the NSDAP. He thereby becomes 'Youth Leader of the German Reich'. He has the position of a Supreme Authority for the Reich with his office in Berlin and is immediately subordinate to the Führer and Chancellor of the Reich.*

4. *The regulations necessary for the execution of, or for additions to, this Law as well as the general directions for its application will be issued by the Führer and Chancellor of the Reich.*

HITLER YOUTH LAW, DECEMBER 1, 1936.

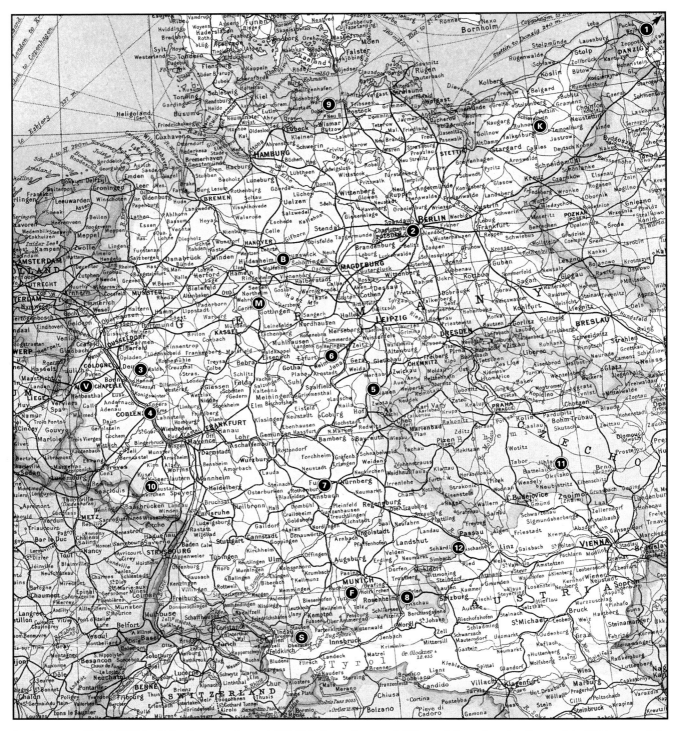

At the outset 12 Adolf Hitler Schools were planned: [1] Tilsit (in East Prussia, off the map), [2] Potsdam, [3] Waldbröl, [4] Koblenz, [5] Plauen, [6] Weimar, [7] Hesselberg, [8] Chiemsee, [9] Heiligendamm, [10] Landstuhl, plus Iglau [11] in Czechoslovakia and Braunau [12] in Austria. None of the planned school buildings materialised in time so, as an improvised measure, the Adolf Hitler School classes (secondary school age groups) were housed in the three Ordensburgen (literally meaning Castles of an Order of Knights). These were essentially Party universities for adult students and were located at Krössinsee [K], Sonthofen [S] and Vogelsang [V]. A Hitler Youth academy was set up at Braunschweig [B], and the elite from SA parents were sent to Feldafing [F]. A youth detention centre was set up at Moringen [M]. When Hitler gave his lengthy 'annual report' to the Reichstag in February 1938 (from which we have quoted earlier), he referred to the progress that had been made: 'At present for the Hitler Youth alone 1,400 homes and a large number of schools are under construction. The Youth Hostels Organisation has 2,000 youth hostels at its disposal; in 1937 some eight million spent a night in the hostels, this figure being over eight times as large as that for all the other youth hostels in the world together. The Naval Hitler Youth comprises 45,000 boys, the Motor Hitler Youth 60,000 boys. As part of the campaign for the encouragement of aviation, 55,000 members of the Jungvolk were trained in gliding for group activities. 74,000 boys of the Hitler Youth are organized in its flying units and 15,000 boys passed their gliding test in the year 1937 alone. Today 1,200,000 boys of the Hitler Youth receive regular instruction in small-bore rifle shooting from 7,000 instructors. In the interests of the health of these boys and girls, 4,000 doctors are engaged in the Hitler Youth, 800 dentists and some 500 chemists, who are assisted by 40,000 ambulance boys and 35,000 first-aid girls. Over 30,000 doctors nominated by the Public Health Department look after the health of the individual boys and girls. The whole German youth is medically examined once a year, i.e. over a million individuals being examined.'

Robert Ley (facing away from the camera), in his position of Reich Organisation Leader, carries out an inspection of the boys at the first Adolf Hitler School opened at Krössinsee on April 19, 1937 — appropriately on the eve of Hitler's birthday. On the left is the 'headmaster', Burgkommandant Otto Gohdes. The building in the background is the Ehrenhalle — the Hall of Honour.

It was intended that each Gau would have its own school, and by 1938 the foundation stones of ten of these schools had been laid, but construction was never completed. The first ten Adolf Hitler Schools were opened at Ordensburg Krössinsee in April 1937, each being represented by a 7th-year class from Tilsit, Potsdam, Waldbröl, Koblenz, Plauen, Weimar, Hesselberg, Chiemsee, Heiligendamm and Landstuhl, all being transferred to Ordensburg Sonthofen in September 1937.

Right: **In this rather grainy shot taken from the second of the two towers, the Ehrenhalle can be seen at the rear of the parade ground.** *Below:* **The hall was destroyed by arson in the post-war years.**

Ordensburg Krössinsee — then and now. This is the main entrance with the symbolic twin towers. Being located within the Soviet zone of occupation after the war, it was taken over by the Red Army and is laterly occupied by the Polish Army.

A further two classes from Wartha and Iglau were added during the war, the schools being accommodated in old buildings, and from 1941-44 pupils of Adolf Hitler Schools from Franken, Moselland and Westmark were moved to Ordensburg Vogelsang. It was also intended to add a BDM school to each Adolf Hitler School, but again these plans were not realised.

The school was beautifully situated on the edge of the lake of the same name. On the left in this picture from 1937 lie Blocks 1-10 of the living accommodation (one hesitates to call them barracks) while the semi-circular area on the right is what was called the 'Thing-Platz'. 'Thing', being an English word, gives us completely the wrong connotation as to what it means in German but, at the same time, it is also a difficult word to translate and understand properly but it basically means a Germanic open-air tribal meeting. Latching on to an already existing Romantic revival of Thing plays — known as the Thing Movement — the Nazis set up Thing things in dozens of places in Germany for the Hitlerjugend and others to perform theatre plays and suchlike. Another example of a Thingstätte (Thing place), in this case situated at Heidelberg, is illustrated opposite.

One of the first Thing theatres was constructed on the slope of the Heiligenberg, the wood-covered hill that towers above the city.

The site at Heidelberg had already been used for religious cults by Teutons, Romans and early Christians. Architect Herman Reinhard Alker designed an egg-shaped amphitheatre rising steeply up the slope of the hill. Construction was started in May 1934, over 1,000 workers being employed, but the problems met in blowing out and removing some 25,000 cubic metres of rock soil delayed the official opening until June 22, 1935, the first play being the specially-written *Der Weg ins Reich* by Kurt Heynicke. The finished theatre could hold 15,000 spectators and was equipped with the latest sound and lighting systems, said to be the largest of its kind in the world, which allowed performances to be enhanced with impressive special effects. Despite its beautiful setting, use of the theatre fell below expectations, being little used after 1939. Neglected for many years after the war, today the structure stands on the protected list.

However, it should be noted that the Adolf Hitler Schools provided an education so dominated by physical training and indoctrination as to be entirely inappropriate for the education of a modern elite. Above all, the ambitions focussed on these new schools were largely thwarted by the fact that the traditional institutions of German education — the secondary schools and universities — remained popular among the traditionalists because they provided a satisfactory education and, since they were fee-paying, tended to reproduce those elites.

To teach Party and state officials and others the Nazi creed, a network of National Political Training Institutions were developed. The goal was to establish a hundred so called 'Napolas' but less then half were in being by the end of the war. Here are just a few examples. *Left:* This was formerly the Prussian High School for Physical Training at Spandau in Berlin. *Right:* After its role as an ideological school ceased in 1945 it became a police training centre named after Joachim Lipschitz. The statue can be seen under the tree on the right.

Above: This is the Napola at Ballenstedt, north-east of Nordhausen, built in 1941. *Below:* Unchanged save for the removal of the insignia above the entrance, the huge complex is currently for sale, with only a small part in use as a sports facility.

Then there were the Napolas, the Nationalpolitische Erziehungsanstalten (National Political and Training Institutions), the first three of which were founded as early as April 20, 1933 (Hitler's 44th birthday) on the sites of the former Prussian military cadet schools at Potsdam, Köslin and Plön. These also had a strong Party bias, but had a standard grammar-school curriculum under the Reich Minister of Education and were designed to produce Nazi-inspired leaders in all walks of life. The pupils, known as 'Jungmannen' were incorporated into the Hitlerjugend, but had their own distinctive uniforms, which implied a continuation of the military cadet school, encouraging traditionally minded familes to apply for the enrolment of their sons.

However, that Himmler had a say and had other ideas than some of the parents is evidenced by this letter to SS-Obergruppenführer August Heissmeyer, Inspector of Napolas:

'I have received your report of April 29, 1940, concerning the expansion of the Napolas. There can be no question of a division of responsibilites. I told Oberst Friessner this personally before the start of the parade of 6,000 officer cadets in front of the Führer.

'Oberst Friessner's suggestion would result in the Napolas being entirely subordinated to the Army Cadet Corps and all their pupils would go into the Army.

'In additon, I strongly object to the particular emphasis placed on officer-type attitudes and behaviour in accordance with normal Army principles. I would be obliged if you would tell the gentlemen during your next discussion

Nationalpolitische Erziehungsanstalt, Backnang

Left: **A contemporary picture postcard of a school with an interesting history. Dating from 1906 this building on Richard-Wagner-Strasse in Backnang, a town north-east of Stuttgart, was initially a teachers' academy until taken over in 1934 by the Nazis for a Napola. When it ceased to be a political college in 1945, it was temporarily used as a field hospital; now it is the Schikhard Realschule together with a kindergarten.**

politely but firmly that I am the one who lays down the lines of policy on education for the Napolas and not the Army.'

In all 100 such schools were planned and 46 were in existence by 1945, including some in the incorporated territories of Bohemia, Sudetenland, Alsace, Luxembourg and the Netherlands, being accommodated in manor houses, castles and even some of Austria's closed-down monasteries. Pupils of the Potsdam and Spandau Napolas took an active part in the defence of northern Spandau in 1945 under the leadership of the Waffen-SS.

Left: **The Napola in Vienna lay on Favoritenstrasse. The building itself dated back to the 1600s. The National Socialists opened it in March 1939 but today *(above)* it is used as a training academy for the Austrian diplomatic corps.**

In addition, the SA had its own special school for exceptional offspring of Party loyalists at the Reichsschule der NSDAP Feldafing. This had been founded by Ernst Röhm in 1934 as the 'Röhm-Schule' with the intention of having a military cadet school to provide officers for his 'Brown Army'. He had selected Julius Goerlitz, whom he had known during the First World War, to head the school and, to this end, Goerlitz was given five years leave of absence from the Reichswehr. When Röhm was executed only six weeks after the school had opened, Goerlitz was given a rough time, but managed to survive the SA purge through Hitler's intervention.

Originally the school was accommodated in four large, attractive villas, with six forms, later expanding to eight in 12 buildings. There was the usual emphasis on sport and character-building, but the school also provided special features, like an annual expedition in the spring (the 7th Form within Germany and the 8th Form a foreign trip), excursions to theatres and exhibitions in nearby Munich, and even exchanges with schools in England, Finland and the USA. The 7th Form had dancing and golf lessons, and the 8th Form had driving lessons that enabled pupils to qualify for driving licences.

The school attracted the sons of Party leaders, such as Martin Bormann, Hermann Esser, vice president of the Reichstag, and SA-Brigadeführer Werner Hans Schwarz, as well as children of rich parents, such as Professor Ernst Heinkel, the aircraft manufacturer.

The pupils had a particularly smart uniform consisting of black trousers with a cherry-red seam and an open-necked brown tunic, worn with collar and tie, that had SA insignia on the tunic collar set on carmine patches, and carmine epaulettes. The Nazi Party armband was worn on the left arm above a cuff armband bearing the title 'NSDAP-Oberschule Starnberger See'.

Children of the party elite — like young Martin Bormann Jr *(below)* in 1940 — were sent to the Reichsschule der NSDAP, the select Party boarding school at Feldafing on the Starnberger See, just south of Munich. It was housed in a series of large villas on the hill overlooking the lake, many of them expropriated from wealthy Jewish owners. When first opened as an SA school in April 1934, the villas were renamed after Party heroes, one for example becoming the Horst-Wessel-Haus. The Parkvilla *(above left)*, here sketched by pupil Hans Fischbach, became the Ernst-Röhm-Haus, but this name was soon quietly dropped after Röhm was done away with just eight weeks later! *Right:* Now all villas are again privately owned.

Above: **This is the Reichsführerschule der Hitlerjugend at No. 66 Neue Königsstrasse in Potsdam just outside Berlin. Its purpose was to hold refresher courses for Hitler Youth leaders.** *Right:* **The building still stands minus the script over the doorway. And of course the flag!**

The Nazis believed strongly in the principle that the young should be led by the young: 'Jugend muss von Jugend geführt werden.' With the turmoil of a constantly growing membership and losses to labour and military service, it was necessary to maintain a regular system of leadership training. Boys and girls showing leadership qualities were selected at the age of 13 as Führer-Anwärter or Führerinnen-Antwärterinnen (potential leaders) and allocated to Ausbildungseinheiten (training units) to prepare them for this task, while established youth leaders attended four to six weekend refresher courses during the winter months. On average every two years the more senior-ranking leaders attended three-week refresher courses in Potsdam either at the Reichsführerschule der HJ at No. 66 Neue-Königsstrasse or at the Reichsführerinnenschule des BDM in the Bergmann-Villa at Nos. 41-43 Neue-Königsstrasse (today No. 90 and No. 62 Berliner Strasse respectively). There were also the Reichsschule für Jungmädelführerinnen in Boyden, East Prussia, the Reichsschule für BDM-Werk-Beauftragte (BDM work supervisors) in Hartenstein, Saxony, and the Ostland-Führerschule for HJ leaders in Marienburg, East Prussia.

Right: **The sister building, running similar courses for the girl leaders of the Bund Deutscher Mädel, also still stands opposite at No. 90.**

Regular conventions of youth leaders were held at Gau or Reich level, and from 1936 onwards all the Bannführer (leaders of groups of 3,000 HJ) held annual camps at either Braunschweig (Brunswick) or Weimar, and the BDM equivalent at the Reichssport-Akademie in Berlin. Then in 1939 a joint HJ/BDM leaders' camp was held in Braunschweig.

However, a permanent institute at academy level was considered necessary and a suitable site found in Braunschweig in the Richmond-Park off Wolfenbüttler Strasse. A design by Erich zu Putlitz was selected and the foundation stone laid in 1936, construction being completed in 1939. Set out among the trees of the park, the Akademie für Jugendführung consisted of a main building with a large and a small lecture hall separated by the Ehrenhalle (Hall of Honour commemorating those Hitler Youths who had lost their lives for the movement in its early days) from the dining, tea and club rooms, and a small indoor swimmingpool. Then there were five separate accommodation blocks, a headquarters building and the parade and sports grounds. The first course was interrupted by the outbreak of the Second World War, with all the students being called up for military service.

Work on a similar academy for the BDM, the Hochschule (later Akademie) des Bundes Deutscher Mädel, was started in Wolfenbüttel, but was never completed. Instead the vacant Braunschweig establishment was used for the first course for 80 Führerinnen aged 19-21 from January to April 1941. This preliminary course proved to be too short, requiring a 54-hour week to encompass the syllabus, so subsequent courses were extended to six months, and the second course for 96 female students ran until December 15, 1941. Then in the spring of 1942 the academy was taken over for the accommodation of war-wounded, reopening in November of that year with five-month courses for war-wounded HJ leaders. Consequently subsequent BDM leadership courses were run in 1942 at the BDM-Führerinnen-

Camps, conventions, rallies and parades — all part of the Hitler Youth programme.

schule at Ottendorf in Saxony, in 1943 at the BDM-Führerinnenschule at Schloss Heiligenberg in Hessen-Nassau, in 1944 at a school in the Moselland part of Luxembourg and again at Schloss Heiligen-

berg. A seventh course was begun in March 1945 but not concluded. It is interesting to note that the 1942 course included a few foreigners from Norway, Denmark, Holland and Belgium.

Left: This college of further education for Hitler Youth leaders was established in Braunschweig. Then it was the Akademie für Jugendführung — now it is the Braunschweig Kolleg and Abendgymnasium (evening school for adults) (above).

For those who did not conform, a Jugendschutzlager (Youth Detention Camp) was established in a former female concentration camp at Moringen, 20 kilometres north-west of Göttingen, in 1940. This camp served as a preliminary to incarceration in mental institutions or concentration camps for the incorrigible or to the Reicharbeitsdienst or military service for the more amenable.

The children of these youth organisations were often used to collect money or contributions in kind for such things as the Winterhilfe (Winter Relief Fund), and when war broke out the Hitlerjugend and BDM became actively engaged in supporting the Reichsluftschutzbund (Reich Air Protection League) as messengers carrying out various salvage and relief duties, and the girls were also often asked to entertain the war wounded in hospitals with concerts.

In September 1940, following the sustained bombing of industrial cities by the Royal Air Force, Hitler ordered the voluntary evacuation of children from these areas and detailed Reichsjugendführer Baldur von Schirach to organise the matter. Consequently the Hitlerjugend provided the necessary Kinderlandverschickung (KLV) organisation to implement evacuation to the countryside of southern and eastern Germany. This was done in three age groups, with children under the age of six and their mothers being found accommodation, six to ten year-olds being allocated to foster parents, and 10 to 14-year-olds being sent to special KLV camps run by the Hitlerjugend with teachers provided by the National Socialist Teachers' League.

In 1942 some 600,000 boys and 1,400,000 girls helped bring in the harvest, and the same year the Hitlerjugend set up three-week pre-military training courses for 17-year-olds at 120 camps with Wehrmacht instructors and a further 42 camps with Waffen-SS instructors. Seventeen-year-olds still at school went to the camps as a class, while those already in employment had

Above: **This is the naughty boys school at Moringen, a small town 20 kilometres north of Göttingen (see map page 274). In actual fact it was far more sinister than that. For youngsters that did not abide with Nazi regulations or ideology, life in Germany was not easy. Refusal to join the Hitlerjugend or simple offences, such as enjoying 'forbidden' jazz music were enough to be arrested. From June 1940, male offenders were sent to this special Jugendschutzlager (youth detention camp) housed in a former workhouse for the poor — a complex of stone buildings and workshops with some wooden huts situated in the middle of the town. Previously, from April to November 1933, the facility had served as one of Germany's earliest concentration camps, holding political prisoners from the province of Hannover. After that until March 1938 it had been used as a concentration camp for women, both from Germany and the occupied countries, among them Jews and Jehovah's Witnesses. The regime at the youth camp was draconic. The boys, ages ranging from 12 to 22 years, were put to hard work and exposed to a harsh 're-education' programme. Some who were considered criminal or anti-social were forcibly sterilised. Many died of hunger or from the cruel treatment by their SS overseers.** *Below:* **Today, the site of the camp is occupied by the Niedersachsisches Landeskrankenhaus, an hospital for psychiatric prisoners, the main building on Langestrasse being the only original one that survives.**

to attend during their holidays. The decision to form a Hitlerjugend Division of the Waffen-SS in 1943 brought about tremendous pressure for youngsters to volunteer for it.

Then in February 1943 the senior schoolboys were sent to man the home-defence anti-aircraft artillery as Luftwaffe or Kriegsmarine auxiliaries in order to release experienced adult gunners for the front and also enable an increase in the home-defence organisation to meet the Allied air offensive.

These boys thus replaced all but a few key adult personnel on the home-defence batteries, while the younger ones assisted the Luftwaffe-Helferinnen (female auxiliaries) with the supporting searchlight, radar and communications systems.

In January 1945 Reichsjugendführer Artur Axmann, who replaced Schirach in 1940, had some of the local Hitlerjugend organised into close-quarter tank-destroyer units to take part in the defence of Berlin and elsewhere. The boys were issued with rifles, grenades and Panzerfausts, and then allocated by their companies to either the various Defence Sectors, to a special Hitlerjugend Regiment which was assigned to guarding the Havel bridges opposite Spandau, or to the Axmann-Brigade, which appeared in the Strausberg area on April 21, and included a tank-hunting group armed with Panzerfausts and mounted on bicycles for mobility.

In committing his charges to armed combat, a criminal act further aggravated by the fact that the Hitlerjugend's age bracket had gradually dropped during the course of the war, Axmann obliged boys of 12 to 16 years of age to take up arms like men and risk dying either from enemy action or being hung from a lamppost as a deserter. Mixed with adult Waffen-SS and Wehrmacht troops, they fought with a fanaticism that appalled their opponents as much as did the callousness of their leaders. Needless to say, they suffered tremendous losses.

We have already seen Ordensburg Krössinsee as temporary accommodation for the Adolf Hitler Youth School; now we see its other face as a National Socialist training college for those destined for high office in the Party — the Nazi noblemen called Junkers.

The Ordensburgen

The Party with its deep contempt of 'intellectuals' found its own solution to a higher education that would provide the leadership to take the nation into the future, as was set out in the Party's Handbook:

'With the assumption of power by the Party, the selection of leaders through trial in conflict naturally ceased. And yet, it is essential that the leadership of the party should continously keep up its former fighting strength and buoyancy, for what is at stake is the task of safe-guarding and firmly consolidating what has been won by hard struggle. There has therefore arisen the question of prospective leaders which, especially as far as the high-ranking, specifically political Party leadership is concerned, is to be resolved as follows:

The house magazine for the New Year in 1944 carried this message from Hitler: 'This year, my comrades, the German leadership has been weighed down by the greatest task that one can ever face. Thanks to the bravery and devotion and readiness to make sacrifices at the front and at home; thanks to the dilligence of our workmen, and with the support of our allies in East Asia and our brothers-in-arms in Europe, we have managed to solve these mighty questions. However — as it has been from the beginning — the main burden in Europe was carried by the German people and the German soldiers.'

BURGGEMEINSCHAFT

Jahrgang 1944   N. S. Ordensburg   Folge 4/5
„Die Falkenburg am Krössinsee"

Ihr wollt meinen Platz wissen? Überall wo gekämpft wird.
(Morgenstern)

In diesem Jahr, meine Kameraden, lastete auf der deutschen Führung die größte Aufgabe, die wohl je gestellt werden kann. Dank der Tapferkeit und Hingabe und dem Opfermut der Front und der Heimat, dank dem Fleiß unserer Arbeiter ist es gelungen, unterstützt durch unsere Verbündeten in Ostasien und unsere Mitkämpfer in Europa, diese gewaltigen Fragen zu lösen. Die Hauptlast aber tragen in Europa — wie von Anfang an — das deutsche Volk und die deutschen Soldaten.

· Der Führer am 1. 1. 44

1) Leading functionaries, and in particular Gauleiters (Regional Leaders), have been instructed to devote the utmost attention possible to prospective leaders.
2) Special castles, called Ordensburgen, have been created. In these castles, valuable Party members from all regions undergo three years' training as prospective leaders. Party members must be aged 25 to 30 and represent the elite, racially, physically and mentally. In this connection, their previous occupation is immaterial. They are to be selected by the Reichsorganisationsleiter der NSDAP (Dr Robert Ley) on the recommendation of their Gauleiters in conjunction with the Head Office for Public Health. Among the subjects taught will be history, social politics, philosophy of life, every kind of sport, as well as deportment, etc. If necessary, training will be continued until trainee leaders can be released into the Gauen (regions) as fully trained political leaders.
3) In the Gauen, it is desirable that at first these Party members should be employed as Ortsgruppenleiter (Local Group Leaders), and that subsequently they should, as and when possible and necessary, work their way through all ranks of political leadership. These Party members will undergo continuous assessment of their abilities as political leaders.
4) It is intended that political leaders thus changed should form a replacement nucleus for the higher-ranking and more-directly politically active Party leadership.'

The trainees, who came from all walks of life, were given the title 'Junker' that normally only applied to Prussian nobility, and had to meet the following requirements:

1) Perfect physical health.
2) Exhibiting no disability, including glasses.
3) Racially pure.
4) Of outstanding character and mental disposition.
5) Free from hereditary tendencies.
6) Minimum height of 160 cm (5ft 3in).
7) 23-26 years old.

Inspection of the praetorian guard on October 13, 1937 . . . by none other than . . . the Duke of Windsor!

Married applicants' families were assured of their subsistence for the duration of the course, the rent being paid and the wife receiving a monthly allowance of RM 80 plus a supplement of RM 25 per child.

It was intended that the Junkers would do a four-year course, spending one year at each castle in turn. Of those established, Krössinsee was to specialise in character training, Vogelsang in extending the racist philosophy of the New Order, and Sonthofen in concentrating on career training in the administrative, political, diplomatic and military fields. Krössinsee became famous as a riding centre, while Vogelsang concentrated on sport in general, and Sonthofen on mountaineering and winter sports.

The prime mover in this field was Dr Robert Ley, who had been appointed Reich Organisations Leader after the murder of Gregor Strasser in the 'Night of the Long Knives' in 1934. This appointment gave him control over all the Nazi Party organisational matters, including the Main Education Office and Main Personnel Office. In his concern with the furtherance and conformity of Nazi ideology, Ley issued a monthly 'Schulungsbrief' (Education Letter) directed at all levels of the Nazi Party. The funds for these projects came from the individual subscriptions of the German labour force, Ley being simultaneously also head of the Deutsche Arbeitsfront (DAF — German Labour Front).

The construction of the first of the four planned Ordensburgen began in February 1934 and three of them — Krössinsee in Pomerania, Vogelsang in the Eifel and Sonthofen in Bavaria — were to be completed within the next two years, but the fourth at Marienburg in East Prussia was never even started.

The first to be ready was Ordensburg Krössinsee to the design of Professor Clemens August Klotz of Cologne. It was sited on the banks of the Krössinsee lake, near Falkenburg in the Pomeranian lake district. On April 24, 1936, Dr Ley formally handed over all three Ordensburgen to Hitler in a ceremony at Krössinsee only two years and two days after work had commenced on the site. Hitler then made a speech, which was recorded on parchment and sealed into the foundations of the water tower. However, it was October 17, 1937, before the first four-year Junker course began there. The first commandant was Paul Eckhardt, who was replaced by Reichsschulungsleiter (Reich Schools Director) Otto Gohdes before the opening.

Stepping it out beside the Ehrenhof, October 1937.

The Hall of Honour has passed away but the steps remain.

The corner of the communal building with accommodation blocks Nos. 2-8 in the background — then and now.

The architecture of the Krössinsee establishment reflected that of the province, having walls of local stone and slate with a mixture of slate and thatch roofs. Local granite was used for the fireplaces and timber taken from the surrounding forests for the wooden pillars of the accommodation block porches and covered ways. Some 600 construction workers were employed on the site until the outbreak of war, further work being partly undertaken by prisoners of war.

The whole layout resembled an enclosure, the centrepiece being a ceremonial square set in a circle with a half-moon of five rows of spectator seating on wooden benches. On either flank stood the accommodation blocks with an ablutions facility behind each third one, except for the last row of four, each of which had these facilities in their cellars.

Each accommodation block had a porch supported by wooden pillars. The first room inside was a reception room of about 30 square metres, which was mainly used as a reading and work-room. Then came two dormitories, each with 20 beds, these being set in pairs divided by a thin partition with a large, two-man locker at the foot, thus forming two-man cubicles. Beyond these dormitories was another recreation room connected by a lobby to a covered walkway linking the blocks with the ablutions, classrooms and other facilities. There were 20 of these blocks, providing accommodation for some 800 Junkers in all.

Between the Junker accommodation and the lake was a sports field, on one side of which was a plinth intended for a bronze sculpture by Professor Willy Meller that was never erected.

To the south-west of the Junker accommodation lay the administrative complex in the form of several connecting enclosed yards. The first contained the community centre and large dining hall. Then came the kitchens, carpenter's shop, apartments for the staff, the laundry, music room, garages and also offices for the team leaders. Somewhat apart, but still connected with this complex, was the canteen. On the right-hand side of this complex was a round water tower.

Opposite the administration complex a broad flight of steps led to a large open space in front of the so-called 'Hall of Honour' (Ehrenhof), a circular, thatched, open structure, the centrepiece of which was a two-metre-high eagle and swastika. This was flanked by two pillars and backed by a further 14, on which were sockets for flaming torches engraved with the names of the Feldherrnhalle 16 of 1923.

To the right of the 'Hall of Honour' was a building containing the main lecture hall and Ordensburg guardroom. Work on this building did not start until after the outbreak of war, but it was usable by 1942, although never completed. Next to the commandant's offices it was intended to build the chancery, library, archives, laboratory and photographic dark room, as well as meeting and conference rooms.

Left: **The German War Athletics Championships held at Krössinsee in 1940.** *Right:* **Professor Willy Meller's relief still remains.**

During the war the establishment was used for a variety of purposes. From 1941-44 it accommodated the pupils of the Adolf Hitler School from Tilsit in East Prussia. Following the invasion of the Soviet Union in 1941, some of the Junkers and staff were assembled at Krössinsee to form Sonderstab 'R', a special political leadership team to work in the occupied Eastern Territories under the Reichsminister responsible, Alfred Rosenberg. Then in 1943 an attempt was made to revive the initial concept with Junkers selected from war-wounded servicemen attending courses of several months duration. In all some 1,800-2,000 pupils and staff took part, the third and last course ending on July 26, 1944, although it was disrupted when a fire broke out in the laundry on June 29 which spread rapidly to engulf several buildings before it could be contained.

Further out on the property there was a parade ground, an exercise ground, a riding school and stables, a saddler's and cobbler's workshop, a sick-bay, dental surgery, commandant's quarters, a large guesthouse, a mess for the female staff, a vegetable garden and greenhouse, a piggery and a sewage plant.

Two thatched-roof boathouses on the lakeside served the Junkers' rowing and sailing interests.

To accommodate some of the many permanent staff needed to run the establishment, the Labour Front had a special housing estate built in Falkenburg with its own shops, post office and connecting bus service.

The first four-year Junker course moved on to Vogelsang for the second year, and was then due to move to Sonthofen for the third in 1939, when the outbreak of the Second World War resulted in the abrupt termination of the programme. As in the preceding two years, the Ordensburgen between them provided a contingent of up to 1,000 Junkers for the Party Day at Nuremberg, and their advance parties were already there when war was declared, some of the original Krössinsee course's baggage being already on its way from Vogelsang to Sonthofen. The Junkers and their instructors were sent home, where most of them were immediately conscripted into the Wehrmacht.

Centre: **Winter 1943-44 with the headquarters building blanketed in snow. Ordensburg Krössinsee (sometimes spelt with a 'C') had been designed by Clemens Klotz.** *Above:* **Crössinsee is today Szczecineck in Poland and the former Ordensburg is now occupied by the Polish Army.**

The second establishment to be completed was Ordensburg Vogelsang. Again designed by Klotz, it was started in March 1934 on the northern slopes of the Eifel mountains above the Urft Dam, not far from Belgium. The foundation ceremony was performed by Dr Ley on September 22, 1934, and the buildings necessary for conducting training were completed within a record two years. The overall construction time was estimated at at least ten years and at a cost of 250 million Reichsmarks. Three local quarries were acquired for building material, which then had to be taken up to the site in carts drawn by oxen. Up to 1,500 workers were employed on the site at any one time.

Ordensburg Vogelsang seen (top) **under construction in 1936 and** (above) **as it is today. A military training establishment under Belgian Army management since 1950, the facility is due to be closed down in July 2005. Its future use is still uncertain.**

'Heil Hitler'. The Führer is greeted by Reichshauptamtsleiter Richard Manderbach at the Kreisleitertagung on April 29, 1937, a conference between district Party leaders.

Vogelsang was commanded by Reichshauptamtsleiter Manderbach, an old soldier, early Party member and friend of Rudolf Hess. On September 18, 1938, when he left to join the Army, Manderbach was replaced by Otto Gohdes from Krössinsee. The commandant had an adjutant and a staff structure that provided leaders for groups of 360 men (Gruppenführer), 100-200 men (Hundertschaftführer), 40-50 men (Kameradenschaftführer) and 13-18 men (Zugführer). In addition there were the principal instructors (Erzieher), reinforced by guest lecturers rotating between the three establishments, and sports masters or company commanders. The order's teaching establishment for all three castles rose from 250 in the first year to 450 in the second. There were also 70 female employees accommodated at Vogelsang.

The main building at Vogelsang comprised a 50-metre-high tower, which also doubled as a water tower, the commandant's office, a 'Hall of Honour' commemorating the 16 dead of the 1923 putsch, the Führer's and castle guard-rooms, the main auditorium and a large dining hall. On the slopes below were ranged ten buildings with dormitories and day room for 50 men, and a further four buildings for 125 men each, thus accommodating 1,000 trainee Junkers in all.

Apart from a full variety of sports facilities, there was also a hospital with 40 beds and an operating theatre, a guest house, riding school, garages, stores, a driving school and even a small airfield. Ultimately it was planned to add a 2,000-bed hotel to each of the establishments, but this was never put into effect.

In December 1944, the RAF attacked the nearby Urft Dam in an attempt to release floodwater to help the American advance in the area. Bombs hit Vogelsang and the entrance building on the right was destroyed.

The Adlerhof. The eagle, in several stylized forms, is a re-occuring theme throughout the architecture of the National Socialist period. *Above:* These are more creations by Willy Meller — one of the birds can be seen behind Manderbach's shoulder in the Eagle Courtyard *(below)*.

This is the comparison of Hitler's inspection. The fountain has gone and the eagle — or what is left of it — has been moved to a new perch in the corner.

Parades by day . . . and night. *Right:* **This is the 1941 torchlight celebration of the Machtergreifung, the eighth anniversary of Hitler coming to power.**

The Junkers' working day at Vogelsang began at 6 a.m. with a loudspeaker reveille. After washing and dressing, the dormitories and living areas were tidied up, followed by early morning sport conducted by the individual 'Classes of Comrades'. Breakfast then took place in the vast communal dining hall. The Junkers then paraded for the flag-raising ceremony at 7.45 a.m., followed by classes from 8 to 10 a.m., and then a two-hour lecture in the main auditorium. The Junkers paraded outside

And this is Hitler's earlier visit to inspect the facilities on November 20, 1936.

again at 12.15 p.m. for mail call and allocation of afternoon duty sports. Lunch was from 1 to 2 p.m., after which all kinds of sports were engaged in, plus basic military and field training, gas defence and shooting. Then came a session of working groups dealing with themes taken from the practical work undertaken by Party leaders. After a communal evening meal, the Junkers were free to use the establishment's recreational facilities, such as the library, bowling, billiards, orchestral clubs, choirs, etc, or choose to walk out, providing they were back for the 10 p.m. 'lights out'.

Since the formation of NATO in 1955, Vogelsang has been used for military training purposes by all its members but this has now all come to an end.

The military then . . . and the military now. Relaxing outside one of the quarters.

Another of Meller's sculptures was the Torchbearer. As we can only see his legs in the photograph *(left)* showing a visit by

Wehrmacht soldiers, we took the comparison *(right)* so that we see all of him. Luckily he still has his head . . .

. . . **unlike the supermen on another relief down by the sports field who have all been decapitated and the eagle and swastika defaced.**

Hitler visited Vogelsang on November 20, 1936, April 29, 1937, and December 15, 1938, as did other prominent Nazi leaders from time to time, showing the importance they attached to these institutions. On each of these occasions, the local SS detachment provided guards of honour.

From 1941-44 three Adolf Hitler Schools from Moselland, Franken and Westmark (Saarland and Palatinate) were moved to Vogelsang, some 250 pupils in all, aged 8-18. In 1942 the female staff quarters were converted into a home for expectant mothers, evacuees from the Rhineland and other parts of the Eifel.

Robert Ley addresses the chosen few at the open-air theatre before a musical concert. The semi-circular Thing-thing overlooking the valley can be seen in both the pictures on page 288.

The establishment was captured on February 4, 1945, virtually intact and without a fight, by the 1st Battalion, 47th Infantry Regiment, US 9th Infantry Division, who used it for a while before moving on. While unoccupied it was plundered by the local inhabitants. With the post-war determination of Zones of Occupation, in June 1945 Vogelsang fell to the British, who decided to use it as a training area until it was handed over to Belgian Army management on April 1, 1950.

The third establishment, Ordensburg Sonthofen, was started in May 1934 at Sonthofen on the Kalvarienberg in the Allgäu mountains, and was to a design by Professor Hermann Giesler of that town. Professor Giesler's plans differed considerably from those produced by Professor Klotz for Krössinsee and Vogelsang. The chosen site was the top of a hill overlooking the town, where he envisaged erecting a modern castle-like structure to the glory of the Party. It was clear from the start that money was no object. Work began on October 4, 1934, with 300 construction workers, and the engagement of leading craftsmen from the area to embellish the finished product. The original plans only catered for 400 Junkers, but when Dr Ley visited the site on April 7, 1936, he gave instructions for expansion to accommodate 1,000. Implementation of the revised plans entailed the removal of some buildings already completed and, in order to maintain the conformity of the design, some buildings erected on the edge of the hill required as many as three unusable underground storeys to support them on the same visual plane as the others. This also involved an increase in the labour force to about 1,200 in the immediate pre-war years.

The basic layout was in the shape of a U with the main entrance located in the bottom left-hand corner and dominated by a massive tower that was linked to the right-hand side by a covered walkway. Abutting on to the tower on the left-hand side of the central parade ground was the headquarters block incorporating a reception hall, an anteroom, a council chamber and rooms for

Ordensburg Sonthofen takes shape, circa 1936. Located in southern Germany close to the Austrian border (see map page 274) it never actually performed the role it was intended, i.e. a Junkers school. Instead it primarily housed three Adolf Hitler schools as well as holding courses for disabled servicemen.

the administrative offices in a 42-metre-high, palace-like structure. An open-sided gallery ran the length of this building alongside the parade ground. Above were community halls for the new accommodation block, and the uppermost storey was laid out as a concert hall, decorated in white and gold, and included an organ for playing the Glockenspiel of 16 bronze bells installed in the tower at the southern end of the palace. (These bells were

It was first entered by French troops on April 30, 1945 who remained in occupation until replaced by Americans on July 9. They then set up a Constabulary School for training soldiers in the maintenance of law and order in the US Zone of Occupation until such time as a civil police force could be made effective. This school was disbanded in 1948 and the premises used for other military purposes until the autumn of 1952. Eventually in 1955 the establishment was taken over by the Bundeswehr with the new title of 'Generaloberst-Ludwig-Beck-Kaserne' in honour of one of the principal participants in the July 20, 1944, assassination attempt on Hitler.

Above: **Roll-call of the Hitler Youth in the 'Schönen Hof' — the Beautiful Courtyard at Sonthofen — in 1941. In the background the mountains of the Allgäu.**

removed in 1942 in a wartime economy drive.) The tower also contained a chapel, presumably in deference to the strength of religious feeling in the area.

The building on the right-hand side of the parade ground contained many special architectural features with its lecture rooms, more communal rooms, a library, a tearoom, a beer cellar known as the Fuchsbau (foxhole) and the Landsknechtszimmer (mercenaries' room) featuring outstanding carvings of mercenaries of the Middle Ages.

Below: **This is the reverse view of the courtyard in front of the semi-circular tribune.**

Having been captured undamaged in 1945, Sonthofen appears today as if time has stood still.

Hitler's visit, along with an entourage comprising Rosenberg, Todt, von Schirach, Dietrich, Goebbels, Wagner and Hess, took place on November 23, 1937.

Although much used for various local Party events, and the housing of the three Adolf Hitler Schools from Kurmark (Brandenburg), Hochland (Munich – Upper Bavaria) and Mecklenburg with initially between 300 and 370 schoolboys, rising to 1,300-1,700 in 1941, Ordensburg Sonthofen never served its intended role in the Junker training programme. Some courses were held for disabled servicemen during the war, and towards the end of the war it housed 2-300 bombed-out children as well as disabled servicemen. Some of the buildings were marked out as a field hospital, but no doctors were available to staff it.

Hitler's only visit to the town and establishment was on November 23, 1937, when 12,000 SA men provided security for the occasion. As construction was far from complete, a wooden façade of the intended gymnasium was erected for his benefit. Despite the jubilation, a sour note entered the scene when he personally degraded 30 Party officials by ripping off their badges of rank and ordering them to go to the station and travel home in their torn uniforms!

The revised plans involved the construction of a large accommodation block on either side of the parade ground, extending the U, and two slightly smaller ones at right angles beyond to the left and right. Part of this construction phase included a large cookhouse, equipped like that of the luxury liner *Bremen*, that could feed up to 1,500 persons at a time. Next to it was a vast dining room with the largest parquet floor in Europe, 109 metres long by 16 metres wide. The dining room was entered by three flights of open steps from the north and had large opening windows on its southern and western sides leading on to a terrace that could be used on festive occasions.

The establishment included all the usual sport and training facilities. Further unimplemented plans included the construction of a hall to seat 2,500 people, a theatre and hospital, a large 100-metre open-air swimming pool with covered spectator stands, and a 2,000-bed hotel for Dr Ley's Kraft durch Freude (Strength through Joy) organisation.

Adolf Hitler School pupils at Sonthofen. They were the selected few, but many parents and teachers of other children complained about the National Socialist Movement's brutalising effect on young people, for it promoted the glorification of military and quasi-military virtues such as duty, obedience, honour, physical courage, endurance, strength, ruthlessness in achieving goals, and only contempt for such values as peace, gentleness, moderation, intellect, moral courage, sensibility and humanity.

Also university students, greatly reduced in number from the pre-1933 days, had to become compulsory members of the Deutsche Studentenschaft and as such were expected to do four months of labour service and two months in an SA camp, as well as three hours a week of sport. By the end of the 1930s a growing number of students were beginning to resent the regimentation imposed on them, the pressures to conform, the anti-intellectual climate, and the crudity and moral duplicity of the regime.

Above left: **Virtually the only alteration at Sonthofen is the omission of the traditional eagle — technically the Hoheitszeichen der NSDAP — which greeted visitors as they entered the Ehrenhall.**
Above right: **As the complex is now dedicated to Generaloberst Beck (shot as a conspirator in the July 1944 plot), the eagle has been replaced with a text by him: 'It shows a lack of greatness and appreciation of one's task when a soldier in the highest position sees his duties and tasks only in the limited framework of his military assignments without becoming alive to his supreme responsibility towards the people as a whole'.**
Right: **Then, the 16 bells were dedicated to the martyrs of the Feldherrnhalle, each bell individually named. The bells rang out the *Hohenfriedberger Marsch* and the *Horst-Wessel-Lied* but they were melted down circa 1942 as part of the Reich-wide handing in of church bells.**

Above: **Today the bell tower dominates the landscape, just as it did 70 years ago during the Third Reich** *(left).*

The Schutzstaffel — The SS

Believing himself to be the reincarnation of Heinrich I who founded the First German Reich, Himmler salutes the tomb at Quedlinburg on the 1,000th anniversary of the King's death.

Although the most colourless character among the Nazi leadership, lacking natural authority and with all the charisma of a pedantic headmaster, Himmler's docile loyalty to Hitler ensured the latter's trust, and the constant expansion of his organisation kept his senior officers too busy to exercise their rivalry within the closed ranks of the Schutzstaffel — the black-uniformed Special Guards of the Party known simply as the SS — so Himmler's position remained secure.

His measures to improve the standards of recruitment bore fruit in that the SS came to be recognised by the public as an elite, offering considerable prestige to its members, thereby also attracting some well-educated and even aristocratic recruits for its upper echelons.

Himmler saw the SS as closed brotherhood, and with Hitler's indulgence he founded an SS Order of Knights for his senior officers — SS-Gruppenführer and above — based on both the Jesuits and the Order of Teutonic Nights of the 12th century, whose symbols and ceremonies appealed to Himmler's fantasies, which included that of believing himself to be a reincarnation of Heinrich I, founder of the First Reich, otherwise known as Henry the Fowler. Every year at midnight on July 2, the anniversary of the king's death, he would visit his tomb to pay silent homage.

Himmler wanted to replace the traditional Christian-based ethic of Western civilisation with a morality based on a new form of religion drawn from the Germanic heritage. One of the first steps was to evolve fresh cults and rituals, including the introduction of an SS marriage service.

King Heinrich's tomb in the cathedral at Quedlinburg (south of Magdeburg in former East Germany) became an SS-Weihestätte — a consecrated place — but it was Wewelsburg Castle, just south of Paderborn, that was to become the SS Shrine of Shrines. *Above:* Here Himmler and Robert Ley are snapped as they approach the castle from the Alme river valley via a minor road from Büren.

Schloss Wewelsburg pictured before the war. Himmler got his hands on it for a peppercorn rent in 1934.

Eventually in 1934 he picked on Wewelsburg Castle as a suitable home for the Order. A triangular-shaped fortress dating back to the early 15th century, it stood on an outcrop of rock overlooking the Alme river some 20 kilometres south of Paderborn. The castle had fallen into decay and the SS were able to obtain a rental agreement from the local authorities for the token sum of one Reichsmark per annum. Himmler charged architect Hermann Bartels with converting it into the 'Reichsführerschule-SS' with the idea of creating a special academy for the senior leaders of the SS.

At first, using the cheap labour provided by 40 members of the Volunteer Labour Service, Bartels had some relatively small rooms fitted out as living accommodation and studies. A castle warden was appointed, SS-Obersturmbannführer Manfred von Knobelsdorff, and three directors of studies were

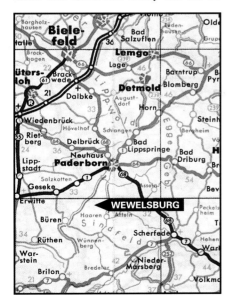

Today, owned by the city of Paderborn, the castle is partly a youth hostel and also a museum.

The first Kommandant SS-Obersturm-bannführer Manfred von Knobelsdorff was forced to resign his post in 1937 when he overreacted to an altercation at a shooting match in the local village. *Above:* His successor was SS-Stan-dartenführer Siegfried Taubert who had joined the NSDAP and SS in 1931. *Above right:* The entrance to the castle — unchanged since the day the SS were tenants. *Right:* An SS squad leaves the castle on May Day 1938.

appointed, but when they arrived they found that there was still no acceptable accommodation, furniture, or schedule of duties available for them, so they had to improvise. These studies involved pseudo-scientific research into Germanic culture, the German ethos, racial matters, prehistoric and early and medieval historic data, and so on, subjects mainly inspired by SS-Brigadeführer Karl-Maria Wiligut, a former colonel in the Austrian Army who also used the pseudonym 'Weisthor', and who was on Himmler's personal staff and had considerable ideological influence, despite having previously spent some time in a lunatic asylum as mentally unstable.

In the spring of 1935 the castle personnel were taken on the establishment of the Reichsführer-SS's personal staff and uniformed accordingly. That autumn Himmler banned any further unauthorised visitors to the castle and changed its title to 'SS-Schule Haus Wewelsburg'.

Left: Taubert with a group of SS-Gruppenführers in June 1941. On the left is Reinhard Heydrich, the chief of the RSHA, soon to be made Reich Protector of Bohemia and Moravia — an appointment which would lead to his death at the hands of British-trained Czech agents less than a year later. *Right:* Now it's Kaffee and Kuchen in the local Alte Mühle teashop!

Left: **A gateway of a different sort — the entrance to Nieder-hagen concentration camp. Himmler had this set up on the eastern outskirts of Wewelsburg to provide free labour for his** grandiose ideas for alterations and enlargement of the castle. *Right:* **Who would guess that this innocuous house was once the gatehouse to an SS concentration camp.**

As time went by, Himmler became more and more intent on the idea of establishing the castle as the ideological and cultural focal point of his Order, but for this he needed funds. Consequently the 'Company for the Promotion and Conservation of German Cultural Monuments' was set up with Himmler as chairman and SS-Obergruppenführer Oswald Pohl as business manager.

The voluntary labour force was replaced in 1938 by a batch of 100 prisoners from Sachsenhausen concentration camp for whom a new separate camp was established nearby with the name of Niederhagen. In due course this had a maximum population of 3,300, all working on the castle, and with a high mortality rate, for 1,285 are known to have died here, including 50 that were on a work-to-death sentence.

Some of the structures from the concentration camp still stand like this former kitchen building now used by the local fire brigade.

Left: **Slave labourers at work on the castle. From September 1941 until April 1943, Niederhagen was the smallest independent SS concentration camp of its kind having a maximum of around 3,300 prisoners. Even so the mortality rate was horribly** high at over one third. On April 30, 1943, the camp was disbanded and the inmates moved to the main camp at Sachsenhausen. Thereafter it was used as a base for training both Hitler Youth and German ex-patriots.

Left: **All building work on the castle then ceased and by 1944 the outer walls had been camouflaged. Then, in 1945 as American forces closed in, Himmler sent in demolition engineers from the Waffen-SS to ensure that his brainchild did not fall** into enemy hands intact. The explosions and resulting fires on March 31 left the structure still standing but gutted internally. *Right:* **Painstaking restoration has returned the castle to its former glory.**

Work began on converting the castle's northern tower into the 'world's epi-centre', where the Order's most solemn ceremonies would take place. There was to be a vast vault for the mourning of dead senior SS leaders, with a main hall above it for their assemblies, and above that again a domed festival hall. In order not to change the classic outline of the castle, it was decided to dig down more than four metres into the rock and cut a staircase through from ground level in the east wing descending more than nine meters into the vault, where a central ornament in the form of a sun wheel (the origin of the swastika) was set in the floor, and 12 pedestals set around the periphery.

Above in the assembly hall, which replaced the castle's chapel, there was a marble floor with another centrally-set sun wheel in gold, and 12 niches in the walls, while marble columns supported the ceiling above. In preparation for reconstruction of the upper works, the existing outside walls were demolished down to chapel floor level, and this was the stage the work had reached by the end of the war.

Even as building work continued, Himmler was still using the castle for his Order's ceremonies and held regular gatherings of his senior officers, of which there were only 12. This magic number, which was the maximum he would allow at table, he admitted was 'like the British King Arthur, who was really a Teuton and copied the idea of his Round Table from the court of Barbarossa.'

He had a suit of private apartments built for himself over the dining hall in the south wing, which included a hall displaying his extensive collection of weapons, a library with 12,000 books, a meeting hall and a courtroom for the senior SS Court. There was also a guest suite for Hitler in the same wing, although Hitler never visited the castle.

The SS had the former castle chapel converted in to a hall for carrying out their own ceremonials. The original marble floor still remains although the central swastika has been removed.

Bartels produced plans for a vast extension of the Wewelsburg facilities, which it was intended to realise after the war. However, on March 31, 1945, on Himmler's instructions a Waffen-SS engineer unit managed to filter through the advancing Americans and reach the castle, where their demolitions created considerable internal damage but without destroying the basic structure.

Apart from the Wewelsburg, the company also claimed interest in Sachsenhain near Verden on the Aller (where Charlemagne had 4,500 pagan Saxons massacred in 782), Kyffhäuser in the Harz mountains and the tomb of Heinrich I in Quedlinburg Cathedral. Bartels was appointed SS-Sturmbannführer and director of the Wewelsburg project, as money began to pour in from the wealthy members of 'Friends of the Reichsführer-SS'.

A circular crypt was constructed in the cellar, its precise purpose unknown although the room is sometimes referred to as the Valhalla — a shrine to the dead. Around the circumference are 12 pedestals which are believed to reflect the number of SS-Hauptämter (head offices) then in existence. A sun wheel — the originator of the former significance of the swastika as a health-giving device — was inset in the floor. *Left:* It has since been removed . . . but *(right)* look up at the ceiling!

Left: **Himmler's SS empire was controlled from No. 9 Prinz-Albrecht-Strasse [1] in Berlin. This was actually the old Prinz Albrecht Hotel which Hitler had often used before he became Chancellor. Since 1931 the SS had its own internal intelligence department called the Sicherheitsdienst — the SD for short. Its chief was Reinhard Heydrich who was installed just round the corner in the former Prinz-Albrecht-Palais in Wilhelmstrasse [3].**

Right: **A totalitarian state needs its secret police force and when Göring was the Prussian Minister of the Interior he established such an organisation in April 1933 called the Geheime Staatspolizei — the dreaded Gestapo. Its headquarters set up next door at No. 8 Prinz-Albrecht-Strasse [2] which was formerly the Arts and Crafts Museum. When Göring handed over to Himmler in 1934, he just moved across the road to the new Air Ministry [4].**

Himmler's offices as 'Reichsführer-SS' and from June 17, 1936, 'Reichsführer-SS und Chef der deutschen Polizei' were located at No. 9 Prinz-Albrecht-Strasse (today Niederkirchnerstrasse) in Berlin, in the former Hotel Prinz Albrecht. Here were accommodated his personal staff and the administrative headquarters of the SS, which originally comprised four main branches: the Allgemeine (General) SS of part-time volunteers, the Sicherheitsdienst, the Verfügungstruppen that became the Waffen-SS in late 1939, and the Totenkopfverbände (Death's Head Units) that guarded the concentration camps.

The headquarters contained the following main offices:

(1) Himmler's Persönliche Stab des Reichsführers-SS (Private Office) under SS-Brigadeführer Karl Wolff, who was to go on to become an SS-Obergruppenführer und General der Waffen-SS.

(2) The SS-Rasse- und Siedlungshauptamt (RuSHA, Race and Resettlement Head Office) under SS-Obergruppenführer Richard Darré, who was also Reich Minister for Food Production, from whose fixed prices he was able to skim off funds to support the SS.

(3) The SS-Gericht (Court of Honour) under SS-Brigadeführer Paul Scharfe.

(4) The SS-Hauptamt (Head Office) under SS-Obergruppenführer August Heissmeyer, who was also Inspector of Napolas and married to Gertrud Scholtz-Klink, the head of the National-sozialistisches Frauenschaft (NSF, National Socialist Women's Organisation).

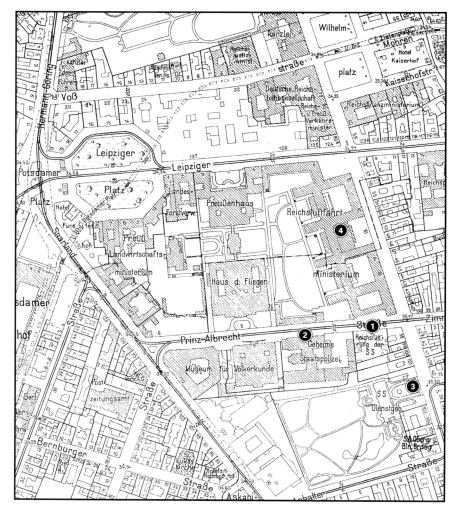

Left: **By the end of the war the Gestapo headquarters was a battered shell which was later demolished and the site levelled . . . but then along came another regime! The kerb on the southern side of the street marked the boundary between the borough of Mitte in the Soviet Sector and Kreuzberg in the US Sector.** *Right:* **This didn't matter much in 1945 when these GIs were pictured outside the front door of No. 8 but things changed when the GDR sealed off East Berlin with the Wall.**

(5) The SS-Führungshauptamt (Operational Department) serving as headquarters of the Waffen-SS under Hans Jüttner.

(6) The SS-Personalhauptamt (Personnel Department) under SS-Gruppenführer Maximilian von Herff.

(7) The SS-Wirtschaftsverwaltungs-Hauptamt (WVHA, Economic and Administrative Head Office) under SS-Obergruppenführer und General der Waffen-SS Oswald Pohl, which ran the vast business empire developed during the war using labour from the concentration and forced-labour camps.

Next door at No. 8 were the Gestapo headquarters in what had been the Kunstgewerbemuseum (Arts and Crafts Museum), cellars of which contained the cells where prisoners were deprived of light and sleep, beaten and tortured to extract information. The role of the Gestapo had been defined in Prussian State Law: 'The Secret State Police have the task of investigating and combatting throughout the state all attempts to endanger the state.' There were no legal means of redress against arrest by the Gestapo, which was a law unto itself, and arrest in most cases led to either summary execution or confinement in a concentration camp.

In fact the SS and law courts were in competition to impose the harshest penalties on enemies of the state, and the SS would sometimes extract prisoners from their cells either before or immediately after sentence and either shoot them or send them to concentration camps to be worked to death. Convicts that had completed their sentences were often then sent on to concentration camps as incorrigible or habitual criminals.

Just round the corner at No. 107 Wilhelmstrasse, adjoining the former hotel, was the Prinz Albrecht Palace, which accommodated the Sicherheitsdienst (SD), the SS's internal police, security and intelligence service founded by Reinhard Heydrich and run by him until his appointment as Deputy Reich Protector of Bohemia and Moravia in September 1941. After the reorganisation of September 27, 1939, this became the Reichssicherheitshauptamt (RSHA) controlling the functions of the SD, Gestapo and Kripo (criminal police) and maintaining lists of the regime's enemies under the categories of Communists, Social Democrats, Freemasons, Jehovah's Witnesses, Jews, Gypsies and Homosexuals. The main departments concerned were:

(1) Personnel under SS-Brigadeführer Bruno Streckenbach, former head of the Hamburg police, who became responsible for establishing both the first ghettos in Poland and the infamous Einsatzgruppen execution squads that committed wholesale murder in the East.

(2) Legal Affairs under SS-Brigadeführer Dr Karl Best.

(3) SD under SS-Gruppenführer Otto Ohlendorff, at one time commander of Einsatzgruppe D, which was responsible for the liquidation of at least 90,000 civilians in southern Russia.

(4) Gestapo under Generalleutnant der Polizei und SS-Gruppenführer Heinrich 'Gestapo' Müller.

(5) Criminal Police (Kripo) under Generalleutnant der Polizei und SS-Gruppenführer Artur Nebe.

(6) Foreign Intelligence under SS-Brigadeführer Heinz Jost and later under SS-Brigadeführer und Generalmajor der Waffen-SS Walter Schellenberg.

(7) Ideological Research under SS-Obersturmführer Paul Dittel.

The wall they built and improved upon over the following years has been retained along this street now renamed Niederkirchnerstrasse although the roadway — the old death strip of raked earth to show up footprints — has now been paved.

Shortly after Hitler took office, Josef 'Sepp' Dietrich set up a special security detachment, hand-picked from the SS, to protect the Führer. They were renamed the 'SS-Leibstandarte (or Bodyguard Regiment) Adolf Hitler' and having expanded to some 2,500 were based some 12 kilometres to the south-west of the main SS HQ in their own barracks in the Lichterfelde district. *Above:* This inspection is taking place on the parade ground at the rear of the main block — now given over to lawn *(right).* The barracks were originally built for Kaiser Bill's cadets, the main building being demolished and rebuilt by 1938 with more modern facilities *(below left).* Seven years later it was under new management.

Left: It was occupied by the Soviets until the Americans took over on July 4, 1945 *(right).* They renamed it Andrews Barracks in memory of the European Theater of Operations commander who lost his life in May 1943 (see *After the Battle* No. 123).

However, one building connected with the SS which has hardly changed at all is the officer's school for the security police.

In April 1937 when the reorganisation of the national police resources under Himmler produced the Hauptamt Sicherheitspolizei (Security Police Head Office), the Führerschule der Sicherheitspolizei (Security Police Officer School) took over the facilities of the Police Institute in the western half of the old Palace Barracks opposite Berlin's Schloss Charlottenburg. This installation comprised four buildings on the south-west corner of Schloss-Strasse and the Spandauer Damm, with gateways on both of these streets, and a garage in the courtyard behind. Here courses were given in criminal sciences and political education, combined with some paramilitary training, that were open to all security police, criminal police, Gestapo and SD officials, as well as candidates for the Kolonialsicherheitspolizei (Colonial Security Police).

With the creation of the Reichssicherheitshauptamt (RSHA) in 1939, the school was placed under the control of Amt I of the RSHA, Division 1B, for which it provided the necessary offices.

Only the absence of the sentry box, soldiery and SS flags give away its change of use from the Sicherheitspolizei to the Bröhan-Museum.

In charge of the school was SS-Standartenführer Erwin Schulz until August 1942, when he became Inspector of Security Police (SIPO) and SD schools, and handed over to SS-Obersturmbann-führer Rudolf Hotzel, who remained in charge until the end of the war. During his term of office in Charlottenburg, Schulz also spent some time with the Einsatzgruppen in Eastern Europe.

Three students posing at the Schloss-Strasse entrance of the SD-Führerschule — then and now.

Members of the Schutzstaffel were deemed by Himmler to personify the true Aryan — the Nazi definition being a person of a Caucasian race not of Jewish descent. As far back as December 1931 he had issued his 'Marriage Order' which forbade any SS man entering into wedlock without his approval, acting on the advice of his 'Race Office'. Any member marrying without such consent would be dismissed from SS service. Provision was then made for the obligatory four children from the union to be born in SS maternity units operated by the Lebensborn organisation. Confinement homes were set up at Hohehorst near Bremen; Klosterheide northwest of Berlin; Kohren-Sahlis south-east of Leipzig; Nordrach in the Black Forest; Schalkhausen south-west of Nuremberg; Wernigerode in the Harz mountains, also at Wiesbaden and Steinhöring north-east of Munich *(right)*. This operated from August 1936 to May 1945 and could cater for 30-50 mothers at any one time.

This statue by H. Anker of the breast-feeding mother once stood outside the Steinhöring home but has recently been cleaned and moved to the garden of what is now a clinic for the mentally handicapped.

Obsessed with ideas on the purity of the race, Himmler also founded the Lebensborn (Fount of Life) association in September 1936 as an extension of the Marriage Order of 1932 under the auspices of the SS Race and Resettlement Head Office, financed by compulsory contributions. This statute charged every SS man to produce four children, whether in or out of wedlock. The children were to come into the world in well-equipped Lebensborn homes, and would be provided with birth documents, basic financial support and would also recruit adoptive parents as necessary.

The Lebensborn was described by Günther d'Alquen in the SS newspaper *Das schwarze Korps* as follows: 'The Lebensborn association consists primarily of members of the SS. It provides mothers of large families with the finest obstetrical treatment in excellent maternity homes, also facilities for rest both before and after confinement. It also affords an opportunity for pre- and extra-conjugal mothers of good stock to give birth under relaxed conditions.'

There were 13 Lebensborn homes in Germany, and a further nine in Norway, each with their motto of 'Every mother of good blood is our sacred trust' and staff selected for their political reliability, as the system did not conform to normal legal or religious standards. Mothers received an allowance of 400 Reichsmarks, which easily met the daily fee of 2-5 Reichsmarks, enabling single women to move in early during their months of pregnancy.

Himmler was so enthusiastic about increasing Germany's stock of healthy Aryans that in 1939 he called on German women and girls of good breeding to become mothers of children of men setting off to war. However the number of children born out of wedlock remained minimal. Later on he encouraged racially acceptable women in the conquered territories that had become pregnant with a soldier's child to give birth in a Lebensborn home so as to enable the child to be Germanised. Consequently nine of these establishments were located in Norway, where

These gates with its Germanic runes was pictured in 1992 by *After the Battle* **reader Mr J. Hearne, but when we revisited the** home for this book the gates had been removed to the rear garden.

the population was deemed 'pure Aryan', which produced 12,000 children as opposed to the estimated 7,500 from those in Germany, only to have the Norwegians wreak terrible revenge on these children after the war.

Himmler also had some 200,000 likely children kidnapped and shipped back to special camps in Germany for examination as to their suitability for adoption or elimination. But for those unfortunate imported female slave labourers of lesser racial groups that were found to be pregnant he ordered compulsory sterilisation.

Whether Himmler's privately circulated offer 'that every unmarried woman who . . . longs for a child can confidently turn to Lebensborn' which would supply her with a breeding helper (Zeugungshelfer) was actually put into practice remains unknown.

In the so-called RuSHA Trial of 14 high-ranking members of different SS organisations by United States Military Tribunal I in Nuremberg in 1948, Inge Viermetz, the sole defendant from the Lebensborn programme, was acquitted.

Most of the Lebensborn maternity units have remained either hospitals or clinics in the medical world. *Above:* **This is the main block at Steinhöring and** *(below)* **an example of one of the older buildings: Heim Harz at Wernigerode. It was originally a hospital and reverted to one again after the war. Today it is named the Harz-Klinikum.**

On September 24, 1934, Minister of Defence General Werner von Blomberg issued a directive outlining the new relationship between the Wehrmacht and SS, which was followed on December 18 that year by the Chief of the General Staff, Generalleutnant Ludwig Beck, issuing an order whereby the Army would establish guidelines for the training of the militarised SS, including the setting up of three SS-Junkerschulen (officer cadet schools). The latter were necessary as the SS then lacked qualified and experienced staff of its own for this purpose. The main establishment was located south of Munich at Bad Tölz — this is an original picture postcard of the period.

The first SS officer cadet school was opened on October 1, 1934. This was the SS-Junkerschule Bad Tölz, which opened its doors for 100 Junkers in the centre of Bad Tölz in southern Bavaria under SS-Standartenführer Paul Lettow, a former colonel of the Reichswehr and a police tactician.

The second academy, the SS-Junkerschule Braunschweig, opened at Braunschweig (Brunswick) in the spring of 1935 under Paul Hausser, formerly a Generalleutnant in the Reichswehr, who was to be appointed SS-Brigadeführer and Inspector of the SS-Verfügungstruppe in October 1936. A third and a fourth academy were established during the course of the war, the one at Braunschweig being destroyed in an air raid.

The Bad Tölz location was conveniently close to Himmler's Tegernsee residence (see page 83) and Party Headquarters in Munich, but in practice proved awkward for both the town and the school, so in 1936 construction began on a new site some six kilometres outside the town.

The architecture of this new site was designed to reflect both the new Nazi image and its hereditary relationship to the Teutonic Knights, its layout being copied from the latters' headquarters castle at Marienberg (Malbork) in East Prussia. Massive twin towers in medieval style flanked an equally massive gateway, the vast parade ground inside was flanked by barrack blocks with walls a metre wide pierced by recessed windows. Steel, concrete, marble and granite created a modern image of a grand medieval castle containing a fully electric-powered kitchen, Germany's first military Olympic-sized indoor swimming pool, a sports field with an electronically-operated scoreboard, an up-to-date vehicle workshop for the garages, a stable for 120 horses, a 400-seat theatre with retractable screen and organ, and a fully automated bowling alley.

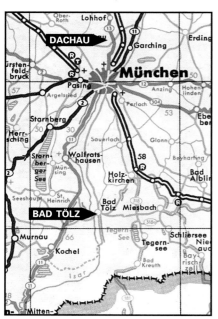

The massive arched gateway was flanked by twin gate-houses.

The entrances to the Junkers' quarters were located at the base of the towers, which contained imposing circular staircases. At the foot of the main entrance was an equestrian statue of Frederick the Great flanked by photographs of Hitler and Himmler. The Junkers' accommodation included semi-private bedrooms, communal toilet facilities, an elegant dining room, music room, lounge, library and even a beer cellar.

Among the sports available to them were riding, archery and fencing in keeping with the knightly image, and also basketball and weightlifting. Their training facilities included electronically-controlled blackboards, audiovisual equipped classrooms, sand-tables for tactical training, and an automated target range.

Not so well catered for were the 50 or so prisoners housed in the cellars, who helped maintain the establishment as a subsidiary of Dachau concentration camp.

During the pre-war era, the SS-Junkerschulen's task was to provide the ideological and military training for an elite vanguard of political soldiers, a professional officer corps for all branches of the SS, including the military element or SS-Verfügungstruppe (SS-VT).

Until July 1936, the recruits for the academies were selected exclusively from the SS-VT, whose strength limited the number of Junkers to about 100. Then, with the introduction of compulsory military service in March 1935, the SS found itself excluded and could only recruit by means of word of mouth in the Party-led Hitlerjugend and Arbeitsdienst.

The applicants had to meet stringent racial, physical and political standards, although level of education and social status played no part. They had to be able to prove pure Aryan descent back to 1800, have a height of at least 1.74 metres (5ft 8in), not wear glasses or be overweight. They also had to produce certificates from the police showing

The academy was taken unopposed by the 141st Regimental Combat Team of the US 36th Infantry Division on April 29, 1945, and thereafter, until the collapse of the Soviet Union, under the name of Flint Barracks accommodated the US Seventh Army NCO Academy and 10th Special Forces Detachment (Airborne) of the US Army in Europe. Today, the complex is owned by the town of Bad Tölz and was undergoing restoration when we visited it in the summer of 2003.

them to be of good behaviour, as well as a character reference from their civilian employer. Any previous contact with 'enemies of the state' meant automatic exclusion. Like their Army counterparts, accepted candidates then had to spend a year in basic military training with an SS-VT unit before being accepted as an officer cadet. Other recruits came direct from the ranks of the SS-VT via a selection board upon the recommendation of their commanders.

With Himmler's appointment as 'Reichsführer-SS und Chef der deutschen Polizei' in June 1936, recruitment expanded into the police service and by 1939 some graduates of the SS-Junkerschulen were consequently being posted to the Ordnungspolizei and SS-Sicherheitsdienst (SD — Security Service).

The new establishment at Bad Tölz opened in 1937 and by 1938 consisted of 49 officers and 240 NCOs and below catering for 250 Junkers. By this stage, however, even after graduating at the academy, the Junkers were expected to complete a three-month platoon leader's course in the practical application of infantry or armoured tactics before being commissioned with the rank of SS-Untersturmführer.

On August 17, 1938, Hitler issued a decree that placed the SS-VT and Junkerschulen under the operational command of the Wehrmacht in time of war. The SS-VT became the Waffen-SS in November 1939 and began to expand rapidly. The Bad Tölz and Braunschweig establishments were then nominated as reserve SS officer corps training centres, the first batch of this kind of cadet arriving at Bad Tölz in January 1941. Then in June 1942 it also became a training and rehabilitation centre for disabled SS officers and cadets who, although unfit for front-line duty, could be assigned to administrative duties in any of the various departments of the SS.

However, there was a limit to manpower recruitment in Germany, to which the Wehrmacht was legally restricted, a restriction that the Waffen-SS could overcome by taking in selected 'Germanic' recruits from western and northern Europe to fight in the 'holy war' against Bolshevism. Consequently some 700 volunteer cadets of this kind were processed through Bad Tölz in four-month courses from May 1943 onwards.

On March 27, 1945, Hitler ordered the cadets at the school to be formed into a new SS-Grenadier-Division 'Junkerschule' under the command of SS-Obersturmbannführer Richard Schulze-Kossens. The division was renamed 'Nibelungen' on April 9 and surrendered to the Americans at Reit-im-Winkel in Bavaria on May 8.

The SS buildings remain much as they were save for the entrance archway.

THE CONCENTRATION CAMPS

I passed through the barrier and found myself in the world of a nightmare. Dead bodies, some of them in decay, lay strewn about the road and along the rutted track. On each side of the road were emaciated faces of starving women, too weak to come outside, propping themselves against the glass to see the daylight before they died.

I saw a man, wandering dazedly along the road, stagger and fall. Someone else looked down at him, took him by the heels and dragged him to the side of the road to join the other bodies lying unburied there. No one else took the slightest notice — they didn't even trouble to turn their heads. Behind the huts, two youths and two girls who had found a morsel of food were sitting together on the grass in picnic fashion sharing it. They were not six feet from a pile of decomposing bodies.

RICHARD DIMBLEBY,
BBC RADIO BROADCAST, APRIL 19, 1945

The concentration camps and incarceration centres established by the police and partly by SA and SS autonomous groups on an ad hoc basis immediately following the Reichstag fire numbered about 50, using such sites as factories and camp buildings. They were mainly located in Prussia and around Berlin, but also in middle Germany, especially in Saxony and Thuringia where there were strong Communist elements, and at places like Lichtenburg, Sachsenburg, Hohenstein, Bad Salza, Colditz and Heuberg, near Stuttgart. Göring, as Minister President of Prussia, set up a centre for his enemies in Berlin where the Columbiahaus became renowned for the cruelties practised on prisoners there. Rudolf Diels *(below left)*, his Gestapo chief, took over control of the Prussian concentration camps in which the SA were getting out of hand, and by April 1934 he had closed them all down except for the Columbiahaus.

Below right: It stood just north of Tempelhof on the Columbiastrasse (now renamed Columbia-Damm) and is today the HQ for Police District No. 5. Once the wild camps had been phased out, the remaining camps came under the authority of SA and SS personnel appointed as Hilfspolizei (Auxiliary Police) until the Röhm putsch of June 30, 1934, when the SS under Reichsführer-SS Heinrich Himmler took over. (As the contents of this book are limited to those aspects of the Third Reich to be found within today's boundaries of the Federal Republics of Germany and Austria, the concentration camps in the countries occupied by Nazi Germany fall outside the scope of this work. This explains why the five main killing centres where most of the Nazi genocide on the Jews took place — Belzec, Chelmno, Treblinka, Sobibor and Auschwitz, which were all located in occupied Poland — are not covered in the present chapter.)

Before we leave Berlin we should illustrate another important building — and one which has been preserved — as it features prominently in the Nazi programme to exterminate the Jewish community in occupied Europe. On the morning of January 20, 1942, representatives from all the main ministries concerned met in this villa at No. 56-58 Am Grosser Wannsee under the chairmanship of Reinhard Heydrich (*above* — see also page 304). He announced that the conference had been set up as he had been given responsibility for working out a solution . . . a final solution . . . to the 'Jewish problem'. He said that 'instead of emigration there is now a further possible solution to which the Führer has already signified his consent — namely deportation to the East'. Although not directly stating that the 'final solution' was a euphemism for mass murder on a grand scale, Hitler, Himmler, Heydrich and SS-Obersturmbannführer Adolf Eichmann *(below left)*, the head of the Jewish Evacuation Office of the Gestapo, and others, were fully aware of what was being planned. Hitler even said as much at his speech at the Sportpalast ten days later on the anniversary of his appointment as Chancellor.

> *I do not even want to speak of the Jews. They are simply our old enemies, their plans have suffered shipwreck through us, and they rightly hate us, just as we hate them. We realize that this war can only end either in the wiping out of the Germanic nations, or by the disappearance of Jewry from Europe. For the first time, it will not be the others who will bleed to death, but for the first time the genuine ancient Jewish law; 'an eye for an eye, a tooth for a tooth' is being applied. The more this struggle spreads, the more anti-Semitism will spread — and world Jewry may rely on this. It will find nourishment in every prison camp; it will find nourishment in every family which is being enlightened as to why it is being called upon to make such sacrifices, and the hour will come when the worst enemy in the world will have finished his part for at least a thousand years to come.*
>
> ADOLF HITLER, JANUARY 30, 1942

Eichmann was the chief organiser for the mass deportation of Jews from all over Europe to the extermination camps in the East, and he had been working in the SS Jewish Affairs office as far back as 1934. However, whereas Heydrich was assassinated in June 1942, Eichmann survived the war but was tracked down in Argentina by the Israeli Secret Service and kidnapped in May 1960. Sentenced to death, he was executed on May 31, 1962. *Below left:* This was Eichmann's office building (nominally RSHA Section IV-B-4) located at No. 116 Kurfürstenstrasse. *Below right:* The site is now occupied by the Hotel Sylter Hof.

Dachau

Dachau concentration camp was from the first an SS camp, being founded by Himmler, then Police President of Munich, on March 20, 1933, on the site of a former gunpowder factory. The first commandant was Hilmar Wäckerle, a brutal but inefficient individual, who was replaced in June 1933 by Theodor Eicke, a former Army paymaster. While Eicke was likewise brutal he was also very efficient. He gave his guards paramilitary training and induced an attitude of fanatical hatred toward the prisoners as enemies of the state, laying down set rules for their conduct and punishment. Prisoners attempting to escape were to be shot without warning, as was any attack on a guard. Punishments included 'free hanging', in which the victim was hung with his hands tied behind his back so that his shoulders became dislocated. Prisoners were also beaten to death or severely injured, driven across the warning strip next to the boundary fences to be shot by the guards in the watchtowers.

Dachau, just outside Munich (see map page 310), was the first true concentration camp to be established by the Third Reich. (We saw one of its early commandants on page 34.) The slogan on the roof, common to all camps, reads: 'There is only one road to freedom and its milestones are Obedience, Zeal, Honesty, Order, Cleanliness, Temperance, Truth, Sense of Sacrifice and Love of the Fatherland'.

Eicke so impressed Himmler with his work that he was appointed Inspector of Concentration Camps on July 1, 1934, and his methods became standard throughout the system. The commandants were masters of life and death in their camps and protected by the SS from any interference by the courts. The delivery and registration of prisoners was the responsibility of the Gestapo detachments allocated to the camps.

Sanitised and memorialised, the horrors of yesterday appear far divorced from the neat beds and gravelled pathways of today. This is the old kitchen [5] on the aerial picture *(opposite).* **After Dachau was liberated by the Americans it was first used as a POW compound, primarily for SS prisoners. Later it became a refugee camp for displaced persons (or DPs). The International Memorial was inaugurated in 1968.**

If we look on Dachau as typical, this overview will help describe the layout which was common to most camps. [1] The Lagerstrasse (the main camp road. [2] Wohnbaracken (barrack huts). [3] Appellplatz (parade ground). [4] Jourhaus (entrance to compound). [5] Wirtschaftsgebäude (kitchen, laundry & storage). [6] Revierbaracken (infirmary barracks). [7] Totenkammer (mortuary). [8] Strafblöcke (penal barracks for escapees). [9] Priesterblock (clergy prisoners). [10] Kantine (the canteen). [11] Desinfektionsbaracke (disinfection block). [12] Plantage (vegetable garden). [13] Stacheldrahthindernis (barbed wire fence and wall). [14] Wachtürme (watchtowers). [15] Bunker (the camp prison). [16] Crematorium. [17] SS guards compound. [18] Entrance. [19] Commandant's office. [20] Officers' quarters. [21] Offices. [22] Barracks. [23] Eicke-Platz. [24] Officers' Mess. [25] MT garages and workshops. [26] Ordnance training workshops. [27] Deutsche Ausrüstungswerke (furniture and clothing workshops). [28] Post-war war crimes trial building. [29] Where the SS guards were shot in 1945.

317

Prisoners new to the concentration camp system were inducted upon arrival by being driven to the registration office with blows and kicks. They were then forced to wait outside squatting in a tight knee-bend with their hands clasped behind their heads for hours, constantly subject to verbal and physical abuse, it not being uncommon to be urinated all over by the guards. Eventually, usually the next day, they would be admitted one by one for registration and for an identity photograph to be taken. They were then stripped of their clothing and possesions and all body hair shaved off them by other prisoners before the striped camp uniform was issued. The badges classifying their prisoner category and their allocated camp numbers were then sewn on the left breast and right trouser leg, and the prisoners allotted to their huts. These badges consisted of triangular scraps of cloth in different colours, red for political prisoners, green for criminals, black for anti-socials, pink for homosexuals and brown for gypsies, while Jews wore two yellow triangles sewn in the form of

the Star of David. From then on the totally humiliated prisoners were just numbers at the mercy and whim of their SS guards and the Kapo supervisors. Towards the end of the war the supply of striped uniforms ran out, so prisoners were issued with normal civilian clothing taken from the extermination camps that had large diagonal yellow crosses sewn on.

The routine in the camps began with reveille at 4.30 a.m. After washing and frugal breakfast came bed-making, to which the SS guards attached great importance. Then came the morning roll-call on the open parade ground in all weathers — at which the absence of a cap could result in the instant execution of the offender — followed by the detailing of the various work-commandos and the march to work at 6 a.m. There was a break from 12 a.m. to 1 p.m. and then work continued until 6 p.m. The prisoners were then marched back for the evening roll-call and to witness the punishments awarded during the day, a process that could last anything up to four hours. They were then

dismissed for the evening meal and were free until 'Lights Out' at 9 p.m.

Prisoners' rations were of the sparsest kind consisting of either a weak milk soup or ersatz coffee for breakfast, a thin soup made from swedes for lunch, to which a slice of bread was added for those on the hardest details. At supper the prisoners were issued with their bread rations for the following day, together with a piece of cheese with margarine or jam. This meagre diet, the thin clothing, poor sanitary conditions and arduous work took a constant toll.

In 1935 Dachau was the largest concentration camp with 2,500 inmates. By the summer of 1939 the number had increased to 6,000 and by August 1943 to 17,000. In all some 200,000 prisoners were registered here, of whom 30,000 died. The number of deliberate executions at Dachau appears to have been limited. Fifty-five Polish intellectuals were shot there on November 11, 1940, an unknown number of Soviet officers in February 1944, and then on April 19, 1945, four French and 11 Czech officers.

The camp gatehouse has been retained but all the original huts have been demolished, save for the replica on the right.

The awful contrast between then and now. This is . . . or rather was . . . the shower block.

The camp was expanded in 1937 as a training facility for the SS, involving a great deal of construction work carried out by the prisoners building barracks and schools for administration, Allgemeine-SS officers, SS medical orderlies and cooks, and numerous other facilities. SS-Totenkopfstandarte I 'Oberbayern', 1,473 strong under SS-Obersturmbannführer Max Sauer was raised here in April 1937, and Eicke returned on November 1, 1939, as an SS-Gruppenführer to form his Waffen-SS Division 'Totenkopf' from part of his Standarte and police units. All the Totenkopf elements of the concentration camp guards now rated as Waffen-SS and could change their distinctive brown uniforms for the same as worn by crack front-line troops.

With the change of emphasis in the camps to war production, in April 1942 the Inspectorate of Concentration Camps became subordinated to SS-Obergruppenführer and General of the Waffen-SS Oswald Pohl's Economic and Administrative Head Office (WVHA), which controlled the SS's vast business empire. However, a strident conflict continued between those SS officers who saw the elimination of Jews as their top priority, and those who wanted to extract the maximum effort from their prisoners in war production before death intervened. In March 1945 Himmler's tasking of the SS Chief Hygienist, SS-Oberführer Dr Joachim Mrugowsky, with the improvement of conditions for the remaining 600,000 concentration camp inmates, of whom 120,000 were now deemed unfit for work, came far too late for implementation.

The attrition rate amongst the ill-treated and overworked prisoners was horrendous at all the camps, Dachau being no exception. At times the two ovens in the crematorium (below) **just could not cope with the number of dead whose emaciated bodies were piled up outside like so much rubbish.**

On April 29, the 1st Batallion of the 157th Infantry Regiment, US 45th Division, entered the SS compound by the back door.

When the GIs inspected the railway wagons they found them full of corpses . . . but there were even worse horrors ahead.

Medical experiments were carried out on prisoners in most of the camps by SS doctors with a horrifying amateurism that failed to produce any results of value, but served to bolster Himmler's image as a patron of science.

For instance, SS doctor Sigmund Rasch conducted freezing experiments on about 300 prisoners at Dachau from August 1942 onwards to determine their reaction to the cold and means of recovery.

Dachau main camp's industry was the production of uniforms for the SS and prisoners, but there were also 125 satellite camps providing labour for various other industries.

Sounds of battle alerted the camp to the imminent arrival of American troops on April 28, and that evening the guards lowered the swastika flags and replaced them with white ones. The first Americans to arrive next day came via the marshalling yards, where they came across 50-odd cattle cars in and around

The GIs were so outraged at what they discovered at Dachau that the SS guards were despatched out of hand. An analysis by Colonel Howard A. Buechner, then a 1st Lieutenant and the first American doctor to enter the camp, explains that of the 560 guards, 30 were killed in combat, 40 bludgeoned to death by camp inmates, 122 shot where they were found and 346 lined up and machine-gunned. Because the execution had been pictured on film by Tech/4 Arland B. Musser of the 163rd Signal Corps Photographic Company, eight officers and NCOs were singled out for court-martial, including Dr Buechner on the grounds that he should have attempted to try to stop the execution. However when the matter reached General George S. Patton, the Military Governor of Bavaria, he called for all the documents and photographs to be brought to his office whereupon he set fire to the evidence in his waste paper basket. The picture *(above)* escaped his purge and was released by the Field Censor with this caption: 'Soldiers of the 45th Inf Div, US Seventh Army, order SS men to come forward after one of their number tried to escape from the Dachau concentration camp after it was liberated by US Forces. Men on the ground feign death by falling as the guards fired a volley at the fleeing SS man.'

of which were the corpses of 2,310 Hungarian and Polish Jews that had been despatched from Birkenau in a journey lasting over a month. The Americans were so enraged by what they encountered in the camp, with dead inmates lying around everywhere and a mountain of corpses outside the crematorium, that when one of the SS watchtower sentries opened fire on the rioting prisoners, the American troops hunted down and killed any SS guard they could find. The remaining guards were then lined up and machine-gunned.

The Americans recorded the liberation of 31,432 inmates, although the International Committee had previously recorded 67,665 inmates on April 26. A further 2,466 inmates were to die after liberation.

The first trial of 42 defendants, including the last commandant Obersturmbannführer Martin Weiss and five doctors, took place at the camp between November 15 and December 14, 1945, and resulted in 36 death sentences but, in view of the rough treatment they had all received from the American guards, none of these executions were carried out.

The mass execution took place here in what was the old SS compound (see page 317) which was taken over and occupied by the US Army until Munich was chosen to host the 1972 Olympic Games. The Bavarian Interior Ministry urgently needed a base close to the stadium for security forces so the Americans agreed to quit the SS compound which was then handed over to the West German police. All requests to picture this spot were refused until we were finally given permission in 2003 to photograph it for this book (For more detail on Dachau, see *After the Battle* No. 27.)

Sachsenhausen

The usual concentration camp motto (see page 316) greeted prisoners at Sachsenhausen — the second concentration camp established by the SS north of Berlin in 1936. A camp for women was opened in May 1939 further north at Ravensbrück (see page 342).

Sachsenhausen concentration camp outside Oranienburg, north of Berlin, was established by the SS in 1936, being constructed by inmates of the Emsland camp in Esterwegen in a triangular shape with a 2.5-metre-high perimeter wall guarded by eight watchtowers. The camp also incorporated a special Gestapo prison, where special prisoners were detained, tortured and executed, including some British officers who had been captured.

The camp commandants were Hermann Baranowski, who died in 1939; Hans Loritz, who committed suicide in the Neumünster internment camp in 1946; Walter Eisfeld, who died in 1940; and lastly Anton Kaindl, who was sentenced to life imprisonment by a Soviet military court and died in captivity.

In 1938 the Inspectorate of Concentration Camps moved its offices out of Berlin to Sachsenhausen.

Of the few original huts remaining, Nos. 38 and 39 were burned down by neo-Nazis in 1992. Part of the so-called 'small camp' within the camp and known as the Jewish huts, they have been rebuilt in their former style and now house the camp museum.

After the war Sachsenhausen was taken over by the Soviets, as were Buchenwald and Ravensbrück, for the detention of their political enemies. Some 65,000 of these are believed to have died of starvation, malnutrition and disease during this period, apart from those executed for various reasons. The remains of 12,500 prisoners were later found buried in mass graves just outside the camp.

Approximately 225,000 Germans were imprisoned here for political reasons between 1933 and 1939, being categorised at first as Communists, Socialists and Centre Party members, to which were later added Jews, Gypsies, 'asocials', criminals, Jehovah Witnesses, soldiers dishonourably discharged from the Wehrmacht, SS members undergoing punishment, Soviet prisoners of war and captives from the occupied territories of Czechoslovakia, Poland, Norway, Holland, Belgium and France. In 1939 an additional 162,000 were being held without trial in 'protective custody', and by the summer of 1943 some 17,300 prisoners, including 1,700 women, had been interned for 'destruction through labour', i.e. to be worked to death. In 1939 the camp population averaged 25,000.

In the summer of 1938 prisoners from Sachsenhausen began work on the world's largest brick factory next to the canal locks at Lehnitz, east of Oranienburg. The purpose of this so-called Klinkerwerk (brickworks) was to provide building materials for the construction of Germania, for which the canals provided a cheap means of transportation. As a sponsoring agency, the SS founded the Deutsche Erd- und Steinwerke GmbH (German Excavation & Quarrying Company) with registered shareholders. Further brickworks were also started that year near the Flossenbürg and Buchenwald camps and in the Neuengamme satellite camp.

From August 1938 onwards about 1,500 prisoners a day were marched to and from the Klinkerwerk construction site, where, as one survivor recorded: 'The SS men far preferred to use us prisoners for shooting practise than ordinary targets, choosing particular prisoners pushing wheelbarrows and shooting straight at them.'

Many lives were lost digging out the two canal docks and draining marshy land to construct a railway line the nine kilometres to Zehlendorf to bring in the clay for brickmaking. However, the clay eventually turned out to be unsuitable for the dry-pressing process planned, and in 1939 the factory had to be converted to the wet-pressing method with artificial drying.

At first the prisoners detailed to the Klinkerwerk squads were those being punished for infringements of the camp rules or because they came from a racially inferior group, such as Jews, gypsies, and homosexuals, that it was intended to work to death. Jehovah Witnesses were also included for their refusal to carry out military service or swear an oath of loyalty to Hitler. Jews were treated with particular severity and were even accommodated separately until their deportation to Auschwitz in August 1942. About 200 homosexual prisoners were worked to death at the Klinkerwerk in a deliberate campaign mounted between July and September of the same year.

In 1941 the Klinkerwerk was awarded its own camp and satellite status from Sachsenhausen. Then in 1942 part of the factory was turned over to the manufacture of grenades and warheads, achieving the production of up to 10,000 grenades a day, although the explosives were added elsewhere. At the same time the re-cycling of scrap metals from all over the conquered continent began, also under tremendous pressure.

The actual number of deaths at the Klinkerwerk is not known. Usually bodies were removed to the main camp, where the SS registry office would issue death certificates falsifying the cause of death and the number of bodies destroyed in the camp crematorium. When the commandant of Sachsenhausen ordered the removal of all the ashes around and in the crematorium in the spring of 1945, some eight to nine tons were dumped in the Hohenzollern Canal.

In 1940 a boot-testing strip was established along the semi-circular rear of the main camp's parade ground where prisoners carrying 35lb loads had to walk ten hours a day testing out military boots on nine different kinds of surfaces.

Over 11,000 Soviet prisoners of war were executed in the mass execution facility within the main camp in Station Z, constructed in 1942, where prisoners could be killed with a shot in the back of the neck, gassed, or executed on the nearby rifle range, and their bodies cremated.

Sachsenhausen had a total of 61 satellite camps with prisoners working at factories such as the Heinkel works in

Now one can come and go as one pleases but for tens of thousands it was a one-way journey.

By the end of the war a total of 700,000 persons had passed through the camp gates of whom perhaps upwards of 100,000 never walked out alive. No doubt Himmler gave Sachsenhausen top marks for efficiency.

Germendorf, the DEMAG works (Deutsche Maschinenfabrik AG) and the Zeppelin Airship Construction Company, which made barrage balloons.

In 1942 a secret detachment of 144 highly-skilled workers, mainly Jews, was set up under SS-Sturmbannführer Bernhard Krüger using huts 18 and 19 in the camp and Schloss Friedenthal in Oranienburg for the production of forged banknotes, postage stamps, passports and other documents. This was 'Operation Bernhard' organised by Generalleutnant der Polizei und SS-Obergruppenführer Dr Ernst Kaltenbrunner, head of the Security Police in the RSHA, on behalf of the German Secret Service. With a view to damaging the British economy by flooding the market with forged banknotes, £134 million pounds worth of £5 and £10 notes were printed, some of which got into circulation. Toward the end of the war the entire unit was moved to Mauthausen and Ebensee concentration camps, where they were liberated by American troops on May 5, 1945. Meanwhile their forged products and equipment had been sunk in the Töplitzsee lake by the SS, from where most were recovered in 1959 and 1963.

Again medical experiments were carried out on prisoners here, the first being deliberate wounding followed by artificial contamination of the wounds in order to experiment with a newly-developed antiseptic in gangrenous conditions, resulting in several deaths. In the summer of 1944, four out of eight prisoners died from experiment of an unknown kind. Then that September experiments were made with poisoned ammunition to test the rapidity of the poison's effect.

In early February 1945 the commandant had the eastern satellite camps vacated, including Bad Saarow, Briesen, Fürstenberg/Oder, Kolpin, Küstrin, Storkow, Strausberg and Trebnitz, the prisoners being driven back by train or on long marches to the main camp. The SS used the evacuation of Lieberose camp as an excuse to massacre the Hungarian and Polish Jews interned there, then murdered a further 1,000 sick and weak prisoners before marching the remaining 1,500 prisoners back to Oranienburg, shooting at least 36 along the way and a large number upon arrival.

Himmler's negotiation with Count Folke Bernadotte of the Swedish Red Cross, resulted in the rescue of 2,176 Scandinavian prisoners by a fleet of white buses which made seven runs during the period March 15 and 29 between Sachsenhausen and a part of Neuengamme concentration camp then under Swedish control.

A labour squad returns to camp. This is the gatehouse of the prisoners' compound, 'Schutzhaftlager' literally meaning a 'protective custody camp'.

324

Above: **The guard towers along the western wall of the camp, with the camp workshops on the outside — then and now** *(below).*

From February onwards, the SS transferred thousands of prisoners on to camps farther to the south or west, such as Mauthausen and Bergen-Belsen, while large numbers of Jewish prisoners continued to arrive from Auschwitz and Hungary. The Berlin satellite camps' prisoners were not transported back to Sachsenhausen until April 20, 1945, and were then marched off to the north-west, when the evacuation of the main camp began on the 21st, the SS having notified the International Red Cross of the impending evacuation two days ear-lier with a request for food supplies. Some 33,000 of the 36,000, including women and children, were set off with

their SS escorts in groups of 500 prison-ers, clad only in their prison garb with wooden shoes and sometimes a blanket. Only the first groups received any rations to take with them. They marched 20-40 kilometres a day in cold, wet weather, dragging wagons loaded with the belongings of the SS men, who shot those who lagged behind or were caught scavenging for food.

By April 23, more than 16,000 prison-ers were concentrated in the Belower Woods near Wittstock, where the Inter-national Red Cross caught up with them, bringing food supplies, and was able to have the order regarding the shooting of prisoners suspended. An

emergency hospital with prisoner staff was set up at Grabow for 800 prisoners, 132 of whom died. The march continued on April 29 and by the beginning of May the surviving prisoners reached the area between Parchim and Schwerin and were finally liberated as they met up with Soviet and American forces.

During the fighting around Oranien-burg, Soviet and Polish troops came across the camp on April 22 and 23 respectively, being enthusiastically greeted by the remaining 3,000 inmates, who had been too ill or weak to march. 300 of these died in the camp after liber-ation. It was then used by the Soviets as an internment camp until 1950.

Buchenwald

Buchenwald concentration camp was established in July 1937 outside Weimar as a replacement for the original Lichtenburg camp. It eventually had 136 satellite camps in central Germany and in the Ruhr supplying slave labour for such firms as Krupp, Hasag, Rheinmetall-Borsig, IG Farben, Junkers, Braunkohle-Benzin, Bochumer Verein and others. The Gustloff-Werke II factory, which was directed by Gauleiter Fritz Sauckel who was to become General Plenipotentiary for Labour Assignment in March 1942, produced rifle barrels at the camp, as did the Walther Weapons Zehla-Mehlis plant. The main camp had the usual Deutsche Erd- und Steinwerke brickworks and adjacent quarry.

'Beech Forest' was the euphemistically-sounding name invented for one of the most notorious camps: Buchenwald. It was built in 1937 just north-west of Weimar, the inmates being used as forced labour in the adjacent quarry and munition works.

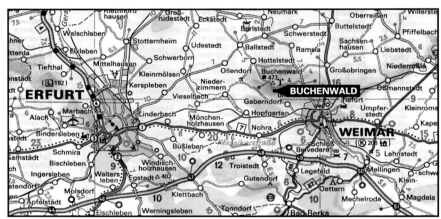

The camp was captured by the Americans on April 11, 1945 but it had to be handed over to the Soviets on July 1, as it fell within their zone of occupation. They continued to use Buchenwald as an interment camp until it was given to the German Democratic Republic in 1950. The GDR then set about converting it into a memorial with a strong anti-fascist theme.

There were two camp commandants: *Left:* SS-Sturmbannführer Karl Koch, who had joined the NSDAP in 1931. He was inducted into the SS the following year in Kassel and had already been in charge of the 'wild camp' in the Columbiahaus in Berlin (see page 314). He was posted to Sachsenhausen in July 1936 and to Buchenwald in July the following year. In December 1941, somewhat ironically, he was arrested by the SS under suspicion of corruption but was released the following day on Himmler's orders. In the spring of 1942 he moved to Maidanek camp in Poland where once again he was accused of corruption. An SS court sentenced him to death and he was executed at Buchenwald in April 1945. *Centre:* His wife Ilse, known as the Witch of Buchenwald, was acquitted of a similar corruption charge but was given a life sentence, later reduced to four years, by a US military tribunal. Released soon after, she was arrested again in 1949 and tried before a German civilian court, the Schwurgericht (Jury Court) in Augsburg, which on January 15, 1951 sentenced her to life. She committed suicide in a Bavarian prison on September 1, 1967. *Right:* SS-Oberführer Hermann Pister had been a member of the Schutzstaffel since 1932. In 1941-42 he was in charge of the SS-Sonderlager (Special Camp) Hinzert (15 kilometres south-east of Trier) and replaced Koch in January 1942. Arrested by the Americans and sentenced to death, he died of a heart attack in September 1948.

Under the commandants Karl Koch and, from the end of 1940, Hermann Pister, some 239,000 prisoners were registered here of whom 56,000 perished. When 2,000 Poles arrived in October 1939 they were placed in an open barbed-wire cage to die of cold and starvation, and only 500 were still alive when the compound was closed down in February 1940. Some 8,483 Soviet prisoners of war were murdered in stables specially converted for the purpose of execution by a shot in the back of the neck. Another 11,000 prisoners were hanged and a further 33,462 were killed in the camp by various means, not counting the fate of women in the satellite camps. In October 1942 all the Jewish prisoners were sent to Auschwitz/Birkenau for extermination.

Among the 35,600 inmates in December 1943 were listed some 12,600 Soviet forced labourers, 11,400 political prisoners, 22,000 Danish policemen and 7,300 Poles.

A group of 43 British and Canadian officers that had been captured while working with resistance groups on the Continent were brought to Buchenwald to be secretly liquidated in 1944, only four of whom survived.

Medical experiments were conducted in the camp, including the infliction of phosphor burns and injections with typhus, yellow fever, typhoid, cholera and old blood plasma. Many inmates were killed in the camp detention hall with injections by SS doctor Erwin Ding-Schuler on the orders of commandant Koch. New vaccines produced by IG Farben were also first tested out on the inmates, and tattooed human skin was used to produce exhibition specimens or useful articles for SS family members, such as lampshades, briefcases, etc.

Centre: **SS-Sturmbannführer Dr. Erwin Ding-Schuler carried out horrible medical experiments on helpless victims in Block Nos. 46 and 50** *(left)*, **which went under the guise of the** 'Hygiene Institute of the Waffen-SS'. *Right:* **The building has been demolished — this is where it stood. Ding-Schuler cheated justice by committing suicide in August 1945.**

Buchenwald was unique as it was the first concentration camp opened to Allied newsmen as Captain Harry Butcher, General Eisenhower's aide, explains: 'He had gone to one of the German internment camps [Ohrdruf] and had seen the horrible treatment given the inmates. He said that their condition beggared description. He had interviewed several through an interpreter and said that their stories of starvation, cruelty, and bestiality were so overpowering that he felt sick. In one room he had seen 20 to 30 naked men killed by starvation. Ike said he had forced himself to see the bodies, as he wanted to be able to have first-hand evidence to combat anyone in the future who would say that stories of the atrocities were "propaganda". I told him I thought we should give responsible people at home an opportunity to see the ghastly scenes for themselves. He is planning to ask the War Department to select a group of editors and publishers to visit the camps.'

These pictures were taken in the yard beside the crematorium which still stands.

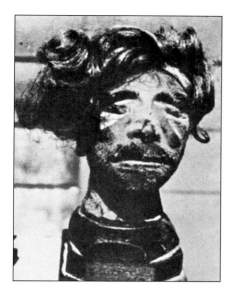

Eisenhower called in a war crimes investigation unit which discovered even more horrific evidence: human heads shrunken and mounted for display and crates filled with tens of thousands of gold teeth.

Corruption was so rife in the camp, such as the theft of inmate property combined with their killing, that Koch himself was tried by an SS court in 1944, sentenced to death and eventually shot in his own camp! His wife and co-defendant, Ilse Koch, known as the 'Witch of Buchenwald', was accused of receiving stolen goods but was acquitted for lack of evidence.

In March and April 1945 the bulk of the prisoners were sent off on death marches, during which an estimated 22,500 died. Then on April 11, two days before American troops arrived, the 21,000 remaining inmates of the main camp liberated themselves under Communist leadership after the SS guards had disappeared. Among them were 904 children and Wing Commander Forest Yeo-Thomas and Captain Christopher Burney, two British SOE agents who had been captured earlier in the war.

A few days later American officers, acting on information obtained from some of the prisoners, discovered a considerable treasure trove of valuables, such as wedding rings and precious stones, taken from the prisoners and hidden in some bunkers in the side of the adjacent quarry.

Apart from the dental gold, jewellery, precious stones and other valuables of the victims were found sealed in nearby tunnels. These assets, together with gold removed from the Merkers mine (see *After the Battle* No. 93) were held by the Inter-Allied Reparation Agency set up in January 1946 to provide funds for the 'rehabilitation and resettlement of persons eligible', notably Jewish victims of Nazi actions. The work of allocating these funds continued for over 50 years. Meanwhile, after the German Democratic Republic came into being, this dramatic memorial was erected. (Although the date on the tower reads 1945, it was unveiled in September 1958.

Buchenwald had been reached by the 6th Armored Division of the US Third Army on April 11, and it was another unit from Patton's Third — the 11th Armored — which two weeks later entered another concentration camp just east of Linz in Austria. A young soldier, Charles Ellington described what he saw: 'No description can do justice to the stench, the filth and the human misery we found at Mauthausen. Those survivors had to be rounded up, calmed, fed, washed and slowly brought back to normality.' We have just read how Eisenhower made an example of Buchenwald in throwing it open to newsmen but, as this SHAEF signal shows, as soon as the camp had been cleaned up the true message was lost, some later visitors even becoming sceptical about the awful conditions reported earlier. And when one visits the clean, neatly-preserved buildings today, it is difficult to comprehend what really took place. *Below:* This is Mauthausen 60 years on; as the guide explains 'the soil of this vast stronghold is soaked with the blood of thousands of innocent people'. *Opposite:* This is the comparison of the courtyard as it was: a hell-hole of humanity . . . where the quick and the dead existed alongside each other in absloute squalor.

Mauthausen, Austria

SECRET   SHAEF   SECRET   93

STAFF MESSAGE CONTROL

INCOMING MESSAGE

DRLS

TOO 082107B MAY

SHAEF 82/9
TOR 090900 MAY
eod, 090916 MAY

THIS IS A REPRODUCTION OF AN INCOMING COM ZONE MESSAGE

S E C R E T

P R I O R I T Y

FROM   :   TWELFTH ARMY GROUP SIGNED BRADLEY

TO   :   ETOUSA

PASSED TO   :   SHAEF MAIN FOR ACTION

REF NO   :   Q-20235 MAY 1945

        This is paraphrase of First US Army message.

        BUCHENWALD concentration camp has been cleaned up, the sick segregated and burials completed to such an extent that very little evidence of atrocities remain.

        This negatives any educational value of having various groups visit this camp to secure first hand information of German atrocities. In fact, many feel quite skeptical that previous conditions actually existed.

        Suggest that further visits - this camp be discontinued.

ACTION   :   G-1 SHAEF MAIN

INFORMATION :   SGS
                  G-2
                  G-3
                  G-5
                  AG RECORDS

SMC IN 2786   9 MAY '45   1030B   SL/ra   REF NO: Q-20235

599   SECRET   S E C R E T   14   COPY NO.

THE MAKING OF AN EXACT COPY OF THIS MESSAGE IS FORBIDDEN

From 1938 to 1945 Mauthausen was a name synonymous with fear and terror. Historian Derek Penton explains that 'it evolved from a ringed enclosure of barbed wire into a citadel consisting of granite gateways, courtyards, watch towers and high-voltage fencing. The camp was constructed by the prisoners themselves over a period of six years from granite blocks hewn in the quarry below. The appearance of Mauthausen was probably more forbidding than any other concentration camp. At night it was depicted by brilliant but sinister floodlights. Such a sight must have struck fear into the hearts of thousands of prisoners as they approached the fortress after a two and a half mile trek from the railway station. The entrance into the camp was through the main outer gateway, under whose arch countless men, women and children passed only once in their lifetime. Newly arrived prisoners were initiated into camp life in the yard just inside the main gate. Here the commandant Franz Ziereis would often welcome the newcomers with the words: "Here is only a marching in; the way out is through the chimney of the crematorium".' *Left:* On May 6, 1945, the inmates had the supreme pleasure in toppling the symbol of Nazism from over the main gate. *Right:* The supports still remain to be seen.

After the Anschluss with Austria in March 1938, Himmler ordered the establishment of the Mauthausen concentration camp near Linz to save the cost of transporting Austrian prisoners farther afield. It was also conveniently close to some granite quarries for development under the Deutsche Erd- und Steinwerke umbrella, the quarries and the infamous 'staircase' access being used extensively in the abuse and working to death of prisoners. The first commandant was Albert Sauer who died in Falkensee in 1945.

At the outbreak of the war the camp held about 1,500 prisoners, and by April 1942 had expanded to 5,500. It eventually possessed 56 satellite camps and, when liberated there were about 50,000 prisoners in the main camp with a further 24,000 who had arrived the previous month accommodated in the main satellites Güsen I and II. More than 30,000 had died in the previous four

The stone watch towers survive but the original electrified fence and floodlighting have gone.

From 1943 onwards the labour force worked in the armaments industry for Messerschmitt AG. Those found unfit for work were eliminated either in the camp's own gas chambers or in a mobile gas van that shuttled between Mauthausen and Güsen, or killed by a lethal injection in the camp infirmary. There was also a special installation close to the camp crematorium for killing prisoners with a pistol shot in the back of the neck.

In 1941 1,000 Dutch Jews were sent here to work in the quarries, as were 600 Italian Jews in 1944 and thousands of Hungarian Jews in early 1945. Among the prisoners were tens of thousands of Spanish republicans who had been interned in France in 1939, deported by the Germans to Mauthausen in 1940, and systematically worked to death in the quarries or shot at random until only 3,000 remained alive by January 1945. Of these 2,163 were killed in the last months. Of 1,000 Polish civilian workers, non-Jews, brought to the Ebensee satellite after the Warsaw uprising in September 1944, only 100 survived.

Below: **The same pathway which leads to the 'Staircase of Death'.**

Above: **Himmler inspects Mauthausen in 1939. L-R: Dr Ernst Kaltenbrunner, later Heydrich's successor as chief of the Reich Main Security Office; Franz Ziereis, the camp commandant; Himmler, and August Eigruber, the Gauleiter of the Upper Danube district. All four got their come-uppance at the end of the war: Ziereis was shot and fatally wounded by an American soldier on May 23, 1945, the same day that Himmler took his own life (see page 85); Kaltenbrunner was executed at Nuremberg on October 16, 1946, and Eigruber hanged by the Americans in Landsberg prison on May 28, 1947.**

months. The camp also held the record for the number of executions carried out — 36,318 — and in September 1944, 47 captured Allied airmen were deliberately worked to death here. The last commandant, SS-Obersturmbannführer Franz Ziereis, once boasted that he had given his son 50 Jews for target practice as a birthday present.

Derek Penton: 'The grandiose plans for the reconstruction of German cities promoted by Hitler and Speer demanded full exploitation of Mauthausen's natural stone. The quarries in which an average of 3,000 prisoners worked became notorious for their high mortality rate. Life expectancy was estimated at six weeks. Because camps such as Mauthausen were to be permanent features of the "Thousand-Year Reich", construction in stone was also applicable.' *Above:* This is the Wiener Graben quarry — then and now — with the infamous staircase on which so many toiled . . . and died . . . in the right background.

The camp was liberated by American troops on April 25, 1945. The death register recorded the deaths of 71,000 prisoners in Mauthausen and its satellites. The Americans found nearly 10,000 bodies in a huge communal grave. Of the 110,000 freed in the main camp and elsewhere, of whom 28,000 were Jews, more than 3,000 died after liberation.

The Third Reich's version of the treadmill of ancient times: 'The granite blocks were carried on hods strapped to the backs of prisoners from the bottom of the quarry to the flat summit of the hill above. Prior to 1942 this was done by means of a boulder pathway up the hillside before being reconstructed as a staircase consisting of 186 steps. This became known as the infamous "Staircase of Death" on which hundreds of prisoners were shot, crushed or beaten to extinction.'

It was Lord Russell of Liverpool who in 1954 set out 'to provide the ordinary reader with a truthful and accurate account' of Nazi war crimes in his book *The Scourge of the Swastika*. 'During the war, on the lowest computation, twelve million men, women and children from the invaded and occupied territories were done to death by the Germans. At a conservative estimate eight million of them perished in German concentration camps. Speaking of these Sir Hartley Shawcross, the chief prosecutor for the United Kingdom at the trial of major war criminals, said in his closing speech, "Twelve million murders! Two-thirds of the Jews in Europe exterminated, more than six million of them on the killers' own figures. Murder conducted like some mass production industry in the gas chambers and the ovens of Auschwitz, Dachau, Treblinka, Buchenwald, Mauthausen, Maidanek, and Oranienburg." To these camps were brought millions from the occupied territories; some because they were Jews, some had been deported as slave labour and were no longer considered fit for work. There they were herded together in conditions of filth and degradation, bullied, beaten, tortured, and starved and finally exterminated through work or "eliminated", as the Germans called it, by mass execution in the gas chambers. The survivors have told of their experiences, and the camps themselves have given testimony of the horrors of which their very walls were silent witnesses. Those who were the first to enter these camps will be forever haunted by the horror of what they saw.'

Photographs can do little to adequately portray what really happened in these compounds, now all scrubbed and pristine so expunging the filth and squalor . . . and the smell. This is the spot where the SS photographed Hans Bonarewitz being hauled to his death. He had been smuggled out of Mauthausen in a crate on a lorry in June 1942. After he was recaptured he was displayed with his crate in the yard for seven days before being taken to the gallows on July 30.

Another camp liberated by the US Third Army was Flossenbürg, this time by the 90th Infantry Division.

Flossenbürg

Flossenbürg concentration camp was established in May 1938 near Neustadt in Upper Bavaria not far from the Sudeten part of Czechoslovakia on a site chosen for its both its inaccessibility and the proximity of granite quarries. It had an initial capacity of 1,600 prisoners, later extended to 3,000, With a change in priority to war production, 85 satellite camps were established for this purpose, 25 of them being for women, accommodating 5,000 prisoners in all. Between 1938 and 1945 some 111,400 prisoners were registered

How can one equate the landscaped gardens and well-trimmed lawns with a place of disease, degradation and death?

at Flossenbürg, of whom 16,000 were women. A total of 22,334 died, many of diseases caused by malnutrition and overwork, but these figures do not include Soviet prisoners of war.

Among those prisoners executed here were the pastor Dietrich Bonhoeffer and Admiral Wilhelm Canaris on April 9, 1945, for their complicity in the July 1944 plot against Hitler.

The camp was liberated by troops of the US 90th Division on April 23, 1945, shortly after 14,000 prisoners had been sent off on death marches in three separate groups, which cost the lives of a further 4,000. Only 1,526 inmates were found in the camp at the time of liberation, of whom a further 120 died shortly after.

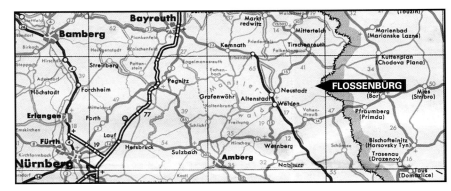

Flossenbürg was located east of Bayreuth down a dead-end road close to the Czech border. Its quarries were conveniently situated to supply the huge Nazi building projects in Nuremberg.

Above: **The punishment cells are [1].** *Below left:* **The laundry [2] has been preserved together with the kitchen block [3].**

Below right: **Although the electrified fence has gone, some posts still survive on the perimeter.**

Liberation at last! Freed prisoners congregate on the Appellplatz to celebrate May 1. The building in the background is the laundry block. Flossenbürg had four commandants: Jakob Weisehorn, who committed suicide in 1939 when his embezzling was discovered; Egon Zill, who was sentenced to life imprisonment in 1955, which was later reduced to 15 years and who died in 1974; Max Koegel, who committed suicide in 1946; and Karl Künster who was killed near Nuremberg in 1945.

View across the Neuengamme roll-call square. When the camp was first built, all prisoners were housed in wooden huts but in 1943 construction began of twin, two-storied accommodation blocks for prisoners, one at either end of the Appellplatz. The southern building seen in the background housed Blocks Nos. 1-4 and the northern one Blocks Nos. 21-24.

Neuengamme

Neuengamme concentration camp was originally established in December 1938 some 30 kilometres east of Hamburg as a satellite of Sachsenhausen, becoming independent in June 1940, providing yet another brickworks for the Deutsche Erd- und Steinwerke company. Of the 106,000 prisoners registered at Neuengamme, 13,500 of whom were women, only ten per cent were actually German nationals, the rest coming from all over occupied Europe. An estimated 55,000 subsequently died in the main camp and it satellites or on the death marches of April 1945.

At first the prisoners were employed building and extending their camp and the facilities for the SS guards, in developing the brickworks and in deepening the canal connecting the brickworks with the Dove-Elbe river. About 300 Russian and Ukrainian prisoners were employed in the latter task, working up to their waists in the freezing cold water, while the brickyard and clay pit work details involved between 600 and 1,200 men.

Workshops for the SS war industries were set up in 1942, including a Walther Weapons Works Zehla-Mehlis plant, and slave labour was hired out to other firms, resulting in some 70 satellite camps being established and guarded by SS, but in some cases (like in satellites of other camps too) also by naval, air force and police units. In 1943 production of pre-fabricated concrete sections for air raid shelters and housing blocks was started, a railway line was constructed linking the camp with the main system, two air raid shelters built for the SS guards, and some brick two-storey prisoner accommodation.

Below: **After the war, the British used the former concentration camp first as POW enclosure and then as internment camp for ex-Nazis. In 1948 the Hamburg prison authorities took over the grounds. The camp's wooden structures were demolished and a detention centre built on the site. A memorial column was erected in 1953, but it stood on the perimeter of the former camp. In 1965, at the suggestion of the Amicale Internationale Neuengamme, the City of Hamburg decided to declare the former camp grounds an official memorial site. Nonetheless, a second prison building was added in 1969 and plans were developed for further encroachments on the historic remains. Under persistent pressure from the Amicale and local German civic action groups, in 1984 Hamburg put the camp's architectural remains under protection as historic sites and in 1989 the major decision was taken to move the original prison elsewhere and develop the site into a proper camp memorial. Now, with the prison gone, the Appellplatz has been restored and work is underway to indicate where the wooden huts stood with low stone profiles.**

Left: **The guardhouse at the entrance to the SS compound of the camp. There was a separate entrance to the prisoner's compound further down on the right, giving direct access to the Appellplatz,** **but this was the camp's main entrance. In the background one can just pick out the northern prisoners' accommodation block under construction.** *Right:* **The guardhouse as it looks today.**

From 1940 until 1942 the camp was commanded by SS-Hauptsturmführer Martin Weiss, who was succeeded by SS-Hauptsturmführer Max Pauly on transfer from Stutthof concentration camp, where he was renowned for his cruelty.

The monthly death rate at the camp was about 500 in 1943, rising to about 1,700 in 1944 and about 2,500 in February 1945. A typhus epidemic in the winter of 1941-42 accounted for 1,600 deaths alone. The bodies were usually cremated in the camp but the dead from the satellite camps were buried in nearby cemeteries. Like all concentration camps, Neuengamme was used by the Gestapo for executions, about 2,000

taking place here. Towards the end of 1942, 448 Soviet prisoners of war were executed by gassing in two batches, and numerous Soviet officers and members of the Wehrmacht were shot by the SS

on their rifle range. Instructions from the RSHA and WVHA led to frequent hangings, including that of 35 Soviet and Polish prisoners on August 9, 1944, and 58 Dutch prisoners in March 1945.

SS camp guards and staff on parade in front of the garages and workshops in the SS compound. The picture was taken on November 9, 1943, so the occasion must have been the 20th anniversary of the Munich putsch.

The photographer stood on the roof of the SS canteen, which no longer exists, so our comparison was taken from ground level.

Left: **From 1940 to 1942 up to 1,600 prisoners were deployed on the broadening of the Dove-Elbe river and construction of a branch canal leading to the camp's brickworks. The Elbe labour squads had the deadliest job of all. Working in deep mud in all weathers, with nothing more than shovels, wheelbarrows and tip-wagons, constantly chased on by their SS guards and Kapos, hundreds of inmates perished during the work. Here, prisoners are toiling on the river dike a few hundred metres north-west of the camp (opposite the spot where the branch canal enters the river).** *Above:* **The same houses still stand along the Neuengammer Hausdeich.**

Left: **Prisoners at work at the camp end of the branch canal. Earth dredged up from the river was loaded onto barges and moved to places where the prisoners then had to unload the silt and distribute it over the countryside. Once the canal and** harbour basin were completed, the barges were used to bring in sand and coal for the camp's brickworks and to carry out the finished product. *Right:* Over half a century later, the jetty is a silent place of pilgrimage.

Then . . . and now. The camp brickworks were built by the prisoners between 1940 and 1942 to replace the small brickyard that lay further west and had been used since 1938. The new plant was extensively automatised, employing only some 100 inmates as opposed to the hundreds doing the manual work in the awful clay pits. As agreed by contract with the City of Hamburg, the clinker bricks produced were to be used for construction of the planned Führer buildings in the city.

In March 1942 construction started of a 1.7-kilometre branch railway to the camp. By early 1943 a station building and double sidings had been completed at the eastern end of the camp. The goods trains facilitated the war industries that had been set up in the camp but they were also used to bring in prisoners from all over Europe and transport prisoners out to one of Neuengamme's many satellite camps or to the extermination camps.

SS doctors and medical orderlies were responsible for the murder of a large number of 'useless mouths' by lethal injection during the period 1942-43, after which such cases were sent off to Auschwitz for extermination. They also carried out experiments on both healthy and sick prisoners alike. SS doctor Kurt Heissmeyer infected 25 adults and 20 children with tuberculosis, the children and their minders being later murdered by hanging in the school at Hamburg's Bullenhuser Damm before the arrival of the Allied forces.

The evacuation of Neuengamme was ordered in April 1945. The camp records were destroyed and 71 Gestapo prisoners from Fuhlsbüttel were hanged in the camp prison. The rest of the prisoners were then sent off on death marches with one or two day's rations of food and water to such destinations as Belsen-Bergen, the prisoner-of-war camp at Sandbostel and the satellite camp at Wöbbelin, where lack of food, rampant disease and appalling sanitary conditions took their toll by the tens of thousands.

Youth camp volunteers cleared and reconstructed the sidings in 1994. A lone boxcar was set up to symbolise the many prisoner transports that arrived here during the war.

One large group was despatched to Lübeck to be loaded on ships which were then to take them out to sea and be scuttled, thereby destroying all evidence of their existence. Some 4,600 prisoners were loaded on the liner *Cap Ancona*, and about 2,000 each on the freighters *Thielbeck* and *Athen*. However, the *Cap Ancona* and *Thielbeck* were attacked by British aircraft while still in the Neustädter Bight on May 3, 1945. The *Cap Ancona* caught fire and sank with the loss of all but 600 prisoners, and the *Thielbeck* sank immediately leaving only a few survivors. The *Athen* survived.

Both commandants were tried and executed in 1946.

Left: **During the first years of the camp's existence, the corpses of prisoners who had died were cremated in Ohlsdorf cemetery in north-east Hamburg. In 1942, with the number of dead increasing rapidly, the SS had a crematorium with two ovens built within the confines of the camp. Before the corpses were burnt, their gold teeth were extracted. The ashes were brought to the camp nursery to be made into** compost and scattered as fertiliser. This picture, taken in 1945, is looking north-west. The buildings visible in the background are those of the Walther arms factory in the camp. *Right:* **A few years after the war the crematorium was demolished but in 1965, when the site of the former camp was first made into a memorial, its foundations were outlined in the greensward.**

Ravensbrück

Ravensbrück concentration camp was opened for female prisoners on May 15, 1939, to replace the Lichtenburg camp in Saxony. It was located beside a lake some 50 miles north of Berlin and surrounded by swamps. It had an original capacity for 6,000 prisoners, but by 1944 it held double this figure, having to be substantially enlarged in 1940 and again a year later. The main camp also had separate enclosures for 20,000 men and 1,000 young girls, the men's camp being a Sachsenhausen satellite. The camp had its own crematorium installed in 1943, and in 1944 the SS added a gas chamber.

With the introduction of war production, the main camp set up nearly 100 satellites to enable the women prisoners to work assembling weapons for the Siemens and Halska firms, in ammunition factories and for Volkswagen and Heinkel.

From 1942 onwards some horrendous medical experiments were conducted in the camp, including infecting prisoners with gangrene, and transplantation experiments with human bones and muscle on Polish women.

Today it serves as the camp museum. A Ravensbrück Memorial was first opened by the East German administration in 1949.

Later parts of the camp were taken over by the Soviet Second Guards Tank Army and a driving school was also located there.

Himmler on an inspection tour in 1941. As he enters the camp, the SS Commandant's office can be seen in the background. The Ravensbrück camp staff included 150 female supervisors (SS-Aufseherinnen), who were either SS volunteers or women who had accepted the post for the sake of better pay and work conditions it offered, compared to working in a factory. In 1942 and 1943 Ravensbrück also had a training establishment for SS female supervisors. The 3,500 women who underwent this training then either served here or at other concentration camps, and often proved even more cruel than the SS guards in the treatment of prisoners.

Every two or three weeks, the SS commandant and his two assistants Johann Schwarzhuber and Hans Pflaum selected ill and weak women for 'the transport to Mittweida', the SS euphemism for extermination in a mobile gas chamber. The treatment of children was particularly

The kitchen and laundry building behind the SS wardresses has since been demolished. What remains is the garage block.

Prisoners were made to work both inside the camp in a large clothing factory, and on hard labour outside. *Left:* These girls are making shoes out of straw. *Right:* The majority of the camp has been demolished — however the workshops survive.

Above: **About a kilometre north-west of the main camp, the SS had set up an experimental farm — the Versuchsgut Ravensbrück. Here women work on the foundations for the concrete** roadway. *Below:* **They made a good job of it because it has stood the test of time. The farm is now privately owned but Herr and Frau Gollan kindly gave us permission to take the comparison.**

cruel. Newborn babies were immediately separated from their mothers and either drowned or thrown into a sealed room until they died, although later some were allowed to survive only to succumb to starvation or the appalling sanitary conditions. Other children were thrown alive into the crematory, poisoned, strangled or drowned.

In all about 132,000 women, some with young children, were registered at Ravensbrück, mostly from Poland and the Soviet Union, but also numerous Jews, and gypsies. It is estimated that of these some 92,000 women and children died in the camp from starvation, execution or weakness.

One of them was Violette Szabo GC, a British SOE operative captured after parachuting into the Limoges area in June 1944 (see *After the Battle* No. 86).

Another SOE operative detained there, Odette Sansom, survived because she pretended to be the wife of Peter Churchill, for whom she worked, and so the commandant took her to be a relative of Winston Churchill, the British Prime Minister. (She was also awarded the George Cross after the war, see *After the Battle* No. 121).

Thanks to the intervention of the Swedish Red Cross, French and Swedish women inmates were handed over in early April 1945, and 2,500 German women set free. On April 27, the day before Soviet troops arrived, the SS guards sent off about 24,500 male and female prisoners on a death march with the usual consequences. Only 3,500 sick female prisoners remained behind.

The camp commandants were Max Koegel, who committed suicide in 1946, and Fritz Sühren, who was executed in 1950.

The cell block *(top)* **beside the crematorium** *(above)* **has been preserved but somehow the places seem unreal. The buildings above are witnesses to the unspeakable horrors meted out to those unfortunates who lived and worked there only to be cast aside when their day was done. It is almost as if the casually-dressed visitors of today are intruding on the sanctity of what is really hallowed ground.**

The Red Army took over the camp for its own troops, and Fürstenberg became a major garrison of the 2nd Guards Tank Army. During the period 1968 to 1972 extensive work was carried out on the existing facilities to accommodate two motor rifle regiments, two tank transport battalions, tank parks and three signals units, along with stores and married accommodation for the permanent staff. With the reunification of Germany in 1990, the Soviet Army ended its presence at Ravensbrück.

Bergen-Belsen

Out of all the camps in Germany, the awful revalations which awaited British troops at the end of this country road in April 1945 shocked and horrified the world. Foreverafter the name Belsen will conjure up depraved cruelty and inhuman suffering.

The Belsen-Bergen concentration camp was established in April 1943 on the Lüneburg Heath ten miles north of Celle (see map page 339) as a holding centre for Jews nominated as potential exchanges for German citizens interned abroad, following consultations between the RSHA and Foreign Ministry on the subject. Originally established for the workers constructing the new barracks to the north, the camp had then been used to accommodate 600 French and Belgian prisoners of war until July 1941 when they were replaced by 20,000 Soviet POWs. Of these some 18,000 had already died of dysentery, typhus and tuberculosis when the SS took over under the command of SS-Hauptsturmführer Adolf Haas.

A Baukommando (construction team) of 500 prisoners from Buchenwald, Niederhagen and Natzweiler concentration camps was then brought in to enlarge the camp and improve its sanitary installations. A small crematorium was also built.

The camp then gradually filled with 'privileged' Jews, the first batch being from Poland armed with South American papers. In August 1943, 441 Greek Jews arrived from Thessalonika with Spanish passports, followed by nine transports of Dutch Jews, totalling 3,670 in all, in September. Some 2,000 of the Polish Jews were sent back to Auschwitz in Ocotber 1943 and May 1944 for elimination. During 1944 smaller groups of 'exchange' Jews arrived at Belsen from

Greece (155 Spanish and 19 Portuguese passports), Italy (200 North African Jews with British passports), France (200 Jewish wives of French prisoners of war), Yugoslavia, Poland, Albania and Germany, and in July 1944 a large group of 1,683 Hungarian Jews.

Daily life in the camp was harsh, but tolerable. The average daily ration consisted of coffee in the morning, 1.5 litres of soup at noon and, if available, 200-300 grammes of bread in the afternoon. Sometimes there would be a little jam or butter, or a small slice of sausage or cheese. A roll-call was held every day at 3 p.m., which could last from one to five hours. In spite of a lapse of social and moral values — marked by petty quarrels, egoism and theft — many tried to

Left: The horrendous conditions found within the camp defy adequate description — so much so that the army erected this sign at the entrance lest later visitors should be in any doubt about the true face of Nazism. *Above:* No sign today at the original entrance, now just an unnamed track into the forest.

The track bisected the camp which extended for over three-quarters of a mile. The main prisoners compound lies on the left, the building in the foreground being one of the cook-houses. The area on the right housed the women's camp.

uphold some sort of standard by engaging in cultural, educational and religious activities. Meanwhile, everyone lived in the hope that they might be released abroad and regain freedom.

Only six group transfers ever left Belsen for the free world, and of these, only two were of the kind originally envisaged. In February 1944, the 441 Greek Jews of Spanish nationality were sent to Spain — not in exchange, but as a 'return' of citizens to a neutral country. Then in June, 222 Jews from Belsen were sent by train to Istanbul where they were actually exchanged for interned Germans from Jerusalem, after which they reached Palestine. In August and December 1944, the 1,683 Hungarian Jews were sent to Switzerland and freedom, not in exchange for

This is the Lagerstrasse today, nature having reclaimed the camp site.

Left: If one had been there on April 18, 1945, this is what one would have seen: British soldiers forcing the German SS guards to load lorries with the pitiful bodies of the thousands of dead to be transported to the burial ground. When one of the SS tried to escape he was gunned down to the cheers of the watching inmates. Above: The small brick buildings stood here within the female enclosure.

However, by then Belsen had assumed an entirely different character. In March 1944 the SS-Wirtschaftsverwaltungshauptamt began sending to Belsen prisoners from other concentration camps who were so ill or exhausted that they were no longer of use to the war industry, making Belsen a dumping ground for ill, sick, starved and emaciated slave workers. The first batch of 1,000 men arrived from the Nordhausen underground V-weapons factory on March 27 and were soon followed by others. No additional food or medical care was provided, and of the 4,000 such persons sent to Belsen in 1944, 1,700 had died before the year was out.

Then in August 1944 some 4,000 Polish women and children captured in the Warsaw uprising arrived, followed by another 8,000 women from Auschwitz by early November. These women were accommodated in large tents erected in the open space beyond the huts.

The SS then divided the camp up with tall wire fences to segregate the various categories of prisoners. The Häftlings-Lager (Prisoners' Camp), which was where the original Baukommando had been housed, and which was administered as a concentration camp with all the brutality that entailed, was used to

An open area in the south-western corner of the main compound (where a tented camp had been in August 1944 to house thousands of new arrivals) was selected for several huge pits to be dug to bury the thousands of dead. Again the SS guards, both men and women, were made to carry out the job of manhandling the rotting corpses without gloves.

Germans but as part of a secret deal between the SS and Jewish rescue organisations to trade people for money and goods, Himmler's main aim being to create a secret opening for secret negotiations with the Western Allies. Then, in January 1945, 136 American Jews were released to Switzerland in an American-German exchange operation. Finally, as late as March 1945, 105 Turkish Jews left for Sweden in another 'return of neutrals' operation.

It is now April 1946 . . . and former prisoners return to mourn at one of the mass graves.

Today the 11 huge graves are neatly landscaped and inscribed with the approximate number of dead contained within each.

The graves contain over 20,000 — this is Grave No. 2 — but there are four other mass graves where the totals are unknown.

The worst sight of all was when urgent steps had to be taken to speed up the burial of the rotting corpses. The first man detailed just could not stomach the job, so Sapper Frank Chapman who had joined the Royal Engineers in 1942, took over. 'The sight was awful and the stench was terrible. The first thing was that I was covered in DDT powder. I didn't think it was right but there was a great risk of an epidemic — you just had to get on with it. There were bodies lying all about so I started to push them in which made the job go faster. It did not take long. We had to wash down with petrol to get rid of the lice and our clothes were burned each night. I used to wear a mask to reduce the risk of inhaling germs and to lessen the smell . . . the dreadful smell of disease and death.' (Frank Chapman died in February 2004.)

accommodate the male sick and disabled brought in from other camps. Here Kapo, Karl Rothe, murdered 200 inmates with phenol injections and was later killed by his fellow inmates.

The Neutralen-Lager (Neutrals' Camp) comprised two huts containing the several hundred Jews who were citizens of neutral states. Conditions here were relatively tolerable, being organised under a Jewish Council and with reasonable rations. A sub-section of this camp, the Sonder-Lager (Special Camp) contained the 350 Polish Jews with Latin-American passports or Palestine Certificates, who were kept separate to prevent them informing the other inmates of the Nazi atrocities going on in the East.

The Ungarn-Lager (Hungarian Camp), also comprising two large huts, was opened in July 1944 to accommodate the 1,683 Hungarian Jews awaiting the conclusion of Himmler's exchange dealings for money and goods. These prisoners wore their own clothes with the Star of David and had Jewish self-administration.

Possibly one of the most shocking pictures from the Second World War was taken on this spot.

These were the lucky ones . . . those that came through. On April 28 this group of political prisoners were on their way to freedom.

The Stern-Lager (Star Camp), consisting of 18 huts, was the largest and most important until the autumn of 1944. Again this was under Jewish administration with the inmates wearing their own clothes with the Star of David, but all were forced to work taking apart leather shoes for recycling in the war industry. Families could mix during the day but were accommodated separately by sex at night.

The Zelt-Lager (Tented Camp) or Frauen-Lager (Women's Camp) was opened in August 1944 and consisted of six large tents until they were blown down in a November gale when new huts were erected. This became a sort of transit camp for female slave labourers sent out as work squads to various camps and factories in northern Germany, mostly outposts of Buchenwald and Flossenbürg.

On December 2, 1944, SS-Hauptsturmführer Josef Kramer relieved Adolf Haas as camp commandant and Belsen was transformed into a concentration camp. At this stage it had 15,257 inmates. The Jewish self-administration of the Star Camp was abolished and Kapos introduced, as well as collective punishments.

From January 1945 onwards, an influx of inmates evacuated from other camps — exhausted from long marches or train journeys in open wagons through the icy winter — reached the camp, and Kramer took over the adjacent 35 huts of Stalag XI B's prisoner of war hospital to accommodate them. This became known as the Grosses Frauenlager (Large Women's Camp) and by January 15 formed Belsen's largest contingent with 16,475 women against 5,811 men. More and more arrived, leading to chaotic conditions, unbearable overcrowding, starvation and raging epidemics with appalling death rates. Vast stocks of medicine and instruments stored in the new part of the camp were left unused and only discovered by prisoner doctors just before liberation. On February 1 the population was 22,000, 7,000 of whom died during the course of that month. The water supply collapsed when the power station supplying the pumping station was bombed. Water was delivered by water trucks to the nearby barracks, but not to the camp.

Belsen was at its worst about three weeks before liberation. Typhus was endemic with about 1,000 people succumbing to it daily, and the crematorium was unable to cope, although working day and night. There was no running water and rations were down to half a pint of soup per day with bread three times a week.

In April the last remaining 'exchange Jews', some 7,000 in number, left in three separate batches for Theresienstadt, but new arrivals kept pouring in. Part of the nearby barracks had to be taken over to accommodate a batch of 15,000 prisoners from Nordhausen. In the first two weeks of April, a further 9,000 died and thousands of corpses lay strewn all over the camp.

On April 11, as part of his attempts to commence negotiations with the Western Allies, Himmler gave permission for the camp to be handed over to the approaching Allied armies. That same day, in a last attempt at a cosmetic clean-up, Kramer ordered the dead to be thrown into huge pits that had been dug for the purpose and for the next four days exhausted inmates were driven to dispose of some 17,000 bodies, working 12 hours at a time without food or water.

On April 12, two Geman emissaries approached the British Second Army's lines on the River Aller under a white flag and were taken to the HQ of the 159th Brigade of the 11th Armoured Division. These were the commandant of the Bergen training area and the deputy to the local combat commander, both full colonels. Their purpose was to inform the Allies of the existence of the camp, described as containing 45,000 internees, including 1,500 cases of typhoid, and to request a local truce so that the camp could be kept isolated to

Left: Meanwhile taken into custody was SS-Hauptsturmführer Josef Kramer, the infamous camp commandant who was shackled and held in an underground cellar prior to being moved to the high-security prison at Celle. Right: There he was pictured with Irma Grese, his notorious 22-year-old

SS wardress. All the SS personnel arrested at Belsen were brought to trial and Kramer and Grese and nine others were sentenced to death. The British hangman, Albert Pierrepoint, was flown over to Hameln jail to carry out the executions on December 13, 1945.

As each hut was cleared it was put to the torch to contain the spread of disease. *Above:* **The last hut was ceremoniously set alight by flamethrower on May 21, 1945.**

prevent the spread of the disease. This was eventually agreed, and it was not until late morning on the 15th that the first British officer entered the camp as 29th Armoured Brigade drove past it on the road to Winsen.

Many of those who took part in the liberation of Belsen were to remain mentally scarred for life, the circumstances were so horrific. Richard Dimbleby, the BBC correspondent who arrived at the camp on the 18th, broke down five times while making the recording of his report, and was enraged when the BBC refused at first to broadcast it without confirmation from other sources, threatening to resign unless they did so. His report was broadcast on the 19th and more than confirmed by the filming of the 10,000 unburied found. A further 13,000 died after liberation. The overall death toll at this camp was estimated at 50,000, plus 30,000 Soviet prisoners of war.

The British war crimes trial of 45 men and women, including Josef Kramer, held at Lüneburg between September 17 and November 17, 1945, resulted in the execution by hanging of Kramer and ten others, including three women, with 19 others sentenced to varying terms of imprisonment. Another four men were sentenced to death and five to prison sentences at a second trial held at Celle and Lüneburg in May-June 1946. Another man received a life sentence at Hamburg in April 1948. By 1955, all those sent to jail at the Belsen trials had been released.

The first memorial was dedicated at Belsen by the Jewish survivors on April 15, 1946 — the first anniversary of the liberation of the camp. The British Military Government had already decided that the site must be retained as a memorial although the foundations of all the huts, the fences, watch towers and the crematorium were demolished. An international memorial was unveiled in 1952 when responsibility was handed over to the government of Lower Saxony. A new entrance was constructed a kilometre further south and an exhibition centre opened in 1966. (For the detailed history of Bergen-Belsen concentration camp, see *After the Battle* No. 89.)

'Earth conceal not the blood shed on thee.' Remembering the dead 50 years on.

The International Memorial, unveiled in 1952, consists of an obelisk and a wall with inscriptions in 14 languages.

THE SECOND WORLD WAR BEGINS

Since the autumn of the past year, and on the last occasion in March 1939, there were submitted to the Polish Government proposals which offered the possibility of a solution of the questions in dispute acceptable to both parties. The British Government are aware that the Polish Government saw fit, in March last, finally to reject these proposals. At the same time, they used this rejection as a pretext or an occasion for taking military measures which have since been continuously intensified.

Already in the middle of last month Poland was in effect in a state of mobilisation. This was accompanied by numerous encroachments in the Free City of Danzig due to the instigation of the Polish authorities; threatening demands in the nature of ultimata, varying only in degree, were addressed to that city.

To this were added barbaric actions of maltreatment which cry to heaven, and other kinds of persecution of the large German national group in Poland which extended even to the killing of many resident Germans or their forcible removal under the most cruel conditions.

This state of affairs is unbearable for a Great Power. It has now forced Germany, after remaining a passive onlooker for many months, in her turn to take the necessary steps for the safeguarding of justified German interests.

ADOLF HITLER, AUGUST 29, 1939

354

Hitler the Warlord

The opening shots of the Second World War were fired by the German battleship *Schleswig-Holstein* at 4.47 a.m. on Friday, September 1, 1939 at Westerplatte, the Polish fortress guarding Danzig.

The timing of Hitler's decision to attack Poland did not tally with Göring's economic preparations for war in the mid-1940s, but there is good reason to suspect that Hitler believed that his health would not last out long enough to see his concept of the Reich achieved if he left it any later. Certainly Hitler's health was to diminish rapidly after he launched his attack on the Soviet Union in 1941.

Below: **We found the exact spot on the Vistula river with the original warehouse still standing on the left and pictured it from a Polish river launch.** *Right:* **The first salvo from the 280mm (11-inch) guns set fire to workshops at the southern end of the Westerplatte peninsula. The ground assault followed at 4.55 a.m.**

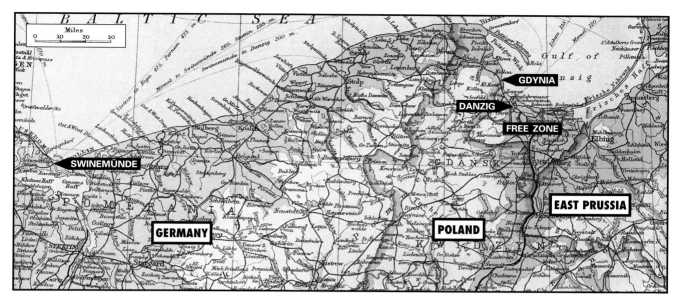

Although Hitler's territorial ambitions (see pages 56-57) had set the war clock ticking, it was the Polish corridor at Danzig which was the final straw. The Versailles Treaty gave Poland — previously landlocked — access to the Baltic but at the expense of cutting off Prussia from Germany. However the Poles were still subservient to the German-dominated legislature in the so-called 'Free port of Danzig', causing them to develop a rival port at Gdynia, so the re-drawing of the map led to discontent on both sides. Hitler wanted both parts of Germany reunited and, even as 'negotiations' were underway back in May, the Germans had given the Polish Government notice of the visit of the *Schleswig-Holstein*, under the pretence of honouring fallen comrades from 1914-18. She left the German Baltic port of Swinemünde on August 24 and arrived in Danzig the following morning. Thousands of spectators lined the banks to welcome the old battleship, a veteran of the Battle of Jutland in May 1916. While her Captain followed diplomatic protocol and presented himself to the Polish Commissioner General, all the time he was awaiting orders to open the attack. These arrived on the afternoon of August 31, ordering battle to commence at 4.45 a.m. the following morning.

From the outset Hitler donned a military type of uniform and followed the troops into Poland on his special train, enthusiastically spending the days touring in an open car, armed with a pistol and an oxhide whip, and with his ADC and valet distributing cigarettes to the troops. But this was a new kind of warfare, not just in the devastating blitzkrieg tactics used with tanks and dive-bombing aircraft to smash a way through, but one directed simultaneously at two completely different kinds of enemies, political and racial. Following up behind the troops came Himmler's six Einsatzgruppen with the task of eliminating 3,500 Polish nobility, clergy and intellectuals, expelling 1,200,000 Poles from territory to be absorbed into the Reich and preparing ghettos in Polish cities to take Germany's remaining Jews, just as Hitler had ordered. The Wehrmacht looked aghast at what was going on but, fatefully, decided it was none of their business.

From now on Hitler played the much propagandised role of 'der grösster Feldherr aller Zeiten' (the greatest field commander of all times) or 'Gröfaz', as it was mockingly condensed to. The attack launched on Poland on September 1, 1939, saw the Polish air force destroyed by September 5. The Soviets moved in from the east and on September 27 Warsaw surrendered. At a cost of 8,082 killed and 27,278 wounded, Hitler had acquired the remainder of Silesia, taken Danzig and added the new Gau of Wartheland to the Reich to form a solid link with East Prussia. Poland was reduced to a rump to be called 'Generalgouvernement Polen' under the brutal governorship of Hans Frank, the Party's legal expert.

Left: The assault troops go in. This is the contest for Danzig's post office which was defended by 52 postal workers. The battle lasted all day and the outcome was only decided when the SS brought up armoured cars equipped with flamethrowers. It was only after the 38 survivors surrendered that the Germans demonstrated the ruthlessness with which the war was to be fought. They were put on trial as non-combatants and all but four were executed. *Right:* The same corner today on Obroncow Poczty Polskiej.

For months we have been suffering under the torture of a problem which the Versailles Diktat created — a problem which has deteriorated until it becomes intolerable for us. Danzig was and is a German city. The Corridor was and is German. Both these territories owe their cultural development exclusively to the German people. Danzig was separated from us, the Corridor was annexed by Poland. As in other German territories of the East, all German minorities living there have been ill-treated in the most distressing manner. More than 1,000,000 people of German blood had in the years 1919-20 to leave their homeland.

I am determined to solve (1) the Danzig question; (2) the question of the Corridor; and (3) to see to it that a change is made in the relationship between Germany and Poland that shall ensure a peaceful co-existence. In this I am resolved to continue to fight until either the present Polish Government is willing to bring about this change or until another Polish Government is willing to do so. I am resolved to remove from the German frontiers the element of uncertainty, the everlasting atmosphere of conditions resembling civil war.

This night for the first time Polish regular soldiers fired on our own territory. Since 5.45 a.m. we have been returning the fire, and from now on bombs will be met with bombs. Whoever fights with poison gas will be fought with poison gas. Whoever departs from the rules of humane warfare can only expect that we shall do the same. I will continue this struggle, no matter against whom, until the safety of the Reich and its rights are secured.

I am asking of no German man more than I myself was ready throughout four years to do at any time. There will be no hardships for Germans to which I myself will not submit. My whole life henceforth belongs more than ever to my people. I am from now on just the first soldier of the German Reich. I have once more put on that coat that was the most sacred and dear to me. I will not take it off again until victory is secured, or I will not survive the outcome.

ADOLF HITLER,
SEPTEMBER 1, 1939

The surprise attack at Danzig, plus a massive assault across the Polish frontier by two army groups supported by 3,000 tanks and the bombing of airfields, was an out-and-out declaration of war which finally led Britain to take a firm line. On the Friday afternoon, the British Prime Minister, Neville Chamberlain, informed the House of Commons that 'unless the German Government are prepared to give His Majesty's Government satisfactory assurances that the German Government have suspended all aggressive action against Poland and are prepared promptly to withdraw their forces from Polish territory, His Majesty's Government in the United Kingdom will without hesitation fulfil their obligations to Poland.' When no reply was received, yet attacks on Poland intensified, a final warning was delivered to the German Minister of Foreign Affairs at 9 a.m. on Sunday, September 3 to the effect that if no satisfactory assurance was received by 11 a.m., then a state of war would exist between Britain and Germany. Twenty minutes after the deadline had expired, von Ribbentrop delivered a blunt rejection.

The battle at Westerplatte lasted eight days (see *After the Battle* No. 65), and by the end of September Polish forces had been vanquished and the country itself divided up between Germany and the Soviet Union which had taken the opportunity to invade Poland's eastern frontier. On September 19 Hitler played the conquering hero in a triumphant entry into Danzig. *Above:* This is the main street called Dluga . . . now pedestrianised *(below)*.

The convoy halts outside the Artushof where Hitler was due to speak.

The historic Guildhall dating from the 14th century is just out of the photo to the left of the fountain.

American CBS correspondent William Shirer was one of those present: 'I had a seat on the aisle, and as he strode past me to the rostrum I thought he looked more imperious than I had ever seen him. Also he was about as angry during his speech as I've ever seen him. When he spoke of Britain his face flamed up in hysterical rage. Afterwards a Nazi acquaintance confided to me that the "old man" was in a terrible rage because he had counted on making today's speech in Warsaw, that he had waited three or four days outside the Polish capital, burning to enter it like a conquering Caesar and make his speech of victory, and that when the Poles inside refused to surrender and each day continued their stubborn resistance, his patience had cracked and he rushed to Danzig to make his speech. He had to talk! We had expected Hitler to offer peace to the West and announce what the future of Poland would be. He did neither, merely remarking that Poland would never be recreated on the Versailles model and that he had no war aims against Britain and France, but would fight them if they continued the war.'

I tried to find a solution. I submitted proposals orally to those in power in Poland at that time. They knew these proposals — they were more than moderate. I do not know in what state of mind the Polish Government could have been to reject such proposals.

You know the developments of those days in August. I believe it would have been possible to avoid war were it not for the British guarantee and the incitement of these apostles of war.

As you know, I have ordered our air force most strictly to limit themselves only to military objectives. But our opponents in the East and West must not take advantage of this. In future we shall take an eye for an eye, and for every bomb we shall answer with five bombs.

We have seen that in England this co-operation between Germany and Russia has been regarded as a crime.

To those Western outbursts I give this answer: Russia remains what she is, namely, Bolshevik, and Germany remains what she is, namely National Socialist. But neither the Russian nor the German Government wants to be drawn into war in the interests of the Western democracies.

Germany's political aims are limited. We shall come to an understanding with Russia about this, as she is the nearest neighbour whom this affects. We shall never go to war about this, because German aspirations are limited. England ought really to welcome an agreement between Germany and Russia, because such an agreement sets at rest England's fears of unlimited German expansion.

I have no war aims against England and France. I have tried to maintain peace between these countries and to establish friendly relations between the English and the German nations. Poland will never arise again in the form laid down by the Versailles Treaty. Not only Germany, but also Russia guarantees this.

If England now continues the war she reveals her real aims, that she wants war against the German Government, and I have the honour to stand here as representative of this regime. It is for me the greatest honour to be regarded in that way.

When England says that the war will last three years, then I can only say that I am sorry for France. If it lasts three years the word capitulation will not arise on our side, nor in the fourth, fifth, sixth and seventh years.

About one thing there can be no doubt — we are taking up the challenge.

ADOLF HITLER, DANZIG,
SEPTEMBER 19, 1939

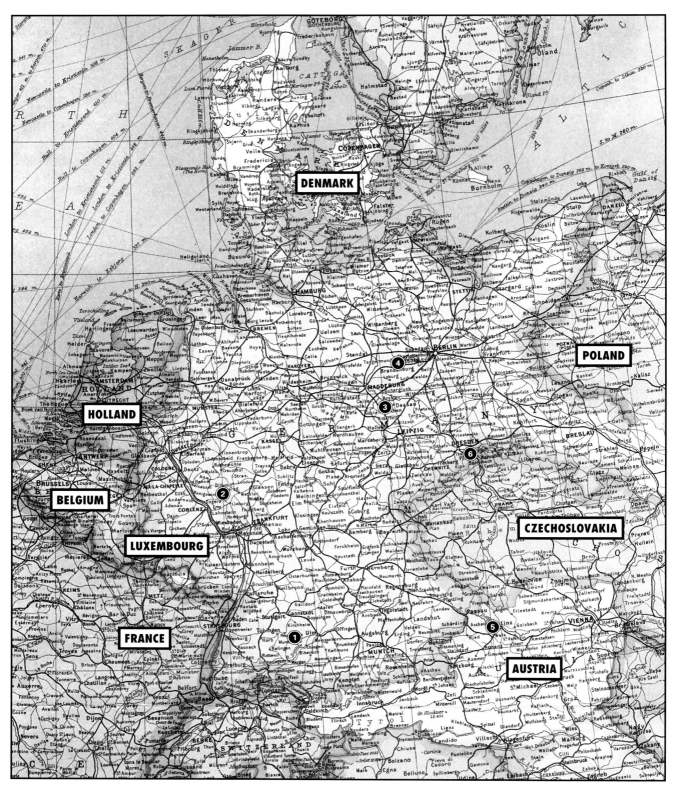

Hitler promptly switched his attention to the West. The declarations of war by France and Great Britain had come as a shock and they had either to be cajoled into a peace agreement, preferably separately so that they could be tackled individually in due course, or attacked before they could build up their forces. On October 6 he made his so-called 'peace appeal' in a speech to the Reichstag, but had already decided upon his line of attack to strike through Luxembourg and Belgium straight for the Channel ports, and on October 9 informed his Wehrmacht chiefs that his war aim was: 'the destruction of the power and ability of the Western powers ever again to be able to oppose the state consolidation and further development of the German people in Europe.' He told them Germany had to

attack now while it could fight on a single front and before the enemy could build up their resources. There would be no return to trench warfare, the blitzkrieg tactics used in Poland would be repeated. The attack would be launched at 7.15 a.m. on November 12. None of the chiefs objected, although all were convinced that their forces were not ready for such a bold move. The only thing to hold them back was that the Luftwaffe reckoned that they would need five days of clear weather to destroy the enemy air forces and ensure air superiority. That criterium was to hold until May 1940. At the same time as he was contemplating an attack in the West, Hitler's thoughts were elsewhere: on six killing centres he was setting up to carry out his programme on euthanasia.

In October 1939 Hitler issued his decree on euthanasia, which he had held back until wartime to facilitate its execution. Initially aimed at children, whose cases were examined by the Reich Committee for the Scientific Registration of Serious Hereditary and Congenital Illnesses to make the life or death by lethal injection decision, the programme was extended to adults. The killings were carried out at six selected asylums that had previously been prepared by specially trained SS teams of physicians and nurses: Grafeneck [1] near Stuttgart, Hadamar [2] near Limburg, Bernburg [3] on the Saale river, Brandenburg [4] on the Havel river, Hartheim [5] near Linz, and Sonnenstein [6] near Pirna.

The victims were killed in gas chambers disguised as shower rooms or in mobile vans into which carbon-monoxide was pumped, and their corpses then incinerated in specially constructed crematoria. As this was taking place within Germany, news leaked out and protests delivered unavailingly to the judicial authorities. Bishop Clemens von Galen of Münster delivered several powerful sermons against the programme.

By the time Hitler called a halt to it in August 1941, 70,273 people had already been exterminated and considerable experience gained in these techniques for its application to the 'Jewish question'.

Euthanasia — or mercy killing from the Greek meaning 'a good death' whereby incurable or terminally ill patients have their lives ended painlessly but *at their request* — is hardly the correct word to use when describing Hitler's death houses where patients were murdered *against* their wishes. The places chosen to carry out this policy were usually existing hospitals or sanatoriums like this one at Grafeneck [1], a tiny village tucked away in the Schwäbische countryside, some 45 kilometres southeast of Stuttgart. Built as a Samaritan Foundation in 1928, it became the location where nearly 10,000 were murdered. Victims were gassed in vans or specially constructed chambers. At Grafeneck, the building containing the gas chamber was demolished after the war to make room for the agricultural farm of what is today again an asylum for physically and mentally handicapped people. The institute's main building *(above)* survives unchanged.

In 1963 the ashes of 270 of those who had been murdered were interred in the cemetery within the grounds.

Left: A psychiatric hospital had been established five kilometres north of Limburg at Hadamar [2] as far back as 1883 and for over 50 years it cared for its mental patients — that is until the Nazis commandeered it in 1940 and converted it into a killing centre. Right: An illegally taken photo showing a coach (circled) arriving with a new batch of candidates.

Left: The grey coaches would drive into this wooden garage at the rear of the building where the patients could be unloaded away from prying eyes. This is an early post-war photograph; today the death garage has been removed (right).

The killing was done in the cellars. Above left: The gas pipes leading to the gas chamber (left) have been cut short and the wall where they emerged repaired with new tiles. Above: The corpses were removed and taken to the far end of this corridor where the cremator stood (replaced now with a photograph).

Another picture taken surreptitiously shows the tell-tale black smoke rising from burning human corpses in the crematorium. The cemetery illustrated *(below)* lies on the hillside on the right. Hadamar is probably the best known of the Nazi 'euthanasia' killing centres but its life was short: from January to August 1941. Nevertheless during that period the recorded deaths number 10,072 giving an average of 40 people killed per day. Today, once again, it is a hospital catering for mentally ill patients and since 1991 the building that was the murder centre has been turned into a memorial museum. The plumbing of the gassing installation and the crematorium ovens were removed after the war in an effort to erase traces of the crime but the murder cellars as such remain.

Left: This is the main entrance to the hospital at Bernburg [3], a large town 35 kilometres south of Magdeburg, as it appeared during the war. It was a killing centre from November 1940 until August 1941 when a total of 9,375 victims had been murdered there. The flue from the crematorium was linked into the main boiler chimney seen today *(right)*.

This is the actual building where the killings took place pictured in August 2003.

The transport coaches would draw into the shelter which stood against this back wall.

Like in all six 'euthanasia' institutes, the killing process at Bernburg was done in a conveyer belt fashion: from the ground floor where they were registered, undressed and photographed, the victims were taken down into the cellars and straight into the gas chamber. The corpses then went via an autopsy room to the morgue and into the crematorium ovens.

Left: The gas chamber. A viewing port was provided for the staff monitoring the killing. *Right:* The small room beyond the entrance door is where the gas cylinders were stored. After the war Bernburg reverted to its former role as a psychiatric clinic for the mentally ill and until 1990, of course, lay within East Germany.

A second killing centre which fell within the Soviet zone of occupation after the war lay in Brandenburg [4], west of Berlin. Unlike the other locations which were centred on hospitals, this one on Neuendorfer Strasse was located in a prison built in 1798. From 1820 to 1931 it served as a penitentiary and from August 1933 to February 1934 as a concentration camp for political prisoners. Then from 1934 to 1939 it served as a police barracks until, on September 1, it was taken over by the Landespflegeanstalt Brandenburg for the euthanasia project. All told, 9,722 were gassed here between January and September 1940. In the photo above the gas chamber is [1]; the cell block [2]; and the concentration camp administrative building [3].

The prison was demolished after the war to be replaced with this memorial which was dedicated on April 27, 1997.

But the Austrian killing centre has been preserved . . . complete with a reconstruction of the coach shelter! *Above:* This picture shows Schloss Hartheim [5] just west of Linz as it looked in 1940-41. It was used to murder victims for a two-year period beginning in January 1940 and by the time it was closed, 18,269 people had passed through its doors on a one-way trip. *Below:* Like all six former 'euthanasia' institutes, Hartheim is today a museum commemorating its victims.

Once the bus entered the enclosure, the victims were passed through the doorway *(left)* **into this corridor** *(right).*

This is the room where the bodies were consumed in the furnace of the cremator. It was surprising that in a totalitarian state, public opinion could make any impact but when word of the forcible killing of handicapped patients leaked out, Bishop Clemens von Galen boldly spoke out against it in sermons in Münster. Hitler ordered the killing to cease in August 1941, possibly because it had achieved its end: not only by the elimination of available patients but also in the pre-selection of suitable individuals who were willing to carry out such measures for employment in the 'Final Solution' without qualms. By the time the euthanasia programme was brought to an end, over 70,000 had been forcibly put to death.

On Wednesday, November 8, 1939, Hitler arrived in Munich for the annual get-together of the National Socialist 'Old Guard' the following evening. He paid his compliments to Paul Troost's widow and then went to visit Unity Mitford recovering from her recent suicide attempt (see page 198). Frau Troost remembered that Hitler seemed on edge, saying that he must talk with Schaub, his driver, about changing his schedule. *Above:* Lunchtime found him at his favourite restaurant, the

Café Heck which stood — as it still does *(right)* — on the corner of Ludwigstrasse and Galeriestrasse, not a stone's throw from the Feldherrnhalle. Heinrich Hoffmann lunched with him and recalled that Hitler 'seemed particularly anxious that I should go to Berlin with him, and in the Bürgerbräukeller, just before he mounted the rostrum to make his speech, he asked me again: "Well, Hoffmann, thought it over? Are you coming?" And when I excused myself he seemed very disappointed.'

On the afternoon of November 8, 1939, as the Bürgerbräukeller in Munich was being prepared for Hitler's speech that evening, Georg Elser, a skilled carpenter and cabinet-maker, slipped in unnoticed and hid behind one of the flag-decorated pillars in the gallery at the back of the speakers' platform, where he had previously cut out a secret panel. Elser, who had recently been released from Dachau concentration camp where he had been held as a suspected Communist sympathiser, waited until the preparations were complete in the hall and the lights switched off before placing the bomb that he had prepared. This consisted of a timing device attached to some sticks of dynamite in a wooden box. Hitler's speech was scheduled to start at 10 p.m., so he set the device for 11.20 p.m., which he reckoned would be about halfway through. He then left the building, again unnoticed.

Hitler arrived on schedule but was delayed in delivering his speech by ten minutes due to the ovation given him. His speech was mainly an attack on Great Britain but at 11.07 he abruptly terminated his speech and left without shaking hands or chatting with old comrades as he would have normally done. That morning Frau Troost had com-

Hoffmann: 'That he was uneasy about something was obvious. His speech was much shorter than usual, and when he left, he did not shake hands with his old comrades, as had been his invariable wont every year at this reunion. Some feeling of haste and urgency seemed to be impelling him forward and "the old guard" watched with disappointment as he turned abruptly and swiftly left the hall. After his departure the hall swiftly emptied, and within a few minutes I myself had packed up my camera and likewise departed. Only a few of the old comrades and the serving staff were left.'

According to the late author John Toland, who in 1971 interviewed Heinz Ruck (a commando with Otto Skorzeny), the first assassination attempt against Hitler was in about 1929, when a disillusioned SS man placed a bomb under the speakers' podium in the Sportpalast in Berlin (see page 216-217), intending to explode it while Hitler was speaking. However, a sudden urge to go to the toilet resulted in him being accidentally locked in and consequently unable to detonate his device. *Right:* The bomb blast in Munich brought down the roof and killed seven. *Below:* A roof truss has been shored up to prevent further collapse.

mented on his apparant lax security and Hitler had decided to take an earlier train than originally intended. The bomb exploded on schedule, killing seven and wounding 63, including Eva Braun's father. The news did not reach Hitler until his train stopped at Nuremberg.

Three years later, Hitler is reported to have talked only about two attempts on his life, explaining that in both instances the failure to kill him was down to pure chance: 'I left the Bürgerbräukeller ten minutes before the appointed time because of an urgent conference in Berlin which it was imperative that I should attend. In the other attempt my life was saved because the would-be killer, a Swiss, who stalked me for three months in the neighbourhood of the Berghof, regularly missed me when I went out, and when he tried to continue his stalking in Munich, he was discovered by a railway official. The man apparently had travelled beyond Munich with a ticket from Berchtesgaden to Munich, and the railway official in question asked for an explanation. The story that he had been in Berchtesgaden for several months, trying to deliver a letter to me, aroused the suspicions of the railwayman, who caused him to be held for interrogation. When the man was searched, a sealed envelope addressed personally to me was found on him, but the envelope was empty, a circumstance which led to a full confession. The confessions of this Swiss interested me in so far as they confirmed my conviction that not a soul could cope with an assassin who, for idealistic reasons, was prepared quite ruthlessly to hazard his own life in the execution of his object. I quite understand why 90 per cent of the historic assassinations have been successful. The only preventative measure one can take is to live irregularly — to walk, to drive and to travel at irregular times and unexpectedly. But that, after all, is merely normal caution, and not prevention.'

Two British agents, Captain Sigismund Payne Best *(left)* and Major Richard Stevens *(centre)* were initially thought to be responsible. The two men, working undercover in Holland, already had a rendezvous with German contacts arranged for Thursday afternoon on the border at Venlo but when they showed up at 4 p.m. they were kidnapped at gunpoint and carted over the frontier into Germany (see *After the Battle* No. 11). Captain Best and Major Stevens survived the war in spite of being held in Sachsenhausen. and Dachau concentration camps. In fact the bomb had been placed in the pillar behind the speaker's rostrum by Georg Elser *(right)*. He was also held in Dachau for several years and was executed just before the camp was liberated.

He immediately jumped to the conclusion that this was the work of two British intelligence officers, Captain S. Payne Best and Major R. Stevens, with whom Heydrich's agents had been playing a game on the Dutch border, and ordered their arrest. They were kidnapped in Venlo and brought across the German border for questioning, eventually surviving five years in concentration camps. Elser was caught on the Swiss border next day and interrogated by the Gestapo, to whom he freely admitted that he had planted the bomb and claimed that he had had no accomplices. However, Hitler did not believe that Elser could have done it, even though Himmler had personally interrogated and beaten the prisoner. Consequently, Elser was never brought to trial but kept as a privileged prisoner in Dachau concentration camp.

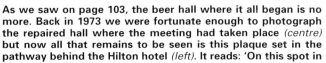

As we saw on page 103, the beer hall where it all began is no more. Back in 1973 we were fortunate enough to photograph the repaired hall where the meeting had taken place *(centre)* but now all that remains to be seen is this plaque set in the pathway behind the Hilton hotel *(left)*. It reads: 'On this spot in the former Bürgerbräukeller, the cabinet-maker Johann Georg Elser tried on November 8, 1939 to assassinate Adolf Hitler. With this he wanted to put an end to the Nazi terror regime. His intention failed. After 5½ years detention, Elser was murdered in Dachau concentration camp on April 9, 1945.'

A timeless comparison in the Odeons-platz. Five days later, the funeral ceremony for the seven victims was conducted by Rudolf Hess, their names being added to the NSDAP Roll of Honour for 1939 together with Hugo Sommeregger, killed in Sachsenburg in January, and Otto Schmidt who would lose his life in Duisburg in December.

The names of the seven killed, Michael Wilhelm Kaiser, Emil Kasberger, Franz Lutz, Leonhard Reindl, Eugen Schachta, Michael Schmeidl and Wilhelm Weber, were added to the roll of honour and the Party propagandist made the most of this event with elaborate ceremonies for the dead at the Feldherrnhalle, for which Hitler flew back to Munich, where Rudolf Hess addressed the mourners. A solemn procession then ensued along Ludwigstrasse and Leopoldstrasse to the Northern Cemetery.

The cortège passes through the Victory Arch of the Bavarian Army on Ludwigstrasse on its way to the Nordfriedhof.

Hitler announced January 17 for the attack on the West, but this had to be postponed once more when a German aircraft strayed across the border and made a forced landing at Mechelen in Belgium with a staff officer carrying the operational plans for the airborne attack on that country.

Germany's essential iron-ore imports from Sweden were mainly dependent upon northern Norwegian ports, Narvik in particular, for shipment. The British and French governments decided to take preventative action and so issued a note to the still neutral Norwegian government on April 5 saying that they reserved the right to deprive Germany of Norwegian resources. French and British expeditionary forces, including Polish troops, were prepared and the Royal Navy started laying minefields off Norway.

Alert to the danger, Hitler wasted no time in pre-empting this move. The landing forces were loaded on to cruisers, destroyers and torpedo boats rather than on slower transport vessels, and the six naval groups tasked to seize Norway sailed from April 7. The capacity of the warships bringing the assault forces was greatly limited and additional transport groups were to bring, at first more supplies and heavy equipment, followed by the bulk of the troops and supplies required for the break-out. Finally, with 500 transport aircraft, the X. Fliegerkorps was tasked to deliver 3,000 troops in the initial assault.

The attack was launched next day. Two German divisions quickly overran Denmark and elements of three further

Five months later, on April 9, Hitler launched his offensive into Scandinavia, invading both Denmark and Norway on the same day. His move was triggered by Anglo-French attempts to blockade the Norwegian ports that handled Germany's vital iron ore shipments from Sweden. Landing from the sea and by air at six widely dispersed places along the Norwegian coast — Oslo, Egersund, Kristiansand, Bergen, Trondheim and Narvik — the Germans quickly overcame Norwegian resistance and successfully resisted counter-landings by French, Polish and British forces at Narvik, Åndalsnes and Namsos. Here troops belonging to Gruppe Oslo Nordwest, comprising the 163. Infanterie-Division and elements of the 69. and 181 Infanterie-Divisions, advance north-west from Oslo towards Hønefoss in mid-April in the offensive to link up with the northern landing groups.

divisions and Generalmajor Eduard Dietl's 3. Gebirgs-Division attacked Norway at Oslo, Egersund, Kristiansand, Bergen, Trondheim and Narvik. Some 500 transport aircraft, 220 bombers and 100 fighters were used in support. There were some nail-biting moments, but by June 10 it was all over. The Allies had withdrawn, taking the Norwegian government with them, and the Norwegian Army had been instructed to lay down its arms. The Germans had lost 3,700 killed to 6,100 Allied troops, but the iron-ore supply was secure. Naval losses had been heavy and about even on both sides, the consequences being far more severe for the much smaller Kriegsmarine. (See *After the Battle* No. 126.)

The British and French withdrew from Norway on June 8 — their intervention having been a fiasco — and the Norwegians capitulated on the 10th. Within two months, the daring 'Weserübung' operation had achieved complete success in spite of the fact that only few forces had been involved. Hitler had specified that this Scandinavian diversion must not weaken preparations for the major land offensive in the West. In his 'Directive for Weserübung' signed on March 1, he had insisted that 'the forces employed will be as small as possible. Weakness in numbers will be made good by skilful action and surprise in execution.' *Left:* The victorious German commanders in Oslo including Kurt Bräuer, the German Minister in Oslo; Admiral Hermann Boehm, Commanding Admiral Norway, and General Nikolaus von Falkenhorst, Commander-in-Chief of Operation 'Weserübung' Nord. *Right:* The National Theatre on Karl Johans Street lies halfway between the Royal Palace and the Norwegian Parliament.

With his northern flank secure, Hitler's attention immediately reverted to an attack on the West. Generaloberst Erich von Manstein produced a daring plan that both met and improved on Hitler's own ideas, and this was the one adopted, despite the High Command's objections that it was too risky.

Hitler arrived at his field headquarters, code-named 'Felsennest', early on May 10, 1940, as his troops swarmed across the borders of Holland, Belgium and Luxembourg, effectually bypassing the Maginot Line. Hitler was particularly interested in the glider-borne attack on Eben Emael that guarded the crossings on the Albert Canal, whose leaders he had briefed personally over a model of the Belgian fortress, and which proved highly successful.

Führerhauptquartier 'Felsennest' was located in a copse crowning a hill just west of Rodert, 30 kilometres from the frontier with Belgium. *Top:* **The nerve centre was this camouflaged bunker.** *Centre:* **Hitler, with Wilhelm Brückner behind, and Rudolf Schmundt on his left, descends the track from the HQ to the village.** *Above left:* **Thirty years ago we visited Felsennest during our research for** *After the Battle* **No. 19 covering all Hitler's headquarters and this was our picture showing the bend in the old track on the right. The foundations for a new road had just been laid.** *Above right:* **Just look at the transformation today!** *Right:* **The HQ was destined to become a National Socialist shrine to one of the most successful military campaigns in history and Hitler wanted it preserved as a monument. Instead it was blown up by the Wehrmacht in 1945, its ruin now mouldering in the undergeowth.**

The rapid advance over the northern Belgian plain effectively distracted attention from the armoured thrust working its way through the Ardennes on the nodal point at Sedan, where German troops crossed the Meuse river on May 13-14, scattering the French 2ème and 9ème Armées. The blitzkrieg tactics brought General Heinz Guderian's armour to Abbeville by May 20, thereby cutting off the Allied forces in the north from the rest of France. The British were obliged to withdraw and start evacuating, the Belgians to surrender. Hitler then made the blunder of holding back the armoured forces closing in on Dunkirk to allow the Luftwaffe to finish off the remaining French and British forces trapped there, but fog and the Royal Air Force foiled the plan.

Above: **The campaign on the Western Front is but seven days old but Hitler's forces have already eliminated Holland, broken the Belgians, and breached the invincible French Maginot Line. Here on May 17 the warlord enters Bastogne.**
Right: **Then the name meant little; not until December 1944 was its place in history assured.**

Dutch resistance to the German invasion was such that an impatient Hitler ordered it crushed, as a result of which the Luftwaffe were sent to bomb the positions guarding the bridges leading into Rotterdam over the Nieuwe Maas river on May 14, but hit the city centre instead, killing over 800 civilians, a figure that was grossly exaggerated by the international press, so increasing the fears of the populations of the countries threatened and adding to their general demoralisation and the traffic chaos caused by refugees.

On June 6 Hitler moved his headquarters forward to the little Belgian village of Brûly-de-Pesche, north-west of Charleville.

Code-named 'Wolfsschlucht (Wolf's Glen), Hitler is pictured there with Hauptmann Gerhard Engel (see page 94).

Sunday, June 16. It was here at Wolfsschlucht that Hitler performed his so-called jig on learning that France had surrendered. In fact all he did was stamp his right foot but a

Canadian film editor, John Grierson, duplicated the original sequence shot by Walter Frentz (one of Leni Riefenstahl's cameramen) to make it look as if Hitler was dancing for joy!

Nevertheless, with northern France cleared, the German Army was able to comb its way south through a totally demoralised France until on June 19 Maréchal Philippe Pétain asked for an armistice. Hitler returned from a brief meeting with Mussolini in Munich on June 18 to sanction the humiliating terms in the same railway carriage at Compiègne on June 19 in which the Kaiser's representative had signed the surrender of the German Army in 1918.

Wednesday, June 19. *Left:* The railway carriage in which the Armistice had been signed to end the First World War is drawn out from its museum building to stand on the exact spot it occupied on November 11, 1918. *Right:* Hitler arrived at the Clairière de l'Armistice on Friday, June 21 after motoring down from Wolfsschlucht. Having taken Maréchal Foch's seat (extreme left)

facing the French delegation, he said nothing as Generaloberst Keitel, standing beside him, read out a prepared statement putting the blame for the new war on the Allies. Göring, Admiral Erich Raeder and Joachim von Ribbentrop have their backs to the camera while Generaloberst Walther von Brauchitsch, the army commander-in-chief, and Rudolf Hess sit at the far end.

'Here on the Eleventh of November 1918 succumbed the criminal pride of the German Empire — vanquished by the free peoples which it tried to enslave.' As a young man bent on seeking revenge for what he called the Diktat of Versailles, under which Germany was to suffer harsh reparations for the damage she had caused in Belgium and France in 1914-18, Hitler would no doubt have heard of the unveiling of a great memorial at Compiègne in 1922. Ten years later on the eve of his ascent to power, Hitler would have read about the ceremony at Compiègne held on November 11, 1932, to commemorate the establishment of the historic site as a French national memorial. Little could he have known that he had less than ten years to wait before he could personally show his contempt. After the ceremony the slab was blown up as was the railway shed (which had been financed by an American benefactor, Arthur H. Fleming, in 1927) and the whole area defaced.

The French delegation stalled the negoti-ations throughout Friday but on Satur-day afternoon Keitel gave them a dead-line and they signed at 5 p.m. Early the following morning Hitler treated himself to something that he had always wanted to do: a private tour of the architectural wonders of Paris. With Albert Speer, sculptor Arno Breker and architect Her-mann Giesler as guides, and Hoffmann to take the photographs, the party was flown to Le Bourget in the early hours of Sunday morning. With Hitler in the lead-ing car, they reached Paris just before 6 a.m. The streets were deserted as the ten-car convoy followed a prepared route to take in the main sites: the Opéra, La Madeleine, Champs-Élysées *(top)*, the Arc de Triomphe *(right)*, the École Militaire, the Dome des Invalides to see Napoleon's tomb, the Palais de Justice, Notre-Dame, Les Halles, Mont-martre, with the tour ending at the Basilique du Sacré-Coeur *(below)*.

Left: Having visited Albert Speer to get him to mark a map with the precise route that they followed, we retraced Hitler's foot-steps — or rather tyre tracks — in 1976 for *After the Battle* No. 14. The only possible time one could freely negotiate the streets of Paris and stop anywhere to take photos was — like on Hitler's visit — early on a Sunday morning when the city shuts down. *Right:* We drove the route at the same time and ended at the Sacré-Coeur by 8.15 a.m. — just as Hitler was leaving. There we found — rather appropriately — two Germans asleep in their car on the same spot where the Führer had stood back in 1940!

Undoubtedly this is Hoffmann's most famous photograph. Speer and Breker are filmed posing with the warlord at the Trocadéro with the Pont d'léna over the Seine in the background.

As Hitler's plane circled Paris for one last look, he confided to Speer: 'It was the dream of my life to be permitted to see Paris. I cannot say how happy I am to have that dream fulfilled today.'

With his victory over France having redressed the balance over what he saw as the iniquities of the terms of the Armistice imposed on Germany after the Great War, no wonder it was all smiles. Now Hitler issued his 'Last Appeal to Reason' to Britain: four-page reports of his Reichstag speech were dropped later over the UK.

Now was time to strike at Great Britain, and the OKW were ordered to plan a seaborne invasion for mid-September under the title Operation 'Seelöwe' (Sea-lion). Meanwhile Hitler had one more attempt at a peace offer in his speech to the Reichstag on July 19. However, the speech, which began with an attack on Winston Churchill, the new Prime Minister of a coalition government united in its determination to defeat Hitler's Germany, fell on deaf ears.

Whether or not Hitler was seriously intending to invade England, or just using these preparations as a diversion from his intention to strike at the Soviet Union, is difficult to determine, for his orders for planning both operations were issued the same month. The Kriegsmarine's surface fleet had been so depleted by its losses off Norway that it could now only muster one battle cruiser, four destroyers and three torpedo boats, thus leaving the launching of 'Seelöwe' entirely dependant upon achieving total air supremacy. Göring launched Operation 'Adler' (Eagle) on August 13, 1940, but when the Luftwaffe failed to achieve air supremacy due to the gallant efforts of the outnumbered 'Few', on September 17 Hitler postponed 'Seelöwe' indefinitely.

The air assault on the United Kingdom up to the end of 1940 had resulted in the deaths of over 22,000 civilians and destroyed a million homes, but failed to disrupt the British war effort. It had cost the Germans 1,800 aircraft with their irreplaceable crews. (The British were fortunate that the Germans in their emphasis on the ground-support role had failed to produce heavy bomber fleets, otherwise the outcome might have been very different.)

A LAST APPEAL TO REASON

BY

ADOLF HITLER

Speech before the Reichstag, 19ᵗʰ July, 1940

I have summoned you to this meeting in the midst of our tremendous struggle for the freedom and the future of the German nation. I have done so, firstly, because I considered it imperative to give our own people an insight into the events passing by history, that lie behind us; secondly, because I wish to express my gratitude to our magnificent soldiers, and thirdly, with the intention of appealing, once more and for the last time, to common sense in general.

If we compare the events which prompted this historic struggle with the magnitude and the far-reaching efforts of military events, we are forced to the conclusion that its general course and the sacrifices it has entailed are out of all proportion to the alleged reasons for its outbreak — unless they were nothing but a pretext for underlying intentions.

The programme of the National-Socialist Movement, in so far as it affected the future development of the Reich's relations with the rest of the world, was simply an attempt to bring about a definite revision of the Treaty of Versailles, though as far as at all possible, this was to be accomplished by peaceful means.

Versailles were intolerable, not only because of their humiliating discrimination and because the disarmament which they ensured deprived the German nation of all its rights, but far more so because of the consequent destruction of the material existence of one of the great civilised nations in the world, and the proposed annihilation of its future, the utterly senseless accumulation of immense tracts of territory under the domination of a number of States, the theft of all the irreparable foundations of life and indispensable vital necessities from a conquered nation. While this dictate was being drawn up, men of insight even among our foes were uttering warnings about the terrible consequences which the ruthless application of this insane conditions would entail — a proof that even among them the conviction predominated that such a dictate could not possibly be upheld in days to come. Their objections and protests were silenced by the assurance that the statutes of the newly-created League of Nations provided for a revision of these conditions; in fact, the League was supposed to be the competent authority. The hope of revision was thus at no time regarded as presumptuous, but as something natural. Unfortunately the Geneva institution, as those responsible for Versailles had intended, never looked upon itself as a body competent to undertake any sensible revision, but from the very outset as nothing more than the guarantor of the ruthless enforcement and maintenance of the conditions imposed at Versailles.

All attempts made by democratic Germany to obtain equality for the German people by a revision of the Treaty proved unavailing.

World War Enemies Unscrupulous Victors

It is always in the interests of a conqueror to represent stipulations that are to his advantage as sacrosanct, while the instinct of self-preservation in the vanquished leads him to recognise the common human rights that he has lost. For him the dictate of an unscrupulous conqueror had all the less legal force, since he had never been honourably conquered. Owing to a rare misfortune, the German Empire, between 1914 and 1918, looked for leadership. To this and to the as yet unenlightened faith and trust placed by the German people in the words of democratic statesmen, our downfall was due.

Hence the Franco-British claim that the Dictate of Versailles was a sort of international, or even a supreme, code of laws, appeared to be nothing more than a piece of insolent arrogance to every honest German; the assumption, however, that British or French statesmen should actually claim to be the guardians of justice, and even of human culture, as mere stupid effrontery. A piece of effrontery that is thrown into a sufficiently glaring light by their own extremely negligible achievements in this direction. For seldom have any countries in the world been ruled with a lesser degree of wisdom, morality and culture than those which are at the moment exposed to the ravages of certain democratic statesmen.

The programme of the National-Socialist Movement, in so far as it freeing the Reich from the innermost fetters of a small subordination of Jewish capitalistic and plutodemocratic profiteers, proclaimed to its...

Germany's demands for this revision were a vital necessity and a matter of the existence and honour of every great nation. They will probably one day be regarded by posterity as extremely reasonable. In practice, all these demands had to be carried through contrary to the will of the Franco-British rulers. We all regarded it as a sure sign of successful leadership in the Third Reich that for years we were able to effect this revision without a war. Not that — as the British and French demagogues asserted — we were at that time incapable of fighting. When, thanks to a growing common sense, it finally appeared as though international co-operation might lead to a peaceful solution of the remaining problems, the Agreement to this end signed in Munich on September 29, 1938, by the four leading interested States, was not only not welcomed in London and Paris, but was actually condemned as a sign of abominable weakness. Now that peaceful revision threatened to be crowned with success, the Jewish capitalist war mongers, their hands stained with blood, saw their tangible pretexts for realising their diabolical plans vanish into thin air. Once again we witnessed a conspiracy by wretched corruptible political creatures and money-grabbing financial magnates for whom war was a welcome means of bettering business and their profit, scattered to no avail throughout the nations began to exercise its disintegrating influence on sound common sense Scribblers concentrated upon deceiving honest men, who wanted peace, as weaklings and traitors, and upon denouncing the opposition parties as the Fifth Column, thus breaking all internal resistance in their criminal war policy. Jews and Freemasons, armaments manufacturers and war profiteers international businessmen and Stock Exchange jobbers seized upon political forelings of the desperate and Hecatombs type, who described war as something infinitely desirable.

It was the work of these criminal persons that spurred the Polish State on to adopt an attitude that was out of all proportion to Germany's demands and still less to the attendant consequences.

In its dealings with Poland, the German Reich has pre-eminently exercised genuine self-restraint since the National-Socialist régime came into power. One of the most despicable and foolish measures of the Versailles Dictate, namely, the severance of an old German province from the Reich, was crying out aloud for revision. Yet what were my requests?

I name myself in this connexion, because no other statesman might have dared to propose a solution such as mine to the German nation. It merely implied the return of Danzig — an ancient purely German city — to the Reich, and the creation of a means of communication between the Reich and its severed province. Even this was to be decided by a plebiscite subject to the control of an international body. If Mr Churchill and the rest of the war-mongers had felt a fraction of the responsibility towards Europe which inspired me, they could never have begun this infamous game.

It was only due to these and other European and non-European parties and their war interests, that Poland rejected my proposals, which in no way affected either her honour or her existence, and in their stead had recourse to terror and to the sword. In this case we once more showed unexampled and truly superhuman self-control, since for months, despite murderous attacks of the minority Germans, and even bespite the slaughter of tens of thousands of our German fellow-countrymen, we still sought an understanding by peaceful means.

What was the situation?

One of the most unnatural creations of the Dictate of Versailles, a populace puffed up with political and military pomp, insults another State for months on end and threatens it to grind it to powder, by light battles on the outskirts of Berlin, to hack the German armies to pieces, to extend its frontiers to the Oder or the Elbe, and so forth. Meanwhile, the other State, Germany, watches this insult in patient silence although a single movement of her arms would have sufficed to prick this bubble inflated with folly and hatred.

On September 2, the conflict might still have been averted — Mussolini proposed a plan for the immediate cessation of all hostilities and for peaceful negotiations. Though Germany saw her armies storming to victory, I nevertheless accepted this proposal. It was only the Franco-British war-mongers who desired war, not peace. More than that, as Mr Chamberlain said, they...

needed a long war, because they had now invested their capital in armaments shares, had purchased machinery and required time for the development of their business interests and the amortization of their investments. For, after all, what do these 'citizens of the world' care about Poles, Czechs or such like peoples?

On June 19, 1940, a German soldier found a curious document when searching some railway trucks standing in the station of La Charité. As the document bore a distinctive inscription, he immediately handed it over to his commanding officer. It was then passed on to other quarters where it was soon realised that we had lighted on an important discovery. The station was subjected to another, more thorough-going search.

Thus it was that the German High Command gained possession of a collection of documents of unique historical significance. They were the secret documents of the Allied Supreme War Council, and included the minutes of every meeting held by this illustrious body. This time Mr Churchill will not succeed in contesting or lying about the veracity of these documents, as he tried to do when documents were discovered in Warsaw.

These documents bear no signal index inscribed by Messieurs Gamelin, Daladier, Weygand, etc. Their carriage at one time be continued or rented by their very gentlemen. They at the very least remarkable evidence of the machinations of the war mongers and war extenders. Above all, they show that those stout-hearted politicians regarded all the small nations as a means to their ends; that they had attempted to tie Finland in their own interests; that they had determined to turn Norway and Sweden into a theatre of war; that they had planned to turn a conflagration in the Balkans in order to gain the assistance of a hundred divisions from those countries; that they had planned a bombardment of Batum and Baku by a ruthless and unscrupulous interpretation of Turkey's neutrality, who was not unfavourable to them; that they had inveigled Belgium and the Netherlands more and more completely, until they finally entrapped them into binding General Staff agreements, and so on, ad libitum.

The documents further give a picture of the dilettante methods by which these political war-mongers tried to quench the blaze which they had lighted, of their democratic militarism, which is in part to blame for the appalling fate that they have inflicted on hundreds of thousands, even millions of their own soldiers, of their barbarous unscrupulousness which caused them ruthlessly to force mass evacuation on their peoples, which brought them no military advantages, though the efforts on the population were outrageously cruel.

These same criminals are responsible for having driven Poland into war.

Eighteen days later this campaign was, to all intents and purposes, at an end.

Britain and France Considered Understanding a Crime

On October 6, 1939, I addressed the German nation for the second time during this war at this very place. I was able to inform them of our glorious military victory over the Polish State. At the same time I appealed to the insight of the responsible men in the current States and to the nations themselves. I warned them not to continue this war, the consequences of which could only be devastating. I particularly warned the French of embarking on a war which would forcibly eat its way across the frontier and which, irrespective of its outcome, would have appalling consequences. At the same time, I addressed this appeal to the rest of the world, although I feared — as I expressly said — that my words would not be heard, but would more than ever arouse the fury of the interested war mongers. Everything happened as I predicted. The responsible elements in Britain and France reviled in my appeal a dangerous attack on their war profits. They therefore immediately began to attack on their every thought of conciliation was out of the question, nay, even a crime, that the war had to be fought in the name of civilisation, of humanity, of happiness, of progress, and — to leave no stone unturned — in the name of religion itself. For this purpose, negroes and businessmen were to be mobilised. Victory, they then said, would come of its own accord, it was in fact, within their easy reach, as I myself must know very well and have known for a long time since, or I should not have broadcast my appeal for peace throughout the world. For if I had had any justification for...

378

When the Luftwaffe failed to achieve air supremacy over Britain — the pre-requisite for an invasion — on October 12 Hitler was forced to postpone Operation 'Sea-lion' until 1941. However by the time spring came, Hitler's eyes had turned eastwards and on March 13 he issued a directive for the invasion of the Soviet Union . . . but first he was forced to intervene in the Balkans. On April 12, Hitler arrived aboard his personal train *Amerika* at the little Austrian station of Mönichkirchen. Here it remained serving as Führerhauptquartier 'Frühlingssturm' (Spring Storm) for the next 14 days until his forces had achieved the upper hand in Greece and the invasion of Crete (see *After the Battle* No. 47) had been launched.

During October 1940, Hitler tried to get the support of Generalissimo Franco of Spain and Maréchal Pétain of Vichy France to support him in his war, but Spain had been devastated by its civil war and Franco refused to commit himself, although later the Blue Division of Spanish volunteers was to fight alongside the Wehrmacht in Russia. Pétain would not go beyond promising collaboration that did not entail waging war. Again French volunteers were to fight on the Eastern Front as members of the Waffen-SS Sturmbrigade 'Frankreich', which later expanded into the Waffen-SS Division 'Charlemagne', remnants of which were to fight until the very end in Berlin.

On December 17, 1940, the General Staff presented its plans for the invasion of the Soviet Union to Hitler, who opposed their view of Moscow as the main objective. The nodal centre of the Soviet Union was of less importance to him than the 'Bolshevik breeding grounds' of Leningrad and Stalingrad, showing his main intent to be not the destruction of the Red Army, but the elimination of Bolshevism, with which he correlated the annihilation of the Jews. He told them: 'The final objective of the operation is to erect a barrier against Asiatic Russia on the general line Volga-Archangel. The last suriving area of Russia in the Urals can then, if necessary, be eliminated by the Luftwaffe.'

In all his dealings with his generals, Hitler's fixations overrode any of their own proposals or ideas. His lightning victories so far had taught him nothing except to confirm his own sense of genius. He believed that the Russian campaign would not last longer than four months. Indeed he was so confident that he issued an order forbidding the production of winter clothing. Then on February 17, 1941, he even ordered plans for a drive on India, seizing the Near East in a pincer movement between the Soviet Union's border with Iran and North Africa.

Mussolini's attacks on British forces in Egypt from Libya in September 1940 and on Greece from Albania the following month both proved disastrous fiascos for the invaders, eventually obliging Hitler to provide some support. Generalleutnant Erwin Rommel was sent to Northern Africa in February 1941 to turn the tide with a precious armoured division and other troops to form the Afrikakorps. In preparing the ground for his attack on the Soviet Union, Hitler had already placed German troops in Hungary and Romania, and persuaded Bulgaria to join the Tripartite pact on March 1, 1941, but Yugoslavia remained a political and military obstacle in his domination of the Balkans and for access to Greece. Attempts to coerce the Yugoslavs into compliance failed, so Hitler had both Yugoslavia and Greece attacked on April 6, 1941. By this time a British expeditionary force had arrived in Greece to meet the threat, but belatedly and too weak to provide more than a delaying action before the Greek forces collapsed and the British were forced to evacuate to Crete, where they came under a massive airborne attack in May, bringing yet another German victory.

The small station remains virtually unchanged, a peaceful spot midst a wooded valley 70 kilometres south of Vienna.

With Germany on the point of launching a massive second front against the Soviets, an unprecedented political problem faced Hitler on the home front when his deputy 'defected' to Britain. This must have been a huge blow to Hitler's prestige and esteem, and a public relations disaster of the first magnitude, as Hess had been his closest confidant since the early days of the Party.

Professor Karl Haushofer had been a close friend of Hess right back to his term of imprisonment with Hitler in Landsberg in 1924. The professor's son Albrecht was adviser on British affairs to the German Foreign Office and the Haushofers did not believe that war with Britain was in Germany's best interests, a premise which Hess thought also accorded with Hitler's own beliefs.

Once Hitler's last appeal to reason in his Reichstag speech on July 19, 1940 had been ignored by the British, the Haushofers began the search for a possible contact in Britain with the ear of the Government with whom peace overtures might be broached. The choice fell on His Grace, the 14th Duke of Hamilton whom Hess said he had met at the Olympic Games in Berlin in 1936.

The date for Operation 'Barbarossa' was now set for June 22, 1941. At a briefing of more than 200 senior commanders on March 30, Hitler told them: 'The war against Russia will be such that it cannot be fought in a chivalrous manner! This struggle is one of ideologies and racial differences and will have to be conducted with unprecedented, merciless and unrelenting harshness.'

Then on June 6 he told Generalfeldmarschall von Brauchitsch to issue a directive for the liquidation of all captured Soviet commissars; whether captured in battle or while offering resistance, they were to be shot at once. When von Brauchitsch objected, Hitler broke in with: 'I cannot demand that my generals should understand my orders, but I do demand that they follow them!'

There was an alarming diversion on May 10, when Hess flew to Scotland in an abortive attempt to get Great Britain out of the war. It was an idea not entirely out of step with Hitler's own desires, but Hess was fully briefed on 'Barbarossa' and his flight was a propaganda coup for the British. A furious Hitler had Hess written off as mentally deranged, but the latter divulged nothing of Hitler's plans to the British, who already were aware of what was going on through 'Ultra' and were passing on the information to Moscow, where Stalin steadfastly refused to believe this and all other similar reports of an imminent invasion.

Against the Red Army Hitler had massed at least 152 German divisions, including 19 panzer and 15 motorised infantry divisions, with an estimated 3,350 tanks and 7,200 artillery pieces, supported by 2,770 aircraft. Then there were 14 Finnish divisions in the north, and 14 brigade-sized Romanian divisions on the southern flank. However, these

impressive figures belied certain critical factors: the new panzer divisions had a paper strength of only two-thirds that of those of 1940, much of the transport for the motorised infantry divisions was unreliable captured material, the bulk of the infantry had to move on foot with horse-drawn supply wagons, and the artillery was also mainly horse-drawn, requiring some 625,000 horses in all.

Although the three main army groups striking toward Leningrad, Moscow and Rostov respectively were spearheaded by armoured formations, the road and rail communications that had enabled

the success of blitzkrieg tactics hitherto were not to be found in the vast open expanses of the Soviet Union. Once the initial breakthroughs had been achieved by the armour and vast numbers of prisoners rounded up, the German infantry still had a long way to go to catch up and the armour and motorised vehicles began to experience severe problems of supply, spares and maintenance as a result of the paucity of the communications available. For the hundreds of thousands of Russians soldiers surrendering to the Germans there was simply no provision.

There was another connection between Hess and Hamilton which it was hoped would give them common ground: their long standing interest in flying. Hess had trained as a pilot in 1918 and although he did not complete his course until the month before the war ended, flying remained a passion and in 1934 he won the annual air race round the Zugspitze. The Duke had been a serving pilot with No. 602 (City of Glasgow) Squadron since 1927 and, while Hess won his accolade for flying over the highest mountain in Germany, the Duke became the first man to fly over the highest mountain in the world. Although banned by Hitler to fly, Hess had still been taking up aircraft from Augsburg airfield where he could discreetly use those belonging to the Messerschmitt works, rather than take the risk of being found out if he had used Luftwaffe machines.

To end up just 11 miles from his intended destination after a solo flight — at night — of nearly 1,000 miles, with the last 400-odd over water and enemy territory, was a remarkable achievement and one of which Hess was later very proud. After reaching what he thought was the Duke's Scottish home, Dungavel House in Lanarkshire, Hess abandoned his aircraft and took to his parachute. He landed on Floors Farm, near Eaglesham, where he was taken into custody. (For the full story of Hess's flight and subsequent incarceration in Britain and Germany, see *After the Battle* No. 58.) *Below:* In May 1993 an elaborate marker was erected on the spot where he landed near Eaglesham but it was quickly smashed to pieces by unknown hands. (See also page 80.)

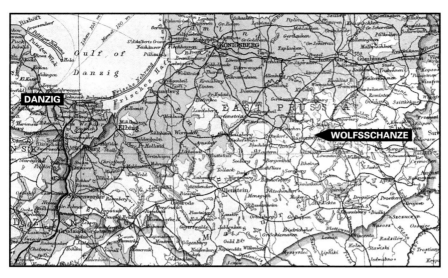

Back in the summer of 1940, a Führerhauptquartier had been constructed just west of Rastenburg in East Prussia, a clear indication of Hitler's intention to mount an offensive against the Soviet Union at some stage in the future. Code-named 'Wolfsschanze' (Wolf's Redoubt), it had its own railway station, Bahnhof Görlitz, and there was an airfield nearby which gave easy access to or from Berlin.

Once Operation 'Barbarossa' was launched on June 22, 1941, Hitler spent a major part of his time over the next three years at Wolfsschanze before he finally left for good on November 20, 1944. *Above:* Here he is pictured with Ribbentrop and Göring. *Right:* There was an outer security perimeter (Sperrkreis II) and an inner top security zone (Sperrkreis I) surrounding the vital nerve centre.

During the summer of 1941 Hitler became seriously ill at his 'Wolfsschanze' Führerhauptquartier at Rastenburg in East Prussia with stomach cramps and dysentery. Dr Morell was constrained to send an electrocardiogram of Hitler's heart back to an expert in Germany for diagnosis and was advised that his anonymous patient had a rapidly progressive coronary sclerosis, although it is unlikely that he informed Hitler of it.

Mussolini, who was still shattered by the loss of his son in an air crash, visited Hitler and together they flew out to inspect a Bersaglieri division at Uman in the Ukraine, but Hitler was not interested in acquiring any more Italian troops, which was Mussolini's motive.

Meanwhile Hitler was in bitter dispute with his field commanders for halting the advance on Moscow and sending its most powerful armoured units to bolster the flanking probes on Leningrad and the Ukraine. It was not until September 5 that he ordered the resumption of the advance on Moscow, using the code-name 'Taiphun' (Typhoon). Confident of an early victory, on October 2 he set off back to Berlin in his special train to make a speech in the Sportpalast next day in which he boasted of his triumphs so far. Back at the Wolfsschanze on October 9 he dictated a press release claiming that the Soviets had been defeated.

However, the delay in launching 'Taiphun' had cut the time factor too fine before the weather changed and heavy rains bogged down the Germans' mobility with seas of mud, and poor visibility robbed the Luftwaffe of the air superiority factor it had won. Then in late October the mud froze and the winter was upon an army, only one in five of whose soldiers was equipped with winter clothing, thanks to Hitler's previous instructions, and whose equipment was not designed for operation in the extreme temperatures they were about to experience.

Despite Hitler's prodding, the attack on Moscow faltered under the appalling conditions, and then Generalfeldmarschall Gerd von Rundstedt was obliged to give up Rostov after having only held it for a week. Hitler replaced Rundstedt with Walter von Reichenau and went to check on the reasons for this retreat with the commander of the Leibstandarte-SS 'Adolf Hitler', only to find that his officers agreed with Rundstedt in the need to retreat from Rostov. By December 5, with the temperature outside Moscow down to minus 31 degrees Centigrade, General Georgi Zhukov counter-attacked along a 200-mile front.

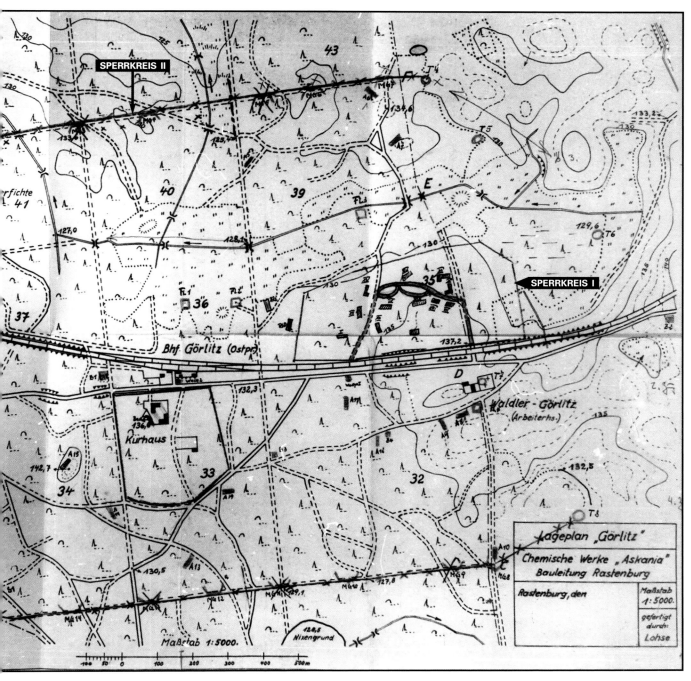

On December 6 a dejected Hitler admitted to Generalmajor Alfred Jodl that victory could not be achieved that year, and it took the news next day of Japan's attack on Pearl Harbor to restore his spirits. Leaving orders for the Wehrmacht to go on to the defensive along the Eastern Front, Hitler set off for Berlin to deal with the new international crisis. Against all advice, and with his fixation of US President Franklin D. Roosevelt as the embodiment of World Jewry, he convened the Reichstag on December 11 to announce his declaration of war upon the United States.

The situation before Moscow continued to deteriorate. On December 19 Generalfeldmarschall Walther von Brauchitsch ventured to tackle Hitler in a private interview, and emerged two hour's later having been dismissed from

his post, for Hitler had decided to appoint himself official commander-in-chief instead with the comment: 'The commander-in-chief's job is to train the army in the National Socialist idea and I know of no general who could do that as I want it done. For that reason I have taken over command of the army myself.' All his field commanders' pleas to withdraw in order to save their troops continued to be rejected. As soon as the generals came face to face with Hitler, he would launch into a lengthy speech before they had a chance to say anything, and they found their resolution eroded, their objections seemingly demolished and their facts in doubt. They all knew that Hitler's arguments were incorrect, but he succeeded in confusing them completely.

Then on February 8, 1942, Hitler suffered a severe personal blow with the

death of his Armaments and Munitions Minister Fritz Todt in an air crash. He decided to replace him with Albert Speer, who was to prove far more efficient.

With the outset of spring, Hitler's health and spirits improved and he began planning a drive on the Caucasus via Kursk under the code-name 'Blau' (Blue). However, heavy rains delayed the launch until June 28. Kursk was taken on July 6 whereupon Hitler decided to move his headquarters forward to FHQ 'Werewolf', a collection of wooden huts a few miles north-east of Vinnitsa in the Russian Ukraine. He then decided to strike at Stalingrad in addition to the Caucasus, thus spreading his resources even more thinly on the ground, and by late August German troops had reached Stalingrad.

Meanwhile the key city of Rostov on the Don river had been taken on July 25, enabling Generalfeldmarschall Wilhelm List's Heeresgruppe A to pass through and turn south and south-east heading for the oilfields at Maikop and Baku. There was also good news from Generaloberst Erwin Rommel's Afrikakorps, who had taken the British supply base at Tobruk on June 21 and pushed on to El Alamein well inside Egypt by July 3.

But toward the end of September, the 'Rote Kapelle' (Red Orchestra) spy ring was uncovered, leading to 46 executions of prominent German citizens who had been passing information to Moscow. This convinced Hitler that he was surrounded by traitors and from then on he pointedly refused to shake hands with any staff officers. On September 9 he summarily dismissed Generalfeldmarschall List for failing to

The war on the Eastern Front. By the end of September 1941, Generalfeldmarschall Gerd von Rundstedt, commanding the southernmost of the three army groups invading the Soviet Union, had surrounded and destroyed over half a million Russians in a giant pocket east of Kiev. *Above:* **Kharkov in north-eastern Ukraine was captured on October 24 although it changed hands three more times.**

break through to the Baku oilfields and took over direct command of Heeresgruppe A himself. Then on September 24 he went on to dismiss the army's chief-of-staff, Generaloberst Franz Halder, replacing him with the newly-promoted Generalmajor Kurt Zeitzler, whom he advanced a further two grades to Generaloberst.

Hitler then returned to Berlin to deliver another speech at the Sportpalast, for the third time that year containing a veiled reference to the annihilation of Jewry, as if preparing his audience for the harsh reality of his dual programme of Lebensraum and Holocaust.

November 1942 was a bad month for Germany. The 6. Armee made no further progress at Stalingrad and Rommel was forced to retreat in North Africa for lack of supplies after the battle of El Alamein, and a vast armada of Allied shipping was sighted off Gibraltar. However, this did not deter Hitler from attending the annual celebration of the 1923 putsch in Munich with his old comrades.

The Soviets recaptured the city in February 1943; the Germans retook it the following month before the final Russian victory in August that year (see *After the Battle* **No. 112).** *Below:* **This was Ploshchad Sovietkoi Ukrainy, now Ploshchad Konstitutii.**

The German offensive by the 6. Armee under Generaloberst Friedrich Paulus (left) against Stalingrad began on June 28, 1942, and by August 23 his forces had reached the city on the banks of the River Volga. Bitter fighting continued over the next three months as the Red Army defended every street . . . every house . . . and every factory. On January 31, 1943, when Paulus surrendered, he was the first German officer of Generalfeldmarschall rank to be taken prisoner in the war —

Hitler having promoted him by radio earlier that day hoping it would stiffen his resolve not to give in. When he did, Hitler was disgusted: 'Paulus did an about-face on the threshold of immortality', he declared. Right: Here Paulus is being interrogated by Marshal of the Soviet Union Konstantin Rokossovsky, commander of the Stalingrad Front (renamed the Don Front), and Colonel-General Nikolai Voronov, the representative from the Stavka (the Soviet High Command).

Then on November 19 and 20, 40 Soviet divisions attacked the weak Romanian forces on the 6. Armee's flanks in an encircling movement that isolated almost 250,000 troops at Stalingrad. Rashly accepting Göring's wild promise that he could supply them by air, Hitler ordered Generaloberst Friedrich Paulus to stand fast at all costs, refusing him the freedom of movement he requested, and summoned Generalfeldmarschall Erich von Manstein from the Leningrad front to form the new Heeresgruppe Don to push through to the 6. Armee's relief. The air supply proved so ineffective that Hitler called in Generalfeldmarschall Erhard Milch in mid-January to take charge, but he too found the task beyond his capabilities.

The relief operation was mounted on December 12 with three armoured and ten infantry divisions, and they advanced to within earshot of the 6.

Armee before being checked. Manstein's attempts to get Hitler to allow a break-out were rejected and Stalingrad designated a 'Festung' (fortress), which meant that it would have to be defended to the last man.

Paulus, just promoted to Generalfeldmarschall, surrendered on January 31, 1943, at the end of a month in which 140,000 of his troops had died. The Soviets took 91,000 prisoners, of whom barely 5,000 were to see their homeland again. The German Army had suffered a shattering defeat, losing nearly a quarter of its strength on the Eastern Front.

At the same time Heeresgruppe A had been pushed out of the Northern Caucasus and back across the Don to reinforce Manstein's Heeresgruppe Don, which now found itself out on a limb and obtained Hitler's reluctant consent to withdraw, as the Soviets launched their offensive with the ambitious aim of clearing the Ukraine. By February 9 the

Soviets had reached Bielgorod and Kursk and were threatening Kharkov, the fourth-largest city in the Soviet Union. Hitler ordered Kharkov to be held at all costs, but the SS-Panzerkorps ignored his orders and withdrew on February 15 rather than be cut off.

On February 17 Hitler flew down to Manstein's headquarters where he was reported upon arrival to be unshaven, his skin slack and yellowish, and his uniform jacket covered in foodstains. He stayed for two days, eventually agreeing to Manstein's plans for a counterattack, which resulted in pushing the Soviets back, costing them 40,000 casualties and over 600 tanks.

The thaw brought an end to the winter campaigning on both sides, but left a vast Soviet-occupied salient around Kursk, about half the size of England, that would be the setting for the next major operation, 'Zitadelle', when the ground hardened.

Left: Victory then . . . and victory today (right). The statue of Mother Russia on Mamajer Hill — more than 230 feet tall — is set midst the graves of thousands of Red Army soldiers who

paid the ultimate sacrifice. The Battle of Stalingrad — the city has since been renamed Volgograd — in 1942-43 resulted in up to 800,000 Soviet and German dead.

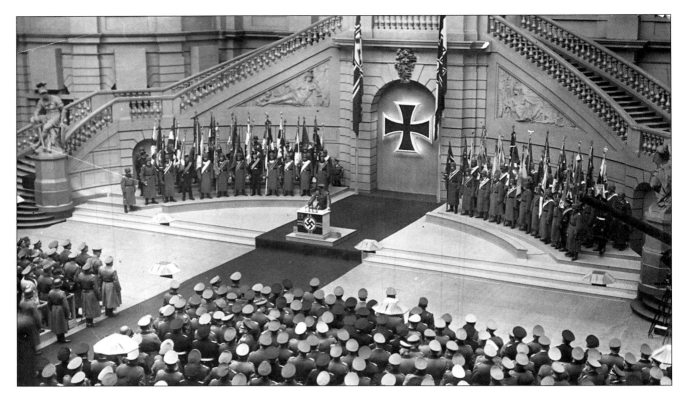

As far back as 1938, senior officers in the Wehrmacht were developing plans for a coup d'état against the Nazi regime. Then, these early deliberations were aimed at preventing war which seemed inevitable. One of the central figures was General Franz Halder who had succeeded General Ludwig Beck (also a plotter-in-waiting) in 1938. Halder was the Chief of the General Staff of the Army until dismissed by Hitler in September 1942 but it was not until March 1943 that the first determined attempt to kill Hitler was set in motion. On Sunday March 21 the Führer was due to speak at the Zeughaus in Berlin, the military museum situated just beyond the war memorial (see pages 236-237) on Unter den Linden. It was Germany's 'Remembrance Sunday' — Volkstrauertag or People's Day of Mourning — which had been established after the 1914-18 war in preference to the hated November 11 when the Allies remembered their dead. In 1934 Hitler changed the name to Heroes' Memorial Day — Heldengedenktag. *Above:* The conspiritors knew that Hitler would give the address in the courtyard of the museum before moving inside where Oberst Rudolf von Gersdorff hoped to be successful as a suicide bomber.

However, another plot to assassinate Hitler was under way, this time by certain members of the Wehrmacht. Generalmajor Hans Oster, Chief-of-Staff of the Abwehr (Wehrmacht intelligence), and his group selected Generalmajor Henning von Tresckow, Chief-of-Staff to Generalfeldmarschall Hans Günther von Kluge, to carry out the assassination. The plan was to plant a bomb aboard Hitler's plane during a visit to the front. On the evening of March 13, 1943, one of Tresckow's staff officers, Major Fabian von Schlabrendorff, gave a member of Hitler's entourage a parcel containing what purported to be two bottles of brandy for delivery to a friend at the Wolfsschanze. However the bomb, made out of English plastic explosive, failed to explode, and there was a panic to recover it before it was discovered. Schlabrendorff succeeded in recovering the bomb whereupon it was found that the detonator had been a dud.

A few days later, on March 20, Schlabrendorff tried again, handing over some plastic explosive to Oberst Rudolf Christoph Freiherr von Gersdorff, Kluge's Chief of Intelligence, at the Hotel Eden in Berlin. The latter's task was to place himself close to Hitler at the Heldengedenktag ceremony at the Zeughaus next day and blow Hitler and himself to pieces. Gersdorff arrived with a bomb in either greatcoat pocket, and when Hitler's speech was over and he moved to the exhibition hall where Russian trophies were on display, accompanied by Göring, Himmler, Keitel and others, Gersdorff broke the acid capsule that set off the fuze, and followed. However, Hitler only stayed a few minutes, not long enough for the ten-minute fuze, so Gersdorff was obliged to find a toilet, remove the fuze and dispose of it.

Having set off the fuze, Gersdorff was mortified to see Hitler quickly leave the building so he was forced to abort his mission. The treasures in the Zeughaus included Manfred von Richthofen's red Fokker Triplane but most of the exhibits were lost during a later RAF raid. The building itself was re-opened in 2004 after many years of restoration. The steps, damaged by bombs, were demolished after the war.

Schloss Klessheim, situated on the western outskirts of Salzburg, was ideally situated as a conference centre as it lay just 30 kilometers from the Obersalzberg and Hitler used it frequently for top-level diplomatic meetings.

Hitler left the Wolfsschanze at the beginning of April for a break at the Berghof, from where he met Mussolini for three days of talks at Schloss Klessheim on April 22. Mussolini was unwell and had serious political problems at home. He had come to ask Hitler to seek peace with the Soviets and allow the return of all the Italian troops, neither of which Hitler could countenance.

Hitler's relentless war against the Jews continued remorselessly. The Jewish uprising in the Warsaw ghetto from April 9 to May 15 came as a shock, for the 'cowardly' Jews displayed considerable courage against overwhelming odds. Of the 56,065 Jews finally rounded up, 7,000 were summarily shot, 22,000 sent to extermination camps and the remainder to labour camps. On June 19 he instructed Himmler to proceed with the deportation of Jews to the East, 'regardless of any unrest it might cause during the next three or four months.' Berlin had been declared 'Jew-free' earlier in the year, after the last of the Jews working on munitions there had been sent to Auschwitz.

Hitler met Mussolini here on May 29, 1942, for what in post-war jargon would be called a Big Two summit conference, to discuss the progress of the war. A second meeting took place in more informal surroundings the following day at the Berghof. They met at the castle again in April 1944 but by then Mussolini was a spent force with his country having surrendered the previous September.

With the castle extensively reconstructed in 1940-42, Nazi eagles still adorn the entrance to what is now Salzburg's casino!

Hitler returned to the Wolfsschanze on May 10, only to learn next day of the loss of Tunisia with the surrender of 300,000 German and Italian troops.

'Zitadelle' was launched on July 4, 1943, in the form of a pincer movement from the north and south. The Germans were fielding their new Panther and Tiger tanks for the first time, as well as their Elephant assault guns. The Soviets had prepared a vast web of defensive positions to absorb the German attack before launching their own armoured counterattack, and confidently outnumbered the Germans in every factor, including the air. By July 10 the northern pincer was stalled after an advance of only eight miles and the southernmost one after an advance of 20 miles. The Germans then renewed their attack in the south in what

Benito Mussolini's reign lasted almost 21 years: from October 30, 1922 until July 24, 1943. *Left:* **In his days of glory he would speak to the crowds in front of the Palazzo Venezia, his headquarters in Rome, where the famous balcony led straight from his palatial office.** *Right:* **Unlike Hitler's Chancellery, the building still stands unchanged as a national museum although the Duce's office is closed to the public.**

became the largest tank battle of the war, losing 400 panzers and 10,000 men, but claiming to have destroyed and crippled 1,800 Soviet tanks.

The Soviet counter-attack was launched on July 12, and that same evening Hitler called off 'Zitadelle'. On August 3 the full counter-offensive began, liberating Bielgorod and Kharkov, and forcing the Germans into retreat along the whole front.

Following the invasion of Sicily by the western Allies on the night of July 9/10, Hitler took his train down to

northern Italy for another meeting with Mussolini, which was held at the Villa Gaggia near Feltre on July 19. In a formal conference setting Hitler harangued a silent Mussolini on the need to continue fighting the war with every possible means, but only five days later the Fascist Grand Council met to discuss Mussolini's conduct of the war and voted for a restoration of a constitutional monarchy, resulting in Mussolini's replacement by Field Marshal Pietro Badoglio, a bitter opponent of the Nazis, and Mussolini's arrest.

Left: **Also closed to inspection is the conference chamber where, on Saturday, July 24, 1943, Mussolini's future was decided by the Fascist Grand Council. Italy, unlike Germany, still possessed a monarchy and, with support for Mussolini on the wane, a motion was passed seeking his replacement,**

which was confirmed by King Victor Emmanuel III the following day. *Right:* **Stripped bare of all its former furnishings, this is the room where the fateful meeting took place. (For a detailed acount about the 'Night of the Grand Council', see** *After the Battle* **No. 77.)**

Mussolini was promptly arrested and shipped out to the island of Ponza and later to a naval base on the Isle of Maddalena, off Sardinia. When news of the Duce's downfall reached Hitler at Rastenburg, he called in a Waffen-SS officer, Hauptsturmführer Otto Skorzeny, to effect a rescue. On July 27 he flew to Rome to set up a forward base and try to find out where Mussolini was being held. It took Skorzeny a month to track his prison down: a hotel *(above)* high in the Abruzzi mountains which could only be reached by cable car. A glider assault was then planned for September 12.

Returning to the Wolfsschanze, Hitler had to face the devastating news of the Hamburg firestorm raids at the end of the month, in which 50,000 were killed and 800,000 rendered homeless. Göring and Goebbels were devastated by these events and on September 10 Hitler taped a lengthy speech at the Wolfsschanze which was broadcast to the nation, promising final victory.

In early September news of the armistice agreed between the Western Allies and the Italian Government prompted Hitler to have Mussolini rescued from the hotel where he was being held on the Gran Sasso, the highest peak in the Apennine mountains north of Rome. For this task he detailed SS-Hauptsturmführer Otto Skorzeny, who led a glider-borne raid on the hotel and then evacuated Mussolini in a Fieseler Storch that managed to land nearby. It was a spectacular feat that earned the admiration of friend and foe alike for its daring, Skorzeny's men getting away by cable-car with their 12 casualties from a glider crash.

Mussolini was brought to the Wolfsschanze on September 14. He wanted to retire from politics, but Hitler had him issue an official communique announcing his resumption of the supreme direction of the Italian Fascist Party, together with four orders of the day that reinstated the authorities dismissed by Badoglio, reconstituted the Fascist Militia, instructed the party to support the Wehrmacht, and ordered an investigation into Members' conduct relative to the July 25 coup that had deposed him.

The Italian guards were completely taken by surprise and overpowered without bloodshed. *Above:* Mussolini was led from the hotel to where a short strip had been cleared so that a Fieseler Storch could land and take both him and Skorzeny to Rome. *Below:* From there Mussolini was flown to Hitler's HQ in East Prussia. (For more on the rescue of Mussolini, see *After the Battle* No. 22).

On February 14, 1942 the Air Ministry issued new instructions to RAF Bomber Command to focus future operations on 'the morale of the enemy civil population, and in particular of the industrial workers', and from now on 'area bombing' became standard RAF policy. The new directive coincided with the appointment of a new chief, Air Marshal Sir Arthur T. Harris, who lost little time in introducing a series of hard-hitting raids against German cities, but it was the raid on the night of May 30/31 that marked a watershed in the RAF's new bombing policy. The ironic code-name — Operation 'Millennium' — and the very idea of a 1,000-bomber raid were characteristic of Sir Arthur's vigorous promotion of the concept of massed attacks against single cities. Harris's choice of target, Hamburg, was also historically symbolic, as he planned to light a 'centenary conflagration' to celebrate the 100th anniversary of a disastrous fire which had destroyed much of the old city in 1842.

However, nature intervened and poor weather over northern Germany dictated a switch of targets to Cologne. Thus Hamburg was spared . . . but only for a year. On May 27, 1943 Harris announced that Hamburg had been specially selected for a series of heavy raids which had been designed to totally destroy the city. 'The Battle of Hamburg cannot be won in a single night', he told his crews before the operation commenced. 'It is estimated that at least 10,000 tons of bombs will have to be dropped to complete the process of elimination. To achieve the maximum effect of air bombardment, this city should be subjected to sustained attack. On the first attack [on July 24/25] a large number of incendiaries are to be carried in order to saturate the Fire Services.' A grim portent of the hoped-for outcome was signified by the choice of the Biblical code-word for the operation: 'Gomorrah' — the city destroyed by fire and brimstone in the Book of Genesis.

Two follow-up attacks took place in July by the US Eighth Air Force before the RAF returned on the night of July 27/28. A chance combination of hot weather, low humidity, accurate bombing, and the absence of the fire brigade still dealing with the earlier raid, produced a cataclysmic thermic firestorm. With a death toll approaching 40,000, the great majority from asphyxiation within the firestorm area, the city authorities faced a major health hazard from the thousands of corpses buried in and under the ruins. It was some six weeks before all the fires were out, and the buildings had cooled sufficiently to enable teams to enter the fire zone, and it was anticipated that it would be many more months before all the bodies could be recovered. The central firestorm area was therefore declared a Sperrgebiet — a prohibited area — and all the roads leading into it were sealed off with walls built of loose bricks salvaged from the bombed buildings. *Above:* This was the entrance to the death zone at the junction of Ausschläger Weg and Eiffestrasse.

At the end of the war it was thought that it would take 25 years to clear all of Hamburg's ruins but in fact the majority had been dealt with by 1953. The new buildings on the left belong to a vocational school for aircraft construction. (A detailed account of the Hamburg firestorm was included in *After the Battle* No. 70.)

After Munich's Bürgerbräukeller was seriously damaged by Elser's bomb (see pages 368-369), an alternative venue for the 'Neunte Elfte' celebration had to be found. This was the Löwenbräukeller on Stiglmaierplatz. His speech on November 8, 1943 was upbeat even though events were moving against Germany on all fronts.

In his annual speech from the Löwenbräukeller beer hall in Munich in November commemorating the 1923 putsch, and broadcast to the nation as usual, Hitler was full of confidence, but the last months of 1943 saw severe setbacks for the Wehrmacht both at Leningrad and in the Ukraine, where they had been driven back to the eastern edge of the Pripet Marshes in the centre, and the remains of Heeresgruppe A had been cut off in the Crimea. Overall, the last year had cost the Wehrmacht some 1,686,000 casualties and replacements were increasingly difficult to find. The Soviets were now fielding over 3,000,000 men against Germany's 2,000,000 and their equipment was constantly being improved at a pace the Germans could not meet. On December 22 the introduction of National Socialist Leadership Officers was announced in an attempt to fire the troops with Nazi ideals.

Then on January 26, 1944, Hitler addressed several hundred generals and admirals assembled at Rastenburg, saying: 'If Providence should actually deny us victory in this battle of life and death, and if it is the will of the Almighty that this should end in catastrophe for the German people, then you, my generals and admirals, must gather round me with upraised swords to fight to the last drop of blood for the honour of Germany — I say, gentlemen, that is the way it *must* be!' But this met with only a deadly silence instead of the cheers he

expected. Affronted, he went on to say he was aware of anti-Hitler sentiment among certain Wehrmacht officers and that some of his Führer Orders were not being obeyed as they should. He was

also aware of the Free Germany movement among certain officers captured by the Soviets. Having lost his original theme, he ended his speech abruptly and walked off.

The beer hall was bombed in 1944; became a food warehouse which was looted in 1945, and was gutted by fire in 1986. Yet it has risen from the ashes having been rebuilt the following year although the architecture of the meeting hall is now totally different. (The celebration of the 'Ninth of the Eleventh' in November 1944 had to be held in the Circus Krone (see page 101) at No. 43 Marsstrasse, Himmler appearing instead of Hitler. In his speech the SS chief appealed for the final sacrifice: volunteers for the Volkssturm — the civilian army — to make a last-ditch stand for Germany.

Hitler feared that the Allies must know the location of the Wolfsschanze and would bomb it, so ordered a vast reconstruction of bomb-proof bunkers there, and moved back to the Berghof for the summer while the work was in progress. However, it was not the Wolfsschanze that was disturbed by bombers, but the Berghof as Allied aircraft flew over from Italy to bomb Munich and other targets in southern Germany. The Berghof's air raid shelter was outside the back door and 85 steps down. Hitler would stand at the entrance to the shelter waiting for the 'All Clear' to sound, not allowing anyone out until they did so, but not realising that soon many of his staff were not bothering to take shelter. During the raids the whole area would be covered in artificial fog. Although well protected with anti-aircraft guns, they were only to fire unless the Berghof was attacked, so held their fire not to disclose the position.

Meanwhile Germany was being pounded from the air, and the Gauleiters kept sending Hitler evidence of the destruction being wreaked on their cities with photographs and reports. By early May the American daylight attacks on fuel plants in southern and eastern Germany were having a direct effect upon war production. Hitler would rail at the failure of Göring and his Luftwaffe to prevent the raids, but did nothing to appease his suffering subjects. To his intimates he would talk about future reprisals, merciless revenge and ultimate victory, but he never visited his devastated cities and travelled through them with the blinds of his railway carriages drawn.

Hitler's health was now markedly worse. It was noted that his knees trembled if he stood for any length of time and that his left hand shook enough to make a cup rattle in its saucer when he held it. He was having severe stomach cramps again and was having to take injections to counter fatigue.

On March 17 he met Admiral Miklos Horthy, the Regent of Hungary, at Schloss Klessheim in a stormy meeting which ended in the admiral reluctantly accepting the presence of German troops in his country, these being Hitler's assurance that Hungary would not seek peace with the Soviets.

By the middle of April the Soviets had completed a four-month operation to clear the area between the Pripet Marshes and the Black Sea, bringing them to fullest extent of their supply capabilities and so to a pause. The fighting to clear the Crimea took another month, during which 151,500 German and Romanian troops got away by sea and air. The failure to stem the Soviet advance resulted in the dismissal of Generalfeldmarschalls Erich von Manstein and Ewald von Kleist.

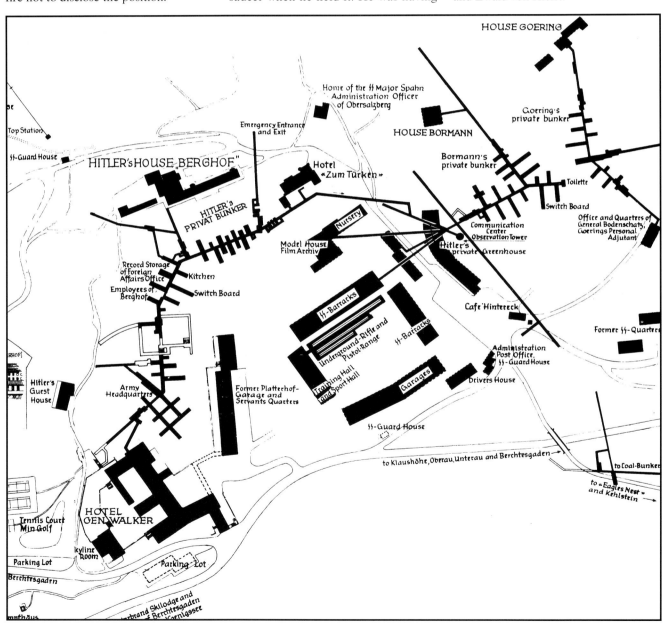

With the Allied air campaign wreaking havoc across Germany, bomb-proof shelters were constructed for Hitler at his three main 'residences': Rastenburg in East Prussia; the Chancellery in Berlin, and the Berghof on the Obersalzberg *(above)*.

On May 18 Hitler appointed Generalfeldmarschall Gerd von Rundstedt Commander-in-Chief West with Generalfeldmarschalls Erwin Rommel and Johannes von Blaskowitz commanders of Heeresgruppe B and Heeresgruppe G respectively. This made Rommel responsible for the supervision of the defence arrangements along the Atlantic Wall in anticipation of an invasion by the Western Allies. Hitler saw the Pas-de-Calais as the most likely invasion point, a point of view reinforced by the successful deception measures used by the Western Allies.

The Allied invasion of Normandy on June 6, 1944, took place while Hitler was still at the Berghof, and caught the Germans fully be surprise. Rommel was at his home in Germany to celebrate his wife's birthday and planning to see Hitler, and many officers were away on exercise

Air raid shelters on the Obersalzberg which were sealed in the 1970s have now been opened up and linked to the new documentation centre (see page 456).

in Brittany. Considerable delay was experienced in getting Hitler's release of the armoured reserves, especially as he was still convinced that the main attack would come in the Pas-de-Calais.

His counter-stroke was the V1 flying bomb, the much-vaunted revenge weapon, which he then ordered into action on June 10. Two days later seven bombs were fired at England from France, four of which crashed immediately and another two disappeared. The V1 campaign caused considerable damage and alarm, killing over 6,000. Eventually over 9,000 V1s were fired against the United Kingdom, of which 5,000 reached their targets.

However, the situation in Normandy had become so desperate that on June

17 Hitler drove out to meet Rundstedt and Rommel at a village near Soissons. Rommel reported that the situation was hopeless under total Allied air superiority and argued for withdrawal to fight a decisive battle beyond the range of the deadly naval guns, but Hitler would have none of it, saying that his V1s would settle the matter in their favour.

Two weeks later Hitler summoned Rundstedt and Rommel to the Berghof for another consultation, refusing Rommel's request for a fighting withdrawal to the Seine. Instead he ordered a counter-attack, which failed, and when he heard that Rundstedt had told Keitel that they should sue for peace, he had Rundstedt replaced by Generalfeldmarschall Günther von Kluge.

SECURITY FENCE

TO AIRFIELD

The reinforcement of the buildings at the East Prussian HQ in 1944 had forced Hitler to vacate the Wolfsschanze which is why he was at the Berghof when the Allies landed in Normandy on June 6. He returned in mid-July by which time the Red Army was only 150 kilometres away. The Führerbunker [1] was still not ready so Hitler was living in the Guest Bunker [2]. This picture was taken shortly after Hitler's return. He is walking westward from the southern wing of the Guest Bunker towards the Lage-baracke [3] where the daily situation conferences were convened. On the right is the path leading to the entrance gate for the top-security Führer's compound (the Führersperrkreis). The Nachrichtenbunker (Communicators Bunker) [4] can be seen beyond the vehicle standing on the road.

Back in 1942 the conferences were held in the Keitelbunker [5] but this lay in the area of the Wolfsschanze that was currently in the throes of alteration, and had poor security bearing in mind the number of building workers present on the site.

Over a period of several years in the late 1960s and early 1970s, Dr Richard Raiber and Professor Peter Hoffmann made several visits to Rastenburg, measuring and mapping the Wolfsschanze — even getting themselves arrested in the process! This is the photo Professor Hoffmann took then of the remains of the Keitelbunker. (Sadly Dr Raiber died in March 2002 but we published his report in 1977 in *After the Battle* No. 19.)

Other important buildings are: [6] Barracks for the SS escort detachment. [7] RSD and SS barracks. [8] Press. [9] Security. [10] Hitler's staff. [11] Secretarial. [12] Post office. [13] Government and service liaison officers, doctors, barbers, etc. [14] Cinema. [15] Garage. [16] Drivers' quarters. [17] Bormann. [18] Hitler's Wehrmacht adjutant and the Army personnel office. [19] Mess. [20] Jodl. [21] Göring. [22] Tea House. [23] Hitler's exercise area. [24] Kriegsmarine. [25] Führer-Begleit-Kommando. [26] Guests. [27] Von Ribbentrop. [28] Guard post. This artist's impression looking north does not show the camouflage which would have hidden the complex from aerial observation. The route taken by von Stauffenberg after leaving his primed briefcase bomb in the conference room in building [3] is shown. He had to pass out through the gate to the inner Führer compound, drive over the level crossing on the railway line, and then pass through the outer gate before leaving for the airfield situated on a plateau six kilometres away.

Left: **Five days before the plot to kill Hitler was sprung, Oberst Claus von Stauffenberg, extreme left, was photographed at the Wolfsschanze. With him are (L-R) Konteradmiral Karl-Jesko von Puttkamer, General der Flieger Karl Bodenschatz (back to camera), Hitler, and Generalfeldmarschall Keitel. They are standing between the Lagebaracke and Guest Bunker in the Führersperrkreis before the afternoon conference. The view is looking east. In the centre distance (beyond the officer walking toward the group) is the west face of the south wing of the Guest Bunker where Hitler was living in July 1944. Note the poles for suspension of camouflage nets.** *Above:* **When Dr Raiber took his comparison, he explained that 'a little hill, origin and function unknown, stands just this side of the truck and makes it impossible to obtain good photographs of the ruins of the Guest Bunker's south wing today.**

The interior of the Lagebaracke following the explosion of the bomb on the morning of July 20, 1944. The device, carried into the conference room by Oberst von Stauffenberg in his briefcase, contained just under a kilogramme of explosive, and it was amazing that, of the 24 people present, no one was killed outright. Dr Heinrich Berger, the shorthand writer who was standing right next to the bomb, lost both legs and died that afternoon. The Luftwaffe Chief-of-Staff, General Günther Kor- **ten, and Oberst Heinz Brandt, senior staff officer with the Army Operations Section, were both grievously injured and died in hospital two days later. General Rudolf Schmundt, the Führer's senior Wehrmacht aide (also head of the Army Personnel Office), who died of his wounds three months later, had been standing at the end of the table — seen here with the end which was nearest the explosion blown off. Here Bormann and Göring discuss the Führer's close brush with death.**

Left: **The table has been pulled outside. L-R: Albert Bormann (younger brother of Martin and one of Hitler's adjutants); Goebbels; Dr Werner Naumann, Secretary of State in the** **Propaganda Ministry; Julius Schaub and Göring.** *Right:* **Shredded trousers from one of the injured, reputed to be Hitler's but most probably from Dr Berger because the Führer always wore black.**

Meanwhile the anti-Hitler conspirators had not given up in their attempts to assassinate Hitler, although four had failed for various reasons during the period September 1943 to February 1944. The lead had been taken over by Oberst Claus Schenk Graf (Count) von Stauffenberg, the Chief-of-Staff under General Friedrich Olbricht commanding the Replacement Army in Berlin, who had lost an eye, his right hand and two fingers of his left hand, but was nevertheless prepared to be the assassin.

He had his first opportunity on July 11 when summoned to the Berghof, taking a British bomb in his briefcase, but found on arrival that Himmler, whom he wanted to kill together with Hitler and Göring, was absent. Four days later Stauffenberg was again summoned to another top level conference, but this time to the Wolfsschanze to where Hitler had moved meanwhile, even though construction of the bomb-proof accommodation he had ordered was still incomplete.

Mussolini was scheduled to visit Hitler on that Thursday and in fact the conference had been advanced by 30 minutes to get it out of the way before he arrived. Hitler's injuries were to his right elbow, which had been resting on the table while cupping his chin in his hand, burns to both legs and perforated eardrums.

Left: **Having left the building (visible in the background), Mussolini is seen talking to Obergruppenführer Karl Wolff, Wehrmacht plenipotentiary in Italy. Martin Bormann stands between the Duce and Hitler, while Himmler is between Hitler and Göring. Luftwaffe General Oberst Bruno Lörzer is to the** **right of Göring, and Schaub is just visible on the extreme left.** *Right:* **The late Dr Raiber's favourite photograph of himself was this one in front of the collapsed roof of the conference building; demolished not as a result of the bomb but from last-ditch demolitions in November 1944 by the Wehrmacht.**

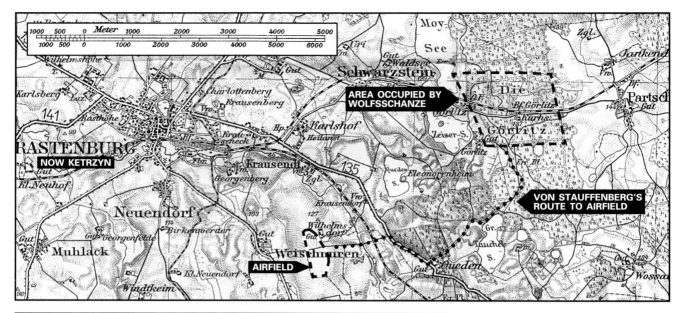

This is the spot where the southern guardhouse ([28] on the plan on pages 394-395) once stood. Von Stauffenberg had reached his car parked outside the inner Führer zone when his bomb went off but, because engineers had been removing trees to expand the camp using explosives, the driver Feldwebel Fischer was not unduly worried. Together with his aide and co-conspirator, Oberleutnant Werner von Haeften, they drove up this road to the airfield, completely unaware that Hitler had survived.

The bomb plot of July 20, 1944, largely failed because the explosive force of the bomb was insufficient. The windows of the brick and concrete building were open, so reducing the blast effect, and the explosion was further dissipated by the roof void. Had the new command bunker been complete, possibly the blast would have been contained, killing everyone in it. Hitler suffered no serious consequences apart from an injury to his elbow, and eardrums, and his pulse was quite normal when checked that evening. In his radio broadcast to the German people that evening, he attributed his escape to divine Providence. That same afternoon he greeted Mussolini upon arrival at the railway station and showed him the ruins of his conference room.

Stauffenberg escaped back to Berlin, but there the plot collapsed and he and his fellow conspirators were either shot, committed suicide or were rounded up in the massive investigation that followed, only to be executed in due course.

As von Stauffenberg would be incommunicado for the two-hour flight to Berlin, General Erich Fellgiebel had been detailed to phone ahead. However when he saw Hitler emerge from the shattered room alive, he was stunned: 'Something terrible has happened. The Führer is alive', he telephoned. As a result, General der Infanterie Friedrich Olbricht, commanding the Home Army, did nothing, waiting for von Stauffenberg who was his Chief-of-Staff, to arrive. He reached Berlin at 4.30 p.m. and insisted that the bomb had gone off and Hitler must be dead. Instead, the SS surrounded the Bendlerblock and six of the plotters who had been identified were put under close arrest. An instant court-martial found them guilty whereupon the nominal leader, Generaloberst Ludwig Beck (far left) was handed his pistol and told to hurry up. Having fired two shots but failed to kill himself outright, he was given the coup de grâce. Left: It happened here: a plaque on the wall of the actual room now part of the memorial museum.

A firing squad was quickly assembled in the courtyard where a pile of sand left over from building work provided a convenient stop-butt. One of the five, Generaloberst Erich Hoepner, pleaded that he had nothing to do with the plot and so he was separated from the other four who were marched downstairs to be shot.

Above: (L-R) General Olbricht, Oberst Albrecht Ritter Mertz von Quirnheim (Chief-of-Staff in the General Army Office), von Stauffenberg, and Oberleutnant von Haeften. *Below:* The memorial in the Bendlerblock courtyard now symbolises the execution.

Left: The bodies were taken to St Matthäus churchyard in Grossgörschenstrasse and quickly interred on this spot but were later exhumed and reburied at a location which has never been determined. *Right:* The first burial place was not far from the Volksgericht, or People's Court, located in the old Prussian

Court of Appeal building in Heinrich-von-Kleist-Park where trials, conducted by the notorious Nazi judge, Roland Freisler, subsequently took place of numerous individuals implicated in the plot. After the war this became the home of the Allied Control Council.

Generaloberst Hoepner, who had pleaded not guilty at the summary court-martial on the evening of July 20, was tried in the People's Court on August 7 along with Generalfeldmarschall Erwin von Witzleben *(left)*, Generalmajor Helmuth

Stieff, Generalleutnant Paul von Hase, Oberstleutnant Robert Bernardis, Hauptmann Karl Klausing, Oberregierungsrat Peter Graf Yorck von Wartenburg, and Oberleutnant Albrecht von Hagen. *Right:* **This is the court room today.**

On July 21 Hitler replaced his Chief-of-Staff, Generaloberst Kurt Zeitzler, who was unwell, with Generaloberst Heinz Guderian, the Inspector-General of Armoured Troops. Guderian promptly issued an order of the day calling for 'the unity of generals, of the officer corps and of the men of the Army.' A few days later he went even further, calling on the General Staff to 'co-operate in the political indoctrination of younger commanders in accordance with the tenets of the Führer.'

In August Hitler summoned his senior commanders for another harangue and ordered that the German salute replace the normal military salute throughout the armed forces.

Germany was now fully entrapped in a two-front war. In the East the next stage of the Soviet advance was Operation 'Bagration', which was conducted north of the Pripet Marshes between June 22 and August 29, 1944, that

All eight were adjudged guilty and taken to Plötzensee prison in Königsdamm for immediate execution. Prior to 1933, death sentences in Germany were carried out by beheading but in Hitler's 'Enabling Act' of March 23 that year, hanging was introduced as an alternative method of execution. *Above:* **At Plötzensee, a girder fitted with eight hooks was installed behind the guillotine above a raised platform. Without a trapdoor giving a drop to break the neck of the victim, the so-called Austrian method of hanging was more akin to strangulation and the executioner often had to hasten the end by hanging on to the victims legs. It is estimated that 2,500 persons or more were either guillotined or hung at Plötzensee during the Third Reich of whom 89 were July 20 plotters.** *Right:* **Today the execution chamber has been walled off from the main prison which is still used. The guillotine was removed by Soviet troops and the raised platform has also disappeared and, for some reason, the number of hooks in the beam has been reduced to five. All told, it is believed that around 600 were arrested in connection with the assassination plot of whom 200 were executed.**

Hitler's health began to deteriorate rapidly after the injuries he suffered on July 20. First came a series of violent headaches, then his stomach problems increased, and he was taking at least five kinds of tablets seemingly indiscriminately, for his orderly would hand over tablets on demand so that Dr Morell had no control over the situation, although the doctor still kept administering his mysterious injections to little effect. Hitler's left arm began to shake uncontrollably and an ENT specialist was summoned from Berlin. Dr Morell himself fell ill and was temporarily replaced by a Dr Weber. Two other doctors then determined that Morell had been giving Hitler enough strychnine with his injections to have fatal consequences if he continued. When reported to Hitler, he flew into a rage and dismissed them both. For a while he confined himself to his room, eating alone, before gradually admitting his intimate circle of his secretaries, his ADC Albert Bormann and Ambassador Walter Hewel, the Auswärtiges Amt (Foreign Office) representative at the Führerhauptquartier, to have tea in his bedroom, where he lay prostrate in bed, almost inert with dull, staring eyes. Eventually he got over this crisis and returned to a more normal routine.

In this picture taken on August 8, 1944, note how Hitler is using his left hand because of the injury to his right arm. He is greeting Wilhelm Schepmann who took over the leadership of the SA after Viktor Lutze was killed in a car crash in May 1943. In 1944 he was made responsible for the military training of the Volkssturm (People's Army).

brought them across the frontiers into the Baltic states and East Prussia, to within a few miles of Warsaw and gave them bridgeheads across the Vistula river south of that city. During this operation Heeresgruppe Mitte was virtually destroyed with 17 divisions totally annihilated and another 50 reduced to half-strength. Then on August 1 the Polish Home Army staged an uprising in Warsaw, hoping in vain to obtain Soviet support.

In the West Lieutenant General George S. Patton's Third Army's armour broke through at Avranches on July 30 and commenced a wide sweep toward Paris, and between August 10 to 19 some 50,000 German troops of 5. Panzerarmee and 7. Armee were trapped in the slaughter of the Falaise Pocket with all their heavy equipment. By the end of the month the Allies were across the Seine, had taken Paris and also landed in the south of France.

The deadly V2 rockets became operational in September but too late to save the day. By the end of the month the Germans had been driven back into Alsace-Lorraine, or the Westgau as they called it, and out of Luxembourg and Belgium. However, an adventurous British attempt to seize a bridge across the Rhine at Arnhem with airborne forces in mid-September failed with heavy losses.

By the end of the month Finland, Romania and Bulgaria had defected from the Axis camp, seeking peace terms with the Soviet Union, and were followed by Hungary, but Hitler had Skorzeny kidnap Admiral Horthy's son and then seize the citadel in Budapest where Horthy and his government were quartered.

Upon his return, Hitler briefed Skorzeny on his role in the counter-offensive from the Ardennes that Hitler was now

planning. Skorzeny and his men would operate behind enemy lines in American uniforms and using American vehicles to capture bridges, issue false orders and generally create confusion and panic.

Amassing 250,000 men in total secrecy, Hitler planned to launch eight re-equipped panzer divisions and a

panzergrenadier division, backed by a further 25 new volksgrenadier divisions to smash through the American lines and retake Antwerp, splitting the Americans from the Anglo-Canadian forces in the north and creating sufficient havoc to enable him to switch his reserves for a counter-offensive against the Soviets.

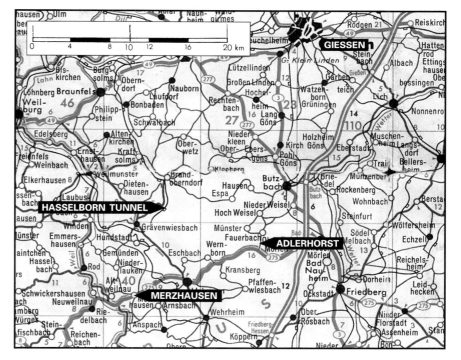

In the summer of 1939, Hitler gave orders for a site for a permanent headquarters to be found in the west — a sure sign of what was on his mind. The site chosen at Ziegenberg in the Taunus mountains was ideal: just seven kilometres fom the autobahn; 15 from the nearest Luftwaffe airfield at Merzhausen; 18 kilometres from the railway tunnel at Hasselborn where the Führer's train could be hidden; 28 kilometres from the OKH headquarters at Giessen, and having good telephone lines to Berlin. This then became Führerhauptquartier 'Adlerhorst'.

Who exactly found the site at Castle Ziegenberg is not clear. Warlimont says it was a staff officer of Abteilung 1 of the OKW; Speer claims it was 'some of my collaborators and myself'; Hoffmann says it was Rommel, together with Schmundt, Engel, Below, Todt and Speer — all travelling incognito in civilian clothes. What is certain from documents is that the first design drawings for 'Adlerhorst' are dated September 8, 1939 and that the castle and its grounds were requisitioned by the Wehrmacht the following day. Had the invasion of Great Britain taken place in 1940, Hitler would have moved back from Brûly-de-Pesche (see pages 374-375), to Adlerhorst and overseen Operation 'Seelöwe' from there. As it was, the headquarters did not come into its own until 1944 when it was ideally situated for masterminding Hitler's last throw in the west: Operation 'Wacht am Rhein' to be launched in the Ardennes. Just like the breakthrough he had achieved in the same area in May 1940, so he hoped to duplicate his success in December 1944.

As usual, Speer's design was functional as well as decorative. This is the garage block.

It survived the war unscathed and was taken over by American occupation forces.

In 1998 the building was converted into office accommodation for the PSB-IT computer software company.

Moving his headquarters to the FHQ 'Adlerhorst', which was camouflaged as a number of pillboxes under trees that were in fact the entrances to underground bunkers, Hitler waited for the bad weather than would negate Allied air superiority. He attacked on December 16, catching the Americans completely by surprise, but the Western Allies rallied and by January 8 the Germans were obliged to withdraw, having suffered 100,000 casualties and lost 600 tanks to 76,000 Allied casualties. During the operation the Luftwaffe launched its last big attack of the war on January 1, 1945, destroying 156 Allied aircraft, mainly on the ground, but at considerable cost in its own aircraft.

Even Speer's ornate petrol station survives, minus the pumps.

Hitler left Berlin for Adlerhorst at 5 p.m. on December 10 and left at 6 p.m. on January 15, 1945. As the Western Front was an OKW theatre of operations, the Chief of the Army General Staff, Generaloberst Heinz Guderian based at Zossen south of Berlin, was forced to commute between the two headquarters to confer with Hitler. For the first few days, the Allies were caught by surprise and poor weather grounded their aircraft. German forces pushed almost 60 miles from their starting point, and spread out over an area of 400 square miles, but by Christmas Day the attack had more or less run out of steam. Nevertheless it was a severe embarrassment to and a failure of Allied intelligence and it took American, British and Canadian forces a month to regain the lost territory. Thereafter the drive on Berlin continued. The loss of reserves cost the Germans dear when the Russians launched their spring offensive, and the ultimate price of failure was the inevitable defeat of the Third Reich. (For chapter and verse on the battle, see Jean Paul Pallud's *Battle of the Bulge Then and Now*.)

The headquarters prepared for Hitler in 1939 was based in and around the castle at Ziegenberg but it seems that in 1944 the accommodation at the Schloss *(above)* and its reinforced bunkers *(below)* had all been earmarked by Generalfeldmarschall Gerd von Rundstedt, the Oberbefehlshaber West, for his own HQ. *Above:* A house has been built on this particular bunker.

So when Hitler arrived on December 10, he occupied a subsidiary complex two kilometres up the road at Wiesental. [1] Guardhouse on the Ziegenberg road. [2] Hitler's living quarters. [3] Kasino (Officers' Mess). [4] Wehrmacht-führungsstab (OKW Operations Staff under Generaloberst Jodl). [5] Generals' accommodation plus switchboard. [6] Bormann. [7] Reichssicherheitsdienst (Security Police). [8] OKW headquarters.

By the look of the smirk on Speer's face it would seem that Hitler was in one of his expansive moods as he confers with Generaloberst Jodl and Generalfeldmarschall Keitel. A picture no doubt taken before the battle was lost.

Left: **Extensive camouflaging made the buildings almost impossible to detect, even at close range. This is the OKW headquarters building [8] — note the sunken guard post roofed with logs in the foreground. In 1957 it became the Gasthof Adlerhorst but is now a private house** *(right).*

Left: **This is the Reichssicherheitsdienst bunker provided for the security detail guarding the compound, again heavily camouflaged midst the trees.** *Right:* **Sixty years later, Wiesental has become a fashionable place to live with few clues remaining to remind one of the drama once enacted here.**

Of Hitler's personal quarters today nothing remains. *Left:* **This is how the buildings looked when captured by troops of the US VIII Corps in April 1945 and** *(right)* **the villa which now stands partly on the same site. Initially, American war correspondents identified Schloss Ziegenberg as Hitler's 'hideout' during the Battle of the Bulge but British reporters correctly identified the Wiesental location as having been the place occupied by Hitler.**

All but the OKW building were demolished, but the thickness of the walls in the cellar of the former Gasthof Adlerhorst provide a clue to its former use. When Hitler left Adlerhorst on January 15 the war had less than four months to run. Save for one short outing to the Eastern Front, Hitler would spend these weeks in his last headquarters: the Führerbunker below the garden of the Reich Chancellery.

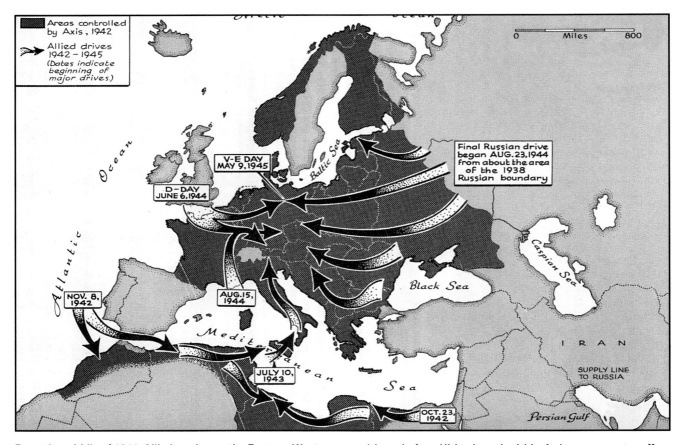

Legend on map:
Areas controlled by Axis, 1942
Allied drives 1942–1945 (Dates indicate beginning of major drives.)

V-E DAY MAY 9, 1945
D-DAY JUNE 6, 1944
Final Russian drive began AUG. 23, 1944 from about the area of the 1938 Russian boundary
NOV. 8, 1942
AUG. 15, 1944
JULY 10, 1943
OCT. 23, 1942

Baltic Sea
Atlantic Ocean
Mediterranean Sea
Black Sea
Caspian Sea
IRAN
SUPPLY LINE TO RUSSIA
Persian Gulf
Miles 0 — 800

From the middle of 1944, Allied armies on the Eastern, Western and Southern Fronts were advancing inexorably on Germany, **and long before Hitler launched his Ardennes counter-offensive, the much-vaunted Siegfried Line had been breached.**

Between January 12 and 14 the Soviet forces massed along the line of the Vistula river south of Warsaw launched a massive assault, smashing through and destroying the German forces opposing them, including the reserves that Hitler had ordered deployed too far forward. By the end of the month the Soviets had taken most of Silesia, the remains of Poland and the Warthegau up to the Oder river, where they were able to establish bridgeheads barely 50 miles from Berlin. However, in doing this they had outstripped their lines of sup-

ply and left aside the area of Pomerania on their northern flank, where Generaloberst Guderian began assembling forces for a counter-attack. To Guderian's dismay, Hitler gave the command of these troops to Himmler, and it was not until they had been defeated that Guderian was able to persuade Himmler, who had withdrawn to a sanatorium at Hohenlychen under the pretext of a bad cold, to hand over command to Generaloberst Gotthard Heinrici, before Guderian himself was replaced by General Hans Krebs on March 28.

In the six weeks that the Soviets needed to deal with these matters, the Germans were able to build up a line of defence along the Oder using ad hoc and Volkssturm (home guard) units reinforced by formations hastily switched from the front in Alsace-Lorraine. Desperate as they were for troops to defend their home country, Hitler refused to allow the evacuation of Heeresgruppe Nord from the Kurland peninsula, where 189,000 troops were left to surrender at the end of hostilities.

The so-called impregnable line of fortifications guarding Germany's western frontier, with its mutually-sited pillboxes, minefields, barbed wire, anti-tank ditches and dragon's teeth, had absorbed one third of the country's cement production **between 1938 and 1940. It was first breached here on the road just north of Roetgen, a small village astride the Belgian-German border, by an American task force on September 13 . . . without firing a shot!**

But the immediate threat was from the Red Army and on Sunday, March 3 — Heroes' Memorial Day — Hitler ventured out to visit his commanders on the Oder front. Travelling along roads choked with dispirited troops, he met with General Theodor Busse of the 9. Armee at Harnekop Castle, 30 miles north of Berlin. Plans for the defence of the Oder-Neisse river line were discussed where around a million defenders were facing a Soviet force of 2½ million.

Operating since January 15 from his Führerbunker deep beneath the Reich Chancellery garden with surprisingly limited communications facilities, Hitler was primarily concerned with events on the Eastern Front, where his constant intervention in the tactical handling continued to cause needless casualties. On March 3 he paid a surprise visit to the 9. Armee, meeting General der Infanterie Theodor Busse at Schloss Harnekop, the headquarters of the CI. Armeekorps, and on April 4 he summoned Generaloberst Heinrici to review the defensive arrangements in detail.

No sooner had Hitler returned to Berlin than Germany's main defensive obstacle in the West — the River Rhine — had been crossed by American forces which had captured the bridge at Remagen intact as it had not yet been demolished.

Hitler was furious. He sacked von Rundstedt and ordered a court-martial for bridge commander Major Hans Scheller and three of his men. They were subsequently shot by firing squad (see *After the Battle* No. 16).

During the bitterly cold winter of early 1945 the Western Allies gradually closed up to the Rhine and on March 7 the bridge at Remagen was captured intact, enabling the Americans to establish a substantial bridgehead there before breaking out into central Germany on March 25, by which time the Lower Rhine had also been crossed by Canadian, British and American forces striking out across the northern plains. Generalfeldmarschall Walter Model's Heeresgruppe B was encircled in the Ruhr and surrendered on April 18, when Model committed suicide. By April 25 the Americans had met up with the Soviets at Torgau on the Elbe, cutting Germany in half.

Left: East and West joined hands at Torgau, 100 kilometres south of Berlin on April 25. *Right:* Repaired after the war, the bridge was blown again by the Germans 49 years later!

On the same day — Wednesday, April 25 — that US and Soviet forces met on the Elbe, the Red Army closed the ring around Berlin . . . and the Royal Air Force visited the Obersalzberg! Uncertain as to Hitler's precise whereabouts, and with the knowledge that the Nazis were reported to be preparing to make a last stand in an Alpine redoubt, a massive knockout blow was planned for Hitler's mountain retreat using over 350 Lancasters from Nos. 1, 5 and 8 Groups including No. 617 Squadron carrying 12,000lb Tallboys — their last of the war. However, target-marking Mosquitoes found reception for their Oboe receivers difficult because of mountains blocking the signals from one of the ground stations.

Low cloud and snow covering the ground also made positive identification of the individual buildings difficult. Compare this picture with the plan on page 392. [1] Berghof. [2] SS Barracks. [3] Platterhof Hotel. [4] Göring. [5] Guest house. [6] Bormann. [7] Hotel Zum Türken (the SS headquarters). [8] Bomb-burst.

Two Lancasters failed to return. Ten members of the crew were captured but four from LM756 of No. 619 Squadron were killed. They were Flying Officer Wilfred De Marco, WO2 Norman Johnston, Sergeant Edward Norman and WO2 Gordon Walker. All are buried in Klagenfurt War Cemetery in Austria.

As American forces of the 3rd Infantry Division closed on Berchtesgaden on May 4, those SS troops remaining set fire to the Berghof, gutting the building. This is how the men of the 7th Infantry Regiment found it.

THIS BUILDING WAS RESTORED/IN USE   * HOTEL ZUM TURKE

Looking up the hill to Bormann's house (see also page 61) with the corner of the Berghof on the right. The flattened building on the left behind the Tallboy crater was the home of the administration officer on the Obersalzberg.

But Hitler was not at home; in fact he had not been back to the Berghof since July 1944 although he had planned to fly there to celebrate his 56th birthday on April 20. Instead he decided to remain in Berlin . . . but just look what a difference six years of war had made. This is how the Chancellery appeared — all new and pristine — on his 50th birthday in 1939 — a day when the might of the Third Reich was omnipotent and the world held its breath over the Führer's increasing demands.

This is the nearest comparison we could find which was taken just a month before his 1945 birthday. Blasted, battered and boarded up, the Chancellery is now a sorry site with an emergency water reservoir having been built on Wilhelmplatz.

On April 16 the Soviets launched their final offensive and within four days had broken through the last of the German defences before Berlin, although at tremendous cost. The leading Nazis called on Hitler to congratulate him on his birthday on April 20, and then all left Berlin while they could, except for Martin Bormann, Reichsjugendführer Artur Axmann and Goebbels, whom Hitler invited to join him in the Führerbunker with his family. Berlin was then surrounded and all Hitler's attempts to bring about a relief operation failed, despite sending Keitel off to urge greater efforts in the field.

Bormann deliberately misinterpreted a signal to Hitler from Göring as evidence of treachery, whereupon Hitler had Göring stripped of all his appointments, but when he heard of his 'faithful' Himmler's secret negotiations with the Western Allies he ordered Himmler to be hunted down and executed.

Berlin, where Hitler would end his days, was a ruin ever since the RAF launched their own 'Battle of Berlin' in 1943 with a devastating raid on the night of November 22/23 which left at least 175,000 people homeless. Over a dozen more massed attacks followed until Bomber Command was diverted to pre-invasion targets, its very last visit to the German capital being on Hitler's birthday in 1945! But as the 76 Mosquitoes made their night attack, Hitler was safely below ground in his back garden shelter. The Chancellery is [1]; Wilhelmplatz [2]; the Propaganda Ministry [3], and the emergency exit from the Führerbunker [4].

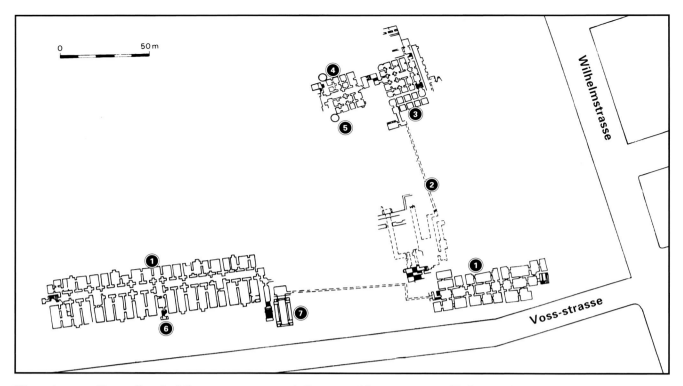

When the new Chancellery building was constructed, Speer made provision for the basement [1] to double up as air raid shelters in time of war. They were linked by a tunnel [2] leading to the cellars of the old Reich Chancellery [3]. With the increasing air raids, these cellars were reinforced in 1943 while a deeper bunker — the Führerbunker [4] — was built alongside, linked to it by an angled staircase. Thereafter the old cellars became known as the Vorbunker, being used as a service area with storerooms, a kitchen, and servants quarters, etc, as well as accommodation for the Goebbels family. An observation tower-cum-pillbox-cum-emergency exit [5] (seen in the picture below) had been built beside a second emergency stairway from the Führerbunker. Two other interesting features of the Chancellery shelters were an exit stairway to Voss-strasse [6], protected by a tilting concrete cover, and also a vehicle lift [7] to an underground garage 25 feet below the surface.

It was the Russians who first obtained an accurate description of the uses of the various rooms in the Führerbunker from their post-war interrogations of former key members of the Reich Chancellery group who were in the bunker in April 1945 and were subsequently captured by them. 'From the old bunker a connecting tunnel to the new was broken through with a stair-case [1], which ended in a small chamber [2] with an armoured door. Behind this door began the broad, two-part passageway of the Führerbunker. In the near half of the passageway [3] stood, on the right wall, cabinets with air raid equipment (gas masks, fire equipment, etc). A door on this wall led to the machinery room [4] and air conditioning plant. The second armoured door led into six adjoining rooms. Here was a telephone station [5] operated by an officer of Hitler's body-guard; a telephone switchboard and a telegraph [6]; Dr Morell's room [7]; a first-aid station [8] where also there was a bed for Dr Ludwig Stumpfegger, the emergency physician; a bedroom [9] for Heinz Linge and orderly officers as well as a social room [10]. On the left wall in the first half of the corridor stood a table and an armchair. A clock hung over the table. Nearby was a telephone station, from which the watch sergeant announced trunk calls to the situation conferences. A door on the left side led to washrooms [11]. There Hitler's Alsatian Blondi had her place. An armoured door separated the first part of the passageway from the second, the reception room [12]. An officer of the bodyguard stood at the entrance to the recep-tion section. Here the participants assembled before the con-ferences and waited for Hitler. Large paintings hung on the wall, mostly landscapes. On the right wall stood 12 to 16 arm-chairs. On the opposite wall was a cushioned bench in front of

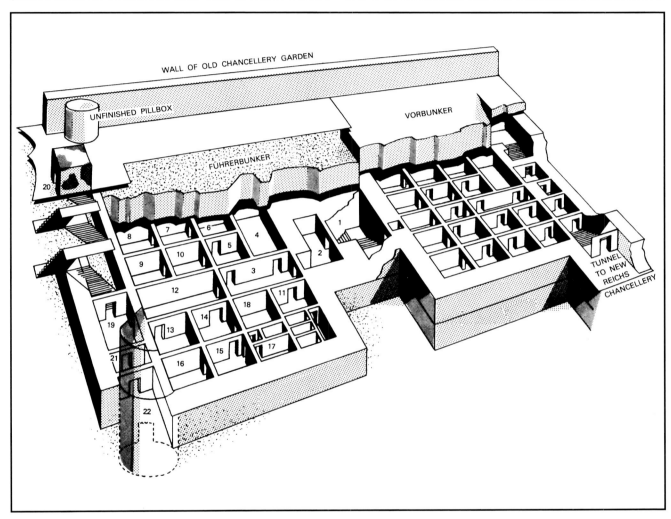

which stood a table with cushioned chairs. To the right and left of the bench were two armoured doors. The left led into the rooms of Hitler and Eva Braun, the right into the situation con-ference room [13]. In front of Hitler's apartment was a little refreshment room [14]. In front of its door stood a screen which blocked the view into the rooms of Hitler and Eva Braun from those in the passageway. Behind the double door of the refreshment room was Hitler's office [15], laid with a thick, soft carpet. On the table was a bronze lamp, ink stand, telephone, world atlas and a magnifying glass and usually the Führer's eyeglasses. Over the table hung one of Menzel's paintings, a half-length portrait of Frederick II in an oval frame. Against the opposite wall stood a sofa, and in front of it there was a table and three coloured silk-covered chairs. A still-life hung over the sofa. To the right of that stood a tea table, to the left a radio receiver. On the right wall hung a painting by Lucas Cranach. A door on the same wall led to Hitler's bedroom [16], whose flooring was likewise laid with carpet. Here was a bed with a night table, a clothes cabinet, a mobile tea table on castors, a safe in which he kept secret papers, bookshelves, and oxygen

apparatus. To the left in Hitler's office was a door to Hitler and Eva Braun's bathroom [17]. From the bathroom a door led to Eva Braun's toilet and bedroom [18]. Here stood at the right of the door a dark couch, a small round table and an armchair. Opposite the couch on the opposite wall stood Eva Braun's bed, a clothes cabinet, and a box for her dog. On the floor was a dark fancy-flowered carpet. The walls were decorated with flower paintings. The second door from Eva Braun's room led into the refreshment room. At the end of the reception section was the so-called "air lock" [19] with armoured door. In the air lock there were to the right and left emergency exits to the garden behind the Reichskanzlei. From the right exit [20] led a winding stairway. A steel staircase, like a fireman's ladder, led to the left emergency exit [21]. This exit likewise was roofed with a dome-shaped tower with machine gun ports, in which was an observation post [22]. SS personnel from the body-guard manned the watch in this tower. The tower had tele-phone communication with the Führerbunker.' It was in room [15] — Hitler's study — that he and his wife committed suicide around 3.30 p.m. on Monday, April 30.

By midday on Monday, Soviet troops were reported right outside in the Voss-strasse and it was obvious that the Chancellery might be overrun at any moment. After taking their formal leave of those remaining in the bunker in the reception room, Eva led the way through the refreshment room to her husband's study. The armoured door was closed and Otto Günsche took up station to prevent any-one entering. After an interval of ten min-utes or so no sound had been heard and eventually Heinz Linge opened the door but, when assailed by the strong smell of cordite and bitter almonds, called for Bor-mann to lead the way. 'Hitler was sitting on the left of the sofa, with his face bent slightly forward and hanging down to the right. With the 7.65mm he had shot him-self in the right temple. The blood had run down on to the carpet and from this pool of blood a splash had got on the sofa. Eva Braun was sitting on his right. She had drawn both her legs up onto the sofa and was sitting there with cramped lips so that it immediately became clear to us that she had taken cyanide.' The Soviets had Berlin all to themselves until July 4 when American and British forces entered the capital to take up occupation duties in their respective sectors. Later that month war correspondent Percy Knauth (rear) was pictured inspecting bloodstains — Hitler's bloodstains — on the settee.

With the end clearly in sight, on April 29 Hitler married his mistress of long standing, Eva Braun, in the Führer-bunker in the company of members of his inner circle. Until then their assoc-iation had been a close secret known only to the Berghof intimates.

He then dictated his Political Testa-ment, nominating Grossadmiral Karl Dönitz as his successor as Reich Presi-dent and Goebbels as Reich Chancellor. Hitler and his bride then committed sui-cide at 3.30 p.m. next day and Goebbels sent General Krebs to try and arrange a

cease-fire with the Soviets so that he could convene the new government. This was refused, so Goebbels and his wife committed suicide on May 1 after murdering their six children, and next morning the remains of the Berlin defence surrendered.

Erich Kempka had already been instructed by Günsche to obtain some petrol to burn the bodies and the jerrycans of fuel had been delivered to the doorway of the emergency exit ready for the funeral pyre. 'Günsche told me that the Führer was dead', related Hitler's driver later. 'A short time after that Linge and Dr Stumpfegger came from the private room of the Führer carrying a corpse wrapped in an ordinary field-grey blanket. One could only see the long black trousers and black shoes which the Führer usually wore with his field-grey uni-form jacket. I could not observe any spots of blood on the body wrapped in the blanket. Thereupon Martin Bormann came

from the Führer's living-room, carrying the corpse of Mrs Eva Hitler in his arms. He turned the corpse over to me. Mrs Hitler wore a dark dress. I did not have the feeling that the corpse was still warm. I could not recognise any injuries on the body. The dress was slightly damp only in the region of the heart. Linge, Stumpfegger and Günsche now went upstairs with the corpse of the Führer to the bunker exit to the garden. I fol-lowed with the corpse of Mrs Hitler. Together with Günsche and Linge I poured the fuel over the corpses until they were saturated. I struck a match and lit a peice of cloth. I threw it on the corpses and within a second a roaring flame shot up.'

On December 11, 1947, the Soviet authorities blew up the emergency exits which still remained standing in the Chancellery garden.

SITE OF FÜHRERBUNKER

VOSS-STRASSE

LEIPZIGER PLATZ

When the Berlin Wall was erected by the East Germans in August 1961, for the next 30 years the Führerbunker lay hidden under a mound of earth in the so-called 'death strip' between the inner and outer walls.

In 1988 work began to build blocks of flats along the Wilhelm-strasse. As a result, the inner wall was moved westwards to provide more land which meant that the Führerbunker now lay within the building site. *Left:* Winston Ramsey, Editor-in-Chief, visited East Berlin that August. Here he is pictured just in front of the three-metre-thick roof slab, then being demolished, with the opening for the emergency exit stairway clearly visible just behind. The bodies were buried in a trench which lay just in front. *Right: After the Battle* reader Peter Thompson pictured with Rochus Misch, the telephone switchboard operator in the bunker, on the same spot in 2001. (For a detailed account of Hitler's last days, see Tony Le Tissier's *Berlin Then and Now*.)

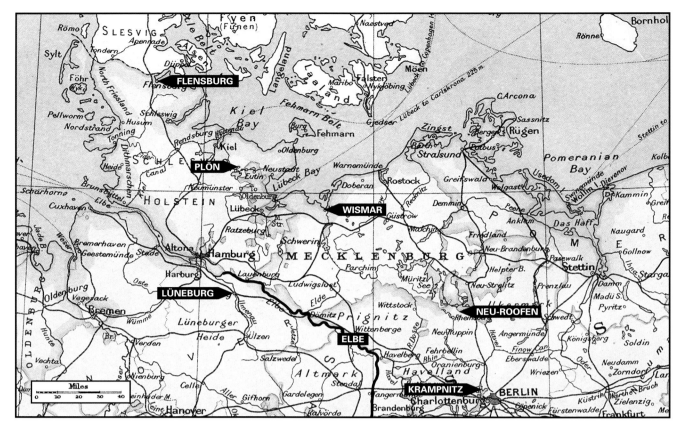

The Flensburg Government

In the final two weeks of the war, the headquarters involved in the German conduct of operations shifted from Berlin to north-west Germany. The map highlights the places prominent in the story.

On April 19, 1945, Grossadmiral Karl Dönitz had his OKM staff move out of 'Koralle', the secret headquarters between Bernau and Eberswalde, north-east of Berlin, to the officer cadet school at Plön when the Soviet break-through from the Oder threatened to overrun them. He himself stayed behind in order to be able to congratulate Hitler on his 56th birthday next day, when Hitler charged him with the defence of northern Germany.

At this point Dönitz was 54 years old, a convinced Nazi and faithful adherent of Hitler. As Commander-in-Chief of the Kriegsmarine, he was determined not to see a repeat of the 1918 naval mutinies and revolution, and continued to enforce ruthless discipline within his service. His U-Boat campaign having collapsed, his main concern was now the supervision of the massive-scale evacuation of soldiers and civilians away from the Soviets over the Baltic.

On April 22 Hitler finally decided to remain in Berlin, so the OKW staff under Generalfeldmarschall Wilhelm Keitel and Generaloberst Alfred Jodl moved to Neu-Roofen, near Rheinsberg in Meckenberg-Vorpommern, where Dönitz visited them on April 27 to appraise himself of the general situation, which by now was hopeless. In order to keep his operational ports open in the Baltic and give room for the influx of refugees pouring into Schleswig-Holstein, Dönitz was particularly anxious that the Allied advance from the west be checked at the Elbe as long as possible.

Grossadmiral Dönitz: In place of the former Reich Marshal Göring the Führer appoints you as his successor. Written authority is on its way. You will immediately take all such measures as the situation requires.

BORMANN, BERLIN, 6.35 p.m. APRIL 30, 1945

My Führer: My loyalty to you will be unconditional. I shall do everything possible to relieve you in Berlin. If fate nevertheless compels me to rule the Reich as your appointed successor, I shall continue this way to an end worthy of the unique, heroic struggle of the German people.

GROSSADMIRAL DÖNITZ, PLÖN, APRIL 30, 1945

Grossadmiral Dönitz: Führer deceased yesterday at 15.30. Testament of April 29 appoints you Reich President, Minister Goebbels Chancellor, Reichs-leiter Bormann Party Minister, Minister Seyss-Inquart Foreign Minister. On the Führer's instructions the testament sent out of Berlin to you and to Generalfeldmarschall Schörner, to assure its preservation for the people. Reichsleiter Bormann will try to get to you today to orient you on the situation. The form and time of announcement to the troops and public are left to you. Confirm receipt.

GOEBBELS/BORMANN, BERLIN, 3.18 p.m. MAY 1, 1945

As the last dramatic hours of the Third Reich were being played out in Berlin, the OKW had already moved out of the capital. On April 22 Keitel and Jodl, with a skeleton staff known as Führungsstab Nord, had moved from Dahlem to Krampnitz, north of Potsdam, and from there on the night of April 23/24 to Lager Neu-Roofen just north-east of Rheinsberg. (Führungsstab Süd went to Berchtesgaden where Generalfeldmarschall Albert Kesselring was in command of the southernmost part of Bavaria, western Czechoslovakia and what remained of Mussolini's puppet state in northern Italy, and the two beleaguered military enclaves in Kurland and around Danzig that he was trying to evacuate.) Meanwhile Grossadmiral Karl Dönitz had also moved his naval headquarters away from the approaching Red Army to Plön. Hitler must have already earmarked Dönitz as his successor — over the heads of Bormann, Göring, Goebbels and Himmler — as he had put the defence of northern Germany under his overall control on April 20 — ten days before the formal announcement.

Meanwhile Himmler was visiting him at Plön daily as Dönitz needed his resources and co-operation in order to maintain effective control within his domain. On April 28 news of Himmler's secret negotiations was released but when questioned by telephone, Himmler claimed that the news was false. That same day Hitler sent the wounded and newly-promoted Luftwaffe Generalfeldmarschall Robert Ritter von Greim to tell Dönitz to arrest Himmler, but Dönitz took no action.

Then at 6.35 p.m. on April 30, Dönitz received a signal from Bormann informing him of his appointment as successor to the Führer in place of Göring, but omitting any mention of Hitler's death, Hitler having committed suicide at 3.30 p.m. that day. Dönitz replied with a message assuring Hitler of his unshakeable loyalty.

Himmler had only just left, but in view of a previous conversation between them on the succession, which Himmler expected to fall to him, Dönitz sent a message recalling him. They then spent the night alone together in discussion. According to Dönitz, Himmler was shattered by the news, but offered to serve as the Number Two man in his State, an offer that Dönitz declined.

At 11 a.m. on May 1, Dönitz received another signal from Bormann informing him that Hitler's testament was now in force, but again not stating clearly that Hitler was dead, although an investigation by his legal department assured Dönitz that this was the case. Then just after 3 p.m. confirmation came from the Führerbunker that Hitler was dead.

At this point Dönitz's rule was limited to his own small area in the north of Germany, including the peninsula of Schleswig-Holstein and Denmark, Norway and western Holland, a completely

At this point, unbeknown to the Germans, other forces now came into play. In mid-April General Eisenhower had instructed the British 21st Army Group to advance as quickly as possible to the Baltic to seal off Schleswig-Holstein and Denmark before the Soviets. He also wanted to cut off the German forces there and halt the mass of refugees who were fleeing westwards from the advancing Red Army. The Elbe was crossed just south of Hamburg on the night of April 28/29 by both the British VIII Corps and the American XVIII Airborne Corps and on May 1 the bridgehead was rapidly expanded. With the news of Hitler's death, German opposition collapsed and Allied forces advanced virtually unopposed, Wismar on the Baltic coast being reached on the afternoon of May 2 (see *After the Battle* **No. 88).** *Above:* **Leading the advance was the 1st Canadian Parachute Battalion mounted on tanks of C Squadron of the Royal Scots Greys.**

separate southern area under the overall command of Luftwaffe Generalfeldmarschall Albert Kesselring.

Dönitz's radio message to the country at large at 10.03 p.m. that evening reported Hitler's death as heroic and appealed for the struggle and sacrifice to continue, saying: 'Against the English and Americans I must continue the fight for as far and as long as they hinder me in the execution of battle against the Bolsheviks . . . The oath of loyalty which you gave to the Führer is now

due from each one of you to me as the Führer's appointed successor . . .'

Himmler returned to Plön on May 2 and was invited for lunch. That afternoon Dönitz learned that the British and American forces had just cut across the base of the Schleswig-Holstein peninsular to the Baltic, taking Lübeck and Wismar, thereby blocking the east-west escape route by land, as well as the Soviet advance on this area, and rendering further resistance in north-western Germany pointless.

They covered the 40 miles to Wismar in record time and beat the Russians to the port by just two hours. This is Diebstrasse.

On the evening of Wednesday, May 2, Dönitz moved his headquarters as far north as possible to Flensburg, right on the border with Denmark. *Left:* There he took over the sports school building of the Naval Cadet School in the suburb of Mürwik. *Right:* In September 2004 the building had just undergone a complete refurbishment and builders were just clearing away the rubbish.

Dönitz decided to move his headquarters to the Marineschule (Naval Cadet School) Mürwik at Flensburg, right up on the Danish border. There he found accommodation on the modern passenger ship *Patria* and set up his government, which met daily at 10 a.m. in a disused classroom.

Johann Ludwig (Lutz) Graf Schwerin von Krosigk, a former Rhodes Scholar, who had been Reich Finance Minister since 1932, reluctantly became Dönitz's Principal Minister, a title he preferred to that of Reich Chancellor, as well as Minister of Finance and Minister of Foreign Affairs. Reichsminister Albert Speer, for whom Dönitz had a lot of respect, became Reich Minister for Industry and Production, SS-Obergruppenführer Dr Wilhelm Stuckart, who had been a State Secretary in the Ministry of Interior, became Dönitz's Minister of the Interior in place of Himmler, and SS-Obergruppenführer Dr Herbert Backe remained Reich Minister for Food and Agriculture.

It was decided that should either Goebbels or Bormann appear, they would be arrested, and Hitler's appointees Alfred Rosenberg, Reich Minister for the Eastern Territories; SA-Obergruppenführer Berhard Rust, Reich Minister for Science and Education; and Dr Otto Thierack, Reich Minister for Justice, were all formally dismissed from their posts. At the same time, Dr Walther Funk, President of the Reichsbank and Reich Minister for the Economy; Dr Wilhelm Ohnesorge, Reich Post Minister; and SS-Obergruppenführer Dr Hans-Heinrich Lammers, Reich Minister without Portfolio and Head of the Reichs Chancellery, were advised to follow Göring's example and surrender to the Western Allies.

On May 3 Keitel and Jodl arrived with the OKW, as did Himmler with his headquarters. On the military side, Dönitz wanted Generalfeldmarschall von Manstein to take over from Keitel, retaining the capable Jodl as his Chief-of-Staff, but Jodl threatened to resign if Keitel was sacked, and Manstein could not be found in his enforced retirement, so he retained both of them.

Here Dönitz is picutred emerging from the building with his personal adjutant Korvettenkapitän Walter Lüdde-Neurath. Hostilities had already ceased in Italy at midday following the unconditional surrender which had been signed in the Royal Palace at Caserta, just north of Naples, on April 29, and Dönitz conceded that any further fighting in north-west Europe was pointless. The British had offered to spare Hamburg as an opening for negotiations so Dönitz agreed to send a delegation to meet Field-Marshal Montgomery, headed by Generaladmiral Hans Georg von Friedeburg, who had succeeded him as head of the Kriegsmarine. He would be accompanied by General der Infanterie Hans Kinzel who was Chief-of-Staff to the Oberbefehlshaber Nordwest, Generalfeldmarschall Ernst Busch.

Lieutenant-Colonel Trumbull Warren, Montgomery's Personal Assistant, witnessed their arrival. 'At 0800 hours on May 3, Colonel Christopher Dawnay [Monty's Military Assistant] received a phone call from Colonel Michael Murphy, [General Dempsey's Intelligence Officer] to say that he had received a delegation of four officers, and although General Dempsey had not spoken to them it was thought that they wanted to try and compromise a surrender if they could get certain terms for Germany. Dawnay went immediately to Field-Marshal Montgomery and reported this to him. He told Dawnay to have Dempsey send them to his headquarters and when this was done to report back to him. He then pushed the buzzer in his caravan, sending for me.'

The Second Army headquarters of Lieutenant-General Sir Miles Dempsey were located at Häcklingen in buildings now occupied by a psychiatric clinic. From here it was only about three miles to Field-Marshal Montgomery's Tactical Headquarters which had been established on the Timeloberg hill on Lüneburg Heath near Wendisch-Evern.

Colonel Warren: 'Very quickly Field-Marshal Montgomery told both of us to get the Union Jack put up; that when the four German officers arrived they were to be lined up under the Union Jack facing his office caravan; that we were to get everyone else out of sight; the two of us were to put on our sidearms, stand at ease to the side about 25 feet between his caravan and the Union Jack, and under no circumstances were we to make a move until he told us. He also asked us to get Colonel Joe Ewart, his Intelligence Officer and interpreter. We expected the Germans to arrive in about 20 minutes. In due course they arrived, escorted by military police, who were immediately dismissed. These four officers were lined up under the Union Jack and being proper officers they stood to attention; two were Navy and two were Army. The Navy officers were dressed in long black leather greatcoats and the Army wore grey greatcoats and the General had the most beautiful red lapels.'

The same day, despite OKW objections, Dönitz sent Generaladmiral Hans Georg von Friedeburg to negotiate with Field-Marshal Sir Bernard Montgomery at his headquarters on Lüneburg Heath with the proposal that German forces in north-western Germany surrender and the remains of Heeresgruppe Weichsel be allowed to retreat to the western demarcation line and surrender to the British. When Montgomery replied that he could not accept the surrender of troops that had been fighting on the Eastern Front, Friedeburg objected that they could not possibly be expected to surrender to the Soviets, whereupon Montgomery interjected that they should have thought of that when they invaded the Soviet Union in 1941!

Montgomery refused to comment on the question of refugees from Mecklenburg, but added that he was not inhuman. He then went on to concede that soldiers from the Eastern Front could surrender to his forces, but warned that he did not have the facilities to cope with a whole army group. He then demanded the surrender of considerably more German forces in the west, including all those in Holland.

'On the right of this line was the senior officer, General Admiral von Friedeburg, Commander-in-Chief of the Fleet. Next was General Kinzel, Chief-of-Staff of the German Army North. He was a magnificent looking officer about 6' 5", in his late 40s, complete with monocle — a real professional Prussian. Next was Rear Admiral Wagner, Flag Officer to the Admiral of the Fleet. Last was Major Friedel. This chap was really something! He was at least 6' 2" and had the cruellest face of any man I have ever seen.'

Friedeburg reported back to Flensburg with these points and then returned to Montgomery's headquarters with the authority to sign the instruments of surrender for all German forces in Holland, Denmark and northern Germany to become effective at 8 a.m. on May 5.

Even while Friedeburg was conducting these negotiations on May 4, Dönitz ordered Heeresgruppen Mitte, Süd and Südost to fight on to prevent as many Germans as possible from 'Bolshevisation and slavery', calling for absolute obedience and iron discipline. 'This was the wish of our dead Führer and in order to save the German people.'

However, Heeresgruppe Südost in Croatia had been left out on a limb by the armistice signed by SS-Obergruppenführer and General of the Waffen-SS Karl Wolff on April 29. This saw the cessation of hostilities in Italy on May 2 with the result that the army group, penned in by advancing American and Soviet troops, was surrounded by Marshal Tito's Yugoslav Army and its commanding general captured and summarily executed, the troops being sent on a death march and eliminated.

With Montgomery's interpreter Colonel Joe Ewart at his elbow (he would be killed in a road accident on July 1), the Field-Marshal reads out the terms of surrender. Major Friedel (just out of the picture to the left) would also be killed in a motor accident two weeks later. Von Friedeburg committed suicide on May 23 and Kinzel (with his back to the camera on the right) shot himself on June 25. (See *After the Battle* No. 48 for a detailed description of all the German surrenders.)

Left: Later Montgomery had an elaborate memorial erected on the spot which he renamed Victory Hill. For ten years a permanent guard was mounted against the monument being vandalised but when this had to be withdrawn in 1955 on cost grounds, the bronze plaque was quickly prised off and replaced with the slogan: 'Due to this victory, Communism could spread in the heart of Europe. After ten years it is time to recognise the common danger. Let us forget the past.' Three years later, as British troops prepared to leave that part of Germany,

it was decided that it would be safer to dismantle the memorial and re-erect it in Britain. Today it graces the New College Square at the Royal Military College at Sandhurst. *Right:* Victory Hill reverted to its original name of the Timeloberg and became a Bundeswehr tank training area. For 40 years one could still see the foundations where the monument had stood . . . but when we checked the site in 1985, German panzers driving about the range had ground the concrete into dust. The memorial stood over on the right.

Left: Ten years later a new memorial was set up at the base of the hill, just outside the entrance to the training area. It, too, was soon vandalised and the inscription defaced and a Nazi

rune scratched across it. *Right:* The stone was simply turned around and the inscription re-engraved: 'Surrender on the Timeloberg — 1945 – 4. Mai – 1995 — No More War'.

The surrender signed at Lüneburg at 6.30 p.m. on May 4 was to take effect at 8 a.m. on Saturday, May 5. That afternoon the 19. Armee in Austria under General der Panzertruppen Erich Brandenberger surrendered his forces to Major General Edward H. Brooks of the US VI Corps. *Left:* The act of surrender was held in the Landsrat building in Innsbruck where, overlooked by a well-armed Colonel Joseph L. Longevin, Brandenberger put pen to paper. *Right:* No formal plaque or memorial was erected to mark the event which took place in this committee chamber of the town hall.

Also on Saturday Heeresgruppe G in southern Germany surrendered to the US 6th Army Group. Ironically the venue was one of Albert Speer's creations — the property of the sculptor Josef Thorak who produced many works for Hitler. The monolithic building near Haar, some 12 miles east of Munich, had been taken over by the US XV Corps as its headquarters.

Being now occupied by the Bavarian government (as a store for the Munich opera house), as expected it was only with some difficulty that we were able to obtain permission to photograph the exterior. Access to the interior was denied.

In May 1945 the Supreme Headquarters of the Allied Expeditionary Force was located in the College Moderne et Technique de Garçons in Reims. *Left:* These German POWs are passing the main entrance on Rue Henri Joliaeur. *Right:* General Eisenhower's War Room has been preserved within the building which remains much as it was when the surrender was signed.

Dönitz next sent Friedeburg to General Dwight D. Eisenhower's Supreme Allied Headquarters at Reims with instructions to negotiate a separate surrender of German forces in the west. However Eisenhower insisted on unconditional surrender on all fronts, with the one exception of an immediate partial surrender of Heeresgruppe G in the Tyrol and Vorarlberg, where he had heard rumours of an 'Alpine Redoubt', which would be a formidable nut to crack should its existence prove to be true. This, however, turned out to be a 'red herring'.

Bad weather on Saturday morning delayed the arrival of von Friedeburg and Oberst Fritz Poleck (from the staff of the OKW) so instead of landing at Reims their aircraft had to divert to Brussels which meant a journey by road of 125 miles. *Above:* They arrived just after 5 p.m. Von Friedeburg's intention was just to surrender the forces facing the Western Allies (as by then negotiations in the Netherlands were already over), but Eisenhower refused to continue discussions unless the Eastern Front was included. It was to be the total unconditional surrender of all German forces and there was to be no bargaining.

When von Friedeburg explained that he did not have authority to surrender both fronts, a message was relayed to Flensburg asking that either he be given permission to sign or the head of the OKW be sent for that purpose. *Left:* Generaloberst Jodl arrived with his aid, Major Wilhelm Oxenius, at 6 p.m. Sunday evening. *Right:* A somewhat frosty face as he passed von Friedeburg in the corridor. The escorting officer is Major-General Kenneth Strong, head of the intelligence section (G-2) at SHAEF.

Dönitz could not accept this and sent Generaloberst Jodl to Reims on May 6 in an aircraft provided by Montgomery and escorted by his Chief-of-Staff to try and get agreement to the surrender in two stages, first in the west, then at least four days later in the east, thus enabling more troops to get away from the Soviets. Jodl tried to put off signing until May 8, but Eisenhower threatened to close the Allied lines to refugees and soldiers who wished to surrender at 0.01 a.m. on May 9 if he did not sign immediately. Dönitz complained bitterly that Eisenhower failed to see the danger

---

Only this text in English is authoritative

ACT OF MILITARY SURRENDER

1. We the undersigned, acting by authority of the German High Command, hereby surrender unconditionally to the Supreme Commander, Allied Expeditionary Force and simultaneously to the Soviet High Command all forces on land, sea, and in the air who are at this date under German control.

2. The German High Command will at once issue orders to all German military, naval and air authorities and to all forces under German control to cease active operations at 2301 hours Central European time on 8 May and to remain in the positions occupied at that time. No ship, vessel, or aircraft is to be scuttled, or any damage done to their hull, machinery or equipment.

3. The German High Command will at once issue to the appropriate commanders, and ensure the carrying out of any further orders issued by the Supreme Commander, Allied Expeditionary Force and by the Soviet High Command.

4. This act of military surrender is without prejudice to, and will be superseded by any general instrument of surrender imposed by, or on behalf of the United Nations and applicable to GERMANY and the German armed forces as a whole.

5. In the event of the German High Command or any of the forces under their control failing to act in accordance with this Act of Surrender, the Supreme Commander, Allied Expeditionary Force and the Soviet High Command will take such punitive or other action as they deem appropriate.

Signed at Rheims at 0241 on the 7th day of May, 1945.
France

On behalf of the German High Command.

Jodl

IN THE PRESENCE OF

On behalf of the Supreme Commander, Allied Expeditionary Force.

On behalf of the Soviet High Command.

W. B. Smith

Sousloparov

F. Sevez -2-

Major General, French Army
(France)

posed by the Soviet Union, but saw no alternative to ordering Jodl to go ahead and sign, which he did at 2.41 a.m. on May 7. However, Eisenhower's Chief-of-Staff, General Walter Bedell Smith, had forgotten that he had the official surrender document negotiated between the Allies secure in his safe and so had to draft a new one.

Jodl's letter of authority from Dönitz used the word 'Waffenstillstand' (armistice) and he tried to explain why an overall capitulation was impossible but this ploy was given short shrift by Eisenhower. Giving Jodl an ultimatum, the latter sent a signal to Dönitz asking permission to agree to the Allied terms of unconditional surrender. The reply was received just after midnight. Jodl put his signature to the document on behalf of the German High Command at 2.41 a.m. Sunday morning. It was then counter-signed by Lieutenant General Walter Bedell Smith on behalf of Eisenhower; Major-General Ivan Susloparoff, the Soviet liaison officer at SHAEF, and Général François Sevez representing Général Alphonse Juin, Chief-of-Staff to Général de Gaulle.

At the conclusion of the signing, General Jodl got to his feet and stood to attention. Addressing General Smith he said in English: 'I want to say a word'. Then he lapsed into German, which was later interpreted as: 'General! With this signature the German people and German armed forces are — for better or worse — delivered into the victor's hands. In this war, which has lasted more than five years, both have achieved and suffered more than perhaps any other people in the world. In this hour I can only express the hope that the victor will treat them with generosity.'

When Stalin heard about the ceremony which had taken place in Reims he was furious. Not only was the Soviet representative not empowered to sign anything but he insisted that the surrender must be enacted in Berlin, the 'centre of Nazi aggression', and before the 'Supreme Command of all the countries of the anti-Hitler coalition'. He instructed the Soviet commander in Berlin, Marshal Georgi Zhukov to organise a re-signing the following day; meanwhile Major-General Susloparoff was recalled to Moscow in disgrace and never heard of again. *Above:* The venue for the ratification ceremony was the Officers' Mess of the Wehrmacht's military engineering school at Karlshorst which had been taken over by Colonel-General Nikolai Bezarin, commander of the Fifth Shock Army, for his headquarters.

Consequently Stalin, enraged that the ceremony had not taken place before senior representatives of the Red Army, (only his liaision officer having been present at Reims) demanded a repeat ceremony at the fortress engineers' barracks at Karlshorst in Berlin on the night of May 8/9 using the correct documentation. He sent the dreaded Andrei Vyshinsky, who had been the State Prosecutor at the pre-war purge trials of the Red Army leadership, from Moscow to supervise the ceremony with a copy of the agreed document. Nevertheless, there were considerable delays while various protocol problems were resoved, and it was just past midnight, Moscow time, before the German delegation could be marched in for the ceremony.

Generalfeldmarschall Wilhelm Keitel was the main German signatory, with Generaloberst Hans-Jürgen Stumpff signing for the Luftwaffe and Friede-burg for the Kriegsmarine. Marshal Georgi Zhukov, Commander-in-Chief of the 1st Byelorussian Front and nominal Deputy Supreme Commander of the Soviet Forces, signed for the Red Army and Air Chief Marshal Sir Arthur Tedder for the Western Allies, while General Carl Spaatz of the USAAF and Général Jean de Lattre de Tassigny of the French 1ère Armée signed as witnesses. This unconditional surrender by the Wehrmacht following the defeat of Nazi Germany ensured that there could be no future allegation of a 'stab in the back' as had occurred in 1918.

Dönitz's procrastination, however, according to one source had enabled some 2,022,602 Germans to escape the Soviets by sea between January 23 and May 8, a considerable achievement. Konteradmiral Conrad Engelhardt, who was in charge of the evacuation, later reported that a 'total of 223 ships out of 366 employed, were lost by enemy action and though no accurate human losses can be given, an estimate of 30,000 lives, i.e. 2 per cent of those taken on board, were lost out of a total of 1,900,000 persons carried'.

The school had been built between 1936-38 and followed typical Nazi architectural lines. After the war it became part of the main Soviet headquarters in Berlin but the mess was opened in 1967 as a combined museum and memorial to the Red Army's achievements in defeating Germany. Since the withdrawal of Russian forces in 1994, the museum has been managed by a combined German-Russian foundation and the display altered to cover relations between the two countries since 1917.

This time the German delegation was headed by Keitel which must have brought joy to the heart of Général de Lattre de Tassigny who was signing on behalf of France as it was Keitel who had dictated the armistice terms in 1940 (see page 375). He was accompanied by the head of the Luftwaffe, Generaloberst Hans Jürgen Stumpff, while von Friedeburg represented the Kriegesmarine. Eisenhower was satisfied with the validity of his ceremony at Rheims and so sent his deputy Air Chief Marshal Sir Arthur Tedder, accompanied by General Carl Spaatz of the US Army Air Force and General de Lattre of the 1ère French Army, to represent the Western Allies at Karlshorst. After some debate and not a little argument over protocol, the approved surrender document was eventually ratified by Zhukov and Tedder at 11.30 p.m. on May 8 on behalf of the Soviet Union and the Western Allies respectively, with Spaatz and de Lattre signing as witnesses. The war in Europe was officially over.

The huge carpet which still adorns the surrender room was removed from the Grosser Empfangssaal in the Reich Chancellery (see page 244).

On May 6 Dönitz summoned Himmler and told him that he had no further use for his services and that his presence was no longer welcome at the headquarters. However, it should be noted that Himmler's escorting party were all issued with naval identity documents with the ranks of petty officers and ratings, and the uniforms to go with them.

Schwerin von Krosigk broadcast to the nation on May 7, announcing the unconditional surrender of the German armed forces, and was followed next day by Dönitz, who pointed out that the Nazi Party had stepped aside and that political power now rested with the occupying powers, who would decide whether or not he would remain in office.

On May 12 a SHAEF Control Party under American Major General Lowell W. Rooks arrived at Flensburg to supervise the OKW. The Americans promptly arrested Keitel but left Jodl in charge with instructions to keep them informed of any orders issued by his office. However, he too was soon arrested, along with Generalfeldmarschall Albert Kesselring, the last Commander-in-Chief West, and General der Artillerie Walter Warlimont, Jodl's Deputy Chief-of-Staff.

The Allies were irritated by Dönitz's continual attempts to stir up trouble with the Soviets, and forbade any exchange of courtesy between the Germans and themselves, which outraged the German officers now obliged to stand to attention in front of their conquerors. Then on May 17 a Soviet delegation under General Truskow arrived and started behaving in a very friendly manner toward the Germans, plying them with vodka and cigarettes.

Dönitz and Schwerin von Krosigk tried to convince the Allies that a central administration was necessary to deal with the problems of food, disease and communications. Dönitz was still besotted with the idea that his government had to preserve 'the most beautiful and best that National Socialism has given us — the unity of our racial community.' The very idea that prominent democrats and trade unionists should be invited to take part in government was totally unacceptable to him and his entourage, for their experience of the Weimar Republic had shown democracy to be unworkable. Albert Speer alone argued that it was essential to form a government acceptable to the Allies, but none of the others could believe that they had done anything wrong under Hitler or that the Allies could possibly object to them. When confronted with the horrors of the concentration camps they merely replied that the German people knew nothing of these crimes. There was no hint of shame, or horror or of repentance at these monstrous crimes against humanity.

Dönitz considered that where concentration camp inmates had been treated inhumanely, the perpetrators should be dealt with by German courts, but in any case most of these people were 'hardened criminals', 'morally degenerate' or 'anti-social elements' that deserved to be incarcerated in such camps.

On the morning of May 23 Dönitz's government was informed of the Allied Command's decision to take them into custody as prisoners of war by General Rooks on the *Patria*. They were allowed to pack a bag each and were then taken under escort to the police headquarters in Flensburg, being treated so crudely by British troops, including meticulous body searches, that Admiral von Friedeburg committed suicide rather than be so humiliated. All were deprived of their valuables before being allowed to dress and then photographed by a large number of pressmen invited to witness the event (see *After the Battle* No. 128).

Dönitz's government had lasted just 23 days.

DE-NAZIFICATION

The National Socialist German Labour Party, its formations, affiliated associations and supervised agencies, including para-military organizations and all other Nazi institutions established as instruments of party domination, are hereby abolished and declared illegal. The Nazi organisation enumerated in the attached Appendix, or which may be added, are expressly abolished. The re-forming of any of the organisations named herein, whether under the same or different name, is forbidden.

All real estates, equipments, funds, accounts, records and other property of the organisations abolished by this law are confiscated. Confiscation is carried out by Military Commands; general directives concerning the distribution of the confiscated property are given by the Control Council.

Until such time as the property mentioned is actually placed under the control of the Military Commands all officers and other personnel, including administrative officials and others accountable for such property, are held personally responsible for taking any action necessary to preserve intact all such property and for complying with the orders of the Military Commands regarding such property.

Any person violating any provision of this law shall be liable to criminal prosecution.

ALLIED CONTROL COUNCIL, BERLIN, OCTOBER 10, 1945

The Allies were determined to see Germany de-Nazified and changed politically to either a democratic or communist government, depending upon their own system. They also wanted varying degrees of reparation, mainly in the form of industrial machinery, and coupled with this was the acquisition of expertise in various fields where German scientists and engineers had proved themselves far more advanced than their opponents.

The British and American military government personnel that had to deal with these problems were hopelessly handicapped by lack of pre-planning by their governments, changes in policy, inter-ministerial department conflicts and lack of co-ordination with their Allied partners. The personnel themselves were often unqualified for their roles and ignorant of the German language and customs, so that they were wide open to deceit and corruption. They were also subject to rapid turnover as demobilsation took place, as well as lack of adminstrative support and facilities. Strangely enough, few of the Germans who had sought refuge from the Nazis in England before the war, for instance, were entrusted with assisting in these tasks. Consequently, a valuable source of people capable of unmasking Nazi hardliners in the civic administration was overlooked.

Although the formal Allied Control Council directive on the de-Nazification of Germany was not promulgated until September 1946, troops carried out their own unnofficial action as soon as they entered Germany. Here Warrant Officer Richard W. Geger has prised his souvenir from the wall of the post office in Krefeld. The new name was very appropriate — replacing one song-writer for another — as Francis Scott Key wrote *The Star-Spangled Banner*!

Francis-Scott-Key Street has since been renamed Sternstrasse and, although the old post office on the corner of Weggenhofstrasse has been demolished, the bar that now stands on the site is named Alte Post — The Old Post Office!

As American troops advanced to capture the birthplace of the Nazi Party — Munich — a variety of unconnected groups of anti-Nazis rose up on April 27 and attempted to take over key buildings and prevent deliberate demolition. SS and loyal troops tried to crush the uprising which was still going on when the 42nd and 45th Infantry Divisions entered the city. Here 'Rainbow-men' of the former unit march down Rosenheimer Strasse although the men appear to be unaware of the significance of the building that they are passing. Even the wartime caption writer got his facts muddled because he said that 'during a party reunion at the headquarters July 20, 1944, an unsuccessful plot against Hitler's life wrecked the historic building' but that 'some attempt to restore it had been made prior to the fall of the city'. The picture was released by the censor for publication on May 5, 1945. The Bürger-bräukeller was taken over by American forces as a mess until April 1948 when the German table-tennis championships were held in the hall. The building was demolished in September 1979 (see page 103).

Near the end of the 'Ninth of the Eleventh' parade route lay the Brown House — or what was left of it, a far cry from its days as the Party HQ (see page 154). It was hit during the last major RAF raid on Munich on the night of January 7/8, 1945.

It lay here on the right-hand side of the road.

The other division was the 45th and, rather ironically, for the first 15 years of its existance it wore as its formation sign an ancient good luck symbol — a yellow swastika on a red background.

However when Hitler adopted that emblem for his Party, the division had to abandon its shoulder patch and for a time wore no insignia at all . . . that is until the 'Thunderbird' was born early in 1939: an American Indian symbol signifying 'sacred bearer of happiness unlimited'.

The Joint Chiefs of Staff Instruction No. 1067 issued to General Eisenhower in April 1945 as Commander-in-Chief of the United States Forces of Occupation and member of the four-power Control Council for Germany, included a paragraph under the heading of De-Nazification, which stated that: 'All members of the Nazi Party who have been more than nominal participants in its activities, all active supporters of Nazism or militarism and all other persons hostile to Allied purposes will be removed and excluded from public office and from positions of importance in quasi-public and private enterprises. No such persons shall be retained because of administrative necessity, convenience or expediency.'

Later in May, a party of US Senators on a fact-finding tour of Germany, inspected the Nazi 'holy of holies'. The officer holding the map on the right would appear to be their guide. Arrangements were already underway to remove the dead and return them to the original graves from which Hitler had had them exhumed in 1935 (see pages 148-149).

An initial directive on the future governing of Germany was issued to General Eisenhower on April 28, 1945, although its contents were not made public until October. The Allied Control Council came into being on June 5 when the 'Declaration regarding the Defeat of Germany and Assumption of Supreme Authority by the Allied Powers' was signed in Berlin by Eisenhower, Marshal Zhukov, Field-Marshal Montgomery and General De Lattre de Tassigny. Its opening paragraph read: 'The German armed forces on land, at sea and in the air have been completely defeated and have surrendered unconditionally and Germany, which bears responsibility for the war, is no longer capable of resisiting the will of the victorious powers.' But it was the conference between Britain, the Soviet Union and the United States held at Potsdam, just outside Berlin, from July 17 to August 2 which produced the agreement covering the Allied policies for Germany during the initial years of occupation.

434

A significant statement in the agreement was that 'all German land, naval and air forces, the SS, SA, SD and Gestapo with all their organizations, staffs and institutions, including the General Staff, the Officers' Corps, Reserve Corps, military schools, war veterans' organisations and all other military and quasi-military organisations, together with all clubs and associations which serve to keep alive the military tradition in Germany, shall be completely and finally abolished in such manner as permanently to prevent the revival or reorganisation of German militarism and Nazism.' Also the aim was 'to destroy the National Socialist Party and its affiliated and supervised organisations and to dissolve all Nazi institutions'. The formal de-Nazification or destruction of permanent structures of the regime was not spelt out at Potsdam; that came later in Directive No. 30. *Right:* **Here the Ehrenmal is wired for demolition in January 1947.**

On and after the effective date of this Directive, the planning, designing, erection, installation, posting or other display of any monument, memorial, poster, statue, edifice, street or highway name marker, emblem, tablet, or insignia which tends to preserve and keep alive the German military tradition, to revive militarism or to commemorate the Nazi Party, or which is of such a nature as to glorify incidents of war, and the functioning of military museums and exhibitions, and the erection, installation or posting or other display on a building or other structure of any of the same, will be prohibited and declared illegal; also the reopening of military museums and exhibitions.

Every existing monument, poster, statue, edifice, street or highway name marker, emblem, tablet, or insignia, of a type the planning, designing, erection, installation, posting or other display of which is prohibited by this Directive must be completely destroyed and liquidated by 1 January 1947; also all military museums and exhibitions must be closed and liquidated by 1 January 1947 throughout the entire German territory.

An object of essential public utility or of great architectural value should not be destroyed or otherwise liquidated when the purpose of this Directive can be achieved either by the removal therefrom of the objectionable part(s) or by some other alternative constituting an effective eradication of its memorial character.

The appropriate military authorities in each Zone will designate responsible local German officials who will be made and held responsible for the compilation of complete lists of memorials in their jurisdiction which are prohibited and condemned to destruction and liquidation by this Directive.

Moreover, should these responsible German officials consider that in any particular case concerning an object of exceptional artistic value an exception to the general rule above should be made, it will be open to them to submit such a request to the appropriate military authorities for forwarding to the Zone Commander for consideration.

ALLIED CONTROL COUNCIL DIRECTIVE No. 30
BERLIN, SEPTEMBER 3, 1946

After the stonework was cleared away, the bases were filled with earth as we saw on page 151.

The caskets had been removed two years earlier when the remains of the 16 had been quietly reburied in their original cemeteries. *Right:* In the first volume of *Mein Kampf,* Hitler wrote: 'On November 9, 1923, at twelve-thirty in the afternoon, in front of the Feldherrnhalle as well as in the courtyard of the former War Ministry, the following men fell, with loyal faith in the resurrection of their people: Allfarth, Felix, businessman, b. July 5, 1901. Bauriedl, Andreas, hatter, b. May 4, 1879. Casella, Theodor, bank clerk, b. August 8, 1900. Ehrlich, Wilhelm, bank clerk, b. August 19, 1894. Faust, Martin, bank clerk, b. January 27, 1901. Hechenberger, Anton, locksmith, b. September 28, 1902. Körner, Oskar, businessman, b. January 4, 1875. Kuhn, Karl, headwaiter, b. July 26, 1897. Laforce, Karl, student of engineering, b. October 28, 1904. Neubauer, Kurt, valet, b. March 27, 1899. Pape, Klaus von, businessman, b. August 16, 1904. Pfordten, Theodor von der, County Court Councillor, b. May 14, 1873. Rickmers, Johann, retired Cavalry Captain, b. May 7, 1881. Scheubner-Richter, Max Erwin von, Doctor of Engineering, b. January 9, 1884. Stransky, Lorenz, Ritter von, engineer, b. March 14, 1889. Wolf, Wilhelm, businessman, b. October 19, 1898. So-called national authorities denied these dead heroes a common grave. Therefore I dedicate to them, for common memory, the first volume of this work. As its blood witnesses, may they shine forever, a glowing example to the followers of our movement. Adolf Hitler, October 16, 1924.' As we have seen (pages 148-149), Hitler had the bodies exhumed in 1935 and placed in sarcophagus in the Ehrenmal where they lay for the next ten years, but in July 1945, as part of the de-Nazification programme, they were removed under the direction of the American military government.

Am 9. November 1923, 12 Uhr 30 Minuten nachmittags, fielen vor der Feldherrnhalle sowie im Hofe des ehemaligen Kriegsministeriums zu München folgende Männer im treuen Glauben an die Wiederauferstehung ihres Volkes:

Alfarth, Felix, Kaufmann, geb. 5. Juli 1901
Bauriedl, Andreas, Hutmacher, geb. 4. Mai 1879
Casella, Theodor, Bankbeamter, geb. 8. Aug. 1900
Ehrlich, Wilhelm, Bankbeamter, geb. 19. Aug. 1894
Faust, Martin, Bankbeamter, geb. 27. Januar 1901
Hechenberger, Ant., Schlosser, geb. 28. Sept. 1902
Körner, Oskar, Kaufmann, geb. 4. Januar 1875
Kuhn, Karl, Oberkellner, geb. 26. Juli 1897
Laforce, Karl, stud. ing., geb. 28. Oktober 1904
Neubauer, Kurt, Diener, geb. 27. März 1899
Pape, Claus von, Kaufmann, geb. 16. Aug. 1904
Pfordten, Theodor von der, Rat am obersten Landesgericht, geb. 14. Mai 1873
Rickmers, Joh., Rittmeister a. D., geb. 7. Mai 1881
Scheubner-Richter, Max Erwin von, Dr. ing., geb. 9. Januar 1884
Stransky, Lorenz, Ritter von, Ingenieur, geb. 14. März 1899
Wolf, Wilhelm, Kaufmann, geb. 19. Oktober 1898

Sogenannte nationale Behörden verweigerten den toten Helden ein gemeinsames Grab.

So widme ich ihnen zur gemeinsamen Erinnerung den ersten Band dieses Werkes, als dessen Blutzeugen sie den Anhängern unserer Bewegung dauernd voranleuchten mögen.

Landsberg a. L., Festungshaftanstalt, 16. Oktober 1924.

Adolf Hitler.

The first reburials took place in the Nordfriedhof on July 6 when Andreas Bauriedl was interred in grave 121-2-26 *(below left)* and Theodor von der Pfordten was laid to rest in grave Mauer Rechts-286 *(below right)*. Oskar Körner was buried in grave 108-4-11 but payment to maintain it ceased in 1946 and, following German practice, the headstone was removed and the space re-used. (From the cemetery records it is not clear if the remains were disinterred or whether the new burial was made on top.) Wilhelm Ehrlich was returned to his home town Gralow in the Warthegau, which is today Gralewo in Poland. Nothing is recorded concerning the reburial of Kurt Neubauer, only that it took place in July 1945. Nordfriedhof is the cemetery where Professor Troost is buried (see page 161) and where Leni Riefenstahl was laid to rest in September 2003 (see page 462).

The majority of burials took place on the following day in the Alter Teil (old part) of Westfriedhof *(above left)*. Here lie seven of the Nazi martyrs: Felix Allfarth (165-2-15); Theodor Casella (40-W-45); Martin Faust (26-3-4); Karl Laforce (188-10-3); Klaus von Pape (17-W-91); Max Erwin von Scheubner-Richter (91-W-23), and Lorenz Ritter von Stransky. He was originally buried in Grave 166-3-6 *(above right)* and later in 54-W-19, but there is nothing marking the graves today. The families have stopped maintenance payments on all these seven graves so the plots have all been re-used at least once. *Below:* Wilhelm Wolf's family grave (155-1-22) is marked with a headstone listing his death on November 9, 1923. He is buried in the Ostfriedhof *(below right)* where Anton Hechenberger and Karl Kuhn were reburied too although their graves (94-17-21 and 24-11-6 respectively) are now occupied by later burials. According to newspaper reports at the time, the brass from two of the caskets was to be melted down to cast a 'peace bell which was to be hung in the square' (Königsplatz) although there is no record that such a bell was ever made.

Johann Rickmers was sent back to Vortlage to be buried on a mill and farm estate on a moated island which lies near Lengerich between Münster and Osnabrück in Westphalia. The road leading to Haus Vortlage was once Johann-Rickmers-Strasse but is today Münsterstrasse.

Zone Policy Instructions were issued to implement Directive No. 30, the ZPI placing the onus of responsibility on local German officials to carry it out: 'The Oberpräsidenten of all Provinces or equivalent German authorities in Länder, should, accordingly, take immediate steps to cause to be rendered unobjectionable, so far as this can be done, any object of a kind

forbidden by the Directive and to proceed to the destruction of all objects not rendered unobjectionable as aforesaid.' Eagles and swastikas were one of the first targets like that on the Feldherrnhalle (page 137) and the Führerbau (page 158) in Munich or the Air Ministry in Berlin *(above)* although several were carried off by the Allies as souveniers.

But if the offending insignia could be dealt with by some other method, this was permitted. *Left:* The Air Ministry provides a

good example of hiding the swastikas with cladding, and the Horst Wessel Hall at Erwitte *(right)* that of obliteration.

In some cases the work to disguise the swastika was borderline . . . like the welding on the Olympic bell *(left)* . . . but never does one see the emblem still intact like the one on this grave! *(right)* SA-Sturmbannführer Dr Hans Probst was killed during the failed Nazi putsch in Austria on July 27, 1934 — just a few weeks after the Night of the Long Knives but well before the Anschluss in 1938. The headstone was spotted by Frans Mekers in Graz and it appears that although it has been brought to the attention of the authorities several times, the Austrians have turned a blind eye to this unique piece of Third Reich history.

However, after 12 years of Nazi rule, there were very few responsible persons left in public or private life that did not fall within these categories. Consequently many were retained precisely because of 'administrative necessity, convenience or expediency', particulary in the British Zone, where the 22,700-strong Control Commission became more concerned with the reconstruction of Germany than handling their own national interests. In contrast, in Bavaria the American military government had dismissed over 100,000 Nazi officials from the civil services by August 1945.

The scale of the problem was such that in late 1945 the Americans introduced the 'Fragebogen' system, a 131-question questionaire, to be completed by every adult in their zone. From this questionaire the individual could then be categorised as to his involvement in the Nazi movement. The British also adopted this system for their zone.

No hiding the National Socialist Memorial in Bayreuth which stood in the Luitpoldplatz opposite the Rathaus. On May 19, 1933, the Nazis had passed the 'Law for the Protection of National Symbols' (Gesetz zum Schutze der nationalen Symbole). Not that it made any difference for the Allied Control Council repealed the law on September 20, 1945 along with 26 other laws enacted by the regime such as that covering the Relief of Distress of the Nation; the law against the creation of Political Parties; the law securing the Unity of Party and State; the law protecting Party Uniforms and insignia; the Reich Flag Law; the law protecting German Blood and German Honour; the Hitler Youth laws; the Prussian law concerning the legal status of the NSDAP, and several laws concerning Jews, their property, eliminating them from economic life, their employment; marking them; and restrictions on their passports, etcetera, etcetera, etcetera.

Inevitably, with the three main 'Nazi' towns of Munich, Nuremberg and Bayreuth being located in southern Germany, all fell within the US Zone of Occupation. American troops had already taken it upon themselves to carry out adjustments to the main stadium in Nuremberg by removing the gold swastika over the tribune in spectacular fashion!

After the Americans had blown off the swastika (the bricks scattered on the steps were left over from German attempts to camouflage the stadium from aerial observation), the tribune remained intact . . . right up until 1967 when Nuremberg itself carried out their own alterations. The official explanation given for blowing up the pillared wall was that it was 'in bad constructional condition' but clearly there were other more-important reasons. In particular, the ceilings by Hermann Kaspar were felt an acute embarrassment by the city authorities. The *Nürnberger Nachrichten* commented that 'the breaks in the pillar gallery's ceiling offer a good opportunity to knock down another piece of National Socialist heritage.'

Nine years later, the abutments at either end were reduced in height citing the same reason: bad structural condition. This picture was taken in 1969 — compare with the present-day comparison on page 178. However Speer's two fire bowls have been preserved: one in the hall under the tribune and the other in Nuremberg's swimming stadium.

By the end of the war the British, French and Soviet Union governments had approved the American concept of a tribunal to try the leading Nazis and had accepted 'conspiracy' and 'membership of criminal organisations' as legitimate charges. At the London conference of the Four Powers in June 1945, the final draft of a plan for the trial system, emanating mainly from the American government, was accepted as the constitutional document upon which the International Military Tribunal at Nuremberg was based, and became known as the London Charter.

However, the very nature of a trial, as opposed to summary execution, implied using rules of evidence, a defence and even the possibility of acquittal. There were four kinds of war crimes trials: the trials of the main war criminals by the International Military Tribunal at Nuremberg; the trials held by the individual military governments in their occupation zones; trials held during and after the occupation by German courts, and trials in countries that had been occupied by Germany during the war for crimes committed on their territory.

The Nuremberg trial – held at the Nuremberg Palace of Justice from November 20, 1945 to October 1, 1946 – involved 22 accused, one of whom,

However, Nuremberg's main claim to fame in the de-Nazification process was its hosting of the main war crimes trial. The International Military Tribunal held its first meeting in August in Berlin but as a suitable undamaged building could not be found in the city, the trial itself was switched to the Palace of Justice [1] in Nuremberg. It had a large court room and, more importantly, an adjoining prison [2] where the defendants could be held securely. The gymnasium where the subsequent executions took place is [3].

Prisoners were watched continuously by individual guards but two of the defendants still managed to commit suicide: Robert Ley hung himself before the trial began using a noose made of rags tied to a toilet pipe, and Hermann Göring took poison the night before he was due to be hung. Cyanide had been given to him by one of the American guards, 1st Lieutenant Jack Wheelis, a fact revealed by the late Ben Swearingen in 1984 (see *After the Battle* No. 44).

The courtroom was on the second floor of the Palace of Justice. A lift enabled each of the accused to be brought directly to the courtroom. Microphones were installed in the dock (on the right) because the trial was to be conducted in four languages, English, French, German and Russian. Every seat in the court, for the accused, judges, lawyers, press and visitors alike, was fitted with headphones and a switch. A group of interpreters would listen through headphones to the proceedings and repeat them in other languages. The translated version of what was said was then relayed to every person.

The historic courtroom at No. 110 Fürther Strasse — now simply referred to as 'Room 600' — is today used for civilian trials but guided one-hour tours are given every Saturday and Sunday for those interested in seeing it.

Twenty-two defendants were on trial although Martin Bormann was absent. (Unbeknown to the court, he had not escaped justice but was mouldering in his makeshift grave in Berlin — see page 63). The 21 accused were (front row L-R): Göring, Hess, Ribbentrop, Keitel, Kaltenbrunner, Rosenberg, Frank, Frick, Streicher, Funk and Schacht. Rear row: Dönitz, Raeder, von Schirach, Sauckel, Jodl, von Papen, Seyss-Inquart, Speer, von Neurath and Fritzsche. All of them were charged with Count 1 of the indictment: 'A common plan or conspiracy to seize power and establish a totalitarian regime to prepare and wage a war of aggression', together with one or more of the following: Count 2: Wage a war of aggression. Count 3: Violation of the laws of war. Count 4: Crimes against humanity, persecution and extermination.

The tribunal comprised four members; one judge from each Allied power with four judges in reserve. *Above left:* The President was British: Lord Justice Geoffrey Lawrence (right), the alternate President being Sir William N. Birkett. *Above right:* The United States judges were Francis A. Biddle and Judge John J. Parker. *Below left:* For France, Professeur Henri Donnedieu de Vabres and Conseiller Robert Falco, and representing the Soviet Union *(below right)* was Major-General Jurisprudence Iola T. Nikitchenko (right) and Lieutenant-Colonel Alexander F. Volchkov. During the proceedings all the judges appeared in the judicial robes except for the Russians who wore military uniforms.

On November 20, 1945, Lord Justice Lawrence opened the proceedings with a short opening statement: 'This trial is unique in the history of the jurisprudence of the world and of supreme importance to millions of people all over the globe. There is laid upon everybody who takes any part in this trial, the solemn responsibility to discharge his duties without fear or favour in accordance with the sacred principles of law and justice.' The following August, after a trial lasting 284 days, each defendant made his final statement before the proceedings were adjourned pending the verdicts which were delivered on October 1, 1946. Armoured cars blocked all streets leading to the court as each man was taken down one by one, to hear his fate. Hjalmar Schacht, Hans Fritzsche and Franz von Papen were found not guilty although they subsequently faced other charges (see page 452).

Martin Bormann, was tried in his absence, his death not having been established. They were all charged with conspiracy to wage aggressive war and as members of one or more of the six nominated criminal organisations: the Reich cabinet, the SS, SA, Gestapo-SD, OKW or the Nazi Party. The conspiracy charges were maintained, but the criminal organisational charges fell through. The trial ended in ten being condemned to death (although Göring cheated the hangman by poisoning himself beforehand), three being given life sentences (only one of whom, Hess, actually served the full sentence), four to lesser terms of imprisonment from ten to 20 years, and three were acquitted.

VERDICTS OF THE INTERNATIONAL MILITARY TRIBUNAL

	COUNTS				VERDICT				
Defendants	*One*	*Two*	*Three*	*Four*	*One*	*Two*	*Three*	*Four*	*Sentence*
Göring	X	X	X	X	G	G	G	G	Death
Hess	X	X	X	X	G	G	NG	NG	Life
Von Ribbentrop	X	X	X	X	G	G	G	G	Death
Keitel	X	X	X	X	G	G	G	G	Death
Kaltenbrunner	X		X	X	NG		G	G	Death
Rosenberg	X	X	X	X	G	G	G	G	Death
Frank	X		X	X	NG		G	G	Death
Frick	X	X	X	X	NG	G	G	G	Death
Streicher	X			X	NG			G	Death
Funk	X	X	X	X	NG	G	G	G	Life
Sauckel	X	X	X	X	NG	NG	G	G	Death
Jodl	X	X	X	X	G	G	G	G	Death
Seyss-Inquart	X	X	X	X	NG	G	G	G	Death
Speer	X	X	X	X	NG	NG	G	G	20 Years
Von Neurath	X	X	X	X	G	G	G	G	15 Years
Bormann	X		X	X	NG		G	G	Death
Von Schirach	X			X	NG			G	20 Years
Raeder	X	X	X		G	G	G		Life
Dönitz	X	X	X		NG	G	G		10 Years
Schacht	X	X			NG	NG			
Von Papen	X	X			NG	NG			
Fritzsche	X		X	X	NG		NG	NG	
	—	—	—	—	—	—	—	—	
TOTALS	22	16	18	18	8	12	16	16	Guilty
					14	4	2	2	Not Guilty

No photographs were taken of the executions on the night of October 15/16, which were carried out by Master Sergeant John C. Wood *(left)*, a professional hangman from Texas.

Three gallows, each eight feet high and eight feet square with 13 steps, had been built against the end wall of the prison gymnasium *(right)*, one being a reserve in case of malfunction.

At 1 a.m., Wednesday, October 16, witnesses were gathered in the gymnasium where short days ago, American security troops had romped spiritedly through a basketball game.

Uniformed men — American, Russian, British and French — paced about with work to do. Chaplains were present to provide last comforts for the doomed. A limited number of correspondents were ready behind small tables to tell the world how beasts die. All stiffened tensely when, at 1.10, the guard outside knocked to announce the arrival of Ribbentrop.

A lieutenant colonel and three sergeants, all of them American, strode to a door at the centre of the long side wall. The first to enter that door was another American lieutenant colonel, who had escorted Ribbentrop across the prison yard. The rat-faced, one-time Nazi mastermind of deception entered the arena of his doom. Two of the sergeants pinned his arms and the third went behind him to remove the handcuffs, quickly tying the hands again with a leather thong. Ribbentrop's eyes glinted with a flash of horror at sight of the three black gallows, and he swung his gaze away to the newsmen, the uniformed officers and men of four nations.

Two guards led him to the Number One gallows. Ribbentrop covered the two yards or so with slow, deliberate steps, apparently trying to prolong his waning time on earth. Waiting beside the gallows steps, an American colonel addressed the official interpreter crisply: 'Ask the man his name.'

The question was asked. The answer came in a clear, mild voice: 'Joachim von Ribbentrop'.

With the same deliberateness, Ribbentrop climbed the 13 steps, his back ramrod stiff, his eyes travelling helplessly up the twin posts to the crossbeam and the metal ring from which the ominous rope dangled with its yawning noose. An American sergeant turned him to face front, while another made ready to draw the black hood over his head. Below the colonel had the interpreter ask the condemned if he had any final words to say.

Ribbentrop looked from face to face of the military witnesses and the eight foreign correspondents. Sharply, in a firm voice, he cried, 'God save Germany!' As the hood was brought close, he reared back slightly, and still fighting pathetically for an extra moment or two of life, said, 'May I say something more?'

The interpreter granted permission with a nod. 'My last wish is that Germany realise its entity and that an understanding be reached between East and West. I wish peace to the world.'

He clamped his lips shut and held his chin firm as the black hood was brought down and fixed over his face. At 1.16 a.m., the hangman, an American sergeant, sprang the trap. Some words of prayer pierced the abrupt silence, and the army chaplain descended the 13 steps.

Two minutes later another knock on the entry door brought in Field-Marshal Wilhelm Keitel. At 63, he was ten years the senior of Ribbentrop but acted younger and stauncher then had the man who now dangled unseen behind the curtain of gallows Number One. He marched in military fashion to the second gallows. Loud and clear he identified himself for the interpreter waiting at the scaffold steps: 'Wil . . . helm Kei . . . tel!'

Scorning the assistance of the guards, he stomped up the 13 steps and turned as if at a review of the troops. He was dressed in his Field-Marshal's uniform, including the black boots he was determined to die wearing. Invited to say what he wished to, he thrust forth his hammer jaw and surveyed the witnessing faces arrogantly.

'I call on the Almighty God to have mercy on the German people! More than two million German soldiers went proudly to death for their Fatherland. Now I follow my sons.'

The black hood was pulled over his head to the murmuring intonations of the chaplain. As the trap was sprung and Keitel was already plunging to his death, his last words soared, all defiance and no remorse: 'Deutschland über alles!'

A clattering thump punctuated the outcry, and echoed into a silence marred by the clearing of dry throats here and there among the cheerless witnesses. All eyes were on the two taut ropes, each piercing the maw of a scaffold with a body at its end motionless and unseen.

Soon an American and a Russian, both army medical officers, went with stethoscopes through the curtain of Number One gallows. The colonel waited outside. At 1.30 sharp the two doctors emerged and spoke briefly to the colonel, who then turned smartly to face the witnesses, snapped to attention, and officially announced, 'The man is dead'.

J. G. RAFFEY, 1963

With the top men — Hitler, Goebbels, Göring and Himmler — all having taken their own lives, it fell to Joachim von Ribbentrop to be first on the scaffold. When the medical officers had pronounced him dead, one of the press witnesses, Mr J. G. Raffey, described how 'some of the witnesses turned their backs as two soldiers arrived carrying a stretcher and took it inside the scaffold. The hangman climbed upstairs to the platform unsheathing a commando knife he wore at his belt. He cut the rope, and immediately proceeded to fashion another noose.' Using the scaffolds alternately, Mr Raffey recounted that 'ten minutes from the thump of Keitel's doom the colonel signalled for the next prisoner to be brought from the condemned block. The two litter-bearers emerged from the scaffold with Ribbentrop's lifeless body, noose and black hood still in place, and carried it behind a stiff black curtain at the end of the room. At 1.36 there was the familiar knock on the door and Gestapo Chief Ernst Kaltenbrunner was brought into the glare of gymnasium lights.'

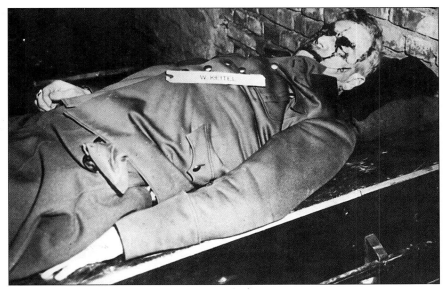

After each body had been cut down, it was labelled and photographed, the pictures being released to the world's press exactly a week later. We saw Ribbentrop's photo on page 91; this is Keitel showing evidence of his face having struck the trapdoor as he fell.

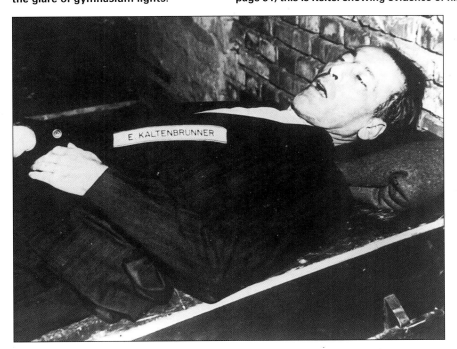

Left: 'Kaltenbrunner wore an old coat with a sweater underneath, and might have looked like any weathered thin man of 43 in the world but for the sabre scars of old duels that made his face hideous. He looked nervously at the various watching faces and, glancing at the gallows, licked his lips. A Catholic chaplain preceeded up the 13 steps. Asked if he had anything to say, he answered in a low voice: "I would like to say a word. I have loved my German people with a warm heart. And my Fatherland. I have done my duty by the laws of my people, and I regret that my people were led, this time, by men who were not soldiers, and that crimes were committed of which I have no knowledge". Kaltenbrunner had taken over from Reinhard Heydrich upon his assassination in 1942, and had proved an even more gruesome hatchet man for the diabolical Himmler. The hood was drawn over the scarred death's-head of a face. Still speaking in a modulated tone, the heinous mass murderer said, "Good luck to Germany". At 1.39 a.m., the hangman sent him on his short plunge to death.'

Right: 'Next was Rosenberg, 53, one-time editor of the *Völkischer Beobachter*. Pasty-faced and lethargic, but firm of gait, he entered the gymnasium at 1.47½ and plummeted through the trap at 1.49, the quickest of all to die. In the intervening minute and a half he gave his name absently, looked once without expression at the chaplain who ascended with him to pray, and answered with a single negative syllable when asked if he had anything to say. For some short moments there was a pause in the proceedings, after which the Russian and American doctors reported to the colonel, who announced that Kaltenbrunner was dead. The body was removed on a stretcher and placed behind the dark curtain. While Rosenberg still hung within the Number Two gallows, the fifth candidate for oblivion was brought across the prison yard and into the gymnasium.'

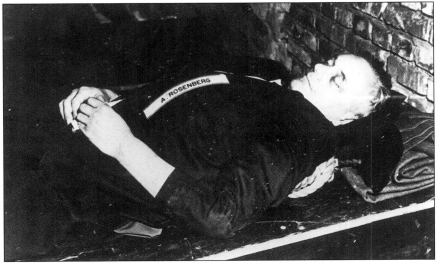

Right: 'Hans Frank, 46, SS general and iron fisted Gauleiter of Poland, smiled benignly as the manacles were replaced by the leather thong, and he smiled as he quietly gave the interpreter his name at the gallows steps. In its pouch of weathered flesh his Adam's apple kept bobbing up and down to indicate nervous swallows, but he never quit smiling and seemed transported in a fervor of religious atonement. He spoke his last words in a humble whisper that was just barely audible: "I am grateful for the kind treatment during my captivity, and I ask God to accept me with mercy". Kind treatment, mercy — concepts that had never tempered the administration of this man who had wiped out entire Polish villages. Kind treatment, mercy — words he could comprehend only in relation to himself. His Adam's apple danced. He closed his eyes as the black hood descended toward them, but he did not surrender the beautific smile. He may have been smiling still when the slam of the scaffold cut him away from humanity.'

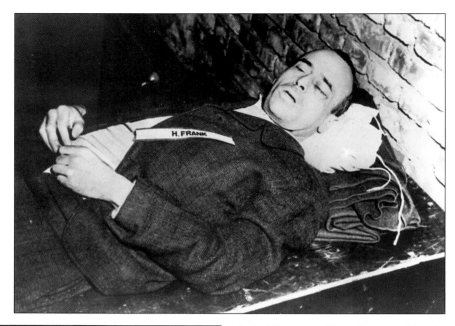

Left: 'The unsettling effect on the witnesses of Frank's behavior, particularly after Kaltenbrunner's performance, was further enhanced by the appearance, next, of a feeble old man in the hall. The colonel had just pronounced Rosenberg dead and the body had been removed when, at 2.05 a.m., Nazi Minister of the Interior Wilhelm Frick, 69, entered the death chamber. The wages of all he had accomplished in the destruction of human dignity and hope were in Frick's ash-grey face. This old man was sick. The plundered faces of all his countless victims seemed to be haunting him to the very marrow. In the short distance to Number Two gallows he stumbled twice. He had to be assisted up the steps. On the last one he stumbled again. Eyeing the black hood, he agreed to say some last words, and all he could say was, "Long live eternal Germany". Hans Frank was pronounced dead. His corpse was removed behind the black canvas curtain at the rear.'

The stage was set for a performance too shocking for any of the witnesses to anticipate. The knock on the door came at 2.13. The two lieutenant colonels faced each other, and then Julius Streicher was inside. The arch Jew-baiter of Germany was an unsightly gnome of a man in worn and misshapen clothes. Sixty-one, bald, with frizzy hair over his ears and a grizzled imitation-Hitler moustache, he looked at one witness after another with a sneer. With his hands bound behind him he trundled over to the Number One gallows, flanked on each side by an American sergeant. There, in a defiant burst of rage, he shrieked from the very bottom of his bitter guts: 'Heil Hitler!' The American colonel angrily snapped, 'Ask the man his name!' The interpreter put forth the question. In yet another shriek, Streicher said, 'You know my name very well!' At the interpreter's insistence, the repulsive little man shouted, 'Julius Streicher!' Then, climbing the stairs, the man whose name was synonymous with every vile obscenity cast at the Jews and whose being was the very symbol of the Jewish persecution and massacre, wailed, 'Now it goes to God!'

At the bottom of the steps the colonel said, 'Ask the man if he has any last words.' The interpreter extended the invitation and, shaking with bitter fury, Streicher yelled, 'The Bolsheviks will hang you one day!'

The black hood was brought down over his face, but apparently Streicher had more to say. In the sudden dark all his defiance evaporated, all his Nazi arrogance and rage. An instant before the trap slammed open beneath him, Julius Streicher let out a whine: 'Adele, my dear wife.'

The mercy of immediate oblivion which had come to the others was not there for Streicher. The rope snapped taut as had the others before it, but then lurched and swung contortedly with hideous groans from the hidden bowels of the scaffold. Every man in the room stiffened in horror to the sounds of strangulation, but one man, the Army hangman, shook himself out of it and sped through the curtain and caught hold of the twisting vessel of agony and yanked down with all his might until the voice and the man went dead.

J. G. RAFFEY, 1963 [For photo, see page 93]

Right: 'The next of the condemned was brought in: Fritz Sauckel. He mounted the steps of the gallows and turned to face front without requiring more than the first push from a guard. Then he met the invitation to say his final words with a shriek as loud and hysterical as Streicher's just before him. "I am dying innocent! The sentence is wrong! God protect Germany and make Germany great again! God protect my family!" The crack of doom sounded for Sauckel at 2.26 a.m., but that was not his exact moment to die. Sharing the hatred of his predecessor, he shared his fate as well. An eerie groan issued from inside the scaffold; the rope, which should have stood as straight and firm, swung from side to side. The hangman darted inside and the groans ceased. The crowning irony had occurred: Streicher and Sauckel, the most loathsome of all these abominable men, had both screamed in sickening self-righteousness and had both been strangled in slow agony by some mysterious fate that would not allow them the mercy of a quick death.'

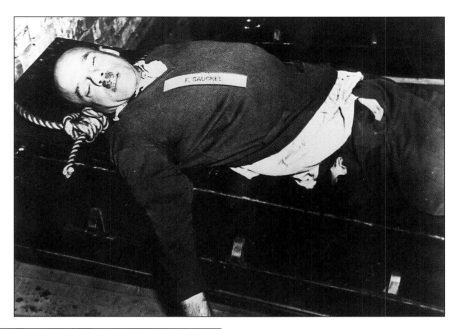

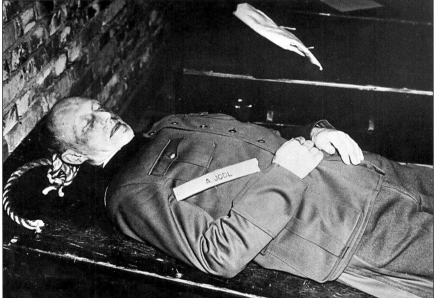

Left: 'Next in line was Jodl. Though he arrived in uniform as had the other professional soldier, this intimate friend and prime tactical adviser of Hitler was completely devoid of Keitel's military pomp and bearing. At 56, he was seven years younger than Keitel, but gave an opposite impression. Jodl's face was pinched and haggard. His tongue kept darting out to wet his lips. Where Keitel had marched as if to a drumbeat, Jodl shuffled pitiably along. Where Keitel had barked his name like a thunderclap, Jodl sounded his like a comedian imitating a timid Swede. He was an abject figure mounting the 13 steps. His words before the trapdoor slammed open beneath him were, "My greetings to you, my Germany". The time was 2.34 a.m. Moments later Sauckel's death was offically announced, and a sigh was audible in the witnessing group, like a sign that only then had the hideous drama of Streicher and Sauckel ended. Some men brought handkerchiefs to their faces as the body was removed.'

Right: 'With Jodl still hanging inside gallows Number One, the last of the condemned entered. Arthur Seyss-Inquart, 54, who went limping on his club foot to the gallows. He licked his lips before giving his name. The guards had to assist him up to the platform. When invited to speak his final words he took a moment to gather them past all sense of guilt into a neat package of lofty and virtuous sentiment: "I hope", he said with the modulated passion of an office-seeker, "that this execution is the last act of the tragedy of the Second World War, and that the lesson taken from this world war will be that peace and understanding should be between peoples." Then, as if to keep from sounding apologetic, and as if to exonerate himself of all the evils he had committed for the Nazis, he drew himself up and said, "I believe in Germany". Seyss-Inquart plummeted to death at 2.45 a.m. He was pronounced officially dead, after the removal of Jodl's body, at 2.57, and the grisly retribution at Nuremberg jail was done.'

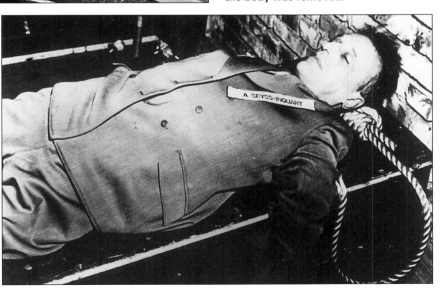

The bodies of the executed men were then cremated under the direction of the US Third Army mortician Rex Morgan who personally disposed of the ashes.

for military prisoners awaiting trial and for political prisoners in transit to concentration camps. Now — and for the next 40 years — it was to perform a new role as a prison for the seven men of the Nazi hierarchy convicted at Nuremberg.

Responsibility for guarding the prisoners was to be split between the Four Occupying Powers: the British taking charge in January, May and September; the French in February, June and October; the Soviets in March, July and November; and the Americans in April, August and December.

Six watch towers stood at intervals around the wall with its electrified barbed-wire fence, and at night the whole area was floodlit. The exterior guard of 32 armed soldiers was reinforced within the building by 18 warders plus ancillary staff, making a total of 78 persons directly involved: a ratio to the prisoners of more than 10 to 1.

Although the trial of the major Nazi war criminals had been carried out in Nuremberg, the incarceration of those sentenced to various terms of imprisonment was to take place in Berlin under the joint supervision of Great Britain, France, the United States and the Soviet Union. The prison selected was located on the Wilhelmstrasse in the borough of Spandau, not to be confused with the other street in Berlin of the same name. This picture was released six days after the seven arrived in July 1947.

On July 18, 1947, an American DC-3 approached Berlin from the south and landed at RAF Gatow late in the afternoon. From it emerged seven men, escorted by armed guards, who quickly directed their prisoners to a waiting bus with blacked-out windows. Then, escorted by Jeeps and armoured cars, the convoy drove east towards No. 23 Wilhelmstrasse in the Spandau district.

There, in 1876, the Kaiser had erected a formidable military prison, built of red brick, with cells for a total of 600 prisoners. Later it became a civil prison but under Hitler it was used both

It had long been decided by the Four Powers that when the last prisoner died — whoever that was — the prison would be demolished to avoid it becoming a shrine to Nazism. Rudolf Hess, serving a true 'life' imprisonment, lived to the ripe old age of 93. After he died in August 1987, the prison was totally demolished, including the perimeter wall, and the rubble buried on the British gunnery ranges at Gatow. The two horse chestnuts beside the prison gatehouse were retained in the grounds of the new Britannia Centre which was constructed to serve the British garrison in Berlin.

Left: **Baron Konstantin von Neurath, 74, was Germany's pre-war Foreign Minister but it was his record as Reich Protector in Bohemia and Moravia which earned him 15 years in Spandau. He was released early in 1954 and died two years later.** *Centre:* **Baldur von Schirach, 40, as well as being Reich Youth Leader was also Gauleiter of Vienna and was found guilty of** aiding the 'resettlement' of the Jews. He received a sentence of 20 years. He died in 1974. *Right:* **Albert Speer was 42 when he was convicted for using forced labour provided by Fritz Sauckel for war production. He, like von Schirach, served his full term of 20 years. He died in 1981 while on a visit to London as a guest of the BBC to record an interview with the historian Norman Stone.**

Left: **The chief of the Kriegsmarine, Grossadmiral Erich Raeder, 71, was found guilty of waging aggressive war, particularly against Norway and the Soviet Union. He was sentenced to life but because of his age was released in 1955. He died in 1960.** *Centre:* **As President of the Reichsbank, Walter Funk was also** given life for accepting personal valuables including gold teeth and fillings from victims exterminated in concentration camps. He was released due to ill health in 1957 and died in 1960. *Right:* **Rudolf Hess also received a life sentence and remained in Spandau until he died by his own hand in 1987 (see page 81).**

Executive power at Spandau was given to the Directors of the Four Powers, who enforced the strict and onerous regime which had been laid down by the Control Commission at Nuremberg. The following is an extract:

'The prisoners must salute officers, warders and senior staff with marks of respect. They must obey all orders and regulations without hesitation, even when these appear to them to be unjust. They must answer honestly all questions addressed to them. The prisoners may approach an officer or warder only if ordered to do so or if they wish to make a request.

'The discipline of the institution provides that prisoners should adopt a standing position. The prisoner must salute an officer, an official or a warder by standing to attention or by passing him in an upright posture. The prisoner must at the same time remove his headgear.

'On admission, the prisoner will undress completely and his body will be carefully searched. The search, which will be in the presence of the Direc-torate will be carried out by four warders. All parts of the body, including the anus, will be searched for articles which might be smuggled into the institution.

'Prisoners will be locked up and guarded in accordance with the verdict of the Nuremberg IMT. They will be addressed by their convict's number; in no circumstances by name. Imprisonment will be in the form of solitary confinement. The cells will be isolated, but work, religious services and walks will be carried out together.

'When awakened, the prisoner will rise immediately and make his bed. He will then strip to the waist, wash, brush his teeth and rinse his mouth. Clothing, shoes and the cell, including furniture, will be cleaned in the time provided for this purpose and in the prescribed manner. Making a noise, shouting, whistling and even approaching the window are forbidden.

'The prisoners may not talk or associate with one another, nor with other persons except with special permission from the Directorate. The prisoner may not have in his possession any articles without permission. If he should find something, he must hand it over to the warder immediately. Equipment, clothing and all articles belonging to the institution are to be treated with care, and used only for the prescribed purposes.

'The Directorate will establish a plan for daily activities, but in principle work will be carried out every day except Sundays and public holidays.'

Because of their age and health, von Neurath, Raeder and Funk were released early in 1954, 1955 and 1957 respectively. Dönitz served his full term of ten years and was released in 1956. At midnight on September 30, 1966 Speer and von Schirach were released at the end of their sentences, leaving Rudolf Hess the sole inmate.

During the next 20 years there were many calls for his release on humanitarian grounds, and much pressure was brought to bear on the three Western Allies to arbitrarily release Hess during one of their periods of tenure of the prison (see page 81).

Although nominated by Hitler as his successor as Head of State, Grossadmiral Karl Dönitz, 55, was found guilty for his role as C-in-C of the U-Boat arm, in particular of ordering the abandonment of shipwrecked sailors and was implicated in the execution of captured crewmen by the Sicherheitsdienst. He served his full term of ten years and was released in 1956. He died in 1980 and was buried in grave L-5 in the Waldfriedhof cemetery in Aumühle near Hamburg.

The Nuremberg courts continued to be used by American Military Tribunals right up until 1949. During that time there were 199 trials resulting in 36 death sentences (18 of which were carried out); 23 sentences of life imprisonment (which in most cases meant seven years), and 102 shorter terms.

Left: August Frank pleads 'Nicht Schuldig' (not guilty) at a trial of 18 defendants on March 10, 1947. *Right:* Still on duty in 1947 — in spite of the fact that we believe the US authorities were well aware of his part in Göring's suicide — none other than 1st Lieutenant Jack Wheelis!

The trials held in the Allied zonal courts subsequently resulted in the conviction of 5,006 individuals for war crimes, of whom 794 were sentenced to death and 486 actually executed. Almost all the remaining accused and imprisoned were released by 1956.

Following the far-from-thorough purge of the German courts in 1945, the Allies re-established the German judicial system. War crimes could then be tried by the German courts, but only using the criminal definitions specified under Allied Control Council Directive No. 10 of December 20, 1945, as opposed to those under German law, which in effect meant using retroactive law, thereby violating their own criminal code, as well as Allied Control Council Directive No. 1, which strictly forbade such a practice. Punishments under Directive No. 10 ranged from death to loss of civil liberties. However, existing German law was fully adequate to cope with crimes by Germans against Germans within the Third Reich, and by the end of 1950 5,228 persons had been convicted, although mainly for minor offences, only 100 sentences having related to murder. The main reason for this was that the whole legal system was still manned mainly by former Nazis who saw these cases differently to the Allied conquerors. Consequently large numbers, particularly of the more senior ranking Nazis were able to lie low and escape justice.

The same attitude persisted after the Allied High Commissioners handed over authority to try Nazi crimes under German criminal law in 1950, for both the judiciary and the public remained reluctant to pursue such matters. Never-

theless, between 1951 and 1955, a further 628 persons, many of them former SS camp guards, were convicted. Then in 1955 the statute of limitations put an end to the prosecution of crimes carrying sentences of ten years' imprisonment or less, and from that point onwards only premeditated murder could be prosecuted. Nevertheless, following the ending of the formal occupation of

Germany in 1955, some trials of the worst mass murderers took place in the late 1950s and 1960s that had far greater public impact. Only those individuals that had already been tried by the Allied courts were immune from prosecution, and among these were many high Nazi functionaries whose cases had been dropped for lack of sufficient evidence at the time of prosecution.

Although military personnel carried out check-ups in the early days of the occupation, official de-Nazification courts were later established which graded offenders in four different categories of Nazi: major offenders, offenders, lesser offenders and followers. The three men acquitted by the International Military Tribunal were subsequently tried under this criteria: Hans Fritzsche received nine years but was released in 1950 and died in 1953; Franz von Papen's subsequent sentence of eight years was rescinded in 1949 and he died ten years later. Hjalmar Schacht also received eight years but was released in 1948. He died in 1970.

The new German government established an office to investigate crimes committed in the conquered territories, which led to the successful prosecution of several of the individuals concerned, and then went on to extend the statue of limitations for murder beyond the existing 20-year limit.

The majority of the fourth kind of trial, those by the countries in which the crimes had been committed, concerned the Soviet Union, which arrested tens of thousands of German suspects for incarceration in former concentration camps and jails, where many died of hunger and disease, and the survivors subjected to military tribunals to receive the customary 25-year sentence for even the most minor 'offence', or execution for more serious charges.

The policy of the Allies, as determined in May 1945, was the de-Nazification, decentralisation and decartelisation of German industry. To their surprise, German industry had not been totally destroyed by the Allied bombing as had been claimed. The US Strategic Bombing Survey discovered that only 20 per cent of Germany's extended wartime industrial capacity had been eliminated, and that only the belated concentration on the destruction of the oil industries and railway network had

Meanwhile, in the Soviet Zone, de-Nazification of a physical kind was going ahead in a big way. *Above:* **By 1949 there was very little left of Hitler's Chancellery and by 1950** *(below)* **it was all gone. Yet the red marble was put to good use in cladding the Soviet War Memorial in Treptow Park.**

finally crippled German production. Consequently post-war industrial assets were much the same as pre-war, and blocking the implementation of Allied policy was a proliferation of factors such as corruption, incompetence, political prejudice, personal self-interest and irreconcilable antagonism, not only between the British and American military government officials but also among the Americans themselves.

The German coal industry was the only one to be effectively de-Nazified, and that resulted from two appalling mine disasters that led to the miners striking in protest against having to continue working under the same supervision that had driven them and slave labour so hard during the war. A protest in the autumn of 1946 by German trade unionists to the British trade unions that IG Farben was still run by Nazis led to an investigation that confirmed the case but resulted in no dismissals of the persons concerned.

For over half a century the Chancellery plot on Voss-strasse remained empty but it was a hive of building activity when we photographed it in August 2003.

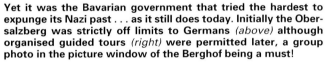

Yet it was the Bavarian government that tried the hardest to expunge its Nazi past . . . as it still does today. Initially the Obersalzberg was strictly off limits to Germans *(above)* although organised guided tours *(right)* were permitted later, a group photo in the picture window of the Berghof being a must!

The Eagle's Nest was under new management — compare with Hitler relaxing in the same easy chair on the right on page 46.

The whole area, including the Eagle's Nest, was designated an American recreation area, reserved solely for members of the occupation forces. Berchtesgaden itself was not restricted and, as the town had always thrived on tourism, it was anxious to see the Obersalzberg opened up to all visitors. By the end of 1951 the US authorities agreed but the Bavarian government were concerned lest the Berghof and the Göring and Bormann ruins become a magnet for followers of Hitler and so, despite strong protests from some quarters, it was decided to demolish all three together with the SS barracks. The big bang came at 5.05 p.m. on April 30, 1952 — but surely it was no coincidence that the date chosen was the anniversary of the day when Hitler committed suicide and the exact time when his body was being consumed by flames!

The garage on the right of the top picture remained intact and *After the Battle* even found the huge door lock just lying inside amongst the rubble in 1973.

But in the mid-1990s came a new wave of demolitions by the Bavarian authorities when what remained of the garage was razed in 1996.

had all been involved in the use of slave labour, and some did not even qualify as scientists. Nevertheless, the whole group were taken to the United States, where they eventually became American citizens and developed the rockets that took man to the moon.

The failure of the de-Nazification process was that the post-war legacy of Nazi Germany was a country still administered in the civil, judicial, industrial and commercial fields almost exclusively by the same people that had supported Hitler and prospered under him. Their retention in office and the deafening silence they imposed on contemporary history led to the student unrest of the 1960s, and it was to take several more decades to bring some degree of comprehension to the population at large of what a monstrous criminal conspiracy these people had been involved in before, during and after the Second World War.

Then the following year, it was the turn of Hitler's guest house, one of the most impressive of the surviving original buildings (which featured on the cover of *After the Battle* **No. 9).** *Above:* **This is how it looked in its heyday and** *(right)* **how we found it in 1973. Two years later American forces quit the area, abandoning the nearby General Walker Hotel.**

Immediately after the war the Allies combed Germany for its scientists, engineers and secrets. The most famous case was that of Dr Wernher von Braun, the German rocket scientist, who surrendered himself and his Peenemünde team, including General Walter Dornberger, to the Americans. By sticking together as an internally disciplined group, they managed to convince their captors of their value and innocence as Nazis, although von Braun was an honorary SS-Sturmbannführer and they

The official reason for the destruction of the guest house was that the Bavarian government wanted to create a 'documentation centre' to counter-balance the over-nostalgic publications for sale at the nearby tourist stands. So in order to record the history of the Hitler era, the historic building was demolished — a seemingly inexplicable paradox illustrating the extreme difficulty the Germans have in coming to terms with their recent history. At the same time the General Walker Hotel (see page 39) — the old Platterhof — was demolished to provide a car park!

The latest example of the State of Bavaria's determination in recent years to erase relics from the Nazi era if they threaten to become a political problem is the case of the summer villa of Rudolf Hess at Reicholdsgrün (see page 79). After Hess's death in 1987, his grave at Wunsiedel (see page 81) became a venue for yearly neo-Nazi demonstrations on his birthday. By then, his house nearby had stood empty and neglected for several years. When it was put up for sale, the real estate agent unscrupulously capitalised on its 'brown' past, openly publicising it as 'the Hess villa' and even advertising it in the right-wing *Deutsche Nationalzeitung*. Several known Nazis showed an interest and it was feared the villa might become a meeting place for old or new Nazis. Others feared the yearly unrest at Wunsiedel might expand to quiet Reicholdsgrün. To prevent all this from happening, the town of Kirchenlamitz (to which Reicholdsgrün belonged) decided to buy the house and demolish it. The estate agent was now asking a hefty price, which stretched the small town's budget, so the State of Bavaria stepped in, subsidising the acquisition behind the scenes. Eventually on July 26, 1999 a demolition firm began knocking down the house. The site was then used to build an underground sewerage clearing tank for the village, and today all that remains of the villa are heaps of bricks *(right)*.

However, something that has escaped, perhaps because it lies in a less sensitive region of Germany (Baden), is the proposed tomb for Albert Schlageter. We read on page 118 how he was re-interred in the cemetery at Schönau but Hitler had even greater plans for him. He had the Schlageter Kreuz memorial erected in Düsseldorf on the spot where he was executed, and on the hillside overlooking his grave the Nazis set about building a mausoleum where their first martyr could lie in the crypt. It was never completed and today, 70 years later, lies mouldering and forgotten — yet it is a unique survivor of the Third Reich era.

Now one final story remains to be told: what happened to Hitler's body? We left the funeral pyre in the Chancellery garden on page 414 just as the building was about to be over-run by the Red Army. As soon as Berlin capitulated, the quest was on either to capture Hitler or trace his body to prove his death. The Soviet search party was led by Lieutenant-Colonel Ivan Klimenko, commander of the Counter Intelligence Section (SMERSH) of the 79th Rifle Corps which had taken over Plötzensee Prison as its headquarters. Klimenko arrived at the Chancellery with three other officers and five soldiers on the afternoon of May 2. In the garden, just outside the emergency

exit, they found two charred corpses which were recognised as being Goebbels and his wife. They were carried on doors to a covered lorry and taken to Plötzensee where Dönitz's liaison officer, Vizeadmiral Hans-Erich Voss, was brought in to make a formal identification *(above)*. The Goebbels' children — Helga 12, Hilda 11, Helmut 9, Holde 7, Hedda 5 and Heide 3 — were not discovered in the Vorbunker until they were found the following day by Senior Lieutenant Ilyin. Their bodies were also taken to Plötzensee together with that of General Krebs who had committed suicide in the bunker. As these bodies had not been damaged by fire, identification was easier.

Voss told Klimenko that although he had not witnessed it himself, he had been told that Hitler's body had been burned in the garden. In spite of the fact that it was now evening, Klimenko took Voss back to the Chancellery where they poked about in the bunker and looked around the garden. Although not fire damaged, one corpse discovered in the pond bore a remarkable likeness to Hitler, but in daylight the following

day it was rejected. Klimenko then began searching again in the area close to the bunker exit where Goebbels had been found, and where one of his men had come across human remains the previous day. *Left:* On May 5, two soldiers, Deryabin and Tsybochin, were set to work and they recovered the remains of two bodies together with that of a German Shepherd dog *(right)*.

The badly burned corpses were put in two wooden ammunition boxes and taken, together with the bodies of two dogs (a second

had been found nearby), to the mortuary (see page 67) at the Surgical Field Hospital No. 496 in the northern suburb of Buch.

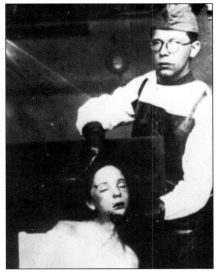

The autopsies were performed by Professor Nikolai Krayevski, chief pathologist of the Red Army, assisted by Dr Anna Yakolevna Marents, the chief pathologist with the 1st Byelorussian Front. *Above:* In this picture taken on May 8, the body of General Krebs is on the dissecting table. *Above right:* Helga Goebbels — the eldest of the six children. *Right:* This is the same mortuary today at the rear of the main hospital. During the post mortem, the jaw from the male corpse was removed complete with the teeth and an associated bridge which was subsequently identified by Hitler's dental assistant, Fräulein Käthe Heusermann, as belonging to Hitler. Cyanide was detected in the internal organs and fragments of glass in the mouth indicated death by poisoning. Part of the cranium was missing and the right side of the head — the side through which Hitler is believed to have shot himself — was more badly burned.

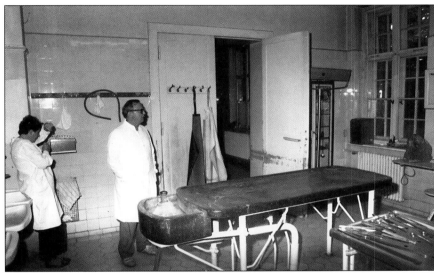

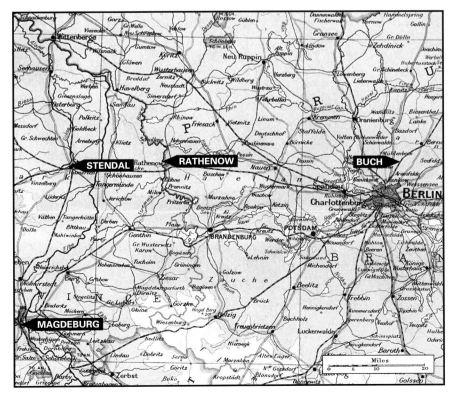

None of this was made known to the Allies, in fact the Russians denied that they had even found Hitler's remains. British investigators from MI5 were hampered by the lack of co-operation as many of those who spent the last hours in the bunker were in Soviet captivity. When Harry Mengershausen, a member of the RSD at the Chancellery, was released in 1955, he revealed that it was he who had dug Hitler's grave in the garden. He also said that he had been taken later to a forest outside Berlin to identify the remains. It appears that Stalin was still having doubts that Hitler was really dead and had ordered a second autopsy. In 1965, the Soviet press agency Novosti released a report by Ivan Klimenko and three years later the Buch autopsies were published in a book by Lev Bezymenski, but it was not until the demise of the Soviet Union that more became known. In 1991, an ex-SMERSH Lieutenant-Colonel, Ivan Blashchuk, who claimed to have been one of those responsible for guarding the corpses at Plötzensee and later at Buch, revealed that they had first been buried in the hospital grounds but when the graves showed signs of being disturbed they were moved to a forest near Rathenow, not far from Stendal to where the SMERSH unit had been transferred.

Blashchuk then claimed that the bodies had been dug up a third time when the unit moved 30 miles to the south to the city of Magdeburg. SMERSH had requisitioned a whole section of Westendstrasse in the Sudenburg district of the city, and he said that the bodies had been buried within the security of the SMERSH compound. Blashchuk gave the name of a second officer who also lived in Moscow although he had not seen him since he had left Germany in 1951. Ex-Captain Ivan Tereshchenko stated that he had been chief of the SMERSH secretariat in Magdeburg and had been given custody of documents confirming the burial and reburial of the remains of Adolf Hitler and Eva Braun at No. 32 *(right)*. Tereschchenko recalled that one document listed the officers present at the final burial.

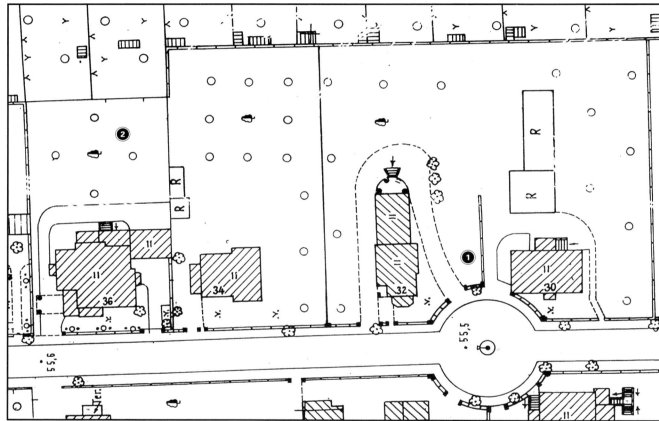

The burials were carried out under the instructions of Colonel Gorbushin, the deputy chief of SMERSH in the Third Shock Army. A large garage then stood beside No. 32, large enough to accommodate five cars, and it was equipped with an inspection pit to facilitate servicing. It was in this pit [1] that Adolf Hitler and Eva Braun were buried. *Right:* Karel Margry, editor of *After the Battle*, pictured the concrete base of the garage in 1991. A third SMERSH officer, Major Vasily Orlovsky, said that he had witnessed the burial of Goebbels and his family, together with General Hans Krebs in the back garden of No. 36 Westendstrasse [2]. When SMERSH — or rather its post-war successor, the NKVD/KGB — vacated the properties in Westendstrasse in 1970, the bodies were removed and taken to Moscow for ultimate destruction.

The Soviet revelations in September 1991 promoted a media scrum of the worst kind. It began when the Foreign Media Affairs (FMA) television company in Holland decided to make a documentary on the fall of Berlin in association with Progress Video of Moscow. As the Soviet officers interviewed had all left Magdeburg in the 1950s, they had no knowledge of the subsequent removal of the remains, so the TV company decided to dig up the gardens. However word got out and several German newspapers got wind of what was about to happen and one of them decided to pre-empt FMA — but dug in the wrong garden! Meanwhile the story had been sold to the British *Daily Express*. However it was the Dutch newspaper *Algemeen Dagblad* which first revealed the existence of the graves whereupon the *Daily Mail*, arch-rival of the *Express*, came out with a 'spoiler' article the next day. Not to be outdone, FMA and the *Express* immediately dug up both gardens during the hours of darkness.

Above: This is our comparison of the garage site after its excavation on July 3/4, 1992 (see *After the Battle* No. 77). *Left:* The Goebbels garden grave behind No. 36 was also dug up. As each bucketful of earth was removed, it was sifted and some pieces of bone were found at a depth of 60cm. Dr Werner Kühne, a local Professor of Pathology, had already been contacted and asked if he could 'be available for consultation by someone from England' although he was not told anything about human bones or Nazi graves. When the fragments were shown to him, his qualified opinion was that they were 'more likely to be from some animal than from a human being'. Nothing further was found in either garden.

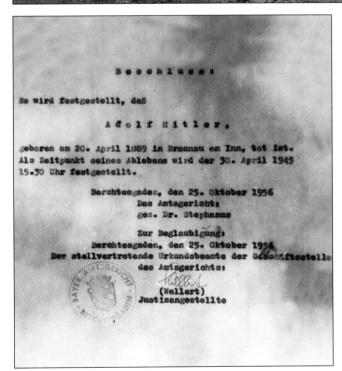

Both FMA and the *Express* tried to put a brave face on it . . . that is until Lev Bezymenski revealed a few days later that the whole exercise had been a complete waste of time as the remains had been removed 20 years earlier! *Above:* Hitler was officially declared dead on October 25, 1956 when notice to that effect was posted in the court at Berchtesgaden.

461

Photographs

Florian Beierl 47 top and bottom left, 60 bottom left.
Bellarchiv 33 all, 34 top right, bottom left, 263 all.
Gerhard Bluhm 51 bottom.
Bundesarchiv 72 bottom left, 105 centre, 109 bottom left, centre and right, 145 top, 206 top, 207 top left, 209 centre left, bottom left, 214 top left, 265 top, 278 centre, 279 bottom left, 282 bottom left, 285 bottom left, 289 top, 290 top right, 306 top, 369 top, 372 top and bottom left, 396 bottom, 397 top right and centre.
Imme van den Berg 32 bottom right, 82 top right.
Henk van Capelle 41 top, 42 bottom, 44 top right.
Jacques Degive 374 centre.
Wilfried Engelbrecht 439.
Helmuth Euler 437 centre.
Michael Foedrowitz Rear endpaper, 7 top right, 69 centre right, 84 bottom, 85 top, 109 centre right, 110 top right, 111 bottom left, 137 top left, 172, 183 bottom right, 221 centre left, 226 bottom right, 227 bottom, 245 top left and right, 369 bottom, 386 bottom.
Berta Geiss 39 bottom.
Hartmut Happel 294 top, 295 top and bottom, 296 top and bottom left, 297 centre.
J. Hearne 309 top left.
Jan Heitmann 6 top right and bottom.
Rob Hopmans 161 bottom left, 399 bottom left, 463.
Imperial War Museum 2-3, 36 bottom right, 37 top, 85 centre right, 312-313, 347 top, bottom left, 348 top and centre, 349 top, 350 bottom left and right, 351 both, 408 both, 417 top, 418 top left and bottom, 419 top, bottom left, 420 both, 421 top, 422 top left.
Institut für Stadtgeschichte Frankfurt 261 top centre.
Kentucky Historical Society 110 centre right.
Volker Knopf 75 all, 76 top left.
Kreismuseum Wewelsburg 298 centre, 300 top left, centre and bottom left, 301 top left and centre, 302 top left and bottom left.

KZ-Gedenkstätte Dachau 316 centre, 319 top left.
KZ-Gedenkstätte Mauthausen 331 top left, 332 top left and centre, 333 top left, centre and bottom left, 334 top.
KZ-Gedenkstätte Moringen 283 top.
KZ-Gedenkstätte Ravensbrück 342 top, 343 top and bottom left, 344 top left and centre.
KZ-Gedenkstätte Sachsenhausen 324 top left and centre.
Landesbildstelle Berlin 24 bottom, 29 top, 31 top left, 36 top left, 63 centre right, 81 top 112-113, 127 top left, 128 top left, 130 top, 204-205, 208 top, 209 top left, 211 top, 215 top left, 231 both, 235 top, 250 top right and bottom left, 273 top, 278 top left, 400 top right, 415 top right, 453 top.
Landeswohlfahrtsverband Hessen 362 top right, centre left, 363 top, 364 top left, 365 top.
Saskia Lelieveld 253 bottom.
Christoph Links Verlag 245 bottom, 252 centre and bottom, 253 top and centre.
Luftbilddatenbank 317, 404 top.
Bernd Mayer 192-193, 194 top, 195 top left, bottom left, 196 bottom left, 197 top and bottom left, 199 top left and right, bottom left, 200 top and bottom left, 201 top, 202 top left and right, centre right, 203 top, 439 centre, 479.
Frans Mekers 439 top right.
Heinrich Meyer 79 bottom.
Andrew Mollo 84 top, 96-97, 103 centre, 105 top right, 106 bottom left, 136 both, 155 bottom left, 158 top left, 161 centre right, 163 top, 214 centre left, 299 top, 310 top and bottom right.
Nederlands Instituut voor Oorlogsdocumentatie, Amsterdam Front endpaper, 7 top left, 10 top left, 11 centre left, 13 top, bottom left, 20 bottom left, 26 bottom left, 27 bottom, 42 top, 52 top, 53 top, 55 top, 65 bottom left, 71 centre and bottom, 76 bottom left, 91 centre left, 99 centre, 100 top right, bottom left, 102 bottom, 106 top left, 107 bottom left, 108 bottom, 109 top

left, 110 top left, centre left, 111 top left, 114 top, 116, 121 bottom left, 122 top, 123 top left, 124 bottom left, 126 top, 127 bottom left, 132 top and bottom left, 135 centre left, 137 bottom, 143 top, 144, 146 centre, 148 both, 149 top and bottom left, 151 centre, 154 top, 158 bottom, 159 top, 160 top left and right, 161 top left, 163 centre left, 164 bottom left, 169 bottom left, 175 top left and bottom, 176 all, 177 both, 178 centre, 179 centre, 180 bottom left, 181 centre, bottom left and right, 190 bottom left, 210 top, 212 top, 213 top left and centre, 215 bottom left, 223 centre, 233 bottom left, 236 bottom, 238 both, 247 top, 248-249, 261 top left, 264 both, 266 centre, 267 top left and centre, 268 top left and centre, 281 top, 286 bottom 290 centre, 291 centre, 297 bottom left, 316 top, 318 top, 319 centre and bottom left, 322 top, 323 top, 325 top, 337 top, 379 top, 386 top, 391 top, 438 top left, rear endpaper left.
Novosti 384 top.
Jean Paul Pallud 19 bottom right.
Anton Plenk 39 second right.
Peter Plenk 49 bottom left.
Sebastian Remus 114 bottom, 118 bottom left and right, 457 centre and bottom left and right.
Rex Features 81 bottom left.
Royal Air Force Museum, Hendon 381 top.
Rolf Sawinski 275 all, 276 all, 284 top and bottom, 285 top and bottom right, 286 top left and right, 287 all, 291 top, 292 top left, centre left and bottom left, 293 centre.
Christian Schmidt 436 bottom left and right.
Keith Spanner 37 bottom.
Stadtarchiv Backnang 279 top left.
Stadtarchiv Erwitte 269 top, centre and bottom left.
Stadtarchiv Nuremberg 170 centre, 178 top, 181 top, 185 top, 441 both, 443 bottom.
Stadtarchiv Wesel 89 centre top.
SV-Bilderdienst 43 top.
Hans Swetlik 92 top right.
Peter Thompson 415 bottom right.
Ullstein, Berlin 55 bottom left, 139 both.
US Library of Congress 70 both, 72 top left and right, 74 top, centre left and right.
US National Archives 77 bottom left and right, 91 bottom left and right, 93 bottom left and right, 228 top, 305 top left and right, 320 top left and centre, 321 top, 328 top and bottom left, 329 top right, 335 top, 336 centre, 346 top, 350 top, 394 top left, 396 top left, 405 top left, centre left and bottom left, 406 bottom left, 407 centre left, bottom left, 409 top, 411, 422 centre and bottom, 423 top left and bottom, 424 top left and right, 425 top, 427 top and centre, 431 inset, 432 top, 433 top and centre left, 434 both, 435 both, 440 all, 442 both, 443 top, 444 all, 445, 446 both, 447 all, 448 both, 449 all, 452 all, 454 bottom, 464 top and bottom, 467.
Volkswagen AG 256 top right, 257 bottom left and right.
Joseph Wotka 307 top left, centre and bottom left.

INDEX

COMPILED BY PETER B. GUNN

Note: Page numbers in *italics* refer to illustrations. There may also be textual references on these pages.

Leni Riefenstahl (see pages 182-183 and 224) died on September 8, 2003 aged 101. She was laid to rest in this beautiful grave in Munich's Waldfriedhof.

The final collapse of the Third Reich. Weapons and uniforms are handed in by German civilians in Stendal on April 13, 1945.

The occupation of Germany begins. Civilians in Schleusingen, which was captured by the US Third Army on April 7, 1945, question military government officials who have set up an open-air office in the town square.

Take your pick. Surrendered pistols and revolvers are sorted and crated ready for shipment to the United States.

Just outside the Sachsenhausen concentration camp lies the building that from 1938-1945 was the main SS nerve centre controlling the entire concentration camp system. Known as the Inspektion der Konzentrationslager (Inspectorate of Concentration Camps), it was housed in what was known as the T-building. It lay close to the Sachsenhausen camp, but was not part of it. After the war it served as a Soviet Army headquarters until the Red Army's departure in 1990-1994. Today the building is occupied by the Stiftung Brandenburgische Gedenkstätten (the agency running the Sachsenhausen camp memorial and other memorials in Brandenburg province) and also the Sachsenhausen municipal finance office. There is a small exhibition explaining the building's infamous past on the first floor.

This is the farmhouse of the SS experimental farm near Ravensbrück concentration camp (see page 344). The present owner Frau Gollan showed us round and pointed out where, on the exterior wall, the word 'SS' has been excised from the inscription carved into the wooden beam *(below)*.

The wording reads: 'Feld und Saaten, Baum und Land, Halt es, Herr, in deiner Hand. 1728 erstmals als Meierei ich entstand, 1753 als Vorwerk bekannt, 1933 zum SS-Versuchsgut erhoben, dem wir treue Dienste geloben.' An approximate English translation is: 'Field and seed, tree and land, keep it, Lord, in your hand. First arisen as a tenant-farm in 1728, by 1753 known as an estate farm, in 1939 I was raised to an SS experimental farm, to which we pledge faithful service.'

Adolf caught on camera! This rarely-seen amateur snapshot brings to mind the recording by Spike Jones (1911-65) of *Der Fuehrer's Face* which featured in the Donald Duck cartoon of January 1943. This was one of five anti-Nazi films released by the Walt Disney studio during the war. The film was originally titled *Donald Duck in Nutzi Land* but when the song was released in advance of the cartoon, it became such a huge hit that the film title was changed to *Der Fuehrer's Face*. The song was written by the Disney studio composer Oliver Wallace and performed by Spike Jones and his City Slickers, the hugely popular musician and comedian of the period. Wartime audiences particularly loved the raspberry sound (somewhat difficult to describe in print) after each 'Heil' in the chorus:

'When der fuehrer says we is de master race,
We heil (*phfft*), heil (*phfft*), right in der fuehrer's face.
Not to love der fuehrer is a great disgrace,
So we heil (*phfft*), heil (*phfft*), right in der fuehrer's face.